Review
of
Biblical Literature

2017

SBL Press

Review of Biblical Literature _____

Editor
Jan G. van der Watt (the Netherlands)

Managing Editor
Christopher Hooker (U.S.A.)
Bob Buller (U.S.A.)

Editorial Board
Rubén R. Dupertuis (U.S.A.)
Mark W. Hamilton (U.S.A.)
Lynn R. Huber (U.S.A.)
James Alfred Loader (Austria)
Christoph Markschies (Germany)
Carol Meyers (U.S.A.)

Volume 19 (2017)
ISSN 1099-0046

SBL Press
825 Houston Mill Road, Suite 350
Atlanta, GA 30329
http://www.sbl-site.org

© 2017 SBL Press

Typesetting by Lindsay Lingo, The Project Company, Loveland, Colorado

Contents

Editor's Foreword

The *Review of Biblical Literature* has established itself internationally as one of the leading review organs for biblical literature and related fields. It has become especially known for being comprehensive, international, timely, and authoritative.

- ✦ *RBL* reviews a wide and comprehensive spectrum of books from publishers large and small—ninety-one different publishers over the past twelve months—across the entire range of biblical studies and its cognate disciplines. To broaden our offerings, *RBL* publishes multiple and contrasting reviews as often as possible.
- ✦ Not only does *RBL* review books written in various languages (e.g., English, German, French, Italian, Spanish, Hebrew); it also invites scholars from a variety of language groups to review for *RBL*. Further, the editorial board overseeing this process consists of leading academics from around the world.
- ✦ *RBL* reviews are published in a timely fashion. As a rule, we attempt to review books within two years of their publication, and we try to place the review within a few months of receiving a book. Finally, we make every effort to publish each review within four or five months of receiving it.
- ✦ *RBL* reviews are written by the most qualified scholars available, whether a member of the Society of Biblical Literature or the broader scholarly guild. In addition, all *RBL* reviews are vetted to ensure their quality by a member of our editorial board.

During the past twelve months, thanks to the cooperative efforts of our reviewers, editors, and staff, *RBL* published 537 reviews. With an average of 4 pages per review, the past year's output would fill more than 2,100 published pages. To take this a step further, the 9,000 reviews published since the beginning of *RBL* through the end of October 2017 would require nearly 36,000 printed pages. This is truly a monumental accomplishment, not least because it has been achieved almost entirely through the contributions of volunteers

As is well known, *RBL* announces the publication of new reviews in a weekly newsletter distributed to over 8,000 member-subscribers and an associated blog (http://rblnewsletter.blogspot.com/). The *RBL* newsletter plays a significant role in leading scholars, students, and interested laypersons to the *RBL* website (www .bookreviews.org), where they can read the latest reviews or search for books reviewed since *RBL*'s creation fourteen years ago. Remarkably, each newsletter generates over 5,000 visits to the *RBL* website within the first four days. Taking all these data into account, it is no stretch to conclude that *RBL* indeed leads the way in providing scholarly reviews of biblical studies publications.

But there is even more to the story than the number of reviews *RBL* publishes and the number of visitors to the website. *RBL* also leads the way in building bridges between biblical scholarship from every region of the world. Over the last twelve months we published reviews by scholars from twenty-five different countries, which underscores our international scope. These countries include: Argentina, Australia, Austria, Belgium, Canada, Finland, France, Germany, Hungary, Ireland, Israel, Italy, Japan, Kenya, Lithuania, the Netherlands, New Zealand, Norway, Puerto Rico, Romania, Russia, Singapore, South Africa, Sweden, Switzerland, Turkey, United Arab Emirates, the United Kingdom, and the United States. This year approximately 44 percent of *RBL* reviews were authored by scholars outside of the United States.

Obviously, our success depends not only on the publishers supplying books but also on hundreds of academics who are willing to share their time and expertise with the readership of *RBL*. We would like to thank them all. *RBL* is a group effort in the true sense of the word, with so many SBL members joining together to make it the success it is.

Thus with gratitude and pride we present this print publication, a selection of 162 reviews published on our website during the latter half of 2016 and the first half of 2017. We hope that this printed selection of reviews published electronically the past year will encourage readers to visit the *RBL* website or the *RBL* blog.

Jan G. van der Watt
RBL General Editor
Radboud University Nijmegen
Nijmegen, the Netherlands

REFERENCE WORKS

The Oxford Encyclopedia of Biblical Interpretation, edited by Steven L. McKenzie and Michael D. Coogan. Oxford: Oxford University Press, 2013. Pp. 1164 (2 vols.). Hardcover. $295.00. ISBN 9780199832262.

Jean-François Racine, Santa Clara University and Graduate Theological Union

According to Denis Diderot's paradigmatic definition of an encyclopedia found in the monumental and trailblazing *Encyclopédie, ou dictionnaire raisonné des sciences, des arts et des métiers* (1751–1772), the goal of an encyclopedia is to gather the various types of knowledge scattered throughout the earth, to expose their systems to one's fellow citizens, and to transmit them to those coming after us in order that works from the previous centuries may not be useless for the next centuries; that our successors, through being more knowledgeable, may become happier and more virtuous; and that the present generation may not pass without deserving some merit from humankind (my translation).

The present work fares well in regard to Diderot's standards, including such a wide array of methods, approaches, theories, interpretations, criticisms, and types of hermeneutics used in biblical studies that the table of contents bears some resemblance to the list of sections found on the program of an Annual Meeting of the Society of Biblical Literature. In the preface the general editor Steven L. McKenzie acknowledges that he built upon the widely used handbook *To Each Its Own Meaning: An Introduction to Biblical Criticisms and Their Application* (Louisville: Westminster John Knox, 1993; 2nd ed., 1999) that he had co-edited with Stephen R. Haynes as well as upon W. Randolph Tate's *Interpreting the Bible: A Handbook on Terms and Methods* (Peabody, MA: Hendrickson, 2006). Ricoeur's three hermeneutical rubrics—the world behind the text, the world of the text, and the world before the text—also proved useful to organize the project and to represent the current proliferation of critical approaches to the Bible attributed to three factors: (1) the abundance of interdisciplinary approaches; (2) the greater dialogue among scholars from various parts of the world; and (3) the recognition of the significance of the reader's situation in the process of interpretation. The editor also acknowledges having had to lump together approaches that exhibit more diversity that some entries may convey. This is the case, for instance, with African biblical interpretation and Central and South American biblical interpretation.

Several entries describe biblical interpretation in various locations, either ethnic (e.g., African, African American, Asian American, Chinese, Cuban, Central and South American, Japanese, Korean, Latina/o, and womanist) or denominational (Conservative Jewish, Orthodox Jewish, Reconstructionist Jewish, Reform

Jewish, Muslim, Catholic, Dispensationalist, Eastern Orthodox, Evangelical, Latter-day Saints, Lutheran, Pentecostal, Reformed, and Wesleyan). Second, this encyclopedia lists 119 contributors hailing from twelve different countries, albeit most of them (95) are located in the United States.

The entries are organized in alphabetical order (see complete list at the end of this review). The diversity of labels—hermeneutics, criticism, interpretation, method, approach, and theory—coupled with the first term of each entry reflects the common state of biblical studies, which have become more interdisciplinary and hence have grown more comfortable with less-defined contours. The format of entries also varies greatly, although each entry provides a working definition of the topic. Most entries also provide a history of the topic, guiding principles, and, in a few cases, an example of its application. Some entries are divided into subentries that focus on the topic in relation to the Hebrew Bible, to apocryphal/ deuterocanonical literature (if applicable), and to the New Testament. This is the case for cultural anthropology, form criticism, historical criticism, orality studies/ oral tradition, redaction criticism, social-scientific criticism, and textual criticism. There is little variation when it comes to the length of the entries: eight to ten pages. This standardization results in significant contractions for some topics. As an example, the *Encyclopedia* has back-to-back eight-page-long entries on patristic interpretation and on Pentecostal interpretation. The latter topic is relatively recent while the former has a long history and has evolved into various traditions. As a result, the entry on patristic interpretation seems compressed in comparison with the one on Pentecostal interpretation. Each entry concludes with a list of related entries and a bibliography. Most entries have annotated bibliographies, which are helpful for anyone who wants to know where to start to learn more on a topic. From that perspective, the entries on feminist biblical interpretation and on the Greco-Roman context stand as models.

The editors are to be commended for having commissioned contributors to write groundwork entries. This is the case with the entry on phenomenological interpretation, which serves as a foundation for entries on most literary and reader-oriented approaches. The same can be said about the entry on postmodern interpretation, which prepares the ground for entries on topics such as deconstruction, LGBT interpretation, postcolonial interpretation, poststructuralist interpretation, and materialist criticism.

I was impressed with the overall quality of the entries. Among these, I highlight a few that correspond to my academic interests: The entry on narrative criticism and narrative hermeneutics covers much ground and elegantly explains the various directions taken by narrative approaches. The entry on structuralist interpretation is similarly outstanding for providing a lucid history of the approach and for exhibiting an encyclopedic knowledge of the multiple facets of the topic. The entry on performance criticism persuasively expounds its significance in New Testament studies. The *Encyclopedia* also makes useful distinctions by having separate entries on empire studies and postcolonial studies as well as separate entries (side by side) on inner-biblical interpretation and intertextuality. Finally, the article on modern translations spells out some directions taken in languages such as Greenlandic, Kikuyu, and Tagalog. I also noted the apologetic tone used to describe some recent approaches less widespread, such as new historicism and mimesis criticism. The latter gives the impression of a limited number of practitioners, even if those are individually prolific, since eleven of the twenty-one works cited in the bibliography are authored by the same scholar who happens to be the author of the entry. The same phenomenon occurs with socio-rhetorical criticism, in which twelve of the sixteen works cited in the bibliography are authored or edited by the author of the entry. I was somewhat shocked with the unusually sober tone of the entry on womanist interpretation, which notes that only a few works so far illustrate this approach. Hopefully, this could serve as an incentive for qualified scholars to augment the number of works written from this angle. Finally, since entries depict the state of the art in biblical interpretation, I was surprised to read that New Testament textual criticism mostly aims at "the analysis of the transmission of the text with a view of identifying variations from the original text" (379) without acknowledgment of the problematic character of what is meant by "original text," considering, for example, how Eldon J. Epp captured and analyzed the problem in "The Multivalence of the Term 'Original Text' in New Testament Textual Criticism," *Harvard Theological Review* 92 (1999): 245–81.

The *Oxford Encyclopedia of Biblical Interpretation* represents a splendid achievement by providing a comprehensive panorama of contemporary biblical interpretation. It shows how works from the previous centuries have initiated trajectories of biblical interpretation that continue today. In that sense, it achieves one of the purposes that Diderot envisioned for an encyclopedia. Diderot also hoped that an encyclopedia would contribute to the happiness and virtue of future generations who would express their recognition to those who assembled it. I will not venture any judgment on the present work's capacity for making happier and more virtuous future biblical interpreters but will readily express my recognition to the editors and contributors of this volume to have so well collected, organized, and made available all this information that makes one realize how diverse and rich biblical interpretation is in the twenty-first century.

Encyclopedia Entries
African American Interpretation
African Biblical Interpretation
Allegory and Allegorical Interpretation
Anti-Judaism and Anti-Semitism in the New Testament and Its Interpretation
Asian American Biblical Interpretation
Assyriology and Biblical Interpretation
Authority of the Bible
Autobiographical and Personal Criticism
Canon of the Bible
Canonical Criticism
Catholic Biblical Interpretation
Central and South American Interpretation

Chinese Interpretation
Class Criticism
Cognitive Linguistics and Biblical Interpretation
Conservative Jewish Interpretation
Cross-Cultural Exegesis
Cuban Interpretation in the Cuban Diaspora
Cultural Anthropology
Cultural Studies
Cultural-Historical Criticism
Dead Sea Scrolls
Deconstruction
Diachronic Interpretation
Diaspora Studies
Disability Criticism
Dispensationalist Interpretation
Eastern Orthodox Interpretation
Ecological Biblical Criticism
Economics and the Bible
Egyptology and Biblical Interpretation
Empire Studies and Biblical Interpretation
Evangelical Interpretation
Exegesis
Feminist Biblical Interpretation
Folklore and Biblical Interpretation
Form Criticism
Formalist Interpretation
Genre Criticism
Geography and Topography in Biblical Interpretation
Gnosticism and Gnostic Interpretation
Greco-Roman Context
Historical Criticism
Historical Jesus, Quest for the
Hittitology and Biblical Interpretation
Homiletics
Ideological Criticism
Inner-biblical Interpretation
Intertextuality
Japanese Interpretation
Korean Interpretation
Latina/o Interpretation
Latter-day Saints (Mormon) Interpretation
Lesbian, Gay, Bisexual, and Transgender Interpretation
Liberation Hermeneutics
Literary Criticism, Literary Theory, and the Bible

Translation Techniques
Trauma Theory
Ugaritology and Biblical Interpretation
Wesleyan Biblical Interpretation
Womanist Interpretation

The Oxford Encyclopedia of the Bible and Theology, edited by Samuel E. Balentine. Oxford Encyclopedias of the Bible. Oxford: Oxford University Press, 2015. Pp. 1200. Hardcover. $395.00. ISBN 9780199858699.

Robert L. Foster, University of Georgia

The Oxford Encyclopedia of the Bible and Theology is the fourth installment in the Oxford Encyclopedias of the Bible. Samuel Balentine and his editorial team have assembled 168 articles written by 156 different scholars, articles ranging from "Adam" to "Worship." As with other installments in the series, the press divided this encyclopedia into two volumes, with the second ending with a topical outline of contents, directory of contributors, and a substantive index (451–558).

Much can be made of the title of a work, and I found the encyclopedia's reference to Bible *and* theology intriguing. In fact, my interest in the *OEBT* arose in part because of the advertisement on the Oxford University Press webpage. The site states that the *OEBT* "will situate itself inside the tension" of issues rooted in the Bible's historical context and issues rooted in the modern world. However, the list of articles does not contain any that clearly address a contemporary issue, including those such as market economics, climate change, or gender/race discrimination, all of which are listed in OUP's advertisement.

Still, this is an encyclopedia of Bible and theology, not biblical theology. So, perhaps one way to measure the success of an article lies in whether the it moves beyond discussing a topic in terms of the Bible's historical context and toward the contemporary context. With this measure in mind, some articles prove more successful than others.

One article I found particularly successful on these terms was Susan Hylen's on "Glory." Hylen surveys the idea of God's glory in the Old Testament, points out the range of perspectives on glory in John's Gospel, and notes that Paul considered glory within the narrative of salvation, including the participation of the believers in the glory of God. Hylen then surveys the use of glory in early church writers, offers a good, if brief, discussion of glory in the theologies of predestination in Aquinas and Luther, and ends with comments on the current political theology of Giorgio Agamben, who sees an economy of glory created and sustained only by human attributions of glory.

Equally successful is John M.G. Barclay's article on "Grace." Barclay begins by discussing the problem of defining a concept based on occurrences of a particular term in ancient texts. Barclay further defines *grace* in a number of ways ranging from its excessive quality to the sense of arbitrariness to the unilateral nature of grace as God's gift. Barclay then looks at the various instantiations of grace in the Hebrew Bible, Second Temple Judaism, and the New Testament without peremptorily restricting expectations of what any text might say about grace. The second part of the article surveys the concept of grace in figures such as Marcion, Augustine, Aquinas, Luther, and Calvin before ending with a nice contrast between post-Reformation Catholic positions on nature and grace and Protestant authors such as Barth and Bultmann, who discussed grace more in terms of Christology and soteriology.

John Pilch is one of eleven authors to write two articles in the encyclopedia. Both of his also do a good job moving from the biblical context to contemporary concerns. Pilch's article on "Hospitality" presents a vision of hospitality from the perspective of Mediterranean cultures. He views hospitality as a possible process of stages moving from evaluating the stranger to taking in the stranger as a guest to the potential transformation of the stranger into a friend or foe. Pilch then uses this perspective to evaluate the modern challenge of immigration and ends by offering two possible avenues of further academic inquiry into hospitality. Pilch's discussion of "Labor" in the Bible runs a bit short, noting that work was originally a gift from God whose fruit was often enough co-opted by conquerors, before closing with some thoughts on the Gospel of John's vision of Jesus as colaboring with God. Most of this article focuses on the postbiblical period, including a discussion of the variously positive and negative views of labor among monastics, Luther's emphasis on labor as worship, and contemporary issues of unemployment and underemployment. Pilch offers some constructive thoughts on a theology of labor, which to his mind must include a theory of social justice and move toward new creation. He concludes this article, much like his first, with several potential avenues for illuminating research on a theology of labor.

Numerous articles in the *OEBT* end with a final paragraph or two assessing the article's topic or a discussion of contemporary developments or the like. On occasion an author offers that the biblical theological perspective does not have much to contribute to contemporary debates. For example, Konrad Schmid's article on "Creation" notes the creation versus evolution debate. Schmid then usefully highlights that the creation visions of the Old and New Testaments cannot contribute to the modern discussion on the origin of the universe, given their outdated cosmologies. He rightly observes that the biblical visions have theological significance in their interpretation of creation as an overarching context for human (and, I would argue, all) life. Deidre Good's article on "Sexuality" concludes with the rather freeing assessment that the Bible really has little interest in sexuality. Good then encourages readers to mind the gap between the biblical text's lack of concern for these issues and the postbiblical needs to regulate sexual behaviors. Good argues that minding this gap may free modern people to intentionally fill this gap in ways that allow for inclusion of different ideas of family and households.

Less successful in terms of theological discussion is Paul Redditt's article on "The Book of the Twelve." Redditt spends a good deal of his allotted space discussing Judean recensions of Hosea, the authorship of certain portions of Micah, the possible reason for the broken acrostic in Nahum, the idea of Hab 3 as a song, and so on. These discussions make the article seem more like it belonged in *The Oxford Encyclopedia of the Books of the Bible* than in the *OEBT*. Similarly, much of Thomas Römer's article on "Historical Narratives (Joshua–2 Kings)" discusses the theory of Deuteronomistic History and the various purposes behind the three major stages of the development of DH he identifies. Ironically, in discussing these three layers the article offers little discussion of the actual contents of Joshua–Kings, touching on a few verses from Josh 5 and 10, 1 Sam 8, 1 Kgs 8, and 2 Kgs 18, 19, 24, and 25. One comes to the end without an understanding of how the portraits in Judges, the David narrative in 2 Samuel, or the Elijah-Elisha narratives of 1 and 2 Kings contribute to the theology of these three layers or to the theology of the whole.

There are a few surprises in the *OEBT*. For example, I found the lack of an article on the Letter to the Hebrews quite surprising. Perhaps this lacuna arises from the fact that many articles on the Bible group material together, and one could not logically place Hebrews with the Catholic Epistles or the Pauline Letters. Still, the fact that the entry for Hebrews says "*See* Atonement *and* Expiation" seems to shortchange the theology of Hebrews, especially in terms of its Christology (I note that Hebrews garners individual attention in the article on "Soteriology" by Jan G. van der Watt). On the other hand, I found Jerry Sumney's article on the "Pauline Letters" quite refreshing in that Romans did not dictate the discussion, and even shorter letters such as 1 Thessalonians and Philippians received substantive treatment. I appreciated especially that his article ended with some discussion of the "fundamental components" of Paul's theology that one may discern from the undisputed letters.

A major contribution to the field of Bible and theology no doubt raises several important questions about the nature of the field. I briefly mention three questions. First, what do we mean by "Bible"? The biggest lacuna in the *OEBT*, to my mind, lies in the lack of an article on the deuterocanonical books of the Catholic or Orthodox Christian traditions. This does not mean that the whole encyclopedia lacks any discussion of these books. For example, Jay Sklar offers some brief thoughts on the Apocrypha and Pseudepigrapha in his article on "Sin." Still, the lack of an article on the deuterocanonical books reminds this reader that, in fact, many theologies exist in part because various canons exist among Jews, Protestants, Catholics, and the Orthodox Churches. But then neither Robert Wall's article on "Canon" nor John Goldingay's article on "Scripture" raise the issue of various canons and Scriptures as issues of concern.

Second, what is the role of the Bible in future developments of theology? Ellen Charry's article on "Biblical Hermeneutics" argues that hermeneutics is an act of guardianship, protecting or shaping a community's beliefs or values and, at times, protecting the community from harmful texts. Charry offers the important observation that "ecclesial interpretation becomes especially necessary when a revered text poses problems for later readers" (1:458). I heartily agree with

Charry's point. One must judge an interpretation of the revered text not only by whether it accurately explicates the text's meaning in the ancient context but also by whether the interpretation influences the ecclesial community to act well in the world. Still, Charry's article, which presents a short history of interpretation of the Christian doctrine of divine election, highlights how, in each of the five cases she presents, a given writer inverts the plain meaning of the text, mediating between the author of the text and the moral and social health of the community to which the interpreter writes. But this begs the question of whether the plain meaning of the text may contribute positively to the ongoing work of theology and, if so, in what measure.

For example, Charry discusses Paul's argument in Rom 9–11 about the place of Jews and gentiles in God's elective purposes, along with Barth's interpretation of these chapters many years later. Charry notes that Paul could not have foreseen the deleterious effects of his reading of the Jews as vessels of God's wrath and gentiles as vessels of God's mercy in the anti-Semitism that arose with the coming of Christian hegemony. However, a disciplined hermeneutic that attends to the rhetoric of these chapters, in the vein of George Kennedy and Wilhelm Wuellner, may note two essential rhetorical elements Charry's article does not discuss: Paul's deep feelings for the Jews (9:1–5) and his imperatives to his gentile audience not to boast over the root that supports their very existence but instead to stand in awe of God (11:18, 20). Thus, a disciplined hermeneutics may show that Paul's argument contributes positively to the push back against Christian supersessionism because, in fact, Paul exhorted against his gentile Christian audience feeling superior to the Jews. Perhaps the need for hermeneutics emerges from the fact that the Bible continues to hold much that may contribute positively to theology, if we listen well.

Finally, what is the future of biblical theology? On the one hand, the "Theology, Biblical" entry is divided into two articles, on the "Old Testament" and on the "New Testament," respectively, written by two separate authors. Most of the rest of the articles in the *OEBT* come from the hand of a single author. Moreover, this division of labor allows for two distinct perspectives on the enterprise. Marvin Sweeney's article on the Old Testament, an excellent survey of the history of Old Testament theology from the Reformation to the present, sees biblical theology as the theological exposition of the Bible defined in terms of each tradition within Judaism and Christianity. Thomas Söding's article on the New Testament, on the other hand, argues that biblical theology seeks the Word of God in the Old and New Testaments, which Söding apparently takes as the idea that unifies the two Testaments. He then defines the Word of God first in terms of Christology ("the Word of God is seen in the face of Jesus Christ" [2:362]). The first half of his article articulates a particular theory of the Word of God in terms of Jesus, the canon, inspiration, and truth, then turns to the question of the relationship of the Old Testament to the New Testament before finally discussing some exemplars of New Testament theology, judging each by its success or failure to integrate the Old Testament more or less fully into its overall theological perspective. These two articles, then, give the reader a sense that, though Sweeney envisions a productive future for biblical theology, the discipline might helpfully explore how to relate the various biblical theologies produced by the varying traditions and that Christian biblical theology in particular must continue to work to embrace the visions of the Old Testament as part of a truly robust biblical theology.

I must conclude that, even with the proviso about the advertisement of the *OEBT*, I thoroughly enjoyed reading the articles in these two volumes. Some proved more promising than others, but one expects some unevenness in any collection of articles. I commend the two volumes to potential readers, knowing that especially the discussions of topics in terms of biblical theology will provide helpful overviews of these topics for students as well as for scholars looking for orientation to particular topics. Further, I think the scholarly guild would be remiss not to note that the production of this encyclopedia offers a subtle reminder that questions of what constitutes the Bible, the relationship of the Bible to theology, and the future of biblical theology are, as always, continuously in process.

The Oxford Encyclopedia of the Bible and Ethics, edited by Robert L. Brawley. Oxford Encyclopedias of the Bible. New York: Oxford University Press, 2014. Pp. xxiii + 541, xi + 556. Hardcover. $395.00. ISBN 9780199829910.

Volker Rabens, Friedrich Schiller University Jena

The Oxford Encyclopedia of the Bible and Ethics (*OEBE*) explores the intersection between biblical sources and ethical issues, both historical and modern, through extensive analytical and constructive treatments of a wide range of topics. *OEBE* is part of the Oxford Encyclopedias of the Bible series, a comprehensive reference work consisting of eight two-volume sets (dealing with, *inter alia*, the books of the Bible and the Bible and gender studies). *OEBE* contains 183 entries ranging in length from 1,500 to 7,000 words. It is organized in an A–Z format. Each entry provides a bibliography for further reading and cross-references to other useful points of interest within the encyclopedia. *OEBE* features a topical outline of contents and an extensive index of 111 pages. By way of comparison with the *Dictionary of Scripture and Ethics* (*DSE*) edited by Joel B. Green (Grand Rapids: Baker Academic, 2011), this index is not a Scripture but a thematic index. Spending so much space and effort on being accessible is a worthwhile venture because *OEBE* has fewer and longer entries than *DSE* (*DSE* has 439 articles, including separate entries, e.g., for Baptist, evangelical, and Lutheran ethics). The contributions are written by a broad range of leading exegetes and ethicists (including German-speaking scholarship, which is missing from *DSE*), combining traditional theoretical frameworks, such as comparative religion, with more recent approaches (e.g., postmodern, queer and gender theory). The topical outline of contents at the end of volume 2 allocates the articles to the categories Biblical Sources, Biblical Themes, Historical and Current Issues, Historical Context and Environment, History of Interpretation/Reception History, Society and

Life Together, and Theories of Ethics. I will discuss several sample articles from each section.

Many of the contributions that fit into the category Biblical Sources are straightforward expositions of the biblical material. Some cover biblical figures such as Paul, describing the figure's life and thought (though in this case with surprisingly little emphasis on the apostle's ethics). Other contributions focus on individual books or even an eminent passage such as the Decalogue or the Sermon on the Mount. A number of articles complement one another. For instance, Ulrich Luz's comprehensive article on Matthew treats various ethical issues, including, of course, the exposition of the Sermon on the Mount. He discusses several interpretative traditions and interacts with different strands of scholarship. In the article "Sermon on the Mount," on the other hand, Ruben Zimmermann approaches the passage mainly from within his innovative methodological framework developed for analyzing ethical texts, called "implicit ethics." Together these two articles form a stimulating introduction to the interpretation of the ethical material in Matthew and the Sermon on the Mount. The article "Matthew" thus fittingly provides a cross-reference to "Sermon on the Mount," though a reference in the opposite direction is missing from the latter article.

The articles that the *OEBE*'s appendix lists in the category Biblical Themes cover topics such as "Spirit" (a helpful analysis by John R. Levison) or "Salvation" (an article that does not draw out explicit connections to ethics). In most *OEBE* entries both Hebrew Bible and New Testament are engaged when "the Bible" or biblical material is presented. However, exceptions are made in the case of topics that occur predominantly in one of the two textual corpora (e.g., "Monarchy") or in cases where authors decide to limit their focus. Thus, somewhat surprisingly, in the case of the entry "Grace and Mercy," which starts off by claiming that "'Grace and mercy' have to do essentially with a Pauline topic" (1:349). The eight pages of the article are then used to investigate the topic primarily from the perspective of Pauline theology (including two pages on "The Jewish Foundation of Paul's Theology of Grace").

A good example of a discussion of critical issues of interpretation and contextualization in this category is Werner Wolbert's article "Holy War." The first half of the article is descriptive, investigating the biblical material relevant for the issue. The second half engages with the ethical problems of holy war. Starting off with a *wirkungsgeschichtliche* analysis of how the holy war traditions of the Hebrew Bible have been employed to justify wars throughout history, Wolbert then mentions two considerations intended to give directions for contemporary explorations of such stories. First, he looks at the pragmatics of the biblical holy war texts. Building on the work of Philip Jenkins (*Laying Down the Sword*, 2011), Wolbert explains that the narratives may not be directed against actual Canaanites but against deviant Israelites whose cultic practices did not conform to Deuteronomic orthopraxy. "What is at stake is Jewish identity.... The subject matter of the stories is monotheism and election. 'The fate of the Canaanites had to be painted in the darkest possible colors because the writers were sending an urgent, eleventh-hour warning to the Hebrew people, to turn back to God or to face annihilation. Israel had to kill the inner Canaanite.... In that sense, later commentators, Jewish and Christian, saw the massacres in allegorical terms' (Jenkins, 2011, 222) as a rejection of anything that distracts or separates from God." Second, Wolbert draws attention to the fact that there is a different view on war in later books of the Hebrew Bible/Old Testament. "War is no longer seen as a fight against evil forces of Chaos, but as a chaotic force itself (Isa 9:4)," and "apocalyptic texts tend to recommend a quietist attitude" (1:377).

OEBE provides a fair amount of articles that describe the ethical material in biblical literature and its cultural and religious context with no explicit interaction with ethical discussions in today's societies (as, e.g., the very nuanced article on "Abortion"). Such contributions have a stronger emphasis on ethics *in* the Bible than on (current) ethics *and* the Bible. Some of the articles that *OEBE* categorizes as dealing with Historical and Current Issues also belong to this group (e.g., "Elderly"). Other articles look further, at the *Wirkungsgeschichte* of ethical material of the Bible (e.g., "Anti-Semitism," "Apartheid"). James Dunn's illuminating article "Antinomianism" starts off with Luther and the Lutheran tradition and then moves back to early Christian history and theology. Dunn concludes that as a term "'antinomianism' seems hardly appropriate, either as a way of denoting Christianity's ultimate separation from Judaism or as characterizing earliest Christianity's attitude to the moral law. Both Jesus' and Paul's exhortation to 'Love your neighbor as yourself' was not a disowning of (the rest of) the law, but explicitly presented as summing up the whole law and as the key to how the law is best and most completely fulfilled (Mark 12:28–31; Rom 13:8–10)" (1:16).

OEBE's appendix lists two shorter categories to which the editors have assigned nine entries each: Historical Context and Environment (for which the article "Honor and Shame" is a good example, providing a descriptive section, a discussion of recent scholarship and its criticism of earlier research on the topic, and some suggestions on using this focus for New Testament studies) and History of Interpretation/Reception History. The latter category encompasses overarching topics such as "Metaethics" and "Metanarrative" as well as more narrowly focused entries such as "History of Interpretation: New Testament" (an article which has no counterpart from the perspective of Hebrew Bible scholarship). We also find analytical essays that discuss the methodological questions of interpreting and appropriating biblical ethics. For instance, Steven L. McKenzie provides a useful overview of the history of interpretative approaches in "Methodology: Hebrew Bible." However, this contribution could have found a place in any general encyclopedia under the heading "Bible: Interpretation of," since it makes no reference to Old Testament ethics or its potential interpretation in the context of canonical or systematic approaches to biblical ethics. On the other hand, in the counterpart contribution "Methodology: New Testament," Stephen Fowl, who is one of the "area editors" of *OEBE* (together with Kathy Ehrensperger, Isaac Kalimi, Ralph Klein, and Jan G. van der Watt), manages to present an intriguing analysis of all these aspects. In his methodological discussion of identifying the lasting value of

New Testament ethics he emphasizes the significance of practical wisdom, Christian formation, and the centrality of faith communities.

The category Society and Life Together comprises a range of different topics covering questions of sociology, economics, and the like. For example, Wolfgang Stegemann's "Egalitarianism" provides a nuanced discussion of the development of egalitarian concepts, starting with the U.S. Declaration of Independence and the French Revolution. In the second part of the article he attends to the biblical material that pertains to questions of hierarchy and equality. After listing a number of texts that are frequently cited in support of (gender) inequality, he explains that the value system of ancient Mediterranean societies was not characterized by the ideal of equality but first and foremost by the values of honor and shame. Biblical authors shared that value system in many aspects. Nonetheless, Stegemann thinks that it is remarkable that both the Hebrew Bible and the New Testament contain basic elements of egalitarianism, which inspired its modern successors. For instance, for Paul the spirit of holiness that has been poured out into believers' hearts (Rom 5:3) was the power of equalization and transformation. Accordingly, Stegemann concludes that egalitarianism as a central idea of the distribution of justice can be traced back to fundamental Judeo-Christian traditions and their further development in societies inspired by them. Another remarkable example in this category is "Justice," by Neill Elliott. In his critical discussion Elliott puts forward that it is more fitting to speak of the disparity or "dispute" of the different biblical voices on justice rather than to invoke metaphors such as a "chorus" of voices. He argues that the "juxtaposition of ... diverse and, perhaps, intentionally contradictory materials within the scope of the Jewish and Christian Bibles required strategies for adjudication on the part of the interpreter and of negotiation by the faith community, even if these have sometimes been the tacit strategies of benign neglect or liturgical marginalization of some texts in preference for others" (1:461).

A final category is called Theories of Ethics, and it has—among others—the article "Theories of Ethics" assigned to it. On eleven pages the late Allen Verhey helpfully expounds major ethical approaches such as normative, teleological, deontological, responsibility, and virtue theories. Subsequent to a critical discussion of "Challenges to Traditional Normative Theory," Verhey turns to the relationship of the Bible and ethics. He provides guidance on how to move from theory to the practice of reading Scripture and to moving from reading Scripture to theoretical reflection. Verhey points out that reading Scripture can prompt the rejection of certain ethical theories such as (quantitative) hedonism. However, he thinks that more frequently reading Scripture inspires readers to revise moral traditions and the theories that arise within particular social contexts. So, for example, "Augustine is indebted to Neo-Platonism and Aquinas to Aristotle, but Scripture forced a modification of the received tradition of eudaemonism and the received account of the virtues." By way of conclusion, Verhey writes: "Let this be the last word, therefore: in reading Scripture as relevant to morality in multicultural contexts and in contexts where people have different views of ethical theory, people in Judeo-Christian traditions should listen hard both to Scripture and to each other" (2:363).

A slightly less optimistic judgement of the critical capacity of Scripture to challenge the reader's prior ethical convictions is reached by Eryl Davies—at least with regard to what is often regarded as a useful hermeneutical tool for applying the provisions of Scripture to the modern world: the concept of "Paradigms." In his article with the same title, Davies builds on the foundation for the paradigmatic approach laid by Christopher Wright, who explains that a paradigm is "something used as a model or example for other cases where a basic principle remains unchanged, though details differ.... A paradigm is not so much imitated as applied" (C. J. H. Wright, *Living as the People of God*, 43, cited by Davies 2:97). As far as the definition of the paradigmatic approach is concerned, however, one needs to be aware that alternative versions of this interpretative method have flourished. In particular, Waldemar Janzen differentiates his approach from that of Wright and the "Western attraction to principles" by stressing that he understands "paradigm" as "a personally and holistically conceived image of a model (e.g., a wise person, good king) that imprints itself immediately and nonconceptually on the characters and actions of those who hold it" (Janzen, *Old Testament Ethics: A Paradigmatic Approach* [Louisville: Westminster John Knox, 1994[, 27–28). Nevertheless, the examples of paradigms that Davies provides fit both approaches: Israel and the exodus are each devoted a separate section in Davies's article. One of the strengths of taking characters and themes of Scripture as paradigmatic is that "readers of Scripture may be afforded guidance on issues of contemporary concern that are not specifically mentioned in the Bible, for while the biblical text may not provide explicit answers to our modern ethical dilemmas, it may at least prove to be helpful in suggesting the parameters of morally permissible behavior" (2:99). However, in the end Davies remains skeptical with regard to the lasting value of the paradigmatic approach to the Bible and ethics. Focusing on Wright's emphasis on principles, Davies remarks that the principles singled out by the reader typically witnesses to nothing else but what happens to chime in with the reader's prior convictions. "The approach thus becomes self-serving, for the message discerned is often no more than a mirror of the interpreter's own preconceived value judgments," and "the obvious meaning of a particular passage" can easily be avoided if that meaning proves too inconvenient. In his view, the adherents of this strategy have generally failed to identify satisfactory criteria for judging the validity of the proposed appropriation of a particular passage (2:100–101).

OEBE editor-in-chief Robert L. Brawley and his team have managed to acquire a remarkable breadth of scholarship for writing this two-volume encyclopedia and to ensure that most of the articles give due attention to both corpora that are mentioned in its title: the Bible and ethics. With the exception of a few articles that hardly discuss ethics explicitly, the great majority of the entries provide a thorough examination of the ethical material in both Hebrew Bible and New Testament. Many of the articles move beyond this descriptive and analytical level to the fields of hermeneutics and (post)modern ethics, sociology and philosophy. *OEBE* provides thorough introductions and thoughtful discussions—it is a comprehensive, interdisciplinary starting point for research on ethical topics belonging to a broad array of categories that is valuable for scholars and students alike.

BIBLICAL THEMES

The Divine Courtroom in Comparative Perspective, edited by Ari Mermelstein and Shalom E. Holtz. Biblical Interpretation Series 132. Leiden: Brill, 2015. Pp. vi + 308. Hardcover. $149.00. ISBN 9789004281639.

Bruce Chilton, Bard College

The Leonard and Bea Diener Institute of Jewish Law at Cardoza School of Law and the Yeshiva University Center for Jewish Law and Contemporary Civilization hosted a conference entitled "The Divine Courtroom," which convened at the Benjamin N. Cardoza School of Law. Two editors, each from Yeshiva University, have skillfully woven the present volume together, sometimes summarizing written notes and sometimes accommodating extensively revised papers. The standard of the editing is in general excellent, if not always aggressive in dealing with oddities of style and the length of paragraphs.

The whole represents a useful discussion of how the divine courtroom emerges as a productive lens for interpreting primary texts, and in this sense the focus is on a "literary phenomenon" (2–3). As the contributions unfold, however, the courtroom emerges also as a "theological phenomenon" (4), part of an attempt "to explain the universe in human terms."

Meira Z, Kensky's *Trying Man, Trying God: The Divine Courtsoom in Early Jewish and Christian Literature* (WUNT 2/289 [Tübingen: Mohr Siebeck, 2010]) provides a point of reference for the project. Her observation that God is on trial when he tries cases proves a fruitful incentive for many of the papers presented here. Although there is a particular value in these studies for those who read biblical texts, the contributors move into the penumbra of the canon, and well outside the canon, in a productive way. The first essay (6–24), by Tzvi Abusch, exemplifies the breadth of the volume, by dealing with *Maqlû*, eight tablets of incantations and one ritual tablet from the first millennium BCE. Abusch identifies a procedural tradition in which "the accuser is able to take the court's knowledge of the witch's guilt for granted and to base the demand that the god kill the witch simply on his own assertion that she bewitched him" (23).

The volume enriches the familiar courtroom scene of Dan 7 by means of comparison with the Book of Giants from Qumran (in particular, Dan 7:9–10 and 4Q530 2 ii 16–20). Joseph L. Angel's essay (25–48) is a necessarily complex analysis, which also factors in 1 En. 14.18–23 and the influence of Ezek 1. The appropriately cautious conclusion emphasizes the broad influence of common apocalyptic traditions among otherwise distinct groups.

Chaya Halberstam takes the discussion is a new direction (49–68) by discussing the issue of "pure procedural justice" in Sifre Deuteronomy. She takes the phrase from John Rawls, who defined such justice as obtaining when "there is no independent criterion for the right result" (Rawls, *A Theory of Justice* [New York: Oxford University Press, 1999], 74). As Halberstam applies the idea, the rabbis in Sifre saw the divine court in such a way, although she is careful to acknowledge other models (since God's justice is scarcely put aside), but argues that "God's ways are made readable through the discourse of law, and specifically through the discourse of procedural justice" (66). Even this view, however, is corrected in Sifre, by "a personal, affective relationship" between God and Israel, "albeit one mediated by law" (68).

Writing in relation to a later period, Warren Zev Harvey deals with Rabbi Nissim of Girona (ca. 1310–1376) and shows that Ran "held there is always an objectively true or just legal verdict, although he also held that that verdict as such has no legal validity" (69–75, 70). This essay is perfectly placed in relation to the last and develops a sophisticated argument. Even in the heavenly academy, rabbis are portrayed as upholding a stricter ruling than God himself in relation to leprosy, while in regard to justice in this world, Abraham is depicted as arguing for mercy on behalf of Sodom and Gemorrah, on the grounds that sparing the lives of the righteous would be cruel, were their city destroyed.

Job Y. Jindo offers a wide-ranging contribution titled "The Divine Courtroom Motif in the Hebrew Bible: A Holistic Approach" (76–93). He considers the topic as "part of a royal model through which God is conceived of as king, the heavenly council as his royal court, and the universe as his dominion" (76–77). He problematizes the notion of metaphor in this connection, observing that it "evokes the sense of 'projected-ness' and, once applied, the *realness* of the image is instantly diminished" (81). Within the paradigm as a whole, the processes of a divine courtroom find their center of gravity.

Meira Z. Kensky, having provided many examples of the divine courtroom from Judaic and Christian sources in *Trying Man, Trying God*, targets Tertullian's *Apologeticum* in this volume (94–127). She explains how apologetic literature combines "classic forensic apology with deliberative or protreptic elements" (97) by way of setting out Tertullian's rhetoric refinement and address of multiple audiences. Ultimately, in this shifting of perspectives, everything transpires under the eye of God, who takes on the responsibility of final judgment, where "body and soul must be restored together in order to face the music" (123). Resurrection, on this view, is less an anthropological hope than a syllogism of theodicy.

Victor Bers and Adriaan Lannu develop an Olympian perspective not only in their choice of primary sources but also in their decision to proceed by survey rather than focused exegesis. They find in "Disqualified Olympians: The Skeptical Greek View of Divine Judges" (128–44) that the gods may be too self-serving, or too abstracted from the exigencies of narrative, to qualify as good judges but also that "gods, by virtue of their immense power and immortal life, lack the seriousness and urgency mortals bring to the task of judging" (144). This raises the question whether mortality is pure proceduralism in a Hellenic key.

Andrew Lincoln takes up the sole topic in the volume related to the New Testament: "The Life of Jesus as Testimony: The Divine Courtroom and the Gospel of John" (145–66). To his mind it was "the Jewish Scriptures in Greek translation, particularly Deutero-Isaiah, that provide the major literary catalyst for the evangelist's use of the lawsuit motif" (149). The particular feature that attracts Lincoln's attention is that in Deutero-Isaiah "YHWH has become the defendant, the one accused by the Judeans in exile and those remaining in Jerusalem" (150). This process is then the "overarching metaphor" that puts Jesus at the center of a "cosmic trial" in which he and the world are at odds (152–53). That trial was intended to vindicate not only Jesus but also those of his followers who had been ostracized as a result of their belief (160).

An application of divine justice is instanced in the story of Naboth's vineyard (1 Kgs 21:1–22:40 and 2 Kgs 9:1–10:11), as developed in F. Rachel Magdalene's essay (167–245). In this treatment, as in Lincoln's and unlike Jindo's, metaphor is central; indeed, "all literature, it seems to me, is metaphorical, and literature about the goings-on in the heavenly realm can never be anything but both metaphorical and mythological" (169). Magdalene discusses the divine court and the issue of the abuse of authority within Mesopotamian and biblical texts, then applies her findings to the case of Naboth's vineyard. She finds that "Elijah speaks for the court, and the Divine Council begins to exact justice from Ahab" (244). The model is applicable to Job: "even where a single human believes that YHWH, himself, has abused his royal and judicial authority—even if mistakenly—YHWH hears and processes the claim" (245).

Carol A. Newsom take up this topic in a different key in "The Invention of the Divine Courtroom in the Book of Job" (246–59), arguing, "Only in the book of Job is the metaphor for a trial with God developed in a such a fashion that it becomes a potential model for organizing a person's relationship with God" (246). To her mind, the strength of Job involves its function as "*generative* metaphor" (252), but having set that up, in the end the book itself finds that "the notion of a trail at law" with God "is a category mistake of the first order" (258).

Eschatology finds its context in issues of judgment, and Mathieu Tillier develops how eschatological warning informs Muslim jurisprudence. He finds that the image of the *qadi* before the final judge was used "to reform the behavior of he judiciary and of the judicial organization" (260–75, 261). References to the similar ethos of the *Didascalia apostolorum* and like sources (263–64, 266–67) are evocative and invite further consideration. This seems especially interesting in light of comparable Christian and Muslim rhetoric and practice designed to keep judges free of entanglements of power (268–71, 273–74).

Dov Weiss contributes the last essay in the volume (276–88), which deals with "Lawsuits against God in Rabbinic Literature." He finds few examples in Tannaitic texts, because they "prohibit protesting God and God's justice system" (277–78, citing Sifre Deut. 307 and Mekhilta de-Rabbi Ishmael, Beshallah 6). By contrast, Amoraic and post-Amoraic midrashim "intensify the anti-confrontational rhetoric" of the earlier sources (278). Weiss gives the examples of Midrash Tanhuma

(Vayyesa 8), where Leah insists to God that, rather than a son, a daughter (who would be called Dina, "judgment") should be born to her; Eccl. Rab. 4:1, where Elijah teaches deceased children punished for their parents' sins how to appeal to God's mercy; and Song Rab. 2:1, where unmerited salvation for Israelites is withdrawn out of fairness for gentiles who are to be punished (280–85). More "a court of appeals than a lower court" (286), the divine sessions revises God's own judgments.

Although the editors are correct to remark that primary texts are the focus of the volume (2), the secondary literature cited is rich; some readers would wish an index of modern scholars. My only concerns have to do with the unresolved tension over the use of "metaphor" as a designation of the courtroom (and related issues) and the lack of partner papers to the fine contribution on Islam. Each of these essays, written by an expert in the field, is worth considering, and in aggregate they are crucial reading.

Reading a Tendentious Bible: Essays in Honor of Robert B. Coote, edited by Marvin L. Chaney, Uriah Y. Kim, and Annette Schellenberg. Hebrew Bible Monographs 66. Sheffield: Sheffield Phoenix, 2014. Pp. xvi + 333. Hardcover. $120.00. ISBN 9781907534935.

Stewart Moore, Cresskill, New Jersey

There are certain constants in a review of a Festschrift. "The essays are of variable quality"—of course, this is true of almost any collection and does not say much. "There is little sense of unity in the book"—I should hope not, as any scholar whose teaching tree is so boringly one-branched as to make thematization simple is probably not worthy of a dedicated volume in the first place. The real question at issue in a review of a Festschrift is whether the book only has one or two essays you will just scan or whether enough entries are relevant and incisive enough for you to consider purchasing the whole volume. While there is nothing all the essays here have in common, there are only a few themes in all, so that the book does tend to cohere. (This despite the editors' democratic decision to list the contributors alphabetically rather than making these themes explicit in the book's organization.)

The first theme is raised by the editors and some of the contributors: interdisciplinary study. Coote is a polymath and a collaborator (the good kind), and four of these essays clearly reflect this. Two essays offer very basic introductions to fields that can fruitfully be applied to biblical studies. Barbara Green presents some fundamental points of genre studies as it has altered the shape of form criticism, while not losing sight—as those who work with genre sometimes do—of the importance of the distinctiveness of a work. John Elliot provides a brief primer on the social-scientific study of both Testaments (with more weight on the Second than the First), with an extensive bibliography that includes all the most essential references. Both essays will do very well for those seeking a short introduction to these subfields.

Two other scholars apply interdisciplinary work to specific texts. Ronald Hendel uses Maurice Halbwachs's concept of cultural memory, combining it with Anthony Smith's idea of myths of origin as the *mythomoteur* of identity, in order to discuss the exodus and its biblical appropriations. However, it is not entirely clear to me what novelty Halbwachs and Smith add to this discussion: memory and identity are already much remarked upon in studies of the exodus. The final interdisciplinary study is by Annette Schellenberg, who uses anthropologist Victor Turner's concept of liminality, combined with appropriations of this idea in theatrical studies, to reconstruct the effect the Song of Songs would have had on its audience. On Schellenberg's reading, the Song both provokes and contains socially restricted feelings, by producing and then dispelling a liminal place. It would be interesting to see what this implies for a *Sitz im Leben*.

The second of our four trends is somewhat related to interdisciplinarity, in the sense that Coote, a noted Hebrew Bible scholar, has here inspired half a dozen New Testament scholars, mostly his colleagues at San Francisco Theological Seminary. The strongest of these are those of Chris Seeman and Antoinette Clark Wire. Seeman's essay takes up the question of why Luke omits a large and essential chunk of Mark. His answer is that by removing that particular piece Luke has omitted Mark's treatment of a mission to the gentiles, precisely for the purpose of delaying that crucial move until Acts 10. Wire takes up the issue of scriptural quotation in Mark and shows clearly through small errors in citation that Mark quotes the Old Greek from memory, not with a text in front of him. This will have interesting consequences for early Christian and Jewish engagements with their authoritative texts.

One New Testament essay brings up an old problem. Herman Waetjen discusses John the Baptist by attempting to contextualize him in a supposed priest-versus-prophet conflict running throughout Second Temple Judaism. The priests, specifically, enforce the purity codes and eventually silence the prophets, until prophets erupt again in millenarian movements that critique the priests. This is a difficult thesis to maintain in the face of the obviously priestly millenarian community of the Yaḥad, which demonstrates no such dichotomy. Further, the division smacks of the old Christianity/morality versus Judaism/purity discourse, which I am sure is not Waetjen's intention, but it remains problematic.

In other essays Eugene Park expands on Gerald Downing's treatment of the resemblances between early Christian missionaries and itinerant Cynics to discuss Jesus's puzzling prohibitions in Matt 10 and Annette Weissenrieder urges us to turn away from a search for a single source, such as a Roman coin, for the image of the woman Babylon in Rev 17 and to focus instead on how John of Patmos constructs the very act of seeing. The last New Testament essay is that of Rev. Chandler Stokes, who produces a charming homiletical exegesis for translating *ekballō* in Mark's description of Peter's reaction to the second cockcrow. The essay is evidence of Coote's broad reach as a teacher and reflects on them both well. It is also a reminder of how much biblical scholarship has yet to do in order to have any real effect on life in our places of worship.

To match the six essays on the New Testament, there are six essays (what other number could there be?) on the Hebrew Bible that are in a less interdisciplinary mode. To begin again with the strongest, Mary Wogec takes up an old assumption—that mother-goddesses are the most invoked in the context of birth—and weighs it against Sumerian and Akkadian ritual texts. In that light, it is clear that healing gods, whatever their gender, are appealed to during birth, not mother-goddesses. The essay is accompanied by a full table of all the relevant texts and is thus an excellent resource for similar studies, such as those investigating women's devotion to YHWH. Emanuel Tov dips into his near-bottomless well of textual-critical knowledge to draw out two interesting observations about the Torah/Pentateuch: legal material shows much less scribal intervention than narrative; the Torah shows so many textual variants not in spite of its holiness but because of it. I would have liked to see these two insights squared, as they seem to me to be in some tension. In other essays Aaron Brody attempts to correlate a specifically Judean ethnic identity at Iron II Tell en-Nasbeh, one inflected by contact with Assyrian imperialism, with the archaeological record of the site, and Uriah Kim discusses the figure of personified feminine evil in 4Q184 and how that text amplifies the language of "Lady Folly" in Prov 1–8 to make her a more formidable conceptual opponent.

The last two Hebrew Bible essays are those of Sarah Schectman and Marvin Chaney. These two are joined by the fact that they both seek to make an intervention in the real world outside biblical studies, which builds a bridge to the last trend in this volume. Schectman surveys the biblical evidence for marriage practices, most of which is quite familiar. The argument she wants to make is that Israelite marriage was a secular custom, not a religious one. I wish that Schectman had spelled out explicitly what consequence this has for the gay-marriage debates she cites in her opening. Chaney's essay returns to well-watered ground in the economic life reflected by the eighth-century prophets. In interpreting the famous charge by Amos that the rich are selling the poor for a pair of sandals, Chaney follows the custom mentioned in Ruth of exchanging sandals upon the conclusion of a bargain in order to argue that one of the things the word "sandals" can mean is a debt instrument. The paranomasia Chaney thus finds in the surrounding verses is detailed and irreducibly literary. This would seem to have consequences for the relationship between the prophet and his text, but these are not drawn out.

The fourth and final theme I find running through this Festschrift is the inveterate, if always stimulating, debate between "maximalists" and "minimalists." Coote having written an important intervention in this debate, *The Emergence of Israel* with Keith Whitelam, this volume is as good a place as any for the next phase of the argument, and three essays take it up. Norman Gottwald begins the discussion by pointing out a truth that is little respected: both sides have a different "teleology"; that is, they are trying to accomplish very different things by their research. Only by making our perspectives and commitments clear, and respecting those of others, can we hope to advance the conversation.

Keith Whitelam contributes a provocative and passionate essay wherein he argues that Mahmoud Ahmadinejad, Israel Finkelstein, and Avraham Faust all have something in common—most surprising! They all assume that the way a nation justifies its existence is by having a history of centralized state rule on the land. All three understand Israel's relationship to such a state in very different ways, of course, but he argues the assumption is still there. This raises the question of what else would justify a nation's existence. Whitelam provides no answer, but this seems to be that rare place where biblical scholars might actually be able to bring something to bear on an intransigent political problem.

Finally, Ernst Knauf takes up Whitelam's challenge from his *The Invention of Ancient Israel* to consider whether a "history of Palestine" could be written. He takes a phenomenological stance: the area south of Syria has throughout history only fitfully been called Palestine, and usually not by a people who would have considered themselves "Palestinians." Thus, Israel cannot "give back" Palestine to the Palestinians because the Palestinians never had it in the first place. Yet Knauf thinks Israel should and will give Palestine to the Palestinians anyway and thus incorporate a state with no prior history. Knauf at least is operating with a different idea of how a state's existence is justified. He does not draw out what that is, but it is in this *aporia*, I think, that the truth lies.

In sum, *Reading a Tendentious Bible* has several good essays, and if you are a polymath like Coote with his interests and commitments, then you may find it worth your while to have this volume on your shelf as well.

By Bread Alone: The Bible through the Eyes of the Hungry, edited by Sheila E. McGinn, Lai Ling Elizabeth Ngan, and Ahida Calderón Pilarski. Minneapolis: Fortress, 2014. Pp. xii + 257. Paper. $29.00. ISBN 9781451465501.

Vicky Balabanski, Flinders University of South Australia

The reality of hunger is the impetus for this collection of essays addressing both a scholarly and a wider audience. The volume comprises ten essays as well as a foreword and introduction, drawn together through reflection on hunger: hunger as a contemporary reality and challenge, hunger as a topic and theme in biblical and extracanonical writings, hunger in its physical and spiritual dimensions, hunger as a *pars pro toto* for poverty, hunger as a consequence of drought and warfare, and hunger as a hermeneutical entry point and lens. As the introduction articulates, "the basic purpose of all the essays is to help the contemporary, first-world reader develop a different field of vision for the biblical texts—one that sees and hears those who hunger, both those mentioned or intimated in the texts and those in our own world today" (6).

The essays are diverse in their methods and foci, yet along with hunger itself, there are other unifying factors to the collection. Many of them stand within the ambit of Catholic social teaching, addressing themselves to contemporary realities in ways that are useful both to the Roman Catholic and other church traditions.

Many of the essays are feminist in their approach and perspective. Some are written by scholars who have firsthand experience of disadvantaged communities and grass-roots engagement with the hungry.

The title is intended to be provocative, jolting the reader to recognize that Jesus's saying about not living by bread alone is misunderstood if it is not read alongside his feedings of the multitudes (2). The subtitle *The Bible through the Eyes of the Hungry* is also to be taken somewhat figuratively, as the authors refract the perspective of the hungry rather than being hungry themselves. There are hints at communal exegesis, but such exegesis predates the written contributions and is not as visible as one might have hoped from the introduction.

The collection was inspired by Kathleen O'Connor's 2009 Presidential Address to the members of the Catholic Biblical Association of America, and this is included as the first chapter. O'Connor draws on Dorothy Sölle's phrase "hermeneutics of hunger," which is also picked up explicitly in the essays by Mary Ann Beavis and Susan M. Elliot. O'Connor's essay is both a nuanced hermeneutical conversation and a careful reading of Gen 11:1–9. In it she seeks to protect the text's strangeness and to value a diversity of readings. Resisting the imposition of uniformity, she takes the baffling of Babel and the scattering positively. It is an elegant and persuasive piece, though the "hermeneutics of hunger" are somewhat kaleidoscopic; at times they seem very close to feminist and postcolonial insights, at others closer to a figurative or spiritual hermeneutical lens. This may be in keeping with the emphasis on contextualization, but it requires a hermeneutical nimbleness that is hard to pin down and hard to replicate.

The essays proceed in something like canonical order. J. L. Manzo offers a study of Isa 58:1–9a with particular focus on the themes of fasting and true worship. Hunger through fasting is a means of opening oneself to the work of God, but this hunger is of no use if it is not matched with love of neighbor. Manzo explores the scriptural provisions for feeding the hungry and with reference to Deut 23:24–25 sets out some important insights in relation to the theology of property: "the right of the human person to receive nourishment takes preceden[ce] over the rights of the property owner. The law, however, does acknowledge the rights of the landlord by prohibiting the removal of provision from the field" (46). Feeding the hungry is shown to be rendering justice, not by bringing everyone to the same economic level but by creating a community of inclusion, humility, and generosity.

Carol J. Dempsey explores hunger not only as a social problem but as an ecological one by examining Jer 14:1–9 with a focus on the implications of drought. She broadens the scope of hunger to notice the animals, herbage, and the ground itself. This text lends itself readily to contextualizing the issues in a contemporary context, but with a caveat that "today's droughts are not the result of divine chastisement" but "of humankind's transgressions flowing from greed, the inordinate use of power, the need to dominate and control, and a failure to care for the common good in a way that is genuine, life giving and life sustaining" (63). Corporate power brokers are particularly in view (65).

The most graphic biblical depiction of starvation is found in the book of Lamentations. Lauress L. Wilkins looks at starvation and famine as a consequence of warfare and as a military strategy. The theological ambiguity of YHWH as Divine Warrior who "devours" the starving inhabitants of Jerusalem develops a rhetoric of hunger, as does the shocking imagery of mothers eating their children in Lam 2:20b. Wilkins articulates the psychosocial dehumanization of Jerusalem's survivors and draws out implications for Catholic social teaching on modern warfare.

After this essay it is something of a relief to turn to the quiet comfort of Ben Sira. Bradley C. Gregory explores the role of hunger in Ben Sira's thought, drawing out similarities to and differences from Proverbs. Ben Sira and his students are encouraged to enjoy the finer things of life, but in moderation. They are not to take their present comfort for granted. For the sage, "wealth is not necessarily a sign of God's blessing; rather, it is a good thing only if it has been acquired righteously. It is striking in this regard that Ben Sira does not blame the poor/hungry for their own condition" (102). He also places no qualifications on assistance to the needy. Gregory shows that Ben Sira "decouples issues of hunger and poverty from the standard sapiential retributive rhetoric concerning laziness and diligence" (110), leaving the reader to draw out the hermeneutical implications of this insight.

In Mary Ann Beavis's essay on Mark's feeding narratives we glimpse something of the communal exegesis behind this essay and the work of the CBA Feminist Biblical Hermeneutics Task Force. She brings the local context of Saskatoon, a small Canadian prairie city, into view prior to her discussion of the Markan material, then connects the ancient and contemporary narratives through a hermeneutic of hunger. Beavis's Markan scholarship is widely known through her commentary in the Paideia series, and this essay is an excellent demonstration of hunger as both a thematic and hermeneutical key.

Linda Maloney gives a short interpretation of Luke's friend at midnight (Luke 11:1–10), inviting us to notice the absence of the woman from the story and wondering whether she will bear the shame for not providing for her family. It invites reflection on property, generosity, and justice—who really bears the cost in the story, and how can this be preached so that it can be heard by those who "have many possessions" (133).

Susan M. Elliott explores logion 97 from the Gospel of Thomas, a saying that likens the "kingdom" to a woman carrying a jar full of meal who walks a distant road only to find as she reaches her house that the handle had broken, the meal spilled out, and the jar empty. In this fascinating essay Elliott challenges us to stare with the woman into the empty jar, to see with God's eyes the reality of physical hunger, also to find freedom in the ability not to consume.

The volume would not be complete without some Pauline studies. Ma. Marilou S. Ibita examines 1 Cor 11:17–34. Using narrative-critical approaches, she argues that Paul advocates that the Lord's Supper (*kyriakon deipnon*) must include the hungry have-nots and that the reference to eating *en oikō* in verse 34 does not mean at home (beforehand) but "in the house" as part of the supper itself.

The final essay, by Sheila E. McGinn and Megan Wilson-Reitz, a fitting conclusion to the collection, persuasively rereads the "idlers" (*ataktoi*) of 2 Thess 3:6–15 not as lazy workers hoping for a free meal but as social climbers who cling to the Roman patronage system and are unwilling to relinquish their privilege of avoiding manual labor.

The collection made me freshly—at times uncomfortably—conscious of the cycle of meals and snacks that I consumed while reading it and of the privileged context in which I live and in which I read and reflect on the biblical texts. I hope that others will share the invitation that this collection offers; I will be inviting students and church leaders to glimpse the text in fresh ways through these essays and to draw on the prophetic and homiletical potential of these perspectives.

Empowering Memory and Movement: Thinking and Working across Borders, by Elisabeth Schüssler Fiorenza. Minneapolis: Fortress, 2014. Pp. xviii + 535. Paper. $49.00. ISBN 9781451481815.

Barbara E. Reid, O.P., Catholic Theological Union

This book is the last in a three-volume project that collects the pioneering feminist critical work of Schüssler Fiorenza. The previous volumes gathered her feminist theological essays (*Transforming Vision*, 2011) and her exegetical and hermeneutical work (*Changing Horizons*, 2013). This final volume traces and locates her work "in the context of a transnational border crossing movement" (xiii). It is "at once an autobiographical and a systemic exploration of both the interface of memory as heritage and as scientific history as well as that of interpretation, movement, and sociopolitical location" (1). Twenty-five of the thirty-four essays have been previously published.

Part 1, "Crossing Borders," begins with an interview with Fernando F. Segovia entitled "Looking Back, Looking Around, Looking Ahead" (17–48), which was first published in a volume edited by Segovia on the occasion of Schüssler Fiorenza's sixty-fifth birthday (*Toward a New Heaven and a New Earth: Essays in Honor of Elisabeth Schüssler Fiorenza* [Maryknoll, NY: Orbis, 2003]). It sets the stage well for the volume, as it highlights the crossings of many borders that have typified Schüssler Fiorenza's work: national, gender and class, disciplinary, methodological, and theoretical. In "Resident Alien/Dual Citizen" (49–64), Schüssler Fiorenza draws on her experiences of racism and nationalism as German and American and proposes that feminist theology must be a resident alien, not at home in establishment theology, whether in universities or churches, and must be as a "native who has moved in," laying claim to the academy and religion as its own and shape them in the direction of liberation (63). In "Fostering Diversity Studies at Harvard Divinity School" (65–73), Schüssler Fiorenza guides students to understand the importance of diversity studies without losing focus on the struggles of wo/men who remain at "the bottom of the global kyriarchal pyramid of exploitation" (73). (Schüssler Fiorenza uses "wo/men" to call attention to the problem of understanding woman in essentialist terms of feminine gender rather than in sociopolitical terms. This fractured form also indicates that women are "not a homogenous social group but are fragmented through structures of race, class, ethnicity, religion, heterosexuality, colonialism, and age" [2 n. 3]. Marginalized men can also be included in this term.) "On Becoming a Feminist Biblical Scholar" (75–89) is an autobiographical reflection that begins with an articulation of the challenges this genre poses for women scholars and concludes with a summary of the four paradigms of biblical interpretation Schüssler Fiorenza has developed that aim to open up opportunities for liberation. In "Feminist Studies in Religion and The*logy between Nationalism and Globalization" (91–100), Schüssler Fiorenza shows how nationalism, gender, and religion are intertwined and how that calls for transnational discourse strategies in feminist the*logy and studies in religion that challenge kyriarchal globalization. (Schüssler Fiorenza uses the*logy to alert readers to the problem of reinscribing gender—Greek *theos* and theology being masculine-defined—while the Divine transcends gender.) "Changing the Paradigms" (101–10) is Schüssler Fiorenza's response to an invitation to write about "how my mind has changed." She sketches not only methodological changes developed over three decades but also the decisive influence on her work from her change in geographical location and academic institution. A lecture tour in Japan prompted "Visiting Japan" (111–31), in which Schüssler Fiorenza explores how the biblical figure of Divine Wisdom and the Asian figure Divine Kannon provide both possibilities and problems for Christian G*d-language and images. "Has G*d Not Spoken with Us Also?" (133–44) contains Schüssler Fiorenza's remarks on the occasion of being presented with an honorary doctorate from the Katholisch-Theologische Fakultät der Universität Würzburg. Her critical rhetorical analysis of texts concerning Miriam lead to reflections on the exclusion of women in academic theology, churches, mosques, and synagogues.

Part 2, "Memory and Movement: History as Heritage," opens with an interview by Annie Lally Milhaven, "The Inside Stories" (147–64), in which Schüssler Fiorenza describes and critiques various directions in the feminist movement in Roman Catholicism and calls for the creation of women-church. In "Beginnings" (165–85) Schüssler Fiorenza shows that it is not only in later years, but from the very start, that "feminist scholars in religion have produced variegated theoretical discourses and developed fruitful new methods, strategies and approaches" (184). In "Feminist The*logy and The*logical Education" (187–91) Schüssler Fiorenza memorializes Sr. Helen Wright, S.N.D., who gathered Catholic feminist theologians in 1978–1980 to discuss feminist theological education. Writing in 2012, Schüssler Fiorenza outlines the great need that still exists for this, as the Catholic feminist movement has had primarily a liturgical and social-justice focus. "Feminist Studies in Religion and a Radical Democratic Ethos" (193–216) was originally delivered in South Africa in 1994 and speaks of the importance of political bases for alliance and the potential for feminist studies in religion to bring about radical democratic transformation of the university. "Feminist Perspectives on Jesus,

Discipleship, and Church" (217–21) is an interview from 1997 with Robert A. Becker, director of public affairs at the National Cathedral in Washington, DC. Schüssler Fiorenza addresses feminist perspectives on the crucifixion, the role of women in Jesus's time, and discipleship of equals, among other christological topics. "Movement Struggles, Wisdom Places, Dreaming Spaces" (223–34) was an address given on the twentieth anniversary of the European Society of Women in Theological Research. Schüssler Fiorenza rallies feminists across the globe to dream together so as to bring about justice and well-being for all. "An Interview with Yoke-Heng Woon for *In God's Image*" (235–49) was given by Schüssler Fiorenza in 2005 while giving lectures and workshops sponsored by the Asian Women's Resource Centre for Culture and Theology in Kuala Lumpur. In "Our Heritage Is Our Power" (251–64), an address given in Chicago in celebration of Wo/men's History Month, Schüssler Fiorenza reflects on the nineteenth-century roots of US feminist biblical studies. This part concludes with an interview conducted by Schüssler Fiorenza's longtime friend and colleague Judith Plaskow on the occasion of Schüssler Fiorenza's reception of the AAR Martin Marty award for Public Understanding of Religion ("'AAR Martin Marty Award' Conversation with Judith Plaskow," 265–89). It traces Schüssler Fiorenza's personal journey to becoming a feminist scholar, outlines the contributions she has made in her books, and concludes with advice for graduate students.

Part 3, "Memory and Theory: Quilting Feminist History," begins with an interview with Alice Bach that originally appeared in the journal *Biblicon* in 1998, using the image of quilting as a hermeneutical key for history writing ("Biblicon Interview with Alice Bach," 293–313). "Re-visioning Christian Origins: *In Memory of Her Revisited*" (315–38) examines the quest for Christian origins as a search for identity and understands its potential to function as a radical critique of prevailing power relations. In "The Quilting of Wo/men's History" (339–50), Schüssler Fiorenza uses Phoebe of Kenchreae to explore how women's early Christian history was produced and transmitted. She proposes replacing the popular understanding of historiographer as one who conveys an objective and unbiased account of the past with that of a "quilt maker fitting together the surviving scraps of historical information into an overall design that gives meaning to the individual pieces" (339–40). "Looking Back and Looking Forward" (351–55) records Schüssler Fiorenza's reflections when she was presented with three different Festschriften to mark her sixty-fifth birthday at the AAR/SBL Annual Meeting in 2003. The ninetieth birthday of Catharina Halkes was the occasion for "Celebrating Feminist Work by Knowing It" (357–66). Schüssler Fiorenza sees such occasions not primarily as celebrations of individuals but as an opportunity to recognize publicly the significance of feminist scholarship and to galvanize feminist scholars for the work that lies ahead. In "Reaffirming Feminist/Womanist Biblical Scholarship" (367–76), Schüssler Fiorenza aims to help "feminists of all colors" to understand how far feminist/womanist biblical studies has come in order to move to a more just future. Schüssler Fiorenza's reception of the Catholic Library Association's Jerome Award was the occasion for "Reviewing my Work in a Roman Catholic Context" (377–81). "Shaping the Discipline: The Rhetoricity/ Rhetoricality of N*T Studies" (383–402) elaborates how critical rhetorical analysis of biblical texts reveals their part in creating and legitimating structures of oppression and domination or engendering sociopolitical acts of liberation. Schüssler Fiorenza shows how ethics and political responsibility are integral to interpretation of Scripture and historical reconstruction.

Part 4, "Scripture as Site of Memory, Struggle, and Vision," sets forth Schüssler Fiorenza's understanding of Scripture "as a site of memory where struggles take place and empowering visions are articulated" (405). It opens with an interview with Michael Norton entitled "Critical Reflections on Philosophy and The*ology" (405–11). In "Biblical Interpretation in the Context of Church and Ministry" (413–21), Schüssler Fiorenza articulates how critical feminist liberationist biblical scholarship needs to become central in empowering Christian ministry "to serve the well-being of an emerging global world society" (421). In "Wo/men in the Pre-Pauline and Pauline Churches" (423–46), Schüssler Fiorenza examines three outstanding women in the Corinthian community—Chloe, Prisca, and Phoebe—as well as their understanding of their faith in terms of Hellenistic-Jewish speculation about Wisdom. The injunctions for women in 1 Corinthians are to be understood in the context of women's leadership in the early Christian communities. "Slave Wo/men and Freedom" (447–70) explores slave women and their struggles in early Christianity and the crippling results when "slavery, submission and obedience—not freedom, equality, and justice" (470) became institutionalized in the church. The book of Revelation has long been an interest and field of research for Schüssler Fiorenza. In "The Apocalypse of John" (471–81), she analyzes apocalyptic language and imagination, imperial counterlanguage, and misogyny and anti-Judaism, then concludes with a hermeneutical reflection on hearing what the Spirit says to us today. In "The Cross as a Central Christian Symbol of Injustice" (483–89), Schüssler Fiorenza advocates that the symbol of the cross not be rejected but that it help us retell the story of Jesus "in terms of justice and not just in terms of internalized love" (483). In "'I Have Not Come to Bring Peace but a Sword' (Matthew 10:34)" (491–511), Schüssler Fiorenza explores how the ideology of the *pax Romana* shaped Christian texts and worldviews, which in turn continues to shape the *pax Americana*. She argues that "peace with justice can be established only in and through the struggles to transform kyriarchal structures and institutions of domination and not through conflict resolution and the transformation of conflict, which leaves its structural kyriarchal underpinnings intact" (511). "The Calling of Mary of Magdala and Our Own" (513–17) is a sermon given by Schüssler Fiorenza at St. Clements in Honolulu in 2006 that invites all to embrace the call into a discipleship of equals as exemplified by Mary of Magdala. The final essay, "Toward a Feminist Future of the Biblical Past" (519–35), provides an apt conclusion, as Schüssler Fiorenza describes the various accents with which she speaks: the*logical, feminist, and emancipatory. She concludes with a rearticulation of her emancipatory paradigms of interpretation and a call for commensurate action that creates conditions for the realization of the biblical visions of liberation and well-being for all.

This collection of essays is a goldmine. It is a compendium of Schüssler Fiorenza's work that is not simply a haphazard collection of unrelated materials; there is a coherence and logic to the three volumes. Some essays have not appeared before in English, and it is a great benefit to English speakers to have them translated for this collection. While there is repetition and overlap, both with the first two volumes and within this one, because of the complexity and depth of Schüssler Fiorenza's thought, most readers will appreciate the repetition, which aids with understanding and retention. While there is historical retrospective, the essays are all still most timely. Recontextualized, they take on fresh meaning. While there have been great advances in critical feminist liberationist work, there is still so much that remains to be done. In Schüssler Fiorenza's words, remembering the past is critical to creating the future.

'Der Herr des Himmels möge lang machen seine Tage und seine Jahre': Religionsgeschichtliche Beiträge; Festschrift für Herbert Niehr zum 60. Geburtstag, edited by Oliver Dyma, Stefanie-Ulrike Gulde-Karmann, and Dagmar Kühn. Alter Orient und Altes Testament 427. Münster: Ugarit-Verlag, 2015. Pp. x + 225. Hardcover. €98.00. ISBN 9783868351712.

Markus Witte, Humboldt-Universität

Mit dem vorliegenden Band ehren Schüler und Doktoranden den an der katholisch-theologischen Fakultät der Eberhard-Karls-Universität zu Tübingen tätigen Alttestamentler Herbert Niehr anlässlich seines 60. Geburtstages. Entsprechend der großen Vielfalt der von dem Jubilar in Forschung und Lehre bearbeiteten Felder enthält die Sammlung Beiträge aus der alttestamentlichen Exegese, der Geschichte Israels und des alten Orients, der nordwestsemitischen Epigraphik und Ikonographie sowie der Religionsgeschichte Phöniziens und Syriens. Jedem der nach Verfassern und Verfasserinnen alphabetisch angeordneten Beiträge ist eine Bibliographie beigegeben. Im Einzelnen enthält der Band folgende Aufsätze:

Florence Berg, „Die vergessene Hauptstadt. Zur Stellung Samarias in der politischen Organisation Israels zur Zeit der Omriden (1. Hälfte 9. Jh. v. Chr.)" (1–28), bietet auf der Basis ihrer Diplomarbeit aus dem Jahr 2014 einen Überblick über die Topographie, Geographie, Archäologie, Soziologie und Ökonomie Samarias. Als wesentliche Faktoren für den Ausbau eines ehemaligen Landgutes zur königlichen Residenz durch die Omriden werden wirtschaftliche und verkehrstechnische Gründe bestimmt.

Hanswulf Bloedhorn, „Julius Euting in Palmyra. Zur Entdeckung der hebräischen Haustürinschriften" (29–44), skizziert anhand ausgewählter Tagebuchnotizen die Reise des deutschen Theologen, Bibliothekars und Orientalisten Euting im Jahr 1882 nach Palmyra sowie die Geschichte seiner Entdeckung und

Identifikation hebräischer Inschriften mit Passagen aus Dtn 6,4–9; 7,14–15; 28,5. Dabei wird auch diskutiert, dass das Gebäude, dem die entsprechende Türrahmung zuzuweisen ist, ursprünglich ein Privathaus aus dem 2. Jh. n. Chr. war, das im 4. Jh. zu einer Synagoge umgebaut wurde. Dem Beitrag sind Abbildungen aus dem Tagebuch Eutings, Zeichnungen und Fotografien der Inschriften sowie ein Grundriss und Fotografien der Synagoge in Palmyra beigegeben.

Oliver Dyma, „Sacharja im Beschwörungskontext. Zu ungewöhnlichen Rezeptionen des Sacharja-Buches" (45–69), beschreibt, ausgehend von einer Exegese von Sach 3,1–10, die rezeptionsgeschichtliche Entwicklung der Figur des Satans „von einer vermutlich menschlichen Figur mit besonderen Aufgaben am Jerusalemer Tempel zu einer Figur der himmlischen Sphäre hin zum Anführer der dämonischen Mächte, derer man sich durch Exorzismen und magische Instrumente zu erwehren suchte" (64). Auch wenn man der These, dass der Satan („der Ankläger") in Sach 3,1–2 ursprünglich ein menschlicher Funktionsträger war, nicht zustimmen mag, so zeigt der Beitrag doch sehr schön religionsgeschichtliche Entwicklungen im Bereich der jüdischen Dämonologie von der Hebräischen Bibel über Schriften aus Qumran (1QGenAp XX, 28–29) und das Henochschrifttum bis hin zu spätantiken/frühmittelalterlichen aramäischen Zauberschalen.

Dagmar Kühn, „The King's Two Bodies (E. Kantorowicz). Ein Konzept zum Verständnis des hellenistischen Herrscherkults im Vorderen Orient am Beispiel Antiochos I. von Kommagene" (71–90), wendet die von dem Mediävisten Ernst Kantorowicz (1895–1963) entwickelte These eines natürlichen, sterblichen und eines übernatürlichen, unsterblichen Leibs des Königs auf die altorientalische und ägyptische Königsvorstellung an. Am Beispiel von Stelen des Antiochos I. von Kommagene (69–36 v. Chr.), unter anderem mit der Darstellung des opfernden Königs vor der Gottheit (*dexiosis*-Relief), sowie an Antiochos' Grabmal auf dem *Nemrud Daği* verdeutlicht sie das Verschmelzen spezifisch altorientalischer und griechischer Traditionen, aber auch spezifischer Ausprägungen der Herrscherideologie des Antiochos.

Matthias Lange, „Umgang mit den Toten in Marquas/Gurgum" (91–110), gibt einen instruktiven Überblick über die funerären Traditionen im syro-hethitischen Königreich Gurgum bzw. seiner Hauptstadt Marquas und seiner Beziehungen zum benachbarten Sam'al. Die mit Ausnahme der phönizisch-assyrischen-luwischen Trilingue auf der İncirli-Stele durchgehend hieroglyphen-luwischen Stelen-Inschriften aus dem 10.—8. Jh. v. Chr. werden historisch verortet sowie ausführlich epigraphisch und ikonographisch diskutiert. Neben strukturellen Parallelen zu entsprechenden Objekten aus Sam'al und Karkemiš lässt sich für Gurgum ein eigenständiges religiöses Symbolsystem im Blick auf den Umgang mit den Toten aufweisen.

Sarah Lange, „Inszenierung eines Familienrituals für die Könige von Akkad. Das *kispum* im Text Mari 12803" (111–26), interpretiert das in dem im Aufsatztitel genannten Mari-Text beschriebene *kispum* des Königs Jasmaḫ-Adad (1795–1776 v. Chr.) für die akkadischen Herrscher Sargon (2334 v. Chr.) und Narām-Sin

(2254–2218 v. Chr.), in dem auch die nomadischen amurritischen Stämme der Ḫanäer und Numḫäer erwähnt werden, als ein zwecks Legitimation des eigenen Thronanspruchs eingeführtes Familienritual. Dabei werden sowohl die verschiedenen Erwähnungen für das *kispum* in Mari als eines für die individuell bekannten Toten begangenen Rituals vorgestellt als auch die unterschiedlichen Dimensionen von Erinnern, Erinnerung und Gedächtnis in dem speziellen *kispum* des Jasmaḫ-Adad herausgearbeitet und dessen Bedeutung für den König und die Teilnehmer an diesem Kultakt rekonstruiert.

Philipp Maier, „ ‚Child Sacrifice' Customs in Ancient Israel and Phoenicia?" (127–42), referiert aus seiner unpublizierten MA-Dissertation, die er im Jahr 2012 an der University of Sheffield eingereicht hat, die These, dass weder der textliche noch der archäologische Befund für die Annahme eines Kinderopfers im alten Israel und in Phönizien sprächen. Bei den immer wieder als „Kinderopfer" angesprochenen Riten, die in der Hebräischen Bibel erwähnt werden, handele es sich um Fruchtbarkeitsriten im Kontext des Totenkults, bei dem Kinder und Feuer eine besondere Rolle spielten. Der punische Terminus *mlk* und die Verhältnisse in Karthago ließen sich nicht unmittelbar auf Israel und den vorderen Orient anwenden. Leider wird der Name des Vaters der These, derzufolge das hebräische Wort *molekh* mit dem punischen Begriff *molk/mulk* zu verbinden und als Opferbegriff zu verstehen sei, Otto Eissfeldt (1887–1973), durchgehend falsch geschrieben. Zudem ist eine ganze Reihe neuerer einschlägiger Untersuchungen nicht berücksichtigt. Beigegeben sind fünf Abbildungen von phönizischen und punischen Grabstelen.

Henrike Michelau, „Der Aspekt der (persönlichen) Frömmigkeit in der Waagschale des Lebens. Zur Deutung der hellenistischen Adorantendarstellungen in der Sepulkralkunst" (143–58), weist am Beispiel der Ikonographie der Yehawmilk-Stele aus Byblos aus dem 5. Jh. v. Chr. und phönizischer Adorantendarstellungen auf Grabstelen aus dem 4. bis 2. Jh. v. Chr. den Wandel religiöser Vorstellungen nach, die gleichsam im Kontext politischer und sozialer Veränderungen stehen. So tritt an die Stelle der Darstellung des Herrschers vor der Gottheit eine einzelne betende oder opfernde Privatperson. Der sorgfältigen epigraphischen und ikonographischen Analyse gehen grundsätzliche religionsgeschichtliche Überlegungen zum Begriff der „persönlichen Frömmigkeit" voran und folgen sieben Zeichnungen der Yehawmilk-Stele sowie diverser phönizischer und punischer Adoranten und Opfertierträger.

Angela Rohrmoser, „Das ‚Widderhorn' in der Webtechnik des Kivrim und als Ornament des Alten Orients" (159–74), zeigt exemplarisch die Bedeutung von Textilien in der experimentellen Archäologie auf. Die Verwendung des „Widderhorns" im Brettchenweben bei Turkstämmen bestätigt eine grundsätzlich in der Ornamentik zu beobachtende hohe Konstanz hinsichtlich der Motivik und Herstellungstechnik innerhalb eines kulturellen Großraums bei gleichzeitigen regionalen und ethnischen Besonderheiten. Ursprünglich habe das „Widderhorn" eine magische Funktion besessen und als sakrales Kennzeichen gedient. Sieben Abbildungen illustrieren die begrifflich wohl auf eine semitische Wurzel *k-b-r* zurückgehende Technik des Brettchenwebens sowie unterschiedliche Verwendungsstoffe und Bildträger für das „Widderhorn" und den „Doppelwirbel".

Gabriele Theuer, „ ,Ihr sollt erkennen, dass ich JHWH bin' (Ex 6,7). Zur Rede von Gott in der Exoduserzählung. Implikationen für unser Sprechen von Gott" (175–96), bietet einen Überblick über verschiedene Gottesbilder in der alttestamentlichen Exodusdarstellung, die sie im Wesentlichen als eine zwischen dem 7. und dem 5. Jh. v. Chr. entstandene Komposition betrachtet und theologisch in der Mitte des Alten Testaments verortet. Der weitgehend deskriptive Durchgang durch die Themen *Offenbarung des Gottesnamens, Plagen als Zeichen und Wunder, Erkenntnis Gottes im Meerwunder, Exilserfahrung als Korrektur von Gottesvorstellungen* und *Bilderverbot* mündet in dem Plädoyer, entsprechend der Vielfalt und Dynamik der alttestamentlichen Sprachbilder „von Gott in Dichotomien" zu sprechen (193).

Joanna Töyräänvuori, „The Beloved as a Title of Royal Legitimation in Ugaritic and Biblical Texts" (197–217), diskutiert das ugaritische Epitheton *mdd il ym* in KTU 1.1 IV 9–32 sowie weitere Belege für das semantische Cluster *mdd, ydd, hdd, dd* und *dwd* im Nordwestsemitischen und im biblischen Hebräisch. Sie kommt zu dem Ergebnis, dass diese Begriffe einen Ersatznamen für den erwählten Kronprinzen darstellten, mittels derer dieser als Geliebter der Gottheit, die das entsprechende Königtum beschützt, bezeichnet worden sei. Dabei habe die königliche Titulatur der Könige von Jamchad, erstmals belegt für Abba-el (etwa 1750–1720 v. Chr.), Pate gestanden. Von dort sei es sowohl nach Ugarit eingedrungen als auch vom alten Israel übernommen worden. Dementsprechend sei auch der Name David (*dwd*) wie der Name Jedidja (*ydydy[h]* (vgl. 2Sam 12,24–25) als Epitheton mit der Bedeutung „der Geliebte" zu deuten.

Ein Gesamtregister, gegliedert nach Sachen, Göttern/Engeln/Dämonen, Personen/ Stämmen/Völkern, Orten/Regionen/Ländern, Bibelstellen, antiken Texten sowie Inschriften und Bildquellen (219–25), beschließt die lesenswerte Anthologie, die für jeden, der an der Kultur- und Religionsgeschichte des alten vorderen Orients interessiert ist, etwas enthält.

Beware the Evil Eye: The Evil Eye in the Bible and the Ancient World: Volume 1: Introduction, Mesopotamia, and Egypt, by John H. Elliott. Eugene, OR: Cascade, 2015. Pp. xiv + 210. Paper. $25.00. ISBN 9781620321478.

Nicole L. Tilford, Atlanta, Georgia

New Testament scholar John H. Elliott is known for his research on evil-eye beliefs in the ancient world. In this book, the first of a four-volume set, Elliott returns to the subject. Although his ultimate goal is to understand references to evil-eye beliefs in the Bible (see vol. 3 in the set), in this volume Elliott treats the ancient Mesopotamian and Egyptian evidence in its own right. In doing so, he has created a helpful resource that biblical studies scholars can refer to when examining the cultural context behind the evil-eye beliefs in the Bible.

The first volume begins with a general introduction (ch. 1) to the evil eye phenomenon around the world. Here Elliott defines *evil eye* as the belief that "certain individuals … possess an eye whose powerful glance or gaze can harm or destroy any object, animate or inanimate, on which it falls" (3). He then surveys the belief throughout time, discusses the belief's key features, and reviews previous scholarship on the topic. In keeping with his other works, Elliott approaches his subject from a social-scientific perspective. For Elliott, the evil eye is not a magical superstition or a psychological illness but rather "a vivid indicator of social relations and interpersonal dynamics" (4). Individuals who possessed the evil eye, he argues, were typically social outsiders (widows, strangers, and the like), and their victims were the young or those undergoing social transition (birth, marriage, death). They lived in societies with limited goods, high mortality rate, and fierce competition between social classes. They were the victims and perpetrators of envy, power, and fear.

The second half of the volume (ch. 2) takes these basic insights and applies them to specific appearances of the phenomenon in ancient Mesopotamia and Egypt. In keeping with previous scholarship, Elliott argues that belief in the evil eye began in Sumeria and spread from there throughout the ancient world. Discussing a number of incantations and amulets from Sumeria, Assyria, Ugarit, Phoenicia, Babylonia, and Egypt, Elliott finds that ancient peoples often believed that the evil eye was an innate ability of a maleficent human being. But they also frequently believed that the evil eye was an independent, hostile entity similar to a dragon, serpent, or demon. Regardless of its human or supernatural origin, the evil eye was a dangerous force that could stop rain, wither crops, and cause illness and death. Individuals therefore used amulets, incantations, hand gestures, or special substances to ward off the influences of the evil eye and cast any associated curses back on the one who wished them ill. Some incantations cited by Elliott, for instance, presume that words alone can break the influence of the evil eye (see, e.g., KTU^2 1.96, cited p. 94). Others call upon specific deities to protect the afflicted (see, e.g., a spell from the Pyriamid Texts, cited p. 125). One even suggests that an evil eye cast by the demoness Lamashtu could be countered by salt and ashes (BM 122691, cited p. 88). Whatever the specific method employed, the evil eye provided individuals an explanation for the ills that befell them and a way to fight back.

Although Elliott does not neglect the physical, historical, economic, social, and cultural contexts of his evidence, he finds a great deal of consistency in the cross-cultural belief. This is apparent in the first half of the book as Elliott compiles the list of common features noted above. It becomes even clearer in the catalog of ancient Mesopotamia and Egyptian beliefs in chapter 2. Rich excerpts of Sumerian, Akkadian, and Babylonian incantations are placed alongside comparative evidence from later Greek, Roman, Jewish, and Christian texts with little consideration for what distinguishes one culture from another. Elliott's description of Egyptian evidence is somewhat more nuanced as he delves into the connection between the evil-eye belief and the eye of the Egyptian god

Horus that is found on numerous protective amulets. Yet even here Elliott does not hesitate to place evidence from over four millennia beside each other and to interject the occasional reference to the Muslim Hand of Fatimah or modern Sri Lanka masks.

Such juxtaposition is at times jarring, but it in no way diminishes the study. Although the reader may wish for more cultural nuance, Elliott includes enough historical and linguistic details for each example to satisfy most readers without obscuring his primary goal: to highlight the cross-cultural similarities of the belief. Indeed, the reader is left with the impression, contra Marie-Louise Thompson ("The Evil Eye in Mesopotamia," *JNES* 51 [1992]: 19–32), that belief in the evil eye was a widespread cultural phenomenon in the region long before Alexander the Great ventured south. The later demonic, envious, and destructive associations of the belief that one finds in the Bible were entrenched early on and only continued to strengthen as time progressed.

In the end, some may dismiss this volume for being a simple reiteration of earlier surveys on the subject from the late 1800s (e.g., by Otto Jahn, Siegfried Seligmann, Frederick Thomas Elsworthy) or the myriad treatments of the subject in the 1900s (e.g., by Clarence Maloney, Thomas Hauschild). The discussion of the "salient features of the evil eye" in chapter 1, for instance, largely follows the conclusions of Clarence Maloney (*The Evil Eye* [New York: Columbia University Press, 1976], vii–viii) and Alan Dundes ("Wet and Dry, the Evil Eye: An Essay in Indo-European and Semitic Worldview," in *The Evil Eye: A Casebook*, ed. Alan Dundes, 2nd ed. [Madison: University of Wisconsin Press, 1992], 257–312). Similarly, most of the incantations discussed in chapter 2 have been published elsewhere. Elliott himself acknowledges his debt to these earlier thinkers and positions his volumes as a continuation of their research (see 57–58).

This fact should not, however, detract from the importance of Elliott's work. As Elliott states, the goal of these four volumes is to "present the *first monograph* treating all the Evil Eye texts of the Bible within the context of the Circum-Mediterranean and ancient Near East, from Sumeria (3000 BCE) to Roman Late Antiquity (600 CE)" (72, emphasis original). If the present volume is any indication, Elliott will achieve his goal. In this volume, Elliott has not only reiterated the work of his predecessors; he has also compiled and updated their work, both in terms of stated evidence and methodological nuance. This volume, and those to come, are therefore well-positioned to become the definitive treatment on the subject. Until all four volumes are released, the reader will admittedly be left wanting. Once all four volumes are published, however, Elliott's study will be a welcome resource not only for biblical scholars but also for those interested in the development of the evil eye throughout history.

Beware the Evil Eye: The Evil Eye in the Bible and the Ancient World: Volume 2: Greece and Rome, by John H. Elliott. Eugene, OR: Cascade, 2016. Pp. xxxvi + 334. Paper. $41.00. ISBN 9781498204996.

Nicole L. Tilford, Atlanta, Georgia

In this, the second of a four-volume set, New Testament scholar John H. Elliott continues his career-long study of the evil-eye beliefs in the ancient world. Picking up where volume 1 ends, this volume explores references to the evil-eye beliefs in Greece and Rome. In it, Elliott has provided another helpful resource by which to understand the cultural context of evil-eye beliefs in the ancient world.

Volume 1 of the set contains a lengthy, seventy-six-page introduction that discusses the theoretical underpinnings of the evil eye phenomenon. The introduction (ch. 1) to the second volume reminds the reader of the key points of Elliott's earlier discussion: the evil eye's association with envy, its presumed connection with demons, its ability to inflict harm and illness, and its particular danger to children and mothers. However, Elliott does not belabor these points at the beginning of this volume. Instead, after this brief, six-page introduction, Elliott proceeds right the topic at hand: evil-eye belief in Greece and Rome.

Although not the earliest appearance of the belief, the Greco-Roman evidence is certainly the "most extensive" (1). Not surprisingly, then, this volume is over one hundred pages longer than its predecessor, with most of the pages devoted to specific examples of the belief around the Mediterranean. Chapter 2 previews the discussion with a survey of the belief from Homer to late Roman antiquity (800 BCE–600 CE). Brief discussions of specific occurrences appear, with special focus on the evil eye's connection with envy. Also noted here are the key terms associated with the belief in Greece and Rome, especially *baskanos, baskainein, baskania, ophthalmos ponêros* (Greek) and *fascinus, fascinare, fascinatio, oculus malus* (Latin).

As with the previous volume in the set, this volume emphasizes that there is a great consistency in how the evil-eye belief has been understood throughout time. One sees this emphasis clearly in chapter 3, which takes up most of pages in the book. Chapter 3 expands the examples from chapter 2 to discuss the salient features of the belief throughout Greece and Rome. Although Elliott does not neglect historical and cultural nuance, his primary aim in this chapter is to highlight the similarities between sources.

The chapter begins with an extensive discussion of Plutarch's *Symposium* (or *Table Talk*; from book 5 of *Quaestiones Convivales*), a lengthy treatise devoted to the evil eye. Elliott uses the treatise in conjunction with Clarence Maloney's list of evil-eye features (*The Evil Eye* [New York: Columbia University Press, 1976], vii–viii) to establish the basic features of the belief in Greece and Rome. Important here is Elliott's point that Plutarch presents evil-eye belief as a rational idea held by educated elites, explainable by the conventional scientific thought of his day; it is not an irrational, superstitious belief of the "uneducated masses" (63), a point Elliott returns to later in the chapter (119–21).

Following the discussion of Plutarch, Elliott uses other Greco-Roman evidence to delineate the main features of the belief: its dependence upon ancient ocular theories (see below), its association with envy, its processes as explained by emic thinkers, its moral implications, its physiological manifestations, its victims, and its protective devices. Interesting here is Elliott's brief discussion of inadvertent activations of the evil eye, the belief that an individual could affect another person unintentionally (see, e.g., 117), and *autofascination*, the belief that individuals could inadvertently afflict themselves (see, e.g., 118, 149). Such occurrences suggest that the evil eye was more a force of nature in Greco-Roman societies than in their Mesopotamian counterparts.

In this regard, one of the most valuable contributions of this volume is Elliott's extensive discussion of ocular theories in chapter 3 (56–59, 72–81, 113–18). As Elliott rightly notes (19), one cannot understand the evil-eye belief without first understanding the way that ancient peoples understood the eye. The evil-eye belief depends on an extramission theory of vision. Unlike other theories of vision, which view the eye as a passive organ that receives external stimuli (the intromission theory), an extramission theory of vision argues that the eye is an active organ capable of affecting the environment by "transmitting particles of ray-like energy" (57). It is through these particles that an individual who possessed an evil eye was thought to damage the weak and vulnerable. In other words, the evil eye was an extension of a natural, human process.

While the content of the volume is commendable, the structure of the book leaves something to be desired. Chapter 2 could easily have been merged with chapter 1 to create a more solid introduction to the volume. The discussion of Plutarch's *Symposium* (47–70) reads as a distinct case study and could have been separated as such for easier reading. Indeed, if the material were offered as a separate chapter, an instructor wishing to provide students with a brief snapshot of the belief in ancient Greece could easily assign just the pages on Plutarch. Chapter 4, on the other hand, spans only two pages. Its distinction as a separate chapter no doubt serves as a way to indicate that the *good-eye* belief, the topic of the chapter, is distinct from the evil-eye belief in Greece and Rome. However, the discussion could have easily been included at the end of chapter 3 without confusing the reader. Perhaps most important, the long excursus on envy in chapter 3 (83–113) is awkwardly placed. From the table of contents, the reader could easily think that all twelve sections following page 83 belonged to the excursus, rather than only seven of them, and the current headings in the chapter do little to divest the reader of that assumption. Moreover, the excursus awkwardly separates the discussion of ocular theories (72–81) and additional emic theories (113–18). The discussion would have been clearer if the envy sections were set off as a separate chapter or placed elsewhere in chapter 3 as a regular section. The second excursus in the chapter is not much better. Presumably it spans pages 170–74, but it might have been clearer embedded as regular discussion within the previous section, rather than set off as an excursus. Perhaps the current structure was designed to lend some continuity to the four volumes. However, a different structure would have better distinguished the different topics and assisted the reader in following the main argument.

That said, volume 2 makes an important contribution to our understanding of the evil eye in the ancient world. With extensive textual discussions and over sixty illustrations, Elliott has catalogued the major evidence of the belief from the Greco-Roman world in one volume. His dependence on previous scholarship, so noticeable in volume 1 (see my *RBL* review of vol. 1), is more subdued in this volume. While he draws upon previous scholarship, here it is clearly Elliott who leads the reader through the vast Greco-Roman evidence. Elliott has set out to provide the "basic context and matrix" (274) for those who wish to understand references to the evil eye in the Bible. He has certainly accomplished that. With access to this volume and the preceding one, the biblical studies scholar is well prepared to analyze the biblical references in their historical contexts.

ANCIENT NEAR EAST

The Lamentation over the Destruction of Ur, by Nili Samet. Mesopotamian Civilizations. Winona Lake, IN: Eisenbrauns, 2014. Pp. xii + 286. Hardcover. $89.50. ISBN 9781575062921.

Ralph K. Hawkins, Averett University

This volume by Nili Samet has a threefold purpose, namely, to present a revised edition of the Sumerian Lamentation over the Destruction of Ur, a new introduction to the literary genre of Sumerian city laments in general, and an introduction to the Ur Lament in particular.

The volume originated as a dissertation written under the direction of Jacob Klein and Shmuel Vargon at Bar-Ilan University from 2005–2008. While the original dissertation was based primarily on photographs of the relevant duplicates, the author later had the opportunity to collate most of the duplicates from their sources, which allowed her to identify new joins and improve upon her original readings. In addition, she added a new introduction and updated the commentary.

The volume consists of five chapters, with the first (1–31) serving as an introduction. In it Samet introduces the special genre of lamentations over the destruction of cities and temples. While the general lament is a well-known genre in world literature, the Mesopotamian laments over the destruction of cities and temples belong to a "unique and almost unparalleled genre," which has "no known ancient parallel outside the ancient Near East" and is "almost exclusively attested in Sumerian and biblical literature" (1). Samet postulates that the uniqueness of these dirges "could be explained by the historical circumstances that gave rise to these laments," which were composed in the wake of the destruction of ancient political regimes by their rivals. The body of Sumerian lamentations consists of two subgroups, known as *city laments* and *cultic laments.* The cultic laments are quite stylized, while the city laments are literarily diverse and rich.

The city laments recount the destruction of the main cities of Sumer during the collapse of the third dynasty of Ur in 2004 BCE. The destruction typically climaxes in the destruction of the temple, the cessation of its cultic rituals, and the flight of the temple's deities. The destruction of the temple bears religious significance in that it comes at the decision of the great gods (3). Samet briefly describes the makeup of the city lament and summarizes the five city laments that are currently known, including: Lament over Ur (LU), Lament over Sumer and Ur (LSUr), Lament over Uruk (LW), Lament over Eridu (LE), and Lament over Nippur (LN) (3–5).

With regard to the dating and historical background of the city laments, Samet notes that their study is plagued by an inherent problem: "if the political regime it mourns has already perished, who would be interested in composing laments over its destruction and in ensuring the transmission of these laments?" (7). She builds on the interpretation of Michalowski, who proposed that the composition of laments to Ur, including an appeal for its restoration, may be part of a royal attempt to present Isin as the legitimate successor of the previous, magnificent kingdom (7).[1] The city laments appear to have originated in cultic settings, which is indicated both explicitly and implicitly in various sources (9–12). Samet explores the question of the city laments as a genre and whether or not ancient peoples classified them as a special form. As it turns out, the ancients arranged them together in archival lists and thus clearly perceived them as sharing common features (12–13). The Lamentation over the Destruction of Ur is the only one of these that can be fully reconstructed, on the basis of ninety-two available manuscripts.

In the final section of the introduction Samet provides a thorough and helpful overview of the Lamentation over the Destruction of Ur (13–31). The 436 lines are divided into eleven *kirugus*,[2] which recount the fall of Ur to the Elamite and Sua people during the reign of Ibbi-Sin (ca. 2006 BCE). *Kirugu* 1 describes the abandonment of cities and shrines by their patron deities (14–17). *Kirugu* 2 describes the bitter lament that erupted over the abandoned cities and temples, with Ur as its central theme (17–18). *Kirugus* 3–4 are devoted to the lament uttered by Ningal before the god, probably Nanna. Her lament has four foci: (1) the "storm-day" that destroyed Ur; (2) Ningal's vain attempt to rescue her city from destruction; (3) the sudden and unexpected decision of the gods to change the destiny of Ur; and (4) Ningal's attempt to change this decision of the gods. *Kirugu* 5 is focused on the main agent of destruction, the storm, which is summoned by Enlil (22–24). The storm's attack, which occurs in the cosmic sphere, is a metaphor for the invasion of human enemies into Sumer in the earthly sphere. *Kirugu* 6 describes the dead silence and devastation that follow the storm. The conditions are such

---

1. P. Michalowski, *The Lamentation over the Destruction of Sumer and Ur*, Mesopotamian Civilizations 1 (Winona Lake, IN: Eisenbrauns, 1989), 5–7.

2. A *kirugu* is a musical notation for a section.

that helpless people are abandoned and children are separated from their parents, both of which are signs of "the breakdown of the most basic social systems" in the land (24). *Kirugu* 7 contains three laments by Ningal, who escaped the city during the catastrophe and now stands outside, wailing, plucking out her hair, beating her chest, and crying. She is portrayed as a victim of the decision of the great gods. Interestingly, the rationale that she offers for the destruction is that it was "false," "built but not well established" (26). *Kirugu* 8 contains an appeal to Ningal that is intended to convince her to return to her city. *Kirugus* 9–10, which constitute a single unit, contain an "incantation-like" appeal for the removal of the storm. Lastly, *Kirugu* 11 contains an appeal to Nanna in the form of a ritual performed before the god, to look with favor upon his people, his land, and the one performing the ritual. At the conclusion of the ritual, the priest bows and expresses the wish that Nanna be praised in his restored city (30–31).

Chapter 2 contains a "Revised Edition of the Ur Lament" (32–52), while chapter 3, "Transliteration and Translation" (54–77), features the transliteration of the text followed by its translation on the opposing page. Chapter 4 features the "Commentary" (78–132), which contains detailed discussions of the text, new joins, and proposed improvements to prior readings. Chapter 5 contains the "Score" (133–233), which gives an account of the extant textual witness. The volume concludes with a bibliography (234–43), multiple indexes (244–53), and twenty-nine plates containing full-color photographs of tablets containing fragments of the Lamentation over the Destruction of Ur.

As noted above, laments of all kinds are well-known in world literature, but the genre of lamentations over the destruction of cities and temples has no parallels outside the ancient Near East. Its predominant attestation is in Sumerian and biblical literature. Since the Lamentation over the Destruction of Ur is the most famous model of the city laments, Samet's presentation of a revised edition of the Sumerian Lamentation over the Destruction of Ur provides an important updated resource for the study of this unique genre. It will be of special interest to students and scholars engaged in the study of ancient Mesopotamian civilizations. However, since the Lamentation over the Destruction of Ur provides a parallel to the biblical book of Lamentations, it will also be of interest to students of the Bible.

Male and Female in the Epic of Gilgamesh: Encounters, Literary History, and Interpretation, by Tzvi Abusch. Winona Lake, IN: Eisenbrauns, 2015. Pp. ix + 236. Paper. $39.50. ISBN 9781575063492.

Susan Ackerman, Dartmouth College

On page 89 of *Male and Female in the Epic of Gilgamesh*, Tzvi Abusch writes of the late Professor Yochanan Muffs that his "understanding of ancient texts [was] almost preternatural"; "one can only marvel," Abusch goes on to say, "at his ability to grasp and to bring to life the emotions and metaphors that govern these texts." The reader of *Male and Female in the Epic of Gilgamesh* might well say the same of Abusch, based on the nuanced and discerning interpretations of the Gilgamesh Epic that Abusch puts forward on almost every page of this book.

Male and Female in the Epic of Gilgamesh brings together nine of Abusch's essays on the Gilgamesh Epic, published over the course of almost thirty years. Indicated here is Abusch's deep and sustained interest in the Epic, particularly— as the volume's title suggests—in issues of gender. Six of the volume's essays take on three major women characters of the Epic explicitly—the goddess Ishtar, the divine tavern keeper Siduri whom Gilgamesh encounters at the ends of the earth, and the courtesan Shamhat who tames the wild man Enkidu in the Epic's Tablet I—and one of the Epic's other women, Gilgamesh's mother Ninsun, is discussed as part of a seventh essay ("Hunting in the *Epic of Gilgamesh*: Speculations on the Education of a Prince," originally published in the Festschrift for Israel Eph'al).

In three of these essays—"Ishtar's Proposal and Gilgamesh's Refusal: An Interpretation of *The Gilgamesh Epic*, Tablet VI, Lines 1–79" (originally in *HR* 26 [1986]), "Gilgamesh's Request and Siduri's Denial, Part I: The Meaning of the Dialogue and Its Implications for the History of the Epic" (originally in the 1993 Festschrift for William W. Hallo), and "Gilgamesh's Request and Siduri's Denial, Part II: An Analysis and Interpretation of an Old Babylonian Fragment about Mourning and Celebration" (originally in the 1993 Festschrift for Yochanan Muffs)[1]—Abusch focuses, as his titles suggest, on the women characters' verbal interchanges with Gilgamesh, especially the subtleties of each woman's speech to Gilgamesh and the interpretation that follows once those subtleties are adduced.

By comparing an incantation text in which Gilgamesh is addressed in his role as the judge of the underworld, for example, Abusch shows that Ishtar's proposal to Gilgamesh, that were he to marry her, "Kings, nobles, and princes shall bow down before you," is really a proposition that he become a netherworld functionary. No wonder, then, that Gilgamesh, so hungry for life, refuses vehemently. Siduri's famous words to Gilgamesh, too, are revealed by Abusch to have previously undetected allusions and implications. More specifically, Abusch argues that, by ending her so-called *carpe diem* speech with the exhortation that Gilgamesh "let a [mortal] wife ever delight in your lap," Siduri counters the notion that Gilgamesh previously put forward in explaining his plight to her: that he sees a way to escape death by marrying her, an immortal goddess, and thereby living forever. Somewhat similarly, Abusch argues that, when Siduri, in the middle part of her speech, urges Gilgamesh to "daily make a festival," she is urging him to transform the banquet of the dead that can be characteristic of ancient Near Eastern mourning rituals—in which Gilgamesh has engaged incessantly since his beloved friend Enkidu's death—into "a feast of this world ... in which the living participate and by which they reaffirm their lives" (117).

---

1. A fourth essay, "Mourning the Death of a Friend" (originally published in 1993 in *The Frank Talmage Memorial Volume*), synthesizes the conclusions of "Gilgamesh's Request and Siduri's Denial, Parts I and II."

In "The Courtesan, the Wild Man, and the Hunter: Studies in the Literary History of the *Epic of Gilgamesh*" (originally published in 2005 in the Jacob Klein Festschrift), Abusch again considers a scene of male-female interaction, but here the male in question is the nascent Enkidu (that is, Enkidu in his wild and untamed state) and the interaction Abusch examines is physical: the courtesan Shamhat's intercourse with Enkidu. Through, again, a very careful and sensitive reading of the text, Abusch proposes we should identify two sexual encounters as taking place, the first an encounter where Shamhat responds to Enkidu's immediate sexual desire by mating with him in an animalistic way and the second, spanning seven days and nights, an encounter where the intercourse is human in character and so serves to transform Enkidu into a human—and eventually Gilgamesh's bosom companion.

Abusch, writing together with Emily West, takes up the episode of Enkidu's encounter with the courtesan again in "The Tale of the Wild Man in India and Mesopotamia: The Seductions of Ṛśyaśṛṅa in the *Mahābhārata* and Enkidu in the *Epic of Gilgamesh*" (originally published in *The Ancient World in an Age of Globalization*, 2014). The title of this essay signals that, in addition to issues of gender, another area that interests Abusch—and that like gender, is considered in several of his essays—is an examination of parallels between the Gilgamesh Epic and other literatures of the ancient world. These literatures include, of course, the older Sumerian compositions about Gilgamesh (see, e.g., 129, 139–40, 171–72); they include as well other ancient Mesopotamian myths (see, e.g., 29, 85, 115, 175) and texts from elsewhere in the Semitic world: preeminently Ugarit (see, e.g., 115) and the Bible (see, e.g., 65, 74, 110–11, 116–18). But Abusch also evokes the literatures of Egypt (see, e.g., Abusch's references to the Egyptian Harper's Songs on 74, 100–104), of classical Athens (see, e.g., Abusch's references to Xenophon's *Cynegeticus* on 173), of Rome (see, e.g., Abusch's reference to Horace's *Odes* on 116), and, as in Abusch's essay with West, the great *Mahābhārata* of India. Most commonly, however, Abusch looks to Homer. He compares Gilgamesh's encounter with Siduri, for example, with the *Odyssey*'s tales of Odysseus encountering Circe and Calypso (29, 68–71, 84–85, 111–15), and he similarly compares Gilgamesh's refusal to give Enkidu's body up for burial with Patroclus's accusation in the *Iliad* that Achilles has failed to accord him proper funerary rites (98–99). In "The *Epic of Gilgamesh* and the Homeric Epics," moreover (originally published in *Mythology and Mythologies: Methodological Approaches to Intercultural Influences*, 2001), Abusch takes on larger questions about the relationship between the Gilgamesh Epic and Homer's texts. These include an exploration of what Abusch describes as ideological parallels, whereby Abusch suggests that the theme he sees dominating the Old Babylonian version of the Gilgamesh Epic—the need for Gilgamesh, the powerful yet somewhat unruly epic hero, to come to terms with the social structures and conventions of manhood (marriage and family life)—defines also the *Iliad*'s characterization of Achilles. Likewise, Abusch proposes, the theme that he sees dominating the eleven-tablet Standard Babylonian version of the Epic—the need for the unruly hero Gilgamesh to come to terms with the

responsibilities entailed in his role as king—defines also the *Odyssey*'s characterization of Odysseus.

Note carefully here Abusch's interest in differentiating the Old Babylonian
version of the Epic and the eleven-tablet Standard Babylonian version, for issues
concerning the literary history and development of the Epic represent another
major focus of Abusch's work. Indeed, already in his original publication on the
Epic, in *HR* 26 (1986), Abusch took up the issue of Ishtar's Tablet VI proposal to
Gilgamesh to become a netherworld functionary (according to Abusch's interpretation) and compared it with Tablet XII and Enkidu's description there of "the
norms and procedures that govern life in the netherworld" (142) in order to suggest that the Ishtar episode in Tablet VI and Tablet XII's commentary, so to speak,
on this Tablet VI episode represent, respectively, the penultimate and ultimate
stage of the literary accretions that resulted in the Epic's final twelve-tablet version.
Somewhat similarly, in his three 1993 articles that dealt with Gilgamesh's encounter with Siduri, Abusch took up issues of the Epic's literary development in order
to suggest that in the Epic's original form Gilgamesh's wanderings ended with
Siduri; only subsequently, according to this reconstruction, was the Utnapishtim
episode added (with the result that Siduri's famous speech resolving Gilgamesh's
dilemma by sending him back to Uruk to start a family was suppressed). Issues of
the Epic's literary development, moreover, take center stage in "The Development
and Meaning of the *Epic of* Gilgamesh," originally published in *JAOS* 121 (2001),
although this is hardly the end of the discussion for Abusch, as he makes clear in
his introduction to this 2015 volume, where he revisits proposals he had made
about the Epic's development in "The Courtesan, the Wild Man, and the Hunter"
(2005), only to disavow them (see 6).

The result of reading these sustained reflections on the Gilgamesh Epic's literary development, and also on the Epic's women characters and its literary parallels
in and beyond the Near East, is to experience *Male and Female in the Epic of
Gilgamesh* as a whole that is greater than the sum of its parts. Moreover, many of
the essays in *Male and Female in the Epic of Gilgamesh* were originally published
in Festschriften (five out of nine), and another two were originally published in
volumes of conference proceedings. Collections of these sorts are not necessarily
the most accessible, especially in institutions with smaller libraries. Eisenbrauns
has thus done a great service in bringing Abusch's thirty years worth of essays on
the Gilgamesh Epic together.

From the Mari Archives: An Anthology of Old Babylonian Letters, by Jack M. Sasson. Winona Lake, IN: Eisenbrauns, 2015. Pp. xx + 454. Hardcover. $59.50. ISBN
9781575068305.

Amanda H. Podany, California State Polytechnic University, Pomona

A number of ancient Mesopotamian and Syrian cities have produced archives
of thousands (sometimes tens of thousands) of cuneiform documents. Many such

archives are made up almost entirely of the kinds of documents only an ancient accountant (or an Assyriologist) could love: administrative texts, lists, contracts, and the like. This is not true, however, of the Syrian site of Mari. The archives that have been discovered there, over the decades since the French excavations began there in 1933, include thousands of letters, mostly between officials and the local kings. Many of them were written during the reign of King Zimri-Lim, a period of just fourteen years. More than two thousand of these letters have already been published, with French translations, in volumes in the series Archives Royales de Mari (ARM). The letters are full of details of policy and intrigue, war and diplomacy, jealousy and generosity. They represent a gold mine for historians.

Assyriologists often bemoan what the many records available to us do not reveal—we know the names of thousands of individuals, we know about events that warranted a royal inscription or a year name, and we even have a precise knowledge of the number of sheep delivered to a temple on a particular day, but the motivations and personalities of the individuals who inhabited that world are hidden from us by the nature of most of the documentation. Who were they? What did they care about? Almost invariably, we simply cannot know. More records survive from Mesopotamia and Syria than from any other ancient civilization, yet we are often in the dark concerning the thoughts behind historic actions.

Except, that is, on the rare occasion when letters survive. The letters from Mari open up a wide window into the ideas, actions, and relationships of a number of powerful men and women living in the eighteenth century BCE. They did not write these letters for posterity. They did not expect to find us, over 3,700 years later, reading over their shoulders. They wrote about pressing matters of state importance or about personal grudges or worries. They wrote about the signs from the gods that had to be heeded or the seating arrangement for a banquet. They wrote for their own time, with only their own immediate goals in mind, not with an eye to the future. Yet the letters survived and can tell us so much.

In Jack M. Sasson, the kings of Mari and their officials have an ideal spokesperson for the English-speaking world. Sasson has written dozens of articles about Mari, over more than forty years, and they have always sparkled with life. Fellow scholars look forward to his talks at conferences because he speaks of the Mari officials as though they were familiar friends with sometimes annoying but forgivable quirks. How fortunate we are, therefore, that Sasson has in this volume invited us in to the Mari archives and taken us on a tour. He is a wise and meticulously organized guide. This book is much more than an anthology. Each of the approximately 750 letters translated here (in whole or in part) is accompanied by a brief introduction and is set in the context of other letters that help illuminate its contents. Better still, the five chapters in which the documents are presented, and many of the dozens of subsections within those chapters, begin with short essays by Sasson and are accompanied by abundant, detailed footnotes that shed more light on the topics. Just about every conceivable aspect of the life, administration, culture, and religious beliefs of the people of Mari is addressed here and illuminated with vivid passages from the ancient letters. In addition, throughout the book Sasson makes references to relevant biblical passages and notes that one of the aims of the book is to "sharpen reciprocally our appreciation and understanding of the ancient world in which the Hebrew Bible took its final form" (19).

The introduction (1–20) provides information that will guide readers, even those unfamiliar with the kingdom of Mari, through the main points necessary to make sense of the letters: the details of the kingdom, its languages, and its archives. One useful feature of the introduction is a "Cast of Characters" (9–12). The letters are full of references to the royal families and civil servants of the Mari kingdom, so the reader may need to return often to this list to be reminded of the relationships and professions of the individuals named in the letters that help explain their actions and words. A list of ancient place names follows, with their modern names (where known) and the names of their most prominent rulers (12–15). Many, though not all, of the places can be found on the map in the inside back and front covers of the book (a few of them are spelled slightly differently in the list and on the map, such as Hazor/Haṣor, Ilan-ṣura/ Ilanṣura).

Chapter 1, "Kingship" (21–118), the longest in the book, includes eight main sections: "Becoming a King"; "The King's Charisma"; "The Wealth of Kings"; "Acts and Behavior"; "Vassals"; "Diplomacy and Treaty-Making"; "Dynastic Marriages"; and "The Marriage of Mari Princesses." Each of these is in turn divided into between three and six subsections, some of which are in turn divided into as many as seven sub-subsections, each constituting a letter. For example, one finds a letter about "Excrement in a Cup" (§1.5.b.ii, 78), under the heading "Whining and Scheming," which in turn is within the subheading concerning "Vassals." (In this particular letter, a vassal who had drunk a cup of friendship with Zimri-Lim later showed his hostility to the king by dropping "excrement into the cup he used"!) In this chapter, as is true throughout the book, Sasson identifies and translates what he terms "letters with juicy contents" (xix) that provide evidence for the institutions and behaviors named in the subheadings. His choices are wonderful and eye-opening, especially when read in combination with the others chosen to illuminate the same topic. For example, §1.7.a, "The Marriage of Beltum of Qatna to Yasmah-Addu of Mari" (under "Diplomatic Marriages," 103–7) includes seven letters. These take us through the negotiations that preceded the marriage, the merging of the houses and royal families of the two kings (the king of Mari and the king of Qatna, father of the betrothed princess), the king's surprising neglect of his new wife, the illness of the princess, and her father's request that she return to visit him in Qatna. These letters were originally published in five different volumes between 1950 and 2000 (in ARM 1, ARM 2, ARM 5, ARM 26, and LAPO 18). Seeing them side by side allows the reader a more nuanced picture of diplomatic marriage in general and of this marriage in particular.

"Administration" is the topic of chapter 2 (119–80). Here the subheadings for the letters are "Provincial Officers," "Palace Officers," and "Notables." The sub-subheadings in this case are all titles of officials, with their responsibilities laid out in further subheadings. The longest section focuses on the crucial role of governor or *šapiṭum* (120–33); it includes twenty-two letters in the main text and short excerpts from eighteen more in the footnotes. These all pertain to provincial governors and their responsibilities, from controlling the local tribes to dealing with swarms of locusts. For the latter (and as an example of the many treasures to be found in the book), Sasson provides a half-page-long footnote that includes biblical references to locusts, varieties of locusts mentioned in the Mari letters, and locusts as food both in ancient Syria (some were more valued than others, and freshness was a plus) and now ("fried in oil or butter, after removal of wings and legs").

Chapter 3, on "Warfare" (181–214), is divided into sections on "War Mentality"; "Casus Belli"; "Armies"; "Combat"; "Siege Tactics"; and "Aftermath." These, in turn, are again subdivided. An interesting section here pertains to the Ḫābiru (194–96), who fall into the category of mercenaries and whose identity and military activities are reflected in six Mari letters in the main text and excerpts from three more in the footnotes. Sasson observes that the term derives from the verb ḫabārum, which meant "to move out (more or less permanently) from a place" (194 n. 26). One of the delightful aspects of the book is seen in the shared attention to major concerns of warfare such as siege strategies (209–11) and glimpses of human experience, such as a group of two thousand soldiers "marching in cold weather" and in desperate need of clothing (193).

The shortest chapter in the book is chapter 4, about "Society" (215–34). This chapter is largely concerned with the judicial system and includes subsections on "Organs of Justice"; "Procedure"; "Crime"; "Asylum Seekers"; "Detention"; "Punishment"; and "Legal Documents." Because the Mari documents were found in the palace, fewer private documents were found there than one might hope. Some aspects that might well have been classified under the category of society, such as social class and marriage, are to be found in chapter 6, "Culture."

Chapter 5, "Religion" (235–93) begins with three ancient lists of deities from Mari (5.1, "Pantheon," 235–37), which are not exhaustive but were created for specific occasions, such as blood sacrifices. The other subheadings in the chapter are "Devotion"; "Rituals"; "Paraphernalia"; "Caring for the Gods"; "Divine Power"; "Communicating the Will of God"; and "Ordeals." One hardly need mention the importance of the letters quoted here for providing a view of ancient Syrian religion as it was actually practiced. Of particular interest are the letters pertaining to prophecy (278–81), visions (282–85), dreams (285–88), and signs (288–89).

Many other aspects of life in Mari are covered in chapter 6 under the broad umbrella of "Culture" (294–342). This includes "Population" (note the section on residents, with subdivisions for the various social classes, 294–99); "The City Mari"; "Court Life"; and four sections about the life cycle: "Childhood"; "Adulthood"; "Health"; and "Death and Burial." Quoted in this chapter are some of the most intriguing letters in the book, and Sasson notes that no monograph has yet been written on society and culture in Mari (294). These letters show that such a study could and should be undertaken; there is a great deal of evidence to work from.

The last chapter, "Reflections" (343–47), begins with the topics of internationalism and ethnic diversity (noting that the society and culture at Mari were both more international and diverse than is often realized), then goes back through the titles of each of the chapters to write more impressionistically about each. For example, under "Kingship" Sasson observes that "combat was endemic, and I cannot point to any appreciable stretch of time in which Mari kings were not embroiled in it, whether it was their choice or not" (344).

More than one hundred pages at the end of the volume are devoted to supporting materials, including an extensive bibliography (348–66), concordances (367–441), a subject index (442–52), and an index of biblical citations (453–54). The concordance of correspondents is particularly interesting. It shows, among other things, that ninety-three of the quoted letters in the book were written or received by twenty-nine different female correspondents. A quick count reveals that fifty-three letters were written by women to men, thirty-three were written by men to women, and seven were written by women to women. Princesses, many of them married to vassal kings, often wrote to their father about matters of state in their husbands' lands, and Zimri-Lim wrote back to them often using the same tone that he employed in correspondence with his civil servants.

Most of the correspondents were princesses and queens, but others include three palace songstresses and a harem woman. Innumerable other letters in the volume, though written between men, discuss matters concerning women. Given how rare it is in any era of history to find documents written or dictated by women, the Mari material quoted here would make a valuable corpus for study in a course about women in the ancient world, for example. The letters nicely belie the notion that women were chattel or property of the men at the time.

If one were using the book in this way, it should be noted that the cast of characters in chapter 1 includes entries for only eleven of the prominent women at Mari. Missing are several of Zimri-Lim's daughters (Baḫlatum, Battaḫra, Belassunu, Belatum, Duḫšatum, Hazala, Inbatum, Partum, and Tišpatum), the king's sister (Nigḫatum), and some regional queens (Azzu-ena queen of Ašal, Lamassi-Aššur queen of Ekallatum, Liqtum queen of Burundum), many of whom wrote or received letters that are found in the book. Citations of the letters that they wrote and received can be found in concordance B.

Of course, the letters compiled in this volume can be used in the study of many aspects of the ancient Near East. The book's organization by topic and the useful subject index allow relevant letters to be easily found.

Sasson is typically self-deprecating in his acknowledgments, noting that this work came into being as a book rather than a short section in a volume of collected primary sources, because the author "lacked the discipline to make a narrow selection when thousands of Mari documents have already been published" (xix). Of course the discipline involved in the translation, organization, annotation, and publication of hundreds of documents is mind-boggling. This is a work that will be of use to generations of students and scholars. Sasson has not only provided access in English to documents from Mari that were previously only available in French; he has also chosen them wisely, has presented them in a systematic way that allows for new insights (on the part of scholars as well as students and general readers), and has done so in a single, amply annotated, and relatively inexpensive volume. Sasson is well-known for being generous with his time and for his willingness to help colleagues; by creating this book he has helped us all to better understand the kingdom of Mari.

Royal Apologetic in the Ancient Near East, by Andrew Knapp. Writings from the Ancient World Supplement Series 4. Atlanta: SBL Press, 2015. Pp. 466. Paper. $59.95. ISBN 9780884140740. Hardcover. $79.95. ISBN 9780884140764.

Danny Mathews, Pepperdine University

This is the first substantial and systematic study of apologetic in the ancient Near East. Past research has been in the form of an unpublished dissertation in 1967 (by Herbert M. Wolf) and influential articles (especially by Hoffner [1975], McCarter [1980], and Tadmor [1983]). Moreover, the subject of past apologetic research has been typically limited to a comparative focus of two texts, such as McCarter's analysis of the David material with the autobiography of Hattusilis III. By comparison, this study provides an overview of sixteen ancient Near Eastern texts followed by detailed analysis of seven texts that are distributed widely both geographically and temporally: the Proclamation of Telipinu and Autobiography of Hattusili III in Hatti during the second millennium BCE, the Traditions of David's Rise and Reign and the Succession Narrative of Solomon during the early first millennium in Israel, the Tel Dan Inscription of Hazael in Aram in the late ninth century, Esarhaddon's apology in Nineveh A in Assyria in the seventh century, and Nabonidus's apology in the Babylon Stela in sixth-century Babylon.

Knapp draws upon the work of rhetorical scholars to define apologetic as "propaganda produced as defense against attacks upon a person's character or conduct" (45). Apologetic is not a genre, in contrast to the assumptions of biblical scholars, but rather a "literary mode (or mood)" that can be a component of a number of genres (41). He uses the example of Heller's *Catch-22*, which has the form of a novel but the mode of satire. This mode of apologetic is rooted not in genre but in the motivation to respond to accusations. This definition provides a much-needed clarity to previous uncritical use of the term and allows for the inclusion of a variety of genres within the scope of the study, such as royal inscriptions and third-person biblical narrative. This view of apology raises the need to reconstruct as clearly as possible the historical situation in order to understand better the specific charges brought against the ruler, and this becomes a major focus of this study.

Following the theoretical discussion and overview of the individual apologies in the ancient Near East, the bulk of the book is devoted to an analysis of the seven texts. A chapter is devoted to each of these texts and is organized into four parts: (1) a historical reconstruction of the circumstances of the ruler's rise to power; (2) a transliteration, translation, and detailed textual and philological notes of each nonbiblical text, with a source-critical analysis given instead for the two biblical texts (since biblical translations are readily accessible); (3) analysis of the apologetic by examining the rhetorical strategy and common motifs intended to response to specific charges leveled against the king; (4) a discussion of the *Sitz im Leben* of the apology.

This analysis reveals common trends throughout the entire ancient Near East. The subjects of all of the extant apologies are kings who respond to typical charges of illegitimate accession to the throne through actions such as assassinating the current king or killing opponents or rivals to the throne. Other apologies respond to more narrow charges, such as being unfit for the throne (Esarhaddon) or a heretic (Nabonidus). By the end of the book this consistent attention to apology as providing specific and immediate response to current charges provides a cumulative and substantial refutation of Tadmor's thesis that apology was rather focused more on future concerns, namely, ensuring a smooth transfer of power to a successor.

In addition to the detailed reconstruction of the historical context, each chapter also analyzes various common motifs and explains how they were used to refute the specific charges leveled against the king. Of these motifs, the most important are (1) divine election, where the king's right to the throne is due to the power and will of the deity (or deities); (2) royal prerogative/affiliation, that is, the will of a predecessor who designated a particular son to be king; and (3) popular acclamation, where the will of the people establishes the legitimacy of the king. Other motifs used in varying degrees include military success, the unworthy predecessor/rival, merciful victor, and passivity.

This is a top-notch resource rooted on a clear theoretical foundation and based on painstaking textual and historical analysis. The study is consistently cautious and judicious in making historical conclusions and is often up front on the speculative and provisional nature of the enterprise of historical reconstruction. What is admirable is the intention to integrate the disciplines of rhetorical, ancient Near Eastern, and biblical studies in a user-friendly format. The one exception is the normalized transliterations of the nonbiblical texts and textual commentary that will be of interest to specialists in Hittite and Akkadian, but this section can easily be skipped without distracting from the main agenda of the study. As a result, this resource will provide a very helpful introduction to scholars who wish to become better versed in the basic context and content of exposure to some of the famous ancient Near Eastern texts.

By way of evaluation, a number of observations can be made. First, it is disappointing that the focus was limited to only seven texts, since Knapp affirms that there are a number of other texts that could legitimately be included. As a result, as Knapp acknowledges, this is by no means an attempt at a comprehensive study. This is fair enough, but it seems that including Darius's Bisitun Inscription, which Knapp describes as the best example of royal apologetic excluded from the study, would have extended the geographical and temporal scope of the study to Persia in the late sixth century or early fifth century BCE.

Second, the chapter on David is the weakest in the book. It occupies some ninety pages and is about three times the length of other chapters. It appears that too much attention is given to reconstruct the historical context surrounding David's rise to power. Given the speculative and provisional nature of this enterprise, which Knapp acknowledges throughout the study, it is not clear how crucial this substantial analysis is for analyzing the individual charges and various motifs. As a matter of practical expedient, it might have been better to adopt a specific historical reconstruction that has been previously published and leave a fresh analysis for another day or to restrict the focus to analyzing the rhetorical situation implicit in the text. This would then have provided more space for including other apologies, such as the Bisitun Inscription. That said, the clear definition of apologetic as shown in the study provides a strong argument for the historicity of much of the material as being issued during the reign of David, since it is difficult to imagine the rationale for responding to specific charges, such as serving as a Philistine mercenary, being offered centuries later after his life. It will be interesting to see how future studies on the historical David respond to this argument.

Third, the preceding shows the need for a clearer discussion of and differentiation between reconstructing the historical context in comparison to analyzing the rhetorical situation. It seems that, in theory, attending to the rhetorical situation, much like the "implied reader," involves a theoretical construct based on the details of the text itself. In some cases, a historical analysis is crucial, such as using the Assyrian annals and texts in the Hebrew Bible to reconstruct the situation underlying the brief and fragmentary Tel Dan inscription, and this results in an advance by identifying the apologetic aspect of this inscription. But in other cases, such as an analysis of the biblical narrative, which presents a whole different set of critical issues, a rhetorical approach that involves reconstructing an implied context might be a more useful way to focus on the use of specific apologetic strategies.

Finally, a very minor quibble is the need for at least some theoretical discussion of the identification and function of a "motif." However, the motifs are clearly identified and their shared traditions in the ancient Near East is well documented and convincingly demonstrated. One exception might be "divine election," since this seems to be a bit too generic and to include other distinct motifs, such as the vanguard motif that uses specific terminology to indicate the deity's presence with or in front of the king, typically in a military context.

These are all minor critiques that should not distract from the quality and usefulness of this study that is now the standard reference for apologetic in the ancient Near East. It is to be hoped that Knapp will extend this study to include the remaining texts in a new or revised edition.

Hittite Scribal Circles: Scholarly Tradition and Writing Habits, by Gordin Shai. Studien zu den Bogazköy-Texten 59. Wiesbaden: Harrassowitz, 2015. Pp. xxiv + 461. Hardcover. €88.00. ISBN 9783447105262.

Yitzhaq Feder, University of Haifa

The reviewed volume is a comprehensive revision of the author's Berlin dissertation on Hittite scribal habits in the Late Empire period, written under the supervision of Eva Cancik-Kirschbaum and Jörg Klinger. It also builds on the author's earlier MA thesis at Tel Aviv University on the prosopography of thirteenth-century BCE Hittite officials, supervised by the late Itamar Singer, to whose memory the volume is dedicated.

The primary aim of this review is not to provide a comprehensive evaluation of the book but rather to focus on aspects of this work that will be of interest to biblical scholars and situate it in relation to the current wave of interest in ancient Near Eastern scribal activity. Although the topic is by no means new, it is clear that research on the specialists responsible for text production has enjoyed an unprecedented upsurge of interest in the past two decades—and rightfully so. Scholars such as David M. Carr and Karl van der Toorn have shown how the vast corpora of cuneiform evidence bearing on scribal production and revision of texts, including questions of authorship and authority, can shed light on key questions bearing on the composition and transmission of the Hebrew Bible. Yet, with all due respect to the Mesopotamian archives that have been the focus of much recent discussion, it may be the works of the Hittite scribes that offer the most penetrating view of a particular scribal culture at work. It is this potential that Gordin's monograph seeks to exploit.

Gordin's attempt to delineate to the extent possible detailed profiles for Hittite scribal circles (specifically those of Walwaziti and Anuwanza) is based on the state of the art of Hittitological research. It employs a "no holds barred" analysis of find spots of tablets, tablet layout, cuneiform paleography and orthography, onomastics of Luwian seals, historical reconstruction, and more. These various pieces of data are used to achieve a first-name basis acquaintance with individual scribes and determine their professional lineages.

Needless to say, large sections of this book (particularly in chs. 4–6) are quite technical and will be hard for the non-Hittitologist to digest. Surprisingly enough, however, much of the discussion—particularly in the opening three chapters—is remarkably accessible and highly relevant for broader discussions of scribal activities in the ancient Near East, including the Hebrew Bible.

Chapter 1 introduces the concepts and aims of prosopography of Hittite scribal culture, that is, to reconstruct to the extent possible the social world of the Hittite scribes. Here the reader might have benefited from a more thorough introduction to prosopography, which appears only in the following chapter. Prosopography is defined there as "a collective investigation of scribes, their duties, and their position in the Hittite state hierarchy" (80), followed by a summary of the types of evidence necessary for this inquiry. Although the scope of the discussion is much broader, Gordin's book focuses on the evidence from the thirteenth century BCE, addressing: "(1) the structure and function of the different scribal families and collegial circles; (2) the writing habits of individual scribes across several documents, and when possible, over time; (3) writing practices shared by individuals working in the same scribal school" (5). Chapter 1 proceeds to survey the types of evidence bearing on the scribal and archival spaces at the Hittite capital of Hattusa (Boğazköy). Here Gordin offers a balanced and insightful survey of the new wave of research on the terminology and realia of Hittite scribal practices, including discussion of different types of tablets and the significance of their layout. Finally, the most direct evidence of scribal activity—manifested in incipits, colophons, and scribal signatures—are discussed in detail (39–49).

Chapter 2 opens with a full list of the 172 tablets from the Empire period (ca. fourteenth– thirteenth centuries BCE) that Gordin was able to identify bearing personal annotations of the scribes. This corpus of evidence serves as a springboard for tackling more general questions. In particular, Gordin addresses the various types of texts represented in the Hittite archives and the problems posed by modern classifications. He offers an up-to-date and critical evaluation of the use of paleography for dating tablets, stressing the need to distinguish between "basic ductus" (sign forms) and "personal ductus" (a particular scribe's handwriting). After summarizing the standard diagnostic sign forms for dating tablets (with a useful visual summary on 90—91), Gordin shows how this scheme is complicated by individual scribe's writing styles, demonstrated directly with high-definition photos of representative sign forms from the actual tablets. This task is taken up more fully in chapter 6.

Chapter 3 is entitled "Tracing Hittite Technical 'Authorship' and Scribal Specialization." At this point Gordin begins the arduous task of sketching to the extent possible an individualized profile of each attested scribe from the Late Empire period. He begins with a tabular summary and onomastic analysis, suggesting the possible ethnic background of each scribe (95–106). He then traces the explosive growth in signed manuscripts from the Old and Middle Hittite periods to the Empire period. Of particular interest is the summary of the percentage of signed manuscripts according to genre (112, based on a representative sample), which demonstrates that personal annotations were far more common for festival (46 percent) and ritual (20 percent) texts than for other genres, for example, texts of foreign origin (5 percent) or historical texts (5 percent). This finding raises the question of why it was more important for the scribes to sign the festivals and rituals. A related topic pertains to the relationship between these scribes and the ritual experts (e.g., the "Old Woman" Tunnawiya) to whom most of the ritual texts are attributed. Aside from the interesting and much-debated question of the authenticity of these attributions, Gordin points out the correspondence between these formulae and those found in "shelf-lists" for archiving tablets, noting that "knowing the name of the author of a composition was a practical concern of the archivist, not merely an indication of the efficacy of the written and spoken words" (115). He also points out that these shelf-lists may serve to determine the "rights" of a particular scribal circle to a composition. More generally, he interprets the surge in scribal signatures in the Late Empire period as an index of increasing scribal specialization and ownership over particular compositions, including defined sections of an extended series (e.g., the tablets for the twenty-ninth day of the AN.TUḪ.ŠUM^{SAR} festival).

In chapter 4 Gordin examines work relationships, for example, between an apprentice and a supervisor, as reflected in textual formulae. He distinguishes between several different scribal titles, discussing the relationship between terms in the cuneiform (Hittite) tablets and hieroglyphic (Luwian) seals. This discussion includes medical practitioners and diviners bearing scribal titles, as well as officials who acquired at least basic literacy (discussed further in 229–37).

Chapters 5 and 6 are the longest chapters in the volume (ca. one hundred pages each), the most substantive in the analysis of hard data and, predictably, the most technical. Chapter 5 attempts to situate each scribe within the two major scribal circles of the Late Empire period, namely, those of Walwaziti and Anuwanza. After describing Walwaziti's lineage (which is known in detail thanks to KBo 4.12), Gordin surveys the major scribal projects of this circle, especially the *ḫišuwa* festival, before proceeding to study lesser-known scribes and identifies several distinctive scribal practices of this circle. Gordin then turns to the work of the scribal circle of Anuwanza. Again Gordin identifies the major projects of this circle and scribal lineages, a task made somewhat easier by this circle's penchant for detailed genealogies in their colophons. This chapter also discusses distinct phases in textual production, specifically the production of a new text edition from varied sources and copying, the former task performed by a more elite scribal position. The chapter concludes with a schematic summary of the major scribal figures, placing them in an approximate chronological framework (240).

Chapter 6 is a detailed analysis of scribal habits as reflected in the paleography and orthography of thirty-eight representative manuscripts from the Late Empire period. In what is probably the most comprehensive survey of this type in Hittitology (and ancient Near Eastern studies in general), Gordin analyzes the personal style of individual scribes and the relationships between their affiliates. The generous use of high-resolution photographs in his detailed analysis of particular sign forms provides the reader with a convenient and unmediated engagement with the data and will facilitate the difficult task of matching unsigned tablets with their scribes in future research.

Chapter 7 is the grand finale. After a meticulous study of individual "trees" in the previous chapters, Gordin steps back to describe the forest, offering a fascinating overview of the development of scribal institutions in Hattusa throughout Hittite history. He suggests that the choice of particular sign forms is not arbitrary but reflects streams of tradition and rivaling claims to authority and prestige for the Walwaziti and Anuwanza circles.

In sum, Hattuša's textual archive has left us with an unparalleled resource for the study of text production in the ancient world, due to the high precision of our knowledge regarding the provenance of the tablets and by virtue of the relatively systematic nature of the scribal signatures from the Late Empire period. While obviously this scribal culture was unique in many of its characteristics, it offers an important vantage point for understanding the world of cuneiform scribes more generally.

Riding the new wave of Hittitological research on scribal activity and taking it to new heights, Gordin's study mines this data to the fullest. Even if one may question occasionally some of his conclusions, the clear presentation of the data, with abundant photographs and tabular summaries, will push current debates into new territory. Upon completing this work one can only be impressed by the author's extraordinary ability to draw from the most scattered pieces of heterogeneous data to create a synthetic picture of the world of the Hittite scribes. As such, this work is a fitting tribute to Gordin's teacher, Itamar Singer, renowned for his ability to integrate disparate philological and archaeological evidence in producing compelling historical reconstructions. In this regard, the author has been true to his own scribal lineage.

LANGUAGES

The Language Environment of First Century Judaea: Jerusalem Studies in the Synoptic Gospels, Volume 2, edited by Randall Buth and R. Steven Notley. Jewish and Christian Perspectives Series 26. Leiden: Brill, 2014. Pp. vi + 457. Hardcover. €161.00. ISBN 9789004263406.

Steven Thompson, Avondale College of Higher Education

This collection of essays contributes to the lengthy debate about the place of Hebrew and Aramaic in Second Temple Palestine and in the language of the Jesus debate, which has run in the background and at times in the foreground among Western Christians for five hundred years. It even entered international diplomacy during the May 2014 visit of Pope Francis to Israel. When his host, Israeli prime minister Benjamin Netanyahu stated that Jesus spoke Hebrew, his Holiness corrected him: "Aramaic!" This debate about the language of Jesus has historically been energized by the wish either to connect Jesus to or disconnect him from his native Jewish culture. During the twentieth century Jesus was assigned an Aramaic language setting in order to add historical credibility to gospel accounts of his words and acts to counter critical theories of their Hellenistic origin and nature.

Despite the book's rather neutral title, the issue of the language spoken by Jesus is raised in each chapter. Considerable new evidence, plus several new arguments for determining the roles of Aramaic and Hebrew in Second Temple Palestine, are employed. The eleven chapters are clustered under three headings: "Sociolinguistic Issues," "Literary Issues," and "Reading Gospel Texts." In my view, however, they belong more naturally in three somewhat different clusters: the Hebrew background of specific gospel expressions; Hebrew and Aramaic in the culture and literature of Second Temple Palestine; and the history of the argument that Jesus spoke only Aramaic.

Four chapters fit into the first cluster. In *"Hebraisti in Ancient Texts: Does Hebraisti Ever Mean 'Aramaic'?"* (ch. 3), Randall Buth and Chad Pierce integrate considerable evidence into their argument that *Hebraisti* and related terms in John and Acts actually refer to spoken Hebrew rather than Aramaic, as is so often asserted. They develop a convincing case that *Hebraisti* in the New Testament always refers specifically to the Hebrew language, never to Aramaic.

In "Non-septuagintal Hebraisms in the Third Gospel: An Inconvenient Truth" (ch. 8), Steven Notley examines ten Lukan passages containing what he designates "non-Septuagintal Hebraisms" (332) because their Lukan occurrences preserve more "Hebraic" contours than do their counterparts in the LXX, which were translated into more idiomatic Greek. This points to a Hebrew source for the Lukan expressions. Notley combs postbiblical Hebrew documents, finding vocabulary and grammatical features that would account for a range of otherwise "strange" Greek expressions in Luke, such as "by the finger of God" (11:20) and "bosom of Abraham" (16:22). His application of this solid, if sometimes late, documentary evidence to explain Luke's expressions certainly enhances the probability that they have a Hebrew background.

In "Jesus' *Petros—petra* Wordplay (Matthew 16:18): Is It Greek, Aramaic, or Hebrew?" (ch. 10), David Bivin counters the widely asserted Aramaic origin for this wordplay, especially Joseph Fitzmyer's vigorous defense of it as Aramaic. Bivin argues that, although Matthew's form of the wordplay is obviously Greek, it had previously entered the Hebrew language through transliteration and therefore qualified as Hebrew. He cites supporting evidence from Genesis Rabbah and other rabbinic sources for occurrences of a Hebraized, transliterated *petros* and the Jerusalem Talmud for a Hebraized, transliterated *petra*, both appearing as personal names in Hebrew-speaking settings. He puts forward this expression as one more strand of evidence supporting the gospel picture of a Hebrew-speaking Jesus.

In the final chapter of this first cluster, "The Riddle of Jesus' Cry from the Cross: The Meaning of *ēli ēli* (Matthew 27:46) and the Literary Function of *elōi elōi leima sabaxthani* (Mark 15:34)," Buth amasses documentary and inscriptional evidence, provides detailed critiques of earlier explanations, then concludes that, while Mark's version of Jesus's cry of dereliction reflects Aramaic rather than the Hebrew echoed in the Matthean parallel, it should be accounted for as one of several instances where Mark deliberately inserted "foreign" Aramaic words into the (assumed) day-to-day Hebrew speech of Jesus in order to achieve a special effect. This effect, argued Buth, was to invoke "a sense of mystery, awe, and spiritual power" (421). By putting this and a limited number of other Aramaic expressions on the lips of Jesus, Mark brought him into line with a Jewish practice of using "foreign" Aramaic expressions to heighten a speaker's authority and power.

Chapters in the second cluster apply considerable new evidence to the debate about the place of spoken and written Hebrew and Aramaic in Second Temple Palestine. In "The Use of Hebrew and Aramaic in Epigraphic Sources" (ch. 2), Guido

Baltes provides a detailed survey, plus catalog, of the large volume of relevant epigraphic material now available. He critically assess its relevance for, and impact on, the debate, finding extensive support for a trilingual (Hebrew, Aramaic, Greek) Palestinian culture. Neither Hebrew nor Aramaic dominate significantly in surviving material, with Aramaic only slightly more prevalent. This is the case for both Judean and Galilean material, countering traditional suggestions that Hebrew was more likely to be spoken in Judea than in Galilee. While recognizing the challenges of extrapolating prescriptive formulas about language use and distribution from epigraphic data, Baltes convincingly demonstrates a healthy presence of various registers of Hebrew, alongside Aramaic, during the Second Temple era.

Chapter 6, "Hebrew, Aramaic, and the Differing Phenomena of Targum and Translation in the Second Temple Period and Post-Second Temple Period," by Daniel Machiela, first reviews the *status quaestionis* of scholarship on Targum dating and provenance and finds that current evidence weighs increasingly against the existence of any of the major ones at the time of Jesus. Machiela then goes further, challenging the widespread view that Targums are translations at all. He supports instead recent arguments that Targums were created "because their authors wanted a non-Hebrew medium in which they might relate extra-Scriptural information about the Hebrew text in synagogal or educational settings" (223). Accepting this model for the composition and survival of Targums would undermine a major support for the argument that Aramaic was the main language of Second Temple Palestine, thus enhancing the probable place of Hebrew.

Presence or absence of specific Hebrew influence in a wide range of Jewish Greek literature is covered by Buth in chapter 7, "Distinguishing Hebrew from Aramaic in Semitized Greek Texts, with an Application for the Gospels and Pseudepigrapha." This is the technical high point of the collection, having been "simmering" in its author's mind for some thirty years (253 n. 15). He provides three tests involving the presence or absence of specific narrative constructions, which he believes can determine whether a Greek text was translated from Aramaic or Hebrew (247). After applying these tests to a range of Jewish Greek texts in order to establish testing validity, he applies them to the Gospels and Acts. While acknowledging that these tests on their own cannot guarantee conclusive results, he finds that, when combined with other evidence, they provide substantial linguistic support for extensive "Hebrew gospel source(s) behind the Greek sources to the Synoptic Gospels" (318).

This second cluster closes with chapter 9, "Hebrew-Only Exegesis: A Philological Approach to Jesus' Use of the Hebrew Bible," in which Notley and Jeffrey Garcia conduct a sophisticated exploration of Jesus's manner of citing the Hebrew Bible in five Synoptic Gospel pericopes. They conclude that in these passages Jesus employed an ancient Jewish exegetical method known as *middoth*, traditionally attributed to Hillel, in which theological pronouncements are generated by deftly combining excerpts from key Hebrew Bible passages. In keeping with this early rabbinic method, Jesus based his *middoth* firmly on the Hebrew Bible, not on an Aramaic translation. Their finding provides at least indirect support for Hebrew as "the original language of the discourse" (374) in accounts of Jesus's exegetical method.

Chapters in the third and final cluster sketch the history of the argument that Jesus spoke only Aramaic, and they disclose the tendency, through Christian history, to employ the argument of language in identifying Jesus as "one of us" or "not one of them." Serge Ruzer in "Hebrew versus Aramaic as Jesus' Language: Notes on Early Opinions by Syriac Authors" (ch. 5) extracts the opinions of early transmitters of the Syriac New Testament about the capacity of Hebrew, Aramaic, and Greek to convey essential religious truths and their comments in passing about the languages used by Jesus in his ministry. While they supported the usual range of languages—Hebrew, Aramaic, and Greek—available to Jesus and spoken by him, none argued that Syriac was his language.

In "The Origins of the 'Exclusive Aramaic Model' in the Nineteenth Century: Methodological Fallacies and Subtle Motives" (ch. 1), Baltes tracks the view that Aramaic was the language of Jesus, starting with Johann Widmannstadt's 1555 publication of the New Testament in Syriac, subtitled "the vernacular of Jesus Christ, sanctified through his own divine mouth and called 'Hebrew' by John the evangelist" (10). He then turns to Heinrich Pfannkuche's 1798 publication arguing for Aramaic as the "Palestinian national language" (12). The "exclusively Aramaic" position was promoted with heightened intensity in the late nineteenth century in publications by Arnold Meyer, Theodor Zahn, and especially Gustaf Dalman, who more than his peers attempted to "extract" Jesus from Judaism and its culturally specific Hebrew language, under the growing political, religious, and social turmoil in Germany, especially growing anti-Semitism. Baltes closes his survey with the frankly and openly anti-Hebraic, anti-Semitic *Babel und Bibel* lectures by Friedrich Delitzsch at the beginning of the twentieth century. In this chapter Baltes attempts the difficult but necessary task of integrating the purely academic enquiry into the languages of ancient Palestine, and of Jesus, into the political, religious, and social tensions that attempted to take over that enquiry and use it to achieve political goals.

All chapters are valuable for their fresh "excavations" of available textual and material evidence for their respective topics. Several also apply current sociolinguistic theories to their topics. Their work is also strengthened by the range of Israeli scholarship from which they draw, especially that published in modern Hebrew and therefore inaccessible to many researchers. One collective aim of the authors, to more thoroughly document Hebrew as a living language alongside Aramaic in Second Temple Palestine, has clearly succeeded.

Detracting from some chapters is lack of reference to relevant published research. Most striking is the omission of James Edwards, *The Hebrew Gospel and the Development of the Synoptic Tradition* (2009), in which he argued at length that the so-called Hebrew Gospel, widely attested in early Christian sources, was employed by the evangelists, resulting in considerable Hebraisms, especially in Luke. Discussions of Lukan Hebraisms in the chapters under review also fail to acknowledge the extensive work of Adolf Schlatter on the Hebraic features in the Synoptic Gospels, especially his *Das Evangelium des Lukas* (2nd ed., 1960), where he argued for Hebrew, or at least highly Hebraized sources, behind at least four of Notley's "non-Septuagintal Hebraisms" in Luke 6:22, 9:44, 15:18, 16:19 (332–45). The Blass-Debrunner-Funk *Grammar of the Greek New Testament* of 1961 is cited several times, but not its German original, which continued to be revised as recently as 2001 by Rehkopf. To have done so could have supported the arguments of some chapters, because Rehkopf abbreviates and thereby seems to downplay accounts of Aramaic influence in Funk's translation. This is evident in §4 of Blass-Debrunner.

There are a very few references to out-of-date editions of standard reference works: Liddell & Scott's *Greek-English Lexicon* of 1843 is cited instead of the current 1968 edition (345 n. 126). The same author elsewhere (325 n. 23) dates the lexicon to 1996, which is the publication date of the lexicon's *Supplement*. The original 1957 Arndt and Gingrich translation of Bauer's *Greek-English Lexicon* is cited instead of the current, significantly revised third English edition of 2000 (376 n. 3).

This essay collection certainly achieves the modest chief aim claimed for it by Buth in his introduction: "to move beyond the … bilingual Greek-Aramaic assumptions" of much gospel study, replacing them with a "trilingual" one that firmly establishes Hebrew among the living languages of first-century Palestine (4–5). While some of the authors' claims for specific cases of Hebrew influence stop short of complete certainty, the extensive linguistic data they cite strongly supports their case for the restoration of Hebrew as one of the three main languages in use during the first century. Because of its immediate relevance for detailed gospel study, this collection of essays should be on the reference shelf and within easy reach of all serious students of the gospels who attempt to encounter the linguistic landscape of first-century Palestine.

Grammatical Concepts 101 for Biblical Hebrew, by Gary A. Long. 2nd edition. Grand Rapids: Baker Academic, 2013. Pp. xx + 213. Paper. $22.99. ISBN 9780801048746.

Hubert James Keener, Wheaton College

In 2002 Gary Long published a book inspired by the pattern used in the *English Grammar for Students of Foreign Languages* (Olivia & Hill Press) intended to help students of Biblical Hebrew.[1] The result was a helpful supplemental textbook that presented English and Hebrew grammatical concepts in tandem, so that English-speaking students could enter into the foreign world of Hebrew grammar by way of a journey through the basics of English grammar. Last year Baker

---

1. Gary A. Long, *Grammatical Concepts 101 for Biblical Hebrew: Learning Biblical Hebrew Grammatical Concepts through English Grammar* (Peabody, MA: Hendrickson, 2002), xv.

Academic published a second edition of the book that has been updated, slightly rearranged in places, and expanded.

In 2010 Miles Van Pelt published a similar book, *English Grammar to Ace Biblical Hebrew*.[2] As a result, many Hebrew professors will wonder which of the two books will serve better as a supplemental text for their students, and interested students may wonder which book they will find more helpful. The review that follows, therefore, will pay special attention to noting how the second edition of *Grammatical Concepts* compares with the 2002 edition of the same book and Van Pelt's *English Grammar*.

Part 1, "Foundations," lays the groundwork for understanding how language works. The first section adumbrates the various "building blocks or hierarchies" that make up language usage, from the most basic unit (phoneme/phone) to the discourse level of the text itself. The discussion here is insightful and serves the dual purpose of helping students to think about the way in which language works while also introducing them to linguistic concepts that they will encounter in the secondary literature if they move on to advanced academic study of the Hebrew Bible. While the terms used in this discussion may be familiar to professors of Hebrew (emic, etic, lexeme, morpheme, etc.), they are likely to be completely new to most undergraduates. In this way, Long's book is markedly different in tone from Van Pelt's, which sets forth a "very basic introduction to English grammar" and steers clear of linguistic terms such as *emic* and *etic* (Van Pelt, 12).

Yet Long's book "is *not necessarily* to be read cover to cover" (xvii, emphasis original); if, for example, some professors think that the material on linguistic hierarchies might be beyond the zone of proximal development for their students, they will still find much material of benefit in the sections on sound production (7–17), syllable (18), and translation (19–25) that make up the rest of part 1. Perhaps the most helpful section here is the brief treatment of translation theory, which provides the student with a brief overview of the sorts of decisions translators must make, introducing the student to the concepts behind "form-oriented" (i.e., literal) and "meaning-oriented" (i.e., dynamic equivalence) approaches and locating several translations on a continuum somewhere between these two poles.

Part 2, "Building Blocks," makes up almost 60 percent of the book and speaks most directly to the "grammatical" concerns that the book is intended to address. As such, the beginning student struggling to master the foreign constructions of Hebrew prose will find this material the most useful. The format is straightforward and practical. Basic grammatical concepts are taken in turn (gender, number, tense and aspect, mood, etc.). Each concept is addressed first from the standpoint of English grammar, then from the standpoint of Hebrew grammar. While this approach is useful, it would be nice to have the English and Hebrew concepts and examples more directly juxtaposed for purposes of reference and

---

2. Miles V. Van Pelt, *English Grammar to Ace Biblical Hebrew* (Grand Rapids: Zondervan, 2010).

illustration, especially in lengthier sections (e.g., the sections on the pronoun [47–67] and mood [115–28]) where the discussion of a grammatical function in Hebrew becomes even further removed from the accompanying discussion of the same function in English.[3]

This section contains many clear and simple visuals that beginning students will find helpful. Most significantly, Long includes illustrative sentences on nearly every page that are accompanied by arrows, lines, and descriptive comments that make it clear to the reader how words in each sentence function grammatically.

Here, while the discussion is not so advanced as to be inaccessible for most students, it tends again to be more technical in tone and content than Van Pelt's book. For example, Van Pelt describes pronouns as "grammatical stunt doubles" and uses the metaphor to explain such basic concepts as antecedent, gender, near and far demonstratives, and the like (47–54). In contrast, Long's section on the pronoun dives directly into a discussion on the anaphoric and cataphoric, or proleptic, uses of the pronoun on the first page (47) and explores the difference between restrictive and nonrestrictive relative clauses (56–57). This is not to say that Long's treatment is helplessly arcane; it is fairly elementary overall but more technical than Van Pelt. Again, which of the two books is better suited for a given circumstance will depend largely upon the situation and the class's or student's background and preferences.

Part 3, "The Clause and Beyond," moves well beyond the basics of grammar and "introduces the learner to the higher levels of language" (xviii). This section surveys the topics of clause, subject, predicate, and semantics, culminating in a brief introduction to discourse analysis (145–97). This last section will be especially helpful to students who, being close to mastering the basics of Hebrew morphology, are ready to move beyond the struggles of identifying and parsing individual words and can pay closer attention to the ways in which words, clauses, and sentences coordinate together to convey meaning in Biblical Hebrew. Since it is not uncommon for a first-year Hebrew course to culminate in the reading of a biblical book such as Ruth or Jonah, this section could be used as supplemental reading that might aid the students as they struggle to understand how the parts fit together to make a whole.

How, then, does this edition of Long's book compare with Van Pelt's slim volume? How one answers this question will depend upon several situational factors, including the background knowledge and interests of the students involved. In my review of Van Pelt's book, I expressed concern that the book might insult the intelligence of its readers (https://www.bookreviews.org/book-detail.asp?TitleId=7536); the very first exercise in the book reads: "Write out, in order, the 26 letters of the English alphabet" (19)! Long's book, by contrast, has a

---

3. This same suggestion has already been made in Perry J. Oakes, review of Gary A. Long, *Grammatical Concepts 101 for Biblical Hebrew* (https://www.bookreviews.org/bookdetail .asp?TitleId=9163).

very different orientation, and his diction is less colloquial. "Within the halls of the academy," Long tells his reader at the outset, "the commonest surroundings I envision for this textbook, I have thought it pedagogically useful to use English's acrolect, its prestige forms" (xviii). On the one hand, then, some students may find Long's book to be more helpful and insightful; it goes beyond a superficial survey treatment of nouns, verbs, and prepositions and introduces the student to valuable linguistic concepts. On the other hand, other students may find Long's language to be arcane, off-putting, and frustrating and may benefit more from Van Pelt's casual and engaging style.

Several modifications have made this edition an improvement over its predecessor. For example, the first edition contained only a very terse treatment of the article, telling the reader that "any [Hebrew] word that does not have a definite article ... ought to be conveyed in English with an indefinite article";[4] the current edition corrects this, expanding the section significantly with a discussion of indefinite, individual, and qualitative nonarticular nominals that is more helpful and nuanced and an accompanying chart comparing the various meanings of articular and nonarticular nominals (33–38).

More subtly, part 2 now contains paradigmatic third masculine singular forms of the *qal* stem using the roots קטל and פקד (the paradigmatic root used in Allen P. Ross's introductory grammar, also published by Baker Academic).[5] This move to synchronize Long with introductory Hebrew grammars is helpful. I respectfully suggest here that future editions of *Grammatical Concepts* would be more user-friendly if such synchronization were carried a step further. Van Pelt's little volume helpfully tells the reader which chapter in Zondervan's *The Basics of Biblical Hebrew* addresses the material covered in a given chapter of *English Grammar*. It would be a great help to student and professor alike if Long were to include a similar system, tagging sections from Long with page numbers of parallel passages from Ross (or other grammars) that address similar material.

This modest suggestion for improvement notwithstanding, Long's book is a helpful volume that learners of Biblical Hebrew will find useful. The organization is clear, the presentation is straightforward and accessible, and the material covered is highly relevant. Not insignificantly, the book provides the reader with a substantive treatment of a variety of topics, from linguistic hierarchies (3–6), to the complex relationship between tense and aspect (102–14), to a helpful summary of discourse analysis (173–97). I would suggest this book to interested learners of Biblical Hebrew, and I have assigned the book to my own elementary Hebrew class. Alternatively, the book could serve as a refresher for a student who has completed one year of introductory Hebrew already, or it could provide helpful supplemental readings for a second-year, intermediate Hebrew course.

---

4. Long, 2002, 29–30. This error was pointed out in Brian L. Webster, review of *Grammatical Concepts 101 for Biblical Hebrew*, by Gary A. Long, *Bibliotheca Sacra* 2006 (163): 491.

5. Allen P. Ross, *Introducing Biblical Hebrew* (Grand Rapids: Baker Academic, 2001).

Reading Koine Greek: An Introduction and Integrated Workbook, by Rodney J. Decker. Grand Rapids: Baker Academic, 2014. Pp. xxxi + 672. Hardcover. $49.99. ISBN 9780801039287.

James F. McGrath, Butler University

Rodney Decker's posthumously published textbook *Reading Koine Greek* is very much a tour de force. I will not make the attempt here to offer a detailed comparison to other textbooks, whether classic or recent, as there have been many, and I would inevitably end up focusing more attention on those books that I happen to own or have used, whether to learn, or for reference, or to teach Greek to others. I will, however, note where Decker's text seems to stand out from most or all textbooks with which I am familiar, not in the interest of claiming that it is in fact unique but in order to highlight where it genuinely seems to be distinctive at least in relation to many well-known and widely used alternatives.

Language learning is approached in two major ways: inductively, by learning equivalents of words and phrases in one's own language and later discovering or being told the underlying rules and more precise nuances; or with a focus from the outset on grammar and the learning of rules for which one will only encounter the application of some elements much later. Decker's textbook is a hybrid of the two: at times it appears closer to the latter approach, but at the same time it nonetheless seeks to incorporate extensive elements of the former. Entirely missing are the artificially concocted sentences that allow simple words to be strung together in simple sentences that one will never encounter in the New Testament or elsewhere. Gone as well are the English sentences that students are often asked to turn into inevitably awkward Greek. Instead, throughout the volume Decker uses examples drawn entirely from the New Testament, the Septuagint, and other ancient Jewish and Christian literature. At the very beginning, sentences made from both English and Greek words are used, which are then replaced with simple sentences from ancient texts with English glosses and footnotes where necessary to help the beginning student read despite as yet unfamiliar vocabulary. The textbook is emphatically not "New Testament Greek" but *Koine* Greek, and it covers vocabulary, grammar, and examples that are irrelevant for those whose interest is solely in the New Testament. As Decker points out, seeking to understand a particular corpus requires knowledge of the broader linguistic and literary context (xx).

The textbook is one that begins at the very beginning in teaching the elements of Greek, while also offering the major components of a reference grammar and also a workbook, all rolled into one. I will not list the sections individually, since there is no need for this review to say more than that it covers the crucial topics and does so in a logical order—although the decision to relegate the vocative to an appendix seemed odd to me. The amount of detail included is also distinctive. Decker's book explains in writing many matters of form as well as apparent exceptions to rules and the reasons for them, and it does so in greater detail than any other textbook I have used or consulted. In most instances, in the context of my own education, the matters covered were addressed verbally by a professor in the context of an exegesis class beyond the introductory level, and then the explanations were offered only when they were encountered in a text, if at all. Often those who teach Greek are not themselves linguists or trained foreign-language instructors but individuals who studied Greek for pragmatic reasons, to allow us to investigate particular texts of interest to us. This being the case, those who find themselves thrust into the role of Greek professor often hope that students will not ask about exceptions to rules, the dreaded "why" to which we often have no better answer than "that's just the way it is." Often, of course, that may indeed be the only possible response. But because there are complex rules governing the interactions between stems and multiple vowel combinations, beginning Greek professors whose background is primarily in New Testament study will often wonder whether there is a better answer to be given in some of the instances. Decker's book regularly offers such detailed explanations, while also taking the time to let students know whether something is worth memorizing and indicating when something may be skimmed or skipped initially and returned to for later reference. I suspect that few who delve into the book—including those who already have a high degree of proficiency in Koine Greek—will fail to learn something new.

Nevertheless, the book aims to be an introductory textbook, even while dealing as comprehensively as possible with questions of form and grammar. In my judgment, it succeeds in its attempt to provide both, although it is difficult for someone with proficiency in a language to evaluate the way a textbook will seem to complete beginners. Be that as it may, *Reading Koine Greek* has all the things that are standard in most if not all textbooks: an introduction to the alphabet, explanation of pronunciation (including the several different approaches to this), charts with paradigms, and explanation of accents—including why those who copy and paste words from an online Greek New Testament are given away when they fail to change a grave accent to an acute (19). Decker adds to these standard features some others that are less common, including images of manuscripts or ones that show what pages in lexicons look like. Wherever possible, analogies to English grammar are provided. But Decker made great efforts to ensure that students do not think there is a one-to-one correspondence between English vocabulary and grammatical categories and their closest Greek equivalent. This is expressed all throughout the book not only in discussions of matters such as tense and aspect but also in the presentation of new vocabulary, which offers a column with definition, in addition to possible English glosses for the Greek word in question.

Another distinctive feature of the textbook is the incorporation of humor into the text, making it much more engaging than any language textbook without a humorous element ever manages to be. There is a song for learning the alphabet in Greek, silly mnemonics, a Yoda reference, a reference to a contemporary Christian song to illustrate the middle voice, and an insistence that readers really do not want to know the full story behind how a particular unusual form ended up the way that it did. In one instance, the choice of one element in the mnemonic was surprising, using "os" in English to help students remember the Greek ending ας (189). But in general these features seem appropriate, helpful, and likely to be effective in aiding student retention.

Decker mentions in the preface that he writes as a Christian who regards the New Testament as authoritative; I suspect this detail will make some would-be users of the book uncomfortable. It was an interesting move on his part and may have been aimed at forestalling concerns both from those who are interested solely in teaching the language and who are liable to be suspicious of someone who taught at a conservative seminary, as well as from those who might view Decker's criticism of popular misuse of Greek in sermons and other ecclesiastical contexts as indicative that he was attacking their faith rather than someone who shares it. Be that as it may, I will say that Decker's book seems to me equally suitable to secular and religious contexts, since its focus is squarely on the language and the acquisition thereof, and indeed, it differs from other textbooks in providing numerous examples from beyond the New Testament. (It is perhaps also worth noting that the production of New Testament Greek textbooks seems to have a long tradition of association with seminary professors, often on the conservative end of the Christian tradition, so this feature does not distinguish Decker's book from alternatives except in its explicitness about the subject.)

Decker also addresses common misconceptions about the aorist and, appropriately for a volume produced in our time, also addresses the use of relevant software as well as other print resources. Decker states quite bluntly in the epilogue, "If you can read a Greek text only by identifying most of the Greek words through use of the program tools, then you do not know Greek" (564). As a final test, students are given a lengthy excerpt from the Letter of Jeremiah to translate, an excellent move since it is a text that few students will have memorized, and thus they must genuinely rely on their knowledge of the language (558).

Decker's textbook is informed by the latest work on language acquisition, and on more than one occasion Decker tells readers that there is more than one way of approaching things and defers to their teachers. One instance when he does not do so is in the listing of cases in their traditional Greek order (NGDA) as opposed to the order more commonly used in the study of modern languages (NAGD). The latter is often considered preferable both because of the logical flow from subject through direct object to indirect objects, as well as because of the fact that it places identical nominative and accusative forms together where these exist, aiding memorization. Arguments can be offered in favor of both options, but I was surprised that the possibility of an alternative ordering was not even mentioned in passing, given the extent to which Decker generally indicates different approaches to teaching and explaining elements of Greek. For some reason the index at the end does not list references to Philo and Josephus, although it does have other ancient authors who are mentioned, such as Polybius and Plutarch (both mentioned on 8). Such omissions are minor matters when one considers that many language textbooks do not have an index at all.

If and when I ever teach Koine Greek again, Decker's textbook would be my first choice. While it would be better, when offering a review of a textbook, to be able to comment on the basis of having used it in teaching, rather than merely having read it, the features it offers make it possible to recommend it with confidence even so. In particular, the integration of reading from the New Testament and Septuagint throughout, and the exclusive use of real ancient texts as readings, set Decker's textbook apart from all others with which I am familiar.

Reading Koine Greek: An Introduction and Integrated Workbook, by Rodney J. Decker. Grand Rapids: Baker Academic, 2014. Pp. xxxi + 672. Hardcover. $49.99. ISBN 9780801039287.

Steven Thompson, Avondale College of Higher Education

Rodney Decker's *Reading Koine Greek* is not actually a "reader" in the conventional meaning of the term. He provided one of those in his 2007 *Koine Greek Reader*. Not even in the subtitle of the volume under review—*An Introduction and Integrated Workbook*— does it become clear that this is a beginner's grammar intended for students of New Testament Greek. Only in the preface is it declared to be a beginner's grammar for New Testament Greek. As an "integrated" grammar and workbook, this volume continues the current *expansive* tendency of beginning New Testament Greek grammars published during the past decade. Its xxxi + 672 pages include thirty-three numbered lessons plus preface, introduction, abbreviations, six appendices, bibliography, and index.

The basic features of Greek are introduced in a sequence typical for introductory grammars, beginning with nouns and pronouns, then finite verbs, which are treated progressively in thirteen separate chapters. Nonfinite verbs are treated in six chapters, followed by *–mi* verbs in chapters 32 and 33. Adjectives, adverbs, conjunctions, and other grammatical components are covered from chapter 6 onward. Syntax is introduced in chapter 8 and continued in chapters 9, 30, and 31. Verbal semantics is first systematically explained in chapter 13. Untypically for beginner's grammars, this one uses chapter and section (§) rather than page number: thus a reference in the index to "1.24," for example, refers to chapter 1 §24. This simple but useful feature equips students later to find their way through standard reference grammars. Paradigms, charts, and tables are employed generously through the chapters and compiled more systematically in appendix A (566–95).

Decker included in this grammar a veritable armory of features designed to engage and activate students. The customary ones expected in a beginner's grammar include "text boxes" containing supplementary, informative notes. Most chapters include "Reading Exercises" (chs. 1–5) or "Reading Passages" (chs. 6–33) and a vocabulary list for each chapter. Less-conventional features of most chapters include sections titled "Advanced Information for Reference," "Key Things to Know for Chapter Z," and "Now You Try It" workbook-type exercises. Another feature, rare in beginner's grammars, is Decker's use of illustrative clauses that blend Greek and English within a single phrase, for didactic purposes. These could be labeled "Τρεεnglish," a sort of Greek-English counterpart of "Franglais!" Their purpose is obviously to ease students into reading a Greek passage before they have acquired sufficient familiarity with all of its vocabulary and grammar features. Another unconventional but practical feature is the grammatical diagramming of selected clauses, beginning in chapter 3. Decker employs this "forgotten art" to great effectiveness to help students visualize the relation of various grammatical components in clauses. This seems especially useful at a time when so many students lack a basic awareness of the grammar and syntax of their own language. Another strength of Decker's approach to the presentation of Greek syntax comes from his position of "grammatical minimalism" (xv), which calls for reduced expectations of meaning arising from individual words in isolation and insists instead that only in their literary context can words reliably convey their author's meaning.

The teacher's spoken voice comes through in this work more than in most others of its genre. Its regular use of first- and second-person personal pronouns *I*, *we*, *you* seems deliberate, from the first *you* on the first page of the preface right through to the appendices. This feature confirms the impression that this grammar, like most of its genre, originated as classroom presentations. Decker acknowledges the grammar's existence "in manuscript form" for several years while being used by a teaching assistant (xvi). While these frequent direct-address pronouns first strike the reader as somewhat "chatty" and require some getting used to, one should grant a concession to the author. Due to terminal illness, Decker spent his final months sitting at the fireside producing this work, which was published half a year after his death. By means of his grammar he "made himself available" postmortem to continue his role teaching beginning Greek.

A volume this size allows the author to incorporate many features that make it suitable for individuals working on their own as well as for those in class. Note, for example, its treatment of conjunctions (some of which are more correctly particles functioning as conjunctions), to which Decker devoted ten pages distributed across four chapters.

Other features, however, might be seen as unnecessary distractions. In common with other recently published beginner's grammars, this one bristles with statistics, mostly counts of word occurrences—probably far more than most beginners need. Also, it employs a series of single-letter abbreviations for standard grammatical categories, rather than the conventional ones employed in the standard lexica and reference grammars. While these are listed and explained (xxi), they seem an unnecessary sidestepping of a useful convention, especially in light of Decker's frequent reference to Danker's *Concise Greek-English Lexicon of the New Testament*, a work he regularly urges students to consult. Also, there are a small number of references to Hebrew language and grammar which, while of passing interest, could distract beginners grappling with Greek (see §2.26 [42 n. a]).

It is surprising that in 8.19 (145) Decker quotes Conybeare and Stock's venerable 1905 *Grammar of Septuagint Greek*: "roughly speaking, it is true to say that in the Greek of the LXX there is no syntax, only parataxis." This is surely a misstatement by Conybeare and Stock because the LXX, like any ancient Greek literary document, is syntactical from its first to its last verse! What Conybeare and Stock surely meant was that the syntax of the LXX contains little hypotaxis (the subordination of clauses after the manner of classical Greek) and much "parataxis" (coordination of clauses, after the manner of biblical Hebrew). Surprisingly, Decker quotes this apparent misstatement without challenging or correcting it, although earlier he clearly and appropriately defined "syntax" as "the way in which a language organizes the various words into phrases, clauses, statements, and larger units" (8.1, 132).

Readers may detect in Decker's grammar subtle campaigning for his preferred "take" on the long-disputed issue of the nature of New Testament Greek in relation to ancient Greek as a whole. It seemed to have influenced his choice of the label "Koine Greek" in place of the long-established "New Testament Greek" or "biblical Greek" for grammars of this genre. *Koine* appears in the title and is justified in the preface: "This text is titled *Reading Koine Greek*, in part to indicate that it covers not just NT Greek but also the wider range of Bible-related Greek, especially the Septuagint (LXX) and to some extent the Pseudepigrapha and the Apostolic Fathers" (xix). Decker at least indirectly acknowledges the unsuitability of *Koine* for his purpose. Appendix B's list of "Common Koine Verbs" (596) is rebadged more correctly "Common Verbs in the New Testament and Septuagint" two pages later. His unconventional and undefended definition of "Hellenistic Greek" on page 5 is puzzling.

Only one typographical mistake caught this reviewer's attention: "the Greek word *yap*" (132 n. 1). The context clearly calls for Greek *gar* at that point. The unintended pun created by this typo, in an already light-hearted reference to a preacher's sermon, provides a smile! Apart from this, Decker and his team appear to have produced a typo-free work, for which they are to be congratulated!

Overall, Decker has produced a richly informative and generously detailed work of high quality in which he devoted considerable effort to introduce and explain the features of biblical Greek that a beginning student would need to know. This reviewer recommends it, especially for students working on their own, who would benefit from hearing a teacher's "voice." It is also well suited for students whose enlarged capacity for learning enables them to absorb and make use of the wide range of information included.

ARCHAEOLOGY AND HISTORY

Small Change in Hellenistic-Roman Galilee: The Evidence from Numismatic Site Finds as a Tool for Historical Reconstruction, by Danny Syon. Numismatic Studies and Researches 11. Jerusalem: Israel Numismatic Society, 2015. Pp. 288. Paper. $75.00. ISBN 9789655558012.

Mark A. Chancey, Southern Methodist University

Danny Syon's remarkably thorough analysis of Hellenistic and Roman-era coin finds in northern Israel is easily the most comprehensive investigation of numismatic circulation ever published for both Galilee and Palestine as a whole. Though it includes discussion of silver and gold coins, its focus is squarely on bronze currency. It synthesizes data for over 15,000 coins minted between 300 BCE and 260 CE and found at 247 sites in Galilee, the Golan, and adjacent areas as well as six outside sites that serve as comparison points (Sia, Pella, Mount Gerizim, Samaria, Jaffa, and Bet Zur). The result is a significantly clearer picture of the growth of monetization, the shifting importance of particular mints, and the various types of coins in circulation. Twenty-nine tables and seventy-two photos and figures (many of the latter maps with miniature pie charts identifying the most strongly represented mints at individual sites) help convey the massive amount of information Syon has assembled. Syon contextualizes his findings within debates over Galilee's ethnic composition, settlement history, religious practices, and economic climate that are familiar to scholars specializing in early Judaism, New Testament, and the archaeology of Palestine.

A scholar with the Israel Antiquities Authority, Syon is well known among archaeologists and historians of Roman Palestine for his earlier publications on numismatics and the city of Gamla. This book reflects a revision and updating of a portion of his doctoral dissertation, "Tyre and Gamla: The Monetary Influence of Southern Phoenicia on Galilee" [Hebrew] (Hebrew University, 2004), which he wrote under the direction of Dan Barag. Though Syon has coauthored excavation reports on Gamla, this is his first monograph.

Methodological concerns provide the focus for the first five chapters. Syon walks carefully through the challenges posed by the very nature of numismatic evidence and the scale and scope of this study, explicitly justifying his own interpretive decisions. His own categorization of the data is based on mint dates. He reasons, "When analyzing data from a large number of sites, then the effects of uncertain stratigraphy and/or of the varying methods by which the coins were collected can be ignored without too great a compromise" (48). Geographically, his study includes the central Golan, which he argues was considered an integral part of Galilee from at least the Hasmonean period onward (50–52). These chapters also include a chronological overview of the region's history, descriptions of hoards, and identification of pertinent issues in Galilean studies and numismatic scholarship.

The sixth chapter offers a site-by-site summary of numismatic finds, some recovered in stratigraphic contexts and some not. Each of the 254 entries includes the number of coins from the focal period; bibliographic information, if available; and, particularly for unpublished coins, the collection of which they are a part (often Israel Antiquities Authority holdings or kibbutz collections). Even in its rawest form, this is an impressive accumulation of information and resource for future research.

The next six chapters divide the region's coins into six eras, with parameters determined by patterns in the numismatic record: Ptolemaic (300–200 BCE), Seleucid (200–125 BCE), Hasmonean (125–63 BCE), Early Roman Period I (63 BCE–70 CE), Early Roman Period II (70–138 CE), and Middle Roman Period (138–260 CE). The book ends at 260 CE because of the cessation of civic minting in the region during the reign of Emperor Gallienus (253–268 CE). For each period, Syon provides charts, maps, and discussion that identifies the number of coins found at individual sites and the primary mints of origin. For example, a map for the Seleucid period (144 fig. 27) illustrates the geographical distribution of 2,427 coins at 147 sites, with color-coded pie charts for each site indicating the proportion of coins from the main mints, Tyre, Ptolemais, Sidon, and Antioch. Syon describes the dominance of the mint of Ptolemais for the early Seleucid era, the emergence of Tyre as the most prolific issuer of bronze for its later decades, and the surprising presence of coins minted by Antiochus VII at Jerusalem.

The book ends with two brief chapters. One examines the extent to which Galilee's numismatic profile correlates to the findings of surface surveys regarding chronological changes in size, number, establishment, and abandonment of settlements, concluding that "a numismatic database [alone] is not a very suitable tool for the analysis of settlement dynamics" (243). The final chapter concisely summarizes the study's major findings. A bibliography and indices follow, and a map of the 247 sites is inserted at the back cover.

As would be expected, Syon frequently tackles technical issues related to particular coin types. For example, he explores the interpretation of the *alpha* inscribed on coins of Hyrcanus II (59); whether Herod the Great issued copies of Tyrian shekels at Jerusalem, as famously suggested by Yaakov Meshorer (70; like most scholars, Syon rejects the theory); and the identification of the minting authorities for coins issued at Tiberias in 53/54 CE and Sepphoris in 66/67 CE (174–77). Although he argues that Richard Simon Hanson's influential *Tyrian Influence in Upper Galilee* (Cambridge: American Schools of Oriental Research, 1980) misidentifies many coins (25), he does not identify the specimens in question, presumably because of space limitations. One hopes that he will make a make a more detailed case for new attributions in a future publication.

But reflection on broader historiographical questions outweighs analysis of individual coins. Syon devotes considerable attention to the import and wide circulation of Hasmonean coinage. On the basis of numerous numismatic finds from the reigns of Hyrcanus I (135–105 BCE) and Aristobulus I (105–104 CE), he suggests that by the end of the second century BCE "Galilee and the Golan were already inhabited by Jews to a considerable extent" (164), though he also acknowledges the impact of Alexander Jannaeus's later conquests circa 83–80 BCE (161).

Syon contends that previous scholarship viewing Tyre as the dominant mint for Galilee for most of the Greco-Roman era has oversimplified more complex realities. In an argument directed at New Testament scholars, he demonstrates that "precisely in the first century CE Tyre had a smaller monetary role in Galilee than in the periods that came before and after" (226). Syon insists that "one cannot infer direct trade with the city that issued a coin from finding it at some site, any more than inferring that cities that did not strike coins had no trade" (49), a point that suggests less direct trade between Galilean communities and Tyre than is often thought.

Syon seems to provide the definitive word on whether Herod Antipas issued his own coins to monetize his tetrarchy's economy. The client king provided only a small share of the region's bronzes, with far more coming from other Herodian rulers, Roman authorities in Jerusalem, Tyre, and other mints. Coins of Antipas are significantly less numerous than older Hasmonean issues, many of which remained in circulation in the first century CE (171–99). Syon concludes that there is little reason to suspect rapid monetization in the Herodian period as a whole (32–33).

Evidence from Syon's Middle Roman Period (138–260 CE) suggests a growing level of monetization. Issues from Tyre, Ptolemais, Caesarea Maritima were the most widespread, but as civic mints proliferated in the Roman East coins from some sixty-three other mints made their way to the region, creating a "bewildering blend of types and denominations" (219). Syon associates this peak in minting with the "massive urbanization that most cities went through under the Severan dynasty" (219). The third-century economic crisis, with its inflation and debasement of silver, brought this diversity to an end as Romans imposed a more standardized currency system.

Syon opens his first chapter with the acknowledgement that "one criticism that will be leveled at this work is that it does not enter more deeply into issues of economy, trade, monetization, and more theoretical issues of value and coin use, as well as related social questions" (21). It is true that presentation of empirical data and interaction with historiographical matters greatly outweigh in-depth engagement with theoretical literature. However, Syon has certainly provided ample new raw material for more theoretically oriented scholars to explore.

Syon's presentation of this daunting amount of material is usually admirably clear, but close reading of the main text is a must for understanding the accompanying graphics. Tables and maps vary on issues such as their inclusion of silver coins or bronze alone and their inclusion or exclusion of coins from hoards. Many readers will naturally and reasonably wonder how the data Syon has amassed would look if analyzed through stratigraphic lenses, but those familiar with the nature of coin finds and their varying states of publication will recognize that such a project is impossible at this scale.

In any case, Syon is quite candid about the strengths and limitations of his methodological and interpretive choices. He knows what he can show for certain, when the data lends itself to multiple interpretations, and when he lacks the information needed to answer questions definitively. The result of his painstaking efforts is what is now the new starting point for understanding the use of coins in Hellenistic and Roman Galilee.

The Sacred Economy of Ancient Israel, by Roland Boer. Library of Ancient Israel. Louisville: Westminster John Knox, 2015. Pp. xix + 308. Paper $50.00. ISBN 9780664259662.

K. L. Noll, Brandon University

Roland Boer's book is a worthwhile study that this reviewer recommends, but it bears a misleading title. *The Sacred Economy of Ancient Israel* rarely mentions ancient Israel, never offers sustained analysis of ancient Israel, and never defines or explores the word *sacred*, instead viewing the ancient Near East's economy through the lens of Marxist materialism. From Boer's perspective, the economy was the social and political matrix of daily life. Sacredness—to the extent that this concept appears in the book at all—is a label for ancient speculations about otherworldly realities, ranging from superstitions about dead ancestors, benevolent local gods, and malevolent demons, to ritual practices of magic and divination. The book offers insightful discussions about many aspects of daily life in the ancient world, but a more accurate title would have been *Ancient Subsistence Agriculture: The Locus of Resistance against Forced Extraction.*

Chapter 1 trudges through the necessary preliminary remarks about theory in which Boer castigates neoclassical economics and offers his Marxist alternative. Neoclassical economics—the great defender of capitalism—is guilty of several sins, according to Boer. First, neoclassical theorists ignore the social dimension of an economy in favor of an unrelenting focus on the individual. Second, these theorists practice an ahistorical intellectual imperialism in which the myth of Homo economicus, flawlessly pursuing rational self-interest, has been projected into all times and places. Curiously, Boer also asserts that neoclassical economics is guilty of "detheologizing or even debiblicizing economics" (11; see also 18). Unfortunately, Boer does not explain what this cryptic accusation means, and his few fleeting references to theology fail to clarify his point. For example, Boer asserts that the "imperializing pretensions" of neoclassical theory reveal "theology at its most pernicious" because it "overtly dispensed with its theological concerns" and somehow abandoned something that Boer calls "the traditional checks of theology" (12). This is a meaningless word soup. Neither neoclassical economics nor Boer's Marxist economic theories have anything to do with theology, and, not surprisingly, no theological discussions appear in the book. On the contrary, like any orthodox Marxist, Boer treats "the sacred" as an ideological veneer cloaking material realities.

After dismissing neoclassical economics, Boer reviews four Marxist or semi-Marxist approaches to economics, two of which receive approval. Boer is not impressed by semi-Marxist theories about economic relationships between core and peripheral regions or theories associated with reciprocity and redistribution. Unlike the two favored theories, these focus on parts of an economy and not the whole. The first of Boer's favored models is Soviet-era Marxist scholarship, which insists that the word *economy* should encompass every aspect of material existence and applies a familiar Marxist thesis that each mode of production contains internal contradictions generating tension, crisis, and eventual collapse. The second of Boer's favored models is the Marxist *régulation* theory (Boer insists on the French word and not its English cognate, asserting that the latter fails to capture what is meant). This is the theory that economic instability is the normal state of human affairs. Therefore, any imposed economic system is a *régulation*, a structure of social, institutional, and ideological forms that work together to maintain an artificial stability. Boer has combined these two models to suggest that every economy is a set of social relations, a *regime* of habits, customs, rules (both written and unwritten), as well as formal institutions that try to make everything work, but always contain internal contradictions that will lead to collapse and a return to the normal state of instability.

These Marxist models provide Boer with the vocabulary of this book, in which aspects of ancient daily life are conceptualized as institutional *forms*, and these forms work together to sustain an economic *regime*. One type of regime is *allocative*. In an allocative economic regime, all participants are producers who share in the fruits of labor. Boer identifies the ubiquitous agrarian subsistence economy as the allocative regime. It contrasts with two other regimes, each of which is an economy of *extraction*, in which nonproducers extract resources and labor from exploited producers. In Boer's model, the allocative agrarian subsistence economy was the ever-present foundation underlying the extractive regimes, and it always emerged unscathed after each extractive regime rose, endured for a while, and inevitably collapsed. Allocation was the default to which human societies returned every time extraction produced the ill effects that spelled its own doom.

Given his model of an enduring agrarian subsistence economy perpetually resisting the extractive regimes that periodically imposed themselves on it, Boer's historical narrative is predictable. During the Bronze Age, the regime of *palace* (*e*)*states* extracted resources from the subsistence forms over which these smaller or larger kingdoms ruled. The Iron Age saw the emergence of a new regime, that of *imperial plunder*, perpetrated by Neo-Assyrian, Neo-Babylonian, and Persian Empires. As the internal contradictions within each regime took their toll, that regime collapsed so that the normal state of affairs, the localized subsistence economies, reemerged. Viewed over the long duration from the early Bronze Age to the late Persian era, these unstable subsistence economies occasionally punctuated by regimes of imposed stability constitute a mode of production that Boer has chosen to call the sacred economy.

In the three-act tragedy that Boer narrates, Israel is nothing more than a minor character who walked onto the stage somewhere near the start of the final act and was quickly defeated by larger imperial players. According to Boer, Israel emerged as an anachronism. It was an Iron Age attempt to reconstruct a Bronze Age regime, the palace (e)state, during an era in which Mesopotamia had moved on to the new regime of imperial plunder. Not surprisingly, Israel and its neighboring anachronisms were devastated by the imperial hordes. Although Boer never discusses why biblical literature exists or how it might have evolved from a loose anthology to sacred scripture, he turns to the Bible occasionally to illustrate points that he has stressed. These occasional references suggest that Boer views the Bible as a repository of narratives and poems that mirror the larger economic trends of their era. Some biblical literatures express resistance in the face of economic extraction, while others either celebrate extraction or construct elaborate fictions influenced by the palace (e)states and imperial regimes.

Boer tends to romanticize subsistence agriculture, but he avoids the error of depicting the subsistence economy as an egalitarian utopia. Rather, he argues that subsistence survival necessitated social forms that could allocate resources effectively, and these social forms imposed hierarchies that effectively enslaved everyone to a socioeconomic system that could not tolerate deviance. It is at this point in the book that Boer covers the usual topics and, except for a Marxist spin, discusses these topics in the usual way. Chapters 2 and 3 treat the economic roles of religious ideology, domesticated animals, domesticated flora, alcohol, land allotments (or, in Boer's view, land-use allotments), flexible kinship ideologies, flexible household spaces, and the varieties of social hierarchy that can be labeled patron–client relationships. Boer moves to regimes of economic extraction in chapters 4, 5, and 6, which present Boer's Marxist interpretation of palace (e)states, class conflict, ideological rationalizations by and for priests and other nonproducers, and, finally, imperial states and their methods of extraction, such as tribute, tax (including tithes), plunder, and exchange, the latter of which, says Boer, should not be construed as primitive capitalism. For specialists, these five chapters will provide useful insights about familiar topics. For nonspecialists—such as the many biblical researchers who did not earn degrees in either economics or social anthropology—this portion of the book is a valuable survey of important topics related to the Bible, and it rewards careful study.

Generally speaking, this is an excellent study of the harsh realities faced by everyone who lived in the ancient Near East, and this reviewer chooses not to quibble over minor details. Suffice it to say that, like any academic publication treating many controversial aspects of research, Boer's book draws minor conclusions here and there that will generate dissent in various quarters, especially those who continue to view data for exchange as evidence of early, or primitive, capitalism. Also, readers who have been misled by the book's title will be disappointed to discover almost nothing about ancient Israel and meager justification for the superfluous labeling of Israel's economy as "sacred." There are, however, two larger failings in this book that demand brief comment.

A significant failing is Boer's obsession with fitting all phenomena into his universalizing Marxist paradigm. Boer is relentless in this respect and might be as guilty of an ahistorical intellectual imperialism as are the neoclassical theorists he despises. In some cases he distorts a phenomenon in order to fit it into his model. For example, Boer strains to convince his reader that patronage—the social relationship in which one individual and his retainers lord it over clients in an uneasy symbiotic relationship—was, in most cases, an allocative economic form and not a form of economic extraction. Although Boer admits that the emergence of a strong man and his entourage could and did lead to extraction, he seems unwilling to admit that extraction is patronage's raison d'être. Similarly, Boer is unwilling to concede that his two theoretical regimes of extraction, palace (e)states and imperial plunder, are really examples of patronage at a level that is more complex than subsistence forms of patronage. I can find no logical reason for Boer's desire to downplay patronage, as it would not have been difficult to incorporate the evidence of patronage into his model in a more convincing manner.

A second failing is Boer's awkward attempt to render his Marxist thesis applicable to our contemporary world. The concluding chapter presents ancient agrarian subsistence economies as a role model for those who desire to resist or reject capitalism. However, Boer is compelled to concede that ancient agrarian subsistence was no picnic. It was unstable and often devastated by natural disasters. It could sustain itself only by means of hierarchical social forms that were xenophobic and "geared toward abuse of the young, of women, and of the elderly" (221). Moreover, its hand-to-mouth existence was not able to produce the necessary environment for intellectual advances (such as biblical literature and Marxist philosophy, not to mention technology, medicine, or the potential for incrementally more egalitarian economic and political structures, such as liberalism). As a result, the subsistence economy that Boer offers as a role model is not one that ever existed in the ancient world. It is a fictional subsistence economy located in Boer's imagination and consists of a few maxims that any capitalist who is concerned about the natural environment has already adopted, such as encouraging human population control in order to make optimal, not maximal, use of resources. Perhaps this reviewer can be dismissed as an unreconstructed nonproducer (university professor) who extracts his livelihood from exploited (tuition-paying) producers, but this portion of Boer's book seems *willfully* naïve. It leaves the reader with a sour taste after the delectable treats of the previous chapters.

Despite its misleading title, *The Sacred Economy of Ancient Israel* is a useful analysis of key factors that impacted the daily lives of ancient peoples. Although the book does not focus on the Hebrew-speaking peoples who lived in Iron Age Palestine, it advances the discussion about the larger environment of which those peoples were a part, an environment that had a profound impact on every individual, from nonproducing kings and priests to the productive agrarian commoners they exploited.

Israel and Empire: A Postcolonial History of Israel and Early Judaism, by Leo G. Perdue and Warren Carter; edited by Coleman A. Baker. New York: Bloomsbury, 2015. Pp. x + 328. Paper. $39.95. ISBN 9780567243287.

Steed Vernyl Davidson, McCormick Theological Seminary

Postcolonial studies has brought greater attention to the imperial realities that lay in the background of the evolution of early Judaism and Christianity. Biblical texts variously keep these realities subsumed or foregrounded. *Israel and Empire* provides a necessary historical accounting that shows the march of these empires as well as how Israel/Judah (and later Judea/Israel) fared in their midst. Applying the postcolonial optic to construct and narrate this historiography, the authors and editor provide readers with a resourceful companion to the biblical texts that paves the way for more heightened postcolonial enquiry into this period.

Structured in six chapters, with five of them dedicated to the major imperial powers of the period, the volume situates itself within the field of postcolonial criticism. Chapter 1 offers a quick summary of postcolonial studies with a critical analysis of the contributions of Edward Said, Homi Bhabha, and Gayatri Spivak to postcolonial studies. The chapter mines their work for their value to biblical studies while trying to glean a stronger resistant voice. This chapter avoids a soft form of anticolonial activity that is limited to abstraction or negotiation with its consideration of issues such as economics and race. While still heavily indebted to this particular triumvirate, the chapter leans into directions that thicken the description of postcoloniality. The writers pay good attention in this chapter to the fact that what is at stake is not merely an intellectual debate but the idea of liberation.

The remaining chapters each follow a similar structure that presents the metanarrative of the respective empire and pays attention to forms of resistance mostly with data from biblical texts and extrabiblical sources. The Neo-Assyrian imperial propaganda of dominance forms the context for examining Yahwistic counterclaims of supremacy through the book of Hosea in chapter 2. The distinction between Hosea as a book set within the Neo-Assyrian period and aspects of the book that date to that historical period is not immediately clear in this chapter. The Neo-Assyrian ideology of control as expressed through its religious system and monarchy allowed for territorial conquest without the expectation of religious conformity. Hosea provides a hidden transcript of resistance that offers a demand for absolute fidelity to YHWH. While the authors engage the language of intimacy that characterizes aspects of the Neo-Assyrian ideology and Hosea, they view these exclusively from the perspective of an ideological confrontation. This narrow focus means that implications of gender as seen in Hosea's marriage and the intersections of gender and foreignness as seen in the treatment of Jezebel in the analysis of the book of Kings receive a less than stout treatment from a postcolonial perspective. The issue of gender deserves more than a footnote (52 n. 37).

Chapter 3 moves on to the Neo-Babylonian Empire with the assertion that Babylonian control required acceptance of their supremacy. Showing the extractive nature of the Babylonian imperial project, the writers focus attention more upon the threat of enculturation faced by those exiled in Babylonia as well as on the diversity of the Judean exilic experience. The chapter offers a cogent description of various exilic communities using Jeremiah and Second Isaiah as textual companions for the exploration of Judean resistance. Jeremiah's oracles against Egypt and Babylon supply a rhetorical aggression against empire, while Second Isaiah develops a "cultural hermeneutics" that rewrites the control of empire.

In chapter 4 the writers deal with the Persian Empire. Here they provide less direct biblical engagement than in the previous two chapters. The narration offers a balance between the benefactions of the Persians in handling a diverse empire and their belligerence when dealing with conquered peoples. The authors provide useful details about the Persian imperial metanarrative, a challenging task given the limited data, in their attempt to show textual resistance to imperialism through a resurgent monarchic sentiment presaged upon Davidic representations in the work of the Chronicler as well as Haggai and Zechariah.

Chapter 5 offers an extensive treatment of what the writers rightly identify as the Greek empires. In order to avoid homogenizing the various actors, they examine Alexander, the Ptolemies, and the Seleucids in turn by narrating the distinctive aspects of their imperial metanarratives. Attention to violence and revolts in this chapter marks an important turn in this volume, even though the narration of the Maccabean revolt and the establishment of the Hasmonean monarchy seems quite tepid for a postcolonial historiography. Antiochus IV receives special treatment as the context for the maneuverings of the high priesthood, and one would think a critical point from which to analyze the evolution of apocalyptic. While the chapter provides an adequate summary of apocalyptic texts such as Daniel and 1 Enoch, they are situated largely within an amorphous notion of resistance rather than the maelstrom of Hellenization and its consequent impact upon Jerusalem religious elites.

Two shifts occur in chapter 5 that continue into chapter 6, unsettling aspects of the book. Beginning in this chapter the text switches to the first person without any identification of the writer. Second, empires and their agents are described as hybrid or creating third space (Herodians in "ambivalent third space," 241; Pompey constructed in the Psalms of Solomon with a hybrid identity, 281). While these instances are never specifically associated with Bhabha's notion of hybridity or ambivalence, the previous use of Bhabha suggests that they should be read in that light. In any event, the concept of hybridity remains troubling in postcolonial studies, and these instances add further to the distortions caused by the use of difficult terms.

The final chapter follows the previous one in its extensive reach into historical data, this time with great help from Josephus. The focus on the Roman Empire pays attention to imperial religion as expressed in textual and monumental productions. As with the previous chapter, the narration paints a vivid picture of the implications of Roman imperialism as it impacted daily living with attention to military activity, taxation, politics, religious/cultural life, and material culture. This chapter as well details instances of armed revolts as its historical reach includes events such as the destruction of Jerusalem (70 CE), the siege of Masada (74 CE), as well as the second Roman-Jewish war. The attention to Herod as a Roman client king parallels the previous chapter's discussion on various comprador groups. The chapter ends with an examination of text production during the period, with heavy attention to the Psalms of Solomon but adequate treatment of Enoch and 4 Ezra. The brief section on Qumran is curious for its brevity as well as its treatment in this chapter rather than in the previous one, where some aspects of the development of Qumran fit historically. While the chapter understandably refrains from placing what would come to be called Christian texts in the foreground of this period, the lack of discussion on the diversity of Jewish expression is noteworthy. The greater ferment among messianic Jews deserved a broader discussion, perhaps one that could have been picked up in the missing conclusion for the book.

Israel and Empire fills a knowledge gap for postcolonial analysis of the history and texts of ancient Israel. The writers provide information as well as an extensive bibliography that combines disciplines that draw from each other but not often enough nor from a common set of sources. This volume sets the stage for a new turn in several aspects of various fields of study compliments of postcolonial studies. Despite a robust introduction to postcolonial studies, the other chapters of this volume provide a restrained application of the postcolonial optic. Dominated by James Scott's notion of the hidden transcripts and Bhabha's mimicry and hybridity, the historiography of this book limits anti-imperial action to mostly discursive resistance. With no specific purpose in mind, several aspects of texts are labeled as offering resistance, leaving in doubt the real impact of these hidden transcripts. If texts are coded to avoid imperial scrutiny, are they part of some organized underground resistance using them as means to enlist further support? Biblical studies has been quite content to avoid the oppositional implications of the postcolonial optic, preferring to settle for abstract analysis. Unfortunately, in this regard, this volume hews to that line.

The volume, though, offers needed attention to two aspects of postcolonial concern: economics and violence. Although lacking the deep analysis of the economics of empire and other state constructions of the ancient world, the writers single out economics as an important feature of empire construction in each chapter. Following the postcolonial dogma of the economic motives that create and sustain empire, this volume variously shows how Israel/Judah suffers from participation in tributary economies, remain marginal to the fortunes of imperial economies, and construct their own internal economies based upon coercion. The discussion on the temple economy in chapter 6 presents a striking picture of the interlocking relationships of various groups within the Roman Empire. The absence of greater analytical details about the operations of ancient economies may find Roland Boer's *The Sacred Economy* an apt companion to fill in some of these gaps.

The treatment of violence in this volume serves as one of the attempts by the writers to deal with the lived aspects of imperialism. To the extent that they can, they occasionally provide the details of imperial aggression. However, the stronger focus in the volume is on "horizontal violence" informed mostly by the thoughts of Bhabha and Fanon. While the writers appropriately cite Bhabha and Fanon on this issue, their attention to horizontal violence as the expression of the limitations of revolt exposes the absence of a narrative of protest, as distinct from resistance, in their historiography. This concern goes to what makes the volume postcolonial. Is attention to imperial history a sufficient basis for postcolonial analysis if that history privileges the empire and presents reactionary responses from the colonized? Is the work postcolonial if the specter of violence concentrates more upon factional aggression rather than imperial belligerence? Is the postcolonial contribution a different analysis of literary texts though arriving at the same conclusions? See, for instance, the assessment of Anathea Portier-Young's reading of Daniel and other apocalyptic literature as missing aspects of the postcolonial optic while offering the same inferences (200–206).

Israel and Empire opens a potential path that writes the history of ancient Israel and early Judaism. The book maps the terrain to be covered, leaving room for more vigorous application of the postcolonial perspective that leans upon a variety of more recent postcolonial insights. Its contribution will be seen in the heightened attention to historical context in future postcolonial biblical criticism.

Geschichte Israels, by Christian Frevel. Kohlhammer Studienbücher Theologie 2. Stuttgart: Kohlhammer, 2015. Pp. 445. Paper. €35.00. ISBN 9783170292284.

Markus Witte, Humboldt-Universität

Dreißig Jahre nach der Publikation der ersten Auflage der zweibändigen *Geschichte des Volkes Israel und seiner Nachbarn in Grundzügen* (GAT 4/1–2; Göttingen: Vandenhoeck & Ruprecht, 1984–1986; 2., durchgesehene und ergänzte Auflage 1995) aus der Feder des in diesem Jahr verstorbenen Herbert Donner (1930–2016) hat Christian Frevel, Professor für Altes Testament an der katholisch-theologischen Fakultät der Ruhr-Universität Bochum (Deutschland) und Extraordinary Professor am Departement of Old Testament Studies der University of Pretoria (Republik Südafrika) erstmals wieder eine umfassende und aktuelle Gesamtdarstellung der Geschichte Israels in deutscher Sprache vorgelegt. Mit 445 Seiten, von denen 77 Seiten auf diverse Register entfallen, ist sie zwar rund 100 Seiten kürzer als das Werk von Donner, aber rund 160 Seiten länger als Dirk Kinets *Geschichte Israels* (NEchtB Ergänzungsband 2 zum Alten Testament. Würzburg: Echter, 2001), der bis dato jüngsten einbändigen deutschsprachigen Gesamtdarstellung. Erwachsen aus seiner Kurzdarstellung der Geschichte Israels, die seit der siebten Auflage ein fester Bestandteil der von Erich Zenger (1939–2010) herausgegebenen *Einleitung in das Alte Testament* (Studienbücher Theologie 1,1. Stuttgart: Kohlhammer, 2008) war, bietet Frevel nun ein ausführliches Studienbuch, das von den Anfängen Israels in der Spätbronzezeit bis zum Bar-Kochba-Aufstand (132–135 n. Chr.) reicht.

Kennzeichnend für Frevels Buch ist seine didaktische, diskursive und problemorientierte Anlage. Durchgehend werden unterschiedliche Forschungspositionen ausgewogen und vermittelnd referiert, kritisch evaluiert und die Leser mit in die aktuelle Diskussion hineingenommen. Als ein Beispiel sei auf Frevels differenzierte Auswertung der gegenwärtig heftig umstrittenen Befunde von Khirbet Qeiyafa (112–14) verwiesen. Selbst wenn sich in bestimmten Fragen der Chronologie des 10. Jh. v. Chr., des Verhältnisses zwischen Israel und Juda in der Zeit zwischen dem 9. und dem 7. Jh. v. Chr., der Kontinuität und Diskontinuität zwischen der neubabylonischen und der persischen Zeit sowie der Bedeutung der hellenistischen Zeit für die Profilierung der antiken Judentümer ein größerer Forschungskonsens andeutet als noch vor 10–15 Jahren, so sind doch zahlreiche Probleme ungelöst und werden es angesichts der archäologischen und literarischen Befunde wohl auch bleiben. Frevel benennt diese Probleme offen und verweist auch dort, wo er selbst Stellung bezieht, auf die Hypothetik der entsprechenden Thesen und Theorien. So betont Frevel von der ersten bis zur letzten Seite immer wieder, dass jede Form der Geschichtsdarstellung Konstruktion und Interpretation bedeute und dass bei der Darstellung der Geschichte Israels des zweiten und ersten Jahrtausends v. Chr. immer drei Ebenen zu unterscheiden seien: die biblische, die archäologische und die historische. Gleichwohl müssten diese drei Ebenen, zumal bei der Behandlung der Geschichte Israels als einer Disziplin im Rahmen der Theologie, aufeinander bezogen bleiben. Frevel, der nicht nur im Bereich der Religionsgeschichte und Ikonographie Syrien-Palästinas sowie der Erforschung des Pentateuchs und der Geschichtsbücher des Alten Testaments bestens ausgewiesen ist, sondern auch viele Jahre auch im Vorstand des Deutschen Vereins zur Erforschung Palästinas war, gelingt beides: die methodisch saubere Differenzierung der drei Ebenen und die stete Korrelation der archäologischen Befunde mit den Ergebnissen literargeschichtlicher Analysen der alttestamentlichen Überlieferung. Letztere ist weder als reine Fiktion aus hellenistischer Zeit zu betrachten noch als eine unmittelbare zeitgenössische Quelle. Diese Erkenntnisse gehören an sich zum Grundbestand alttestamentlicher Wissenschaft, es schadet aber nicht, angesichts bestimmter Fehlentwicklungen in der Forschung immer wieder einmal daran zu erinnern.

Das Buch selbst gliedert sich in zehn unterschiedlich lange Teile, mit jeweils bis zu elf Kapiteln. Jedem Kapitel ist ein Block vorangestellt, in dem klassische und aktuelle Sekundärliteratur repräsentativ aufgeführt ist. Auf Fuß- und Endnoten ist verzichtet worden. Einschlägige altorientalische Quellen zur Geschichte werden im Fließtext zitiert, zumeist nach dem von Manfred Weippert bearbeiteten *Historischen Textbuch zum Alten Testament* (GAT 10; Göttingen: Vandenhoeck & Ruprecht, 2010). 62 Schwarz-Weiß Abbildungen lockern den Text auf und bieten zusätzliche Veranschaulichungen. Neben Grundrissen des eisenzeitlichen Vierraumhauses, des Jerusalemer Tempels oder eisenzeitlicher Stadttore und Kapitelle finden sich hier zahlreiche Siegel- und Münzdarstellungen, Umzeichnungen von Inschriften auf Stelen und auf Ostraka, Abbildungen judäischer Pfeilerfigurinen und Reiterfiguren, phönizischer Kerubenthrone, des Leuchtturms von Pharos oder der in den Höhlen von Qumran gefundenen Tonkrüge und vieles andere mehr. Ebenso in den Fließtext integriert sind kleine Zeittafeln, Listen altorientalischer, israelitischer und judäischer Könige, der Jerusalemer Hohenpriester aus der Zeit des Zweiten Tempels und der Stadthalter der persischen Provinzen Samaria und Jehud sowie Übersichten zur Stratigraphie einzelner Ortslagen und zur Siedlungsgeschichte Israels-Palästinas.

Kap. 1 ist Grundsätzen der Historik und der Quellenkunde gewidmet (17–41). Kap. 2 behandelt, einsetzend mit der Spätbronzezeit, die Vorgeschichte Israels in der Spannung von Urbanisierung, Tribalisierung und Reurbanisierung in einem vielfältigen Wechselspiel von klimatischen, sozialen und politischen Veränderungen in der Levante und in Ägypten, wobei hier auch knapp auf den literarischen Charakter der Erzählungen über die Erzeltern und den Exodus eingegangen wird (42–65). Kap. 3 stellt auf der Basis einer sehr ausgewogenen Kombination unterschiedlicher Modelle zur „Landnahme" von Albrecht Alt und William Foxwell

Albright bis hin zu Israel Finkelstein die über einen Zeitraum vom 12. bis zum 10. Jh. v. Chr. verlaufende und regional zu differenzierende evolutionäre Entstehung Israels *in* Palästina dar (66–92). Kap. 4 beschreibt die Entwicklung von regionalen Häuplingstümern zur Entstehung eines überregionalen Königtums und eines Staates in Israel und in Juda, wobei viele Elemente der David- und Salomoüberlieferung erst Entwicklungen des 9./8. Jh. v. Chr. widerspiegelten. Mit der Reduktion des geschichtlichen Anteils Davids und Salomos, an deren grundsätzlicher Historizität nach Frevel nicht zu zweifeln sei, wächst einerseits die Bedeutung des vordavidischen Jerusalem, andererseits die Bedeutung der Omriden, was jeweils dem archäologischen Befund entspricht (93–171). Kap. 5 thematisiert die Geschichte Israels und Judas vom 9. Jh. v. Chr. bis zum babylonischen Exil. Für die Zeit bis zur neuassyrischen Eroberung Samarias 722/720 v. Chr. rechnet Frevel, unter anderem ausgehend von der Identität der namensgleichen Könige Israels und Judas, Joram, Ahasja und Joas, damit, dass Juda ein Filialkönigtum des wirtschaftlich und kulturell höher stehenden Israel war. Erst in der Zeit nach 722/720 v. Chr. hätten Juda und Jerusalem aufgrund des sukzessiven Zustroms von Bewohnern des „Nordreichs" und im Schatten der *pax Assyriaca* eine besondere Eigenständigkeit und wirkmächtige Bedeutung erlangt. Wie im Fall des Exodus oder Davids reduziert Frevel hier das von der biblischen Überlieferung geprägte Bild, ohne dass er zum Beispiel der These von einer Josianischen Reform 622 v. Chr. oder einer ersten, die Geschichte Israels und Judas zusammenfassenden Version der Königebücher unter Josia den Abschied gibt (172–286). Kap. 6 behandelt die Geschichte Israels in der Perserzeit. Hier werden unter anderem die demographischen und ökonomischen Auswirkungen der neubabylonischen Zerstörungen Judas diskutiert, die sogenannte persische Toleranzpolitik und die Datierung des Wiederaufbaus des Zweiten Tempels (schon unter Darius I. oder erst unter Artaxerxes I.?) problematisiert, die grundsätzliche Historizität des Kyrus-Edikts verteidigt sowie die umfangreichen archäologischen und epigraphischen Funde auf dem Garizim, die Papyri aus den Archiven auf Elephantine (5. Jh. v. Chr.) und im Wādī d-Dālīye Archiv (375–332 v. Chr.) ausgewertet. Die Perserzeit erscheint demnach als die formative Periode des späteren Judentums, wobei in der materialen Kultur eine hohe regionale Diversität und interne Pluriformität besteht (287–327). Kap. 7 und 8 sind schließlich der weiteren Entfaltung der perserzeitlichen Entwicklungen in der hellenistischen und römischen Zeit gewidmet. Das Phänomen der Hellenisierung Israel-Palästinas bereits vor Alexander dem Großen (356–323 v. Chr.) und die Bedeutung der jüdischen Diaspora kommen hier ebenso zur Sprache wie die Urkunden des jüdischen Politeuma im ägyptischen Herakleopolis aus der Zeit zwischen 144/3 und 133/2 v. Chr., religiöse Gruppen im Judentum seit dem 2. Jh. v. Chr. und die Politik Herodes des Großen (37–4 v. Chr.) und seiner Nachfolger (328–366, 367–382).

In allen Kapiteln, die auch je für sich gut lesbar sind, geht es Frevel um den Aufweis von Strukturen des Geschichtsverlaufs, um die Skizzierung regionaler Entwicklungen und um eine Zusammenschau der wirtschaftlichen, klimatischen, politischen und religiösen Faktoren, die geschichtliche Ereignisse bedingen. Als ein verschiedene Phasen der Geschichte Israels (und seiner ostjordanischen Nachbarn) übergreifendes Muster wird ein Nord-Süd- und ein West-Ost-Gefälle herausgearbeitet, demzufolge wesentliche ökonomische, politische und religiöse Entwicklungen von Syrien über Israel nach Juda und Jerusalem bzw. von den phönizischen und philistäischen Küstenstädten nach Israel und Juda verlaufen sind. Ein Glossar ausgewählter archäologischer, exegetischer und soziologischer Fachbegriffe, eine knapp kommentierte Übersicht wichtiger Quellensammlungen zur Geschichte Israels und Gesamtdarstellungen, elf Karten zum Vorderen Orient und zu Israel-Palästina, eine Liste der im Buch erwähnten Ortsnamen in Israel-Palästina mit Angabe der Koordinaten sowie Register zu antiken Autoren, biblischen Texten, Inschriften, Namen und Sachen beschließen das sehr gelungene Lehrbuch zur Geschichte Israels und Judas in alttestamentlicher Zeit, das angemessen auch immer wieder auf zentrale Fragen der Religionsgeschichte wie die Ursprünge der Yhwh-Verehrung, die Bildlosigkeit und die Pluralität des Yhwh-Kultes oder den jüdischen Monotheismus eingeht.

Ashkelon 5: The Land behind Ashkelon, by Yaakov Huster. Final Reports of The Leon Levy Expedition to Ashkelon 5. Winona Lake, IN: Harvard Semitic Museum, Eisenbrauns, 2015. Pp. xv + 222. Hardcover. $49.50. ISBN 9781575069524.

Carol Meyers, Duke University

The Leon Levy Expedition has been excavating the prominent coastal site of Tel Ashkelon for more than thirty years. Full publication of the excavation materials began in 2008, and Yaakov Huster's *Land behind Ashkelon* is the fifth volume in the final-report series. Rather than presenting materials from the tel, this volume is a collection and analysis of data from the area around the tel in fulfillment of the expedition's commitment to understanding the site within its regional context. Having been district inspector of the Ashkelon region for the Israel Antiquities Authority for many years, Huster is uniquely situated to present and interpret the results of all the surveys and excavations (mostly salvage ones) in this region; he considers this volume the "culmination of a lifetime of observation" (xi). His work appears in three of the book's five chapters, with several Ashkelon project staff members contributing the other two chapters.

In the first chapter, "Introduction" (1–11), Huster reviews previous surveys of the region and describes his goals: (1) identifying settlement patterns, from the Paleolithic through the Ottoman periods, and noting changes in those patterns over time; and (2) examining the relationship between Tel Ashkelon and the sites (on map sheets 87, 88, 91, 92, and 96 of the Archaeological Survey of Israel) in the area in a 15 km radius around the tel. His identification of sites improves the work of previous surveys; by taking deposition patterns and other factors (e.g., lack of structural remains) into account, he eliminates many "nonsites" or "artifact scatters" listed as sites on earlier maps. The site maps by period (in the second chapter) are thus more accurate; according to Huster's reckoning, the number of sites, especially in the Iron II to Roman periods, is generally smaller than what older surveys indicate.

Huster's second chapter, "Survey of Settlement Patterns by Period" (13–88), is the core of the book. It presents the location and nature of human activity in the area over many millennia—from the Lower Paleolithic through the medieval period (ending in 1516, with the termination of Mamluk rule in the Levant). Most periods are presented in separate sections, accompanied by maps locating the sites. However, Neolithic and Chalcolithic are combined. Similarly, the subdivisions of Early Bronze are considered together, as are the Late Bronze subdivisions, but Middle Bronze I (or Early Bronze IV or Intermediate Bronze) and Middle Bronze II appear separately, as do Iron I and Iron II. For the later periods, Persian and Hellenistic are combined, and the medieval section includes the Crusader period and both Early (Fatimid, Ayyubid) and Late (Mamluk) Islamic periods.

As would be expected, the data are scant for the earliest periods, although there are clear lithic remains of the Upper Paleolithic, from east of the *kurkur* ridges parallel to the coast, and the Epipaleolithic, mainly from along the coast. Scattered Neolithic and Chalcolithic deposits are also close to the shore and also along some east–west drainage basins. The rather sparse settlements in the Bronze and Iron I periods were mainly inland. Ashkelon lacked a "true hinterland" (30) in these periods; as an urban center its primary role was as a maritime power and international port. Its economy was tied to East Mediterranean trade rather than local agrarian productivity, thus exemplifying Stager's "port power" model (34). Settlement in the region was still sparse in the tenth–ninth centuries but increased somewhat in the eighth century, especially along newly established roads, perhaps because of Assyrian interests in maintaining communications networks in its far-flung empire. Settlement numbers receded in the Persian and Hellenistic periods, even as Ashkelon itself was thriving because of its maritime functions. In the Roman period and especially in the Byzantine period, a marked increase in settlements, many in places never previously settled, can be observed. The hinterland became a highly developed wine-production area, as did much of Palestine in this period. The site hierarchy that emerged differs from the more diffuse settlement pattern of earlier epochs and reflects an "integrated economy based on wine production and export" with an explicit "synergy between the many churches in the region and the wine trade" (53). Settlement patterns of subsequent periods (Early Islamic and medieval), known more from archival materials and other texts than from surveys and excavations, continued the Roman-Byzantine pattern but with a gradual decline in settlement number and size. The numerous mosques and *welis* in the region attest to the Islamic presence, especially in the Mamluk period.

Chapter 3, Michael Press's "Identification of Ottoman Sites" (89–107), supplements the preceding chapter by providing data about Ashkelon's hinterland in the Ottoman and also Mandatory periods. Textual sources as well as survey and excavation materials abound and testify to the continued decline in the number of settlements. Those still inhabited were almost entirely agricultural settlements producing a variety of crops—but not wine. Most of the chapter (95–107) consists of two appendixes identifying Ottoman period sites.

In the fourth chapter, "Ashkelon as Maritime Gateway and Central Place" (109–23), George A. Pierce and Daniel M. Master build upon Huster's foundational work in chapter 2 to offer theoretical suggestions (e.g., Stager's port-power model, already cited in ch. 2) about Ashkelon's relation to its hinterland. Human habitation was sparse in the prehistoric periods. When it developed in the historic periods, it evinced two discrete settlements patterns. From the Early Bronze through the end of the second millennium BCE Ashkelon dominated the rather sparsely settled area, focusing on maritime trade and also functioning as a regional gateway. Then in the late Iron II period through the Crusades, Ashkelon became a "dynamic gateway" with a much closer relationship to hinterland sites, which increased in number—perhaps at first because of a subtle climate change that improved the agrarian potential of the hinterland and ultimately because of the development of the wine industry concomitant with the expansion of Christianity in the Levant. The hinterland eventually became less populated, with the decline of wine production after the Islamic conquest and especially after Ashkelon was destroyed in the thirteenth century. Settlements nonetheless continue; the westward orientation of Ashkelon as a port meant it had relatively little connection to hinterland sites, which thus were not dependent for survival on a maritime regional center.

Chapter 5, "Regional Archaeological Survey: Map of Sderot (96)" (125–207), is Huster's detailed presentation of one of the map sheets showing Ashkelon's hinterland. His brief description (125–31) of the map area includes a summary of research and an archaeological overview of map 96 by period (Lower Paleolithic through the Mandate). Figures illustrating each period and three appendixes—Index of Site Names; Index of Sites Listed by Period; Index of Map of Sderot (96) Sites—make up the bulk of the chapter (132–207).

Huster and the other authors are to be commended for this rich collection of information about Ashkelon's region and their compelling theoretical framework for understanding settlement patterns and the changes in those patterns—in the location and number of settlements—over time. The book is greatly enhanced by its many figures, mainly in chapters 2 (eighteen maps) and 5 (twenty-four artifact drawings [pottery, lithics, metal, and marble], fourteen photos, and sixteen maps). The maps especially, many in color, are highly effective in conveying the pattern and size of settlements. Similarly, the ten tables, one in the first chapter and nine in the second, provide convenient access to the comprehensive data upon which Huster's analysis draws.

If this volume is to be faulted at all, it is for what has been omitted. Settlements patterns are determined in many ways by geomorphological features, many of which are mentioned. However, no map locates them, making the discussion difficult to follow at times. A description in chapter 2 of geological and geographical features of the hinterland would have been helpful, but such information, and only briefly for map 96, does not come until chapter 5. Also, the front matter includes a list of tables but does not list the eighty-five figures (maps, photos, drawings), making it difficult for the reader to consult overlapping aspects of the book's content without flipping through several chapters, page by page. Finally, the implications for settlement theory of the overlap of Ashkelon's hinterland with that of the nearest urban centers (e.g., Ashdod to its north) within its 15 km radius are not considered. But these omissions are hardly sins and do not seriously detract from the value of this addition to the Ashkelon reports.

Antioch on the Orontes: A History and a Guide, by Jørgen Christensen-Ernst. Lanham, MD: Hamilton Books, 2012. Pp. xiv + 203. Hardcover. $44.00. ISBN 9780761858638.

Mark Wilson, Asia Minor Research Center

Christensen-Ernst's volume is a welcome addition to the guidebooks now appearing for individual sites in Turkey. The book consists of two sections: Part 1 covers the history of Antioch in ten chapters; part 2 provides a guide in four chapters to the sites in Antioch, modern Antakya. After chapter 4 ten figures are included: a map of ancient Antioch and nine black-and-white photographs. Nine appendices, a bibliography, and an index conclude the book. The author's journalistic, academic, and linguistic experience in Turkey as well as residence in Antakya make him well qualified to write this guidebook.

In his introduction the author warns potential visitors that not much of the ancient city remains to be seen, but he rightly notes that one can still feel the spirit of the place. Even though the so-called Church of St. Peter is the most popular pilgrimage site, it is highly doubtful, and rightly so, whether the cave "has anything to do with the early Christians" (xi). Yet with its variegated ethnic and religious makeup, Antakya is indeed a city of tolerance, perhaps even a "small Jerusalem."

Chapter 1 examines the beginnings of the city. The name of the modern province Hatay is derived from the original inhabitants, the Hatti or Neo-Hittites. The local historians John Malalas and Libanius are utilized as sources throughout the book. This brief two-page overview ends with the arrival of Alexander the Great in 333 BCE. This early history could have been enhanced by including Tell Ta'yinat and Alalakh/Atchana, where there are ongoing excavations by Canadian and Turkish archaeologists. Finds from these Bronze/Iron Age sites are now prominently displayed in the new archaeology museum in Antakya.

Chapter 2 cover the Seleucid history of the city. The capital of the empire was transferred from coastal Seleucia Pieria to Antioch in 285 BCE after the death of Seleucus I. The geographical relationship of the two cities, with Antioch situated ten miles inland, figures in the account of Paul's first journey from Seleucia (Acts 13:4; cf. 14:26). The urban area with its Hippodamian grid plan developed between the Orontes River and Mount Silipius. The modern Kurtuluş Street is built over the ancient cardo maximus. The statue of Tyche sitting on Mount Silpius with the river god Orontes swimming at her feet became the city's iconic symbol and the most famous Tyche of the Greco-Roman world. In this chapter the arrival of the Jewish community is also described, particularly the role of Antiochus IV and the Maccabean rebellion.

Chapter 3 summarizes the Roman period starting with the visit of Julius Caesar in 47 BCE. When Augustus made Syria an imperial province around 27 BCE, this capital city gained new prominence. The visits of various emperors are chronicled, including the near death of Trajan in 115 CE when an earthquake struck the city. The rise of Christianity is likewise surveyed, and Antioch's significance is affirmed as the launching point for Paul's three missionary journeys. The tradition that Peter was the church's first bishop is rightly questioned, and several excellent reasons are suggested why the cave church would not have functioned as a gathering place for persecuted Christians. The provenance of the Didache is probably Antioch; however, there is no discussion of Antioch's possible connection with Titus or Matthew's Gospel. Ignatius and his bishopric are briefly summarized.

Chapter 4, on the Byzantine period, discusses various personages, including John Chrysostom and Theodore of Mopsuestia. Simeon Stylites the Younger took up residence on a pillar on a hilltop southwest of the city whose remains can still be visited. However, the identification is confused in part with that of Simeon Stylites the Elder, who resided on the pillar at nearby Qalaat Semaan.

Chapter 5 describes the arrival of Islam in 637 CE with the Omayyad dynasty. With the capital located in Damascus, Antioch lost much of its former glory. In 969 the Byzantines recaptured the city. An insightful feature throughout is quotations from various eyewitnesses, such as the Iraqi Christian writer Ibn Butlân's description of the city in 1051.

The Crusades, discussed in chapter 6, is a particularly dark period in the city's history. The siege of 1097–1098 brought famine and pestilence, and when the Crusaders finally gained access, they massacred Christians and Muslims alike. The Norman Principality of Antioch, surveyed in chapter 7, covers the period from 1098 to 1268. When the Mameluke commander Baibars captured Antioch, the city was burned, 17,000 killed, and 100,000 taken prisoner. The chapter closes ominously: "The dark years of Antioch had begun" (112).

Chapter 8 briefly covers the Mamelukes. In 1401 Tamerlane again sacked the largely ruined city. The Ottomans, the subject of chapter 9, captured the city in 1515. The city remained subservient to nearby Aleppo, however. During this period Western travelers, familiar with the city's rich history from literary sources, began to visit Antioch. Christensen-Ernst well documents how Antioch's profile slowly began to rise in the late Ottoman period.

Chapter 10 summarizes Antakya's history after World War I and the founding of the Turkish Republic in 1923. The Hatay region was under a French mandate and claimed by Syria, but Atatürk succeeded in forcing a referendum in 1939 to determine the region's national status. The Turks outvoted the Arabs so Hatay became part of Turkey, even though some maps of Syria still show the region within its borders. Antakya's long and complicated history continues today with the crisis with Syria and the shooting down of a Russian fighter jet to its south in 2016. The guide in part 2 has four sections. Chapter 11 features seven tours of the city and region. For this practical section most people would purchase the book; however, its seven pages are too brief. The major site on the first tour, the archaeology museum, has now relocated to a large new facility north of the city. This museum with its large collections of mosaics is now one of the preeminent archaeological museums in Turkey. Because there are so few things to see in Antakya, most tour groups also visit Seleucia. That site is spread out and somewhat complicated, so a fuller description as well as a map would have been useful. An eighth tour to visit Atchana and Tell Ta'yinat also should be included.

Chapter 12 surveys the religious mixture of the city: Sunnis, Alawis, Orthodox, Catholics, Jews, and Protestants. All have places of worship in Antakya today. The Catholics run a guest house under the leadership of the long-serving priest Father Domenico. The Jewish community has dropped from the forty members estimated by the author to eighteen members today. So it is sometimes difficult to find a minyan at the historic synagogue in the city. Chapter 13 covers various myths and legends related to the city's history.

Chapter 14 presents a picture of Antakya drawn in 2011. Surprisingly, there is no mention of Mustafa Kemal University north of Antakya with its 25,000 students and whose archaeology department is active in local excavations. Also strikingly absent is mention of Antakya's famous dessert, künefe, known throughout Turkey. Shops featuring this cheesy shredded-wheat sweet are clustered especially in the city center. Visitors today will find two new shopping malls, each with a Starbucks. Because of the war in Syria and the many refugees in the city, tourism is almost nonexistent. Various governments, including the United States, have advised against travel to the Hatay region. My visit in September 2015 to see the newly opened archaeology museum found life in Antakya as normal with no safety issues. The marvelous hospitality, noted by the author, was still on display despite these challenging times.

Appendices discuss the following subjects: (1) "Lord, God and Logos"; (2) "Monarchianism"; (3) "The School of Antioch"; (4) "The Church of St. Peter"; (5) "Topography"; and (6) "Languages." The book closes with a bibliography and index.

The endnotes to each chapter and the bibliography are useful for further research. A significant omission is *Antioch: The Lost City*, edited by Christine Kondoleon (Princeton, 2000). This volume, consisting of ten essays and a three-subject richly illustrated catalogue, remains the best scholarly book on the city. *Antioch on the Orontes: Early Explorations in the City of Mosaics* was published by Koç University Press in 2014. Edited by Scott Redford, this bilingual volume features three essays on Antioch's history, archaeological research, and other excavations in the area. The numerous photographs documenting the American excavations in the 1930s are especially interesting. Another popular guidebook, similar to Christensen-Ernst's, was published in 2013. Entitled *Antioch on the Orontes: An Illustrated History*, it was written by a retired American professor Kevin M. McCarthy. Not only does it contain more and better quality photographs, but its price is a third of the volume under review.

HEBREW BIBLE/OLD TESTAMENT: GENERAL

The Last of the Rephaim: Conquest and Cataclysm in the Heroic Ages of Ancient Israel, by Brian R. Doak. Ilex Foundation series 7. Cambridge: Harvard University Press, 2012. Pp. xxiii + 288. Paper. $17.96. ISBN 9780674066731.

Debra Scoggins Ballentine, Rutgers, The State University of New Jersey

Brian R. Doak provides thorough analysis of biblical giant traditions and situates this fascinating understudied topic within broader Mediterranean literary use of giants. He balances critical treatment of specific examples with reconstruction of the roles of giants within narrative themes, specifically flood cataclysm, divinely enabled "conquest" of the land of Canaan, and war on the cusp of the Davidic monarchy. Doak corroborates his proposed roles of giant peoples as well as individual giants through comparative analysis of the relevant Mediterranean and ancient West Asian exemplars. Overall, Doak accomplishes several central aims of a scholarly monograph: he provides not merely a digest but analysis of relevant data, which scholars may use to study further this and related topics; he explicitly locates the theories and interpretive strategies undergirding his study; and he makes clear the payoff of his comparative study, identifying shared aspects of biblical and Mediterranean giant traditions as well as how giants contribute to biblical stories of cataclysm, "conquest," and combat distinctly.

Published by the Ilex Foundation and Harvard University's Center for Hellenic Studies, this monograph is a revision of Doak's dissertation, and the positive influences of his committee members, Peter Machinist, Jon Levenson, and Gregory Nagy, are palpable. The comparative nature of this project contributes to recent progress among scholars of the Hebrew Bible and its ancient cultural milieu toward critical comparative study. A current leading figure is Carolina López-Ruiz (*Gods, Heroes, and Monsters: A Sourcebook of Greek, Roman, and Near Eastern Myths in Translation* [Oxford University Press, 2013]; *When the Gods Were Born: Greek Cosmogonies and the Near East* [Harvard University Press, 2010]). I was pleased to learn that she fostered the comparative aspects of Doak's work, which bears critical and creative contributions. Doak writes clearly, and his rhetorical use of questions throughout effectively engages the reader.

Deuteronomy 3:11, which specifies that the large king of the Bashan is the only remnant of the Rephaim, peaked Doak's interest in biblical giants (xi). While size makes a giant, Doak argues that the figures have abstract connotations. Before he explores the relationship of biblical giants to heroes, various *ethnē*, and the Rephaim, his first chapter provides scholarly context for study of biblical giants, including literary use of giants from antiquity to modernity. Rare occurrences of physical gigantism grow within folklore to become giant peoples, and, remarkably, travel journals as late as the 1930s reported the giant stature of the original inhabitants of Canaan as historical (3–5). Doak develops the notion of a pan-Mediterranean *koinē* of customs, materials, religious phenomena, and symbols, including giants, reasonably based on "the historical fact that Greece and the Near East had significant contact with one another from a relatively early period, and that this contact must have meant something for the development of society, culture, and religion in each realm" (26, 45). He engages Eliade and J. Z. Smith regarding comparative methodology, a topic to which Doak returns in his conclusion (47–50).

Chapter 2 discusses biblical examples. The three prominent branches of biblical giant traditions are the origin story of nephilim and gibborim in Gen 6; giants among the residents of Canaan, who are dealt with in stories about the Israelites obtaining this territory; and David's defeat of Goliath. The biblical anthology exhibits the notion both that giants are strikingly large individuals and that, ethnologically, whole groups of peoples might be giants. Doak proposes several symbolic meanings of giants' oversized nature: Gen 6:1–4 associates giants with "sexual transgression against divine boundaries" (53, 223); stories of the Israelites securing the "promised land" portray giants as intimidating residents who must be displaced and, theologically, embodiments of "everything wrong that Israel will put to right when they occupy their promised home" (88, 93, 223); the narrative of David's rise to prominence and kingship, Doak explains, features giants embodying anarchy, the threat of which is quelled by establishment of David's monarchy (117, 224). As Doak emphasizes, it is intriguing that giants do not appear in biblical historiography after the tales of David and several of his warriors defeating particular giants and sons of giants. The utilization of giants within narratives of the two most significant social developments featured in the biblical foundation story, possessing the land and establishment of the Davidic monarchy, suggests that the category giants comprised useful character-types, ethnos-types, and symbols.

In his third chapter Doak presents comparative analysis of the literary pattern of flood cataclysm as divine response to an unbearable rise of objectionable behavior. He proposes that biblical notions of a generation of giants are thematically parallel to Greek notions of a heroic generation. He argues that both biblical giants and Greek heroes are associated with transgression and hubris. The problem of these generations is quelled by divinely mandated flood, war, or a mixture thereof. He discusses the Greek works *Cypria*, *Iliad* 12, *Works and Days*, and *Catalogue of Women*; Mesopotamian traditions such as Atrahasis, Gilgamesh, and Assyrian inscriptions describing flooding of Babylon; Hebrew Bible flood and battle-as-flood passages; and a few targums and rabbinic commentaries.

Chapter 4 proposes that biblical giant traditions exhibit a "narrative sublimation of heroic dualities," that is, explicit utilization and intentional diminishing and suppression of heroic themes (xv, 153, 196). Doak interrogates how one might explain biblical presentations of giants as peoples who reside in Canaan in a narrative-historical context as well as figures of the netherworld. He finds that Greek hero cult traditions, in which heroes are present in epic battles and cultic otherworlds, might illuminate the significance of biblical giants maintaining two narrative locations. Doak soundly generalizes: "we, as modern readers, are not getting the complete picture that ancient Israel's oral and written traditions had to offer. … Israel's giants represent fragments of local memory and tradition, not all of which have been preserved, and … these giants played an even larger role for ancient audiences than we find in the Hebrew Bible—where their function is often large enough" (153).

In his fifth chapter Doak proposes that the demise of biblical giants "constitutes a moment of historiographic organization for the Deuteronomist and other sources" (xv, 200). He proposes that giants are utilized as a "counter-identity" such that the Israelites follow the "corrupt generation of giants," who thus serve the literary construction of positive Israelite "identity" (212). He associates biblical "sublimation" of giants, as well as presumed rejection of epic, with biblical notions of coalescing various types of power: political power in the Davidic monarchy and capital; cultic institutional power in one temple and city; and divine power in one "Universal God" (xvi, 221).

In his conclusion Doak begins by summarizing the dual meaning of the German word *Riese* as "giant" and "hero" in late fifteenth-century German literary discourse, including Martin Luther's sermons. This dual meaning is comparable, Doak explains, to biblical examples of "transpositions between the categories of 'giant' and 'hero'" (222). As a literary, historical, cultural, and theological classification, giants are intertwined with heroes, not simply as opposing foe categories, but rather with overlapping characteristics, strengths, and roles. Doak employs Eliade in his articulation of the narrative possibility of giant figures reappearing in present temporal settings while belonging to mythic, epic, or "marvelous" times (225–26). He returns to J. Z. Smith's influential methodological discussion of the comparative enterprise to bolster his case for "the participation of both Greek and Israelite authors in a Mediterranean *koinē*, a shared religious, historical, and cultural discourse" (226). I appreciate that Doak frames "the emergence of giants as a visible religious category in the Hebrew Bible" as resulting from Israelite literary creativity that shares aspects with Greek tradition, rather than using notions of borrowing or suggesting that biblical giant traditions are less creative or "native" than literary types or tropes that are "historic" rather than "epic" or "mythic" (226).

Doak explicitly engages theorization of giants by Walter Stephens, Timothy Beal, Jeffrey Cohen, and Susan Stewart. Theorization of giants overlaps with "monster theory." There are connections, both thematic and genetic, between biblical "monsters" and how biblical notions are used in subsequent literature featuring monsters. Discussion of how storytellers use monster-types involves literary analysis as well as psychologizing interpretation. Psychologizing interpretations speak to the minds of modern interpreters and readers. With the ancient cultural milieu, we must take care to avoid retrojecting anachronistic notions. With biblical texts, due to durative theological interpretations, which represent the views of interpreters within their own historical contexts, we must be all the more cautious lest we present psychologizing interpretations, which might assume postbiblical theological notions, as if they are historical. Doak largely avoids this methodological risk in that his citations and discussion show he is in conversation with scholars

who explore psychologizing interpretations in a self-aware fashion. Throughout his study Doak's careful treatment of specific cases shows layers of meaning
within biblical giant traditions. Occasional generalizations about potential theological functions of giants run at cross-purposes with Doak's careful specificity
and the sophisticated dynamics he uncovers. Giants are obviously intimidating
"larger than life" threats to preferred sociopolitical arrangements that are presented as proper order. Doak further suggests stark symbolic meanings such as
"mythical spirit opposing the pristine order of creation," "principal demon of
disorder who reigns on the open battlefield of the Philistines," "inherent excess
or surplus," "*Chaosmächte*" (227). While specialists will recognize which meanings are case-oriented and which are more speculative, some readers might not
understand that modern notions of "faith," "madness," and "hell" (terms that are
not central to Doak's study but that he uses in the conclusion) are anachronistic
and ill-fitting for the ancient cultural milieu (229). Doak notes that he draws on
Levinson's understanding of biblical *Chaoskampf* traditions, and throughout this
echoes in the notion that giants are "symbols of a chaotic peril," acting "as a sort of
earthly parallel to descriptions of the *Chaoskampf*" (52). While I fully agree that
traditions of divine combat are central within biblical historiography, theology,
and myth, in the case of biblical giants, explanation via *Chaoskampf* distracts from
Doak's nuanced analysis. Doak's descriptors of giants as representative of what is
disorderly, overgrown, and wild, particularly in moments of historical and political crisis, are more specific and communicative.

*The Responsive Self: Personal Religion in Biblical Literature of the Neo-Babylonian
and Persian Periods*, by Susan Niditch. Anchor Yale Bible Reference Library. New
Haven: Yale University Press, 2015. Pp. 200. Cloth. $50.00. ISBN 9780300166361.

Carol Newsom, Candler School of Theology, Emory University

This slim volume by Susan Niditch investigates two related concerns. One,
which I take to be the major interest, is in "lived religion," that is, how individuals
made use of religious practices, objects, language, and concepts as they negotiated
their individual lives, with all the attendant hopes, fears, and desires of existence.
The practice of lived religion is a human constant, and Niditch's examples appropriately range over many centuries. The difficulty in pursuing this topic is, of
course, the limitations of our sources. We lack the ability of researchers of contemporary cultures to embed with our subjects and be participant-observers of their
worlds. Material culture offers tantalizing hints of practices and beliefs, though
these are often difficult to interpret. Thus we are largely dependent on textual
sources. The analysis of these texts leads Niditch to her second focus, the increasing evidence for a concern with the individual and with personal experiences in
the literature from the time of the exile through the Persian period. While Niditch
is careful to distinguish her claim from what she sees as an older tendency to differentiate preexilic Israel as oriented to the "community and shared culture," as

though "somehow exilic writers discover the individual or invent the self" (135), she does attribute the increasing focus on individual experience in some way to the changed social structures and worldviews that develop in the wake of these traumatic events. Though the claim seems inherently plausible, Niditch's seeming ambivalence about the extent to which she wishes to make a strong chronological argument inhibits a sustained and detailed analysis of the ways in which these phenomena may be understood as responses to historical trauma.

The book is structured as a series of seven brief case studies. The first, which focuses on the proverb about "sour grapes" that appears in both Jeremiah and Ezekiel, I found to be the least satisfying, or perhaps the least clear. I think the point of the argument is that the prophets take a proverb used by the people as an attempt to make the unfairness of events comprehensible and recast it as a statement about "God's fairness … in his treatment of individuals" (27). They respond with formulations that insist that at least in the future each person will be judged on individual behavior. The concern for fairness and the individual is more clearly present in the second case study, "Personal Religion in Ecclesiastes and Job," where not only the question of just desserts but also the theme of death looms large in a way that is not characteristic of earlier literature. Equally important are the literary changes that Niditch details, the more extended depictions of emotion, the prominence of the first-person pronoun, especially in Qoheleth, and the foregrounding of inner dialogue and self-reflection and evaluation. Even though these are highly literary texts, these elements suggest a growing cultural concern for personal experience.

The third case study, "From Incantation and Lament to Autobiography," explores related issues. Incantations and personal laments are powerful examples of religious practices used by individuals to negotiate the problems of everyday life. Though laments are structured by traditional and conventional language, Niditch argues persuasively that they might be customized to fit individual circumstances. Although we lack access to the practice of everyday Israelites, even literary texts suggest how this might work, as Jonah's prayer is framed to fit his situation and Jeremiah's confessions articulate elements of his own dilemma. Niditch shows the limitations of the old alternatives of seeing laments either as romantic expressivism or wholly conventionalized forms. The most intriguing aspect of the chapter is her argument that aspects of the lament influence the shaping of Nehemiah's memoir. The narrative form allows the writer (who may or may not be Nehemiah) to individuate the motifs in ways that construct something of an autobiography.

In "The Negotiating Self," the fourth case study, Niditch turns away from issues of interiority and self-fashioning to the issues of individual agency as they are expressed by the vow. Like the incantation and the lament, the vow is undoubtedly an ancient practice. Focusing on the Nazirite vow in particular, Niditch attempts to historicize some of the changes that occur in the Persian period, as these are reflected in the priestly regulations of Num 6. The temporary nature of the vow, the role of the priests, the role of sacrifice, and the inclusion of women as those who may make the vow for themselves are examined in terms of economic and social issues (possibly as a sign of status and a show of prosperity), as a negotiation between institutional and private religious interests, and as a way of both acknowledging and controlling women's religious agency. Though much must remain speculative, Niditch's analysis is richly suggestive and perceptive.

Similarly, her investigation of the Khirbeit Beit Lei burial site in chapter 5, "Material Religion, Created and Experienced," is an attempt to analyze the grave site with its objects, drawings, and inscriptions in terms of the religious practices and experiences of individuals. As she observes, however, though the drawings (a figure with a lyre, one with arms upraised, one with an ibex headdress, two ships, abstract designs) invite speculation about the roles of music, prayer, the journey of the dead, and practices of protection, we simply do not know if these figures are even related to the burials at all. The verbal inscriptions do suggest protective practices, as well as personal requests and responses from the deity. Though there are no closely related biblical texts, the symbolic ritual actions in early Persian period vision reports and the long tradition of prophetic sign acts may speak to a broader culture of material actions by individuals to engage with divine powers for particular ends.

The sixth case study, "Experiencing the Divine Personally: Heavenly Visits and Earthly Encounters," turns to the literary evidence for dreams and visions. In practice, these are deeply experiential events, though the possibility of delusion and fakery made them subject to a persistent cultural ambivalence. Niditch again draws attention to the tension between the existence of cultural templates and the intriguing differences in detail and mode of presentation, especially in the later ones, to suggest that these preserved reports may also be windows into individualized experience, despite their literary framing.

The final chapter treats "Characterization and Contrast: Dynamics of the Personal in Late-Biblical Narration." Comparing the stories of Tamar and Ruth, Niditch persuasively demonstrates the increasing attention given to dialogue, representation of inner thoughts, motivation, emotion, and the quality of personal interaction in the story of Ruth, characteristics that are also present in the story of Jonah. These shifts in narrative style bespeak a growing interest in interiority. Though Niditch does not discuss the psalms, one might also note in the Second Temple period addition of superscriptions to many of the psalms, so that they provide the text of things that David might have said at certain points in his life, Ps 51 being among the most telling.

If a reader has a sense of frustration upon finishing this book, it is simply the obverse of an appreciation of its richness. So many different topics are covered in less than 200 pages. Any one of the chapters might have been the subject of an entire book. Because the discussions are so compressed, many issues that cry out for further development are only touched upon. Especially to the extent that the argument does involve a claim about change over time, one would have liked to have had more extensive comparison of earlier and later texts, so that more specific signifiers of change could be identified. But perhaps because they are so brief, these chapters will inspire other scholars to take up the challenge and develop some of these suggesting leads with the depth they invite.

On Biblical Poetry, by F. W. Dobbs-Allsopp. New York: Oxford University Press, 2015. Pp. xxii + 575. Hardcover. £47.99. ISBN 9780199766901.

Benjamin D. Sommer, The Jewish Theological Seminary

This excellent book combines literary and philological approaches to provide a sensitive, insightful, and comprehensive study of biblical poetry, its forms, its analogues in the ancient and modern worlds, and its interpretation. The book is divided into four parts that examine the nature of the line in biblical poetry, the variable rhythms employed in biblical poetry, the lyric nature of biblical verse and its relation to music, and the importance of understanding the oral nature of biblical poetry. A final chapter applies the methodological insights of the book to a close reading of one short biblical poem, Psa133.

Following several literary theorists (Barbara Herrnstein Smith, James Longenbach), Dobbs-Allsopp regards the line as the sine qua non of all poetry: what distinguishes verse from prose is the consistent practice of the former to interrupt its discourse with frequent pauses on a more or less regular basis and thus to divide itself into short units of speech that can be represented typographically or chirographically as lines. Not all these lines have parallelism, Dobbs-Allsopp tells us; what makes a group of words a poetic line is not a semantic correspondence with the previous or following line but simply the fact that one pauses at a line's end before moving on to the next. (By *line* Dobbs-Allsopp means what some others call the verset, the colon, or the half-line; what some others call the two- or three-part line of biblical poetry Dobbs-Allsopp refers to as the couplet or triplet. By focusing more on this shorter unit in a manner matching the NJPS translation's approach to lineation, he succeeds in emphasizing its relative brevity and frees himself from the need to worry about the ways it parallels the preceding or following line.) Dobbs-Allsopp stresses repeatedly the oral nature of the line: whether it was reduced to writing or not, it was heard in the ancient world rather than seen, and it was often composed orally as well. He argues that the relative brevity of biblical poetic lines results from the limits of human memory processing. He notes that poetry from cultures in which poems are typically composed and read in written form often has longer lines and that some late biblical poems show longer line lengths as a result of the increasing role of writing in ancient Judah. His attention to the oral nature of biblical poetry is salutary; it encourages interpreters to attend to features that stood out in oral recitation, such as occasional longer lines that emphasize central ideas or mark the close of a poem or a stanza.

Dobbs-Allsopp stresses that biblical poetry had no meter; its varying rhythms resemble those of modern free verse. Dobbs-Allsopp makes clear that he is not the first to make this comparison: Benjamin Hrushovski spoke of the free rhythms of biblical verse already several decades ago, Gay Wilson Allen wrote during the 1930s of the influence of biblical verse on Walt Whitman's creation of free verse, and Whitman himself described the Bible's unrhymed and unmetered poetry as an inspiration. But Dobbs-Allsopp examines this analogue at length and to an extent not seen in previous scholarly literature. Discussions of non-metrical poetry in modern English (and also of alliterative nonmetrical poetry in Old English) lead Dobbs-Allsopp to discuss important but often neglected topics such as the role of enjambment and end-stopping in biblical poetry, the ways changes in rhythm and line-length signify areas of emphasis and textual segmentation, and the relationship between the paratactic structure of successive lines and the associative rather than discursive or narrative structure of biblical poems. To give but one example from among many dozens that shed significant new light on old problems: Dobbs-Allsopp shows that parataxis characterizes not only the syntax of sentences that often coincide with couplets or triplets but also the overall structure of whole compositions. It is this associative, list-like rather than narrative structure that explains one of the most common (and, at least for me, hitherto baffling) features of biblical laments and hymns of praise: their tendency to jump back and forth among their constitutive themes (complaint, plea, etc.).

An especially original and promising feature of this work is its use of visual material. Several illustrations exemplify the varied ways that ancient texts did or did not indicate the lineation of poems. Dobbs-Allsopp provides illustrations from Qumran scrolls, Septuagint manuscripts, Akkadian, Egyptian, and Ugaritic texts, as well as early masoretic manuscripts. Wall paintings, statues, stelae with inscriptions alongside illustrations, ostraca, and bas reliefs also enrich points that Dobbs-Allsopp makes throughout the book. Alas, the fifty-two illustrations (grouped together in the middle of the book) are so small that often the points Dobbs-Allsopp wants them to make are difficult and, at times, all but impossible to appreciate. Happily, this problem can be easily solved. I very much hope that Dobbs-Allsopp will make all the illustrations available at a website where readers can increase their size at will. In theory a website at Oxford University Press would make sense, but it will probably be quicker and easier for Dobbs-Allsopp to make them available at a site of his own.

The range of literature this book cites is extraordinary. Dobbs-Allsopp productively utilizes work by literary theorists, scholars of several poetic traditions (Greek, Latin, Old English, as well free verse of the nineteenth and twentieth centuries), psychologists who specialize in cognition, and anthropologists who study folk literature and orality—all this in addition to biblical, Assyriological, Ugaritological, and archaeological scholarship, including a good deal of rarely cited but enlightening German-language scholarship dating back roughly a century. The integration of all this material, along with useful discussions of modern poets (above all Whitman but also William Carlos Williams and W. S. Merwin) is exemplary. Further, while all biblical scholars know of the seminal work of the eighteenth-century scholar Robert Lowth on biblical poetry, and some have read snippets of it, Dobbs-Allsopp has studied Lowth closely. He rehabilitates Lowth's work, showing it to be more varied, more subtle, and of much greater worth than contemporary summaries or critiques of Lowth realize.

In regarding parallelism as merely one feature of biblical poetry rather than its essence, Dobbs-Allsopp resembles James Kugel, who made a similar argument in *The Idea of Biblical Poetry* (1981). Both scholars, however, have a somewhat surprisingly narrow view of what constitutes parallelism. Dobbs-Allsopp seems to confine the term to semantic-lexical parallelism. But as scholars who brought the work of Roman Jakobson into biblical criticism have shown, all poetry is based on parallelism of one sort or another, whether semantic-lexical, phonological, or rhythmic. Thus all lines of iambic pentameter are rhythmically parallel with each other, even though they usually have no lexical parallelism. As a result, many of the examples of couplets or triplets that Dobbs-Allsopp claims have no parallelism are in fact, full of parallelism as Jakobson (and biblical scholars cited by Dobbs-Allsopp, such as Alan Cooper, Stephen Geller, and Adele Berlin) understand it. Dobbs-Allsopp differs from Kugel on a different issue: Dobbs-Allsopp rejects the view that there is a continuum between prose and poetry in the Bible. Poetry consistently has lines of relatively short length; prose does not. But Dobbs-Allsopp does not address the liminal texts that Kugel describes, which have fairly clear lines that do not appear consistently and are sometimes rather long. It would be interesting to know how Dobbs-Allsopp regards a text such as Gen 1:1–2:4a, which has parallelism of various types that suggest the presence of lines, though these lines are not found in all sections of the text; further, even when lines are consistently present, they are longer than what one usually finds in biblical poetry.

Dobbs-Allsopp speaks of the need for specialists in literary theory and comparative literature to understand the nature of biblical poetry and to recognize the plausible claim of ancient Near Eastern poetry to be one of the first examples of free verse, and he hopes his book will be accessible to scholars outside biblical studies. At times, however, he assumes the reader already knows a fair amount about biblical studies and its terminology. This excellent study is not the first book one would want to read on the subject; it is pitched at a fairly high level that may make it difficult for people outside our own guild to benefit from parts of it. Even biblical critics will find it hard going at times. The book is frequently redundant. In a section on the lens provided by X, Dobbs-Allsopp will discuss the way that X relates to Y; later in a section on the lens provided by Y, he discusses the way Y relates to X, often citing the exact same literature in the footnotes to both sections. Thus there are subsections on parallelism in chapters 1, 2, and 4 whose content is heavily overlapping. Similarly, Dobbs-Allsopp tells us that biblical poetry is not metrical on pages 9, 10, 15, 56, 115–16, and he also devotes all of chapter 2 to the issue of this corpus's nonmetrical nature, including a section on pages 99–103 with the title "Biblical Hebrew Poetry Is Not Metrical." He does not err on page 120 when, introducing yet another paragraph on the nonmetricality of biblical poetry, he admits, "I belabor the point." The significance of biblical poetry's orality and the types of evidence for it (short lines, a lack of radical enjambments, paratactic syntax) are discussed at some length many times in the three chapters that precede the chapter specifically devoted to that subject. A further stumbling block that may put off some readers involves his syntax. Many a sentence is interrupted by multiple parenthetical statements, some set off by commas, others by dashes, and a few by parentheses; between an adjective and the subject it modifies, one or even two parenthetical clauses or lengthy phrases may intervene; several more will appear (some nested within others) between the subject and the verb; and another may intervene between the verb and its object. All this makes for difficult reading. Of course, the discovery of turgid prose in academic writing in the humanities is hardly news. In most cases, however, the overly complex syntax serves a clear purpose, which is to disguise the absence of original, interesting, or sometimes even coherent ideas in the article or book in question. But Dobbs-Allsopp's book is full of new, compelling, and outstandingly well thought out ideas of real significance, and it is a shame that some readers may fail to read the whole book because of the prose.

This criticism is relevant only because Dobbs-Allsopp's book is in fact so deeply informative, even for scholars who specialize in biblical poetry. I, for one, wrote a book on literary allusion in one poetic corpus (Isa 40–66); I am currently writing a commentary on the Psalter; I regularly give a graduate-level seminars on biblical poetry, as well as another, on Psalms, that focuses heavily on questions of biblical prosody. Yet in every one of this book's four sections I learned new perspectives for understanding biblical poetry as well as more sophisticated and sensitive ways of applying older perspectives. Further, when I already held the same view as Dobbs-Allsopp on a particular point, I frequently found that he articulated the idea in question with greater clarity and learning than I could have before reading his analysis. This book is lengthy and requires some time and effort, but that effort will recompense the reader very handsomely.

The Hebrew Bible: A Critical Companion, edited by John Barton. Princeton: Princeton University Press, 2016. Pp. xii + 613. Hardcover. $45.00. ISBN 9780691154718.

Phil J. Botha, University of Pretoria

According to the Library of Congress Cataloging-in-Publication Data (as stated on page iv), this book of 613 pages is a "general-interest introduction to the Old Testament from many disciplines." This is an apt description, but it does not do justice to the fine quality of academic expertise brought together in this interesting and creative overview of the current status of research into the Hebrew Bible. This book is not yet another introduction to the Hebrew Bible. Instead of the traditional way of introducing the Hebrew Bible book-by-book, the publisher or editor (or both) opted for a thematic approach. The book is also valuable for people with more than a "general" interest, although lay people will also find it informative and understandable. John Barton does state in the introduction (ix–x) that the aim was to produce a guide that is accessible to the "nonspecialist reader" (ix) and for readers from any religious background, since it was given a "nonconfessional character" (x), but students and academics will find it useful for orientation regarding the history of research on a multitude of disciplines, with a special focus on the current state of research.

In addition to providing insight into the nature and context of the biblical books, one of the important aims of book is to help dissolve the isolation traditionally accorded to the study of the Bible. It is thus designed to reintegrate the Hebrew Bible "into a wider framework of human literature and culture" (x). As such, it will also open up new vistas of understanding for students in the humanities (other than theological students), whether their areas of interest may be literature, human history, philosophy, social science, or language.

Experts, mostly from universities in the U.K., Europe, and the U.S., but also from Ireland, China, Malta, and Israel, were asked to work together on this publication. The result is twenty-three essays grouped together in four parts. Most of the essays refer the reader to the essential literature on the particular topic through extended endnotes and very helpful bibliographies of relevant sources. The book will therefore also be of value to beginning researchers in various fields of study of the Hebrew Bible by providing a useful overview of the current issues.

All the essays are worthy of a detailed discussion, but in view of the constraints of space only a sentence or two can be accorded to each. Part 1 is on "The Hebrew Bible in Its Historical and Social Context." Editor John Barton contributes chapter 1 to this section, "The Hebrew Bible and the Old Testament." Barton discusses the problem of the name of this collection of books from the perspective of the people by whom it was regarded as sacred, the languages used in it, the ancient translations of the Bible that also enjoy canonical status to a greater or lesser degree, the "apocryphal" books not included in the "Hebrew" Bible, and the order of the books in the different versions. In "The Historical Framework: Biblical and Scholarly Portrayals of the Past," Francesca Stavrakopoulou points out that "history" is a *portrayal* or a *version* of the past, not an accurate "record" or description of events (26). It is a difficult task to disentangle objective reality from the subjective, tendentious, and male-dominated ideology in which it is enshrined in the Hebrew Bible. When the biblical version is compared to nonbiblical artifacts and known events, a rough framework of political events emerges, but it is up to each historian to decide whether the major gaps and uncertainties that remain can and should be reduced by considering the biblical evidence on these matters. Katherine Southwood's "The Social and Cultural History of Ancient Israel" reviews the advantages social-scientific investigations have had for gaining information on Israel's social and cultural history. She discusses the methodological difficulties in reconstructing the society and culture in early Israel, inter alia, in terms of ethnicity, kinship, the role played by women, and hospitality. Chapter 4, Anthony J. Frendo's "Israel in the Context of the Ancient Near East," discusses the role that archaeological remains from Egypt and the ancient Near East play to help us contextualize the texts of the Hebrew Bible. He is much more positive about the value of the biblical narratives for filling in the gaps in our knowledge of ancient history than, for instance, Stavrakopoulou is in chapter 2.

Part 2, "Major Genres of Biblical Literature," introduces the biblical books but groups them together according to genre. Thomas Römer was tasked with writing about "The Narrative Books of the Hebrew Bible." He points out that about half of the content of the Hebrew Bible is narrative. He compares the contents of the Enneateuch (Genesis–Kings) to material from the ancient Near East and points out how the biblical writers made use of narrative traditions from Sumer, Ugarit, Assyria, Babylon, and other places. He also provides valuable insight into the research about the formation of the Pentateuch, the so-called Deuteronomistic History and the so-called Chronistic History. A final paragraph is dedicated to the emergence of the Jewish novellas Ruth, Esther, parts of Daniel, and the Joseph story. In "The Prophetic Literature," R. G. Kratz. Kratz discusses the phenomenon of prophets and their function in the ancient Near East. He explains how understanding the phenomenon can help us to understand not only the role of biblical prophets but also how prophetic oracles came to form the kernel of prophetic books that are in essence reinterpretations, adaptations, and actualizations of the original oracles. Kratz also gives an annotated list for further reading (155–59). Assnat Bartor's "Legal Texts" (those in the Pentateuch and other texts dealing with legal issues or that refer to the Pentateuch) discusses the influence of other, older law codes from the ancient Near East and the fact that the so-called law codes should be recognized to be primarily literary texts that reflected divine law and justice and only much later were transformed from moral advice to binding decrees. Jennie Grillo's adds the chapter on "The Wisdom Literature" and Susan Gillingham's that on "The Psalms and Poems of the Hebrew Bible." Grillo points out that there is no separate category such as wisdom literature in the Old Testament but rather material from widely divergent times that share "a pool of family resemblances" (182). Thus Proverbs, Job, Ecclesiastes, and wisdom elsewhere in the Old Testament are discussed. Gillingham's overview of the book of Psalms and the research on it since the time of Gunkel and up to the recent growing interest into the reception of the Psalms is masterful. She treats the origins of the psalms, the use of the psalms, the compilation of the Psalter from the oldest compilation of fragments to the book as a whole, and poems outside the Psalter in the Hebrew Bible and those found at Qumran.

Part 3, on "Major Religious Themes" in the Hebrew Bible, has seven chapters. Benjamin D. Sommer's "Monotheism" tackles the difficult debate about whether preexilic Israel was monotheistic or basically polytheistic. Building on the work of Yehezkel Kaufmann, Sommer argues on the basis of the consistent omission of unambiguous polytheistic themes in biblical texts, thus a "legitimate" argument from (conspicuous) silence, that *monotheism* is a useful term to describe the difference between Israel and its neighbors. In "Creation: God and World," Herman Spieckermann's explication of creation as represented in Genesis is particularly enlightening; he also discusses creation motifs in the Psalms, the prophetic books, and the wisdom books. Hilary Marlow chapter on "The Human Condition" investigates the Old Testament perspectives on humanity and its relationship to God and one another; the meaning of life, and questions of ecology. In "God's Covenants with Humanity and Israel," Dominik Markl follows this theological concept in its development in the Pentateuch, Prophets, and Writings against the back-drop of treaties and covenants of loyalty in the ancient Near East. C. L. Crouch tackles the topic of "Ethics" (ch. 14, in which she considers the influence of history and genre on the variety of moral opinions found in the Hebrew Bible), while Ste-phen C. Russell's "Religious Space and Structures" describes the religious function and graded sanctity, linked to religious time, that were accorded to houses, gates, open-air altars, high places, temples, and the like. Finally, in "Ritual: Diet, Purity, and Sacrifice" Seth D. Kunin convincingly demonstrates how the various rules regarding food, purity, sacrifice, and feasts all form part of a cohesive, meaningful structural system.

Part 4, "The Study and Reception of the Hebrew Bible," also contains seven chapters. In "Reception of the Old Testament," Alison Gray explains the impor-tance of this fast-growing approach that involves anthropology, sociology, and hermeneutics and that also urges exegetes to consider the ethical consequences of their research. Christoph Bultmann's "Historical-Critical Inquiry" describes the origin and growth of historical criticism and the differences between it and modern historical-critical inquiry into the Hebrew Bible. David Jasper gives an overview of "Literary Approaches," beginning with the Bible as literature and work-ing through deconstruction and postmodernism. R. W. L. Moberly's "Theological Approaches to the Old Testament" advocates a new paradigm that continues the twentieth-century work on Old Testament theology but that is more responsive to newer interpretative dimensions. Eryl W. Davies tackles "Political and Advo-cacy Approaches." This refers to newer approaches and methods applied to the study of the Old Testament, such as feminist biblical criticism, liberation theol-ogy, postcolonial criticism, and queer criticism, while some of these approaches are illustrated in a concluding paragraph with reference to the interpretation of the book of Ruth. Carmel McCarthy describes "Textual Criticism and Biblical Translation," and Adrian Curtis offers the final chapter, "To Map or Not to Map? A Biblical Dilemma." McCarthy's overview is a useful, up-to-date description of the need for and the concerns as well as the methods of textual criticism, while Curtis discusses the problem that maps aiming to aid the Bible reader's understanding of biblical texts can have the undesired effect of suggesting that the biblical accounts are more historically accurate than they really are. In view of all the advantages provided by maps, he concludes ("with appropriate caution," 571) that maps are indeed needed.

The book has a useful index of Scripture (575–88) that also includes texts from the New Testament, apocryphal/deuterocanonical books, and pseudepig-raphal books (only one reference, to 1 Clem. 11:1). There is an index of modern authors (589–95) and a useful index of subjects (596–613).

As a result of its thematic approach to the Hebrew Bible, and as one could predict beforehand, a measure of overlap occurs between various essays. The same books or chapters in books and the same theological issues are sometimes tra-versed in different essays. Contradictory points of view are sometimes expressed, but this does not detract from the value of the book. It merely underlines the notion stressed a number of times within the book that the multifaceted nature of the Hebrew Bible itself makes it improbable and even undesirable that complete consensus on any particular issue will ever be achieved. Some scholars who have dedicated much energy to research on the Hebrew Bible will no doubt feel that the scope covered by the book is not exhaustive enough (e.g., critical spatiality is not represented), but in terms of the stated aim to introduce the Hebrew Bible "as one of the great texts of our culture" (x) to a wider audience, the book is a great success and can be recommended confidently for a broad audience of Jewish and Christian believers, students of theology and the humanities, and teachers and researchers.

Wrestling with the Violence of God: Soundings in the Old Testament, edited by M. Daniel Carroll R. and J. Blair Wilgus. Bulletin for Biblical Research Supplements 10. Winona Lake, IN: Eisenbrauns, 2015. Pp. xiii + 178. Hardcover. $37.50. ISBN 9781575068282.

Eric A. Seibert, Messiah College

Throughout the history of biblical scholarship, far too little attention has been paid to divine violence in the Hebrew Bible. While there has been a notable increase in publications devoted to this topic over the past decade, much work remains to be done. For that reason alone, it is gratifying to see a collection of essays exploring violent portrayals of God in Scripture.

Wrestling with the Violence of God had its origins in the Old Testament Theology session of the Evangelical Theological Society's Annual Meeting in 2012. The book includes an introduction followed by seven essays, each focusing on divine violence in a different passage or book of the Old Testament. After briefly summarizing these chapters, I will offer some evaluation.

In the introduction, M. Daniel Carroll R. and J. Blair Wilgus orient readers to the nature of the problem, noting that the God of the Old Testament has been critiqued by believers and unbelievers alike. Carroll and Wilgus believe a *comprehensive* response to these critiques requires utilizing five "fields of research": comparative studies, history of reception, theological foundations, textual readings, and virtuous sensitivity (8–11). This volume is primarily concerned with only one of these, namely, textual readings.

Paul Kissling's opening essay, "The Near-Sacrifice of Isaac: Monstrous Morality or Richly Textured Theology?," focuses on Gen 22:1–19. Kissling believes those who accuse God of issuing an immoral decree—or who fault Abraham for being willing to carry it out—fundamentally misread the text. These problems fade away when the text is read rightly, which for Kissling means reading it "*empathetically*" and contextually (15–16). Kissling attempts to demonstrate this by engaging in a close reading of the text (exploring literary techniques such as naming, repetition, wordplay) and by drawing upon insights gained from placing this narrative in its literary, historical, and interpretive contexts.

Daniel Block explores a number of exceedingly troubling texts in "How Can We Bless YHWH? Wrestling with Divine Violence in Deuteronomy." Rather than trying "to justify divine destructiveness and belligerence in the Hebrew Bible," Block says his goal is just "to understand it as the book of Deuteronomy portrays it" (31). To that end, he considers both the "forms" divine violence takes in Deuteronomy and its "targets." He also explores the motivation for divine violence, looking first at God's response to Israel's "moral offenses" before turning to a more extensive discussion of God's violence against Canaanites (41–50). Ultimately, Block stresses the need to view divine violence against the backdrop of divine grace (39, 41, 50).

Hélène Dallaire's essay, "Taking the Land by Force: Divine Violence in Joshua," begins by recognizing how terribly problematic the violent portrayal of God is in Joshua. Her essay includes a short historical overview of the interpretation of the book of Joshua, an exploration of various reasons why some believe the book was included in the canon, a discussion of God as warrior, and an investigation of the meaning of ḥērem. Dallaire believes "The book of Joshua should ... not be read as an exact description of the events but rather as historical national literature in which the accounts reflect the literary traditions of the day, the rhetoric of military records, and the theological language of Israel" (72). This, she contends, mitigates some of the inherent problems with a strictly literalistic reading of the book.

In "Cries of the Oppressed: Prayer and Violence in the Psalms," David Firth focuses on imprecatory psalms. After offering a hermeneutical approach for reading these psalms, Firth then gives extended attention to two individual psalms (Pss 109 and 69) and two communal psalms (Pss 137 and 79). A key insight he derives is "that justice is something only God can enact" (88). Firth believes Christians can still pray imprecatory psalms despite the tension that exists with other parts of Scripture, such as Jesus's command to love one's enemies in Matt 5. What these psalms teach, according to Firth, is that we must rely upon God to do justice and must leave our violence in prayer (89).

Heath Thomas's contribution, "Suffering Has Its Voice: Divine Violence, Pain, and Prayer in Lamentations," problematizes divine violence in the book of Lamentations. Thomas's detailed analysis demonstrates how God's presence and absence in the wake of Jerusalem's destruction are perceived as expressions of divine violence. (Thomas uses the language of divine passivity, distance, and presence.) The appropriate way to negotiate this violence, according to Lamentations, is through prayers of confession and complaint. As Thomas puts it, "Lamentations provides a context for a spirituality that takes divine violence back to God in prayer to await his response" (109).

M. Daniel Carroll R. finds recent treatments criticizing God's violence in the Prophets lacking and seeks to offer a corrective by focusing on the issue of divine judgment in the book of Amos. In "'I Will Send Fire': Reflections on the Violence of God in Amos," Carroll R. stresses that God's justice upon Israel's sin requires judgment but that this judgment should not be regarded as mean-spirited or capricious. Rather, when God judges, it is "with deep sorrow" because of the connections God has with the people of Israel, the creation, and humanity in general (127). Carroll R. emphasizes God's judgment as purposeful and compassionate and writes, "Judgment is not the work of an impulsive, vindictive, heartless, or detached deity; it is a step toward blessedness and salvation" (129).

In the final essay, "Toward an End to Violence: Hearing Jeremiah," Elmer Martens attempts to balance the violent images of God in Jeremiah with others that are more positive and pleasant. The stated purpose of his essay "is to present a portrait of God from the book of Jeremiah that at a minimum tempers the portrait of a violent God, and more maximally highlights a trajectory into the New Testament that envisions an end to violence" (134). Martens attempts to accomplish this by contextualizing God's anger vis-à-vis the covenant and by highlighting portrayals of God's benevolence, love, and loyalty throughout the book.

I commend the editors and contributors for devoting sustained attention to the topic of God's violence in the Old Testament. These difficult and unsavory characterizations of God must not be ignored. Given the way violent Old Testament passages have often been abused, I was glad various contributors stated that these texts should *not* be used to inspire or justify acts of violence today (28, 47, 53). Clear statements like this should appear frequently when biblical scholars deal with texts that have been—and continue to be—used to justify violence and killing.

In spite of the limited number of contributions, this volume does a good job of covering a wide range of important Old Testament texts across the canon that contain divine violence. The essays are characterized by a close reading of the text, and many readers will benefit from this careful analysis.

According to Carroll R. and Wilgus, "The core belief of the contributors to this volume, and *perhaps the most important component of this work*, is that the issue of God's participation in violence found in the Hebrew Bible can be addressed and understood without jettisoning belief in the Bible as the word of God" (vii–viii, emphasis added). They also claim this book "is motivated at least in part by the desire to offer an alternative voice to those who currently … diminish the theological and ethical value of the Old Testament and question its presentation of God" (12). This gives some essays an apologetic flavor as contributors attempt to reassure readers things are not as bad as they seem. The book also seems to operate with the assumption that those who do "question" or challenge the Old Testament's portrayal of God are thereby guilty of denying the Old Testament as Scripture—an assumption I would strongly dispute.

With the possible exception of Dallaire (71–73), the writers also seem to assume that God said and did what the text claims and that this accurately represents God's character. In my opinion, this assumption significantly limits the usefulness of this volume, since it prevents contributors from engaging in an ethical critique of "God's" violent behavior. Instead, they analyze and generally accept the text's view of God without challenging it. Embracing such portrayals is extremely problematic, *especially* for those who wish to use the Hebrew Bible to think about what (the living) God is actually like, since God is portrayed as behaving in ways that appear unethical and immoral on numerous occasions.

To illustrate some of my concerns more specifically, I will briefly comment on two essays. Martens's essay on Jeremiah helpfully reminds us that, when speaking about God in the Old Testament, it is always important to consider the wide range of images included there. Less helpful is his attempt to use positive images of God to neutralize more problematic ones. The rhetorical effect of the essay is to say to readers, "Yes, God sometimes behaves violently, but don't be overly concerned because such actions are always in the service of a greater good. Besides, the text reveals many other facets of God's character that are highly commendable. These trump all else and should be your primary focus" (see, e.g., 139–40, 149). Arguments that use the ends to justify the means are unpersuasive, in my estimation, since they allow virtually anything to be justified. Moreover, regardless of how many positive images of God one finds in the book of Jeremiah, their presence alone is not enough to overcome the enormous moral and theological problems raised by the frequent portrayals of God terrorizing, killing, and destroying countless people in Jeremiah and throughout the Hebrew Bible.

Block's chapter on Deuteronomy provides helpful categories that can be used to sort through the vast volume of material in the book dealing with divine violence. My concerns are with his discussion of why God commanded the slaughter of Canaanites. Block puts forward many standard arguments offered by conservative scholars grappling with this issue (e.g., eliminating Canaanites was necessary for the salvation of the world; killing Canaanites was justified because they were wicked, 46). The problem with arguments such as these is that they raise serious questions about divine justice and goodness, especially when one considers that unarmed civilians—including infants and toddlers—were among those slated for destruction. In light of that, it is unsurprising to hear Block say, "I am pessimistic that we will ever find a satisfying answer" (43). From my perspective, there can be no satisfying answer for those who assume God actually issued this dreadful divine decree. It simply is not possible to justify such indiscriminate killing.

A better approach begins by acknowledging that God never commanded Israelites to kill Canaanites in the first place, and there are many good reasons to accept this position (see, e.g., Randal Rauser, "'Let Nothing That Breathes Remain Alive': On the Problem of Divinely Commanded Genocide," *Philosophia Christi* 11 [2009]: 27–41). While the violent portrayal of God in parts of Deuteronomy and elsewhere throughout the Hebrew Bible are understandable given the cultural and historical context in which they were written, they do not reflect God's true character (see further my *Disturbing Divine Behavior: Troubling Old Testament Images of God* [Minneapolis: Fortress, 2009]).

In sum, those who agree with the assumptions that undergird this collection of essays will undoubtedly find much in this book to appreciate. Those who do not agee will find its usefulness more limited. Still, all can benefit from the very careful readings of biblical texts found throughout the book. The contributors of this volume deserve our thanks for helping us in this regard and for not allowing us to sidestep some of the most theologically challenging portions of the Old Testament.

Patterns of Sin in the Hebrew Bible: Metaphor, Culture, and the Making of a Religious Concept, by Joseph Lam. Oxford: Oxford University Press, 2016. Pp. xix + 308. Hardcover. $74.00. ISBN 9780199394647.

Ryan P. Bonfiglio, Columbia Theological Seminary

In this study Joseph Lam offers a thorough and thoughtful linguistic analysis of the Hebrew Bible's language about sin. In contrast to other approaches to the same topic, this study does not primarily focus on etymologies of individual terms such as ʿāwōn ("iniquity"), ḥēṭʾ ("sin"), and pešaʿ ("transgression"). Rather, Lam endeavors to identify and describe the metaphorical patterns that underlie a wide range of biblical expressions that describe sin's effects, consequences, and remedies. In doing so, Lam offers detailed and fresh insight into the concept of sin in ancient Israel's scriptures.

Like many other studies in biblical metaphor, this book begins with a discussion of theory and terminology. Two ideas are crucial for Lam's subsequent analysis. First, he emphasizes that the study of metaphors can be a means of gaining access to cultural assumptions behind certain concepts. These assumptions tend to be expressed not through isolated metaphors but rather through broader patterns of expression that are systematically interrelated through a common concept or theme. In the case of the Hebrew Bible's language about sin, Lam finds four pervasive root metaphors: sin as burden, sin as divine account, sin as path or direction, and sin as stain or impurity. Lam devotes a chapter to the analysis of each of these root metaphors with the goal of elucidating the full range of nuances in how biblical authors characterize the notion of sin.

Second, Lam contends that "metaphor is not an intrinsic quality of a linguistic expression but, rather, a mode of construal" (6–7). As such, it is context that ultimately determines whether a given term functions as a metaphor or as a literal statement. When a metaphor is used repeatedly and in predictable ways, the original metaphorical sense of the term can fade, and, as a result, it can become incorporated into the lexicon as a nonfigurative expression. Lam refers to this process as the "lexicalization" of a metaphor. The notion of lexicalization enables Lam to more finely parse the distinction between the literal and the metaphorical, a point he deems to be essential in certain aspects of his study.

The metaphor of sin as burden dominates the Hebrew Bible and is the subject of Lam's lengthiest chapter (ch. 2). In this metaphor, sin is portrayed as a physical object that burdens, weighs down, crushes, and immobilizes the sinner. The burden includes not only the sin itself but also its results: the forensic guilt, divine punishment, and putative psychological effects associated with sin. This root metaphor gives birth to a variety of entailments, including descriptions of sin being placed upon a person (Judg 9:57); descriptions of the severity of sin in terms of "heaviness" (Isa 1:4); the sinner falling (Prov 11:5) or being bowed down (Ps 107:17) under the weight of sin; and sin as a yoke (Lam 1:14).

The most common expression of this metaphorical pattern involves the use of the verb nāśāʾ to indicate either the "bearing" of sin or, conversely, the lifting off or "forgiving" of sin. The former usage, which is the more typical formulation, high-lights the ongoing responsibility of an individual for his or her own sin, although in some isolated cases people can bear the sins of others (Exod 28:38). In the latter usage, emphasis is placed on the ability of the offended party (God or another human) to absolve the sinner from the consequences of sin. Lam notes that all but one instance of *nāśāʼ* meaning "to bear" occurs in the Priestly sources (P, H) of the Pentateuch or in Ezekiel, while instances of *nāśāʼ* meaning "to forgive" exclusively are found in non-Priestly literature.

How can this patterning be explained from a historical-linguistic point of view? Lam proposes that through time the use of *nāśāʼ* as "to forgive" became disassociated from the spatial-physical meanings of "lifting, bearing, or carrying" and thus was lexicalized as a term denoting the act of an offended party pardoning the sin of another. The use of *nāśāʼ* as "to bear" in Priestly literature thus reflects a subsequent linguistic innovation that "revivifies" the original metaphor of sin as burden. Lam speculates that this development coincided with the tendency of the Priestly writers to use *sālaḥ* ("to pardon, forgive") in place of the lexicalized sense of *nāśāʼ*.

Chapter 3 turns to metaphors that depict sin as entries in an individual's heavenly account. The underling notion is that of a divine judge who fastidiously keeps record of all human deeds. This pattern includes expressions about the writing down (*kātab*) and the erasing (*māḥāh*) of sin as well as the reckoning (*ḥāśab*), remembering (*zākar*), and not forgetting (*lōʼ šākaḥ*) of sin in the mind of God. The sin as account metaphor also includes expressions that depict God's repayment or requital of sin as is especially evident with the verbs *šillēm* ("to recompense") and *hēšîb* ("to send back"). In both cases, sin is thought to create a debt in an individual's heavenly account that God must balance by providing a punishment for the sin in proper proportion. Importantly, Lam notes that God is almost never described as ransoming people from sin—the debt is owed to God, not "the clutches of sin itself" (153). Also relevant to this metaphorical pattern is the much-discussed verb *pāqad*. While Lam recognizes that in the Hebrew Bible this term is well on its way to becoming lexicalized with the meaning "to punish," its original metaphorical sense had to do with the attributing of sin to an individual's heavenly account.

The metaphor of sin as path or direction (ch. 4) maps elements of spatial movement onto an understanding of the moral life. Sin can be the target of the movement of a moral agent (1 Kgs 8:32), but more common are descriptions of the path itself as being evil (Jer 18:11) or as leading one astray (Prov 12:26). This metaphorical pattern also makes it possible to talk about the forsaking of sinful behavior in terms of "turning away" (*šûb* + *min*) from iniquity or "turning aside" (*sûr*) from evil. Also belonging to this pattern are the group of metaphors from the book of Kings that speak of walking in the (sinful) way of one's father (1 Kgs 15:26).

Chapter 5 focuses upon the complex and oft-debated relationship between the concepts of sin and impurity. In light of Lam's focus on metaphors, what is of note is that overt portrayals of sin as stain are not common in the Hebrew Bible.

Nevertheless, there are instances in which sin is described by means of imagery related to stained clothing (Isa 1:18–20) or shed blood on one's hands (Ezek 23:37). In other texts, the sinner is said to be washed from the stain of sin (Isa 4:3–4). Still other instances involve descriptions of Israel's sin in terms of metal impurity (Mal 3:2–3) and menstrual impurity (Isa 64:5 [Eng. 64:6]). In each case the metaphor presents sin as a type of intrusion into a defined space or as a pollution of a pristine state.

In his conclusion (ch. 6), Lam summarizes his earlier findings and offers a brief discussion of the development of metaphors for sin in postbiblical Hebrew texts. While this latter topic represents a potentially rich area of study, its sparse treatment here (only three pages) unfortunately feels something like an afterthought in an otherwise masterful study.

Overall, there is much to like about *Patterns of Sin in the Hebrew Bible*. For a technical monograph, its prose is refreshingly lively and accessible. It is packed with hundreds of biblical references (in both English and transliterated Hebrew) that help to concretely illustrate aspects of the discussion. I also appreciate that, while Lam's work is theoretically informed, he never gets bogged down in the tedium of cognitive metaphor theory. Due to its accessibility, this book would work well in an undergraduate or seminary classroom—indeed, I have already added it to the syllabus for my own course on biblical metaphors.

Despite the thoughtfulness of Lam's study, two minor points of critique are of note. The first is methodological. Not without good reason, Lam's study of metaphor focuses exclusively on linguistic forms of discourse in the Hebrew Bible. However, literary evidence is not the only means of gaining access to the cultural assumptions that lie behind a concept such as sin. In fact, in recent years an increasing number of scholars have begun to turn to ancient art or iconography to shed additional light on the conceptual background of the biblical world. Iconographic evidence has been especially illuminating in studies of divine metaphors and other imagery in the Hebrew Bible. Yet except for one tantalizing reference at the outset of chapter 2, a discussion of ancient iconography is lacking in Lam's study. This observation does not mean Lam's text-centered approach is misguided. Nevertheless, if one truly wishes to examine "the ancient Israel concept of sin" (ix), then considering the rich repertoire of Syro-Palestinian iconography might well enhance and expand what one gleans from the textual evidence alone.

Second, while Lam's study excels at the detailed analysis of the four metaphorical patterns in question, comparatively less is said about the relationship between these patterns and how they map onto different parts of the Hebrew canon. For instance, what theological or rhetorical conclusions might be drawn about why certain root metaphors tend to cluster in particular literary settings? What insights might be gained by comparing how sin is patterned in, say, the book of Proverbs with the Priestly sources of the Pentateuch or the postexilic prophets? In other words, what meta-patterns become observable when the analysis of sin in the Hebrew Bible zooms out to a broader canonical context? To be fair, these sorts of questions likely lie beyond the scope of Lam's project, and for practical reasons it might well have been judicious for Lam not to have ventured into this terrain. Yet in my estimation, answering these questions represents a potential next step in the study of the concept of sin in the Hebrew Bible. The fact that Lam's study prompts such questions serves as further evidence of its valuable contribution to the field of biblical studies.

PENTATEUCH

[Re]reading Again: A Mosaic Reading of Numbers 25, by Anthony Rees. Library of Hebrew Bible/Old Testament Studies 589. London: Bloomsbury, 2015. Pp. x + 191. Hardcover. $104.00. ISBN 9780567554369.

L. Michael Morales, Greenville Presbyterian Theological Seminary

In this revision of his dissertation at Charles Sturt University, Rees attempts to address a perceived crisis in biblical studies, particularly regarding the discipline's entrenched divide between historical critics and postmodernists, as well as the discipline's general irrelevance with regard to world affairs. He seeks a reconfigured biblical studies with a new end, one that will engage significant cultural issues such as religious fundamentalism, exile, human trafficking, the imbalance of world resources, and the like. With Num 25 as a test case, and utilizing the mosaic art form as the guiding metaphor for his approach, Rees explains his aim "to read a passage of scripture using a variety of methods now common in biblical studies" in order to demonstrate the strengths of diversity (8–9).

An introductory section offers an orientation to the present rift in biblical studies, tracing scholarly discussion on the nature and end(s) of biblical criticism. Rees begins with John Barton's *The Nature of Biblical Criticism* (2007) and highlights various other voices such as George Aichele, Peter Miscall, and Richard Walsh's "An Elephant in the Room: Historical-Critical and Postmodern Interpretations of the Bible" (*JBL* 2009), along with John Van Seters's response (*JHS* 2009). Roland Boer's manifesto (*Rescuing the Bible*, 2007) is noted, in which he calls for an ideological alliance between the secular left and the religious left. Hector Avalos (*The End of Biblical Studies*, 2007), alternatively, urges a postscriptural world whereby the Bible is abandoned, and R.S. Sugirtharajah ("Critics, Tools and the Global Arena," 2000) suggests reestablishing the discipline of biblical studies by turning its attention to significant world issues. Rees then commends his publication as an attempt at a new biblical studies where the old and new talk together, forging a way of overcoming the discipline's emergent rifts; he endeavors not to privilege any one method over another but rather to demonstrate how each individual reading may enrich our understanding of the text. The introduction concludes with the author's translation of Num 25:1–18 (textual-critical issues are not addressed).

The first two chapters of *[Re]reading Again* briefly survey the history of interpretation, covering the precritical and postcritical eras, respectively. Contributions from Philo, Josephus, Origen, the Talmud, Rashi, and the Samaritan Chronicle are rehearsed in the first chapter. Here Rees notes how narrative gaps in the text were imaginatively filled in by early interpreters. Equally pertinent though not under-scored, however, is the rather *consistent* interpretation of Num 25 throughout this history. The second chapter examines contributions by Calvin, Keil and Delitzsch, George Buchanan Gray, Martin Noth, Philip Budd, Jacob Milgrom, and Baruch Levine. Rees points out that critical work by the likes of Astruc and Wellhausen opened up the Pentateuch and moved scholarship forward, even while spawning a diversity of theories and approaches to the text.

Rees offers a historically oriented reading in chapter 3. Labeling the source-critical division of the text as "at best arbitrary," he nevertheless affirms that it "does shed some light on this chapter and the narrative development of the embedded themes" (72). He fruitfully explores intertextuality between Num 25 and Exod 34, as well as with Ps 106. Reading Ezra 9–10 into the text, he remarks that the banned foreign wives following the exile "join the catalogue of women who are a threat, most dramatically portrayed by Cozbi" (88). In a bit of circular reasoning, he asserts that, since Moses's wife was a Midianite, ethnic purity must not have been a consuming issue for the wilderness generation; references in the text that do show such a concern, therefore, must have been retrojected by later hands to justify their exclusionist and isolationist stance (88–89). The core issue of Yahwism (versus ethnicity), in the instances where converts like Rahab and Ruth were not excluded, is not discussed.

Chapter 4 turns to a literary reading of Num 25, offering a brief history of the enterprise beginning with Robert Alter's *The Art of Biblical Narrative* (1981) and highlighting the work of Jan Fokkelman, Shimeon Bar-Efrat, and Yairah Amit, among others. Rees's analysis touches on the beginning and ending of the liter-ary unit, spatiality (covering Shittim, the tent of Meeting, Zimri's tent, Peor), the manipulation of time, the narrator, plot, and characters (Moses, Phinehas, Zimri, Cozbi, Yahweh).

In chapter 5 Rees offers a feminist reading. Again, he provides a brief orien-tation to the chapter's approach, noting the "hermeneutics of suspicion," which explores the oppressive values that have silenced women's voices and presumes an androcentric system whereby evil is gendered as female and goodness is described in male terms, and "imaginative identification," which imagines the presence of women wherever the text does not explicitly deny it. Inconsistent treatment of data is evident throughout this section. For example, on the one hand, the phrase "sons of Israel" confirms suspicions that "this is a male-centric text" that sup-presses women (121), while, on the other hand, when the presumably more inclusive terms "Israel" or "the people" are used it is, Rees suggests, in order to divert the blame away from the direct perpetrators, the sons, and toward the females whose presence is implied by the inclusive terms (122). Is this really so? Rees's consideration is incomplete inasmuch as it is the male leaders who are to hang as offenders (Num 25:4), Moses commands the judges each one to "kill his men" (25:5), and it is specifically "one of the sons of Israel" who engages in the flagrant act (25:6). Similarly, Cozbi is at one point praised for being an opponent too formidable for Israel, comparable to Eve for her ability to converse, reason, and act independently, wielding power over men (132); however, when it comes to blameworthiness, Cozbi is regarded as entirely passive and powerless, having left the safety of her ancestral home against her own wishes (138–39).

A postcolonial reading, founded upon the seminal work of Edward Said's *Orientalism* (2003), is offered in chapter 6. Here the Bible is largely sentenced as guilty by association, since biblical themes "lurk stealthily behind" the ideology of invasion (150). Rees here decries the Old Testament narrative's portrayal of Canaanites as unclean, abhorrent, and expendable. There is, unfortunately, neither a discussion of the particular context of the ban nor on the wider emphasis of blessing to the nations within the pentateuchal context of Numbers. Along the same lines, not enough emphasis is given to the *mis*appropriation of the Bible, a point that makes room for the contribution of biblical studies, when the discipline aims for the simple sense of the text as one of its ends. As this chapter steers toward a discussion of aboriginal women in Australia, there is a marked paucity of interaction with the text. Although the book's introduction provides fair warning (11), I was nevertheless disappointed inasmuch as the chapter is still entitled a "reading."

In a brief conclusion, Rees renews his call for a pluralistic approach to biblical studies, one that forgoes the idea of "plain sense" and embraces diversity while resisting the temptation to exercise control over others.

Generally speaking, the basic message of *[Re]reading Again* is obvious enough and without controversy: various perspectives and differing methods can contribute to one's overall understanding of the text and should be appreciated. Since Rees's own perspective (essentially feminist) marks each of his readings, however, this project may have been more successful as a collection of essays by various scholars. In the literary approach chapter, for instance, he refers to the text's "vilification of women," whereby Zimri's "befriending" a foreign woman is portrayed as shameful, whereas to kill one is an act of no small merit (113; see also his comments in the history of interpretation chapters, 30, 40). While complete objectivity is not possible, highly opinionated remarks and loaded terms tend to detract from the typical professionalism of a scholarly work. Phinehas's action and the war on the Midianites, for another example, are often depicted with terms such as "murderous," "barbaric," "extreme brutality," "savage," and "maniacal rage" (85–87, 107, 114–16, 118, 176). Lacking here are the characteristics for which Rees commends Gray's commentary: his restraint when it comes to emotional language and moral judgment (51).

As a result, one comes away from this book sensing quite clearly what its author is about, although the same is not necessarily the case with reference to the text and characters of Num 25. For a recent work, there is also an evident gap of interaction with current scholarship on this particular text (even from among feminist scholars). The following studies on Num 25, to name a few, are absent from the discussion and bibliography: J. M. Cohen (*JBQ* 2013); L. A. Monroe (*VT* 2012); J. Fleurant (*JSOT* 2011); D. Lincicum (*BBR* 2011); P. Steinberg (*JBQ*

2007); K. Pomykala (*Israel in the Wilderness*, 2008, 17–36); D. Bernat (*JJS* 2007); J. J. Collins (*JBL* 2003); B. Organ (*CBQ* 2001); S. Weingarten (*JBQ* 2001); and M. Douglas (*In the Wilderness*, 1993, 191–207). This deficiency, along with the book's noticeable movement away from Num 25 as it progresses, would seem to justify the question as to whether or not using a text as the pretext for discussing current issues makes biblical studies more relevant after all. For the reader whose primary interest is in understanding the text itself, its redaction or background history, or even the text's *application* to current issues, readings that are not text-centered will not likely be reread again. These remarks notwithstanding, the author's aim to promote irenic engagement is to be commended.

Aufbrüche zur Exodustheologie, by Matthias Ederer. Stuttgarter Bibelstudien 231. Stuttgart: Bibelwerk, 2014. Pp. 195. Paper. 27,50 Euro. ISBN 9783460033146.

Kristin Weingart, Eberhard Karls Universität Tübingen

Num 33,1–49 ist auf den ersten Blick kein Text, der größere Spannungsmomente oder tiefsinnige theologische Reflexionen erwarten lässt. Die Aufzählung von 42 Stationen der Wüstenwanderung macht einen reichlich schematischen Eindruck, wird doch nahezu durchgängig mittels der formelhafte Abfolge von „aufbrechen" (נסע) und „lagern" (חנה) Ortslage an Ortslage gereiht. Die Untersuchung von Matthias Ederer (Regensburg) zeigt jedoch, dass an diesem Text, der in der bisherigen Forschung v.a. für Fragen der Lokalisierung bestimmter Ortslagen herangezogen wurde, durchaus narrativ-strukturelle, exodustheologische sowie kanonhermeneutische Entdeckungen zu machen sind.

Die Studie setzt mit methodischen Grundlegungen (Abschnitt I, 11–30) ein, die sie als Beitrag zur „Biblischen Auslegung" (der Ansatz firmiert häufig auch unter „kanonisch-intertextuelle Lektüre") im Sinne eines rezeptionsästhetischen Zugangs ausweist (14f.). Ziel ist die wissenschaftlich gesteuerte Erhebung der *intentio operis* des auszulegenden Textes. Dabei sollen insbesondere die Sinnpotenziale im Fokus stehen, die sich durch den Nachvollzug der im Text angelegten Bezüge zu anderen Texten ergeben (Intertextualität). Den primären Referenzrahmen hierfür bildet der biblische Kanon, der zum einen eine Gewichtung der eingespielten Intertexte durch die vorgegebene Leserichtung und zum anderen als „identitätsstiftende Basisurkunde einer Glaubensgemeinschaft" (15) eine spezifische Textpragmatik vorgibt. Num 33,1–49 wird zunächst durch eine knapp kommentierte Arbeitsübersetzung, Beobachtungen zu Struktur und Gliederung sowie durch die Einordnung in den Kontext in Num 25,19–36,13 erschlossen (17–30). Dabei ergeben sich grundlegende Weichenstellungen für die weitere Untersuchung: Ederer betrachtet Num 33 nicht als Liste sondern aufgrund der weitgehend durchlaufenden Reihung von *wayyiqtol*-Formen als narrativen Text. Dabei gewinnen diejenigen Abschnitte an besonderem Gewicht, in denen die Narrativkette unterbrochen wird, d.h. vv. 1–2; vv. 3–4; vv. 6–9 sowie vv. 38–40. Den Hauptteil der Studie macht denn auch eine Darstellung intertextueller

Bezüge dieser Abschnitte aus, wobei die jeweiligen „Hypotexte" (die eingespielten Texte) präsentiert und analysiert werden, um schließlich das Sinnpotential zu erheben, das sich aus der Text-Text-Beziehung für den auszulegenden Text („Hypertext") ergibt.

Als zentrale Hypotexte zu Num 33,1–2 nennt Ederer Num 9,15–23 (Ex 40,34–38); 10,11–28 sowie Ex 6,1–7,7 (Abschnitt II, 31–97). Num 9,15–23 sowie 10,11–28 werden dabei als Entfaltungen einer verbindenden Thematik gelesen—der Führung Israels durch JHWH während der Wüstenwanderung. Num 9 entwickele mit dem Modell, dass die Stellung der Wolke über dem Begegnungszelt Israel entweder zum Aufbruch oder zum Lagern auffordere, ein Sinnbild göttlicher Führung, das in 9,23c auf die Mosetora als bleibender Repräsentation des Gotteswillens in Israel hinauslaufe. Num 10 reflektiere das Führungsgeschehen in Aufnahme von Num 9 weiter und stelle dem Bild der Wolke die Lade als Bundessymbol zur Seite. Die Aufnahme der genannten Hypotexte in Num 33,1–2 zeigt sich für Ederer an Stichwortverbindungen über die Wurzeln נסע und חנה sowie besonders die Phrasen מסעי בני ישראל sowie על פי יהוה. Auch ohne dass zentrale Stichworte aus Num 9f. (so etwa ענן oder משמרת) in 33,1f. genannt würden, bereichere die intertextuelle Beziehung Num 33,1–2 um wichtige theologische Aspekte; so symbolisiere die Beibehaltung der Marschordnung aus Num 10, dass Israel seine Verfasstheit als Bundesvolk bewahre und zugleich werde durch die Aufnahme von Num 9 jeder genannte Aufbruch Israels als Reaktion auf JHWHs Weisung dargestellt und so die Wüstenwanderung insgesamt als „gelingendes Beziehungsgeschehen" charakterisiert (71). Die Vermeidung von zentralen Stichworten sei sogar Programm, sie wehre der eindeutigen Identifikation eines einzelnen Referenztextes und halte somit eine Vielzahl von Bedeutungsebenen offen. Auf Ex 6f. (und Ex 12,41f.) schließlich führten die Stichwortbezüge über יצא und צבאות. Über die Einspielung dieser Texte werde der in Num 33,1 thematisierte Aufbruch an das Exodusgeschehen zurückgekoppelt und die Wüstenwanderung als „verlängerter Exodus" (96) gedeutet.

Abschnitt III (98–170) ist den intertextuellen Bezügen von Num 33,3–49 gewidmet. Für Num 33,3–4.5 findet Ederer Hypotexte im Exodusbuch, insbesondere in Ex 12,1–13,16, aber auch Ex 14,18 u.a.m. Die Verbindungen ergeben sich auch hier über Stichwortverbindungen (zum Beispiel הכה בכור, ביד רמה u.ä.). Im Unterschied zur Aufnahme von Ex 6f. bzw. Num 9f. in 33,1–2 sieht Ederer in diesem Fall eine andere Art der Bezugnahme. Wurden dort durch den Rekurs auf die Hypotexte erweiterte Sinnpotentiale für Num 33 eingespielt, ziele der intertextuelle Konnex hier auf eine Präzisierung des Prätextes im Blick auf die Zeitangaben und bezüglich der Zeichnung Ägyptens, dessen Niederlage am Schilfmeer bzw. der korrespondierende Erweis der Macht JHWHs hier bereits in die Zeit des Aufbruchs projiziert werde. Im Itinerar selbst hat die Art und Weise, wie die einzelnen Angaben präsentiert werden, für Ederer eine leserlenkende Funktion; dort wo lediglich Ankunft und Aufbruch an einem bestimmten Ort notiert sei, würden denkbare Hypotexte, d.h. andere Itinerarangaben zum selben Ort oder dort lokalisierte Geschehnisse lediglich „versteckt" eingespielt, wäh-

rend Abweichungen vom vorherrschenden Schema „dezidierte Lesehinweise"
darstellten und u.a. erkennbare Neuakzentuierungen der Hypotexte vornähmen
(123). So werde z.B. Num 33,6–8 unter Bezugnahme auf Ex 12–15 als Übergang
von Ägypten zur Wüste, in Num 33,9–37 aber die Wüste selbst als „Lern– und
Praxisraum der Identität und Gottesbeziehung Israels" (139) inszeniert. Num
33,37–41 berichten schließlich von Geschehnissen am Berg Hor und weichen
wiederum stärker vom Grundschema ab. Als aufgerufene Hypotexte benennt
Ederer Num 20,22–29; 21,1–3. Auch hier vermutet er eine Leserlenkung, die auf
eine Akzentverschiebung für die Hypotexte abziele. Im Falle von Num 20 liege sie
in der stärkeren Betonung der Chronologie und der Konzentration auf Aarons
Tod unter Ausblendung der Sukzession. So werde Aarons Tod mit dem des Mose
parallelisiert. Aus Num 21,1–3 betone Num 33 v.a. die kanaanäische Herkunft
des Königs von Arad und sein „Hören" des Kommens Israel. Aus den genannten
Aspekten schließt Ederer, dass mit diesem Abschnitt zum Berg Hor das Ende der
Wüstenzeit und der Beginn der Landnahme markiert werden solle. Ganz entsprechend modifizierten die verbliebenen Itinerarangaben in Num 33,41–48.49 ihre
Hypotexten derart, dass der Weg zwischen Berg Hor und Jordan als Zug durch
ein Gebiet außerhalb des Kulturlands erscheine, gleichsam als „Übergangsraum"
(166) zwischen Wüstenzeit und Landnahme.

Ein eigener Abschnitt (IV, 171–183) thematisiert die Verschriftungsnotiz
in Num 33,2, die für Ederer signifikante Unterschiede zu anderen Verschrif-
tungsnotizen aufweist (nicht auf einen gesetzlichen Stoff bezogen, ohne
Rezeptionsanleitung, ohne klare Identifikation eines Textbestands). Daher werde
Num 33 mittels 33,2 gerade nicht als Text des Mose, sondern als Text eines Erzäh-
lers vorgestellt und darin ein hermeneutisches Modell für die nicht-gesetzlichen
Stoffe der Tora (zumindest für Ex-Num) insgesamt entwickelt: Mose, der nach
33,2a die Stationen von Israels Wüstenwanderung niederschrieb, markiert den
Anfang der Tradition, die in der Rezeption und Applikation von Israels Grün-
dungsgeschichten in der Hand späterer Erzähler nach dem Vorbild und in der
Autorität des Mose münde (182f.).

Die Studie Ederers zeigt eindrücklich, dass auch ein derartig sperriger und
bezüglich des theologischen Gehalts zunächst wenig versprechender Text wie
Num 33 eine gründliche Analyse verdient und bei genauem Blick auf seine
Strukturen und seine literarische Gestaltung weitgreifende Interpretationsspiel-
räume eröffnet. Zu weitgreifend? In der Interpretation von Ederer wird Num 33
geradezu zu einem theologisch-hermeneutischen Schlüsseltext für Exodus und
Wüstenwanderung, mithin einem zentralen Erzählbogen der gesamten Tora.
Diese Sinnpotentiale ergeben sich denn auch nicht aus Num 33 selbst, sondern
erst im Zusammenklang mit den „eingespielten" Texten, wobei im methodischen
Zugang der „Biblischen Auslegung"—unter Ausblendung jeder literargeschicht-
lichen Fragestellung—grundsätzlich das gesamte Alte Testament, wenn nicht der
gesamte Kanon, als Resonanzraum des Einzeltextes in Frage kommt. In dieser
Weite liegt aber zugleich die Gefahr einer Überhöhung des Einzeltextes. Die derartige Sinnpotentiale begründenden intertextuellen Bezüge konstituieren sich

nach dem zugrundegelegten rezeptionsästhetischen Ansatz in der Interaktion zwischen Text und Leser. Hier ist Vieles möglich, die Varianz möglicher Text-Text-Beziehungen (Aufnahme, Anknüpfung, Neuakzentuierung, Korrektur u.v.a.m.) zeigt sich bereits in Ederers Interpretation. Was aber ist vom Text her, im Sinne der *intentio operis*, angezeigt? Für eine derartige Leserlenkung ist die Frage der Markierung intertextueller Bezüge zentral. Reichen Stichwortaufnahmen— zumal bei verbreiteten Lexemen wie חנה, נסע oder יצא—aus? Zielt die Nennung eines Ortsnamens notwendig auf das Einspielen eines oder mehrerer Texte, die diesen Ort nennen oder wird hier u.U. textexternes Wissen abgerufen? Dass derartige Verknüpfungen durch die Rezipienten möglich sind und interpretativ fruchtbar sein können, ist unbestritten, inwiefern aber der Text sie tatsächlich „einfordert" (115 u.ö.) oder gar zu ihnen „zwingt" (Klappentext), wäre methodisch noch genauer zu begründen.

Beigegeben sind Text und Arbeitsübersetzung von Ex 40,34–38; Num 9,15–23 sowie Num 10,11–28.

Reading Deuteronomy: A Literary and Theological Commentary, by Stephen L. Cook. Reading the Old Testament. Macon, GA: Smyth & Helwys, 2015. Pp. xvi + 260. Paper. $17.60. ISBN 9781573127578.

Timothy M. Willis, Pepperdine University

Stephen Cook's commentary on Deuteronomy is the latest installment in a series being produced by Smith & Helwys (Reading the Old Testament). The goal of the series is to provide "a close reading of the final form of the text" without going into verse-by-verse analyses (xiii). Such an attempt to simplify the daunting task of interpretation by focusing on a book's ultimate message (chronologically speaking) is difficult to maintain with a work like Deuteronomy. The reference to "final form" anticipates a synchronic reading, yet Cook feels compelled to interpret the book in light of considerations that are diachronic in nature, and rightly so. Scholars of the Hebrew Bible generally agree that what eventually would become Deuteronomy constituted "the book of the law" retrieved from the Jerusalem temple in the days of King Josiah (2 Kgs 22 // 2 Chr 34). There is significant disagreement, however, about the degree to which the primary shape and message of Deuteronomy was already set when Josiah's people found the book in the temple or whether it received a significant reshaping later in Josiah's reign and/or in a subsequent (post)exilic generation. This is an important issue, because message and immediate audience are closely intertwined. Cook subscribes to the view that one or more Judahite historians took the "Hilkiah edition" of the scroll— "the book of the law," consisting of Deut 6–26, 28—and expanded it with most of chapters 1–4 and chapters 27, 29–34, as they transformed the work into the opening events of a historical narrative running through Joshua, Judges, Samuel, and Kings (6–9). Cook acknowledges other reconstructions of the text's history, yet he focuses primarily on the theological message the book would offer to late preexilic and exilic audiences, without resolving all the interpretive issues related to subsequent historical situations that might have altered the book minimally before it reached its actual "final form." The result is a compelling exposition of several plausible and provocative interpretations of a very important piece of the Hebrew Bible, yet not without unanswered questions and unexplored possibilities for alternative conclusions. I am left intrigued and wanting more, which is a good thing.

The relatively brief introductory chapter (1–23) does an admirable job of balancing the richly nuanced interplay of literary features, sociopolitical influences, and theological message that one must navigate in any interpretation of the book. There are eleven sections; the first section, the last section, and one other lay out the main functions Deuteronomy has performed and continues to perform in the life of Christian and Jewish communities; three scattered sections highlight theological issues, three address literary matters, one compares literary form with theological form, and two in the middle deal with considerations of historical and sociological circumstances. It soon becomes clear, however, that theology is Cook's principle concern. He writes with much greater confidence about the theological message and how it speaks to the changing social and political situations in Judah than he writes about the significance of literary features in conveying that message. A prime example of the latter (which I discuss further below) is his simultaneous presentation of two ways for organizing the structure of the book. He shows a similar ambivalence regarding the importance of attributing certain passages in the book to a late redaction layer (see below on Deut 26:16–19). In a nutshell, the subtitle of the book is only partly accurate, because this is much more a theological commentary than a literary commentary. I find myself agreeing with many of the theological conclusions Cook derives from the book, yet I am uncertain of the validity of some of his supporting arguments because he does not engage in sufficient treatment of literary features to substantiate adequately some of his theological conclusions. Again, I generally like what I see, but I want more.

Since the theological message is his main concern, I will turn first to that aspect of the commentary. Cook presents Deuteronomy as a challenging and corrective voice in the biblical corpus. Its authors and editors write collectively as "the literary and theological figure of Moses," but their words do not represent the words of that historical figure (6). Drawing from existing laws (now in Deut 12–26), the prophetic oracles of Hosea and Micah, the liturgical witness of Asaphite psalms, and familial traditions passed down through village and clan leaders, one or more writers in the first half of the seventh century produce what we might call proto-Deuteronomy. These Deuteronomic traditionists advocate for a broad-based distribution of covenant responsibilities and blessings. The laws of God as they compose them downplay the role of the monarchy and the political and cultic institutions it administers, and they promote a more visible role for local groups and their leaders in fulfilling the covenant, thus making the benefits of a relationship with Yahweh directly available to everyone. Such benefits are not earned; rather, they are natural components of lives lived in communion with Yahweh, in the land he has designated for his people (19–21).

Cook builds from this general framework to show how various laws and teachings consistently convey the details of Deuteronomic theology, even as secondary and tertiary hands expand and reshape the contours of the book. At many points along the way he offers helpful correctives to what he sees as common misrepresentations of the teachings of the book (and the entire Hebrew Bible). For example, he regards the rhetoric about the impending occupation of Canaan as "no land-grab by xenophobic opportunists" but a call to establish a covenant community, a land whose citizens treat everyone—Israelite and alien, male and female alike—as full members of an extended family (30–31, 68–69). The land is a place of rest for all (65), as authority and privilege are distributed throughout the people, empowering those in the periphery along with those in the center (137–45). The direct presence of Yahweh in the land, among the Israelites, furthers this perception. The Deuteronomists speak of this presence as Yahweh's "name," which, Cook argues, does not designate a substituting hypostasis for Yahweh but "the very presence of God's person" (34–35). This special presence accommodates the "exceptional proximity" of Yahweh's entire people—not just the king and his priests—to Yahweh (105–16). Yahweh's "name" is placed over the whole land, and this reflects Yahweh's personal connection to the names by which landholding lineages assert their claims to specific parcels of land (20–21, 67–68). It is on the basis of the direct and personal connections between Yahweh and the people of Israel that obedience to the laws is expected. Readers also misunderstand the writers' intent if they regard Deuteronomy's laws as substantiating a simplistic quid pro quo retribution system (19–20, 35–36). This misperception ascribes to the book "a rigid system of rewards for righteousness and punishments for sin" (91). The viewpoint reflected in the book is more complex than that. The laws reflect the will and the ways—the righteousness—of Yahweh, with whom the people commune in the land in a special relationship. Disobedience is a dishonoring of Yahweh's very person. Obedience entails hearing and serving Yahweh, and these should flow naturally from those who love the God with whom they commune in a "reciprocal commitment" on a daily basis (73–79, 193–94). Considerations by Cook of selected details bear out this general picture.

I find much to commend Cook's characterizations of the teachings of Deuteronomy. His perspective on the "Deuteronomic retribution theology," just summarized, is a good example to consider. Cook points to Deut 8 as Exhibit A of his nuanced understanding of divine retribution, one that is truly relational in nature and played out on a multigenerational, community-wide level. The portrayal of Yahweh's character in the so-called Deuteronomistic History (Joshua–Kings) supports the understanding of retribution that Cook perceives in Deuteronomy. Yahweh does not reward or punish in a strict and mechanical sense on the basis of someone's most recent actions. He often shows undeserved mercy to kings and their subjects "for the sake of David." He ordains punishment for sinful behavior, but the punishment is often delayed or modified in light of repentant human responses.[1]

I find similar appreciation for Cook's perspective on the divine "name theology" in Deuteronomy. The notion that Yahweh's name exists in the Jerusalem temple in place of Yahweh does not comport fully with what we find in texts such as 2 Sam 6–7 and 1 Kgs 8. The purpose of the temple is not to provide a place for a substitute for Yahweh but to represent the permanence and surety of Yahweh's special dwelling among his people. At the same time, the Deuteronomists do not wish to convey the notion that Yahweh's people—even his appointed king and priests—have control over his presence among them (the story of Uzzah in 2 Sam 6 is a good example here), so Cook is correct when he speaks of an inherent tension between the *presence* and *absence* of Yahweh expressed in his "name." Solomon's prayer in 1 Kgs 8 assumes this tension. Yahweh hears prayers "in heaven," yet this is not to imply that he is not on earth, because even heaven cannot contain him (1 Kgs 8:27).

Unfortunately, the skill and understanding that Cook exhibits regarding the theological message of Deuteronomy is not always matched in his treatment of supporting evidence from literary features in the text. One can see this at the macro-level in his discussion of the overall organization of the book and at the micro-level as he argues points from specific passages. The former is most obvious in his introductory discussion of the organization of Deuteronomy. He gives not one but "two literary organizations of the book [that] overlap and do not fully cohere with one another" (17). One organizational point of view regards Deut 12–26 as the main body, with chapters 1–3 + 31–34 and chapters 4–11 + 27–30 providing corresponding layers of a bipartite prologue and epilogue frame around the laws. An inherent weakness in this organization is that it denies any structural significance in the book to the speeches of Moses, which seem to be one of its key literary features. The disconnect between form and content is so jarring, I wondered at times why Cook even included this organization in his discussion. It is more a distraction than a help. The second organizational point of view (which Cook clearly follows in the commentary) derives primarily from the speeches of Moses, and so it is much more defensible on literary grounds. At the same time, it exposes problems when we consider how Cook relates his reconstruction of the book's redaction history to his treatment of the theological message. For example, a key component of Deuteronomic theology from the beginning is the relational aspect of the covenant (see above), yet some of the most crucial passages for conveying this component are not introduced until after the discovery of the book of

---

1. One could actually make a stronger case for "Deuteronomic" retribution theology in Chronicles, where divine responses seem more direct, immediate, and explicitly proportionate. This, in turn, prompts questions for interpreters about shifts in biblical teachings and whether they might be related to shifts in the social environment of the earliest readers (in this case, from a preexilic Deuteronomy to a postexilic Chronicles).

the law during Josiah's reign. His treatment of Deut 26:16–19 gives clear evidence of this unevenness (193–94). He identifies this passage as the "concluding book-end to the entire torah," which forms a frame with Deut 12:1. Within 26:16–19 he finds some of the clearest statements of mutuality, "reciprocal commitment," "the bilateral nature" of the covenant, and so forth. But Cook places this passage among those added by redactors subsequent to the scroll's discovery by Hilkiah and his associates (14). This makes it unlikely that Josiah and his court—and any prior readers—would have heard the message of the book in the way that Cook presents it. They would not have heard this passage as the concluding bookend of the torah, and they would not have been impressed by its emphasis on personal commitment to the covenant with Yahweh. What is more, if Josianic redactors are creating a new literary frame for the central law code, it is possible they were also rearranging and revising the laws within the code. It is even possible that they are responsible for shaping the central code so that it mirrors the Decalogue. This is not to deny that Deuteronomy promotes the understanding of covenant that Cook describes for it, but it does expose uncertainties about when it received its current shape and why the book of the law had the impact on Josiah that Cook attributes to it, if some of the book's central theological features were not present at the time it was discovered. This requires further explanation.

Cook should similarly be commended for the theological significance he accords to the idea of "today" (or "this day") as one encounters it in the book. He rightly observes that Deuteronomy is "pulsing with immediacy" (1), and the repeated use of "today" creates an unrelenting demand for individual and community accountability before God (19–20). One is left wondering, however, how Cook understands "today" in the light of the book's literary development. He speaks at one point of "Deuteronomy's first readers" (2), by which he means Israelites who lived during the days of Assyrian hegemony prior to the reign of Josiah. But we have to ask whether we can really speak of Deuteronomy the book at that time, because as Cook reconstructs the book's history this is before the Josianic redaction. Of particular significance is the importance placed on "today" in Deut 4, a chapter that Cook assigns to multiple redactional layers without explaining how the meaning of "today" might have changed as the historical context changed from redaction to redaction. Was the theme of "today" introduced to the text as part of a call to undivided devotion to Yahweh in the face of Assyrian polytheism, to affirm the reforms of Josiah, as a response to destruction and exile, or all of the above? Further explanation would be appreciated.

Finally, one important example of weakness in Cook's literary analysis at the micro-level will have to suffice. In his comments on the Shema in Deut 6:4 and its surrounding context (73–75), he argues that the descriptor "one" in relation to Yahweh is the key term in the passage, communicating the holism of Israel's God in contrast to the multiplicity of non-Israelite gods. Yahweh's name is *one*, his people worship him at *one* shrine, the shrine is located in the *one* land, and he has willed the land to his *one* people. This seems like a valid point, but some of Cook's supporting arguments from literary features are suspect. He asserts that, in the theology of Deuteronomy, the people "find their own community reintegrated" into a unified group (*one*) through their relationship with Yahweh and as a mirror image of the oneness of their God. What is more, he says that the text conveys the oneness of the people by referring to all the hearers collectively with the singular "you." This can be said of the Shema proper, but one of the well-known literary features of the book of Deuteronomy is the unpredictable alternation between singular and plural forms in reference to the assumed Israelite audience. Just within Deut 6 there are four sentences that shift from singular forms to plural forms (vv. 1, 14, 16–17a, 20). One can see the weakness in the argument more clearly in Deut 12. Cook cites this chapter as the hallmark example of the oneness of the shrine, which in turn implies the oneness of Yahweh and facilitates in the reintegration of the people into one in their relationship with him. But if the oneness of the people is supposed to be communicated with singular pronouns, Deut 12 fails miserably, because the text refers to the people with plural forms in more than half the clauses of Deut 12:1–12. If Cook were to be consistent, he would have to conclude that these clauses convey the idea that the people who worship around the central shrine are not unified. This runs directly contrary to his understanding of the chapter's message. So, while I want to agree with the theological ideas Cook draws out here, I do not always find him supporting them well in his literary analysis of the texts.

Despite these criticisms, I believe that this work deserves to be in the library of everyone who sets out to teach or preach from Deuteronomy. It must be read in dialogue with other studies that provide more critical and detailed treatments of individual passages. But the theological perspective reflected in Cook's commentary is a healthy one, and, in my estimation, it is a perspective that more accurately represents the main teachings of Deuteronomy than many commentaries that have preceded it.

The Book of Exodus: Composition, Reception, and Interpretation, edited by Thomas B. Dozeman, Craig A. Evans, and Joel N. Lohr. Supplements to Vetus Testamentum 164. Leiden: Brill, 2014. Pp. xx + 669. Cloth. €204.00. ISBN 9789004282650.

Jeffrey L. Morrow, Seton Hall University

The editors of *The Book of Exodus* are to be commended in having brought to fruition such a diverse grouping of essays on such a vast array of topics and themes, all dealing with the book of Exodus, its origin, its historical milieu, the narrative context of its many themes, its reception in ancient Jewish and Christian interpretive traditions, as well as contemporary theological approaches to the book. In what follows, I briefly go through the various essays contained in the volume, including more comments where I have some critique or some special praise.

The book is divided neatly into four parts: (1) "General Topics" (1–87); (2) "Issues in Interpretation" (89–301); (3) "Textual Transmission and Reception

History" (303–562); and (4) "Exodus and Theology" (563–609). In the first part, the volume begins with William Johnstone's "Reading Exodus in Tetrateuch and Pentateuch" (3–26), which argues that "the reminiscences in Deuteronomy enable the recovery of a matching account of events in Exodus and Numbers that a later edition has overlaid" (3). Johnstone uses the Decalogue and the wilderness journey as case studies. Konrad Schmid, in the second essay, "Exodus in the Pentateuch" (27–60), seeks to reopen the discussion of the place of the book of Exodus within the Pentateuch. He notes some problems with the traditional Documentary Hypothesis, especially as it has been applied to Exodus, and especially regarding the J and E sources. Schmid argues further that, despite their composite nature, Genesis through 2 Kings represents a "continuous narrative."

The third essay, Lester L. Grabbe's "Exodus and History" (61–87), is the only one in the first part that includes the views of evangelical scholars such as James Hoffmeier, Kenneth Kitchen, John Bimson, and Bryant Wood. Grabbe's essay is an attempt to render a late dating of the book of Exodus possible by situating its knowledge of Egypt and related details from the seventh to fifth centuries BCE. Many of the points he brings up, however, have been dealt with by the very scholars he mentions, and he often does not take their responses into consideration. For example, he mentions the fact that in Exodus the pharaoh is not named, which was standard practice in the second millennium.[1] He notes that "the duties given to the Israelites, such as making bricks, do not match the types of work in which Asiatics were normally employed" (64), yet we have visual depictions of just such Semitic Asiatics involved in various forms of labor, including precisely that of making bricks.[2] Moreover, despite the debates concerning identification of sites and the fragmentary nature of the archaeological record, Grabbe reverts, at points, to using the absence of archaeological evidence as if it were positive evidence of absence, as when he states, "No event of the size and extent of the exodus could have failed to leave significant archaeological remains.... Yet we find nothing" (79). In the end, Grabbe, who concedes some possible retention of early material in the exodus narratives, asserts that the exodus narrative as we have it is "clearly based on and inspired by much later events," prime among them the return of exiles in the sixth and fifth centuries, in particular the Assyrian exile (83). He observes that "references to Egypt often function as a metaphor for Assyria, and Assyrian deportation ends with a return just like the exodus from Egypt" (83), but then does not recognize that such a "metaphor" would only work if there was a prior pattern in place on which to base it.

---

1. As pointed out, e.g., in James K. Hoffmeier, *Israel in Egypt: The Evidence for the Authenticity of the Exodus Tradition* (Oxford: Oxford University Press, 1996), 87–88 and 111–112, a book Grabbe cites (70 nn. 32 and 34, 71 n. 40, 73 n. 51, 74 n. 58, and 76 n. 69).

2. See, e.g., figures 8–9 in Hoffmeier, *Israel in Egypt*, in between pages 76–77. Figure 8 includes Semites, whereas in figure 9 it is not clear that the POWs are Semites.

Jan Christian Gertz's essay begins the book's second part. In "The Miracle at the Sea: Remarks on the Recent Discussion about Origin and Composition of the Exodus Narrative" (91–120), Gertz takes the example of the miracle of the parting of the sea in order to reexamine the question of literary sources underlying the text. Gertz's starting point is the discussion of the resurgence of Wellhausen-style New "Documentarians," scholars such as Joel Baden, who resist modification of the basic classical Documentary Hypothesis with its four component sources. Gertz's study underscores the near impossibility of reconstructing this section of Exodus with the classic four-source (here, three) approach. In the end, Gertz's investigation indicates that there are only two major sources at work in this narrative: a Priestly source and a non-Priestly source.

Next comes Thomas Römer's "From the Call of Moses to the Parting of the Sea: Reflections on the Priestly Version of the Exodus Narrative" (121–50). As with Gertz's earlier essay, Römer begins with the many challenges that have assailed the classic expression of the Documentary Hypothesis. Reflecting the shift in German biblical scholarship, which has not yet replaced the prominence of the Documentary Hypothesis in the world of English-speaking scholarship, back toward an earlier fragmentary hypothesis, Römer's piece seeks to elucidate some commonalities between these reigning approaches. The main point of intersection is the near universal acceptance of the role of a Priestly source.

In "Wilderness Material in Exodus (Exodus 15–18)" (151–68), Rainer Albertz examines the wilderness portion of Exodus in light of its hypothetical compositional history, interpreting that history as expressing Israel's maturation process. Next we turn to Wolfgang Oswald, "Lawgiving at the Mountain of God (Exodus 19–24)" (169–92), who examines the Sinai narratives in Exodus, emphasizing how the notion of law is inextricably bound to the narrative. He argues that portions of the text are Deuteronomistic and are thus linked with Deuteronomistic goals. In "Decalogue" (193–219), Christoph Dohmen walks through the various commandments of the Decalogue, including comparison with the versions in Deuteronomy, and discusses their reception in light of the broader pentateuchal context.

David P. Wright's "The Origin, Development, and Context of the Covenant Code (Exodus 20:23–23:19)" (220–44) is a very interesting essay that takes a look at the Covenant Code in Exod 20–23. He examines the texts in light of the two major hypotheses of composition, that of "gradual redactional growth" and the less common approach of viewing this as originating "as a relatively unified composition" (220). Wright makes special comparison with the Laws of Hammurabi, which lends strength to the unified compositional theory. In the end, Wright argues that the unified compositional theory has more strengths than the redactional growth theory. This is especially the case with the increasing evidence of "close and intricate correlations" (242) with second millennium legal corpora such as the Laws of Hammurabi, but also with a Middle Bronze legal corpus discovered at Hazor.

The penultimate essay of this portion of the volume is Suzanne Boorer's "The Promise of the Land as Oath in Exodus 32:1–33:3" (245–66), in which she examines Exod 32 and the land oath in light of its proximate context, as well as in relation to Deuteronomy. She argues, among other things, that it helped provide hope to the people in God's promise, despite their failures, as in the golden calf episode. The final essay in this section is "Tabernacle" (267–301), in which Helmut Utzschneider examines the tabernacle texts in Exodus. One interesting observation is how "the vestments of Aaron and the high priests are closely, indeed exactly, coordinated with the spatial concept of the tabernacle" (288–89). A number of biblical parallels are made with the tabernacle plans and construction, including with creation in Gen 1, but also with Solomon's construction of the temple in Jerusalem. Utzschneider provides a wonderful discussion of the Exodus tabernacle texts, as well as a useful summary of three different ways scholars understand its "priestly" origin.

The volume's third part begins with Sidnie White Crawford's "Exodus in the Dead Sea Scrolls" (305–21). In discussing the importance of the book of Exodus for the Dead Sea Scrolls, Crawford points out that eighteen Exodus manuscripts were discovered at Qumran (as well as another manuscript from Wadi Murabba'at). Two of the manuscripts follow the textual tradition represented by the Samaritan Pentateuch (with the exception of the command concerning Mount Gerizim's altar construction). A number of other texts from Qumran make some use of content from the exodus tradition. In the end, Crawford concludes that Exodus plays an important role in the Dead Sea Scrolls, including its serving "as a key exegetical text in the documents of the Qumran collection" (320).

Next comes Leonard J. Greenspoon, "Textual and Translation Issues in Greek Exodus" (322–48), where in brilliant fashion he examines the Septuagint edition of Exodus, particularly focusing on the Decalogue. He raises ten intriguing questions, then speculates, eruditely, as to what might be answers to those questions. Jerome A. Lund's "Exodus in Syriac" (349–69) examines the three different but related Syriac translations of Exodus: that of the Peshitta, Paul of Tella's Syrohexapla, and Jacob of Edessa's translation. Lund's essay is a fascinating comparison of these textual traditions; importantly, among other things, it shows evidence of Palestinian Jewish translation influences, particularly for the Peshitta.

In "The *Vetus Latina* and the Vulgate of the Book of Exodus" (370–86), David L. Everson compares the Latin translations of Exodus in the Vetus Latina with that of Jerome's Vulgate. One conclusion is that the Vetus Latina more often favors the Septuagint, whereas Jerome follows the tradition represented by the Masoretic Text more closely. Bruce Chilton's "The Exodus Theology of the Palestinian Targumim" (387–403) comes next, in which he shows how the Aramaic targumic tradition dealt with the book of Exodus and in particular the Passover. He observes this in regard to the Jewish tradition of the four nights of redemption as found in the targumim: "it opens up the commemoration of Passover as the central liturgical celebration not only of Israel's departure from Egypt, but of creation, the covenant with Abraham, and the coming of the Messiah. The theology of Exod 12:42 flowers into a comprehensive account of the divine economy" (387). This is especially interesting in light of the use of the poem of the four nights in Targum Neofiti.

The next essay is Gregory E. Sterling's "The People of the Covenant or the People of God: Exodus in Philo of Alexandria" (404–39), in which he looks at Philo's use of Exodus. The only biblical book Philo relies upon more than Exodus is Genesis, which plays a far more significant role in his thought. Philo retold the exodus story in his *On the Life of Moses*. Sterling concludes with an appendix of citations and allusions to the book of Exodus in Philo's *Allegorical Commentary* and also his *Exposition of the Law* (426–36). We next turn to Craig A. Evans, "Exodus in the New Testament: Patterns of Revelation and Redemption" (440–64), which explores the vast topic of the role of Exodus in the New Testament. After reviewing just some of the many allusions and quotations from Exodus in the New Testament, Evans explains the overall significance. Specifically, he observes how Exodus "established patterns and typologies by which Jesus and his teaching successors understood what has taken place in their time and are able to articulate a theology and an ethic that will guide the Church in the centuries to come" (460).

Paul Spilsbury's "Exodus in Josephus" (465–84) takes a look at the use of Exodus and its importance in Josephus. Especially prominent here is the figure of Moses. This study makes clear Josephus's familiarity with the book of Exodus, despite our inability to determine precisely which translation and textual version he used, as well as with modes of Jewish traditions of interpretation. After Spilsbury's essay comes Lutz Doering's "The Reception of the Book of Exodus in the *Book of Jubilees*" (485–510), which looks at the role of Exodus in Jubilees. Especially significant here is Doering's emphasis on the ways in which the book of Exodus aided in Jubilee's reception of the book of Genesis and in particular creation.

Joel C. Elowsky's "Exodus in the Fathers" (511–34), is a fine essay on the role of Exodus in the early Christian exegetical tradition. Rather than walk through key church fathers, Elowsky takes several themes from Exodus and examines some of the ways several fathers understood these themes, always in light of Christ. Most importantly, and regrettably missing in so much scholarship, Elowsky underscores the mystagogical nature of much of early Christian interpretation and the liturgical context to such exegesis. As he states at the outset, "When trying to understand the profound effect Exodus had on the Fathers, one need look no further than the church's liturgy, its preaching and its teaching" (511). Further, "The events of the Passover and Exodus, more than any other event in the Hebrew scripture, formed the church's life and liturgy, shaped by the Fathers [*sic*] typological and allegorical exegesis" (512). Elowsky clearly understands the "spirit of early Christian thought" (the title of Robert Wilken's 2003 Yale University Press book) and studies early Christian use of Exodus within that context.

Elowsky's essay is followed nicely by "Exodus in Rabbinic Interpretation" (535–62), in which Burton L. Visotzky explores Exodus among the rabbis in their first thousand years (roughly second to thirteenth centuries CE). Visotzky examines the beginning chapter of Exodus in the thought of some of these rabbinic sages, followed by rabbinic traditions concerning Exod 2–11, and by a number of texts concerning the exodus event itself in rabbinic thought. His essay helps show the great diversity of rabbinic thinking and yet at the same time the centrality of Exodus to that thought.

The fourth and final part of the book begins with Walter Brueggemann's "The God Who Gives Rest" (565–90). Brueggemann seeks to show "how God is rendered in the book" of Exodus (566), and he does so with his characteristic eloquence. His main argument, beautifully illustrated throughout this chapter, is that "the God given us in the Book of Exodus is the God who gives rest, who authorizes, permits, and insists upon Sabbath and who wills emancipation from social arrangements that refuse Sabbath" (566). The volume concludes with Terence E. Fretheim, "Issues of Agency in Exodus" (591–609). Fretheim demonstrates the many ways God works through the mediation of various agents. This is a lesson he culls from Exodus, but is able to apply more broadly to how God operates throughout history.

This volume makes an important contribution to the field, especially to the important discussion between scholars of various hermeneutical approaches. There were some omissions but only one worth mentioning. In light of the discussions regarding P, Ezekiel's knowledge of these and related traditions (especially Ezek 20), the failure to mention the arguments in Scott Hahn and John Bergsma's 2004 article on Ezek 20 and its relationship to the P, H, and D traditions is unfortunate.[3] My critical comments notwithstanding, this volume belongs on the shelf of every college, seminary, and university library and will be of interest to any scholar interested in the book of Exodus, Hebrew Bible/Old Testament textual traditions and translations, as well as early Jewish and Christian traditions of interpretation. It is to be hoped that many more such volumes are produced, representing such broad scholarly collaboration on related texts from such diverse methodological backgrounds.

See Me! Hear Me! Divine/Human Relational Dialogue in Genesis, by Elizabeth B. Tracy. Contributions to Biblical Exegesis and Theology 75. Leuven: Peeters, 2015. Pp. x + 169. Paper. €46.00. ISBN 9789042930483.

Karolien Vermeulen, University of Antwerp

Elizabeth Tracy's book is a concise study of the dialogue between humans and the Deity in Genesis. In search for a model of the human-divine relationship within these texts, she analyzes the relevant dialogues in the book of Genesis. Her analysis sheds a new light on these dialogues and shows how the investigation of textual structures, such as adjacency pairs and turn taking in the particular case of dialogue, is a way to elucidate relationships that are shaped by these structures.

---

3. Scott Walker Hahn and John Sietze Bergsma, "What Laws Were 'Not Good'? A Canonical Approach to the Theological Problem of Ezekiel 20:25–26," *JBL* 123 (2004): 201–18.

Tracy opens her book with a short motivation for the selected topic and corpus, followed by a clearly stated threefold aim: to identify latent elements in human-divine dialogues; to present a "potential formula" for these dialogues; and to understand the relationship between human and divine better through the joint results of the first two aims (1–5). The introduction then gives an overview of form-critical and narrative-critical approaches in biblical studies (5–18). It is not always clear why Tracy gives more attention to certain scholars than to others in this section. She could have elaborated more on the contribution of the selected works with regard to the central question steering the book. She leaves it to the reader to fill in why the majority of Israeli scholarship, predating the 1990s, is left out of the overview. After an explanation of key terms, Tracy discusses her selection of passages. She uses clearly delineated parameters that lead to a comprehensive set of examples (19–34), but, given the results of her study, she would do well to return to the excluded examples after all, in a separate article. Can a dialogue between a human being and God about another human being (as in Gen 18) not reveal something about the divine-human relationship? Further, why should the inclusion of a personal name be a *conditio sine qua non*? Does God only know and care about human beings he mentions by name?

Chapter 2 analyzes what Tracy calls "the circumstances of dialogue" (35–89). Each dialogue is treated in the same structured way, discussing both the broader and more immediate narrative setting, the parameters for the dialogue, a translation, and the structure of the conversation in table form. This chapter is largely based on previous research and a stepping stone to the next chapter, where the dialogues are discussed. Whereas the separation of this section from the actual discussion may seem somewhat artificial at first, it accommodates the reader, especially in the third chapter, to draw parallels between the insights gained from the different dialogues. Tracy does not include the original Hebrew text. Instead, she offers readers an annotated translation, concisely touching upon some grammatical or semantic issues that do not fit in the later discussion but may nevertheless influence the interpretation of the dialogue. Whereas the reader versed in Biblical Hebrew may miss the original text, the translation can reach a wider audience. The annotation bridges the gap between both audiences.

Chapter 3 is not only presented as "the essence of dialogue"; it also is the essence of the study (91–160). Here Tracy presents the textual analysis for which she prepared in the previous chapter. In the same structured and clear way as before, she guides the reader through the initiation of the dialogues, the role of the personal names in them, and the actual dialogue in terms of adjacency pairs and turn taking. Although she warns that she will "dislodge" the dialogue from the overall narrative (112), Tracy stays true to that narrative. The analysis is in sync with the broader narrative, which is sometimes briefly mentioned. The chapter becomes particularly interesting in the concluding paragraphs of the analysis of each of the dialogues. In these paragraphs Tracy summarizes insightfully and engagingly what the structure of each dialogue reveals. In a concluding point (160), she lays out two tendencies that are present in all human-divine conversations in Genesis. On the one hand, the dialogues present a God who truly knowns the human being with whom he is talking. In the conversation this human being is the primary focus of God's attention. As Tracy states, "for the length of the conversation there is no other Divine/human personal relationship as important as that of the named individual" (160). On the other hand, the human perspective on the events is foregrounded in the dialogues, no matter how limited or shortsighted this viewpoint is. God's response is both kind and encouraging: "The Divine does not belittle these relatively trivial concerns. Instead, the Deity, explicitly addressed almost every trepidation with a wider possibility—a future or perspective the human did not have the capacity to perceive" (160).

These two main findings are reformulated and supplemented with more specific findings for each of the dialogues in chapter 4, the conclusion of the book (161–62). This chapter leads the reader once more through the whole study, starting from its question over the analysis to its possible answer.

Whereas the importance of the book's contribution to scholarship is beyond doubt, it suffers from some minor flaws, the main one being the near absence of the author's voice or viewpoint. Apart from the short summary paragraphs in the discussion of the dialogues and the conclusion (both appearing near the end of the book), it is hard to hear Tracy's voice amidst the concatenation of names and quotes. The usual suspects of form and narrative criticism fill a substantial amount of the pages, not only with their ideas, but also with their literal words. Moreover, the extensive citation is not limited to the body of the text but recurs in the footnotes as well. Tracy has an interesting point to make, and it is a shame that she did not foreground her insights more openly. The quotative style also interrupts the flow of the text. Tracy must tweak sentences, adding conjunctions between brackets or changing verbs in order to fit them into the phrase she started in her own voice. In addition, she has marked each of these changes with the expression "added by ET." It must be my lively imagination, but I could not but wonder what ET (far from home) had to do with these quotes by biblical scholars. The author (with a film and television production background, 1) should have considered the unfortunate resemblance of her initials with a movie character before deviating from the standard way of indicating changes in quotations.

This said, these points of critique should not overshadow the value of the work. Elizabeth Tracy has written a well-argued and accessible book that offers new insights into divine-human dialogue and divine-human relationships in the book of Genesis. Her findings are the result of a careful blend of literary methods and theological concerns. They prompt the reader to ask further questions that arise from the answers already given (as noted in the discussion of ch. 1). As such, the study itself is an open-ended dialogue with existing research and research still to be done.

Exodus 1–15, by Helmut Utzschneider and Wolfgang Oswald. Internationaler Exegetischer Kommentar zum Alten Testament. Stuttgart: Kohlhammer, 2013. Pp. 372. Cloth. € 69.90. ISBN 9783170222229.

Danny Mathews, Pepperdine University

This study of Exod 1–15 is one of the first contributions to a pioneering new commentary series that seeks to overcome the fragmentation and hyper-specialization that characterize much of biblical scholarship by offering a collaborative and interdisciplinary study aimed at a broad and ecumenical readership including scholars, pastors, and interested nonspecialists. What is innovative for this series is an intentional collaboration from a synchronic and diachronic perspective. While these two approaches have tended to represent polarized options in past scholarship, this work showcases in a neutral and candid way the strengths and limitations of each approach as well as noting how attending to different frames of reference of interpretation can enhance one's overall view and appreciation of the rich complexity of Exodus. As such, this volume not only represents an outstanding introduction into the current state of Exodus scholarship but also provides a solid engagement with the benefits and pitfalls of the two major ways of reading and evaluating biblical texts in modern scholarship.

For each section of Exodus, the commentary follows a basic format of presenting a translation with brief notes followed by separate sections treating the text from a synchronic and a diachronic approach, then concluding with a synthesis that evaluates the different results yielded by these two approaches. At the same time, the commentary is clearly tilted a bit more to the synchronic dimension—this is the first approach to the text, both in the introduction as well as in the exposition of each delineated unit in Exodus. In contrast, a number of textual units in the commentary lack sections on the diachronic analysis and synthesis. This is not necessarily a glaring weakness, since a synchronic approach is probably more of a user-friendly entrance into the interpretative issues of a text for lay readers. Still, one is left wanting just a bit more on the diachronic and synthetic dimensions, especially in terms of relating these two approaches with each other.

The commentary is organized around a synchronic understanding of the text as a "novel of action" that is structured into six narrative phases (30–32). Each narrative phase comprises a number of episodes, each of which in turn is made up of a series of scenes organized by an "action-oriented" plot. While the bulk of Exod 1–15 is action-oriented, involving rapid narrative movement, several lengthy dialogues have been included that slow down the narrative time and function as major turning points in the narrative (Exod 3:7–4:17; 6:2–8; 11:4–8; 12:1–13:16). This action novel functions politically to provide hope in situations of oppression by making the theological claim that all political events are subject to Yahweh's will. Interestingly, from a synchronic perspective the commentary notes two discrete conclusions to the narrative begun in Exod 1. The first conclusion is the etiology of the Passover-Matzot Festival in Exod

12:1–13:16 that narrates the transformation of Israel from forced "service" to Egypt to celebrating the "service" of the Passover-Matzot Festival. The second ending is the deliverance at the sea and two hymns in Exod 13:17–15:21 that serves to refocus the account as a "*Tehillah* narrative" that is understood, based on Ps 78:3–4, as a narrative praising the glorious acts of Yahweh. Both endings serve to immortalize the events of the exodus in cultic and hymnic contexts. This raises the question of the precise subject of inquiry from a synchronic approach. The series editors define the synchronic approach as a study of a discrete textual layer ("*auf einer bestimmten Stufe* seiner Entstehung" [13, emphasis original]). It would seem, then, that the synchronic approach as employed in this study is not simply to be equated with an analysis of the final redacted or canonical form of a text but can also involve a study of hypothetically reconstructed versions underlying the canonical text, such as examining one or both endings of the exodus narrative. As such, the synchronic and diachronic dimensions would essentially be two intertwined approaches that should not be completely unraveled.

The diachronic aspect of this commentary seeks to provide a historical and social context for the various stages of textual development inferred by difficulties and tensions in the text. This study continues the trend in recent Exodus commentaries by assuming a post–documentary hypothesis context (e.g., Dozeman, Albertz, Johnstone) and adopts a "compositional" model by viewing Exodus as a combination of independent narratives. The study identifies five discrete compositions. (1) An older exodus narrative (*Die ältere Exoduserzählung*) is embedded in most of the major texts beginning with the notice of oppression and multiplication in Exod 1:11–12 and concluding with Egypt's downfall in Exod 14. These texts reflect a context of vassalage—deportations of part of the population in conjunction with forced labor and tribute—experienced by the Judean state under Assyrian, Egyptian, and Babylon hegemony during the seventh-sixth centuries BCE. The older exodus narrative directly confronts this ongoing situation by advocating the legitimacy of rebellion under the initiative and guidance of Yahweh as the Lord even over the powerful overlord of the day. (2) The exodus–mountain of God narrative (*Die Exodus-Gottesberg-Erzählung*) includes sections of Exod 3–4, 15, 16, and 18–24. As a nameless mountain without a specific geographical location ("Horeb" and "Sinai" were added later by D and P), the "mountain of God" functions as a symbol of God's real mountain at Zion that has now become a "heap of ruins." (Hence, the Hebrew underlying the standard translation "to Horeb" in 3:1 is translated instead as "in the wasteland" [*in die Ödnis*]). The exodus–mountain of God narrative represents a new polity of Israel that enacts a new justice and legal system that is adopted by the consensus of the post-587 community, which is no longer a nation-state under a king with a temple. (3) The Deuteronomistic History includes all the well-known sections marked by Deuteronomic style. The authors, however, fail to describe the precise meaning of this term. Although the book of Deuteronomy is the main source of comparison with the Exodus counterparts, the consistent use of the abbreviation

DtrG gives the impression that these sections were the work of the same tradents involved in the Deuteronomistic redactions of the books of Joshua to Kings. It is unclear how this composition in Exodus is related precisely with Deuteronomy and the Deuteronomistic History. In Exod 1–15, this composition links the narrative beyond Exodus to Joshua in texts dealing with the gift of the land and regulations for festivals to be observed in the land (e.g., Exod 3:8–9; 12:21–27; 13:3–16). In a preview of the next volume, the introduction to the study argues that the Deuteronomistic History composition invalidated the Exodus–Mountain of God constitution in Exod *19–24 by inserting a frame in 19:3b–8 and 24:4–8 and including new prohibitions of images that serves to recontextualize the polity as a vassal treaty with a new contract of obligations in Exod 34:11–26 probably in the mid-fifth century. (4) With regard to the Priestly composition, the commentary adopts the approach of Blum in viewing these texts neither as a source or redaction but rather as a "composition." This work reflects Aaronide ideology and extends the originally independent narrative backward to Genesis and forward up to Joshua. Exodus is now framed with explicit references to Genesis within a context of creation theology (Exod 1:7 // Gen 1:28 and 17:2; Exod 24:16; 40:17 // Gen 1:1–2:3). The Priestly composition was produced in stages in dialogue with Deuteronomistic texts from the mid-fifth century and probably composed before P texts in Joshua in the middle of the fourth century. (5) Finally, the latest collection of texts that is typically classified as "post-Priestly" is more precisely described in this study as the torah composition. These are a collection of texts that are very late. They assume a discrete Pentateuch created by the separation of Deuteronomy from Joshua and emphasizes the uniqueness of Moses and the torah (e.g., 4:10–17; 14:31; 15:25b–26; 19:9 as well as references to the staff of Moses throughout the plague account and crossing of the sea). Earlier inappropriate views of Moses are corrected (such as Exod 17:1–7 in reaction to Num 20:1–13). This composition is situated in a cosmopolitan context where the people of Israel are on friendly terms with foreigners, such as the Egyptian midwives, the daughter of Pharaoh, and the Midianites (Exod 1:15–22; 2:4, 7–10*; 4:20–21, 24–31).

Each diachronic section in the commentary begins with a chart that classifies each section of the text with one of these five compositions. Working carefully with each textual segment will give a solid inductive exposure to actual practice and results of working from a diachronic perspective.

The commentary rejects the view of Van Seters by arguing that the text is not the work of a conscious historian with a clear understanding of a temporal distance between the past and present. Rather than a critical reconstruction of a past era, the narratives in Exodus instead actualize elements of tradition to address current needs, much like a sermon. The diachronic approach, then, is useful in showing the various ways how past traditions are actualized to address new situations. In addition to the exodus–mountain of God narrative that addresses the destruction of the Jerusalem temple, another example is the exodus tradition itself. The authors locate the earliest context for the exodus broadly to the Nineteenth or Twentieth Dynasty in Egypt, when the campaigns of Merenptah or, later, the civil war during the change in dynasties probably resulted in prisoners of war being taken to Egypt who later escaped. But these traditions were actualized by the older exodus narrative much later in the context of Judean vassalage to Egypt during the Saite period in the late seventh century.

These precise political concerns emerge when considering the texts in their initial stage of composition. A synchronic approach would then attend to how the combination and reconfiguration of these discrete compositions in the current biblical text present these issues in a more general manner that preserves the potential for ongoing actualization. The authors provide a nice modern example of how Martin Luther King Jr. actualized the basic principle of opposition of political abuse of power by using elements of the sea-miracle narrative in Exod 14 to critique British colonialism and racial segregation in America.

The commentary does have several shortcomings. One is the inconsistent use of the diachronic and synthetic sections as noted earlier. Second, although the commentary engages with just about all of the most important and recent scholarly work on Exodus, the omission of any critical engagement with the work of William Johnstone and his reconstruction of Exodus into a D-edition and a P-work is disappointing, especially since his work is based on a careful critical comparison of Exodus with Deuteronomy and could have contributed especially to the study of Exod 12:1–13:16 and 4:18–26. Also, the Exodus commentary by Terence Fretheim gives major attention to creation theology and divine pathos and could have been used in the discussion of these topics. Finally, the emphasis on plot and action seems to have resulted in less attention to a systematic examination to the role of character in Exodus. At various points in the commentary, helpful observations are made on the portrayal of various characters, especially Moses, Aaron, and even God, but it would have been helpful to include an initial systematic sketch of the major characters, especially of Moses.

These, however, are minor issues that pale in light of the quality of the study. Although a coauthored volume, the commentary is consistent in style that is quite readable. The discussion of each text is user-friendly by presenting a selection of topics for discussion in a concise but substantive manner that avoids overwhelming the reader. Especially helpful is an indication of the topic of discussion in the margins, which allows one to use the book like an encyclopedia by quickly locating a discussion of a topic such as circumcision, the pathos of God, canal construction by Neco II, fear of God, to name a few. Most admirable is the clear explanation and critical evaluation of a number of weighty and technical works on Exodus (e.g., Blum, Gertz, Levin, Schmidt) that makes this volume an excellent introduction to current trends in Exodus.

Abschied von der Priesterschrift? Zum Stand der Pentateuchdebatte, edited by Friedhelm Hartenstein and Konrad Schmid. Veröffentlichungen der Wissenschaftlichen Gesellschaft für Theologie 40. Leipzig: Evangelische Verlagsanstalt, 2015. Pp. 220. Paper. €38.00. ISBN 9783374033614.

David M. Carr, Union Theological Seminary in New York

This volume contains the published form of presentations on the character of the Priestly stratum that were originally presented at a May 2012 conference in Stuttgart-Hohenheim, Germany. None of the seven essays fundamentally critiques the idea of a cross-pentataeuchal Priestly strand, even though the title for the volume takes its cue from an earlier volume of essays that fundamentally critiqued the idea of an early, non-Priestly "Yahwist" spanning Genesis and the Moses story (*Abschied vom Jahwisten: Die Komposition des Hexateuch in der jüngsten Diskussion*, 2002). Instead, they offer perspectives by several leading European scholars on the current state of the debate about the basic nature and background of the Priestly material in the Pentateuch. Does that material (or the bulk of it) originate in a separate source; is it all a stratum composed to supplement/expand upon some sort of pre-Priestly precursors (whether a proto-Pentateuch [e.g., J] or separate non-P blocks); or should we work with another model such as Blum's blended model of a broad Priestly "compositional" supplementary stratum that built—at particular points such as the flood and Red Sea narratives—on originally separate Priestly sources/sketches?

The volume starts with a strong defense of a more traditional source perspective on P by Christoph Levin, "Die Priesterschrift als Quelle: Eine Erinnerung" (9–31). Levin recognizes that a source approach to P is difficult to sustain in cases such as the Jacob and Joseph story, where material assigned to P is fragmentary and lacks context, and he—like other authors in the volume—notes the problem posed by the lack of an introduction of Moses in P before he is treated as a known individual (6:2ff.) in a P source generally reconstructed as Exod 1:13–14; 2:23b–25; 6:2ff.). Nevertheless, Levin argues that numerous data militate against an approach to P as a purely supplementary stratum: particularly extensive doubling and contrasting conceptual systems in loci such as Gen 1–11 and Exod 6–14, back-references in P to material no longer preserved in the Pentateuch (e.g., Gen 8:6b), and the way P forms a readable strand even in loci, such as the early part of the Abraham story (P in Gen 12:5; 13:6, 11b–12bα; 19:29abα), where P materials are relatively isolated. Overall, Levin argues that a source approach to (much of) P best explains how specifically P materials present a picture of the *gradual* introduction of divine designations and sacrifice, even as the non-Priestly material has *not* been revised in accordance with these pictures by the hypothesized Priestly redactor/supplementer. In light of this data, Levin concludes that much Priestly material originated as a separate Pg source, albeit one written with knowledge of its pre-Priestly precursor source. This separate Pg source was often imperfectly preserved by an "Endredaktion" (R, *not* RP) that sometimes used elements (often incomplete elements) of P to supplement J and sometimes vice versa. In this sense, Levin affirms a basic source model behind the Pentateuch but attempts to explain why P (and non-P)—though originating in large part as a separate source—often seems to function like a supplement to the other. Moreover, like the other authors in the volume, Levin believes a large bulk of the P and non-P material to have originated in post-Priestly supplements to a P/non-P Pentateuch, so that, in this sense, much of the Priestly stratum is both post-Priestly and supplementary.

Erhard Blum's "Noch einmal: Das Literargeschichtliche Profil der P-Überlieferung" (32–64) provides a state of the art summary of his blended position that the broader P stratum is supplementary, even as it incorporates blocks of originally separate Priestly compositional sketches about the flood, Red Sea, and so on. Blum builds a case for this broader supplementary perspective on P by focusing particularly on the weakest textual locus for a source approach (to P), Gen 19–50. He surveys numerous cases where Priestly material about the ancestors is fragmentary, lacks context, and even seems to function primarily in relation to non-Priestly material. For example, the Priestly system of תולדות labels (e.g., "these are the descendants of Jacob," 37:2) introduce *non*-Priestly material (Gen 37:3ff.). Indeed, this is true even to the point that there is no תולתות אברם ("descendants of Abraham") superscription, since such a label would best introduce a section about Isaac, and the only such material in Genesis, a non-Priestly section in Gen 26:1–33, is embedded in a broader story that already focuses on Isaac's descendants ("the descendants of Isaac," 25:19ff.). In addition, Blum repeats and refines his 1984 argument that the Priestly story about Jacob at Bethel (Gen 35:9–15) only makes sense as a correction of the non-Priestly Bethel tradition (28:10–22). Blum argues that this story was *composed from the outset* to function in its non-Priestly context, since it so obviously presupposes that non-P tradition, yet is not placed at the outset of the Priestly Jacob story (instead, see the P beginning in Gen 28:1–5), where it would stand if it were written to be part of a separate Priestly source. In light of the complexity of the data, Blum, like Levin, believes a mixed model must be adopted. On the one hand, he believes that the books of Genesis through Leviticus contain blocks of Priestly material—labeled P^0 by Blum—that originated as separate Priestly sketches ("Entwurfen"), that were only later conflated with their non-Priestly precursors (e.g., in the flood narrative of Gen 6–9). On the other hand, Blum distinguishes this P^0 level of tradition from the use of such sketches as part of a broader sharp Priestly revision of its non-Priestly precursor, a compositional stratum that Blum (still) labels KP (for Priestly "Komposition"). According to Blum, this model best accounts for the complex data surrounding P in the Pentateuch and renders irrelevant recent discussions about an original "end of P" in Exod 29 or 40 or Lev 9 or elsewhere.

These two more detailed examples show how much of the discussion about P has progressed from simple P-as-source versus P-as-redaction dichotomies that were prominent up through the 1980s. Two other essays in the volume offer contrasting redaction/supplement and source approaches to a similar block of chapters in Exodus. In his "Der literarische Charakter der Priesterschrift in der

Exoduserzählung (Ex 1–14)" (94–133), Christoph Berner builds on his earlier analysis of the formation of Exod 1–15 (a Göttingen Habilitationschrift published as *Die Exoduserzählung: Das literarische Werden einer Ursprungslegende Israels*, FAT [Tübingen: Mohr Siebeck, 2010]) to argue that the earliest layer of P at the outset of Exodus (Pg 1:13–14; 6:2–7:7; 12:1–13, 28) was a supplement to an extremely slender non-P precursor (starting in Exod 2:1–11a), which was then followed by numerous layers of late Priestly and post-Priestly (non-Priestly) redaction. Berner even believes himself able to maintain this approach with the case of the Red Sea, where he acknowledges that the Priestly Red Sea narrative shows clear signs of having existed separately from the non-P Red Sea narrative with which it is combined (124–25). He does so by arguing, citing his Habilitationsschrift, that all the non-P Red Sea narrative materials are *post*-Priestly (125–31). Meanwhile, Thomas Römer's "Von Moses Berufung zur Spaltung des Meers: Überlegungen zur priesterschriftlichen Version der Exoduserzählung" (134–60) arrives at quite different results while covering similar textual ground in Exodus. With Levin, he finds it odd that a Priestly supplementary layer would feature ideas such as the gradual revelation of different divine designations (Exod 6:2–3) only in specifically Priestly supplementary materials and not adapt the pre-Priestly material being supplemented. Moreover, he is struck by the relative readability and coherence, even if imperfect, of the Priestly plague and Red Sea materials standing separate from surrounding non-P materials, and he thinks the nonintroduction of Moses (in P) before Exod 6:2 can be explained by the fact that the author presupposed in his readers a knowledge of Moses or the (pre-P) narrative (145–46). This leads him to posit an originally separate Priestly source that extended up through at least Exod 29 (151).

Scholars often have noted how the source approach to the Pentateuch was originally developed by scholars such as Astruc and Eichrodt on the book of Genesis but that the evidence for such an approach is far less strong for the books of Leviticus, Numbers, and Deuteronomy. The other essays in the volume well illustrate this truism. Jan Christian Gertz's "Genesis 5: Priesterliche Redaction, Komposition oder Quellenschrift?" (65–93) both offers his latest and most refined analysis of Gen 5 (83–90) and more broadly engages arguments (mostly by Blum) for the supplementary/compositional character of P across parts of Gen 1–11. Echoing a comment in his 2000 book on Exodus (and citing a more extensive similar approach in Jakob Wöhrle's *Fremdlinge im eigenen Land: Zur Entstehung und Intention der priesterlichen Passagen der Vätergeschichte*, FRLANT 246 [Göttingen: Vandenhoeck & Ruprecht, 2012]), Gertz concludes, that, though Blum's compositional model may hold for the Genesis ancestral narratives, it does not work well for Gen 1–11.

Meanwhile, the two concluding essays, Eckart Otto's "Priesterschrift und Deuteronomium im Buch Levitikus: Zur Integration des Deuteronomiums in den Pentataeuch" (161–85) and Christophe Nihan's "Heiligkeitgesetz und Pentateuch: Traditions- und kompositionsgeschichtliche Aspekte von Levitikus 26" (186–218) argue in different ways that materials once assigned to a pre-Priestly

H/Holiness source (in Lev 17–26) actually represent a post-Priestly layer linking non-Priestly and Priestly blocks of the Pentateuch. Otto summarizes decades of work on the development of P and on potential exegetical/inter-textual relations that Otto sees between H materials in Lev 17–26 and non-Priestly legal materials in the covenant code and D. Nihan builds on, yet modifies his earlier work on Lev 26, answering queries posed by the current reviewer (*Formation of the Hebrew Bible: A New Reconstruction* [New York: Oxford University Press, 2011], 298–303) about whether Holiness materials like H were composed in relation to but to stand separately from non-P materials or whether they were written from the outset *as part of* a P/non-P composition. Nihan sees evidence, particularly in the reference to a Sinai *covenant* at the end of Lev 26 (26:45), that Lev 26 must have been composed as part of a P/non-P Pentateuch that included the non-P Sinai covenant (P^G is generally agreed not to feature a covenant at Sinai). As Nihan well knows, this reference in Lev 26:45 is only relevant to Lev 26 as a whole if a number of prior scholars are wrong in seeing it and other verses toward the end of Lev 26 as secondary to the chapter as a whole, and Nihan attempts to refute their arguments (212–14). He also argues in a more general way that the final exhortation in Lev 26 is composed as a balance to the (P/non-P) opening of the Sinai pericope in Exod 19, a concluding part of a post-Priestly "Leviticus redaction" consisting of many materials once understood as H (215–18).

I am particularly ill-suited to claim objectivity in evaluating these essays, since I have long argued that many Priestly materials originated in a source, one written with some knowledge of its non-Priestly precursor materials, but originally standing separate from it. Nevertheless, I can say that this volume well illustrates the textual nodal points and broader issues around which the debate still swirls. The critics and advocates of a source approach to (much of) P in this volume agree that we lack a fully preserved Priestly source. Most are acutely aware of places where the data for a source approach to P is stronger (e.g., Gen 1–11; parts of Exodus) and weaker (e.g., Gen 25–50) and vice versa (for a supplement or mixed approach). Much depends on whether one believes a source approach can plausibly account for a given gap in P (e.g., the lack of an introduction of Moses in P before Exod 6:2) or explain how originally separate Priestly materials could come to function vis-à-vis non-P materials in the present text (e.g., the toledot label system of Genesis or Gen 35:9–15 vis-à-vis 28:10–22). More and more scholars appear open to mixing a source approach to some sections (e.g., Gen 1–11; Exodus 1–14; Blum's P^0 sketches/Entwurfen there and elsewhere) with a supplement/redaction/composition approach to P in other sections (e.g., Gen 25–50; Leviticus–Numbers). The emerging question does not seem to be whether P overall is a redaction or a source but how best to conceive of P's origins and linkage/coordination with non-P material in different parts of the Pentateuch (indeed, Hexateuch) in light of the complex and different textual data in those different parts. This suggests that the textual data and scholarship on this question are not completely chaotic. Instead, years of research have helped us reach not only a remarkable consensus on the existence and basic contours of a Priestly stratum distributed across the Hexateuch but also a consistent set of questions and range of possible solutions regarding its character.

Oracular Law and Priestly Historiography in the Torah, by Simeon Chavel. Forschungen zum Alten Testament 2/71. Tübingen: Mohr Siebeck, 2014. Pp. x + 353. Paper. €99.00. ISBN 9783161533419.

Benjamin D. Sommer, The Jewish Theological Seminary

In this learned and rigorous study, Simeon Chavel investigates four Priestly narratives: Lev 24:10–23 (concerning the man who curses God), Num 9:1–14 (the alternate Passover for those ritually impure during the regular holiday), Num 14:32–36 (straw-gatherer on the Sabbath), and Num 27:1–11 (the daughters of Zelophehad); Chavel also discusses a fifth text, Num 36:1–12 (which emends the ruling from the narrative about the daughters of Zelophehad). In each, Israelites approach Moses to describe a problem or legally ambiguous situation; Moses brings an oracular inquiry to God concerning the problem or situation; God responds with a ruling on the specific case at hand, a statutory law for the future, or both. Chavel shows that these texts share a good deal in terms of structure and theme, but they are sufficiently distinct from each other to suggest they do not belong to a single Priestly hand. Chavel refers to these texts as "novellas," explaining the term as fitting in two respects: they are short narratives, and each adds something new to divine law. The novellas represent a thematic and form-critical group of their own within the Priestly literature of the Pentateuch, but, Chavel demonstrates, they also reflect core themes of P as a whole. Rather than standing apart from the rest of P, they are quintessentially P.

In their original Priestly context, the four novellas introduce new laws dealing with situations not contemplated by existing laws, rather than clarifications of law. (One receives a different impression when one reads at least one of these texts in the context of the redacted Pentateuch: a law regarding cursing God appeared already in a non-Priestly legal collection [Exod 22:27], so that in the redacted Pentateuch the Priestly narrative seems to modify or elucidate that law.) All these narratives highlight "the deity's responsiveness to developments on the ground even within the highly detailed [legal] system he himself devised" (16). They "illustrate law as an ongoing affair, the verbal, dynamic mode by which Yahweh continues to interact with Israel and its changing fortunes" (20). Thus these laws point toward the dialogical nature of lawgiving in P, which regards the legal system as being, at least to some degree, human-driven and not just top-down. For instance, Chavel shows that in "the novella about inheritance … the daughters petitioning articulate the solution, and Yahweh expresses his unqualified acceptance of it, rules on the case in precisely their terms, and declares the ruling to serve as a precedence ever after" (263). Chavel stresses the "deep continuity" (269) between the novellas and P generally, for from the very beginning P describes God as altering laws or adding to them on the basis of developments on the ground. This occurs in P already right after the flood, when God, first recognizing the nature of humanity's blood lust, promulgates rules to deal with this unfortunate tendency of his creatures. Exodus 34:29–35 and Num 7:89 also describe Moses as repeatedly consulting with God on matters of law (in contrast to E and D, in which lawgiving was a punctual event rather than an ongoing process). For P, divine law is not perfect, but it is amenable to improvement. Indeed, Chavel points out, P "does not portray the deity as one who considers and anticipates every single eventuality and preemptively accounts for them all, but as one who … comes to recognize … that to maintain his creation he will have to adapt himself to its variability and unpredictability" (269). Here Chavel's conclusions match conclusions about Jewish tradition more broadly found in another recent book, Christine Hayes's *What's Divine about Divine Law?* (Princeton University Press, 2015). That two scholars utilize different approaches and discuss a different though overlapping texts to come to such similar conclusions underscores the strength of their shared thesis. In light of Chavel's work, it also becomes clear that P is a predecessor to a stream of rabbinic and medieval Jewish thought described in Yoḥanan Silman's book, *Qol Gadol Velo Yasaf: Torat Yisrael bein Sheleimut Lehishtalmut* (Magnes, 1999). The convergence between two books treating very different corpora points to the breadth and importance of both.

Chavel maintains that the four novellas, in their combination of law and narrative, "represent the template and features that make up the Priestly history stripped down to their essentials…: narrative organized around a legal climax; community organized around divine rules; and a deity who issues rulings in response to newly emergent facts and circumstances" (18). Because P describes lawgiving as a process rather than an event, P can move back and forth between narrative and law. But Chavel points out that the interdependence of law and narrative is also observable in D and in the non-P, non-D material in the Pentateuch. Consequently, "the interweaving of law and narrative that characterizes the Torah already exists in most of the prior literary works that were combined to create it" (269), just as this interweaving endures in later Jewish literature in the Second Temple period and in rabbinic Judaism from its classical era through today. As with both his analysis of P's law as imperfect but ever subject to becoming more perfect and his description of P's God as growing in knowledge over time, Chavel's discussion of law and narrative bears significant implications for religious thought that go well beyond the philological and historical analysis that make up most of this book. Chavel articulates these implications eloquently in the book's final pages as he describes how this combination of law and narrative recur not just in P but throughout Jewish tradition.

Most of the book consists of detailed and exacting analyses of the four novellas. When Chavel discusses their literary development, he refrains, happily, from laying all four into a procrustean bed. He argues that Lev 24:19–23 and Num 15:32–36 are literary unities, while Num 9:1–14 and 27:1–11 resulted from complex processes of textual development. He also treats the diverse ways in which the novellas relate to their current placement in the longer trajectory of the P source; he lays out how the novellas rework, and serve as sources for, other biblical texts; and he delineates the ways they shed light on other biblical laws they interact with or call to mind. Chavel's analyses draw upon a deeply impressive variety of secondary literature not only from modern biblical criticism but from related fields and from traditional Jewish exegesis. How often in scholarly literature does one come across a footnote that puts Mary Douglas and the *Netziv* right next to each other: the former a Catholic cultural anthropologist of the twentieth century, the latter a nineteenth-century ultra-Orthodox *rosh yeshiva*? Pairings such as this one, which posthumously but appropriately transforms these two thinkers into colleagues, are typical of Chavel's deft hand with secondary literature.

The detailed analysis of the four novellas, it must be said, can make for challenging reading. Chavel presents his intricate argumentation inductively: he asks a question and proceeds at length to break the question down and refine it; he then presents, examines, and refutes various answers from scholarly literature; finally he develops his own approach. As a result, a question and its answer can be separated by many pages, and the reader must join Chavel for a journey without knowing where the journey is headed and often without initially knowing why an issue discussed for several pages is in fact relevant. This sort of structure works well for a dissertation, whose three or four readers are paid to read the whole work; it is less appropriate for a monograph, whose more numerous readers are not necessarily committed to reading each page. Stating theses of lengthy and complex subsections at their beginnings rather than close to their ends would serve readers well.

Space does not permit me to summarize, much less to engage, the rich array of individual insights concerning each novella. One assertion regarding the last novella (Num 27) and its countersuit (Num 36), however, deserves comment. Chavel claims that the latter text "supersed[es]" (260) the former by forcing a daughter who inherits from her sonless father to marry a man from the pool of men who would have inherited the land in question had the father died childless. As a result, Chavel maintains, the countersuit in Num 36 "dramatically curtails" the rights of the women in question (247), rendering their ability to inherit from their deceased father all but meaningless. But this is not the case. Numbers 27:8 allows daughters to inherit if the deceased man has no sons. Verses 9–11 go on to rule that if the man has neither sons nor daughters, his brothers inherit his wealth; the verses then provide an ordered list of increasingly distant male relatives who inherit if the closer male relatives are lacking. According to Num 36, the daughter who wants to inherit must marry someone from a clan that is in her own tribe. But she is not required to marry the male who would inherit in her absence. It may be that her uncle or first cousin would be first in line to inherit if she were not alive, but she is free to marry her second cousin or a fourth cousin twice removed, so long as he is still from her tribe. The uncle or first cousin whose ability to inherit was voided by her marriage to the fourth cousin would hardly agree with Chavel that Num 36 "in effect completely effaced the ruling of the original oracular novella" in Num 27 (260). He would similarly disagree with Chavel if the woman never married—which would mean in effect that she enjoyed a life estate from the property. Granted, when she died childless, the next male from the list would inherit, but by that time the uncle or first cousin might have long been gathered to his kin. In that case, the Num 36 law barred him from the inheritance while guaranteeing the woman the benefit of the wealth. Further, the requirement that she marry a man from her own tribe has little practical effect on her marriage prospects: a woman from, say, Manasseh did not meet men from, say, Naphtali through J-Date (I-Date?), nor did men from Judah flirt with women from Zebulun in a college cafeteria far from home. People chose, acquired, or were given marriage partners from their own village, or from the village two hills over, or from a larger town across the valley. Those marriage partners were likely to belong to their own clan or to some other clan in the same tribe. Thus the restrictions of Num 36 simply direct daughters without brothers to marry someone from what was the most likely pool of suitors in any event. To be sure, women in this situation were likely to know a few men not from their own tribe; think of the non-Benjaminite man who lived in Gibeah in Judg 19 or of women growing up in a village near a tribal border. In that sense, the law in Num 36 does restrict the pool of suitors somewhat. But her ability to inherit independently of the first close male relative in the list from Num 27:9–11 remains unimpaired.

No doubt other readers can find exegetical judgements with which to quibble as well. Such quibbles do nothing to undermine the value of this work, which is a learned, subtle, well-reasoned contribution not only to the study of Priestly literature in the Pentateuch but to the study of biblical law and even of biblical theology more broadly. Scholars from many subfields of biblical studies, along with not a few scholars of rabbinic law and Jewish thought, will profit greatly from this volume.

The Pentateuch: A Social-Science Commentary, by John Van Seters. 2nd edition. Cornerstone Series. London: Bloomsbury, 2015. Pp. 224. Paper. $29.95. ISBN 9780567658791.

Jean Louis Ska, Pontificio Istituto Biblico

"The governing assumption of this guidebook is that the interpretation of the Pentateuch cannot dispense with the initial task of understanding its compositional history" (183). This seemingly innocuous statement will probably provoke some disaffections among readers, especially those favoring more canonical or synchronic readings of biblical texts. But John Van Seters may lose other members of his readership along the way, among others neo-documentarians, supporters of redactional criticism, several specialists of biblical law, or those who said "farewell" to some classical sources, especially the Yahwist. However, this second edition of a very readable and well informed introduction by an exegete who has been called sometimes the "enfant terrible" of pentateuchal research, deserves a careful reading until the end. The author's positions are well-known, and he did not change much in this slightly revised edition of a handbook published for the first time in 1999 (see the review by Jan A. Wagenaar in *RBL* 2000). Modifications are not really significant. The author himself signals that he changed his mind on two occasions. He admits now, for instance, that the meeting of Isaac with Abimelech in Gerar (Gen 26) contains a text older than the story of the encounter of Abraham with the same Abimelech (Gen 20:1–7; 21:25–31a). The second change has to do with Exod 33:1–7, which is interpreted as the origin tradition of the synagogue, a place of prayer and of possible communication with the deity. The "tent of meeting," a lay institution proper to the Jewish community in exile in Babylon and described by the author's Yahwist (J), is to be opposed to the cult of the Second Temple reconstructed by priestly groups. The difference between the author's Yahwist and the Priestly Writer (P) has therefore to do with two main conceptions of the cult, the lay institution of the synagogue, a place of prayer, and the temple, the place of priestly cult and sacrifices. On this point, see the author's recent article "Dating the Yahwist's History: Principles and Perspectives," *Bib* 95 (2015): 1–25. The most substantial addition, however, is to be found in chapter 4 on the new currents in pentateuchal studies in a paragraph entitled "New Developments since 1999."

Let us say that the title of the book is somewhat misleading. It has little to do with what is usually called "commentary," and I did not find many elements of social science in it either. Titles are often chosen by the publisher, but the choice in this case is unfortunate, at least in my opinion. This volume is an introduction to reading the Pentateuch, and a classical one in its intent and shape. The author's ideas are personal and original, of course, and a different title could have brought this better to the fore.

The book contains nine chapters, every one provided with a short bibliography and a few endnotes. The first chapter explains the purpose of the book, intended not for specialists, but for the student and the novice (xi), and some major concepts about the study of the Pentateuch. The second chapter describes the main features of the Pentateuch as a whole, the problem of sources, and the "three basic models for compositional reconstruction," the fragmentary, the supplementation, and the source model. The third chapter is dedicated to a "Survey of Historical-Critical Research on the Pentateuch." We find a short exposition of the major authors such as de Wette, Wellhausen, Gunkel, von Rad, Noth, Albright, with interesting critical remarks, especially on the Albright and Cross school and their (uncritical) reliance on oral traditions. Let me say that Alexander Geddes is (wrongly) presented as a "fragmentist" (17). See, on this, John Rogerson, "Was Alexander Geddes a Fragmentist? In Search of the 'Geddes–Vater Hypothesis'" (in *The Bible and Enlightenment: A Case Study: Alexander Geddes 1737–1802*, ed. William Johnstone, JSOTSup 377 [London: T&T Clark, 2004], 157–67).

The fourth chapter is perhaps the one that deserves a more careful reading. It is occupied by a presentation of the new trends in pentateuchal studies since 1975. With Rolf Rendtorff and Hans Heinrich Schmid, shortly presented in the first pages, Van Seters was one of those who influenced pentateuchal studies after

1975. I will dwell a little more on the pages dedicated to recent developments in the field since 1999. First, Van Seters discusses the thesis put forward by Albert de Pury, Thomas Römer, and especially Konrad Schmid in his *Genesis and the Moses Story* (Siphrut 3 [Winona Lake, IN: Eisenbrauns, 2009]), that the patriarchal narratives and exodus represent two separate traditions united for the first time by the Priestly writer in Exod 6:2–8. Van Seters rejects vehemently the idea, stressing that his Yahwist created a connection between patriarchs and Moses before P in Gen 15:12–15; 46:1–4; Exod 1:6, 8. These texts are often considered late, redactional additions. This position leads Van Seters to end with a note written in his inimitable style, "One can prove anything by so easily eliminating any evidence against this thesis advocated by Schmid" (64).

A second paragraph unfolds the author's ideas about "the use and abuse of the redactor in Pentateuchal studies." John Van Seters defends—forcefully, as usual—the existence of authors and the inexistence of redactors and editors in antiquity. He introduces here one his major ideas, that biblical authors were historians like Herodotus, more precisely "antiquarians," writers of "antiquities," or popular form of histories that "began with the earliest generations of mankind and traced the generations of national ancestors and heroes down to the establishment of cities, states and nations" (65). Van Seters goes on explaining how this form of literature arrived in Israel and was used by the writers of the Bible, especially his Deuteronomist and Yahwist: "There is good reason to believe that this form of Greek antiquarian historiography was derived from the Phoenicians (Canaanites) along with their alphabet, and it is most likely that this was the case for the Israelites as well" (65–66). If I am allowed to add a personal note, it seems to me that we are here in the field of conjectures and that pieces of solid evidence are not much present. To put in other words, I have the impression that the author is substituting F. M. Cross's *Canaanite Myth and Hebrew Epic* with *Canaanite Antiquities and Hebrew History*. The comparison with Herodotus is also debatable. Herodotus may have gathered information from oral traditions, as several biblical writers did. He is, however, a self-conscious author who introduces himself and explains his project in the prologue of his *History*. Moreover, when he exposes different versions of the same event, he tries to distinguish them critically and to decide which one is more dependable. It is hard to find similar features in biblical literature.

The following section deals with the so-called neo-documentarians (Baruch Schwartz, Joel Baden, Jeffrey Stackert). In these pages the reader will find Van Seters's answer to Joel Baden's criticism rather than a real presentation and evaluation of the latter's position. A third section treating recent developments in the studies on biblical law is again almost completely limited to a justification of the author's own publication in the field, *A Law Book for the Diaspora: Revision in the Study of the Covenant Code* (Oxford: Oxford University Press, 2003). As the title indicates, Van Seters considers that the so-called Book of the Covenant (Exod 20:22–23:33) is the work of his exilic Yahwist and not the earliest law code of the Pentateuch. This Yahwist, "a gifted scribe" (69), knew the laws contained in the Deuteronomic Code and in the Holiness Code (in this case, J is later than P, it seems) and had also access to old Mesopotamian legal traditions, such as the Hammurapi Code, which "was almost certainly available in Aramaic translation and script, the official language of the empire" (69). To my knowledge, however, there are many copies of the Hammurapi Code, but up to now no one has found any fragment of such a translation. Even the fragments found recently in Tel Hazor are written in Akkadian.

A last section is a summary of Van Seters's latest publication, *The Yahwist: A Historian of Israelite Origins* (Winona Lake, IN: Eisenbrauns, 2013). This presentation often looks like a pleading *pro domo*. There is also a fair amount of repetition in chapters 3 and 4, as in some other parts of the volume.

The next chapters expose Van Seters's views on Deuteronomy (ch. 5), the Yahwist (ch. 6), the Priestly writer (ch. 7) and the law in the Pentateuch (ch. 8). The order of the chapters is a clear reflection of the author's theory of "supplementation." Deuteronomy, followed by the Deuteronomistic History (D), is the first literary composition of the Pentateuch. A northern origin, a connection with Josiah's reform, and the influence of Neo-Assyrian vassal treaties are ideas common to many scholars in the field. Van Seters's Yahwist is an antiquarian who provided the Deuteronomistic History with a long preface beginning with the creation of the world and followed by the patriarchal narratives and Moses's mission. This Yahwist was thus in touch with an ancient Phoenician/Canaanite antiquarian tradition, read Aramaic documents (an Aramaic version of the Hammurapi Code), but wrote in classical Hebrew, in a variegated style, different, however, from that of the Priestly writer, who composed his work some years later and remained anonymous in spite of all his (or her?) outstanding personal qualities.

The Priestly writer is the successive supplement to this combination of D and J, adding different views on Israel's origin, especially in the field of the cult. This priestly theology is centered on the Second Temple and corrects the lay theology of J. Law in the Pentateuch is the subject matter of chapter 8. After a short exposition on the different kinds of biblical laws, Van Seters proposes his own chronology of the main biblical law collections, with the Covenant Code (Exod 20:22–23:33) following the Deuteronomic Code (Deut 12–26).

These chapters reproduce almost completely those of the first edition and were well summarized by Jan A. Wagenaar in his review mentioned earlier. The volume contains a bibliography (which could have been slightly updated), an index of references, and an index of authors.

The volume is assuredly very instructive, especially about Van Seters's own positions. The presentation of other scholars' theories is sometimes one-sided or incomplete. As an introduction to the Pentateuch, I would recommend that one use it with some other classical handbook to have a more balanced and complete view on the field. Many questions remain open, admittedly, and it is not certain that this plea will convince John Van Seters's colleagues, and this in spite of all my sympathy for the author.

FORMER PROPHETS

Power and Politics in the Book of Judges: Men and Women of Valor, by John C. Yoder. Minneapolis: Fortress, 2015. Pp. xiv + 273. Paper. $30.89. ISBN 9781451496420.

Gregory Mobley, Andover Newton Theological School

The terms we use to understand the protagonists of the book of Judges are misleading. *Judges* they certainly were not, unless Judge Roy Bean comes to mind. Neither were they pious soldiers crusading against Saracen-like Ba'alists. According to John C. Yoder in *Power and Politics in the Book of Judges: Men and Women of Valor*, Israelite leaders in the early Iron Age were or aspired to be warlords of the variety commonly found in preindustrial, kinship-based societies. Yoder, professor of History and Political Science and director of the Peace Studies Institute at Whitworth University in Spokane, is a learned and sympathetic outsider to biblical studies. Yoder has resided and traveled in and studied sub-Saharan Africa. This biblically steeped Old African Hand utilizing the tools of social anthropology has a great feel for the material, and his reconstruction of the so-called judges as godfather-like figures vying for power, managing networks of patronage, and obsessed with honor has verisimilitude and brings them to life.

The study is thematically organized around four questions. (1) "Power and Knowledge" (chapter 2, after an overview) considers what constituted "indigenous knowledge," the intellectual skill set needed for achieving and maintaining power in the era of the Judges. (2) "Power and Trust" asks about the formal and informal bonds of social cohesion at work in a society that lacked centralized authorities to enforce fidelity to pacts. (3) "Power and Honor" seeks to discover on what scales self- and social esteem were measured. (4) "Power and Wealth" attempts to go beyond the counting of camels in order to understand the social and cosmic economics of tribute, gifting, and sacrifice.

In an introductory chapter Yoder locates himself in biblical studies. Susan Niditch's analysis of the literary-historical development of Judges provides Yoder with a historical frame. Sketches of early Iron Age patriarchs and patrimonies by David Schloen, Niels Peter Lemche, and Norman Gottwald compose the outlines of the social structures into which Yoder fills in details based on his study of and experiences in Africa.

In "Power and Knowledge" Yoder seeks to articulate the skill set for leadership in a traditional culture such as Iron Age Israel. Yoder refers to these qualities as "indigenous knowledge" (46), a term borrowed from Jane Guyer, a social anthropologist whose fieldwork is in sub-Saharan Africa. A leader in Judges needed to be a psychologist of the first rank in order know whom to intimidate and whom to indulge in his patronage network, a lawyer of sorts who could settle disputes among clients (Deborah) and negotiate covenants with other warlords (Jephthah), a battlefield tactician (Abimelech), and an oracular specialist who could both divine the will of and conduct business with the Powers (Gideon).

"Power and Trust" is about the codes that governed loyalty and trustworthiness in a society held together by kinship and covenants that, in effect, created fictive kinship, binding strangers together into pseudo-families. For the most part, patronage was the grease that kept the social machinery running, though patriarchs occasionally had to stage violent performances, shock-and-awe barbarities—Jepthtah's immolation of his daughter, the dismemberment of the woman from Bethlehem, the total war tactics of *herem*—to demonstrate that they were serious men. To his credit, Yoder acknowledges the theological projection of this system: this is how the heavenly Father managed his network, too, blessing loyal client servants and cursing the disloyal.

"Power and Honor" is Yoder's strongest chapter. Drawing on anthropologists such as Julian Pitt-Rivers and J. G. Peristiany and biblical scholars such as Zeba Crook and Saul Olyan, Yoder details story by story how honor was the currency of virtually every social transaction in Judges. As he writes: "For many of the characters [in Judges], honor was more important than life itself. In addition to stories featuring honor, throughout the book honorific terms, praise names, titles, and conventions of greeting reflect a preoccupation with honor" (118).

The diction of Judges includes many terms that treat honor as if it were measurable. Words related to the ascription or possession of honor include *kabôd*, "social mass, significance," *kabēd*, "to honor," and *tip'eret*, "dignity." Words related to dishonor connote diminution: *knʿ*, "to humble," *qll*, "to treat with contempt," *ʿanah*, "to disrespect."

In "Power and Wealth" Yoder addresses his final theme, the economy of ancient Israelite patriarchy. Using Goran Hyden's term "economy of affection" (169), Yoder depicts "a preindustrial and precapitalist society where plunder, tribute, and gifting—not markets—dominated the exchange of material goods" (166). Patriarchs sought to outdo each other in potlatch-like competitions, raised their social status through public displays of sacrifice, and cemented the bonds of their social networks through generosity to clients in their kin-based networks. Feasts such as that hosted by Samson were the public occasions for this kind of patrimonial performance of power, not unlike the contemporary fund-raising banquets among the swells chronicled in our society-page photographs. Yoder parses the difference between the "plunder" of social bandits and warriors, the seizure of goods, territory, and "tribute," the normalization of economic coercion enforced by the threat of violence. The brief anecdotes about the "minor judges" are explicit about what made a patriarch rich: the number of sons sired, camels owned, and villages dominated. Wealthy men also served as patrons of family tombs and religious shrines, the latter presided over by the patriarch himself (Gideon) or a hired priest (by Micah in Judg 18). Once again, sacrifices and offerings represented a projection of these practices and idea onto the celestial realm.

Yoder has crafted a gem of a study. It has some flaws, mainly its terminological infelicities such as in the subtitle *Men and Women of Valor*, which sounds like the title for a religious couples retreat. His translations, based on those of Susan Niditch, of Biblical Hebrew *ʾiš hayil* and *ʾešet hayil* are tone deaf to the coarse folk outlaw ballads found in Judges and to Yoder's own analogical cast of warlords and chieftains. The terms *'iš ḥayil* and *gibbor ḥayil* are difficult to translate into English; they refer to men or warriors *with something*, whether status, equipment, or crews. A *gibbor ḥayil* such as Gideon is part of a kin-based organization with enough structure to last, though not for long, beyond his death. But "men of valor" is too abstract and sounds way too virtuous. I also grew tired of the terms from the anthropological literature that Yoder borrows, such as "Big Man" or "Strong Man," to describe male traditional leaders from African societies. Why not describe them simply, analytically as patriarchs or patrons, avoiding pidgin constructions?

There are many good ideas in this book, and though its primary audience is undergraduate and graduate students, this scholar found Yoder's parallels between ancient and contemporary traditional cultures stimulating. By viewing the characters in Judges primarily as political actors rather than religious figures, this political scientist is able to reimagine them in fresh ways. The messengers of YHWH who come to Gideon and the wife of Manoah become itinerant shamans instead of angels. Yoder audits Gideon and discovers that he—slave owner, polygamist, shrine patron, threshing floor manager—was quite wealthy. Through Yoder's social-scientific lens, we see the structure of the protection racket Abimelech operates in and around Shechem and the crew of empty men he hires to be his muscle. Yoder also has an interesting take on Samson, not unlike Stephen M. Wilson in *Making Men: The Male Coming-of-Age Theme in the Hebrew Bible* (Oxford, 2015) as a young warrior who should be in the employ of a warlord who could harness the Danite's chaotic aggressiveness.

"Und das Königtum war fest in der Hand Salomos": Untersuchungen zu 1 Kön 3, by Martin Nitsche. Beiträge zur Wissenschaft vom Alten und Neuen Testament 205. Stuttgart: Kohlhammer, 2015. Pp. 254. Paper. €90.00. ISBN 9783170299078.

Herbert H. Klement, Evangelische Theologische Fakultät, Leuven

Bei der vorzustellenden Studie handelt es sich um eine Dissertation, die im Wintersemester 2014/15 von der Katholischen-Theologischen Fakultät in Erfurt angenommen wurde. Sie trägt die Charakteristika einer solchen frühen Qualifikationsarbeit. Ihr Ziel ist eine rein synchrone Lektüre des im Titel angezeigten Textes. Sie gliedert sich in sechs recht ungleiche Kapitel A bis G: Nach einer Einleitung (Kap. A, 19 S.) folgt unter B eine Vers für Vers durchgehende exegetische Untersuchung von 1. Kön 3 (113 S.). In Abschnitt C geht es um „Begriffliche Entfaltungen" zu dem König und der Weisheit (43 S.). Es folgen Überlegungen zu „Salomobildern, die es in 1. Kön 3 nicht gibt" (Kap. D, 13 S.), den Ägyptenmotiven in dem untersuchten Kapitel (Kap. E, 16 S.) und zu ironischen Aspekten (Kap. F, 8 S.). Mit Kap. G als Abschlussfazit (3 S.) schließt die Studie, gefolgt von einer Literaturliste und einem Bibelstellenregister.

Die Arbeit möchte den Versuch unternehmen „den wichtigen und prominenten Text 1. Kön 3 zunächst für sich zu verstehen, also geschützt vor vorschnellen Vereinnahmungen durch … Kontextbezüge und redaktionelle Zusammenhänge".

So wird das Kapitel als Text ohne Kontext interpretiert. Die Studie ist zudem geprägt von einer gewissen Skepsis, „ob ein theoretisches Konstrukt wie ‚der kanonische Salomoʻ, letztlich sinnvoll ist." Der Autor will für die Herausarbeitung der Salomofigur deskriptiv ausschließlich bei dem eingegrenzten Kapitel bleiben und andere Aspekte zur Würdigung des Königs nicht berücksichtigen. Gleichzeitig verzichtet die Arbeit auf eine ausführliche methodische und hermeneutische Diskussion der zugrunde gelegten Arbeitsweise und springt direkt in eine Auslegung von Kap. 3, das nach Meinung des Verfassers einen „der prominentesten Texte im Alten Testament" (11) und die „populärste Erzählung über Salomo" (14) bereit stellen soll.

Der zu untersuchende Textbestand wird allerdings nicht ganz auf Kapitel 3 beschränkt, vielmehr wird er als „syntaktisch angemessener" bereits ab 1. Kön 2,46b gelesen. Aus diesem Vers, der für den Rezensenten besser mit der Tradition als Abschluss des voraufgehenden Kapitels zu lesen wäre, ist auch der Titel der Arbeit entlehnt. Wie der Anfang erweitert wird, so wird auch am Ende der folgende Vers 1. Kön 4,1 als Abschlussnotiz hinzugenommen. Während es für die summarische Notiz am Ende des zweiten Kapitels, das die Unsicherheiten der Anfangszeit der Herrschaft endeten und das Königtum in Salomos Hand gefestigt war keinen Hinweis im hebräischen Text gibt, markierten die Masoreten mit einer Setuma jeweils vor und nach 4,1 diesen Vers als nicht notwendigerweise zum Folgenden gehörend.

Die so bestimmte Einheit 2. Kön 2,46b–4,1 wird nun zunächst ohne jeden Kontextbezug versweise untersucht. Hatte synchrone Exegese meist immer auch auf Beobachtungen zu Sinneinheiten, Szenen, Gliederungsmarkern oder Erzählbögen geachtet und daraus Erkenntnisse abgeleitet und Verknüpfungen gefunden, die in einem Text Tiefenstrukturen freilegen können, so wird das Kapitel hier formal grob in drei Abschnitte gegliedert: Erzähleinstieg in 1. Kön 2,46b–3,3, gefolgt von den Abschnitten „Opfer und Traum" in 1. Kön 3,4–15 und „Das hörende Herz auf dem Prüfstand" in 1. Kön 3,16–4,1. Bei der anschließenden Übersetzung gehören gelegentliche Erläuterungen zu Übersetzungsentscheidungen nicht zum Textbestand, sie finden sich nur in den Fußnoten. Unter der Überschrift „Historische Rückfrage" werden weiter nicht etwa Fragen der Historizität des Berichteten oder historisch-kritisch Konstruktionen von möglichen Textgenesen behandelt, sondern lediglich textkritische Fragen, insbesondere werden Abweichungen des MT zur LXX angesprochen.

Das ausführlichste Kapitel B setzt unmittelbar mit einer Vers-für-Vers Textwahrnehmung ein, Lexeme werden häufig besprochen, gelegentlich werden hier Übersetzungsentscheidungen erläutert. Am Ende der drei Gliederungseinheiten finden sich jeweils die Beobachtungen zusammenfassende Abschnitte. Im Blick auf das Ganze der Untersuchung wird ausgewertet, dass der erste Abschnitt eine Einleitung bildet, „vor allem durch Nennung von vier Themenkomplexen (Verschwägerung, Bautätigkeit, Gottesbeziehung Salomos, Höhenopfertätigkeit), die mit dem gesamten Komplex 1. Kön 3–11 und nicht nur mit diesem Kapitel zu tun haben" (136). Der Abschnitt „Erzählung von Opfer und Traum" bilde das

Kernstück von 1. Kön 3 und sei „kunstvoll komponiert", in der Salomo Weisheit zugesagt bekommt. In der „Erzählung vom hörenden Herzen auf dem Prüfstand", gemeint ist Salomos Urteil zu dem Kind der beiden Frauen, folgt „gewissermaßen die Probe aufs Exempel". Als zentrale Themen werden „Die Gottesbeziehung", „Der König" und „Die Weisheit" festgehalten. Unter „Historischen Rückfragen" wird dieses Mal konstatiert, dass die vorgeschlagene Struktur des Textes „auch mit Mitteln der historisch-kritischen Methode abgebildet werden" könne, ohne dass dazu eine detaillierte Diskussion geführt wird oder irgendeine Variante solcher Textgenese favorisiert oder beschrieben würde.

Auffällig an dieser Studie zu einer eng begrenzten Texteinheit ist, dass sie meint, sie nach ihren Lexemen, Sätzen und Versen tatsächlich angemessen verstehen zu können, ohne zu erkennen, dass es sich um einen Teiltext in einem wie auch immer eingegrenzten Gefüge handelt. Für den Rezensenten ist so ein Ansatz wenig überzeugend. Die hermeneutische Einsicht sollte leitend sein, dass jeder Text Prätexte hat, mit denen er dialogisch korrespondiert. Solche Prätexte sind für ein angemessenes Verstehen konstitutiv. Kanonisch wäre der Einstieg bei 1. Kön 1 als wichtiger und die Leserichtung leitender Vortext naheliegend. Die „literarischen Beziehungen zu 1. Kön 1–2 und dem Salomobild dieser Texte" werden allerdings vom Autor „als weniger bedeutsam" eingestuft und gar nicht erst diskutiert bzw. „als schwieriger Zusammenhang" (53) gewertet. Was daran schwierig sein soll, ist es arbeitstechnisch nicht wirklich. Es bezieht sich wohl auf die vom Autor intendierte reine und positivistische Salomointerpretation, die durch den Vortext problematisiert würde und die dann deutlich differenzierter hätte ausfallen müssen. Mit Verweis auf ein Papstzitat, das Salomos Bitte um ein „gehorsames Herz, zu verstehen, was gut und böse ist" (1. Kön 3,9) als vorbildlich für heutige Regierende erwähnt, versucht der Autor, in diesem Kapitel eine Salomogestalt zu erarbeiten, die ungetrübt von allen kritischen Anfragen als ein zeitloses Paradigma guter und idealer Herrschaft leuchtet. Der Preis für eine solche Lektüre ist allerdings die Verstümmelung des Textes um seine Kontexte, sowohl die im gegebenen Erzählzusammenhang wie die thematischen Kontexte.

Die Abtrennung der ersten beiden Kapitel vom Rest der Salomodarstellung wird traditionell textgenetisch mit der so genannten Thronfolgegeschichte Davids begründet, deren Ende meist in 1. Kön 2,12 angenommen wird. Diese durchaus kritisch zu wertende, jedoch lange dominante Interpretation, ist offensichtlich der Arbeit nicht bekannt. Der Begriff oder eine entsprechende Diskussionen tauchen in der ganzen Arbeit an keiner Stelle auf.

Als narrativer Solomozyklus wird dann 1. Kön 3–11 bestimmt. Damit wird der untersuchte Text zu dem Eingangsportal, das einen strahlenden, idealen König und seine Herrschaft präsentiert, der dann nur im Alter in 1. Kön 11 an Weisheit und geistiger Unterscheidungsfähigkeit einbüßt, aber insgesamt den Prototyp eines guten Herrschers repräsentiert. Ausgewertet wird dieser angenommene narrative Zusammenhang bei der Lektüre 1. Kön 3 jedoch nicht. Sie erfolgt, als gäbe es einen solchen Zyklus nicht. Lediglich im Nachhinein werden Überlegungen zu den Kap. 4 und 5 und 11 vorgetragen. Sie stehen nach der kontextlosen Textwahrnehmung von 1. Kön 3 unter D „Salomobilder, die es (in 1. Kön 3) nicht gibt", sind damit nicht Teil einer Gesamtdarstellung, sondern für das Verständnis des untersuchten Textes als nicht relevant aussortiert und kontrastieren ihn bestenfalls. Die Diskussion zu diesen Kapiteln bleibt in der Tendenz bei der Sicht eines eher positivistischen Herrscherbildes. Selbst in der Neuordnung der Verwaltungsstruktur in zwölf Regierungsbezirke zur Finanzierung des wachsenden Staatshaushaltes, die die alte Stammesstrukturen ablöst, kann keine implizite Kritik erkennt werden. Dies erstaunt, liegt hier doch der Beginn derjenigen Staatsform, die wegen der Versklavung des eigenen Volkes zu den Aufständen und zur Spaltung des Reiches unter dem Nachfolger Rehabeam führt. Auch die dem Traumgesicht 1. Kön 3 explizit parallel gestellte Erzählung 1. Kön 9,1–9 findet keinerlei Erwähnung: „Da erschien ihm Jhwh zum zweiten Mal wie er ihm erschienen war in Gibeon". Eine Diskussion der Spannung zwischen diesen beiden Träumen wäre literarisch aufschlussreich.

Das Recht einer deuteronomistischen Interpretation wird einerseits formal bestätigt, allerdings ohne dass auch nur im Ansatz erkennbar wäre, welche Variante dieses Theorems denn dabei im Blick sein könnte. Im Ergebnis wird in der Arbeit ein Text isoliert wahrgenommen, jedoch weder als Teiltext einer größeren Gesamtaussage noch als Antworttext auf eine Problematik oder Fragestellung. Ersteres wird als vom Autor nicht gewollt von vorn herein abgelehnt, letzteres ist gar nicht im Horizont der Arbeit.

Für den Rezensenten stellen dies jedoch erhebliche Schwächen dar. Begriffsanalysen und lexikalische Bestimmungen können ohne einen Textzusammenhang nicht wirklich sinnvoll ausgewertet werden. So sind die *bamot* im Königbuch durchaus überwiegend als eine negative Größe gewertet, die von Jhwh trennt. Salomos Opfer auf solch einer Höhe reiht sich ein in die spätere Praxis der Könige, die im selben Buch dann explizit negativ gewertet ist. Will man synchron lesen, dann lässt sich dieser Sachverhalt nicht ausblenden, die Erwähnung solcher Opfer enthält implizite Kritik. Diese bleibt gleichzeitig ambivalent, da Jhwh Salomo in seiner Opferpraxis erhört. Diese Ambivalenz verleiht dem Text in 1. Kön 3 geradezu seine Spannung. Sie jedoch zu leugnen, wie es in dieser Arbeit geschieht, kann nicht überzeugen. Ebenso ist die Erwähnung der Verschwägerung mit Ägyptens Pharao kaum nur ein Hinweis, der Salomos Größe positivistisch feiert. Vielmehr werden, wie die folgende Versklavung des eigenen Volkes bis zur Reichsteilung zeigt, damit unausweichlich Bezüge zur Exodustradition lebendig. Der Autor kann und will solche Interpretationszusammenhänge, die dem Text Tiefe geben, nicht gelten lassen.

Den Rezensenten kann die in dieser Arbeit gewählte kontextlose Lektüre eines biblischen Textes nicht wirklich überzeugen. So lohnend eine Studie zu 1. Kön 3 auch ist und sein kann, die vorliegende Arbeit hätte in vielerlei Hinsicht noch erhebliches Verbesserungspotential.

Die Grundschrift des Ezechielbuches und ihre Botschaft, by Yoo Hong Min. Forschungen zum Alten Testament 2/81. Tübingen: Mohr Siebeck, 2015. Pp. xvii + 396. Paper. €94.00. ISBN 9783161538582.

Sven Petry, Frohburg, Germany

This monograph is the revised version of Yoo Hong Min's dissertation, written under the supervision of Christa Schäfer-Lichtenberger and submitted to Kirchliche Hochschule Wuppertal/Bethel in 2013. The study seeks to reconstruct the basic edition, or *Grundschrift*, of the book of Ezekiel and to interpret its message in its historical context (15). Min identifies and analyzes originally independent textual units within the book and then seeks to explain how they got linked to form a consistent composition—a method he calls *Kompositionskritik*. The situation of exile and the temple theology of the official cult of the kingdom of Judah are presupposed as hermeneutical keys to interpret the *Grundschrift* (17). After giving an introductory outline of the scope and the methodology of his study (ch. 1) Min develops his arguments in five main chapters followed by a summary of his findings and conclusions (ch. 7), bibliography, and indexes.

Chapter 2, titled "Die Entstehung des Ezechielbuches: eine forschungsgeschichtliche Betrachtung" (18–50), presents various models of the origins and the development of the book of Ezekiel. Min particularly discusses the works of G. Fohrer, W. Zimmerli, J. Garscha, K.-F. Pohlmann, and A. Klein. With the latter three he concludes that the book's coherent appearance is the result of redactional work, but he rejects a "late," that is, postexilic, dating. Min finds his assumption of an exilic background of the book of Ezekiel supported by theological and linguistic observations as well as by comparison with other Old Testament writings and traditions, explicitly Jeremiah, P, the Holiness Code, and postexilic prophecy. It seems a bit strange, however, to find him first (correctly) stating that the book of Ezekiel essentially needs to be dated by determining its historical and theological position within the Old Testament by comparing it with other writings (44) but then concluding that, due to the state of scholarly debate, this comparison does not lead to clear results (50).

Chapter 3, "Strukturanalyse der Textkomplexe" (51–132), provides a structural analysis of the textual units that were used to compose the book of Ezekiel. According to Min, these units can be categorized as either prophetic speech or visionary account except for Ezek 33:21–22, which belongs to neither of these two categories. While the visionary accounts provide the storyline that makes for the book's coherent appearance, the prophetic speech units seem to be woven into this composition. Min argues that the origins of the basic structure of prophetic speech go back to Jeremiah, namely, to the Deuteronomistic redaction of the book of Jeremiah (87). Only later (but still during the exile, between 550 and 539 BCE) the structure of prophetic speech was fully developed in Ezekiel. For Min, the basic theological message of the prophetic speech units and the purpose of their structure is to portray the God of Israel as the sole ruler of world history (99).

In chapter 4, "Die kompositorischen Zusammenhänge" (133–208), Min analyzes the links that make for the coherent composition of the book of Ezekiel. Essentially these are descriptions or specifications of place and time of events. Min concludes that these specifications do not belong originally to the textual units to which they are now related and hence are redactional. Citing Fohrer and Zimmerli, he deems the time specifications or dates, which relate the content of the book to historical events, to be reliable. Finally, Min deals with themes and motifs that overarch the book of Ezekiel: Yahweh's glory as well as Ezekiel's captivity, his silence, and his office of being a watcher.

In chapter 5, "Die Grundschrift des Ezechielbuches" (209–72), Min seeks to reconstruct the basic composition (*Grundschrift*) of the book of Ezekiel. Min gives a brief overview of previous attempts to reconstruct an original or "older" prophetic book (Th. Krüger, J. Garscha, K.-F. Pohlmann) before developing his own. According to Min, the *Grundschrift* came into being when an older collection or composition of visionary accounts, which both in structure and themes resembles the paradise story of Gen 2, was combined with prophetic speech units (217–24, 229). Min describes the *Grundschrift* as some form of autobiography that contained at least Ezek 1:1–3:15; 3:16a, 22–5:17, 8–11; 12:1–16; 14:1–11, 20 (except for 20:27–29); 24:15–24; 33:21–22; 37:1–14; and the core of 40–48 with 12:1–16 originally placed after Ezek 24:15–24. Within this composition, Ezek. 20 is of special importance, as this chapter offers a broad theological reflection on the history of Israel. Given the combination with other narrative features, Min finds the closest Old Testament parallels to the *Grundschrift* in the historical narrative of the Pentateuch (259). Hence he compares the *Grundschrift* to the exodus story to discover various parallels especially with regard to the Priestly exodus narrative. He does not explain their nature, however, but hints at coincidence, shared traditions, or literary relations as possibilities, since that would go beyond the scope of his study. Although Min admits that lacking clear reference to historical events the *Grundschrift* cannot be accurately dated, he is convinced that it was composed between 571 and 539 BCE in Babylon, probably not by Ezekiel himself but by people who passed down Ezekelian traditions.

Chapter 6, "Die Botschaft der Grundschaft" (273–354) explores the *Grundschrift*'s message. According to Min, it aims at resolving the crisis the official Judean cult underwent after the fall of Jerusalem by developing a picture of future salvation. Especially Ezek 20 seems to look at the pentateuchal perception of the covenant between Yahweh and his people from an eschatological perspective. The covenant still needs to and will be fulfilled. Actually, Israel did not lose the promised land because the people never left the desert: for the composers of the *Grundschrift*, the exodus, the wandering in the desert, the histories of the kingdoms of Israel and Judah, and the exile all belong to this same period of Israelite history. The fulfilment of Yahweh's promise is still to come. Hence the Zion traditions are rejected because the preexilic temple in Jerusalem never had been Yahweh's eternal dwelling place. In portraying the God of Israel as the ruler of history and king of the gods, the *Grundschrift* disempowers the gods of Babylon.

As it does not deny their existence, the theology of the *Grundschrift* is still just on the way toward monotheism. I do not see, however, why the portrayal of God as heavenly king would be an argument against monotheism. One can surely debate what the theological concept of monotheism actually is, but if the only god of a monotheistic religion cannot be addressed as king, Jesus's proclamation of the kingdom of God is not monotheistic either.

Min's extensive study is clearly structured and offers many valuable observations. His conclusion that the long-noticed relations between the book of Ezekiel and the narrative traditions of the Old Testament, especially the Priestly traditions within the Pentateuch, reflect that both traditions address the same theological questions, albeit from different perspectives (Ezekiel: prophetic-eschatological; P: priestly-covenantal), is persuasive. However, taking Min's premise of a pre-539 BCE origin in Babylon into account, I find it difficult to see whether the extent of his reconstructed *Grundschrift* determines its message or vice versa. Further, when it comes to making commitments regarding the nature of the relations between Ezekiel and P or their dating, either relative or fixed, I get the impression that Min more than once simply refuses to cross the Rubicon.

I consent that the relations between P and Ezekiel are complex, in many cases debatable and due to the nature and volume of the texts hardly to be assessed in a single study. But for specific and limited sections it can be done. And for Ezek 20, the chapter that is central for the theology of Min's *Grundschrift* and the Priestly Exodus account, specifically the revelation of Yahweh in Exod 6, there have been attempts. As I have argued elsewhere, the relations between Ezek 20 and prophetic, Priestly, and (late-) Deuteronomistic traditions are obvious, and Min's study fails to convince me that this observation could be more plausibly explained by the assumption of Ezekelian priority. But if Ezek 20 is younger than P, the priestly cannot be what Min apparently wants it to be: exilic. Showing that Ezek 20 plays a central role for the theology of the *Grundschrift* and claiming all visionary accounts for it actually makes a postexilic dating more likely.

Still, dating is not everything, and some inconsistencies in the conclusions do not devalue the observations provided in this study. If one is interested in the composition history of the book of Ezekiel, one should consider reading it.

Dismembering the Whole: Composition and Purpose of Judges 19–21, by Cynthia Edenburg. Ancient Israel and Its Literature 24. Atlanta: SBL Press, 2016. Pp. xiv + 424. Hardcover. $71.95. ISBN 9781628371246. Paper. $51.95. ISBN 9781628371246.

Edgar W. Conrad, University of Queensland

Cynthia Edenburg has written a jaw-dropping book that left me in admiration of the thoroughness of her research and her close reading of the text of Judg 19–21. Her purpose is twofold: to clarify the growth of the book of Judges and to understand its place in the Deuteronomistic History. Judges 19–21, unlike the preceding chapters, do not recount the rise of a warrior hero to deliver the people from an enemy. The internecine warfare arising from the rape of a Levite's concubine is distinctive. Edenburg presents an intricate and clearly developed methodology and application. The study, however, represents the apogee of an historical-critical method that first developed in the late nineteenth century but seems no longer to offer great promise in the twenty-first century. Her *wissenschaftliche* endeavor is that of the detached observer that no longer seems compelling at a time when there is almost universal recognition of the inevitability of the interpreter's profound involvement in the act of analysis.

Edinburg's argument is developed in four chapters. The first chapter focuses on authors, the second on the geographical background of the authors, the third on the language of the authors, and the fourth on the authors' use of prior texts. Each chapter contains an initial section in which Edenburg establishes the criteria that guides her quest for authorial identity, background, language, and relationship to earlier texts. The chapters are arranged so that each chapter adds further force to her thesis that Judg 19–21 is an early Persian composition (both author and redactor) and therefore a late addition to the Deuteronomistic History. She further concludes that the book of Judges emerged during this time as an independent book.

Chapter 1 argues that Judg 19–21 is primarily the work of a single author, whom Edenburg designates N^1 and a redactor whom she calls R^2. She argues that identification of underlying sources on the basis of variations in terminology (e.g., בני ישראל versus איש ישראל) that characterized past research has "no significance for compositional analysis" because the variations can be explained as redactional in nature. She adheres to "the a priori assumption of textual unity" (10). She argues that a "continuous narrative strand runs throughout Judg 19–21" and encompasses "all the major plot elements of the text in its final form," thus concluding that the text is the work of a single author N^1 (75–76). She does, however, identify and reconstruct an earlier poetic source underlying N^1's narrative of the decisive battle in 20:29–28. The secondary material, she suggests, is the work of a single redactor R^2, whose hand can be seen as "midrashic in nature," evident in the tendency to expand the narrative.

Edenburg focuses on the "virtual space" of the story (Bethlehem, Gibeah, Mizpah, Bethel, Jabesh-Gilead, and Shiloh) in chapter 2. She asks whether the portrayal of these cities reflects the premonarchic period where the author places the events or, on the other hand, exposes the geographical reality of another time (the time of composition). She also raises the question of whether the description might be purely fictive. To answer these questions, she turns to current archaeological data and concludes that the references to Bethelehem, Gibeah, Mizpah, and Bethel fit the situation in Judah during the occupation of Babylonia and the early Persian period, not premonarchic times. The geographical area from Bethel to Bethlehem, she states, reflects the area of habitation at this time. Furthermore, the reason that the Levite may have avoided Jerusalem on his return trip from Bethlehem to Mount Ephraim is that Jerusalem, under the control of Babylon, would not have been a place to seek refuge. The setting in Gibeah, where most of the activity occurs, may derive from the earlier poetic source. The story display-ing the inhospitality shown to the Levite at Gibeah and the hospitality offered by the father-in-law in Bethlehem may prepare the reader for the rise of kingship in I Samuel, where the failed king Saul is associated with Gibeah and the triumphant David is associated with Bethlehem.

Edenburg uses linguistic evidence in chapter 3 to bolster her thesis that Judg 19–21 was a late Babylonian/early Persian composition. If the text uses Late Bibli-cal Hebrew (LBH), this language usage based on external evidence will bolster the dating suggested by the geographical setting. She assembles her data accord-ing to morphology, syntax, and lexica and further refines these categories into what is typically LBH and what is possibly LBH. Typical LBH is found primarily in fifteen LBH lexica (155; I found only fourteen) used twenty-seven times, and many of these (e.g. זכר) are found primarily in P (the Priestly source). There is one instance of typically late syntax (the predicate use of the infinitive in להפקד in 21:3) and five instances of late morphological use (five uses of masculine plural forms in conjunction with feminine referents). Possible LBH lexica, syntax and morphology are more numerous. The possible and actual LBH occurrences are specified by their percentages of usages in the various chapters, another indication of the attention to detail in this study. Typical and possible LBH is not confined to either N^1 or R^2, suggesting that both were influenced by linguistic usage in the late Babylonian/Persian period. R^2 was probably only a generation later than N^1. A more significant finding, however, is that all the Priestly LBH lexica are found only in R^2. How closely related he was to priestly circles Edenburg considers open to question.

Chapter 4 focuses on the way in which the authors used earlier texts in their composition. Edenburg argues that the use of earlier texts is another indication of the early Persian dating for the composition. While a number of authors have used the term *intertextuality* to refer to this interrelatedness of texts, she considers this poststructuralist term useless for historical research: "poststructuralist critics hold that intertextuality is characteristic of the process of reading and not inherent in composition," and "the use of this fashionable term stripped of its ideological charge only results in obscuring the nature of the specific literary phenomena per-ceived in the text" (164). She develops clearly stated criteria for concluding that an author intended an allusion to an earlier text. Readers are alerted to the way authors use earlier texts by what Edenburg calls "textual markers": a verbal ele-ment, pattern, or structure ... from another text" that is "planted" in the new text (168). This marker is further identified when the reader perceives it as "foreign" in its new context because it disrupts the "narrative grammar and hampers the superficial comprehension of the text's overt significance." While these markers may go unnoticed by a reader

the probability of success improves when the alluded text belongs to a recog-nized literary canon and when the readers' literary competence approaches that of an author, for then they will draw upon approximately the same stock of texts used by the author in formulating the allusion. From this, it is clear that allusion represents a diachronic literary dependency, since it serves as a device for reactualizing a prior text. Thus use of allusion is significant for determining both the diachronic relations between texts, as well as the authoritative standing of the alluded text. (169)

The earlier texts in the "literary canon" used by the authors include the Abraham and Lot narrative (Gen 18–19), the battle of Ai (Judg 17–18), the Saul narratives (1 Sam 10–14), the laws of Deuteronomy, the prologue of Judges (Judg1:1–2:5) and the story of Micah (Judg 17–18).

Edenburg's criteria for establishing allusion to earlier texts raise a number of questions. How can one judge that a reader's literary competence approaches that of an author? Further, while there is a literary canon that we recognize, it may not have been the literary canon of the author—or at least they might have differed. It seems that Edenberg wants to have it both ways. Her claim is that sophisticated readers recognize these links because of the limited canon of which Judg 19–21 is a part, and this linkage means that the alluded texts must have had authority at the time of the author. Readers may have similar issues with other stated criteria in the argument. How convincing is an argument about the different historical background in language usage, given the sparse amount of material and the distinctions that in some instances only encompass a generation?

From her study, Edenburg concludes that the following stages in the development of the book of Judges emerged out of an earlier continuous narrative of the Deuteronomistic History:

stage 1—Judg 2:7–12:15 was added before 1 Sam 1–3;

stage 2—the Micah and Dinah narrative (Judg 17–18) were added;

stage 3—the outrage of Gibeah story (Judg 19–21) was devised to fit the context between Judg 17–18 and 1 Sam 1–3; and

stage 4—the prologue to the book of Judges was added, severing it from the book of Joshua and making it an independent work. (R[2]'s revisions to the prologue produced a virtual frame for Judges as a separate and inclusive book.)

As a biblical scholar, I am not inclined to read biblical texts in an attempt to reconstruct diachronic development. However, if I did I would find no better example of how to go about it than Edenburg's detailed study and close attention to methodological procedure. My criticism of this study relates to broader issues of how readers in the twenty-first century interpret ancient texts. Can poststructuralist concerns about the death of the author and the role of the reader be dismissed as ideological baggage? Indeed, the impressive work of Edenburg with detailed discussion of criteria for identifying authors, redactors, geographical background along with the dating of language usage and an author's intentional use of earlier texts are themselves conscious attempts by a reader to reconstruct the diachronic development of texts for an ideological reason that is not acknowledged. Can a reader be objectively detached from a text? Is not the reader, when cutting into a text, sharing the pain of the incision? The obsession for reconstructing the development of texts carries with it an ideological agenda that has prevailed in biblical studies since the nineteenth century. The search for the historical development and background of an author has become an increasingly desperate attempt to find some kind of history (as, in this case, in Judg 19–21) where the narrative itself has been found to be historically inaccurate.

While I was reading Edenburg's dismembering of Judg 19–21, I found it difficult to block from my mind the dismembered corpse of the concubine, the internecine warfare, the virgins of Jabesh-Gilead offered to the Benjamanites, and the encouragement given to the Benjaminites to abduct the young women for brides at the festival at Shiloh. It was very difficult for me to become interested in N^1 and R^2 and their intentions for adding these chapters to the Deuteronomistic History. It did not help me to learn that there is a precedent in Saul's dismemberment of oxen as a way of mustering the people. Gang rape and death, young virgins given as trophy wives, the encouragement to ensure posterity by abducting young women who are enjoying the festivities at Shiloh, and the horrifying slaughter, including "the little ones" (21:11), are so repulsive that it is difficult to sanitize the literature by thinking about what an anonymous author and redactor might have been conjuring up in the sixth century BCE.

There is a kind of intertribal warfare among biblical scholars, and each group often shows inhospitality toward the other. It is important that we learn to be welcoming to one another in order to avoid intellectually violent conflict. I began this review by saying I admire Edenburg's meticulous and detailed accumulation of data that she has brought to her announced methodological pursuit for determining the composition and purpose of Judg 19–21. That is abundantly the case. However, the method itself is one to which I can no longer give allegiance. When Edenburg cuts into the text to see how it was put together, I do not see incisions but the creation of new texts. Readers of texts are not detached observers of how something dead has been put together, like a frog on a biologist's lab table. Readers make texts breathe, so to speak. The authors and their intentions have long since died. Whatever a hypothetical N^1 or R^2 might have been thinking, whatever their intentions might have been in reshaping a hypothetical Deuteronomistic History, any speculation about such matters quickly fades into the background in my reading this literature about violence in the context of the brutal world I myself know, where increasing numbers of refugees seek sanctuary and where women face sexual violence in mob-driven aggression. The kind of careful and thoughtful study she has undertaken, however sophisticated and painstaking in its rendering, however superb as an application of the method employed, however irresistible to historical impulses, may in some sense be an escape from the stories, a way of avoiding the literature itself and the horror it depicts, a means of skirting the responsibility of reading the story as it is in its final form and instead covering the brutality with a blanket of technical argumentation that muffles the cries of the characters and perhaps even the voices of the ultimately unknowable authors and redactors.

Judges 1-12: A New Translation with Introduction and Commentary, by Jack M. Sasson. Anchor Yale Bible 6D. New Haven: Yale University Press, 2014. Pp. xx + 593. Cloth. $100.00. ISBN 9780300190335.

Victor H. Matthews, Missouri State University

Biblical commentaries reflect the personality, interests, and expertise of the writer. That is certainly the case in the commentary on Judg 1–12 written by Jack Sasson. As an established expert on the Mari texts and other ancient Near Eastern literature, Sasson is quick to inject parallels throughout his commentary. As a seasoned interpreter of and commentator on the biblical text, he is attuned to examples of intertextuality, especially drawing on materials in Genesis, Deuteronomy, and Joshua. As a scholar interested in the way in which the biblical texts are reinterpreted in the light of ancient manuscripts, the Septuagint translation, Josephus, and medieval rabbinic works, for the most part Sasson is able to pull these sources quite skillfully into his commentary without overloading his prose or his own interpretative point. In addition, there is at times a charming style that includes his own musings about the text, occasional witticisms ("spiffy" ambassadors in 2 Sam 10:4 [228]), and the interpretations of other scholars.

As is the case with other major commentaries, this volume serves as a reference work rather than as a narrow monograph exploring a particular issue. Its purpose, aside from providing a fresh translation, is to examine each interpretative issue or philological conundrum and, where possible, to suggest a solution. At times Sasson's study of the text also draws him into theological speculation, as in his summary statement about the "fickle devotion" of the Israelites. Sasson shows his sense of humor here by admitting that, while both the Israelites and God learn just how far each can be pushed in terms of their devotion, he says that "God is likely to blink first" (195).

Sasson, knowing that not every perplexing passage can be successfully parsed, shows his strength in diligently dissecting the Hebrew text and, when no solution presents itself as completely plausible, admitting that is the case. An example of his thinking process can be found in his examination of various texts (139–41) that indicate both that Jerusalem was captured by the tribe of Judah (Judg 1:8; contra Josh 15:63) and that the Benjaminites failed to capture the city from the Jebusites (Judg 1:21). Instead of concentrating on the contradiction, Sasson chooses to explore a philological argument over the relative level of destruction of the city based on the terms for "burn" and "capture." Similarly, instead of joining the chorus that proclaims in mock humor that Eglon is a truly "fat" king of Moab (Judg 3:17), Sasson chooses to call him a "very imposing figure," whose personal strengths made him less likely to depend on a retinue, so that he became a victim of his own vanity when facing Ehud (229).

At times Sasson's propensity for etymological exploration seems to exhaust all possibilities, as in his recital of all of the suggested meanings of *šōfēṭ* (186–87). However, he does intersperse these technical comments on the Hebrew with an occasional excursus based on Near Eastern parallels. A good example is found in his examination of Othniel's "zeal for the Lord" (Judg 3:10). Drawing out the various meanings for the Hebrew word *rûaḥ*, he turns to Assyrian texts from the reign of Adad-narari II, who claims to have been invested him with a "royal nimbus" (*melammu*) that elevated him above his people and gave him the character to lead them to conquer other peoples (212).

It is this propensity for injecting material from ancient Near Eastern texts and using comparative Semitic linguistics that separates Sasson's commentary from many others. In that way, while not urging that the Judges material represents historiographical data, he is able to show that the text has a cultural foundation and is not simply a work of fiction intended to entertain. One point along this line is his discussion of the various site names that appear in the text. He notes that evidence for a site having more than one name in antiquity plays into the notion that the biblical writers wished to remind their audience that the land that had been promised to them was "not a wasteland" but "a choice land that had given much prosperity" to its inhabitants before falling prey to the Israelites (151).

He makes excellent use of the Sumerian King List to illustrate the literary pattern in Judges that never has two judges operating at the same time. By showing how Mesopotamian tradition solidifies the notion of divinely regulated, royal authority passing from one city state to another over time, Sasson provides a logic for the organization of the book of Judges (223). With so many references to the Mari texts throughout the commentary, it seems natural to expect them to appear in Sasson's comments. For example, when discussing the origin of the name of Heber the Kenite, he points to a Mari document that uses the term *ḥibrum* for a "nomadic unit that has not settled down" and thus provides a "back story" for why Heber has separated himself from his people in Judg 4:11 (262).

Where Sasson's commentary falls short, however, is in its failure to stay current on archaeological data. This is not to say that he ignores archaeology. However, often his references are twenty or more years old (140, 144), and in fact his bibliography has no citation more recent than 2012. Given the explosion of information that has appeared as a result of the excavation of the Philistine cities and the area of the Shephelah over the last decade, one would have expected him to update his discussion of site names and new finds. He provides little information on the disruption of the Near East by the invasion of the Sea Peoples or on the culture of the Philistine city-states. When he does reference these rivals to the Israelite settlements, it is in the context of the "unconquered peoples" listed in the biblical account (202). There is a nice excursus on the origins of the Amorites (163–64), tracing their roots back to the third millennium, but while that anchors textual references (Judg 1:34–36; 3:5), it does little to place the materials in the context of the Late Bronze Age.

One additional point worth noting is the near absence of references to methods that have drawn scholars to consider feminist, colonialist, or social-scientific interpretations of the text. There is occasional, brief discussion of works by Mieke Bal, Altjaya Brenner, or Gale Yee (275, 315, 322), but the commentary quickly returns to Sasson's comfort area. While he does explore social protocols such as the elements of the hospitality ritual (266), he does not include discussion of social-scientific interpretations of the violations of the protocol. Of course, no commentary can include every possible method or interpretation, but, given the growing importance of recent cultural studies in the exploration of the biblical materials, one might have expected a bit more attention to them.

Overall, this commentary on Judg 1–12 is a solid piece of scholarship that will serve the needs of those who are particularly interested in the philological and comparative aspects of the text. It contains a wealth of information that student and scholar will find useful and enlightening. A companion volume dealing with the remaining chapters in the book is anticipated. It should be an equally helpful reference work; one hopes it will also include a more inclusive discussion of recent archaeological and methodological materials.

Reading David and Goliath in Greek and Hebrew: A Literary Approach, by Benjamin J. M. Johnson. Forschungen zum Alten Testament 2/82. Tübingen: Mohr Siebeck, 2015. Pp. xiv + 270. Paper. €79.00. ISBN 9783161540462.

Joseph McDonald, Texas Christian University

This monograph is a revision of Johnson's dissertation, completed in 2012 at the University of Durham under the supervision of Walter Moberly (vii). Chapter 1 introduces the study, discussing several preliminary matters before describing the author's approach. The narrative of 1 Sam /1 Kgdms 17, centered on the confrontation of David and Goliath, exists in two primary variant literary editions: a longer version, as preserved in the MT; and a shorter version, as represented in LXX Vaticanus (LXX^B). The relationship and priority of these editions are matters of ongoing debate, as Johnson details (2–12). Although his discussion is selective, these sections might have been digested further, given that the broader study does not depend on a resolution of these questions. A final section justifies approaching the LXX as a text in its own right, while not avoiding the fact that this text arose from a desire to communicate the content of another. Johnson's aim is to hold these competing factors in tension, reading the narrative in LXX^B as it stands, then comparing this version to that of the MT (13–14, 16–17). Here, in interaction with the work of Theo van der Louw, Johnson makes an important point regarding a literary reading of the Septuagint with respect to its departures from the MT: the source of these discrepancies (intentional changes, a different *Vorlage*, scribal errors, and so on) has no bearing on the literary significance of the resulting narrative elements, considered of themselves in their own native habitat (16; cf. 150–51). Thus Johnson proposes to read the LXX^B narrative "as its own communicative act," not ignoring the fact of its translational nature but also not focusing solely on its transformations of its *Vorlage* (18–20).

Chapter 2, "Seeing David: 1 Reigns 16," provides a verse-by-verse reading of the story of David's anointing by Samuel and David's subsequent provision of musical therapy to Saul. Johnson's stated primary aim is to focus on the text of LXX^B (22), although this is complicated by this version's rather minor differences from the MT (63), and there is much comparative work here as well (31, 33, 38, 47, 63–64). Occasionally debates engaged in the body may have been better consigned to the notes, as with Johnson's evaluation of variants found only in the Peshitta (31, 33), as this is a reading of LXX^B, not of a putative original text. Finally, Johnson summarizes themes common to both Hebrew and Greek variants, as well as notes found only in the Greek, emphasizing the latter's expansion of a common theme of the importance of "seeing" and slight changes in David's characterization.

With chapter 3, "David and the Giant in μονομαχία: 1 Reigns 17," Johnson enters the heart of his study, analyzing the shorter Greek version of the story of David and Goliath's encounter as preserved in LXX^B. Here Johnson is clearer about his aims—to read the Greek as it stands, though with reference to its presumed *Vorlage*, without dwelling on the large OG minus/MT plus in the middle of the chapter (MT 17:12–31)—and his critique benefits as a result. The irony of the king's court musician taking up the challenge of the enemy champion is a nicely observed artifact of the Greek's direct move (as regards David's presence in the discourse) from David's therapeutic playing to his audacious pledge to fight (90). The play of ἀφαιρέω in the various "removals" here (David's pledge to remove Israel's shame, the removal of Saul's armor from David, and David's promise and fulfillment of the removal of Goliath's head), much amplified in the Greek, is also developed to good effect (126–27). As in chapter 2, Johnson summarizes the narrative's important themes and notes elements brought forward in the Greek version; among the more interesting of the latter is the tendency of the Greek to cast the central duel in terms of the Hellenic μονομαχία, or single combat (137).

Chapter 4, "The Love of David: 1 Reigns 18," treats the aftermath of David's victory over Goliath, which represents the beginning of David's ascendancy and Saul's opposition to his rise. Here again Johnson mostly leaves the several MT pluses to the side in his reading of the shorter Greek text. Johnson makes a number of nice moves here, including noting the chiastically linked summaries of Saul's fear of David as contrasted with the people's love of him (vv. 15–16, 28–29), which is a play confined to the Greek (176, 181), though the discussion occasionally bogs down in textual questions that do not seem entirely relevant to a reading that is not seeking an original text (144, 146).

Chapter 5, "Reading David and Goliath in Greek and Hebrew," presents a comparative reading of the narrative's two primary variant literary editions, considering among other things the effects of the MT pluses that were left aside earlier. Johnson seems to hit his stride here, bringing out interesting connections such as the possible ironic play in the MT between Goliath's shield bearer, who goes before the champion but plays no role in the fight, and Saul's armor bearer,

David, whose decisive role also involves preceding, and, in fact, replacing, Israel's proper champion the king (197). Also well-observed is the foreshadowing in the suspense-building MT episode where David's brother Eliab accuses the shepherd boy of "pride" and an "evil heart," a charge not borne out in the immediate context but one that sets the stage for much later episodes in David's story (192–93). Johnson's detailed attention to both editions demonstrates clearly that the differences between the traditions in LXX^B and the MT have important material effects on their respective presentations of David's story, despite other critics' assertions to the contrary (220).

Johnson concludes in chapter 6 by summarizing his literary findings, then offering a few thoughts on reading the LXX in its own right. His advocacy of an approach that regards "the existence of multiple versions of a biblical story not as a problem to be solved but as a literary richness to be explored" is welcome; Johnson might have gone further, in fact, in asserting the relevance of such an approach to the Septuagint more generally (227–28).

This study provides a good resource for those engaged in text- or narrative-critical examinations of these narratives. Johnson offers a detailed analysis of these chapters, and in general the varied dynamics of the Greek and Hebrew are handled ably. The discursive, verse-by-verse commentary style of his presentation may lend itself best to consultation on specific verses or pericopes, though the summaries of themes and special emphases of the Greek edition in chapters 2–4 are helpfully synthetic. One might also read the comparative chapter 5 first, then explore points of interest in Johnson's earlier, close readings of the Greek.

Something I would have liked to have seen in Johnson's literary study is formal reflection on his narrative poetics or explicit methodological engagement with the work of biblical (or other) narrative critics. Although Johnson notes that his is a "close literary reading" (e.g., 13–14, 17), Johnson does not unpack this much, beyond citing Robert Alter's brief definition of "literary analysis" (15). Johnson accesses the work of Alter, David Gunn, Adele Berlin, Meir Sternberg, Shimon Bar-Efrat, Yairah Amit, and others in the course of his readings and exhibits literary sensitivity in his critique, but some conscious reflection on the poetics of these or other critics at the outset may have tightened things up a bit. When Johnson mentions "the narrator," for instance, whom does he have in mind: Alter and Sternberg's perfectly reliable and authoritative narrator or a kind of character-narrator whose perspectives and views may emerge under interrogation, as in the work of Gunn or Alice Bach? Further who is "the reader" here? Johnson mostly adopts the scholarly first-person plural or speaks of "the reader" in the third person (43), but this particular reader resists always being taken along in this way. On a related note, some brief but deliberate reflection on the bounds of the study would have been welcome. Given its title, it comes as something of a surprise that Johnson's reading encompasses not only 1 Sam/1 Kgdms 17, where David takes on Goliath, but chapters 16 and 18 as well. The justification for including this material should probably have been unpacked in the body of the introduction rather than consigned to a brief note (13 n. 50; though see 22).

These remarks aside, this monograph may be recommended as a conversation partner for those engaged in close work with either or both of these variant literary editions.

LATTER PROPHETS

Zechariah and His Visions: An Exegetical Study of Zechariah's Vision Report, by Lena-Sofia Tiemeyer. The Library of Hebrew Bible/Old Testament Studies 605. London/New York: Bloomsbury, 2015. Pp. xvii + 305. Hardcover. $120.00. ISBN 9780567658555.

Albert M. Wolters, Mount Hope, Ontario, Canada

This latest monograph by Lena-Sofia Tiemeyer, Senior Lecturer in Hebrew Bible at the University of Aberdeen, elaborates on themes already adumbrated in a number of her earlier publications on Zechariah, focusing especially on the question: How real were Zechariah's visions? Did he actually have visual and auditory experiences like those described in the eight "night visions" of Zech 1–6, or are the latter simply literary creations based on similar accounts found elsewhere? Essentially, Tiemeyer argues that this is a false dilemma: it is plausible to conclude that Zechariah's vision accounts are based on authentic experiences, but this conclusion does not rule out the possibility that these accounts were also shaped by the traditions and interpretations that were current in the prophet's religious environment.

Tiemeyer distinguishes between what she calls the "vision report," which includes all of the eight night visions, and the "vision account" of each vision individually. These vision accounts are also to be distinguished from the nonvisionary "oracles" that occasionally interrupt the vision cycle. The present volume focuses on the visions themselves, as distinct from the oracles. Another volume is promised in which Tiemeyer will focus on the oracles and their relationship to the vision accounts. In her view, the latter constitute the basic textual layer of Zech 1–6, whereas the oracles are later additions (279–80).

Drawing on a wide array of primary and secondary literature, Tiemeyer discusses the visions in twelve well-documented chapters, the first four of which are of a broadly context-setting nature, while the remaining eight deal with each of the night visions in turn and interact in detail with the scholarly literature on the main exegetical issues. The result, as Tiemeyer herself puts it, is that her work "falls between a monograph and a commentary" (4).

Prefaced to the twelve chapters is a section called "Preliminary Matters," in which the author gives an overview of the book as a whole and stresses the point that visions, by their nature, are *polyvalent*; that is, they lend themselves to multiple interpretations.

Chapter 1, "Dreams and Visions in the Hebrew Bible," makes the point that in the biblical material dreams and visions are often not distinguished at all and can be interpreted in similar ways. In chapter 2, "Dreams and Visions in Ancient Near Eastern Texts," Tiemeyer deals with the relevant comparative material, specifically as found in the Mari letters, various Neo-Assyrian and Ugaritic texts, and the Balaamite inscription of Deir 'Alla. She concludes that they generally did not make a clear-cut distinction between dreams and visions either.

Chapter 3, "Visions and Culture," explores the relationship between what is seen in a vision or dream and the shared assumptions and expectations of the culture to which the visionary or dreamer belongs. Here Tiemeyer includes in her discussion many postbiblical mystical accounts, Jewish and otherwise. Rather provocatively, she here defends the pointed aphorism that "we see what we expect to see."

The last of the programmatic first four chapters has the somewhat misleading title "The Structure of Zechariah's Vision Report." The word *structure* here does not refer to the chiastic pattern that many interpreters discern in the vision report (surprisingly, Tiemeyer never discusses this) but rather to the three levels that she believes can be distinguished within it: level I (where the prophet reports what he sees), level II (where the prophet and the "interpreting angel" have their dialogue), and level III (where the "visionary world" is revealed that Zechariah and the angel see, discuss, and occasionally enter). Tiemeyer equates these levels with distinct levels (or "states") of consciousness and argues that the verb יצא, which occurs frequently in the vision accounts, refers to a transition from level II to level III or vice versa.

In the remaining eight chapters, which deal in detail with the exegesis of each of the individual night visions, Tiemeyer follows a standard format: an opening section, entitled "The Interplay between Image and Speech," explores the relationship within the vision accounts between the pictures that the prophet sees and the words that he hears. (In chapter 8 this section is prefaced by a brief discussion of "the unique character of Zechariah 3," while in chapter 11 it is omitted altogether.) This opening section is followed by the body of the chapter, entitled "Exegetical Issues," while a concluding section of the chapter deals with the "message" of the vision in question. It should be noted, however, that this "message" component does not seek to articulate the basic religious point or kerygmatic thrust of the relevant periscope but simply draws together the various strands of the foregoing exegetical argument.

It is not possible within the confines of this review to summarize the very rich and detailed exegetical discussion that these chapters contain. I will simply highlight a few of the more unusual and provocative proposals that Tiemeyer puts forward. Many of these have to do with her basic point that we cannot expect visions and dreams to be realistic.

Re vision 1: the words of 1:11 are spoken by the horses themselves, not by their presumed riders (80). Furthermore, Tiemeyer gives the phrase במצלה of 1:8 the unusual meaning "at dusk" (73, 247) and combines this with her view that the vision cycle began at nightfall and ended at daybreak (72–73). On page 84, however, she inadvertently reverts to the more traditional rendering of במצלה

as "in a shady place." Re vision 2: Tiemeyer argues for a conjectural emendation that removes much of 2:4 (102). Re vision 3: the measuring line of the surveyor describes the same object as Ezekiel's measuring reed (108). Re vision 4: this account may be both an integral part of the vision cycle and a secondary addition by Zechariah himself (117). Re vision 5: the two olive trees do not stand alongside the menorah but rather hover above it (154, 178, 180, 184). Re vision 6: the dimensions of the flying scroll (10 by 20 cubits), apply not to the scroll itself, but (as Freeman has suggested) to a column of writing in this scroll, imagined to be partially unrolled (190–91). Re vision 7: its message is simultaneously about social justice and idolatry. Re vision 8: the horses that normally pull a chariot are here depicted as being *inside* the chariot.

Tiemeyer's work as a whole is impressive, both as regards the enormous amount of literature that she draws on and interacts with and as regards the many fresh and provocative proposals she puts forward. All subsequent commentators on Zechariah will have to reckon with it. In my opinion, she is essentially right about her main point, that it is plausible and fruitful to treat the night visions as based on genuine experiences and that this assumption does not preclude an element of literary and interpretative shaping. In my judgment, she is also right in stressing the inherent polyvalence of visions.

But many of Tiemeyer's proposals are likely to be met by a skeptical reaction. Should all dreams and visions, whether "mystical" or otherwise, as well as all manner of trances and hallucinations, really be treated as essentially the same kind of phenomenon? Should we really distinguish between levels II and III in the vision accounts, and if so, can these levels really be equated with levels of *consciousness*? Should we really understand the eighth vision as picturing the horses as being *inside* the chariots rather than attached to them?

One point that I found particularly confusing was Tiemeyer's use of the terms *oracle* and *oracular material*. Sometimes these terms refer to the nonvisionary sections in Zech 1–6, which she promises to treat in a subsequent volume (4, 7–11, 93, 103, etc.), but very often they also refer to the divine speech that is reported as part of the visions, what is *heard* as distinct from what is *seen* (58, 85, 113, 118, etc.).

Unfortunately, the book also contains quite a few minor philological errors. Mistakes are made in translating Greek (17, 83, 211, 237) as well as German (97, 107, 155, 163, 185, 197, 252, 261). As for Hebrew, there is the curious mistranslation of (5:2) חבל מדה as "measuring stick" (108, 110, 112, etc.). Here and there Tiemeyer also contradicts herself, as when she translates (3:9) ומשתי את as "will depart with" in one place (144) but as "will remove" in another (216), or when she first translates (5:7) ככר as "disc" (226) but later as "talent" (238). An especially bizarre mistake occurs on page 250, where she misreads the initial letter of the adjective ברדים ("dappled") in 6:3 as the preposition ב. But these minor philological blemishes should not be allowed to obscure the really original and creative contribution that Tiemeyer has made to the study of the night visions of Zechariah. Overall, it is a very solid addition to the exegetical literature.

Egypt as a Monster in the Book of Ezekiel, by Safwat Marzouk. Forschungen zum Alten Testament 2/76. Tübingen: Mohr Siebeck, 2015. Pp. xvi + 289. Paper. €79.00. ISBN 9783161532450.

Amy Kalmanofsky, The Jewish Theological Seminary

Monsters must be taken seriously. They haunt all forms of popular media, shape the rhetoric of political discourse, and lurk within many religious narratives and foundational myths, including the Hebrew Bible. Monsters certainly terrify and entertain. They also adhere closely to the etymology of the word *monster*: they reveal or show (*monstrare*) deep-seated fears and anxieties, and they warn (*monere*) against real and perceived threats. This is what makes them powerful religious symbols.

In a revised version of his dissertation, Safwat Marzouk examines the motif of the monstrification of Egypt in the book of Ezekiel. Expertly combining contemporary horror theory with historical-critical and close textual analyses, Marzouk considers the components that constitute and characterize the portrayal of Egypt as a monster in the book of Ezekiel. He addresses Ezekiel's unique portrayal of Egypt and asks "why the imagery of a monster in particular seems to be appropriate for Egypt" (3). Marzouk's intriguing thesis is that Ezekiel's Egypt is constructed as a distorted image of Israel's self, a monstrous double, which reflects Israel's fears of losing its unique identity, defined by its relationship with YHWH, and therefore warns against religious assimilation. Egypt, argues Marzouk, "symbolizes religious chaos in which Israel loses its distinctive identity" and, as a monster, "represents transgression of religious boundaries" (3).

In chapter 1, "History of Scholarship: Egypt as a Monster in the Book of Ezekiel in Light of the Exodus Tradition and the Historio-Political Context of the Sixth Century BCE" (15–44), Marzouk provides an overview of the scholarship related to the monstrification of Egypt broadly within the Bible and specifically within the context of Ezekiel. He situates Egypt as monster within the context of the *Chaoskampf* motif and considers whether Ezekiel portrays Egypt as a monster because of the memory of Egypt's oppression of Israel and of YHWH's salvation of Israel at the parting of the sea, as the prophet Isaiah does in Isa 51:9–10. Marzouk concludes that Ezekiel portrays Egypt as a monster not because of the memory of oppression but rather "because Egypt posed and continues to pose a threat to the boundaries that constitute Israelite identity" (29). A Judean-Egyptian alliance against Babylon, attested in biblical and extrabiblical sources, *partly* explains the monstrification of Egypt, since Ezekiel viewed the Babylonian exile as a judgment from YHWH. An alliance against Babylon therefore would be seen as a rebellion against YHWH. Marzouk perceptively adds to the historical-political contexts and concludes that Egypt becomes for Ezekiel a monstrous symbol of idolatry that reflects Israel's susceptibility to apostasy and that works to strengthen Israel's identity in contrast to Egypt (37).

Chapter 2, "Monster Theory" (45–69), offers a comprehensive and clear overview of monster theory. Marzouk pays particular attention to the work of

Michel Foucault, René Girard, and Julia Kristeva, which informs his conception of Egypt as a monster. Marzouk defines monsters as hybrid, interstitial creatures that inhabit the borders between "*double* and *Other, same* and *different, Heimlich* and *unheimlich*" (47). According to Marzouk, a monster's "difference" is expressed mainly through its deformed, abnormal, or grotesque body. The transgressive monstrous body, which breaches and threatens the perceived laws of nature, must be punished. Its punishment testifies to the power of the normative (55–56) and warns against transgression. The punished monster's body also stands for that which exists just outside the normative—a monstrous reflection of it—and that which must be rejected in order to maintain the normative. Using Kristeva's language, Marzouk considers the monster to be abject; he writes: "The monstrous and the abject suffer the drastic association with utter Otherness, yet they are not a complete Other, because prior to the initiation of abjection they were part of an imaginary union with the self" (65–66). In order to maintain order, abject monsters must be contained, but, Marzouk contends, they can never totally be destroyed. Abject monsters hover between sameness and otherness, chaos and order. Rejected from the normative and ordered world, they help to define its borders, while threatening to break through them.

Chapter 3, "*Chaoskampf* in the Ancient Near East" (70–114), brings to bear the monster theory outlined in the previous chapter onto the figure of the monster attested in the *Chaoskampf* motif found throughout ancient Near Eastern literature. Marzouk offers a more nuanced perspective on the typically understood oppositional relationship between order and chaos and the gods that represent them, noting that "keen analysis of literary works on chaos and order reveal another layer of relationship between the two poles, that of a shared aspects of a common identity" (85). He perceives a "complexity in the relation between the gods and the monster gods" (90) and suggests that monster gods, who represent chaos, "embody otherness within sameness" (93). The gods of order defeat the monster gods and dismember their bodies, thereby turning the monstrous bodies into sites of inscription that communicate a threefold message of the sovereignty of the patron god, the weakness of chaos, and the consequences inflicted on those who rebel against the established order (112).

Chapter 4, "Egypt as a Monstrous Double in Ezekiel 20 and 23" (115–53), argues that "Ezekiel portrays Egypt as a monster because Egypt represents the threat of religious assimilation" (117). Egypt, as Israel's monstrous double, "threatens the order of Israel's relation with YHWH" (117). Marzouk claims that Ezekiel establishes a commonality between Israel and Egypt by using similar terminology to describe them and by associating both with the sin of idolatry and with its associated impurity. Israel also shares a history with Egypt. In Ezek 23 the prophet portrays Jerusalem and Samaria as lascivious women whose first illicit sexual relationship was with Egypt before marrying YHWH. Marzouk contends that, for Ezekiel, "the constitution of Israel as a nation took place in Egypt while Israel is engulfed in the chaos of idolatrous practices" (147). The unique relationship between Israel and Egypt, their shared history and the common elements of identity, make Egypt Israel's monstrous double (153). Egypt represents the religious chaos out of which Israel emerges and to which Israel easily could return.

Chapter 5, "Egypt as Abject: Embodying Egypt as a Monster and the Dismemberment of Its Body" (154–201), shows how Ezekiel ascribes to Egypt an abject monstrous body and how YHWH will dismember and defeat this monster. Ezekiel "describes the body of Egypt as an excessive entity" that "transgresses the norms" (171). Egypt has a large phallus (Ezek 16:26) that issues liquid like a horse (Ezek 23:20). Marzouk posits that the "amalgamation of a human being with animalized sexual characteristics creates a *grotestque* image" (172). Ezekiel also addresses Pharaoh as the sea monster Tannin, who lies in the Nile and perpetuates chaos. In this way Marzouk draws an interesting distinction between Ezekiel's description of Pharaoh as monster and the prophet's description of Egypt as a monstrous body. Both need to be contained and defeated in order to protect Israel's distinct identity and its relationship with God. YHWH hunts and publicly dismembers monster Pharaoh (Ezek 29:4; 32:4–5). YHWH also defeats the "body politic" of Egypt by drying up the Nile, and turning Egypt into a desolation (Ezek 29:9–10). Marzouk claims that Egypt's defeat affirms YHWH's cosmological power and serves as a warning to those who would challenge it. Above all, Egypt "becomes a repugnant and repulsive abject" (200) through which Ezekiel sets Israel apart from Egypt.

In chapter 6, "Putting the Monster under Check: Geopolitical Minimization of Egypt (Ezek 29:12–16) and Pharaoh's Descent into Sheol (Ezek 32:17–32)" (202–37), Marzouk observes how YHWH defeats but does not destroy Egypt. YHWH relegates Egypt to its proper place in Sheol among the uncircumcised and restores Israel to its land, thereby establishing a clear boundary between Israel and Egypt, between life and death, and between purity and impurity. Notably, monstrous Egypt is contained but not obliterated. Egypt continues to exist on the periphery of the known and ordered world and could make its way back into that world. As Marzouk observes, of the seven nations condemned in Ezek 25–32, "Egypt is the only nation that is promised a return from the exile and a continuing existence" (203). Marzouk asserts that Israel needs Egypt to continue to exist because Israel needs an "Other against which it can reconstruct its identity" (204). He concludes: "Having Egypt at the periphery and restoring Israel to be at the center of the earth enables the Israelite community to formulate its identity over against the excluded monster that is Egypt. However, the fact that the monster is not completely annihilated but rather put under check testifies to the vulnerability of the cosmos and the ordered world" (237). Likewise, the continued existence of Egypt testifies to the vulnerability of Israel. Most likely, Israel will face its monstrous double again, yet the continued but contained existence of monstrous Egypt ensures that it will have the strength to do so.

Overall, I found Marzouk's study to be comprehensive and illuminating. I have done a fair amount of work on monsters and have applied monster theory to biblical texts. Marzouk's thorough application of the theory and his attention to historical context and textual expression convinced me that this remains a fertile field of study. I imagine scholars interested in monsters and monster theory from a variety of disciplines will find this book useful. Not only does it provide a clear overview of the theory, but it also offers an excellent model for how to apply contemporary theory to an ancient text without it appearing forced or anachronistic. I particularly appreciate Marzouk's definition of monsters and his emphasis on their "sameness" as opposed to their "otherness." As Marzouk himself notes, this is an important corrective to a rhetoric that often is used politically or religiously to construct and alienate an other. In this important study, Marzouk reminds us how much we need monsters in order to define ourselves and how much monsters are more like us than we care to admit. Recognizing an affinity with monsters may terrify some readers, but for Marzouk this realization is "an invitation for us to see how our identities should not necessarily be constructed in opposition to the Other but in dialogue and out of our need for the Other, so that we may put an end to the cycle of violence" (244).

Maleachi, ein Hermeneut, by Jutta Noetzel. Beihefte zur Zeitschrift für die alttestamentliche Wissenschaft 467. Berlin: de Gruyter, 2015. Pp. x + 352. Hardcover. €99.95. ISBN 9783110372694.

Thomas Hieke, Johannes Gutenberg-Universität Mainz

Interestingly enough, this book starts with a picture. Jutta Noetzel introduces her work with a full-color reproduction of Paul Klee's painting *Angelus novus* (1920/32; now in the Israel Museum, Jerusalem; see Wikipedia). Although Malachi is not Klee's *Angelus novus*, the elusive drawing with watercolor and oil pastel illustrates the hermeneutical function of "Malachi." Malachi appears as a historical prophet and is received as such in Sir 49:10 and the passage related to him in the pseudepigraphic *Vitae prophetarum*. However, although "Malachi" transmits the "word of the Lord" (Mal 1:1), the figure is *not* a prophet in the historical or conventional sense. The "messenger" reestablishes the connection between the "sender" Yahweh and the "sons of Levi" and thus introduces a completely new kind of prophecy. The historical "prophet" or author of the prophetic writing entirely vanishes and no longer has an identifiable shape—the *new messenger* (Latin: *angelus novus*!) no longer communicates a new piece of divine revelation that he originally received from God in an individual vision. The *new messenger* has a hermeneutical function and becomes the mediator, interpreter, or exegete of the new medium of revelation: the written Torah. In the words of Jutta Noetzel: "Der Bote ist nicht mehr Offenbarungsmittler, sondern Hermeneut der am Sinai ergangenen, schriftlich fixierten und anerkannten Offenbarung" (see 5).

Here lies the basic hypothesis of Jutta Noetzel's dissertation. She wrote this fine book under the supervision of Arndt Meinhold, Uwe Becker, and Ernst-Joachim Waschke. Its German title, "Maleachi, ein Hermeneut," is difficult to grasp even for a German-speaking audience. The very unusual term *Hermeneut* provokes a longer process of reflection and is thus consistent with the disturbing otherness of the book of Malachi. As several scholars have already stated before, the kind of prophecy articulated in this last writing of the Twelve Prophets follows a new understanding. *Prophecy* becomes application and interpretation of the Torah. According to Noetzel, this idea is the basic core of the writing and the organizing principle in the formation of the book. After reading the first five pages of the book (ch. 1.1), one understands what the term *Hermeneut* stands for and in which way the writing (!) of Malachi represents an *angelus novus*.

After that very helpful introduction, Noetzel proceeds rather conventionally by unfolding the outline and method of her study. The basic approach follows a synchronic line, using text-critical, linguistic, and intertextual tools in order to interpret the final form of the text. Many intertextual indicators point to an intensive relationship of the Malachi text to the Jacob tradition in the book of Genesis and to passages in Deuteronomy. From the intertextual viewpoint, one necessarily turns to questions of the canon, hence Noetzel dedicates a shorter chapter (ch. 5) to the issues of the epilogue (Mal 3:22–24 [Eng. 4:4–6]), the embedding of the epilogue and the entire writing within the *corpus propheticum*, the Tanak, and the Septuagint. According to Noetzel, one can clearly see that "Malachi" is not an original unity but rather an edited text. Thus, she also applies diachronic methods and in chapter 6 adds a redaction-critical proposal for the origin of the writing of Malachi. By the way, following a recent convention that this reviewer adopts as well, Noetzel does not call Malachi a "book" (*Buch*) but reserves this term for the Book of the Twelve, while the twelve single parts of this book are labeled "writings" (hence: *Maleachischrift*). The last part of the introduction (ch. 1.3) summarizes the results of the research on Malachi within the last thirty years (thirteen pages).

Chapters 2 and 3 focus on the broader picture. In chapter 2 Noetzel tries to draw an outline of the understanding of prophecy within the Book of the Twelve. She uses the occurrences of the Hebrew term נָבִיא as a point of departure. In the struggle of competences between priests and prophets, it becomes clear that in the end Moses appears as the prototype of the נָבִיא: all types of prophecy must in some way or other relate back to Moses. Noetzel convincingly demonstrates that in the final form of the Book of the Twelve all prophets who are called נָבִיא (Habakkuk, Haggai, Zechariah, and, implicitly, Amos) stand in the *successio mosaica* and proffer the heritage of Moses. However, this kind of prophecy comes to an end in Zech 13; hence, the following Malachi is no longer a נָבִיא. Thus, chapter 3 considers the writing as a whole and identifies the overall concept by discussing the heading (Mal 1:1), the question of genre, and the inner structure of the entire composition.

The bulk of Noetzel's study is dedicated to a detailed analysis of the six discussion speeches (ch. 4: 81–239). This part more or less resembles a normal commentary. Noetzel presents her own German translation with text-critical notes (especially referring to the Septuagint version). She structures each unit according to formal criteria and identifies the usual patterns such as *inclusio*. Then she turns to the question of meaning and offers suggestions for the interpretation of the content of each unit. Depending on the length of the discussion speech, at times Noetzel introduces subsections for the interpretation of single verses and motifs. For each discussion speech the concluding paragraph analyzes the position of the unit within the entire writing; that is, the function of the section for the whole and its relationship to the other discussion speeches are clarified.

As already noted, the epilogue is treated in a separate chapter (ch. 5) that nevertheless applies the same steps: text, structure, meaning, position. The subsection "position" discusses the function of the final three verses for the entire *corpus propheticum*. Noetzel carefully differentiates between the Tanak and the Septuagint. The Septuagint changes the sequence and places Mal 3:22 (Eng. 4:4; LXX 3:24) last: "Remember the law of Moyses my slave, as I commanded him at Choreb with ordinances and statutes for all Israel" (NETS). According to Noetzel, it is not necessary to apply a diachronic explanation for this transition; rather, the change is required by the differing canonical sequence of the Septuagint. As the book of Isaiah (Esaias) follows the Dodekapropheton, the transition from Malachias to Esaias needs to be adapted: the announcement of eschatological return of Elias the Thesbite cannot be followed by the appearance of Esaias; hence Elias becomes the herald of the day of the Lord, and the admonition to remember and obey the law of Moyses becomes the final criterion for curse and blessing at the day of the Lord and thus the final verse of the Dodekapropheton in the Septuagint.

Chapter 6 presents a suggestion for the diachronic formation of the writing of Malachi. Noetzel expressly states that she understands her redaction-critical hypothesis as a "glass bead game" (*Glasperlenspiel*) with no claim of historical truth. It is only the search for the idea that might have led the authors to pin down (and pen) their "active reading," that is, how they received texts and developed them further. After presenting the *status quaestionis* on the literary growth of Malachi within the formation of the Book of the Twelve, she summarizes the source-critical evidence for different layers or stages of origin of various verses. Noetzel's own model consists of a *Grundschicht* that was enhanced by two layers of active readings. In order to illustrate her hypothesis about the formation of Malachi, she presents a chart on pages 287–93: the *Grundschicht* and the two enhancing layers are subsequently indented. For example: The first discussion speech (Mal 1:2–5) belongs to the second active reading, hence it is indented by about two centimeters. The first verses of the second discussion speech are the beginning of the *Grundschicht* (hence 1:6, 7b, 8 start on the left margin), while 1:7a, 9a are first additions (active reading I) and thus indented by about one centimeter. Although one gets a fine impression about the wording and contents of the *Grundschicht* and the subsequent additions and thus about Noetzel's idea about the growth of the writing, the layered display of the German translation has a different effect on the reviewer: for me, the diachronic model is not convincing. The attempt to read the *Grundschicht* as a text of its own without the additions does not provide a coherent whole. Especially Mal 1:6 does not work as an appropriate beginning (according to my view). Maybe the diachronic suggestion is the weakest part in Noetzel's study, and she was well advised not to base her interpretation on it. On the contrary, it was wise to put the redaction-critical model as a mere suggestion at the end, marking carefully the hypothetical character of the endeavor, and to start the overall interpretation of Malachi from the final form of the text. However, one should not overlook a very helpful feature of the chart with the layered translation: in the column on the right-hand side, for each verse many verse references to other texts of the Tanak are listed. These references are used in the redaction-critical argumentation; however, they also provide a fine resource for further intertextual studies.

The final chapter (ch. 7) summarizes the convincing hypothesis of Noetzel's work: prophecy as exegesis (*Prophetie als Schriftauslegung*). Malachi, the "messenger," is an *angelus novus*, not a conventional prophetic figure. The messenger has no shape (if he were to take on a certain shape or appearance, he would be fallible and contingent). Thus, the messenger is a hermeneutical function, the interpretation of the revelation—revealed in the past, fixed in writing, and authorized by the divine, a revelation for the present according to the divine will. After the end of conventional prophecy (Zech 13), legitimate prophecy consists of Torah exegesis. Deuteronomy 17–18 and Mal 2:4–8 share the same basic idea of "prophecy as interpretation of scripture" (Torah). Thus Malachi becomes a programmatic manifesto regarding revelation and the transmission of revelation: the exegete of scripture takes over the task of the former prophet. The messenger becomes the interpreter (*Hermeneut*) of the written Torah, which itself becomes the new medium of revelation. Several figures can slip into the role of the messenger: Moses (the prototype), Elijah (Mal 3:23 [Eng. 4:5]), the priest (Mal 2:7). The new understanding of prophecy is accompanied by a new understanding of religion: the writing of Malachi shows a tendency to the phenomenon of a secondary religion (Theo Sundermeier) or universal religion. The cult at the temple of Jerusalem becomes less important for a universally conceived Judaism, while "Yahweh Sabaoth" becomes the universal king of the entire world. Becoming a follower of this unique God is the decision of the individual; getting closer to the salvific presence of this deity is no longer limited to the participation in the centralized cult in Jerusalem; the criterion for salvation is the normativity of the written revelation in the Torah (see 303). Thus, in the end everything becomes Torah, even the Psalms and the Prophets.

Noetzel's diachronic view of Malachi will remain a controversial point, but this discussion should not detract from the valuable insights gained by her synchronic analysis of the final form of Malachi. Her understanding of Malachi as a cipher or code for a new understanding of prophecy (prophecy as exegesis, the messenger as interpreter, *Hermeneut*, of the written Torah) is a convincing approach. It explains in a plausible way the characteristics of the last unit in the Book of the Twelve and pays full attention to the canon-hermeneutical function of this part of the Hebrew Bible. Hence, Noetzel's contribution is not only essential for those scholars interested in the Book of the Twelve and its single parts but also important for the religio-historical development of the idea of canon and the understanding of the concept of scripture.

Zechariah, by Al Wolters. Historical Commentary on the Old Testament. Leuven: Peeters, 2014. Pp. li + 475. Paper. €74.00. ISBN 9789042930074.

Anthony R. Petterson, Morling College

This impressive commentary on the book of Zechariah, with which Wolters was engaged for more than twenty years, breaks new ground. It is the eighteenth volume released in the HCOT (Historical Commentary on the Old Testament) series by Peeters, whose contributors are largely from the Netherlands or South Africa. Wolters hails from the Netherlands but has taught for many years at Redeemer University College, Ontario, Canada.

In the introduction Wolters explains that his commentary has four foci of interest: philological aspects of the text; the history of interpretation (as the title of the series indicates); intertextuality; and Christian theological interpretation (3). I will return to comment on Wolters's treatment of each of these.

The introduction also acknowledges the difficulties that the book of Zechariah poses (1–2) and offers a brief historical background to the postexilic period (4–7), a longer discussion of the nature of the Masoretic Text of Zechariah, and an assessment of the character of Zechariah's Hebrew (7–11). The remainder of the introduction is then given to a discussion of the content, genre, structure, and dating of the book, tracking the differing views of these things through the history of interpretation (11–27). As would be expected, a significant section is given to surveying the history of attempts to date Zech 9–14. Wolters distinguishes and traces five broad traditions on dating these chapters since the mid-sixteenth century, identifying some who date parts of these chapters as early as the eighth century BCE, to others who date all of them to the third century. As well as documenting these traditions, Wolters explains the reasons for such views. He concludes the survey by showing how the broad critical consensus has come back to an early postexilic date for these chapters, although many are still hesitant to attribute common authorship for the whole book (21).

Wolters indicates up front that his own view is that the prophet Zechariah is the author of the entire book; this is in keeping with the major interpretative tradition that goes back to rabbinic and patristic times and is consistent with his evangelical Christianity (3). After his survey he concludes that the history of scholarship demonstrates no decisive argument against it (22). In addition, he documents many features of the text that fit well with it (23).

In the introduction Wolters also admits that he has little confidence (and therefore little interest) in diachronic approaches that seek to reconstruct the growth of the Book of the Twelve (including Zechariah): "Whatever editorial shaping these writings may have undergone I consider largely unrecoverable to the modern scholar. Consequently, I do not interact with the many competing theories on offer today" (3).

The book of Zechariah is traditionally divided into two sections (1–8; 9–14). However, Wolters understands the book to have three independent sections: Zechariah A (1:1–6:15); Zechariah B (7:1–8:23); and Zechariah C (9:1–14:21).

Zechariah A contains an initial warning (1:1–6), eight night visions and episodes (1:6–6:8), and the crowning of Joshua (6:9–15). Wolters thinks it is confusing to designate the nonvisionary parts of Zechariah A as "oracles" (preferring to call them "episodes"), and he welcomes the trend to read them in their canonical context. Yet he still sees these episodes as interrupting the description or interpretation of the visions. He deals with two of them in separate chapters in his commentary (2:10–17 [ET 2:6–13]l 3:8–10). A third episode (4:6b–10a) he deals with as part of the fifth vision (ch. 4), arguing that it is an early insertion by the prophet into the cycle of night visions (117) and marking it in his translation with bold text (110).

Wolters also sees a three-part structure in Zechariah B: a prologue (7:1–3), the fasting sermon (7:4–8:19), and an epilogue (8:20–23). This section contains many verbal links with Haggai, which Wolters enumerates (14–15) and then explains by suggesting that Haggai's prophecies had been written down early so that Zechariah "was intimately acquainted with his fellow prophet's messages" (16). While many commentators closely link Zechariah A and Zechariah B, Wolters notes that a significant minority of commentators link Zechariah B with Zechariah C (e.g., Conrad, Sweeney, Webb), but he contends that the differences between these sections are as great as the differences between Zechariah A and Zechariah B and that each section is best treated in its own right.

While most commentators divide Zechariah C into two "oracles" (9:1–11:17; 12:1–14:21), Wolters again divides this section into three, seeing Zech 11 as a central section (comprising the shepherd narrative [11:4–16] framed by two curses [11:1–3, 17]). He finds attempts to determine an overall literary pattern to Zechariah C as unsuccessful (e.g., Lamarche), but at the same time he believes that it is not "a haphazard collection" (253).

Returning to the four foci that Wolters identifies for his work, the first two (philology and history of interpretation) are certainly the dominant features of his commentary, and it is in these areas that he makes his greatest contribution. His proficiency across ancient and modern languages is remarkable and adds a breadth and depth to his research that makes his commentary a standout. He engages a vast literature (the bibliography runs to over forty pages) and regularly includes quotations and translations from German, French, Italian, Swedish, Spanish, Latin, and Dutch (his mother tongue). As well as early interpreters from rabbinic and patristic times (e.g., Jerome), he also interacts with medieval Jewish commentators (e.g., Kimḥi and Rashi), the Reformers (particularly Luther and Calvin), and influential interpreters of the eighteenth and nineteenth centuries (e.g., Delitzsch, Eichhorn, Gesenius, and Wellhausen). Naturally, the majority of interpreters he refers to are from the twentieth and twenty-first centuries. Here Wolters regularly identifies more recent interpreters who thought they were making a new contribution but were really only reviving an interpretation from an earlier time. Ecclesiastes 1:10 seems apt!

In terms of philology, the detailed discussion of the various translations of the Hebrew in a commentary on Zechariah is unparalleled (only the two-volume commentary by Carol and Eric Meyers comes close). In each chapter Wolters provides his own translation based on the Masoretic Text, but in dialogue with the early versions where appropriate. While he is reluctant to depart from "the Masoretic consonantal framework," he feels "free to adopt different word divisions or vocalizations" (10). Wolters regularly challenges traditional lexicographical decisions that lie behind modern translations and either recovers a past reading or provides his own suggestion. It is here that he often breaks new ground (the instances are far too numerous to document and assess in this review). His criticisms and alternative translations seem generally valid and chart a way through often-perplexing interpretative issues, but occasionally his suggestions seem as tenuous as those that he seeks to overturn. Future Zechariah scholarship will have to engage with his proposals.

Concerning the other foci of his commentary, intertextuality is certainly a feature, but Wolters does not make explicit his methodology for determining Zechariah's use of earlier scripture. An example of the way that he brings intertextuality to bear is with his translation of Zech 10:7, "and they will see their children," which is usually translated with the children as the subject: "and their children will see (it)" (so KJV, JPS, NAB, NIV, NRSV, NLT). Wolters argues for an intertextual link with Gen 50:23, which guides his translation, where "Joseph saw Ephraim's children of the third generation" (NRSV). He says: "Since the present pericope is about Joseph (vs 6) and Ephraim (vs 7), the reference to 'seeing their children' is no doubt an allusion that other passage about Joseph and Ephraim" (330). But intertextuality can be notoriously subjective. My question simply concerns the methodology that leaves "no doubt" about an allusion.

While Christian theological interpretation is present in the commentary, it is difficult to see that it is a focus. This is perhaps surprising, given some of Wolters's other writings. I counted only about a dozen instances when brief comments were made about the use of Zechariah in the New Testament. I would have appreciated Wolters's more developed thoughts on how the book is taken up in the New Testament and contributes to Christian theology, particularly Zechariah's presentation of a suffering messiah, but this may have been outside the scope of the series. As an aside on this note, a deficiency of the series is the lack of indices to track these kinds of things.

Some chapters of Zechariah receive much more detailed treatment than others (Zech 4's fourteen verses received forty-five pages; Zech 14's twenty-one verses received twenty-four pages). This is probably because Wolters offers such a radically different translation of Zech 4, which required a longer treatment. However, some significant words and phrases were passed over in Zech 14 (e.g., vv. 1, 2, 7, 9, 11). Still, Wolters gives us far more on Zech 14 than Luther did in his first commentary, whom he cites as saying: "Here in this chapter I give up. For I am not sure what the prophet is talking about" (452).

This is a very important commentary on Zechariah with a focus on philology and the history of interpretation that is almost unparalleled. Wolters has done a great service in bringing so much useful material together and charting a way

through it. Future researchers and translators of Zechariah will have to engage
Wolters's many translation and exegetical proposals.

The Prophets Speak on Forced Migration, edited by Mark J. Boda, Frank Ritchel
Ames, John Ahn, and Mark Leuchter. Ancient Israel and Its Literature 21. Atlanta:
SBL Press, 2015. Pp. xii + 224. Paper. $34.95. ISBN 9781628370515. Hardcover.
$49.95. ISBN 9781628370539.

James S. Lee, International Theological Seminary

This volume is a collection of selected papers presented by the Exile-Forced
Migrations Group in the 2009 SBL Annual Meeting. It is a sequel to *By the
Irrigation Canals of Babylon: Methods in the Study of the Exile*, which was published in 2012. In keeping with the same methodological approach from the
first volume, the current book seeks to address the theme of forced migrations
in exilic prophetic literature (Deutero-Isaiah, Jeremiah, Ezekiel, Zechariah)
through sociological, literary, and theological lenses. The editors explain that
the presenters represent North American and European perspectives, as in the
previous volume, in an effort to bridge scholars from the two continents (1).
I would imagine the inclusion of perspectives from other continents, such as
Asia, Africa, and Latin America, would have enriched the conversation, as these
continents have been affected by forced migrations and displacements as much
as Europe and North America, if not more. Exile is an important subject in postcolonial readings of the Hebrew Bible. Voices from minority groups who have
suffered the plight or are familiar with it may have proven insightful to the interested audience.

David L. Petersen, in "Prophetic Rhetoric and Exile," defines exile in three
different forms: forced migrations, voluntary migration, and incarceration. Upon
the examination of historical evidence, he sees that the exile of Judahites carried
by the Neo-Babylonians was much smaller in scale than the one by the Neo-
Assyrians; the Neo-Babylonians were more focused on tribute and taking booty
during Nebuchadnezzar's military campaigns. Petersen argues that the prophetic
rhetoric regarding the Neo-Babylonian exile as found in Jeremiah and Ezekiel
was shaped by the exilic experience under the Neo-Assyrians as well as the Neo-
Babylonians, thereby hinting at the evolution of exile as a literary trope already
attested in the exilic prophetic literature.

Christopher R. Seitz's "Provenance as a Factor in Interpretation" explores the
canonical logic behind the book of Isaiah, with particular attention to Isa 40–55,
whose provenance has been often attributed to the Babylonian exile. Instead of
addressing the issue of the provenance of the chapters on literary, historical, and
form-critical grounds, he questions the adequacy of "second exodus" typology
as an attempt to extricate Isa 40–55 from the preceding and following chapters.
Contrary to this typology, Third Isaiah does not end on a high note of entry to the
promised land. Instead, it lapses into sin and disobedience. Thus, Seitz argues for

the foregrounding of Zion as the central locus of scattering and returning for the entire book.

Ulrich Berges discusses the identity of the Servant in Isa 40–55 in "You Are My Witnesses and My Servant (Isa 43:10): Exile and the Identity of the Servant." He argues for deported Jerusalem temple singers as the authorial group for the writing. The group's prophetic claim is akin to Chronicles' characterization of the liturgical singing of the sons of Asaph as prophetic (1 Chr 25:2, 3). The projection of the group's collective experience into the singular figure of the Servant is a technique also found in the character of Job and the suffering person of Lam 3. The group believed itself to be the true Israel in its search for identity in the midst of exilic crisis. Calling upon its eponymous hero, Jacob/Israel, the group asserts the renewed divine election of Israel.

Stephen Cook's "Second Isaiah and the Aaronide Response to Judah's Forced Migrations" begins with an inquiry into the priestly characteristic of Second Isaiah and an attempt to connect the authorial group of Second Isaiah to the Aaronides, the tradents of the Priestly Torah (PT). Cook sees the concept of the PT's covenant as unilateral and unconditional and sin as a contagious force. Adopting such concepts enables Second Isaiah to cope with Israel's breach of the covenant. The metaphor of husband-redeemer (גאל) is a representative example of God's unconditional love for Israel found in Isa 54. Divine incomparability is another common theological thread Cook sees in the PT and Second Isaiah. The royal imagery of the Israelite community as the legitimate heir to the Davidic line is invoked by Second Isaiah (Isa 55) and through the PT's portrayal of Abraham and Sarah as a royal couple, progenitors of many nations and kings (Gen 17). The ancestral couple is presented as an example and basis of God's eternal covenant with Israel.

Konrad Schmid addresses a seemingly inaccurate and unfulfilled prophecy of Jeremiah regarding Jehoiakim (36:30) in "Nebuchadnezzar, the End of Davidic Rule, and the Exile in the Book of Jeremiah." Jehoiakim Schmid argues for Jer 36:30's dependence on similar prophecies regarding Jehoiakin in 22:18–19 and 22:30. He finds significance in the dating of the prophecy in Jer 36. Jehoiakim's demise and the end of the Davidic monarchy are prophesied in the fourth year of the Judean king and the first year of Nebuchadnezzar. Schmid sees a scribal reasoning regarding God's ordained universal history continuing through Nebuchadnezzar even after the Davidic line. He notices a discrepancy in 27:1 in that the verse dates the first year of Jehoiakim as the beginning of Nebuchadnezzar's world dominion. The dating has to do with the scribe's literal interpretation of the seventy-year prophecy—counting from the first year of Jehoiakim, 609 BCE, to 539 BCE leads to the number 70.

Mark Leuchter explores an "antecedent event" that may have opened the possibility of a new perspective on Mesopotamia as a sacred space in "Sacred Space and Communal Legitimacy in Exile: The Contribution of Seraiah's Colophon (Jer 51:59–64a)." He sees the evidence of the view in Seraiah's colophon, which is affixed to the oracle against Babylon (Jer 50–51). He cites the phrase "this place (המקום הזה)" in verse 62 and claims that the phrase indicates the sacredness of the place (i.e., Babylon). It is not clear to me how he makes the inference. Perhaps there is an intertextual connection he is thinking of. However, it is not explained or clarified in the essay. The comparison of Seraiah's sign-act (public reading of the oracle and deposition of the scroll in the Euphrates) with the ancient practice of depositing sacred texts in a temple is more fruitful and convincing. The subversive function of Seraiah's colophon as a temple foundation inscription affirms both a temporary sanctity of the Euphrates and Mesopotamia and the eventual demise of Babylon. An early version of Jer 1–25 plus the oracle again the nations, in which the colophon is embedded, serves as a prophetic "charter collection" for the exiles of 597.

In "Ezekiel 15: A משל" John Ahn investigates the symbolic nature of a vine branch being burned on both ends and the middle. He argues that the threefold scorching refers to the successive forced migrations the Judahites experienced in 597, 587, and 582 BCE. The literary context of Ezek 15 makes the interpretation likely, as Ezek 17 contains allegorical references to the 597 and 587 destructions of Jerusalem, and Ezek 19:4 echoes the episode of the bandits who assassinated Gedaliah fleeing to Egypt. According to Ahn, Ezek 15 evidences the view that the irreversibility of divine judgment is sealed by the defilement of the land, when the 582 community carries out its proimmigration or integration policy toward foreigners before its exile. Ahn cites Jer 40:9–11 for the possible evidence of such conjecture, which reports the homecoming of Judahites living in Moab, Ammon, Edom, and other surrounding nations. In light of the exiles' open attitude toward the gentiles exemplified in Esther and Daniel, I would think that the earlier generations of the exilic community, which had experienced and known the harsh life of exiles on a foreign soil, would have been more receptive to a peaceful coexistence with other ethnic groups (e.g., Jer 29:4–7).

Corinna Körting in "The Cultic Dimension of Prophecy in the Book of Ezekiel" traces the amalgamation of two distinct traditions, prophetic and cultic, in Ezek 14:1–11. The phrases נשא עון and כרת מן connect Ezek 14 to sacral law in Lev 17. A prophetic exhortation to repent using words such as בוש and בל in Ezek 14 points to the chapter's departure from the cultic tradition and evidences interweaving of a distinct, prophetic tradition. Körting also sees the scene of Israel's elders coming and sitting down before Ezekiel as akin to a cultic situation (Judg 20:26; 21:2), which ends with Ezekiel's priestly warning against defilement. The text attests to the exilic community's self-perception as a cultic community looking for the teaching of torah newly mediated and interpreted by a priestly prophet. It also illustrates an enlarged role of prophet, which includes priestly tasks.

Louis Stulman portrays Ezekiel and YHWH as a traumatized prophet and a traumatized God, respectively, in "Ezekiel as Disaster/Survival Literature: Speaking on Behalf of the Losers." Employing recent studies on trauma, Stulman seeks insights into the experience of the prophet and the book of Ezekiel, which he regards as "literature of resistance" for the exilic community. As a victim of trauma, Ezekiel bears the pain and scars of war and disasters, which is also symbolic of the deprivation of his community. The prophet directs his condemnatory rhetoric toward the fellow victims of the community instead of the perpetrators of violence. Similarly, YHWH vents his anger at Israel rather than Babylon. Nevertheless, hope is found in YHWH belonging together with the community in the liminal place. Against the despair over divine absence in the midst of exile, YHWH promises to return and dwell in the new temple, thereby affirming divine presence even in human suffering.

Frank Ritchel Ames, in "Forced Migration and the Visions of Zechariah 1–8," applies the sociological model of forced migration to study its impact on an exilic Judean community addressed in Zech 1–8. Outlining the consequences of forced migration, Ames lists: (1) the loss of resources such as domicile, land, property, and domestic animals; (2) increased morbidity and mortality; and (3) communities' response to the crisis by becoming more inclusive and inclusive to outsiders. Turning to Zech 1–8, Ames finds the three consequences of forced migration present in the literature. Zechariah's visions contain YHWH's promise to undo the damages done by the exile. The prophet also envisions Jerusalem without walls, where people of many nations will flow (Zech 8:20–23).

Mark J. Boda's "Scat! Exilic Motifs in the Book of Zechariah" is a delineation of exilic motifs found in Zechariah. He understands exile or forced migration to be the movement of a person or population moving away from the ancestral home. He divides the essay into two sections: one on human exile and the other on divine exile. In 2:1–4 (Eng. 1:18–21), he sees the vocabulary such as horns, plowers (farmers), scattering, terrifying, and throwing as the motifs of human exile. In 2:10–13, words such as שלל (to plunder) and נגע (to touch) attest to exile. In prose sermons, echoing the Deuteronomic covenant, terms such as קללה (curse), שמה (desolation), חרפה (reproach), חרב (ruin), and שרקה (object of hissing) appear. As for divine exile, the penultimate vision (5:5–11) records the return of a female divinity called wickedness to the land of Shinar. Zechariah also speaks of YHWH's return to Jerusalem (e.g., 8:3), which indicates the current exilic state of the deity.

I welcome the engaging discussion around the theme of forced migration in this volume. The issue of forced migration is becoming increasingly a pressing concern in the contemporary international community. I hope this timely and important conversation will bring more awareness of the issue to a wider audience and help us appreciate the unique hope that was born out of the similar struggles the Judahites experienced in their displacement.

First Isaiah, by J. J. M. Roberts. Hermeneia. Minneapolis: Fortress, 2015. Pp. 554. Hardcover. $69.00. ISBN 9780800660802.

H. G. M. Williamson, University of Oxford

In his introduction Roberts tells us that he has been "seriously working on this commentary for about thirty-five years." During this time he has published numerous articles on a wide variety of passages within Isa 1–39, so that his basic stance on most fundamental critical issues is already familiar. (I noted only a very occasional modest revision of opinion.) The whole is greater than the sum of its parts, however, so let my first word be to congratulate Roberts on seeing this stupendous task through to completion. Perhaps only those engaged in a similar enterprise are in a position to appreciate what is involved here.

The format of the commentary follows that with which we are by now familiar in the Hermeneia series, save that the introduction is uncharacteristically brief (eight pages). Within that framework, however, Roberts has exercised his freedom to write what is very distinctively his own commentary. I shall try to describe some of its particular features.

As is to be expected, there are more extensive detailed text-critical notes following the translation of each separate passage than in most other standard commentaries. On the whole these represent a careful presentation of relevant textual evidence with generally cautious conclusions. Roberts reports quite fully on the LXX especially and the other versions where relevant when they appear to depart from an expected rendering of the Masoretic Text. He also documents variant readings in the Qumran Scrolls, but in a slightly inconsistent manner. In some passages he restricts himself to commenting on readings indicative of a genuinely different text, whereas in other passages he seems to attempt to document variants fully, even when they represent nothing more than orthographical differences, which are of no text-critical value. Since these are simply listed without comment and since they add nothing to the task of textual criticism (however interesting they may be for other purposes), this strikes me as a distraction at best; the space taken might have been better used.

Needless to say, this kind of detailed work demands the highest degree of accuracy, and for the most part Roberts is to be commended in this regard. There are occasional lapses, however, so that readers will always need to check for themselves if they wish to take any assessment further. At 12:4, for instance, he says that MT has the plural form for "you will say" whereas 1QIsa^a has the singular. "The versions support MT's plural." In fact, LXX translates with a singular form, and it should have been mentioned as well that 4QIsa^e also has the singular. All three early witnesses to the Hebrew text thus agree against MT—an unusually strong combination—so that there are far stronger grounds for emendation here than Roberts (and, indeed, any other commentator) has realized. This detail has important ramifications, in my opinion, for the contested question of the literary unity of chapter 12 as a whole.

As a rule, Roberts is hesitant to accept emendations, though he does so when there are strong grounds in favor, so that his stance is far from biased. Quite often he dismisses proposed emendations on the ground that they do not enjoy versional support: "MT is supported by the versions" is almost a mantra. Given this cautious approach, my jaw would have dropped had I not already been aware of the position from a previously published article when looking at the commentary on 7:8–9. Here, most certainly without any versional or indeed other textual support, Roberts suddenly indulges in a radical reconstruction of the Hebrew text not just in his textual notes but in the main body of the commentary as well. Now, in principle there is nothing wrong with this. We know from all sorts of evidence that occasionally texts could get mangled during the long course of their transmission, and if this happened during the first few centuries of their existence (i.e., before the translation of the LXX) it is obvious that no textual evidence can have survived. In my opinion, a bold conjecture that removes a serious problem in the text and that makes good sense is often preferable to a convoluted attempt to explain the text that we have or something very close to it in a way that amounts to special pleading. So perhaps Roberts is correct in his conjecture (though personally I am not so persuaded that there is a problem here that needs solving in the first place; the usual view that 7:8b is a late gloss is simpler). If so, however, Roberts has clearly undermined his frequent appeal elsewhere to the versions as a means to defend MT against other conjectural emendations. Sound method in textual criticism requires consistency, not an eclectic mix to favor personal preference.

When we come to the commentary proper, several features stand out. First, Roberts is purposefully light on discussion of form and redaction criticism. He often draws attention to such matters in a brief introductory section to each passage, expresses his opinion on authorship and setting there, then proceeds to his exegesis without further engagement with the subject. Second, the exegesis itself does not proceed according to a marked verse-by-verse principle but in a more flowing style, albeit proceeding through the passage in order. Third, in neither section does he refer to or interact much with secondary literature, although the bibliographies at the end of each section indicate his wide reading. Nowadays it is impossible to be fully comprehensive on this, and readers will find some gaps here and there, but he cannot be faulted for ignoring what others have written; on 7:10–17 (the Immanuel passage), for instance, the bibliography is longer than the commentary itself! However, as Roberts explains in his introduction he does not find helpful those commentaries that set out every possible position on a given topic. His preference is to read those other scholars themselves and to focus here on a positive presentation of his own understanding of the text. (His main dialogue partner is Hans Wildberger, but only as indicative of mainstream scholarship; he rarely actually engages with his arguments.) Finally, the particular strength of his approach is its extremely well-informed focus on the historical setting of each section, with attention to its wide ancient Near Eastern context where appropriate. Attention to that sometimes dominates the analysis at the expense of discussion of other matters.

While appreciating the wealth of scholarship on offer as a result, it stands to reason that it depends on agreement with his dating of the material in the first place, and here Roberts is very much more conservative than many other commentators; it is at this point that his failure to engage with alternative points of view is most troubling, for without good arguments to bolster his starting point many may be tempted to dismiss his historical exegesis as resting on an unfounded assumption. He agrees that a few passages must be later than Isaiah's time, notably chapters 13, 24–27, and 34–35, and he also allows that a passage that was written for one setting during Isaiah's lifetime may have been reread in relation to some other later event. He also speculates that Isaiah himself may have moved an oracle for one reason or another to a literary setting other than its original one, so that again there are two historical levels to be considered, albeit both within Isaiah's own lifetime. Nevertheless, given the diversity of opinions on this subject it is sometimes frustrating to find that he defends Isaianic authorship for reasons that elsewhere he uses to criticize those who take a different opinion. At 14:28–32, for instance, he argues at considerable length on the basis of context that the one who "smote you" (Philistia) must be Ahaz, despite the fact that every historical source we have available is silent on such an eventuality and speaks only of the Philistines invading or defeating Judah. To assert that "there is no substantive basis to deny categorically that Ahaz ever smote the Philistines" despite the lack of any single thread of positive evidence is hardly a secure basis on which to proceed as an historian; on such grounds one could rewrite much familiar narrative, and Roberts is justifiably dismissive of attempts to hold less conservative positions on such a foundation.

In terms of the material that he accepts as post-Isaianic, he does not seem to consider that anything is postexilic; the latest date he allows relates to Isa 34–35, which might come from the same author as Isa 40–55. Elsewhere there is some possible confusion, possibly reflecting the length of time this commentary has been in the making. In introducing Isa 24–27 Roberts is engagingly honest when he admits that "for years I vacillated between different dates, frustrated and with little confidence that I had any real grasp of what was going on in these chapters," this because of the lack of firm historical data (a problem indeed for a commentator on a poetic text). However, in the end he settles for a late preexilic date: "late seventh and very early sixth century." In the introduction to Isa 13, moreover, he thinks it probable that that chapter had the same author as 24–27, though he dates Isa 13 to the exilic period, the first half of the sixth century. While the same author could span this period (perhaps as much as fifty years), it seems unlikely, and it remains strange to link two passages from two such radically different political settings.

The commentary is somewhat uneven in terms of the detail of its coverage. It is, of course, a strength not to write about subjects on which the commentator has nothing valuable to say, but sometimes readers may be disappointed if they want to look up some particular detail. Let 4:2–6 serve as an example. Here, in defense of the position that "the original could be Isaianic," he spends most of the commentary discussing the meaning of *tsemach yhwh*, "the sprout of the Lord" (v. 2). Thereafter the whole of the rest of the passage is covered in a single paragraph of thirteen lines despite the wealth of religiously significant material that it includes, much of which would also usually be considered considerably later than the eighth century. This unevenness can also be readily discerned simply by noticing the considerable difference of length of commentary on one passage compared with another.

Finally, in his introduction Roberts states that he writes "unapologetically as a Christian interpreter of the text," so that, when appropriate, he will add some reflection for contemporary Christian believers. My appetite thus whetted, I was not disappointed in the early chapters; there is an extensive reflection of nearly three columns, for instance, on the "swords to ploughshares" passage in 2:2–4. But the inclusion of such reflections soon peters out, and apart from a few lines in the introduction to Isa 36–39 I could not find any after Isa 9 even where it might be expected, such as 11:1–9 or 25:8.

In sum, there is much of great value in the commentary, but it is uneven in terms of the topics on which it focuses. I shall appreciate it highly for what it offers as its distinctive contribution, while, like Roberts himself, I shall go elsewhere to find discussion of the topics that he has chosen to pass over.

Amos: Justice and Violence, by Walter J. Houston. Phoenix Guides to the Old Testament 26. Sheffield: Sheffield Phoenix, 2015. Pp. ix + 112. Paper. £12.95. ISBN 9781909697966.

Karl Möller, University of Cumbria

Houston's volume on Amos is a contribution to the Phoenix Guides to the Old Testament, a series aimed primarily at undergraduates studying the book for the first time in an academic setting. However, as the blurb rightly suggests, more advanced readers will also benefit from Houston's guide.

Following a brief introduction, which includes annotated lists of the most important commentaries available in English as well as of other key sources for the study of Amos, the book divides into three parts. Part 1, the longest, consisting of five chapters, is entitled "Reading Amos." Chapter 1 explores the nature of the book, its genre and style, the book's small units, the presence of poetry and prose, imagery, and wordplay. Unfortunately, and a little confusingly at first, the layout of the headings does little to help readers distinguish between sections and subsections.

The second chapter looks at Amos's structure, beginning with its formulaic series, such as the oracles against the nations (1:3–2:16) and the visions (7:1–8; 8:1–2), which have led to a widely held three-part division (chs. 1–2, 3–6, and 7–9). There is a brief discussion of chiasms and *inclusio*s, with particular consideration of the important chiasm in 5:1–17. The chapter concludes with some general observations on the identification of rhetorical units, focusing especially on opening formulas (e.g., "Hear this word…").

Chapter 3 investigates Amos's aim, seeing its main theme clearly expressed in 8:2: "the end has come upon my people Israel." Asking whether there is a continuous argument or movement of thought in the book, Houston notes its intensifying tension and the "rising curve in the specific disasters forecast," concluding that it "is clearly arranged to lead up to the final rejection of Israel and destruction of Yhwh's enemies" (27). Other questions considered include the likely addressees of Amos's judgment message and whether that message of doom is conditional or nonconditional. The latter question needs to be—and is—asked both in connection with Amos's oral ministry in Israel and the book's subsequent purpose in a Judean setting. However, perhaps due to the brevity of the discussion, I found that the distinction and significance of these two settings is easily lost on the reader. As for the epilogue in 9:11–15, Houston maintains that it is "not a convincing conclusion to *the prophecy of Amos* as presented by the book" (32).

Chapter 4 considers the book's ethical ideas, looking at the social context addressed by Amos and clarifying the meaning of the terms *justice* and *righteousness*, whose combination Houston sees as referring to "social justice." There is an analysis of the nature of the injustice and oppression condemned by the prophet, a brief section on justice between nations (as addressed in 1:3–2:3), and a discussion of the relationship between ethics and the cult. Houston also considers the ground of Amos's ethics, which, following John Barton ("Amos's Oracles against the Nations," in *Understanding Old Testament Ethics* [Louisville: Westminster John Knox, 2003], 77–129), he finds in "the universal, taken-for-granted moral beliefs that everyone accepted" (41).

The last chapter of part 1 is devoted to the book's theology, including its portrayal of God as both creator and, first and foremost, destroyer. YHWH's relationship with Israel is discussed, as is YHWH's action against injustice: the exercise of "violence against violence" and the "unrelenting determination to destroy." An important, though brief, section asks whether YHWH acts justly. It is good to see Houston taking issue with the judgment on injustice leading to indiscriminate death and destruction. As he says, "there can be no *unthinking* resort to Amos in discussions of justice" (48).

Part 2, "Writing Amos," discusses the formation of the book of Amos. Chapter 6 explores the historical, religious, and social contexts in which this happened. For some reason, in this chapter only the sections are numbered and subsections are readily identifiable as such, a practice that would have been helpful throughout. Houston here reassesses the reign of Jeroboam II, which, archaeological finds suggest, already saw evident impoverishment, and he comments on the presence of Israelite refugees in Judah who might have brought the materials now included in Amos with them to the Southern Kingdom.

In line with Amos's strong focus on social injustice, Houston devotes a considerable amount of space to the social context. He is concerned to offer a nuanced assessment, arguing, for instance, that the exploitation condemned by Amos was likely to have been limited to the cities, whereas the independent peasantry in the hill-country villages would have been largely unaffected by these troublesome developments. Houston generally sees the exploitative practices as individual abuses of patronage, unauthorized exactions by corrupt officials, and distortions of the judicial system, and he cautions that we should not "write off Israelite society as totally corrupt and exploitative" (65). If he is correct, we would have to conclude that Amos's rhetoric has an even stronger hyperbolic edge than is usually recognized.

Chapter 7, one of the longest in this guide, explores how the book of Amos came into being. It opens with some comments on Amos the man, before considering three perspectives on the making of the book, that it all goes back to Amos, that it is a purely literary construct based, at best, on some eighth-century fragments, and that it is the result of a process of redaction. Relying largely on Tchavdar S. Hadjiev's assessment in his *The Composition and Redaction of the Book of Amos* (BZAW 393; Berlin: de Gruyter, 2009), Houston rules out the first two options before offering an account of the redaction-critical study of the book. This rehearses the main theories available in English, those of Hans-Walter Wolff, Joachim Jeremias, Robert Coote, and, most recently, Tchavdar Hadjiev. There is also a brief discussion of the more recent trend of seeing Amos's redaction as being tightly linked to that of the Book of the Twelve as a whole.

Part 3, "Amos Read," features only one chapter, which looks at the book's reception history. Here Houston begins by surveying how it has been read in ancient and medieval times, looking, in turn, at the Dead Sea Scrolls, the New Testament, rabbinic literature, and early and medieval Christianity. He gives particular attention to Girolamo Savonarola, whose reading departed from earlier interpretations in systematically relating Amos's message to social and political abuses of his own time, before moving on to Luther and Calvin. This is followed by the "historical-critical revolution," which led to the modern focus on Amos as "*the* prophet of social justice" (90) rather than seeing him as a witness to Christ, as most Christian readers had done up to that time. A section on "Amos as Inspiration in Struggles for Social Justice" includes a brief discussion of liberationist interpretations, while the treatment of the hermeneutics of suspicion alludes, again briefly, to feminist interpretation of Amos. Houston ends by endorsing David J. A. Clines's important criticism of many commentators' uncritical adoption of Amos's perspective, which ascribes Israel's destruction and the deportation of its citizens to an avenging God. As Clines ("Metacommentating Amos," in *Interested Parties: The Ideology of Writers and Readers of the Hebrew Bible*, JSOTSup 235 [Sheffield: Sheffield Academic, 1995], 76–93) rightly maintains, this is neither scholarly nor human.

Each chapter features a brief further reading section, while a bibliography and some indices conclude this important and helpful guide to the critical study of the book of Amos. Published almost exactly thirty years after A. G. Auld's earlier volume in the Old Testament Guides series (*Amos* [Sheffield: JSOT Press, 1986]), it offers a welcome update that will serve students well as an introductory companion.

To be sure, I did find myself disagreeing with Houston at times. To mention only one example, when he rejects Mark Daniel Carroll R.'s suggestion (*Contexts for Amos: Prophetic Poetics in Latin American Perspective*, JSOTSup 132 [Sheffield: JSOT Press, 1992]) that the cult at Bethel functioned to legitimize the monarchy and state apparatus, arguing that "the image of the people and its ruling institutions presented in the cult will be an ideal, morally unimpeachable" (35), does he not dismiss the danger of civil religion, of institutionalized religion succumbing to the temptation of becoming subservient to the political system, a little too rashly?

More important, however, some recent developments in the study of Amos deserve more extensive treatment. This is true, for instance, for the redaction-critical investigation of Amos as part of the Book of the Twelve. It is even more true for the discussion of liberationist interpretations and the hermeneutics of suspicion. As Houston himself says, "quite a number of recent writers have adopted a more suspicious viewpoint" (94). Sadly, this is not well reflected in his brief treatment, and more should have been said about liberationist readings as well. For this, readers will have to consult Carroll R.'s *Amos—The Prophet and His Oracles: Research on the Book of Amos* (Louisville: Westminster John Knox, 2002).

The Book of Zechariah, by Mark J. Boda. New International Commentary on the Old Testament. Grand Rapids: Eerdmans, 2016. Pp. xxiii + 911. Hardcover. $58.00. ISBN 9780802823755.

Anthony R. Petterson, Morling College

Mark Boda has been at the forefront of Zechariah scholarship for well over a decade. His earlier NIV Application Commentary on Haggai and Zechariah was published in 2004. This much more detailed NICOT commentary reflects his rigorous scholarship and mature reflections on this challenging and inspiring prophetic book. At over 900 pages, the level of detail in this commentary rivals the two-volume Anchor Bible commentary on Haggai and Zechariah by Carol and Eric Meyers (1987, 1993) but obviously reflects another quarter of a century of scholarship on the book. It looks set to be the standard commentary on Zechariah for the coming decades.

The introduction contains information on the text of Zechariah and its transmission; the "referential history" of the book, which sketches the contours of world history as it relates to the Jewish community from the fall of Jerusalem to the time of Artaxerxes; a substantial section on the compositional history of Zechariah (see further below); comments on the book's literary form and structure; its use of inner-biblical allusion (a key feature of the commentary); a summary of the book's main themes: God, leadership, sin, restoration, Zechariah for today; and a nine-page bibliography that includes a page and a half of Boda's own publications.

While many have treated Zech 9–14 as a literary unit with little connection with Zech 1–8, Boda follows the more recent trend to return to dealing with Zech 1–14 as a single book (28). He demonstrates several points of connectivity between the two parts, including their similar intertextual strategies and thematic developments, which "suggests that the ancient practice of identifying these fourteen chapters as a book within scribal tradition is related to the latter's recognition of an original editorial intention" (29).

Boda structures the book into four main parts, which his commentary follows: 1:1–6; 1:7–6:15; 7:1–8:23; 9:1–14:21. Each part is subdivided and sometimes divided further still. For each point of major division, he provides an introduction to the section that helps to orientate the reader. These introductions discuss issues of genre and form, structure, "intertextuality" (106, 420) and "inner-biblical allusion" (522), historical background, development of themes, and key differences of interpretation when relevant. The smallest subunits contain the commentary proper, which begin with Boda's own translation in italics, along with comprehensive and unrivaled translation notes in smaller font discussing variant readings and significant points of Hebrew grammar and syntax. Then follows a verse-by-verse analysis that includes explanation of lexical matters, often comprehensively tracing word usage across the Hebrew Bible in order to see the semantic range and to determine the most appropriate meaning in context. Boda observes and discusses the way in which Zechariah uses forms and themes from earlier biblical traditions (within the Torah, Former Prophets, and especially the Latter Prophets); this is an invaluable feature of the commentary, since it so often clarifies the interpretation. Where appropriate, documents from other cultures across the ancient Near Eastern world are referred to in order to elucidate practices referred to in Zechariah (for instance, those surrounding the construction of sacred shrines and patterns of divine warfare). This is all done in conversation with relevant secondary literature, often in the footnotes. The commentary is a rich mine of information, as Boda fairly summarizes the state of current Zechariah scholarship and carefully argues his own point of view, making numerous distinctive contributions of his own. There is almost no comment on the use of Zechariah in the New Testament and no direct Christian application, but this is understandable given it was a key focus of his earlier application commentary (well worth consulting in tandem).

It is impossible adequately to summarize the content of Boda's commentary in this review. Some of his more distinctive and/or significant lines of interpretation include the following points. The introduction in 1:1–6 depicts an initial positive response to Zechariah's call to repentance (84). The second vision is of four horns who "represent at least Babylon, if not Assyria," who are driven away by four farmers who "represent either the Persians or Yahweh's spiritual forces which enacted judgment on Babylon" (156). In the oracle in 2:10–13, Zechariah is sent to the nations to enact Jeremiah's mission of judgment (200). The visions in Zech 3–4 do not seek to bolster the priestly role; rather, they "highlight the important role that prophets will play in this new era" (225). In this regard, the "standing ones" in 3:7, whom Joshua is given access to, refers to prophets and "may refer specifically to Zechariah himself" (249). The "two sons of unmanufactured oil" in 4:14 are prophetic figures who participate in the divine council (315). The lamp itself may be associated with the endurance of the line of David (cf. Ps 132:17; 1 Kgs 11:36; 15:4; 2 Kgs 8:19) (317), with priests excluded from responsibility for its care (319). The two vision reports of Zech 5 make it clear that the initial penitential response in 1:1–6 did not last (323). The woman in the basket is most likely "a goddess or her idol" who is returned to a place of destruction (349). The vision of the flying scroll indicates that the normal systems of law and order have broken down (336). The final vision has two chariots tracking north, one tracking south, with a fourth chariot possibly remaining "to protect the divine portal" (377). In the sign-action of 6:9–15, two crowns are made, one for Joshua and one for the "sprout" figure (394). The sprout is a Davidic figure, "the most likely candidate being Zerubbabel" (408). Similarly, in 3:8 the expectation of the sprout in the imminent future "suggests that Zerubbabel is the figure in view" (258). Chapters

7–8 highlight key emphases in chapters 1–6 and Haggai in order to serve an ethical agenda, calling for repentance (see 1:1–6; 6:15) (420). The triumphant return of the Lord in 9:1–8 "has been shaped in some way by both earlier literature and historical realities, even as it describes a unique future hope" (531). Concerning the king of 9:9, this verse likely joins Hag 2:20–23 "in creating high expectations for Zerubbabel's rule" (565). The human shepherds in 10:3; 11:3–17; 13:7 are difficult to identify but are probably those associated with the Davidic line after the end of Zerubbabel's reign (609). The good shepherd in 11:4–16 is likely Zerubbabel and the bad shepherd Elnathan (652–53). The figure in 12:10 is Yahweh, rather than a human/kingly figure (717).

Boda proposes a complex compositional history of the book, which I will summarize since it helps to explain aspects of his interpretative approach. He argues that the two-year period between the dates in 1:7 and 7:1 implies that the visions and oracles in this section represent the experience of the prophet over this time, rather than a single night (17–18). The oracles that are found among the vision reports are sometimes integrally related to the vision scene, which suggests they were part of the visions at an early stage (2:8–9[4–5]; 5:4). Yet three of these oracles stand outside the vision cycle: 2:10–17(6–13); 4:6b–10a; 6:9–15. The language and style link these with each other and also with 7:1–8:23. Boda suggests that these units were "a collection of oracles created by the prophet" (19). Hence there appears to be two lots of source material: one related to the visionary experiences of the prophet and the other related to the nonvisionary experiences of the prophet (oracles, sermons, and reports of a sign act) (23). The one(s) responsible for the larger complex of Zech 1–8 brought this source material together, while introducing some elements and reworking others (such as 1:8–17, which echoes elements of 1:1–6). Boda believes this happened shortly after the date in 7:1 (7 December 518 BCE), before the temple was completed. He states: "the book would have provided a countertestimony to any idealistic hopes attached to the completion of the temple, reminding the readers of the multidimensional renewal outlined by Zechariah" (33).

The rest of Zechariah is divided into two sections: Zech 9–11 and 12–14. The first section comprises two prophetic collections (9:1–17 and 10:4–12) and focuses on Judah and Joseph, while the second section also comprises two collections (12:2–13:6 and 14:1–21) and focuses on "inner-Judean identities … while ignoring northern identities" (23). The second section also employs the phrase "on that day" much more frequently. At the same time, the two parts are joined by common literary features and themes that suggest that, while they "may have different points and sources of origination, they have been drawn together into a unified literary collection" (23). At the boundary between the two sections is "the sign-act allegory" of 11:4–16, which Boda contends explains the discontinuities between 9–11 and 12–14, and the smaller shepherd units (10:1–3a; 11:1–3; 11:17; 13:7–9), which were part of the editorial activity that brought the originally disparate units together (25). Explaining this historically, Boda argues that 11:4–16 and the smaller shepherd units are to be linked to the end of Zerubbabel's tenure as governor over Yehud (ca. 510 BCE) and to the rise of Elnathan/Shelomith to power (35, 37). Before this time (between 515 and 510) there was hope for the reunification of the nation and the renewal of the Davidic throne, reflected in Zech 9–10. Boda states that "hope for renewal of the Davidic house endures in chs. 12–13 (12:7–8, 12–13; 13:1), although there appear to be modifications to the hope, including a greater focus on the broader Judean community (12:7–8)" (36; cf. 766). There may be a further shift in chapter 14 with the reference to the kingship of Yahweh (14:9). He later states that chapters 9–14 are "ultimately tracing the demise of all hope for reestablishment of [Davidic royal] rule, looking instead to the rule of Yahweh alone" (521). Boda believes "the most likely period for Zechariah 12–14" is 445–433, during the period of Nehemiah's governorship, but he does not clearly state who he thinks is responsible for these final chapters. He concludes, "this also would be the date for the first readers of the combined book of Zechariah and, shortly after this, a collection comprised of Haggai–Malachi and possibly an early version of the Book of the Twelve existed" (37). The final form of the book first addresses those in the mid- to late fifth century.

Boda's reconstruction of the compositional history is very stimulating but, like all such theories, rather subjective. He clearly makes important observations of literary connections between passages, but discerning different sources and then extracting them from editorial additions and discerning directions of influence is an enterprise fraught with uncertainty, evident in the fact that there are several competing theories of composition that offer quite different scenarios (compare for instance, the recent proposals of Jakob Wöhrle, Martin Hallaschka, and Lena-Sofia Tiemeyer). For the most part, Boda's reconstruction is only in the background of the commentary, but occasionally it seems to me that the proposed compositional history derived from one part of the book drives the exegesis in other parts. Since the sign-actions in Zech 11 play such a pivotal role in his theory of composition of Zech 9–14, it is surprising that Boda does not directly address the view of Carol and Eric Meyers, Michael Stead, Barry Webb, and others, that rather than reflecting contemporary tensions and disappointments in the community, the first sign-action in 11:4–14 portrays Israel's history to the time of the Babylonian exile to explain the people's present adverse circumstances. This interpretation can be traced back to the Targums and leads to quite a different perspective on the material in Zech 12–14. This alternative interpretation provides a much more coherent reading of the final form of the book of Zechariah, meaning that, rather than later parts of the book standing in tension and/or contradicting earlier parts (particularly concerning the hope for a future reunion of Judah and Israel under a Davidic king), the book can be read in a way that all the parts are consistent, even if they have different emphases. Furthermore, the need to date Zech 12–14 later than Zech 9–11, at the time of Nehemiah, dissolves. It also means that the Davidic hope in Zech 12–14 need not be read as negatively as Boda does and results in an interpretation that fits more consistently with the expectations of "the earlier prophets" and more readily with the way that New Testament authors read these later chapters of the book.

The comments in the previous paragraph, however, are "majoring on the minors" (to misuse a title of Boda's). Mark Boda has taught me a tremendous amount about the book of Zechariah in his publications and at various conferences at which he has presented. I am grateful to him for the terrific work he has done in producing an outstanding commentary that brings much of this work together and offers more. I completely agree with David Petersen's comment on the dustjacket: "Anyone interested in the book of Zechariah will need to consult this volume."

Reading the Poetry of First Isaiah: The Most Perfect Model of the Prophetic Poetry, by J. Blake Couey. Oxford: Oxford University Press, 2015. Pp. xiv + 247. Hardcover. $110.00. ISBN 9780198743552.

Daniel J. Stulac, Duke University

This volume is a reworking of the author's dissertation, written under the supervision of F. W. Dobbs-Allsopp and other committee members J. Lapsley and J. J. M. Roberts, at Princeton Theological Seminary. The study is divided into three main chapters, framed by an introduction and conclusion. A bibliography, author index, text index, and subject index are also included.

First and foremost, Couey performs a close examination of particular Isaianic texts deemed "attributable" (18) to First Isaiah, which he defines as "either the eighth-century BCE prophet Isaiah of Jerusalem or the prophetic speeches in Isa 1–39 that most probably represent his work" (2). Unlike the majority of commentaries devoted to Isa 1–39, Couey's work takes seriously the text's formal poetic features. Thus the volume's primary purpose fills an important gap in modern Isaiah scholarship: to interpret portions of First Isaiah's poetry *as poetry.* Secondarily, it offers graduate-level students a valuable introduction to the questions that arise when attempting to understand ancient Hebrew verse.

It is crucial that readers engage Couey's introduction with care, as their understanding of the volume's contribution to Isaiah studies depends on a precise grasp of how he *defines the Isaiah text* and consequently how he *approaches the interpretive task.* As Couey rightly observes, few modern commentators have been willing or able to combine the literary insights of J. Kugel, R. Alter, and A. Berlin with their assessments of Isa 1–39 (9–11). That he attempts a literary reading of certain Isaianic passages, however, does *not* mean that Couey attempts a synchronic reading of the book as a whole. In fact, he is careful to distinguish his approach from those scholars who assume the book's literary coherence, noting that synchronic readings of Isaiah frequently discuss the text in terms of a "plot or drama, which seem ill-suited to a book comprised almost entirely of non-narrative poetry" (12). Following J. Barton, he argues that "it is not self-evident that an ancient work such as Isaiah was meant to be read sequentially from beginning to end, as many final form treatments insist" (12). Rather, Couey sees Isaiah as a "collection or anthology" (13) of poetic statements that must be interpreted in light of the historical contexts pertaining to their original moments of composition. "A literary reading of Isaiah," he observes, "need not be a final form reading" (13). In this way Couey actively resists what he perceives to be an "ahistoricist impulse" and a "backlash against the traditional threefold division of the book" at work in Isaiah studies today (15).

Each of the following three chapters, which make up the body of the study, "explore[s] a different aspect of First Isaiah's poetic style" (18): (1) the line, (2) poetic structure and movement, and (3) imagery and metaphor. In each case Couey discusses characteristics of Hebrew poetry by using a wide variety of examples taken from Isa 1–39. In turn, his close attention to Isaiah's poetry *as poetry* often yields fresh observations regarding the rhetorical function of the verses he cites. At the end of each chapter he balances these smaller examples with a lengthier analysis of what he deems to be a "complete poem" (19): Isa 22:1b–14; 3:1–15; and 1:2–20. Couey recognizes that scholars hold a range of views on the compositeness of each passage but nonetheless maintains "the possibility of considerable, if not total, original unity in these poems" (19). That said, he also posits that his analyses of these three poems "do not finally demand a particular view of their composition" (19).

Chapter 1, "The Line in First Isaiah," examines the problem of lineation in a text whose ancient manuscripts do not offer a great deal of guidance on this front. Couey focuses on parallelism, arguing that the colon (not the bicolon) is the most fundamental unit of Hebrew verse. He also explores rhythm, line length, and syntactic constraints as important indicators of the poetic line. His analysis is everywhere anchored in well-chosen examples that repeatedly demonstrate how line determination and interpretation go hand in hand. As a result, the study frequently yields important insight into the rhetorical character of a particular text. For example, Couey translates Isa 14:26 as follows:

> This is the plan that is planned concerning the whole earth,
> and this is the hand that is outstretched over all the nations. (49)

Couey observes that "the conspicuous length of the two lines creates a sense of expansiveness appropriate for the grand theological claim" (49). To conclude the chapter, he translates and interprets Isa 22:1b–14.

Chapter 2, "Structure and Movement," deals with the "network of relationships among lines that ultimately constitutes the poem" (68). Couey begins with the couplet, which Kugel, Alter, and Berlin showed is basic to these sorts of relationships. He skillfully explains how the poetry in question may demonstrate both narrative and nonnarrative progression between parallel lines. From here he moves on to discuss triplets, quatrains, larger groups, and single lines. Throughout this discussion Couey's detailed attention to Isaiah's poetry *as poetry* continues to yield fresh interpretive results. For example, he translates Isa 18:2 (a "larger group") as follows:

> Go, swift envoys
> to a nations tall and smooth,

to a people feared from there to yonder,
a nation of strength and trampling,
whose land is divided by rivers.

Here Couey argues that "Isaiah appears to take delight in describing the exotic prowess of the Cushites, heaping up phrase after phrase to emphasize the point" (104). Again, his careful analysis of the verse's poetic structure contributes to our understanding of its rhetorical significance. The chapter also discusses poetic devices that bind larger poetic units together, such as distant parallelism, repetition, and catalogues, and concludes with a reading of Isa 3:1–15.

Chapter 3, "Imagery and Metaphor," focuses on the form and function of imagery in First Isaiah, specifically agricultural and animal metaphors. Here Couey relies on the work of G. Lakoff and M. Turner, who understand metaphors as "cognitive devices" (141) that rely on "shared cultural understanding and individual experience" (143). Reading historically as well as literarily, Couey attempts to bring to life the cultural context in which Isaianic imagery was composed. For example, in analyzing Isa 16:8–10, which describes the destruction of Moab's vineyards, he resists the allegorical interpretation some commentators give this passage and instead associates the passage with the "destruction of agricultural industries, including vineyards, [that] was standard military practice in the ancient Near East" (151). Moving to animal imagery, Couey discusses three conceptual metaphors found in First Isaiah: the depiction of conquered cities as animal habitat, nations and leaders as animals, and Yhwh depicted as an animal (165). He concludes the chapter with a reading of Isa 1:2–20.

The strength of this volume stems from Couey's keen insight into a significant gap in modern Isaiah scholarship: the need to examine Isa 1–39 in ways that remain responsible to its poetic language. At the same time, Couey's attempt to differentiate his work from ahistorical tendencies within Isaiah studies is a welcome feature of his approach. Indeed, such readings frequently fail to account for the fact that Isaiah is composed and transmitted within the material *realia* native to ancient Israel. In other words, Couey is correct that the way forward in Isaiah research must combine literary analysis with historical considerations; the two are not mutually exclusive modes of inquiry. Again and again, his work reminds scholars that Isaiah's poetry is grounded in real experience; interpretation that slices away the text's basis in its material past only impoverishes our understanding of it.

The weakness of this volume, however, lies in the fact that it perpetuates serious methodological confusion common to our discipline. In assuming that the book of Isaiah is a "collection or anthology" (13), Couey strongly implies that final-form readings of Isaiah are inherently anachronistic to the text, in that such readings inevitably treat Isaiah as a modern novel while recusing themselves of serious engagement with the text's history of composition. While true of some scholarship, this characterization appears to misunderstand B. Childs's primary *historical-critical* insight: the Bible in general, and Isaiah in particular, is a kind of literature generically distinct from nonscriptural literature. This distinction is relevant *not* because later readers frequently discuss theology with reference to biblical texts but because Isaiah has been written up to be a "scripture" in its "original," written iteration. The only text to which we have access has been constructed for a reception community that is ancient and historical but also one that moves forward in tradition. In treating Isaiah's poetry "in much the same way as other poems" (14), Couey reads the text as if it were a transcript of the prophet's own words, originally uttered in the late eighth century BCE and preserved in hypostasis since that time. Redaction scholars have taught us that this assumption does not hold water. Isaiah has been constructed and reconstructed again and again for an ongoing audience, not an audience lodged at one specific point in time. Certainly Couey is correct that historical knowledge enriches biblical analysis, but this fact does not automatically mean that Isaianic poems are best understood by mapping them onto a hypothetical set of circumstances pertaining to their earliest strata of composition. The Bible simply does not relate to historical events in the way that Couey imagines.

The category mistake identified above results in a serious procedural problem affecting all parts of this study. Couey regularly assigns a given text to a specific set of historical-political circumstances before he completes his poetic analysis of it. For example, in his reading of Isa 18:2 cited above, Couey speculates that the poetic "heaping up" of "phrase after phrase" represents the historical prophet's *sarcastic intent* (104). Problematically, there is nothing about a "larger group" of five cola that warrants such a conclusion, nor is it anywhere clear that the historical prophet's psychology should determine the meaning of Isa 18. Thus the interpretation Couey finally offers is predetermined by the historical *Sitz im Leben* that he imagines the text to represent rather than the rhetorical function that the poetry *as poetry* performs relative to its *Sitz im Buch*. Couey readily acknowledges that Isaianic poems take on new meanings in the larger book but frames the reading task as one in which original poems must first be isolated and dated before they can be understood in association with other texts. If redaction scholars are correct, however—if Isaiah is an edited scripture and not an artifactual inscription—then Couey performs a kind of methodological "bait and switch" whereby he offers historical solutions to the literary questions he raises. As noted above, with reference to the longer poems that conclude each of the three main chapters, Couey maintains that his poetic analyses "do not finally demand a particular view of their composition" (19). On the contrary, his assumption that Isaiah is a "collection or anthology" invariably drives his interpretations. The sort of literary analysis he attempts finally stands at odds with the historicist impulses underpinning his approach.

J. Blake Couey's *Reading the Poetry of First Isaiah* makes an important contribution to Isaiah studies and, more generally, to the study of Hebrew poetry. The reader of this volume does well, however, to reflect carefully on the author's understanding of the *nature of the text* and also his perception of the *interpretive task* and to judge his conclusions accordingly.

Jesaja 1—Eine Exegese der Eröffnung des Jesaja-Buches: Die Präsentation Jesajas und JHWHs, Israels und der Tochter Zion, by Joachim Eck. Beihefte zur Zeitschrift für die alttestamentliche Wissenschaft 473. Berlin: de Gruyter, 2015. Pp. xviii + 410. Hardcover. €119.95. ISBN 9783110402933.

Richard Bautch, St. Edward's University

Joachim Eck's study of Isaiah's first chapter, based on his 2013 dissertation directed by Burkard Zapff at the Katholische Universität Eichstätt-Ingolstadt, provides analysis of the text's structure, poetics, tone, and overall message. With a significant engagement of prior scholarship, Eck develops several new perspectives for the interpretation of the opening to Isaiah. These viewpoints, Eck argues, cohere in an understanding of Yahweh as universal Lord who reigns over the cosmos by means of prophetic words that manifest his divine kingship. The king's subjects, however, have departed from his orderly realm, the sphere of life, and have allied themselves with other powers that are chaotic and deadly. In this scenario of material and spiritual devastation, the daughter of Zion appears as a remnant of the past but also as representative of an unmerited final opportunity for the people of Judah to turn toward salvation. This constellation of themes, in Eck's analysis, reverberates through the subsequent chapters of the book of Isaiah.

Eck's study comprises four chapters. The first serves as an introduction with attention to issues that have arisen in Isaian scholarship relative to the book's opening discourse. These include dating, literary structure and the possible role of a redactor subsequent to the historical Isaiah in the eighth century BCE. The second chapter is also introductory in that it provides the Hebrew text of Isa 1:1–31 with the author's translation and text-critical notes on select verses. Included here are several references to variants in 1QIsa^a, but not to the manuscripts from Cave 4 at Qumran (Isa 1:1–3 is attested in 4QIsa^a; Isa 1:1–6 is attested in 4QIsa^b; Isa 1:10–16 is attested in 4QIsa^f).

Chapter 3 establishes Eck's interpretive point of view on several seminal questions. First, Eck reads the superscription in Isa 1:1 typologically based on the first word, "vision." In a visionary type of superscription, he argues, the prophet is an active mediator of divine revelation. Isaiah 1:1 is said to exemplify the visionary type of superscription and present Isaiah as a prophet who proclaims in his own words what he has seen and whose oracles endure through a series of earthly kings. Second, Eck challenges the view that Isa 1 is a covenant lawsuit that follows the *rîb* pattern. This genre designation is found in Isaiah studies past and present. Eck argues that Isa 1 and certain other texts do not in fact fit the *rîb* pattern, understood as the essential characteristics of the situation at court. In addition, Eck rebuts a corollary argument that Isa 1 is a covenant lawsuit by virtue of Deuteronomic discourse that some interpreters identify in the text. Third, Eck engages in a verse-by-verse exegesis of Isa 1:2–9 that adduces meaning piecemeal but presents these verses as an integral unit. Eck groups the verses in micro-units that are examined philologically, literarily, and, when warranted, historically. Each unit is connected to related materials elsewhere in Isaiah to demonstrate the overture-like quality of Isa 1:2–9. Specifically, the presentation of the divine king of the cosmos in 1:2a links to the scene in God's heavenly throne room in Isa 6 and to the future vision of a new heaven and new earth where all humankind worships God (Isa 66:22–23); the ten sins of the nation in 1:2b–4 link to the ten imperatives for salvation in 1:16–17a, 18a; the bodily devastation in 1:5–7a that results from sin, guilt, and sanction links to the failure of the cultic system in 1:10–15; daughter Zion in 1:8 links to more positive references to this figure in 37:22, 49:22–23, and elsewhere. Thus the exegetical portion of Eck's study enjoys intertextual breadth while achieving depth through the author's close attention to detail.

The fourth and final chapter involves a theological recapitulation of the study's salient points. First, Isaiah is compared to Moses and located within the prophetic tradition associated with Israel's great leader. Eck indicates similarities between Isa 1 and both the Song of Moses (Deut 32) as well as other elements of the Mosaic tradition (e.g., the motif of heart-hardening) to conclude that Isaiah could be considered a successor of Moses. Next Eck considers the motif of sin as it functions in Isa 1:2–7 and following; he notes that ethical misconduct (1:4, 16–17, 21–23, 27) fuels Israel's revolt against Yahweh. The people's corrupt way of life implies a breach of the parental relationship with God, a rejection of the divine kingship over Israel, and a profanation of God's holiness (Isa 1:2–4; cf. 5:16). Finally, the figure of Daughter Zion is related to the Isaian understanding of salvation. In short, the fourth chapter fuses together exegesis and theology, with the latter building cleanly on the former.

Eck's project, a new approach to Isa 1, hinges on his rejecting the chapter's designation as a covenant lawsuit that follows the *rîb* pattern. His work in this regard is convincing. He observes that Isa 1 does not manifest the juridical elements that constitute this genre, namely, summons-indictment-punishment. Typically a covenant lawsuit contains these elements in this sequence, at times with minor variations. Although Eck does not note it, if one considers the covenant lawsuit in Isa 3:13–24, his analysis of Isa 1 becomes more cogent. Isaiah 3:13–24 shows that Isaiah or the early Isaian authors were skilled at using the covenant lawsuit as a literary device, and had they intended to compose Isa 1 as a covenant lawsuit (with the juridical elements of summons-indictment-punishment) they likely would have done so. Eck is on solid ground, too, when questioning the argument that Isa 1 is a covenant lawsuit because of terminology that may be traced back to the Deuteronomic covenant. To show on lexical grounds that a text is covenantal, the word *bərît* or a closely related term such as *ḥesed* should be attested, but neither of these covenantal terms appears in Isa 1.

One of the insights that arises in Eck's reading of Isa 1 has to do with the enumeration of sins in 1:2b–4. These verses contain several different subjects (sons in 1:2; Israel/the people in 1:3, 4) with one thing in common: all act sinfully. Crucially, the sins are ten in number, and Eck correlates the ten sins to the ten imperatives for salvation in 1:16–17a, 18a. He thus shows how the biblical writer unifies the text in a somewhat dialectical fashion while emphasizing salvation in a way that evokes the book's namesake. In a related move, Eck forges a connection between the sin/salvation portions of Isa 1 and 6:9–13, the prophet's oracle about hearing but not understanding God's word; whereas in Isa 1 Israel rebels but is granted a second chance to be saved, in Isa 6 things have deteriorated to the point where a prophetic demand to do justice according to God's will no longer heals but, to the contrary, increases the people's inability to perceive things as they are. Eck suggests that Isa 6, when taken as a reference to Judah's leaders who oppress the poor, is comparable to the situation of Pharaoh enslaving the Hebrews until God hardens his heart. Eck's interpretive moves could be extended even further in light of the larger biblical discourse of deeds and misdeeds, where the number ten is characteristic. There are, for example, the ten words of Exod 20:2–17 (and Deut 5:6–21), along with Pharaoh's ten trials in Exod 7–12 and the ten chances that the wilderness generation is given to meet God's demands (Num 14:20–23). When Eck compares Isaiah's oracle about hearing but not understanding God's word (6:9–10) to Pharaoh's hardness of heart, the comparison could be developed in greater depth by connecting Pharaoh's ten trials to the ten sins of Isa 1:2b–4. Ultimately, the intertext from Exodus about the oppressor Pharaoh resonates with both Isa 6:9–13 and Isa 1:2–4b/1:16–17a, 18a.

In summary, this study is carefully researched and written, and it offers many exegetical insights. The approach is largely diachronic but not rigidly so. Eck's contribution, in fact, exemplifies the trend of reading across the sixty-six chapters of Isaiah as opposed to following the tripartite division of the book that is traced back to Duhm. Indeed, Duhm is never cited, and terms such as Deutero- and Trito-Isaiah are absent as well. Eck's work reflects a newer approach to Isaiah and to its first chapter, and while certain readers may quibble with a few of Eck's conclusions, the volume as a whole will be read with great interest by all who work in Isaiah.

Micah: A Commentary, by Daniel L. Smith-Christopher. Old Testament Library. Louisville: Westminster John Knox, 2015. Pp. xxxiii + 268. Hardcover. $50.00. ISBN 9780664229047.

Claude F. Mariottini, Northern Baptist Seminary

Smith-Christopher's commentary on Micah is a replacement for James Luther Mays's, which was published in the Old Testament Library series in 1976.[1] Mays's commentary was widely used in colleges and seminaries and provided a solid interpretation of Micah's message and ministry. Smith-Christopher's work is a worthy replacement that continues the tradition established long ago for commentaries in this series.

There are different ways of interpreting the book of Micah, based on how one identifies the prophet and his message. Hans Walter Wolff believed that Micah

---

1. James L. Mays, *Micah*, OTL (Philadelphia: Westminster, 1976).

was one of the elders of Judah who was addressing the situation created by the military occupation of the Shephelah.[2] Delbert Hillers proposed that Micah was part of a movement of revitalization, a "millennial" movement. George Pixley believed that Micah was a revolutionary,[3] and George L. Robinson called him "the prophet of the poor."[4]

One of the most refreshing aspects of Smith-Christopher's commentary is his willingness to declare the social-political context from which he reads and comments on the words of Micah. He says that he chooses "to be explicit about my own approach to Micah" (2). Smith-Christopher interprets Micah out of his Quaker background and as one who has been deeply influenced by the biblical scholarship found within the Mennonite tradition. The Religious Society of Friends, a Christian movement also known as the Quakers, promotes peaceful principles; that is, they are committed to nonviolence. Some Quakers also object to participating in wars. The Mennonites are known for their commitment to pacifism and for their belief that war is not the solution to solving the world's problems.

Smith-Christopher's Christian commitment to nonviolent social changes influences the way he looks at the book of Micah: "If I am asked whether my commitments as a Christian devoted to nonviolent social change have 'influenced' my reading of the book of Micah, I can only reply that I certainly hope so" (3). It is out of this tradition that Smith-Christopher seeks to study the impact of militarism in society, past and present. This sociological and theological perspective is found throughout as he interprets Micah's oracles in light of his commitment to nonviolence. He is committed to the historical-critical approach of biblical scholarship, to a movement that seeks equitable distribution of the earth's resources to people who have been denied this kind of access in the past, and to the movement that seeks to accomplish these goals without using violence. In his exposition of the text, Smith-Christopher addresses the concerns of minority communities whose voices have not been heard and whose causes have not been championed. Smith-Christopher also believes that Micah's message reflects a populist movement that rejects militarism, similar to other populist movements in recent history that promote political resistance and antiwar sentiments.

According to Smith-Christopher, Micah's book reflects the tradition of prophetic condemnation of war policies. Micah was "an ancient Israelite critical populist" who was highly critical of the Jerusalem elite (1). His message was a "regionally oriented and political challenge to the oppressive economic and military interests of the central elite of Jerusalem" (21). While Isaiah was closer to the political power located in Jerusalem, Micah was critical of the policies of Hezekiah

---

2. Hans Walter Wolff, *Micah : A Commentary* (Minneapolis: Augsburg, 1990).

3. George Pixley, "Micah—A Revolutionary," *The Bible as the Politics of Exegesis: Essays in Honor of Norman K. Gottwald on His Sixty-Fifth Birthday*, ed. David Jobling, Peggy L. Day, and Gerald T. Sheppard (Cleveland: Pilgrim, 1991), 53-60.

4. George L. Robinson, The *Twelve Minor Prophets* (Grand Rapids: Baker, 1952).

and the political elite who governed from Jerusalem. Micah's strong criticism was against the military preparation against an eminent Assyrian invasion of Judah. The reason for Micah's "populist antimilitarism" was because Jerusalem's policies affected the people, whom Micah called "my people," who lived in the villages. These were the people who suffered the most at times of war and who had to pay a heavy price for the military adventures of those who lived in Jerusalem.

Micah ministered during one of the most political turbulent periods in the history of Judah. His message came out of the many political crises brought about by the presence of Assyria in Israel and in Judah. The Syro-Ephraimite War, the fall of Samaria, and the invasion of Sennacherib during the reign of Hezekiah in 701 BCE resulted in major destruction of life and property. Judah's war against Assyria disrupted many lives and displaced thousands of people, primarily the people who lived in the Shephelah, as the Assyrian army marched toward Jerusalem.

The book of Micah reflects the economic pressure placed upon the citizens of Judah caused by the "policies of destructions" (67) established by the government in Jerusalem and the military elite of Judah in order to deal with the Assyrian menace. Micah was concerned about the terrible disruption in the villagers' lives caused by war policies of the elite in Jerusalem in their attempt to maintain their own economic power during the political crisis facing the nation as well as benefit financially from a resistance against Assyria. In order for Judah to be able to pay the yearly tribute to Assyria and for the elite in Jerusalem to keep their lifestyle, they needed more money, which came from taxation and the exploitation of the poor: "The prophet's anger is especially incited by what he perceives as the calculated cruelty and exploitation" of the citizens in the villages of the Shephelah (81).

The result of this "planned wickedness" was the oppression of the poor by the greedy elite of Jerusalem, the seizing of land from those unable to pay their debts (Mic 2:1–2), the eviction of families from their homes (2:9), the taking of bribes by the political and religious leaders of the nation (3:11), the cheating of the people by merchants and wealthy businessmen using inaccurate weights and measures (6:10–11), and people becoming rich through extortion and violence (6:12).

Smith-Christopher identifies four different contexts that are present in the book of Micah. These contexts influenced the ministry and proclamation of the prophet and influence the reader and the interpreter of the words of Micah. The first context was the international context reflected in the time of Micah by the policies of the Neo-Assyrian Empire. The nations of the eighth century had to deal with the prospect of violence and terror and the painful impact of Assyria's policy of terror and mass deportation, which impacted the citizens of the conquered lands. The impact of these policies caused much disruption in the life of the villagers who suffered the brunt of the impact of an invasion. Smith-Christopher offers a good description of the impact of Assyrian policy in the lives of the people in Judah.

The second context was the regional context of the eighth century and the policies of the kings of Israel and Judah in light of the Assyrian menace. The heading of the book of Micah indicates that the prophet ministered under kings who ruled at the time when Assyria was trying to establish hegemony over the territory that included these kingdoms. The policies of Assyria caused serious economic and political upheaval in them. The imposition of taxes to raise revenues to pay the annual tribute to Assyria brought much hardship to the peasant population of Judah.

The third was the local context. In his discussion of Moresheth as a frontier town, Smith-Christopher offers a description of the economy of the Shephelah and how the military policies of Jerusalem affected the people who lived in the villages of Judah. The place where Micah lived was a place where frontier violence was a fact of life, since it was located near the Philistine cities and it was where invading armies spread violence and destruction.

The fourth context was the "antimilitary populism as the ideological context for reading Micah" (20). To emphasize the antimilitary message of Micah, Smith-Christopher lists thirty-one references in Micah to violence, weapons, and warfare (22–23). Micah's ministry represented a revolt of the Judean peasantry against the military aspirations of the elite in Jerusalem. According to Smith-Christopher, the use of Micah's oracle in Jer 26:16–19 shows that Micah's political message was similar to Jeremiah's. Just as Micah opposed military engagement against Assyria, Jeremiah resisted military engagement against Babylon.

While most scholars see Micah's oracles divided among judgment and salvation oracles, Smith-Christopher says that this arrangement presumes Micah's loyalty to the house of David and the preservation of the monarchy as it existed in the eighth century. Smith-Christopher proposes that Micah is advocating a more radical break with the political realities of his days. Micah's prophecy of a new David in Mic 5 indicates that, by going back to Bethlehem, God was looking for a replacement for the present political leadership in Jerusalem.

Some scholars believe that the oracles of judgment in Mic 1–3 are "fundamentally out of step" with the "swords to plowshare oracle" in Mic 4:1–4.[5] However, Smith-Christopher says that the judgment of Jerusalem in 3:12 is compatible with the antimilitaristic view of Micah. According to Smith-Christopher, Micah is actually saying that "Jerusalem will be plowed—and we want to pound our swords into the very plowshares that will help us do the job" (43).

The book contains two tables and eight excursuses. Table 2 (19) offers a list of the many acts of violence that occurred in the Shephelah. The excursuses deal with issues found in the text and raised in the exegesis. The book includes a lengthy bibliography, an index of Scripture and other ancient sources, and an index of subjects and authors.

I enjoyed reading Smith-Christopher's commentary because I identify and sympathize with the ways in which he approaches and interprets the book of Micah. As one who understands the plight of minorities and who has served and ministered among the less fortunate, the message of Micah has much to say to

---

5. Norman K. Gottwald, *The Hebrew Bible: A Socio-literary Introduction* (Minneapolis: Fortress, 1985), 376.

the villagers who lived in the lowlands of Judah and to people who live in similar social and economic conditions in our own day.

WRITINGS

Consider Leviathan: Narratives of Nature and the Self in Job, by Brian R. Doak. Minneapolis: Fortress, 2014. Pp. xxviii + 302. Cloth. $39.00. ISBN 9781451469936.

Katharine Dell, University of Cambridge

Doak sums up his thesis well when he writes, "On many levels the book of Job repeatedly links self, land, plant and animal with God's activity in the world" (93). Doak begins with the point that the human relationship with "nature" has always been in tension, there being good, harmonious experiences in human experience intermingled with frightening, overwhelming ones. Doak uses Job as the representative of the individual human self in interaction with nature's own individual selves (plants and animals) as well as the elements, the stars, and the cosmos. A key concern is to draw out the plant and animal metaphors used within the dialogue (Job 4–37) as participants set up the primary terms of the debate. However, it should not be forgotten that the dialogue is preceded by the prologue, which lays down some initial images for future interaction later in the book. Indeed, it is the "divine speech" that overwhelms with animal descriptions in particular. According to Doak, in the context of the late sixth and early fifth centuries BCE with its geographical concerns about the land, this speech "points its audience directly into the savage paradoxes of their new efforts to cultivate and control their space" (xix).

Chapter 1 begins with a consideration of the link between nature and morality, and Doak argues that "nature" in terms of animals and plants constitutes a primary metaphor in the book of Job in the discussion of the prosperity/suffering nexus. Doak leads us on to a consideration of selfhood and of the self's own relationship to other living "selves" in the natural world. He cites Ricoeur's point that the self is about one's individual narrative. Here, then, we have Job's individual narrative that takes place in the actual political, economic, and theological situation of the early postexilic period. A review of scholarship on the history/nature debate within biblical studies is included here.

Chapter 2 looks at the wider use of animal and plant metaphors across the Hebrew Bible. Doak discusses definitions of metaphor and favors the Aristotelian model of "transformative metaphor." He argues that animal and plant behaviors act as a correlative to human moral states. He explores ancient Near Eastern parallels in the onomastica of Egypt, the Wisdom of Ahiqar, and the Babylonian Theodicy. He cross-refers to Genesis (1:26 in particular) and Deuteronomy for its link of the covenant to animal and plant success or failure in the land. He looks at "parables" using plants and animals in proverbial and prophetic literature and even considers Qoheleth's ideas of a royal garden and his exploration of human decay in Eccl 12.

Chapter 3 draws out the full extent of the plant and animal imagery in Job. The prologue introduces hedge and animal themes, but it is the dialogue that opens up various metaphors, many of which, interestingly, have psalmic parallels. Each of the friends uses nature analogies in differing ways, but while for them the images are congenial ones, for Job his "nature narrative" is a cursed and ecologically unfriendly cosmos. His is a broken world. Doak writes, "The picture Job proceeds to lay out in 12:13–25 is a dystopian vision of a broken world, a devastated un-created earth upon which humans stagger like drunkards (12:24–5)" (151). The dialogue of voices of the friends and Job means that "micro-narratives" of nature are crafted by the human characters in the book. The friends (including Elihu) compete to characterize nature and gesture toward other narratives of nature as found in Proverbs and Deuteronomy.

Chapter 4 leads us to the climax of the divine speech. Doak maintains that the image of God is, as mainly in the prophets, that of a storm god. The tension between nature being "upheaved" by God (e.g., by a whirlwind) and yet God's provision for nature is upheld here. Doak writes, "In chapters 38–41 we find a deity whose majestic self-revelation amounts to a kind of zoological lecture and a meditation on the earth's physical wonders" (190). He also comments that "the animals of the Divine Speech are not ideas, they are animals in dynamic relation to the suffering human" (199). Just as the ostrich crushes her eggs, so Job's family are "crushed" in the prologue. The same harsh deity acts in each case. Doak points out that, unlike the transformation of chaos into order (as in the creation narratives), here in the divine speech there is a kind of creation reversal, with order giving way to chaos. God's role as "master of the animals" controls chaos, and we meet wild versions of Job's domesticated animals from the prologue in some cases. Animals, though, are self-sufficient, they are survivors, and they are parents. Doak writes, "the human moral universe interacts with and can be compared to animal failures, negligence and alienation" (218). The chaos is represented by the monsters Leviathan and Behemoth. These invincible creatures are ultimately conquered by God, but they exist outside the usual moral categories. Doak sees interest in the fact that Leviathan has already been mentioned by Job in the dialogue (3:8–9) and also finds an echo of Behemoth earlier in Job's wish for "bones of bronze" (6:12). Doak sees a deliberate link made here across the book. These monsters highlight the menacing God who exists outside the covenant with nature. Doak writes, "This is the shock of the book. It is not shocking to think that God is a creator, or that God is high above us, with ways not our ways, and so on. It is shocking to think that we might look at nature's fractures and see God's pleasure" (231).

In the final chapter Doak seeks to link the Joban "self" to the historical situation of Israel immediately postexile. He notes that this was a transitional period of ecological crisis. A new view of the individual was emerging and an accompanying sense of divine freedom in the context of a changed land, also in crisis. There was an accompanying crisis in the economy, in society, and in theology. Texts from a similar time are examined, for example, Haggai, and Zechariah and Isa 40–66 for their ideas about the natural world. Genesis 1 and Deuteronomy are also consulted. Doak airs wider issues of the nature of "natural theology" here. He argues that Job is representative of the "little community" of Judah "struggling in its land" after the exile. Doak writes, "In his own suffering body, unsure about how he relates to his land, animals, and plants, Job embodies Israel's story no less powerfully or meaningfully or prescriptively than do other embodied Israel's in miniature, such as Abraham or Jacob or David" (283). In this sense Job is as much about state formation as about the individual—it is deeply communal. The book of Job, in its deliberate disorientation, functioned to challenge its audience, to inculcate the message that deeds are not always rewarded and that "the God of the universe participates in the construction of the paradoxes and violence of the natural world" (287). In the light of this discussion, the Job epilogue is a rather embarrassing afterthought; it does not fit with the bold challenge of the rest of the book; the "ecological transition" for Israel seems to have been reversed. Doak senses "some kind of avoidance or coverup" (291) in the epilogue.

This study approaches the book of Job with an important armory of questions about the moral universe and the place of humans and nonhumans within it. The drawing out of the imagery of nature, particularly in the dialogue and across the book, is a good and timely achievement. Doak's work is very wide ranging in its concerns: we move from anthropology to sociology to theology to history with a good smattering of philosophy thrown in. He could be criticized for trying to do too much here: perhaps the final chapter trying to link it all up historically is an unnecessary bridge too far, in that the important metaphorical language of plants and animals that he highlights works without any strict grounding in a historical situation. Also, the treatment of the epilogue is a little disappointing. However, Doak's attention to detail and to scholarship from many disciplines is impressive, many footnotes being extremely informative as well as the main text. This is a new synthesis of material through a fresh lens; it brings a neglected theme to our attention and puts it in the context of the ecological interests of our own age. It is an impressive achievement and is to be commended to a wide audience.

Job the Unfinalizable: A Bakhtinian Reading of Job 1–11, by Seong Whan Timothy Hyun. Biblical Intepretation Series 124. Leiden: Brill, 2013. Pp. x + 243. Hardcover. $127.00. ISBN 9789004258105.

Emily Gravett, Trinity University

Applying the insights of philosopher and literary critic Mikhail Bakhtin to biblical texts, especially the book of Job, is nothing new. Carol Newsom's *The Book of Job: A Contest of Moral Imaginations* (2009), for example, has already done so to great effect. But Seong Whan Timothy Hyun seeks to build on this tradition in his *Job the Unfinalizable* (2013), a revised version of his 2011 dissertation. Where Hyun parts ways with predecessors such as Newsom is by perceiving Bakhtinian dialogism *within* the various genres of the book of Job in addition to the interaction *among* the different genres. Specifically, his aim is to examine each voice in

Job 1–11 (which includes the prologue and the first cycle of the dialogue sections) to reveal how their interactions produce variant meanings for Job and his suffering within a book that "seems to continue to offer questions and problems and to remain *unfinalized*" (1).

In the introduction Hyun lays out the two concepts from Bakhtin that are most important to his project: "dialogism" and "chronotope." Dialogism, or polyphony, is the plurality of voices within a single text, indeed, within even a single word. Chronotope, which is what Hyun is adding to existing scholarship, means "time space," that is, "the intrinsic connectedness of temporal and spatial relationships that are artistically expressed in literature" (7; quoted from Bakhtin's *The Dialogic Imagination*, 84). Hyun intends to use the concept of chronotope to analyze the voices therein.

Chapter 2 details "Job in the Chronotope of the Prologue." Hyun moves through what he calls the prologue's six "scenes" (1:1–5, 6–12, 13–22, 2:1–7a, 7b–10, and 11–13), focusing on the textual ambiguities that a Bakhtinian lens allows him to find. For example, the first scene (in which the narrator describes Job) problematizes the narrator's own reliability, the connection between Job's piety and his possessions, as well as the relationship between the sin of Job's children and their saying *brk*. Through such ambiguities, "the narrator provides time and space for his or her readers to consider their own point of view concerning Job as a character" (43). The prologue also includes multiple voices—those of the narrator, but also *hassatan*, God, Job's messengers, Job's wife, and even Job himself—all of which attempt to finalize Job. They ultimately fail, however, instead heightening readers' expectations to hear other voices and provoking readers into participating in the act of trying to finalize Job as blameless, upright, a fearer of God, and a shunner of evil.

Chapter 3 elucidates "Job's Speeches in His New Chronotope," that is, the "dialogues" (Job 3, 6, 7, 9, and 10). In the third chapter of the book of Job, Job's speeches reveal that he understands himself in a new chronotope, and he responds by trying to reshape language, such as the temporal "day" or the spatial "womb," to reorder his shattered course. In the next four chapters, just as he reshaped words, Job attempts to reconfigure his relationship to his body, God, and his friends. Yet these reconfigurations are still not enough to finalize him. Rather, his speeches provoke his friends' voices to emerge to interact with and respond to his. It is in this section that some of Hyun's most illuminating analyses occur, not necessarily based upon the concept of chronotope but rather on, for example, Paul Grice's four maxims for successful communication (e.g., that of "quantity," wherein speakers should "make [their] contribution as informative as is required," 111).

Chapter 4 shifts the focus to "The Voices of the Three Friends." In this chapter Hyun explores how these voices respond to Job's voices as well as echo those from the prologue, *hassatan's* in particular. Their responses are organized under the five themes of Job's identify, fate, words, piety, and knowledge. Eliphaz, for instance, thinks Job naturally suffers and is susceptible to sin because he is a man, but that he is nevertheless righteous and will eventually be restored by God. There is still hope for Job, Eliphaz offers, as he attempts to re-create Job's narrative into a better one. In contrast, Bildad doubts Job's piety, warns him to examine his own sinfulness, and suggests that he needs to humbly ask for favor from God again. Each voice, according to Hyun, reveals the friends' distinct ideological perceptions concerning who Job is, though all agree that he is not perfect or blameless, as no man is.

After exploring how each voice plays a role in defining Job, within the prologue and the dialogue, respectively, the fifth chapter turns to a more familiar, overarching dialogism: "The Dialogic Relationship between Voices in the Prologue and Those in the Dialogue Section." Hyun argues that all voices are essential in providing a definition of Job, that is, of attempting to 'finalize' him. Metaphorically extending Bakhtin's concept of "great time" (time in which words have no limits in the dialogic context), Hyun examines several key words from the prologue, such as "dust," "knees," and "the day," to show how they later echo in the voices of Job, Eliphaz, Bildad, and Zophar in the dialogues. The words repeat but change meaning; they become, as Hyun puts it, "creatively renewed" (167). Hyun ultimately contends that "the prologue and dialogue together depict the kind of man Job is and create a definition of him for readers in *Job*" (168)—that of a pious man.

The final chapter, the conclusion, wonders whether the various voices in the whole book succeed in finalizing Job. It is here that Hyun briefly brings in later chapters from the book of Job, such as Job's speech in chapter 28, Elihu's in 32–37, the divine in 38–41, Job's responses in 40:4–5 and 42:1–6, and the epilogue. For example, because the second and third dialogue cycles are followed by Job's speeches in chapters 27–31, Hyun claims that "Job's three friends have failed to finalize Job" (208). Ultimately, the book ends with the idea that "Job is unfinalizable as long as readers of [the book of] *Job* read, communicate, and dialogue with him. At the same time, as long as Job is unfinalizable, the text dialoguing with readers is unfinalizable" (219).

Many of Hyun's readings throughout the book are quite compelling. For example, he suggests that when we choose to translate *nefesh* as breath and throat, it helps us realize that they are "the minimum that must be preserved for [God and *hassatan*'s] test to have any meaning. If Job no longer had a voice, he could not *brk* God and neither God nor *hassatan* could claim victory in the text" (73). Similarly, when Hyun explains that Job's wife's speech "ends the game without fulfilling the readers' desire to hear Job's responses" and that "Job's ability to answer is the essential component that gives the book of *Job* a unity between the poetic section and epilogue" (78–79), it helps us better understand why Job might have deemed her a "foolish woman" in 2:10.

Other analyses, however, seem more prosaic. Hyun claims, for instance, that the narrator's introduction in Job "provokes readers to ask questions" because it "omits certain key elements that are often used to introduce characters in the Hebrew Bible" (31). That the Hebrew Bible is elliptical—often on key points— should surprise no one. It also does not require Bakhtin to conclude. In fact, Hyun's own readings often reveal how frequently he does not need the concepts of dialogism or chronotope to proceed. He notes that Job is unaware of what has been discussed in the heavenly realm—ignorance he claims is "due to [Job's] chronotopic limitations" (68). While this may be true, scholars have not needed chronotope to recognize that there is an irony here, in that we (the readers), God, and *hassatan* are all privy to information that Job is not. At times, the application of the concept is even a stretch. For instance, language of the body (e.g., breasts or mouth) is called "spatial language," which fits a chronotopic framework but also seems a bit odd.

More generally, I think a few problems occur when trying to apply Bakhtin to a biblical text. For one, Bakhtin is usually referring to novels, like those of Fyodor Dostoevsky, when he is quoted by biblical scholars (see above from p. 7), which Hyun acknowledges but does not fully address. How is the book of Job like and unlike a novel, a genre that emerged only several hundred years ago? I must also note that, paradoxically, chronotope is a concept that Bakhtin used to underscore the significance of, as Hyun writes, "the important relationship between a literary text and its social and political context or unique historical condition" (7). This is a significance that may well be elided when we project modern genres such as the novel, and all of our accompanying generic expectations, onto texts composed thousands of years ago under vastly different conditions.

Most importantly, as Hyun himself admits early on, "Bakhtin himself argues for the existence of monologic literature and sees the Bible as a prime example" (18). While I am persuaded, by Bakhtin, that utterances and words can carry within them multiple voices and even that "truth" is found in the plural, rather than the monologic, we must query how applicable these concepts can be to texts canonized in the Hebrew Bible. After all, its authors (or implied authors) seem to align themselves with God, who to a great extent represents the authoritative voice. Certainly, to a contemporary sensibility, making a bet with *hassatan* over some man's life may strike us as reprehensible, but the biblical text does not present God's actions as such. Even when it turns out that Job was right (and his "well-meaning" friends were wrong in reaffirming retributive justice), God still comes out with the last word; God gets to say who was right and who was wrong. By approaching this book through a Bakhtinian lens, scholars like Hyun must imply that God's voice is simply one among many, which—though it makes for some interesting literary readings—remains problematic, particularly in the context of an argument attempting to demonstrate the unfinalizability of a biblical book.

Invitation to the Psalms: A Reader's Guide for Discovery and Engagement, by Rolf A. Jacobson and Karl N. Jacobson. Grand Rapids: Baker Academic, 2013. Pp. viii + 184. Paper. $17.99. ISBN 9780801036446.

John E. Anderson, Presentation College

Rolf Jacobson, associate professor of Old Testament at Luther Seminary, and Karl Jacobson, assistant professor of religion at Augsburg College, invite readers to experience the psalms as opposed to schooling them in all matters of analysis and psalms interpretation. The title of the book is especially telling. This is not yet another introduction to the psalms but rather an *invitation* to the psalms that serves as an entry point for novice readers to learn to read the psalms well. As such, the Jacobsons do not focus on the intricacies of debate in psalms scholarship, though both are no doubt capable of doing so, or with exhaustive footnotes "filled with dizzying displays of our dazzling grasp of the secondary literature" (4). With this volume they opt to wear the hat of guide rather than guru. Despite this participatory posture, the formative elements of the last few centuries of psalms scholarship are evident with chapters addressing poetry and parallelism, *Gattungen*, *Sitz im Leben*, and theology.

The book is divided into six chapters and an introduction. The introduction is brief (five pages) and unpacks the title of the book. The Jacobsons compare what is offered in the book to a "tour-guide pamphlet" with the objective being "to familiarize the reader with the landscape of the Psalter, so that the reader will be set loose to explore the Psalter and roam widely among its poems" (2–3). As such, the intended audience, they note, is "the interested nonspecialist student— the student who does not read biblical Hebrew or who has only passing familiarity with Hebrew" (3).

Chapter 1 is entitled "Why Is My Bible Repeating Itself? Learning to Understand Hebrew Poetry." After a brief introduction to parallelism, the authors define this Hebrew poetic phenomenon as "*the repetition of elements within a grammatical unit*" (9, emphasis original). What follows are discussions and examples of the various ways in which parallelism can appear in the psalms: within a single line of poetry, between lines of poetry, between verses, between entire sections of a psalm, and between two entire psalms. Synonymous, antithetic, and synthetic parallelism are briefly defined, though the Jacobsons register their hesitancy with such labels, noting that "*there is a problem with trying to categorize art!*" (12, emphasis original). The "really destructive thing" about such classifications, they note, "is that it limits the imagination of readers.... It presents readers with a way of labeling the poetry but does not show them how to digest the poetry" (12). Toward this end, the authors describe parallelism as echoing or extending, or more often doing both.

The second chapter, "What Is a Psalm? Learning to Understand Different Psalm Genres—Part 1," introduces the idea of genre within the psalms. The important point is made that genre has two types: those psalms that are similar on the basis of form and those that are similar on the basis of content. Chapter 2 treats genre as defined by form. Psalm forms discussed include lament, hymns of praise, trust, and thanksgiving. Further subsections for each psalm focus on the situation and audience addressed in the psalm and the language employed. For example, for lament psalms the primary audience is identified as God and the secondary audience as the human community, while the language is divided into complaint, request for help, expression of trust, promise to praise. Those well-versed in form criticism will readily recognize that the language sections are breaking the psalm down into its structural/formal components; this is true for the other psalms in this chapter as well.

Chapter, 3, "What Is a Psalm? Learning to Understand Different Psalm Genres—Part 2," focuses on genre as defined by common themes or content. A number of psalm types are profiled here: royal, enthronement, wisdom, creation, historical, Zion, imprecatory, penitential, and liturgical. Discussions of each type are rich with insights and awareness to the challenges of reading each one. For instance, the Jacobsons ask in regard to imprecatory psalms, "What are these prayers doing in the Bible? Why are God's people asking for others to be harmed?" (82). In response they focus on four points: (1) the humanness of such poems "give[s] voice to genuine human emotions"; (2) the pray-er does not act in violence but leaves that with God; (3) these psalms remind us of the chaos of various societies in history; (4) readers should be mindful "that someone out there might be praying this prayer against *us*" (83). I did find the label "liturgical psalms" confusing and potentially unhelpful; accepting Gunkel and Mowinckel, are not most/ all psalms liturgical at some level or another?

Chapter 4, "What Is a Psalmist? Learning to Understand the Voice and Life Situations of the Psalms," explores the idea of persona in reading the psalms. Given the anonymous nature of the psalms, authorship is unknown. Reading, then, becomes an imaginative invitation in trying to deduce the type of person the author of the psalm was given internal clues. Not only does identifying a persona for the psalm assist in interpretation; it also allows the reader to try out or "put on" that poem's persona. Similarly, readers are invited to muse over the imagined setting in life (what Psalms scholars call *Sitz im Leben*) as a means of getting at the "spiritual" feelings in the psalm or what situation has prompted such a prayer. Both the physical/social and the spiritual warrant attention. The Jacobsons caution rightly against "get[ting] too fixated either on getting it exactly right or insisting that your particular view is the only (or even the best) way to imagine who the psalmist was" (92). Attempting to deduce a psalm's persona requires not only imagination but also humility. Insights into how the psalms, with their locus being the ancient Israelite temple, might inform Israelite religion, as well as some discussion of the dual individual/communal nature of the psalms round out the chapter.

In chapter 5, "Is God a Rock, a Light, or a Shepherd? Learning to Understand Metaphors, Imagery, and Symbolism in the Psalms," the Jacobsons treat metaphor as a vital component to understand for the way they are tied to "psalmic thinking" (119). They describe metaphor as "a picture that is painted in words" (120). They also advance the necessary, though oft-neglected, caution that metaphors are culturally specific and conditioned. After a focused and sustained survey of metaphor, the discussion turns to metaphor specifically in the psalms. Metaphors are used within the Psalter, the authors suggest, in relation to the human situation and God, among others. The authors conclude the chapter thusly: "The poetry of the psalms creates meaning by painting word pictures through which the reader can make sense of life, develop a robust theological imagination, and connect not only to the ancient world out of which the psalms arose but also make sense of the present world in which the psalm reader now lives.… Metaphor both requires and empowers imagination in interpretation, which makes reading the psalms both a challenge and a joy" (146).

The final chapter is "Who Is the King of Glory? Learning to Understand the Theology of the Psalms." This chapter asks the fundamental question "Who is the God of the Psalter?" (150). Noting that there will be a plethora of ways in which readers answer this question, the Jacobsons liken the portrait of God in the Psalter as "more like a mosaic than an oil painting" (150). They then move to propose their own unifying theological umbrella comprising all 150 psalms: that *"the Lord is a God of loving faithfulness"* (152, emphasis original). An attempt to unpack the thorny Hebrew word *hesed* follows, as do individual sections treating this overarching theme in each of the psalm types identified in chapter 2. Bringing this chapter to a close are four responses to the initial question of "who is the God of the Psalter. The Psalter witnesses to a God who (1) is committed to all creation, (2) does not mind being challenged, (3) works through others, and (4) is active in the world (167–73).

Invitation to the Psalms achieves its stated aims. It invites readers into the beauty and raw reality of the life of faith evident in the Psalter and equips them with the tools to become more thoughtful readers of the Bible's prayerbook. Or, to use the authors' own words, they have succeeded in preparing readers not to plumb the depths of the Psalter but to "waterski across the surface" (8). They achieve this with an engaging (and oftentimes humorous) writing style, an ability to distill complicated ideas from a long history of psalms scholarship into something accessible for their intended audience, sidebar discussions tying the point under consideration to contemporary music and poetry, as well as the participatory nature of the book itself. On this final point, there are several fill-in-the-blank exercises in the actual body of the text, which not only fuels readers' imaginations but also forces one to slow down in reading and take a more active role in learning about the psalms.

At the end of each chapter is a "Going Deeper" section with questions and exercises for readers to consider. These range from explaining Hebrew parallelism in an understandable way to a friend to writing your own imprecatory psalm over someone you are angry with … and then ensuring you destroy it! Also rounding out each chapter is a section entitled "For Further Reading," which offers a handful of accessible resources on the topic considered in that chapter. These tools help extend the invitation to the psalms beyond the scope of simply reading this book; this is an invitation the Jacobsons hope will continue to lead the reader on the path of discovery and engagement.

Additional strengths abound. The authors should be lauded for their emphasis not simply on identifying form but focusing on *how* the form means. Moreover, one definitely cannot accuse the authors of failing to show their work. Countless examples from the Psalms, both short and extended, fill each chapter with thorough explications to make the relevant point stick for the reader.

Given that this book has much to commend it, I do wish the authors had included a listing of their own classification of the psalms, sorting them by type. To be fair, one could arrive at such a list by combing through the numerous examples they offer, and they do share in a footnotes in chapter 2 an incipient classification. They note that "different scholars categorize psalms differently" (40 n. 3) in introducing a tentative list of prayers for help, and they identify hymns of praise in another footnote (46 n. 6), as well as trust psalms (51 n. 12) and thanksgiving psalms (57 n. 15). Given one cannot always trust an academic to read the footnotes, it seems odd to bury this important information, despite the notes themselves being quite minimal. If the volume, however, desires to allow readers to "waterski across the surface" of the psalms, erring on the side of ease would prove preferable, especially given their proper emphasis on how vital genre is as a hermeneutical step.

I also believe it would be advantageous to have included some treatment of reading the Psalter as a book. What is the overarching metanarrative of the Psalter? What is the effect of reading the psalms in order from 1 to 150? Such debates have been prevalent in scholarship since the seminal work of Gerald Wilson, and since the authors leave a lot of interpretive room open for the novice reader it would be interesting to allow them to construct their own sense of what it means to read the Psalter as a book, all the while being guided by the Jacobsons with some sense of possibilities scholars have advanced. They edge toward this discussion a few places, once noting (in line with Wilson) that wisdom psalms seem to be placed at critical junctures in the book (66), as well as in the final chapter on theology and the faithfulness of God. But again, inviting readers into this still formative discussion would equip them with yet another tool for discovery and engagement with not just the psalms but the book of Psalms.

A few years ago I was invited to teach a multiweek adult Bible study at my church. I chose the Psalms, assuming people of faith would have an interest in learning more deeply about the prayerbook of the Bible. While the study went well, there were some participants who expressed their frustration at not being able to "get into" the Psalms. Still others wanted a resource to guide them in self-study after our time together ended. For both of these audiences, I wish I had had this book to share with them.

Psalm Studies, by Sigmund Mowinckel. Translated by Mark E. Biddle. History of Biblical Studies 3. Volume 1: Atlanta: SBL Press, 2014. Pp. xii + 491. Paper. $59.95. ISBN 9781589835085. Hardcover. $79.95. ISBN 9781589838017. Volume 2: Atlanta: SBL Press, 2014. Pp. x + 424. Paper. $53.95. ISBN 9781589835108. Hardcover. $73.95. ISBN 9781589838024.

Phil J. Botha, University of Pretoria

Sigmund Mowinckel's original six separate "Psalm Studies" in German (later collected and reprinted in two volumes) are translated in these two very user-friendly and readable English volumes. Volume 1, comprising xii + 492 pages, contains "Psalm Studies 1: 'Äwen and the Psalms of Individual Lament" and "Psalm Studies 2: YHWH's Enthronement Festival and the Origin of Eschatology." Volume 2 contains another x + 414 pages, but the main pages are numbered consecutively from 493 to 904. In it one finds "Psalm Studies 3: Cultic Prophecy and Prophetic Psalms"; "Psalm Studies 4: The Technical Terms in the Psalm Superscriptions"; "Psalm Studies 5: Blessing and Curse in Israel's Cult and Psalmody"; and "Psalm Studies 6: The Psalmists." Both volumes have contents pages providing the page numbers to every section and subsection in the two volumes, so that one can locate a particular paragraph within the context of the whole series of studies (bearing in mind that volume 1 ends at more or less page 500). Volume 2 has an index of sources (869–904) listing references to the Hebrew Bible, Deuterocanonical and pseudepigraphical works, the New Testament, rabbinic works, and Josephus (which has only one reference).

As someone who has on numerous occasions consulted Mowinckel's *Psalmenstudien* when working on a particular psalm but has never had the necessary determination to read the two German volumes from beginning to end, I would like to state unequivocally that the translator has done the English-speaking academic community a favor with this meticulously translated English version of the original. Mark Biddle has included a translator's note (1:xi–xii) in which he mentions the problems faced by someone who has to translate Mowinckel's Norwegian-influenced German (sometimes verging on what Biddle describes as near-pidgin "Germwegian"). Sensitivity for gender-inclusivity and multiculturalism was, as one could expect, of no concern in Mowinckel's day. Biddle says that he settled for a compromise in his translation: not obscuring Mowinckel's cultural setting but sometimes translating into a more idiomatic English than the German original warrants (xi). The result is a great success: many academics who have had to rely on summaries of Mowinckel's arguments now have direct access to the complete arguments in his peculiar, almost discursive, style of writing in these early studies of his, which have been seminal in Psalms research in many ways and for quite some time. It is now easier to see how Mowinckel's thought was influenced by Gunkel but also in which respects and how often he differed from Gunkel and criticized Gunkel's position.

It should be noted that these pioneering investigations of Mowinckel, which appeared in the years 1921–1924, were meant to be innovative and even provocative and that Mowinckel later reconsidered some of his points of view and published a more mature restatement in his 1951 Norwegian publication, *Offersang og Sangoffer*, translated and published in 1962 by D. R. Ap-Thomas as *The Psalms in Israel's Worship I–II*.[1] Mowinckel himself confessed that he later took up a more conservative position in comparison to his earlier views, and Ap-Thomas

---

1. See D. R. Ap-Thomas, "An Appreciation of Sigmund Mowinckel's Contribution to Biblical Studies," *JBL* 85 (1966): 315–325, here 316.

speculates that this retraction may well have been influenced by the "excesses, as he would regard them, of some of his followers of the 'Scandinavian school.'"[2]

Mowinckel wanted to "liberate what is new in Gunkel from its bondage to older views" (3). What he meant by this, it seems, was, first, that Protestant theologians in general had a negative view of cultic religion and had to come to a proper appreciation of the cult in religion (see 5). Gunkel understood the psalms to have originated in the cult but maintained that most of the psalms were the compositions of private individuals from the postexilic period and that they reflected the social and religious tensions of Judaism in the Persian period. Mowinckel saw this as the result of a negative view of the Israelite cult among Protestant theologians and wanted to demonstrate that the psalms were composed by temple officials during (mostly) the monarchic period (see 796–815). According to him, many psalms originated in the cult during the monarchic age, some even before the time of David. This would be applicable especially to those psalms that in his view displayed traces of a festival that celebrated YHWH's enthronement (379).

Second, Mowinckel thought that one had to appreciate the worldview and thought patterns of "primitive human beings" (*primitive* not being meant derogatorily, 3). From Heinrich Zimmern's translations of Babylonian psalms of penitence (*Babylonische Busspsalmen* [Leipzig: Hinrichs, 1885]), Mowinckel picked up the idea that the lives of ancient Israelites must have been dominated by their fear of evil and their attempts to get access to the power that would protect them against this constant danger. He criticizes Assyriologists who would refer to Babylonian cultic procedures simply as "magic and sorcery" and who thus caused theologians to underestimate the role of the cult in providing protection against the dangers that beset the lives of Israelites every day (5–6 n. 1). Mowinckel was also influenced to a large extent by Vilhelm Grönbech's study of primitive cultures, *Vor Folkeaet I Otilden*,[3] and this probably determined his own interpretation of *aun* (as he describes the "original pronunciation" of אָוֶן) as a potency exerted by a certain class of people in ancient Israelite culture (6). The פֹעֲלֵי אָוֶן are those who "do *aun*," and he understood this and synonyms that refer to opponents in the psalms such as נבלים, כסילים, אוילים, חללים, אנשי דמים, מרעים, and רשעים as referring to a group of people who use magical incantations to attack the upright in the Psalter (see 34, 100). Many of the psalms were, in his view, composed with the purpose to protect "decent, peaceful people" against efficacious acts and formulas, thus magical incantations, that were used to make people sick, steal their property or take their lives (66–67). From the analogy of Babylonian lament psalms and also from "direct" evidence that he finds in the "*aun*-psalms and most of the other individual psalms of lament" (101), he infers that the enemies were sorcerers who

---

2. Ibid., 317.

3. This work was published in four volumes in Copenhagen by Pio between 1901 and 1912. See 4 n. 4. Mowinckel attended a series of lectures by Grönbeck on the nature of the primitive cult in 1916, and this proved to be an important stimulus. See 176.

caused illnesses among believers. The believers would come to the temple to make a sin offering and pray for protection against the enemies. When a person was healed, he or she would return to the temple to pay specific vows with a cultic thanksgiving offering, for which purpose a psalm of thanksgiving could then be used (129).

Mowinckel was also convinced that, although they are rarely mentioned in the Psalter, demons helped the magicians, and he finds traces of them in certain psalms (e.g., the description of the enemies in Pss 22 and 59) (70–79). Mowinckel thus interprets most of the individual lament psalms as prayers for help against sorcerers and assumes that in most cases the enemies caused an illness. He explains the fact that there are so many requests for help against enemies and so rarely requests to be healed from sickness as a result of the fact that deliverance from the enemies would include healing *eo ipso* (110). This is one example from many in these two volumes where Mowinckel seems to be so convinced of his interpretation that various features in the text, even the absence of evidence, are called upon to corroborate his view and he seems to lose his objectivity. This is a constant danger that threatens every researcher, but it becomes a real problem when adjustments to the text are made or certain parts are considered to be interpolations in order to make the text fit one's interpretation (see 32, 107, 168, 170, etc.).

In Mowinckel's view, the majority of psalms thus originated in the preexilic period, and he asserts that there is not a single Maccabean psalm in the Psalter (166, 784). They were written by temple singers (843), Levites attached to the temple, and were intended for public use and were later collected to serve as the hymn book of the worshiping community in the cult of the Second Temple (807). Individual psalms of lament could thus be reinterpreted later and used for a different cultic purpose (166). Originally, however, the laments were intended to be prayers related to the rites of purification and healing and to the sin offering such a person would present. They must consequently rather be called "individual sin-offering psalms" (808).

In addition to the idea that the enemies were sorcerers and that the individual psalms of lament were compositions that were used in the cult to free the upright from these evil powers, Mowinckel's second major contribution to the study of the Psalms was to argue that there is evidence in the Psalter of a major annual Israelite festival that was celebrated in the cult in order to commemorate the kingship of Yahweh. The whole of Psalm Studies 2 (175–491) is dedicated to proving the thesis that YHWH had a yearly recurring enthronement festival. In a preface to Psalm Studies 2 (175–80), Mowinckel describes the development of his ideas and the influence of Hugo Gressmann, Heinrich Zimmern, Vilhelm Grönbeck, and Johannes Pedersen on various aspects of his theory. Based on his knowledge of the yearly cultic celebration of the enthronement of a new god in Babylonia–Assyria, as well as the cultic interpretation of Ps 47 by Duhm and Gunkel's interpretation of Ps 24 as a processional psalm, Mowinckel began to conceptualize an annual feast celebrating YHWH's enthronement in Israel. As such occasions were celebrated in Babylonia, in his view this festival must have been the old New Year's festival. The connection between the enthronement psalms and eschatology, he says, appeared to him suddenly "almost like a flash of lightning" in 1917 (176). Mowinckel understood the autumn festival as the major one and thought that concepts and psalms originally associated with it were later transferred to Passover. The celebration of YHWH's enthronement was a sacred drama that produced reality. He describes it as "the shared experience of the new creation of the king coming to save," and this is the root of all eschatology (178–79).

In addition to the more restricted group of psalms narrowly associated with the enthronement festival (Pss 47; 81; 93; 95–100), Mowinckel also saw lines of connection (such as points of view, cultic myths, and practices) that led to many other psalms. So, for example, the idea of a cultic procession with the ark of the covenant in Ps 47:6 suggested to him connections to Pss 24 and 132 as well as to the songs of ascent. The central concept of YHWH's incipient sojourn in Jerusalem in the "enthronement psalms" in turn led him to include Pss 46 and 48 in his investigation of the enthronement festival. In this way he came to use psalms from various genres as sources for his theory about YHWH's cultic enthronement; Pss 8, 15, 20, 24, 29, 33, 46, 48, 50, 66A, 75, 76, 81, 82, 84, 87, 114, 118, 132, 149, as well as Exod 15:1–18, came to be involved in an ever-widening circle of association (184). They were further expanded by the inclusion of the psalms of ascent (Pss 120–134), Ps 85 as a "substantial parallel" to Ps 126, and "harvest and fertility psalms" such as Pss 65 and 67 (185). In Mowinckel's view, these psalms (to a greater or lesser extent) celebrated the establishment of YHWH as king: YHWH came to establish his world-encompassing kingdom. Israel was his chosen people and would thus serve as his highest officials. The other nations had to serve Israel, and YHWH had to be considered the only God and king in the universe (189).

Mowinckel's third major innovation was to recognize the role of prophets in the cult. He identified pieces of direct divine speech in the psalms and linked this to cultic prophecy. Because he considered the psalms to have originated in the cult, such instances of divine speech must naturally have been oracles pronounced by cultic prophets (rather than priests, who would be consulted for simple yes or no answers), he argued (see 495–505). The prophetic oracles could be sacramental elements connected to the great New Year's Festival (e.g., in Pss 12; 14; 50; 75; 81; 82; 85; 87; 89:29–38; 95; 132), connected to occasional worship services, oracles addressed to the king (e.g., Pss 2:6–9; 45; 72; 110), or oracles given in private cultic procedures (e.g., Ps 91). He infers that some of the temple singers must then have been inspired prophets (519).

Mowinckel's interpretation of the Psalms has been criticized from various perspectives. His early work on the Psalter was predetermined by his view about the threat of magic to ancient Israelites and of the individual psalms as compositions prepared for use against magicians during the monarchical period, or otherwise to celebrate the kingship of YHWH at recurring yearly festivals. He was convinced that Israel's cult must have served similar purposes and contained similar texts as those of Assyria–Babylonia and was perhaps too optimistic in his attempt to reconstruct the Jerusalem cult from the individual psalms themselves. Mowinckel had no knowledge of or regard for the work of editors in the postexilic period who adapted psalms, rewrote them, or composed new ones and who arranged them in clusters and books so as to create a literary collection of texts that could be used to reenact the prayers of David or trace the history of Israel from lament to praise. Why would one then want to buy these translations of works that are almost a century old? Because they have been so influential in the interpretation of the Psalter for so long. One can, for instance, not read a commentary such as that of Artur Weiser without coming under the impression of how vast the influence of Mowinckel was. From this translation, one can also discern the factors that influenced Mowinckel and appreciate his individuality in reconstructing the cult of Israel. Mowinckel may have been mistaken in many of the conclusions he made, but in my view there is still great value in his recognition of similar motifs between various psalms. The YHWH-*malak* psalms, for example, probably do not give us direct access to a preexilic cultic festival that celebrated the kingship of YHWH, but in their function of focusing on YHWH's role as the only creator and sole ruler of the cosmos in the postexilic (kingless) era, it is important to read these psalms against the background of Babylonian notions about divine kingship. In this regard, Mowinckel's work can still be put to good use. These two volumes are therefore recommended as necessary, perhaps even indispensable, reading for all who want to understand the book of Psalms.

'Perhaps There Is Hope': Reading Lamentations as a Polyphony of Pain, Penitence, and Protest, by Miriam Bier. Library of Hebrew Bible/Old Testament Studies 603. London: T&T Clark, 2015. Pp. xv + 249. Hardcover. $120.00. ISBN 9780567658388.

Amy C. Cottrill, Birmingham-Southern College

Miriam Bier has produced a lucid and well-argued analysis of the book of Lamentations from a Bahktinian perspective. Her main argument is that Lamentations is a polyphony that contains diverse theological perspectives that are in tension with one another throughout the book and never merge into one coherent, monologic theological voice. Bier also analyzes past interpretations of Lamentations with its multivocality. Despite the recognized presence of diverse theological perspectives in Lamentations, interpreters have emphasized one perspective over others, Bier argues, producing readings that have not done justice to the polyphonic nature of the book. Readers have often monologized Lamentations, finding theological coherence in Lamentations where there is none. Her book is, as she says in the first sentence, "both a reading of Lamentations, and a reading of *readings* of Lamentations (1)." While the "reading of readings" aspect of the book does not amount to a full-blown history of interpretation of Lamentations, it analyzes prominent tendencies in recent scholarly treatments.

Bier begins by introducing the major theological influences in Lamentations and discussing the tendencies among recent interpreters toward theodic or antitheodic readings. In line with previous scholarship, especially that of Bertil Albrektson, Norman Gottwald, Adele Berlin, and Jeffery Tigay, Bier argues that Lamentations reflects multiple theological traditions, "including Deuteronomic understandings of retribution in covenant context, Davidic or Zion theology, priestly purity paradigms, prophetic motifs, and wisdom discourse" (11). Read synchronically, Lamentations is a dialogue between these theological influences and ideological paradigms. The problem, according to Bier, is that many, though not all, interpreters of Lamentations have diminished the plurality of voices and theological influences by privileging one over the other, crediting one perspective with the truth to which the interpreter places the other voices into submission.

The first major category that Bier names is theodic interpretations. Theodic readings take up the question of God's justice in punishing Jerusalem for her sins: "The question for interpreters is whether there is sufficient 'good cause' for the full measure of fury unleashed upon Jerusalem, or whether the measure of anger she has experienced is greater than the measure of her sins" (13). Theodic readings by Philip Ryken, Jože Krašovec, Michael Guinan, F. B. Huey, S. Paul Re'emi, Robin Parry, and Paul House emphasize the ultimate goodness of YHWH and the voices in Lamentations that find that Jerusalem's suffering is commensurate with her sin. Key to many theodic readings is Lam 3:21–39, a confession of sin and acceptance of culpability that seems to justify God's actions against Jerusalem. Bier notes that theodic intepretations tend to construe these verses as determinative of the theology of Lamentations, rather than allowing these verses to stand as one perspective among many in the book.

The second category of interpretation encompasses antitheodic readings that challenge orthodox assertions of God's ultimate goodness in Lamentations. In contrast to theodic readings, antitheodic interpretations refuse to justify God's actions in Lamentations. These readings highlight the places in Lamentations where God's actions against Jerusalem are questioned and contested. Johanna Steibert, for instance, argues that God is often brutal and vicious in Lamentations, far from the merciful portrayal that theodic readings emphasize (19). In this category Bier briefly discusses the works of Stiebert, Tod Linafelt, Carleen Mandolfo, Kathleen O'Connor, Chip Dobbs-Allsopp, and Alan Cooper.

Bier recognizes the presence of theodic and antitheodic tendencies in Lamentations but refuses to allow one perspective to represent the whole. Rather, these theological tendencies are unresolved, truly in tension with one another throughout. The bulk of Bier's analysis of Lamentations, therefore, undertakes a demonstration of what it looks like to read the book as polyphony, resisting the urge to place one voice in control of the other. Bier undertakes an "as if" reading, interpreting each chapter of Lamentations in turn as if it were a polyphony.

In each of the following five chapters Bier discusses a single chapter of Lamentations and its theodic and antitheodic potential. While she recognizes that a particular chapter might lend itself to theodic or antitheodic readings more easily, her goal is to resist giving one voice precedence over the other. For instance, Lam 3 does have the most theodic potential in Lamentations, according to Bier (140), though antitheodic interpretations have correctly noted the elements of protest also present in this chapter in which the speaker justifies God's actions against Jerusalem. However, Bier does not think it is enough merely to recognize antitheodic tendencies that are present in an otherwise dominantly theodic chapter. Rather, Bier treats the antitheodic voice in Lam 3 as its own theological center, a voice that is not in submission to any other perspective. A polyphonic reading "raises the possibility of more expansive" interpretive possibilities, seeing both of these tendencies as distinct theological hubs that are unmerged and remain in tension with one another (140–41).

Chapter 7 treats Lamentations as a whole. Chapters 2–6 has read *as if* Lamentations is polyphony. In chapter 7 Bier returns to the possibility of reading monologically. Her question is, If one were to look for one prevailing point of view in this poetry, where would one find it? There are several options, considering the multivocal composition of the book: the voice of YHWH, the prophet, the omniscient narrator, the lamenter, the author, Zion, or the community. If the interpreter is not persuaded by the centrality of one of these voices, she might argue that the form and structure of Lamentations itself offers the central theological perspective of the book; Lam 3 as the center chapter of the book, Lam 5 as the concluding chapter of the book, or the placement of Lamentations within the canon as a whole might provide a controlling perspective for interpretation. This section of the chapter is an effective demonstration of the possibilities from which the interpreter must choose in order to create a monologic interpretation; the sheer number of options highlights the role of the interpreter in constructing a monologic reading. The many possibilities for reading monologically are not presented here to deride or undercut those who have and will undertake such readings. Bier does not present the possibilities for reading monologically merely to shoot them down but to demonstrate that Lamentations does not present itself as a coherent theology. Rather, monologic readings of Lamentations are products of a methodological habit within biblical studies to find the dominant perspective of a book, as opposed to the dialogic tension that may exist unresolved within texts: "Indeed, the very impulse toward finding coherence in a text is itself a false assumption on the part of biblical scholars, betraying an expectation that biblical texts should conform to some unity, even when that text is unable to agree with itself" (207).

Bier excels at demonstrating the effect of reading polyphonically. For Bier, this is not only a methodology that better recognizes the theological tension in the book of Lamentations, but it is also a reading practice that recognizes the complexity of readers who bring multiple, unmerged, ambiguous, and tensive theological commitments to the practice of interpreting texts. Bier herself holds together a dynamic tension between evangelical Christian and feminist commitments (39, 215). To be sure, some biblical texts are not polyphonic. Paul's letters, for instance, may not lend themselves to this type of reading (214), yet Bier asks biblical scholars to check their own tendencies to seek and find coherence, a habit of mind that might impede us from recognizing the deep dynamism within biblical texts *and* within biblical readers. This is an important book for the study of Lamentations and also for ongoing conversation about the intellectual heritage of biblical scholarship and the role of readers in creating readings that fit within preconceived notions of monologic truth.

Ruth: A New Translation with Introduction and Commentary, by Jeremy Schipper. Anchor Yale Bible 7D. New Haven: Yale University Press, 2015. Pp. xvii + 221. Cloth. $75.00. ISBN 9780300192155

George Savran, Schechter Institute for Jewish Studies

Jeremy Schipper has made a significant contribution to the Anchor Bible commentary series (now the Anchor Yale Bible). His volume on the book of Ruth is one of a new round of updated commentaries on the Hebrew Bible, the earlier volume having been written by Edward F. Campbell in 1975. Where Campbell concentrated more intensively on the idea of the Hebrew storyteller, Schipper focuses on a variety of textual and interpretive issues that give his commentary a wide scope and an important critical perspective. The structure of Schipper's commentary is in keeping with the rest of the Anchor Bible series: a lengthy introduction and an up-to-date bibliography, a new translation of the book, detailed textual notes on many of the verses, and an interpretative essay at the end of each section. The book is well produced, carefully edited and accurate in transliteration—I noticed only a few small errors on pages 20, 35, and 134. The font chosen is clear and quite readable, albeit smaller than that used in other volumes in the series.

The author presents a detailed discussion of the text, most often agreeing with the Masoretic Text but careful to weigh the evidence of the ancient versions. The translation reads smoothly and contains a number of nuanced interpretations that Schipper explains in his notes. Elimelekh went to "*reside as an alien in the territory* of Moab" (1:1). When Naomi leaves Moab her daughters-in-law were "*under her authority*" (1:7). Orpah is instructed to return to "her people and *her ancestors*" in 1:15. When Ruth gleans in Boaz's field, she requests that she be allowed to "*gather* [the sheaves] *into bundles*" (2:7). Boaz is identified by Naomi as "one of our *kindred redeemers*" (2:20). At night on the threshing floor, Boaz "was *troubled* and *turned himself about*" (3:8). In 4:12 the narrator describes the necessary custom "regarding redemption and *substitution*." Finally, the female neighbors in 4:16 proclaim "*For Naomi* a son has been born." All of these, as well as other interesting turns of phrase, are given adequate support in the textual notes. Schipper's aim is to be as accurate as possible in his translation, foregoing style in favor of precision as he deems necessary.

Rather than attempt to address the many interesting observations about the text and its interpretation that Schipper discusses in his comments on each section, the review will focus primarily on Schipper's introductory essay, in which he lays out his deeper understanding of the book of Ruth as well the critical positions that inform the rest of the commentary. Beginning with textual matters, Schipper briefly discusses the textual witnesses that serve as the basis for his translation. In his outline of the structure of the book, Schipper examines a number of possible divisions of the text and explains the logic behind his own decisions about such divisions. Schipper makes a point of marking 1:16b–17 and 1:20–21 as poetic texts despite the fact that the MT treats them as prose. I agree with his decision but would add Naomi's speech in 1:11–13 to the list of poetic sections. In addition to the interweaving of poetry and prose, Schipper is sensitive to the creative use of language in the book with regard to alliteration and paronomasia. For example, the word *'ephah* in 2:17 resonates nicely with the word *'epho'* in 2:19. The unusual term *herayon* for pregnancy may have been chosen because of its proximity to and similarity with other names—Hezron, Nahshon, and Salmon—and as a contrast to Mahlon and Kilyon. It is Schipper's sense that this interplay between sound and meaning is a central aspect of the book's unique diction. Other points that occur in Schipper's notes are developed into significant literary insights. Since the name Boaz "forms a consonantal anagram with the word 'abandon' ('azab)" (8), it suggests a close connection between the name and the man "who has not abandoned his kindness with the living and the dead" (2:20).

The second section of the introduction addresses literary contexts for Ruth, discussing the question of canonical placement, ancient Israelite literary tradition, and the issue of genre. In each of these matters Schipper exercises caution in refraining from reaching a definitive conclusion. Neither the location of the book after Judges (LXX) nor its position in the Writings (MT) can be seen as decisive. On the matter of authorship and dating, Schipper argues that the amount of Late Biblical Hebrew in the book is balanced by an equivalent use of Standard Biblical Hebrew elsewhere, leaving the reader to choose from among the suggestions of different critics. He agrees that the book was a relatively late composition but states this position only tentatively ("one could place its date of composition in at least the early Persian period" (22). Nor can theology provide a clear indication of date, since the same texts have been used to argue for both an early and a later provenance.

Cautiousness is indeed a central characteristic of this commentary. Schipper argues that the narrator of Ruth most often speaks with a neutral voice and does not offer insights into the motives behind the characters' behavior; such deductions about intention are entirely the work of the individual commentator. "Disguising one's interpretive choices as descriptions of the goals of Ruth's author or narrator" (23) often allows the interpreter to present his or her own reading as if it were the objective stance of the narrator. In light of this, Schipper is careful to present different sides of a given interpretive issue in order to show how the narrator's statements can support a variety of readings. In his eyes, narrative ambiguity and selective representation are central aspects of this narrator's style, and the reader should be aware of the extent to which his or her own interpretative stance influences his reading of the text. Schipper demonstrates this clearly with regard to gap filling (What does Ruth think about Orpah's decision to return to Moab?), characterization (To what extent does the poetic speech of Ruth and Naomi indicate the characters' interiority?), and intention (Why does Boaz think or tell Ruth not to be seen leaving the granary in 3:14?). In each of these situations Schipper feels that no objective answer can be found.

The next section of the introduction clarifies Schipper's positions with regard to a number of central issues in the book. His purpose here is to provide a corrective to what he sees as a tendency toward unwarranted assumptions on the part of many commentators. In the matter of specific acts of *ḥesed* and divine activity in general, it has become nearly commonplace to assert that God acts behind the scenes to control events in the book of Ruth. Contrary to this, Schipper notes that "the narrator explicitly attributes to God only things that are beyond human control" (31), namely, the blessing of fertility in 1:6 and 4:13. *Ḥesed* in Ruth is used primarily to describe human actions, but the reasons for the performance of such acts is not explained by the narrator. While these acts of *ḥesed* often result in blessing, the narrator does not describe what motivates Ruth or Boaz in their actions. In a similar fashion, there is a predisposition among certain commentators to attribute sexual desire to Ruth and Boaz, yet very little in the text hints at the presence of such desire. The story does not say if Ruth was physically attractive, if she had intercourse with Boaz in the granary, and if so, whether this reflected sexual desire, romantic feeling, or some other motive. While such assumptions may be understandable in the larger context of the Bible, Schipper maintains that the reader of Ruth should be more circumspect: claiming heterosexual desire on the parts of Ruth and Boaz should require "the same standard for textual evidence that is often demanded of those who map queer desires" onto the characters (37).

In his extended discussion of exogamy and ethnicity. Schipper shows how these matters in Ruth resonate with broader tendencies in biblical practice and understanding. Regarding the relationship of Judahites and Moabites, he points out that instances of Judeans marrying out were not uncommon: Judah in Gen 38:2; Ibzan in Judg 12:8–9; David in 2 Sa. 3:3; Solomon in 1 Kgs 3:1, among others. In light of this, the book of Ruth should not be understood as condemning or condoning such marriages. Moreover, the ostensible connection between Ruth the Moabite and the line of Lot can be read negatively as a critique of her lineage or positively as a reunion of the Abrahamic line that divided in Gen 13. Even Ruth's identification as a foreign woman should be qualified by her relationship to Naomi, since "with" in 1:7, 11, 22 indicates that she was "under the authority" of Naomi. She is therefore in the unusual position of being a foreigner (*nokriyah*) who is nonetheless a member of Naomi's clan ("Boaz is close to *us*. He is one of *our* kindred redeemers," 2:20). Schipper's discussion of household organization reveals similar complexities, such as the use of the term *bayit* to describe "two types of households" (48): in chapter 1 it refers to a limited family structure (*bet 'ab*), while in chapter 4 it implies a more extensive configuration of multiple clans (*bet 'abot*). This has significant implications for the statuses and roles of various characters in the book, but especially for Ruth, whom Schipper describes as "an alien (*ger*) who works under the authority of a wealthier clan member for wages" (48). These distinctions are helpful in understanding how the notion of redemption in Lev 25 relates to the situation of Ruth and Naomi. "Rather than romanticize the inclusion of Ruth in the Judahite clan structure, one should note how her status … may leave her vulnerable to exploitation" (49). The ambiguity of Ruth's situation is brought out further in a brief but insightful discussion of the role of gender in these power relationships. Schipper points to the undeniable success of the patriarchal vision of women's roles in Ruth but notes that there remains a significant degree of gender fluidity within that patriarchal model.

From the standpoint of this reviewer, there could have been greater emphasis upon the literary design of the book as well as attention to the shifting dynamic of interpersonal relations, particularly those between Ruth and Naomi. Nevertheless, Schipper's careful distinctions and critical comments serve as an important corrective to critics who overstate the role of God in the story and are insufficiently attentive to nuances of family structure and foreign identity. His commentary is a welcome addition to the critical literature on Ruth and can be read and studied with benefit by all serious students of the book.

Proverbs, by Ernest C. Lucas. Two Horizons Old Testament Commentary. Grand Rapids: Eerdmans, 2015. Pp. xiv + 407. Paper. $28.00. ISBN 9780802827104.

Ryan P. O'Dowd, Ithaca, New York

It is partly due to the aesthetic sophistication of a thousand interwoven sayings, but it is also the neglect of wisdom literature in early modern biblical studies that together make Proverbs such a fruitful source for fresh readings and new angles of research. This volume in Eerdmans's Two Horizons Old Testament Commentary series charts is own path in order to introduce Christian scholars, pastors, and leaders to a biblical interpretation of Proverbs that is grounded in "theological exegesis and theological reflection" (i). The specific religious focus should not deter non-Christian readers. In keeping with the series format, *Proverbs* divides almost evenly between standard commentary (198 pages) and essays that address theological and hermeneutical issues targeted by the editors (183 pages). These sections are reviewed separately below. The prose is clear and engaging, and Lucas writes comfortably within the text of Proverbs and its history of interpretation.

The introduction (1–47) provides synopses of the main topics in Proverbs study: the concept of wisdom in the Old Testament/Hebrew Bible and the ancient world, wisdom literature, structure, authorship, date and origin, literary forms, and relationships between Proverbs and other ancient Near Eastern wisdom literature. Lucas mostly summarizes dominant views and only occasionally interjects his own opinion. In his discussion of authorship, Lucas at first grants that Solomon may well have had a hand in writing and compiling some sayings, even though the very nature of a proverb suggests a long history of uncertain origins and many editors. He describes the probable social background as "the moderately well-off rural farmer and the urban artisan," *not* a member of the courts (7). But why not? In later discussion of ancient Near Eastern wisdom, Lucas indeed acknowledges that it can be presumptuous to marry content to source (41). That is, there is no reason why someone of royal status could not write poetry about agricultural and family life or a peasant about statecraft. The history of literature is full to the brim with evidence to the contrary, and Lucas's main discussion of authorship would have benefited from his more nuanced qualifications later on.

Although Lucas mostly avoids technical debates, he treats readers to an engaging analysis of strings and clusters in Prov 10–29 (14–22). He begins by juxtaposing arguments by Bruce Waltke and Knut Heim, who claim to see groupings of sayings throughout chapters 10–29, with arguments by Michael Fox and Tremper Longman, who hold a minimalist view about strings and clusters in Proverbs. In an effort to move beyond contemporary impasses, Lucas provides a sample analysis of clusters he finds in Prov 10–11 alongside those of Waltke and Heim, concluding that "there is some encouragement in this degree of agreement to think that the smaller clusters are not just subjective creations by the commentator" (19). Lucas readily grants that "there is indeed a measure of subjectivity in the choice of criteria for linkages." But he adds, "in the natural sciences there is recognition of the importance of 'inter-subjective verification' as a way of ameliorating this." Indeed, research always involves a careful balance of speculation and skepticism, and in its jealousy of the credibility given to the sciences, biblical studies too often mimics naïve caricatures of how science actually works, both epistemologically and socially. This is a prime example. Research into clusters and structure in Proverbs is in its infancy on the whole, and Lucas cautions readers against premature judgment to allow this new path of inquiry to develop.

The main textual commentary is brief, usually moving through individual chapters in three to four pages of printed text. Lucas rarely offers close readings of individual sayings and, even then, seldom departs from consensus opinions about translation and meaning. He nevertheless highlights major points of difficulty where one would expect it, such as the metaphorical and archaeological significance of the water sources in 5:15–20; the woman's sacrificial offerings in 7:14; possible meanings of qānanî (8:22), 'āmôn (8:30), and šlšm (22:20); and various translations of the beginning of Agur's oracle in 30:1.

Lucas follows the so-called consensus view of Proverbs' dependence on Amenemope in 22:17–22:42. More could have been said to acknowledge the contingent nature of this consensus and to alert readers to scholarly reservations about the existence and degree of such dependence. Lucas's voice betrays the tentativeness of the arguments, frequently resorting to phrases such as "could be regarded" (36), "it is arguable" (36), "general agreement," (37) and "it is plausible" (twice on 37). He also acknowledges that "close similarities with Amenemope come to an end" after the tenth saying (155). Vague similarities in content do not equate to borrowing or even demand a common origin.

Almost half of the commentary is devoted to ten essays organized under the "Theological Horizons of Proverbs." In "Acts and Consequences in Proverbs," Lucas confronts outdated characterizations of Proverbs as naïve wisdom against which Job and Qoheleth pen their "protest literature" (198–219). In an article in *JSOT* (2016) Anne Stewart critiques this same outdated position, labeling it the "simplicity thesis." Lucas similarly reminds readers that sentence literature speaks in generalities and not absolutes and that the variety, sophistication, and internal contradictions within the sayings (e.g. 17:17–18; 26:4–5) demonstrate how "the sages [in chs 10–29] were well aware that the character-consequence nexus was only a 'rule of thumb' with regard to developing life-skills, with many exceptions" (218).

"Characters in Proverbs" summarizes terms for major figures in the book: wise, righteous, simple, fool, scoffer, sluggard, and—the most frequently mentioned—wicked. Lucas ends with a discussion of the polar relationships between these characters and the liminal presentation of the "two ways" of wisdom and folly. "Family, Friends, and Neighbours in Proverbs" similarly highlights words and phrases for familiar people. While the family features in the background of the book, Lucas observes that it is imagined in full only twice (Prov 5 and 31) and that brothers are mentioned rarely. The friend and neighbor are far more common.

In "God and Proverbs," Lucas questions what many regard as an outdated assumption, that Proverbs is secular literature with little or no connection to Israel's religious and cultic life. Such views emerged within early reconstructions of Israel's social history and increasingly disputed polarizations of old wisdom and new wisdom—not, as Lucas believes, on the basis of the self-understanding of Proverbs as a literary whole. Proverbs mentions God ninety-four times, after all (246; see also 55), and Yahweh's hand in creation in Prov 1–9 has been carefully matched by his identity of the maker of human beings in Prov 10–29 (247).

"The Personification of Wisdom in Proverbs" begins with a discussion of the literary and historical background for the feminine metaphors for wisdom in Prov 1:20–33; 8:1–39; and 9:1–6. The essay ends with a study of the feminine figures in Prov 1–9 and 31 and several pages of commentary on womanist and feminist responses to Proverbs.

"The Spirituality of Proverbs" explores the devotional and religious potential of the sayings. While Lucas focuses on the benefits to Christian readers, his essay nevertheless sheds light on the religious life of the sages. In conversation with Gerhard von Rad, he argues that modern scholars have too often imported post-Enlightenment dualisms of secular/sacred, faith/reason, and mind/body into a culture in which such worldviews were foreign.

Lucas begins "Wealth and Poverty in Proverbs" with the claim that wealth and poverty feature more prominently in Proverbs than any book in the Old Testament/Hebrew Bible (291). The chapter then helpfully summarizes and evaluates recent contributions on wisdom and poverty by W. J. Houston (2003), L. P. Kimilike (2008), and T. J. Sandoval (2005).

The essay "Wisdom and Christology" rehearses the intersections between wisdom in Proverbs, the Old Testament Apocrypha, and the New Testament. Within Christian theology this intersection of texts has led to various understandings of Jesus as a sage and Jesus as either created in time or else eternally begotten and co-author of creation. Lucas argues that the Old Testament and apocryphal wisdom books are poetry and that, on their own, they offer insufficient grounds for establishing doctrines of Christology.

Wisdom Christology sets up Lucas's final two essays. In "Wisdom and Creation" Lucas bridges Yahweh's use of wisdom in his creation of the cosmos (3:19–20; 8:22–31) with Yahweh's role as creator in Prov 10–29, which serves as a motive clause for care for the poor (14:31; 17:5; 29:13), an explanatory device, and a source of wonder (16:4, 11; 20:2; 27:23–27; 30:18–19). Such connections provide a basis for understanding human ethics and conduct as matters of living within a divinely created order. Finally, "Words in Proverbs and the New Testament" summarizes proverbial sayings about speech and their parallels in the New Testament.

This commentary generally steers clear of theory, whether of literature, metaphor, or paremiology (proverb folklore). This is partly justified by the desire to bear fruit in Christian theology rather than new threads in scholarly research. But the omission is also surprising, given the relevance of these disciplines for a commentary concerned with ancient and modern horizons of interpretation. One would, for example, want to know more about how figures of speech and concepts differ between ancient and post-Enlightenment cultures.

Of almost three hundred cited works, I found seventeen published in the last ten years and only six published since 2010. Of note, Lucas overlooks Knut Heim's recent *Poetic Imagination in Proverbs: Variant Repetition and the Nature of Poetry* (2013), which would have helpfully nuanced his arguments about clusters and strings. Nancy Nam Hoon Tan's *The 'Foreignness' of the Foreign Woman in Proverbs 1–9* (2008) would have similarly added valuable insights to his discussion of feminine figures in Proverbs, especially "The Strange/Foreign Woman" (264–73). Lucas strangely omits discussion of the relationship of wisdom and law, thus excluding important works such as Franz Delitzsch's *Proverbs* (1872) and recent titles such as Bernd U. Schipper and D. Andrew Teeter, *Wisdom and Torah* (2013) and Bernd U. Schipper, *Hermeneutik der Tora* (2012). The relationship of wisdom and law is particularly relevant within the Two Horizons series, given their controversial role in historical studies and Christian theology.

Still, these are minor points in light of the broader focus of the Two Horizons series. There is a great pleasure in reading *Proverbs*, which arises from Lucas's ability to play the role of sage narrator whose personal opinions rarely seem to intrude on a fresh hearing of the sayings. There are treasures in this volume for readers of every stripe.

The Return of the King: Messianic Expectation in Book V of the Psalter, by Michael
K. Snearly. Library of Hebrew Bible/Old Testament Studies 624. London:
Bloomsbury, 2016. Pp. 248. Hardcover. $112.00. ISBN 9780567664334.

Richard Bautch, St. Edward's University

In this study, a dissertation written at Golden Gate Baptist Theological Seminary, Michael K. Snearly takes a decided approach to the book of Psalms. His
premise is that the Psalter can be read as a unified text with a consistent storyline.
In his view, material in book 5 of the Psalter about royal/Davidic promises relates
to Pss 1 and 2 at the beginning of book 1 and to other significantly positioned
psalms such as Ps 89 at the seam between books 3 and 4. Snearly concludes that the
unified Psalter exhibits an abiding interest in kingship, both that of Yahweh and
of Yahweh's earthly proxy, with book 5 articulating renewed hope in the promises
made to the Davidic line. Snearly's work is in step with those scholars currently
exploring book 5's treatment of the Davidic monarchy and the Davidic covenant,
over and against the well-established view that in books 4 and 5 a sole concern
for God's kingship supplants interest in Davidic figures and renders David's line
a vestige of the past. A view related to the latter position is that kingship was
democratized in the process of shaping the psalms into a collection, such that in
the later psalms the promises made to David are understood to be fulfilled in the
people. Snearly opposes both of these views and instead reads book 5 as reassert-
ing the Davidic king within the greater storyline of the psalms.

The book's opening chapters provide discussions of methodology. Chapter
2 reviews the critiques of Snearly's chosen method, editorial criticism, which is
a version of the canonical criticism associated with Brevard Childs and Gerald
Wilson. There have been cogent critiques by Norman Whybray, Roland Murphy,
and Erhard Gerstenberger, among others, including Gerstenberger's charge that
emphasizing the canonical final form of the Bible devalues the historical origins
of the faith traditions within the psalms. Snearly responds to Gerstenberger by
expanding the definition of historical-critical study to include lexical and syntactical work with a (psalm) text, which is the stock-in-trade of editorial criticism.
By Snearly's definition, such textual work engages the "historical context" (as he
distinguishes it from the "historical background") and shows that editorial critics
do not eschew history outright (14). Chapter 3 attempts to put editorial criticism
on positive footing. Interacting with scholarship, Snearly introduces the concept
of key-word links that connect psalms together into distinctive groupings. He
maintains that key-word links form groups on the basis of parallelism, an effect
of which is cohesion and coherence among the psalms in question. Chapter 4
pursues this line of thinking by arguing that, if parallelism exists at various literary levels, it could be possible to demonstrate parallelism "at the highest literary
levels: groups of poems and books" (48). That is, key-word links that are attested
in different books of the Psalter provide the cohesion and coherence to unify the
collection as a whole. Snearly concludes the chapter by outlining his approach to
book 5: he identifies lexical repetitions and parallels to establish a set of key words

that are then used to create hypothetical groupings and psalm-group boundaries (52). He later posits five such groupings of psalms within book 5, each defined by the key-word links that are common to the psalms in that particular group.

Given the central role that key-word links play in this study, it is noteworthy that the Hebrew text included in the volume contains dozens of errors (which could have been introduced at the typesetting stage). There are instances where a *śin* appears instead of a *šin* (68, 95, 117, 142, 153), where the vocalic pointing is reversed (95), where triliteral roots are misspelled (117, 123, 124, 126, 131, 133), and where the Hebrew syntax is twisted (105, 113, 141, 180). The quantity and variety of these errors impede the central argument that is based on key-word links. It is difficult to follow the author at those points where the lexical evidence crucial to his case is distorted.

Snearly applies his methodology to biblical texts in chapters 6 and following. In this the crux of the study, a number of valuable points are made and fresh perspectives emerge. That said, there are also points on which some readers may well take issue.

Chapter 6 seeks to show that certain key words are discernible in Pss 1, 2 (*melek, tôrāh, ṣîôn*), and 89 (*ḥesed, ʿôlām*) such that all three texts are ultimately connected with the psalms in book 5 and help to explain the structure and collective message of those later compositions. In the course of this discussion, Snearly claims that Pss 1 and 2 jointly form the introduction to the Psalter because they share royalist overtones. The feature in question, however, is not self-evident in Ps 1. Rather, Ps 1 is generally regarded as a wisdom psalm that contrasts the ways of the just and the wicked. The psalm's imagery drives home the contrast by casting the just person as a flourishing tree (Ps 1:3) and the wicked as chaff (1:4). Snearly endeavors, nevertheless, to interpret Ps 1 as a psalm about the figure of the king. He notes first that some scholars have aligned Ps 1 with the kingship law in Deut 17:14–20. This parallel, however, is quite weak when the texts are compared closely, as there is no common phrasing, and the perspectives are markedly different. The individual in Ps 1 is likened not to a king but to a tree that bears fruit and prospers (1:3). In a second attempt to identify royalist overtones in Ps 1, Snearly addresses the arboreal imagery of 1:3, again through secondary sources and the views of other scholars. He suggests that the image of a tree evokes a holy plac; if said holy place is the (presumably Jerusalem) temple, then the figure in 1:3 is identical to the king established on Mount Zion, the site of the sanctuary. Here the evidence is circumstantial while the argument is tendentious. Of equal concern is Snearly's appropriating the argument uncritically to conclude that there are royalist overtones in Ps 1 that link it to Ps 2, with the two psalms jointly serving as the introduction to the Psalter.

Chapters 7–11 subdivide book 5 of the Psalter into groups of psalms formed by key-word links common to all the psalms in the group. The groupings include Pss 107–118, 119 (a grouping of one), 120–137, 138–145, and 146–150. With Pss 107–118, the designated key words are *ḥesed* and *ʿôlām*; each word appears at least once in each psalm, although they both appear together in only four of the eleven psalms in question. The grouping includes three psalms with Davidic superscriptions, and Snearly leverages this feature of Ps 108–110: "David becomes a prominent figure again. Even the placement of the Davidic psalms (at the beginning of the group) implies that they are meant to influence that which follows. The message is: David is back!" (127). In Ps 119 Snearly discerns a royal emphasis alongside the psalm's interest in torah. He claims that themes of torah and torah study in Ps 119 recollect "the royal figure of Psalm 1, who is portrayed as a devoted student of Yahweh's Torah" (137). This claim lacks a firm foundation inasmuch as it builds upon the problematic argument that there are royalist overtones in Ps 1. Subsequently, Snearly cites lexical data common to Pss 1 and 119 or to Deut 17:14–20 and Ps 119, but the Hebrew words indicated relate generically to torah study, not to the monarchy or the king. Needed here is direct evidence to support the claim that Ps 119 has a monarchic focus, in contrast to the typical appraisal of Ps 119 as a wisdom psalm. With Pss 120–137, the ascent psalms (Pss 120–134) are extended by three. Psalms 135–137 are understood as a cohesive unit based on another dissertationist's "compelling" (144) work that is cited (as opposed to engaged). Snearly designates five key-word links clustered in Pss 120–137 to make those psalms a group. One key word in particular, *ṣiôn*, becomes the group's witness to a Davidic figure, as in Ps 132:13–18. With Pss 138–145, nine key-word links are discussed as well as the Davidic superscriptions at the beginning of each psalm. Snearly concludes that the links allow these psalms to cohere as a group and that the superscriptions "suggest that the 'I' of these psalms is a royal figure, thus bringing the themes of Yahweh's kingdom and his appointed king into the foreground of Psalms 138–145" (162). Psalms 144–145 are said to round out book 5, with Pss 146–150 understood as the conclusion to the Psalter.

In the book's final chapter, Snearly locates the Davidic references that he discerns in book 5 in a larger context, which he refers to as messianism in comparable Jewish literature; here it would have been helpful to define the complex idea of messiah and discuss the issues around it. He speaks of "a post-exilic redaction [of the Psalter] sometime during the second temple period, ... when there is no Davidic king on the throne" (190). He cites restoration texts such as Amos 9:11 and Jer 23:5 before asserting that 1–2 Chronicles has a close affinity to the perspective on David that he has identified in book 5 of the Psalter. Not all will find Snearly's reading of Chronicles persuasive. Messianic functions such as requiting evildoers and delivering God's people from suffering are not associated with the Davidic line in Chronicles. Chronicles rather presents a templocentric vision of Israel in which David and his line play a key role but not that of a royal messiah. Even David's defeat of the Philistines in 1 Chr 14 is but an aspect of the greater narrative about bringing the ark of God to the central sanctuary in Jerusalem. The significance of Judah's king in Chronicles should be stated with nuance, especially in reference to the exile. Snearly summarizes 2 Chr 36:9–21 as "acknowledging the bitter reality of the exile and the absence of a Davidic king on the throne of the nation" (191–92), although the biblical passage shows no sympathy for Kings

Jehoiachin and Zedekiah when they are exiled and reports rather that God "had compassion on his people and his dwelling place [i.e., the temple]" (2 Chr 36:15).

In sum, this book has its strengths and shortcomings. The analysis involving key-word links is intriguing, but it does not always establish a clear literary relationship among a group of texts or between texts in different parts of the Psalter. The arguments in general would benefit from more detailed textual analysis, especially at critical junctures where another scholar's position is cited and simply adopted. As Snearly's thesis regarding the Davidic promises in book 5 is wide ranging and indeed bold, it requires a close exegetical reading of the psalms to support it. *The Return of the King*, to be sure, makes a contribution in turning our collective attention to the Davidic material in book 5. These psalms contain an undeniable interest in the Davidic legacy and in kingship more generally, although it is expressed piecemeal and in a variety of ways (consider, too, that the LXX and 11QPsa^ conclude with a version of Ps 151 relating key events in David's life). This diverse body of evidence calls into question the longstanding view that books 4 and 5 understand God alone to be king and is, thankfully, spurring new lines of research such as that reviewed here. At a session of the 2015 International Meeting of the Society of Biblical Literature in Buenos Aires, Jerome Creach considered changing views of monarchy in the Persian period with reference to Pss 89 and 138–145 (the final Davidic collection). Recognizing that the king is presented as a frail human with limited capacity, Creach carefully explored the continued expressions of hope for the Davidic monarchy in book 5. At the same session, W. Dennis Tucker presented Achaemenid texts such as Naqši Rustam to suggest that books 4–5 of the Psalter reframe the notion of monarchy in terms of creation and kingship, an approach consonant with the Persian practice of conceiving kingship in terms of creation, kingship, and deity. Tucker locates the late royal psalms in a broader historical context that is plausible and promises to yield new insights into Judean thought about the Davidic legacy in the Second Temple period. Psalms scholars and those in related fields will want to take note of these emerging developments in our assessment of the Davidic material at the conclusion of the Psalter.

APOCRYPHAL/DEUTEROCANONICAL AND OTHER JEWISH WRITINGS

Reincarnation in Philo of Alexandria, by Sami Yli-Karjanmaa. Studia Philonica Monographs 7. Atlanta: SBL Press, 2015. Pp. xvi + 309. Paper. $42.95. ISBN 9780884141204. Hardcover. $57.95. ISBN 9780884141228.

Justin M. Rogers, Freed-Hardeman University

The work under review is the first-ever academic monograph on reincarnation in Philo of Alexandria (ca. 20 BCE–50 CE). The author wrote both his master's thesis (University of Helsinki) and doctoral dissertation (Åbo Akademi University) on the subject, and the present work is a revised and abbreviated version of the latter. Philo is often taken to be a primary witness to "Middle Platonism" (e.g., John Dillon, *The Middle Platonists*, rev ed. [Ithaca, NY: Cornell University Press, 1996], 139–83), and the present work seeks to show that Philo followed the Platonic theory of the soul, including psychic preexistence and reincarnation.

When the theme of the present work was announced to the Philo Seminar at the 2015 Annual Meeting of the Society of Biblical Literature in Atlanta, quite a number of Philonists raised a skeptical eyebrow. Can we actually believe that Philo as a Jew endorsed the reincarnation of souls? Yli-Karjanmaa would answer with an enthusiastic yes, although most modern scholars of Philo would be inclined to disagree. The author shows, however, that his contention is far from novel in Philonic studies.

The monograph retains the basic structure of a doctoral thesis, with only four chapters. The first chapter provides an introduction to the study, a description of the author's methodology and a history of research that serves both as a point of departure and a point of contention for the author's proposed research question.

Chapter 2 discusses the Platonic (and Middle Platonic) context of reincarnation and gives an overview of Philo's psychology, anthropology, and eschatology to show that reincarnation fits within his intellectual system. Philo was not, however, dependent upon a Middle Platonic source but derived the doctrine from Plato himself.

After a survey of Philo's basic eschatology, Yli-Karjanmaa concludes that, "while Philo has no explicit and systematic teaching of the hereafter, he does not express explicit agnosticism about it, either" (111). Such a statement seems to invalidate the premise of the work altogether, for it would at least reduce reincarnation to one of several eschatological options known to Philo. But in the second part of the chapter Yli-Karjanmaa marshals a number of passages to demonstrate that Philo frequently utilizes reincarnational language. His conclusion then becomes much stronger: "His [Philo's] anthropology would well be able to accommodate the doctrine, as would his soteriology as well as what can be inferred of his individual eschatology" (128). The second chapter is essential to the thesis, for Philo's repeated failure to endorse reincarnation explicitly (a significant objection to study's premise) is dismissed as unimportant. Yli-Karjanmaa assumes that Philo's reincarnational language would have been sufficiently recognizable to Philo's audience that he consciously "ran the risk" of being judged as endorsing the theory.

The third chapter discusses four passages taken as direct endorsements of reincarnation in Philo: *Somn.* 1.137–139, *Cher.* 114; *QE* 2.40 and fragment 3 (from the lost *Leg.* book 4, printed in J. Rendel Harris, *Fragments of Philo Judaeus* [Cambridge: Harvard University Press, 1886], 7). Only the first of these passages has received widespread scholarly attention as a testimony to reincarnation, as Yli-Karjanmaa's discussion reflects. There is also a question as to whether the last passage is authentically Philonic, but after a thorough linguistic analysis he concludes that it is genuine (189–95).

Yli-Karjanmaa systematically analyzes each of the four passages and provides a valuable discussion of virtually every detail. The discussions are biased, of course, by the confessed presupposition to prove Philo's endorsement of reincarnation (131). The reader will not be surprised that each passage is judged in approval of the doctrine.

The fourth and final chapter is a "synthesis" that offers additional Philonic passages that Yli-Karjanmaa wishes to fit within a reincarnational framework. Essentially, an attempt is made to demonstrate how certain Philonic texts can be read more insightfully if we assume his endorsement of reincarnation.

The monograph concludes with three appendices, the first on the subject of παλινδρομέω in Philo, the second a text-critical analysis of *Cher.* 114, and the third a text-critical analysis of *QE* 2.40. These are followed by a bibliography and general indices.

The work contains some typographical, grammatical, and spelling errors. For example, "ch. 30" ought to be ch. 3 (19, 85), "changing into animal in Philo form" ought to be "changing into animal form in Philo" (28), "lead" ought to be "led" (56), "may taken" should be "may be taken" (132), and "some Philo's references" should be read as "some of Philo's references" (159). There are also formatting errors. For example, a space is improperly added before a closed parenthesis (109), a footnote has been inadvertently split (157 n. 50), and there is inconsistency between italicizing and not italicizing *QG* and *QE* (72, 78, 83, 85, etc.). On the whole, however, the work seems well edited.

The book deserves some measure of content criticism as well. First, the author concludes that Philo's doctrine of reincarnation was an "esoteric teaching" (247). Philo, it is claimed, did not wish "the references to reincarnation to be immediately understood by *anyone* (*Somn.* 1.139 is an exception) [but] he did not want to hide his position so well that *nobody* can find it" (245–46, emphasis original). Unfortunately, the reader is never introduced to Philo's so-called esoteric audience, nor do we receive an explanation of *why* Philo would need to suppress his theory among his exoteric readers. Yli-Karjanmaa simply states that Philo was reticent to endorse the doctrine explicitly perhaps because it was absent from the Bible, then insists that a longer explanation "would merit a study of its own" (246). Such comprehensive assertions about Philo's audience should surely be backed with more evidence.

Second, Philo is primarily a biblical exegete deeply committed to his ancestral religion. Yet references to Jewish literature in the work are scarce, and little consideration is given to how Hellenistic Jews in Alexandria would have received the doctrine. David Winston seems to reach his conclusion that Philo did not affirm reincarnation because it would offend his Jewish commitments (*Logos and Mystical Theology in Philo of Alexandria* [Cincinnati: Hebrew Union College Press, 1985], 42). Yli-Karjanmaa, however, simply brushes off Winston's objection, asserting that the traditional Alexandrian Jewish view of reincarnation cannot be known with certainty (246). It is equally true, however, that we cannot know how Alexandrian Judaism felt about Platonic eschatology. Further, it is impossible to distinguish the accepted doctrines of Philo's exoteric and esoteric audiences, as Yli-Karjanmaa wishes to do.

Third, Yli-Karjanmaa claims that he is not attempting to argue "for or against Philo's acceptance of the doctrine of reincarnation" (xi), yet he concludes, "This study has found that, beyond reasonable doubt, Philo of Alexandria accepted the tenet of reincarnation" (243). These statements cannot coexist. It appears that in his attempt to marshal evidence in favor of reincarnation, Yli-Karjanmaa's initial skepticism melted away, and he came to assume what the study is required to prove.

Criticisms notwithstanding, the work is admirable in its scope. Yli-Karjanmaa leaves no stone unturned as he seeks to locate the doctrine of reincarnation where it is not obvious and to establish that reincarnation was the preferred eschatological option for Philo. Yli-Karjanmaa also forces the reevaluation of familiar questions such as Philo's doctrine of psychic preexistence (which a number of modern scholars reject) and the death of the soul (which Yli-Karjanmaa insists is "moral corruption that has incarnation as its *result*" [59, emphasis original]).

Yli-Karjanmaa has marshaled an impressive array of evidence to support a doctrine that Philo "neither rejects nor adopts … in so many words" (3). The monograph is a stimulating reassessment of an important Platonic theory in Philo that, if accepted, would require a thorough reevaluation of the psychology and eschatology of Philo in particular and of Hellenistic Judaism in general.

Sapientia Salomonis (Weisheit Salomos), edited by Karl-Wilhelm Niehbuhr. Scripta Antiquitatis Posterioris ad Ethicam Religionemque pertinentia 27.Tübingen: Mohr Siebeck, 2015. Pp. xiii + 350. Hardcover. €79,00. ISBN 9783161528088.

Helmut Engel, S.J., Philosophisch-Theologische Hochschule Sankt Georgen

Der Herausgeber gibt zunächst in seinem Vorwort (vii–ix) einen inhaltlichen Überblick über die recht unterschiedlichen Beiträge und erläutert seine Absicht bei ihrer Zusammenstellung zu diesem Band. In einem ersten Teil des Buches „A. Einführung" (3–37) nennt er mögliche erste Zugänge zur *Sapientia Salomonis* (SapSal) als Teil der christlichen Bibel aus neutestamentlicher Zeit und als Zeugnis des Griechisch sprechenden Diasporajudentums und hellenistisch-römischer Kultur. Gelegentlich würden Leser wohl eine präzisere Ausdrucksweise erwarten; z.B. „gelangen" die griechischen „Zusätze" (zu den masoretischen Textformen) in den Büchern Ester und Daniel nicht erst durch das Konzil von Trient in die Bibel der Kirche (7), sondern befanden sich bereits in den ältesten erhaltenen Septuaginta-Handschriften (so Pap. 967 aus dem 2./3. Jh.) darin. Zu Recht hatte Niebuhr ja erwähnt, dass die Christen „die autoritativen Schriften Israels in ihrer griechischen Gestalt" übernommen hatten (9). Wäre Niebuhr wirklich „den Gliederungssignalen an der Textoberfläche" gefolgt und hätte dabei „die Redeformen berücksichtigt" (19), wäre er nicht zu der unwahrscheinlichen Zweiteilung des Buches in Kap. 1–8 „Die erste Rede des Herrschers (an seine Herrscherkollegen) und 9–19 „Die zweite Rede des Herrschers (an Gott)" gelangt. Mehrere tatsächlich an den literarischen Formen und Gliederungssignalen des Textes orientierte (nicht: „thematisch-inhaltlich begründete") Gliederungsvorschläge, die völlig anders lauten, werden zwar erwähnt (21, Anm. 38), aber nicht diskutiert. In Abschnitt „4. Gattung" (22–24) gibt Niebuhr einen guten, knapp über die internationale Fachdiskussion zu dieser Frage informierenden Überblick. Behutsam und überzeugend werden in „5. Literarische Integrität und Intention" (24–30) literarkritische Versuche abgewiesen, die „Schichten" und Redaktionen, vielleicht sogar verschiedener Verfasser, entdecken wollten. „Der Einheitlichkeit im Rededuktus – von der Mahnrede" (an die, die die Erde richten) „über die Lobrede auf die Weisheit hin zum Lobpreis Gottes im Gebet – entspricht die Kohärenz der Aussageintention" (28). Im Abschnitt „6. Datierung und Herkunft" (30–33) trägt Niebuhr einige der in der Forschung immer wieder genannten sprach- und kulturgeschichtlichen Argumente zusammen und hält die frühe römische Kaiserzeit (1. Hälfte des 1. Jh. n. Chr.) als Entstehungszeit für am ehesten vorstellbar; als Entstehungsort innerhalb des Griechisch sprechenden Diasporajudentums seien auch andere Städte mit starkem jüdischen Bevölkerungsanteil außer dem von den meisten Autoren bevorzugten Alexandria denkbar. Gegen Griechisch als Originalsprache liegen „keine philologisch begründeten Argumente" vor (33–34). In den abschließenden Ausführungen „8. Bedeutung" (34–35) hebt Niebuhr den wichtigen Beitrag der SapSal zum besseren Verständnis der spezifisch „christlichen" Überzeugungen des frühen Christentums (innerhalb des Judentums) hervor und plädiert für eine stärkere Wahrnehmung der SapSal bei der Erfassung der vielfältigen religiösen Welt der hellenistisch-römischen Antike in der frühen Kaiserzeit.

Im zweiten Teil des Bandes „B. Text, Übersetzung und Anmerkungen" (40–134) wird, entsprechend den editorischen Vorgaben der Reihe sapere (Schriften der späteren Antike zu ethischen und religiösen Fragen), jeweils auf den geraden Seiten (links) der griechische Text mit Versnummerierung und auf den ungeraden (rechts) eine deutsche Übersetzung von Heinz-Günther Nesselrath, ebenso nummeriert, abgedruckt (40–111). Für den griechischen Text bleibt natürlich die kritische Edition von Joseph Ziegler unersetzbar. Wenig hilfreich, gelegentlich auch irreführend, sind die in die deutsche Übersetzung kursiv eingefügten Überschriften und die dadurch erfolgenden Textunterteilungen: Z.B. handelt es sich in 1,16–2,24 nicht um „Die Rede der Gottlosen gegen die Gerechten" (43), als habe sich die Sprechsituation nach 1,15 verändert, und es setze eine neue Rede ein, vielmehr bietet der Text ein durch Beurteilungen des Sprechers von 1,1–15 gerahmtes fiktives „Zitat" einer so natürlich nie gehaltenen Rede der Gottlosen; in 8,17 liegt kein literarischer Einschnitt vor, auch handelt es sich in Weish 9–19 nicht um eine „zweite Rede", vielmehr leitet Weish 8,21– bei unveränderter Sprechrichtung seit 1,1, – ein (fiktives) *Zitat* des Gebetes „Salomos" (9,1–18) ein. Die in dem zitierten Gebet natürlicherweise eingenommene andere Sprechrichtung (auf Gott hin) bleibt dann prägend für den weiteren Text des Buches. „Salomo" führt also in dem Text, der an das Zitat seines Gebetes anschließt, für die seit 1,1 Angesprochenen aus, durch welche betende Meditation der biblischen Erzählungen er zu seinen Mahnungen im ersten Buchteil (Kap. 1–6) gekommen ist. Die internationale Forschungsdiskussion und deren Ergebnisse wurden jedoch für die Gliederung und die Überschrifteneinfügungen nicht zu Rate gezogen. Dass die „Anmerkungen"

(112–34) erst am Ende von Text und Übersetzung stehen, macht ihr Studium mühsam. Sehr viele dieser „Anmerkungen" enthalten wertvolle Hinweise. Im Unterschied zu einem Kommentar greifen sie aber nur unsystematisch dieses und jenes heraus; einige erscheinen eher assertorisch, wo eine sorgfältige Aufnahme der internationalen Diskussion angebracht und eine Auseinandersetzung damit weiterführend gewesen wäre; z.b. hätte eine Beachtung des Artikels von José Ramón Busto Saiz, „The Meaning of Wisdom 2,9a," SCSt 31 (1991) 355–59, den Text überzeugend erklärt und die Interpretation von „λειμών als ‚Feuchtgebiet'" unnötig gemacht; der umfangreichste und gründlichste neuere philologische Kommentar zum Buch der Weisheit von Giuseppe Scarpat wird, wie auch der Kommentar von Chrysostome Larcher, zwar im Literaturverzeichnis genannt, scheint aber nicht eingehend konsultiert worden zu sein; auch mit den philologischen Erläuterungen zum Buch der Weisheit in Band II der „Septuaginta Deutsch. Erläuterungen und Kommentare" (Stuttgart 2011) findet keine Diskussion statt, sie scheinen den Verfassern sogar noch unbekannt zu sein.

Den dritten Teil des Bandes „C. Essays" (137–316) eröffnet der informationsreiche Beitrag von Heinz-Günther Nesselrath, „Zur Sprache und Stilistik der *Sapientia Salomonis*" (137–154). Zu einer späteren Nutzung wäre ein griechisches Register und die Aufnahme von einigen dort behandelten Begriffen in das Namens- und Sachregister des Bandes hilfreich gewesen.

Mareike V. Blischke, „Zur Theologie der *Sapientia Salomonis*" (155–73), deren „mehrstufiges literarkritisches Modell nicht zur Grundlage für die übrigen Beiträge gemacht werden konnte" (vii), trägt hier erneut ihre bereits in ihrer Dissertation (2007) wenig plausiblen Vermutungen über eine „Grundschicht" und mehrfache „Ergänzungen" und „spätere Eintragungen" vor. Damit gelangt sie nicht über eine Auswahl von ihr wichtig oder interessant erscheinenden Gedanken hinaus. Infolge ihrer Nichtbeachtung der literarischen Gestalt des Buches bringt sie das Verständnis der SapSal kaum voran, sondern bleibt erheblich hinter dem in der Forschungsdiskussion erreichten Stand zurück.

Friedrich V. Reiterer, „Die *Sapientia Salomonis* im Kontext der frühjüdischen Weisheitsliteratur" (175–89) legt dar, inwiefern sich die SapSal im Vergleich mit anderen biblischen Weisheitstexten und vor allem Sir den griechischen philosophischen Traditionen genähert hat, ohne die eigene jüdische Identität aufzugeben.

Eine kenntnisreiche und anhand von Belegen gut dokumentierte Darstellung bietet der Beitrag von Walter Ameling, „Die jüdische Diaspora im hellenistischen Ägypten" (191–218), der auch die internationale Forschung umfassend berücksichtigt und einbezieht.

In seinem zweiten Beitrag „Die *Sapientia Salomonis* im Kontext hellenistisch-römischer Philosophie" (219–56) stellt Karl-Wilhelm Niebuhr mit Recht fest, dass „die in der SapSal aufgenommenen Gedanken und Motive der zeitgenössischen Philosophie ... philosophische Mittel zum paränetischen Zweck sind" (230). Er gibt zunächst einen durch kundige Literaturverweise gestützten Überblick über die wichtigsten Schulen und Denksysteme der griechischen Philosophie bis in die hellenistisch-römische Zeit, insbesondere in Alexandrien, und erörtert dann den großen Einfluss vor allem der platonischen und stoischen Philosophie auch auf nichtphilosophische Gattungen der Literatur. Anhand von jüdischen Schriften aus hellenistischer Zeit wie Aristobulos, Philon von Alexandrien, Ps-Phokylides und 4 Makk zeigtNiebuhr, dass „die Hauptintention dieser Werke nicht bei der philosphischen Lehrdiskussion liegt, sondern bei einer religiös orientierten Rezeption und Aktualisierung biblischer Überlieferungen" (232). Abschließend erörtert Niebuhr an Beispieltexten der SapSal, wie dort „philosophische Themen und Topoi aufgegriffen und der Intention der Schrift dienstbar gemacht werden" (246). Mit seiner „Integration philosophischer Denkweisen, Begriffsprägungen und Themensetzungen in die biblisch-jüdische Überlieferung ist der Autor der *Sapientia* ... prägend geworden für die Rezeption der alttestamentlich-biblischen Tradition im antiken Christentum" (255–56).

Maren R. Niehoff, „Die *Sapientia Salomonis* und Philon – Vertreter derselben alexandrinisch-jüdischen Religionspartei?" (257–71) beschreibt aus ihrer profunden Philon-Kenntnis eingehend und in mehrfacher Rücksicht das Verhältnis der SapSal zum umfangreichen Schrifttum Philons sowohl in seiner Übereinstimmung (z.B. in der Ethik und in der Überzeugung vom Geschaffensein der Welt als Eckpfeiler des Monotheismus) als auch in seiner Verschiedenheit (z.B. bezüglich der Eschatologie). Die beiden ungefähr zeitgenössischen Autoren gehörten wohl verschiedenen sozialen Schichten in Alexandrien an.

Folker Blischke, „Die *Sapientia Salomonis* und Paulus" (273–91) zeichnet mehrere parallele theologische Vorstellungen und Argumentationsformen in der SapSal und in den Paulusbriefen nach, die es ihm vorstellbar erscheinen lassen, dass Paulus die SapSal gekannt habe, auch wenn er nie daraus zitiert.

Alfons Fürst, „Die Weisheit als Prinzip des Seins und der Erkenntnis. Zur Rezeption der *Sapientia Salomonis* im antiken Christentum und zu ihrer Auslegung bei Origenes" (293–316) macht deutlich, dass die SapSal wie die Schriften Philons von Alexandrien „in das geistes- und religionsgeschichtliche Umfeld des Urchristentums" gehört (295). Ausführlich behandelt er sodann die Verwendung der SapSal für die Entfaltung der Theo- und Christologie des Origenes und für sein Menschen- und sein Weltbild.

Der vierte Buchteil „D. Anhang" (317–50) enthält das Literaturverzeichnis (319–29), ein Stellenregister (331–39), ein Namens- und Sachregister (341–47) und eine Vorstellung der Autoren dieses Bandes (349–50).

Götter für die Toren: Die Verbindung von Götterpolemik und Weisheit im Alten Testament, by Sonja Ammann. Beihefte zur Zeitschrift für die alttestamentliche Wissenschaft 466. Berlin: de Gruyter, 2015. Pp. ix + 332. Hardcover. €99.95. ISBN 9783110364101.

Christl M. Maier, Philipps-Universität Marburg

This slightly revised PhD thesis was submitted to the University of Göttingen and written under the guidance of Reinhard G. Kratz. Sonja Ammann's study explores the relation between biblical idol polemics and wisdom by taking Gerhard von Rad's slim chapter in his *Wisdom in Israel* (1970) as a starting point. In thoughtful analyses of passages from Second Isaiah (ch. 2), Jer 10 and related texts (ch. 3), and the Wisdom of Solomon (ch. 4), Ammann uses the term *discourse*, which is rooted in the sociology of knowledge, as a hermeneutical key. The term *idol* designates the object of the polemics as construed within the discourse; it does not represent any precise statue or deity but an adaptable concept used to denigrate various forms of worship in changing historical contexts (300). Chapter 5 offers a concise synthesis, the gist of which is presented in a brief English summary (ch. 6, 298–303).

In a poignant introduction (ch. 1, 1–17), Amman defines *discourse* as "a structured correlation of statements through which social knowledge is (re)produced" and thus "a collectively shaped product" (3, trans. mine). Applying a discourse-analytical approach modeled by the German sociologists S. Jäger and R. Keller, she assumes that the texts about worshiping other gods and their images contain in their specific statements and forms of argumentation fragments of a discourse that may or may not be related to the discourse on wisdom, its ideas, or its worldview. In a redaction-critical differentiation of the respective texts, she traces statements of idol polemics and their possibly sapiential argumentation, thus elaborating in what way and at which level the discourses on other gods and on wisdom interrelate.

Chapter 2 (18–106) offers a detailed analysis of Isa 40:12–31 and 41:21–29 that concludes that both passages originally described YHWH's sovereignty in history and creation without employing idol polemics. The verses that argue against other gods or their images (40:19–20 and 41:24b, 27, 29b) are considered later additions that relate to different aspects of the basic layer and thus seem to have been written for their specific literary contexts. Because of the widespread theory of a redactional layer of idol polemics in Second Isaiah, Ammann also treats Isa 41:6–7; 42:8–9; 45:14–17, 20–21; 46:1–17; and 48:3–5. As these passages differ in terminology, motifs, and focus, she does not ascribe them to one redaction but interprets them as selective expansions (*Fortschreibungen*) that aim at strengthening Israel's trust in YHWH in an ongoing situation of competing deities. In the most salient polemics against other gods in Isa 44:9–20, she also detects different layers: while 44:9–11 criticizes the men who create images of deities, 44:12–13, 18 judges these artisans as unwise and neglecting YHWH, thus introducing sapiential thought into the discourse on idols. Another expansion in 44:19–20 interrelates both discourses by criticizing the erroneous idea of worshiping other deities.

Chapter 3 (107–91) analyzes Jer 10:1–16 (MT and LXX), Ps 135, and the Epistle of Jeremiah. Ammann distinguishes in Jer 10 a base layer (10:12–16), two successive expansions (10:2–3a, 10:3b–5), the Aramaic verse 11 that connects verses 2–5 and verses 12–16, and a gloss in verse 9, the position of which differs in LXX and MT. The idol polemics in this chapter is only partially taken from Second Isaiah (especially vv. 3b–5). For Ammann the base layer of Jer 10 comments on the wisdom topic of Jer 9:22–23, so the combination of wisdom and idol polemics is not dependent on Second Isaiah but represents another strand of the broader discourse. The following expansions do not amplify sapiential elements. Only the late additions to MT in Jer 10:6–8, 10 transpose the polemic against foreign gods into a polemic against foreign wisdom. Although Ps 135:7 cites Jer 10:13, Ammann assumes that its idol polemics derives mainly from Ps 115 and thus continues a strand of the discourse distinct from wisdom. The Epistle of Jeremiah, written in the third or early second century BCE and designed as a letter of Jeremiah to the Babylonian golah, takes up the idol polemics of Jer 10 rather selectively. Whereas Jer 10 contrasts YHWH as creator god with the gods venerated in idols, the concept of creation plays no role in Epistle of Jeremiah, and idols seem to be an issue of the foreign nations only. Using the genre of wisdom instruction, Epistle of Jeremiah argues mainly that the Babylonian gods and their idols are ineffective and powerless; it invites its readers to reach this insight by reason and empirical observations.

Chapter 4 (192–253) treats Wis 13–15 as an excursus within the Wisdom of Solomon that highlights the damnability of Egyptian idol worship by using motifs and terminology of the idol polemics discourse. Ammann distinguishes a base layer of two parts (13:1–9 and 15:14–19) and five consecutive layers that focus on specific elements of idol worship or add narrative examples. The polemics addresses all sorts of idols, among them wooden anthropomorphic or zoomorphic figures (13:11–19), images of rulers (14:16–20), clay figurines (15:7–13); the text even refers to mystery cults (14:15, 23). In the course of subsequent additions, the polemics against the worshipers of idols grows more aggressive by depicting them not only as stupid but also as evil, so that the latest expansions characterize venerators and makers of idols as godless and immoral. Thus the idol worshipers are categorized in sapiential patterns and stand in contrast to the wise and YHWH-fearing in-group. Ammann relates this heightening of judgment to the sociohistorical situation of Jews in Roman period Alexandria (248–49), who during the reign of Augustus lost their privileged status and tax-exemption (24/23 BCE). While earlier passages in Wis 13–15 condemn Egyptian cults, the later ones defame Roman cults and mores. According to Ammann, the thorough integration of idol polemics into sapiential discourse in the Wisdom of Solomon is influenced both by the tradition of Hebrew wisdom and by Greek philosophy (252–53).

The synthesis in chapter 5 (254–97, with English summary, 298–303) reconstructs the interrelation of wisdom and idol polemics in the course of the tradition in five phases, although the progress is not just linear but winding:

(1) What Ammann deems the base layer of Second Isaiah (40:12–18, 21–31; 41:21–29*) does not contain explicit idol polemics but presents YHWH as the creator god and master of history who is more powerful than all other deities. These passages mirror the exilic situation of the authors and their knowledge of Babylonian gods.

(2) Ammann finds the earliest exponents of the idol polemics in a series of secondary additions to Second Isaiah that do not show any sapiential features.

Some of them tie in with the demarcation from other gods in the base layer by denigrating these gods as mere images and relating the idols' lack of power to their human origin (40:19–20; 42:8–9). According to Ammann, this repudiation of foreign deities is too general to be located in a specific Babylonian context. The polemic targets worshipers rather than gods. Other additions to Second Isaiah (41:24b; 46:3–4; 48:5) draw on the Deuteronomistic discourse on foreign gods and the interdiction of images.

(3) A fusion of the discourse on idol polemics with the discourse on wisdom appears first in expansions from the late Persian period (Isa 44:12–13, 18, 19–20; Jer 10:12–16). They present an idol polemics influenced by sapiential ideas characterizing the idol worshiper as lacking knowledge and insight. The idol worshiper as fool serves as a negative foil to those who worship YHWH.

(4) Passages from the Hellenistic period direct the polemics at the nations, particularly the Babylonians (Jer 10:6–8, 10 MT+). They present the worship of idols as the misguided behavior of the nations (Isa 45:15–17; Ps 135; Ep Jer). Most of these late passages "draw on wisdom discourse in order to exalt the creator god and to conceive of idol worship as an intellectual failure" (300). Ammann also refers to parallels of such idol polemics in Jewish-Hellenistic writings such as Jubilees and the Letter of Aristeas.

(5) The latest texts (e.g. Isa 44:18, 19; Wis 13:1–9) tie the issue of idol worship versus worship of God explicitly to reason: the worship of other gods appears as a sign of stupidity and reliance on superficial impressions. In Wis 13–15 the different aspects of idol polemics form an integral part of the wisdom discourse. In these latest texts, which have parallels in Philo's writings (*Decal.* 52–81; *Contempl.* 3–9), the worship of idols merely demonstrates the intellectual inferiority of the nations and thus serves as a starting point for the idea that other religions are less reasonable.

The study is an excellent example of German redaction-critical analysis that argues in detail for successive textual expansions (*Fortschreibungsmodell*). While Ammann's reasoning is clear-cut and mostly persuasive, it shares the model's weakness, namely, that the small additions can be related to sociohistorical situations and specific authors or redactors only with difficulty. Ammann's poignant observations and meticulous analyses, however, demonstrate the broad range of idol polemics, its widely differing arguments, and thus the intricacies of a discourse that is multivoiced and chronologically elongate. In her textual studies she gathers valuable observations on the material and fabrication of cult images. Especially her delineation of different concepts of characterizing foreign gods and their images helps to distinguish the strands of the discourse on idol worship and the different lines of reasoning. Her overall thesis that idol polemics is not originally a wisdom topic but has been influenced by sapiential thinking from the late Persian period onward is convincing. Therefore, she fully achieved her aim to investigate the issue more thoroughly than Gerhard von Rad. Scholars who study idol polemics in the Hebrew Bible, the Septuagint, or the New Testament will gain manifold insights from this book even without endorsing all of Ammann's redaction-critical decisions.

SEPTUAGINT

The Bible in Greek: Translation, Transmission, and Theology of the Septuagint, by Siegfried Kreuzer. Septuagint and Cognate Studies 63. Atlanta: SBL Press, 2015. Pp. 336. Paper. $44.95. ISBN 9780884140948. Hardcover. $59.95. ISBN 9780884140962.

W. Edward Glenny, University of Northwestern–St. Paul

This book is a collection of previously published essays on the Septuagint by a seasoned Septuagint scholar. The essays, which are in English and German and are organized in four sections, are intended to give "an overview on important stages, developments, and problems of the Septuagint and the research related to it" (vii).

The five chapters in part 1, "Background and Beginnings," serve as a helpful introduction to the topic of the Septuagint and to the discussion of the Old Greek and Recensions in part 2. The first chapter addresses the subject of the "Origin and Development of the Septuagint in the Context of Alexandrian and Early Jewish Culture and Learning." It follows a chronological development from the pre-Hellenistic era to the beginning of the Roman era, and it covers cultural developments, including both general developments and inner-Jewish religious and spiritual trends that were important for the Septuagint. Much of this chapter is devoted to explaining the place of the kaige and the Lucianic/ Antiochene texts in the transmission of the Septuagint.

In chapter 2, "Entstehung und Publikation der Septuaginta im Horizont frühptolemäischer Bildungs- und Kulturpolitik," Kreuzer takes up again some of the topics in chapter 1, maintaining that the emergence and publication of the Septuagint was because of the need for a Greek translation of the Torah in the Jewish community in Alexandria. Jews in schools/study centers connected with synagogues made the translation, and the Letter of Aristeas probably reflects the Jewish desire for the translation to be accepted and read by non-Jews. It is likely that the Pentateuch was translated and published one book at a time, with Genesis being the perfect first book, since it demonstrated the high quality of the Jewish literature and also legitimated the Jews' presence and importance in Egypt.

In "From 'Old Greek' to the Recensions: Who and What Caused the Change of the Hebrew Reference-Text of the Septuagint?" (ch. 3), Kreuzer builds on the fact that Old Greek underwent several recensions and explains that the major source of the differences between the various recensions or revisions was not translation technique but rather recourse to a different Hebrew text-type. He argues that, after the Syrian-Hellenistic crisis in 164 BCE, the new political and religious elite brought their own Scriptures, the pre-Masoretic text (sometimes called prerabbinic), with them to Jerusalem. The chronological system in this text tradition was later changed so that its goal was the rededication of the Jerusalem temple in 164 BCE. This text tradition, which was thoroughly established in the temple during the Hasmonean period, became the reference text for the kaige and other recensions of the Septuagint. The Letter of Aristeas was written to defend the Old Greek.

Kreuzer draws on his experience as coordinator and editor of the translation of the historical books for *Septuaginta-Deutsch* in chapter 4: "Translation–Revision–Tradition: Problems and Tasks in the Historical Books." He gives helpful observations and analysis from Joshua, Judges, Ruth, Kingdoms, 1 Esdras, and 2 Esdras. He also presents evidence that the Antiochene text is the oldest preserved textual form and the one closest to the original Septuagint in Samuel–Kings and Chronicles and points out that the significance of this text is one of the most important and most difficult questions in Septuagint studies.

In chapter 5, "'Object of Great Care': The Prologue of the Wisdom of Jesus, Son of Sirach, in the Context of Its Genre," Kreuzer surveys the genre of prologue, then investigates the function of the prologue of Ben Sira. Using especially the prologue to *Evagoras* from Isocrates, he concludes that in the prologue to Ben Sira the grandson sought to underscore the literary achievements of his translation of his grandfather's wisdom book from Hebrew into Greek.

Part 2, "Old Greek and the Recensions," focuses on one of Kreuzer's main interests. Using his work in the historical books and his interaction with the work of Brock, he supports the argument of Barthélemy that the kaige texts are the result of a formalistic Hebraizing revision and, more significantly, that the Antiochene/Lucianic text represents the original Greek with some corruptions. There is a fair amount of repetition in the chapters in this section, and they would be more effective if they could be combined in one sustained argument.

Chapter 6, "Toward the Old Greek: New Criteria for the Analysis of the Recensions of the Septuagint (Especially the Antiochene/Lucianic Text and the Kaige Recension)," focuses on the problem of developing criteria "to differentiate between the Lucianic recension and the older contents of the Antiochian text so that we can get closer to the Old Greek" (114–15). Kreuzer first discusses the characteristics of the Lucianic text and the evidence from Josephus, Qumran, the New Testament, and indirectly from the Old Latin that it dates to a time long before Lucian. Then he discusses again the kaige text, which Kreuzer argues was rendered "according to its isomorphic rule that the Greek text should represent the look of its Hebrew reference text" (124). This understanding of the kaige text explains why this recension differs from the Antiochene text, which actually for the traits Kreuzer examines (e.g., its addition of the article and explanatory words) "represents the original Greek" (125). Thus, by opening up the traditional assumptions about the Antiochene text and considering the hermeneutical principles employed in the early Jewish period, Kreuzer finds new criteria for evaluating the text and the development of the textual traditions, especially for Samuel and Kings (127).

Chapter 7, "Textformen und Bearbeitungen: Kriterien zur Frage der ältesten Textgestalt, insbesondere des Septuagintatextes, an Hand von 2Sam 12," employs 2 Sam 12 and 2 Sam 15 (Kreuzer uses both passages several times in the book) to again make the case that the Antiochene text is old and close to the earliest Septuagint text of Samuel and Kings. Thus the evidence suggests that there was not a major recension of this text in the time of Lucian, and there is also little evidence for a proto-Lucianic recension; such should not be simply postulated without strong evidence.

Kreuzer's main point in chapter 8, "Translations and Recensions: Old Greek, Kaige, and Antiochene Text in Samuel and Reigns," is that the presupposition that the Antiochene/ Lucianic text is the latest one and that differences between it and other ancient text forms and against the critical editions are the result of a Lucianic redaction are not correct and need to be abandoned. Kreuzer argues that, if we are willing to abandon these false presuppositions and consider the hermeneutics and procedures employed in the kaige recension, the differences between the Antiochene text and the kaige in the older historical books can be consistently explained. This also leads to the conclusion that the Antiochene text is older than the kaige, going back to at least the first century BCE, and following Barthélemy Kreuzer finds evidence consistent with the fact that the Antiochene text is basically identical to the Old Greek, although with corruptions.

In his important ninth chapter, "Lucian Redivivus or Barthélemy and Beyond?," Kreuzer offers the "first detailed evaluation" of Sebastian P. Brock's 1965 (published in 1968) paper "Lucian *Redivivus*" (191). In his short paper Brock had questioned Barthélemy's evaluation of the Antiochene text as basically identical to the Old Greek, although with corruptions, and he offered limited examples to support his arguments. Kreuzer's description of the background and context of the presentation of Brock's paper are intriguing and draw the reader into the story. Brock's division of Barthélemy's theses is also an important part of the story, accepting Barthélemy's evaluation of the kaige and not accepting his conclusions concerning the Antiochene text. Kreuzer argues that Brock's examples are not convincing; some of them present possibilities, but they do not refute Barthélemy, and they actually confirm Barthélemy's connection of the kaige and the early date of the Antiochene text. Going beyond Barthélemy, Kreuzer argues that the nonkaige sections of Vaticanus (in Samuel and Kings) have undergone a milder Hebraizing revision than the kaige sections.

Much of chapter 10, "Old Greek und Semi-kaige: Zur Frage hebraisierender Bearbeitung in den Nicht-kaige-Abschnitten der Samuel- und Königebücher," is repetition of material found elsewhere in this section of the book. New is the discussion of the sources in the nonkaige sections, especially focusing on 2 Sam 6:10–16 and arguing that the Antiochene text is the best witness of the Old Greek in the nonkaige sections.

Chapter 11, "Old Greek, Kaige, and the *Trifaria Varietas*: A New Perspective on Jerome's Statement." focuses on the meaning of Jerome's statement in his preface to Chronicles about the three text forms of the Septuagint that were in use in his time: the Hesychian text in Egypt, the text of Lucian from Constantinople to Antioch, and in Palestine the text of Origen, which Eusebius and Pamphylius had brought to wide reception. On the basis of the widely recognized facts that after the original Greek translation there was a revision of many books toward the Hebrew, Kreuzer argues that the situation Jerome had before him when he wrote this famous statement was the time when that revision was spreading, probably from Palestine, and becoming the dominant tradition. Its spread was gradual, and, although it was dominant in Palestine, the older, original textual tradition was still dominant around the fringes of that area: in northern Syria (so-called Lucianic text), in the west (Old Latin), and in Upper Egypt (Sahidic translation). These text traditions on the fringes represent more closely the original Septuagint, and Jerome connected them with famous men, but these connections do not mean that these famous men were responsible for a redaction of the text that was used in their areas.

Part 3, "The Septuagint and New Testament Quotations," contains a single chapter. Building on the previous essays, Kreuzer tests his ideas concerning the Septuagint text in terms of New Testament quotations from the Septuagint in chapter 12: "The Place and Text-Critical Value of the New Testament Quotations from Dodekapropheton in the Textual History of the Septuagint." One of the main principles he applies in his analysis of Septuagint quotations is Paul Lagarde's proposal that "if there is a reading close to MT and a reading different, the reading that differs from MT is the original one (and the other one is revised toward the Hebrew text)" (233). On the basis of his study of quotations in the New Testament from the Twelve, Kreuzer concludes that quotations in the New Testament can mirror the development of the Septuagint from the Old Greek through its isomorphic-Hebraizing revision, and thus New Testament quotations can provide important witnesses to the textual history of the Septuagint long before the time of the major codices.

Part 4 covers "Two Important Textual Witnesses." Chapter 13 is a fascinating introduction to one of the most famous papyri of the Septuagint, Papyrus 967. Kreuzer helpfully shows how p967 provides insights into bibliology, textual history, and the canon history of the biblical text. Codex Vaticanus, which since the sixteenth century has been the most highly esteemed manuscript for Septuagint editions and research, is the topic of the final chapter of the collection: "B or Not B? The Place of Codex Vaticanus in Textual History and in Septuagint Research." Codex Vaticanus (B) contains both kaige and nonkaige sections in the older historical books. In the kaige sections the text has obviously undergone a Hebraizing revision, and Kreuzer argues that in the nonkaige sections there is also evidence of a Hebraizing revision that is not as strong as in the kaige sections. He calls the nonkaige sections of the historical books a semikaige text. (He prefers the term *semikaige* to *nonkaige*, because the chronology of the revisions is not known.) In the semikaige sections, as well as in the kaige sections of the historical books, Kreuzer argues that the text of B represents the revised text, and the Antiochene text is the one that is closest to the Old Greek. He values both the text of Vaticanus and the Antiochene text, and the two texts are close, although there are many differences between them that he argues must be explained by intentional reworking according to the specific rules he sees driving the Hebraizing revisions.

This book contains important interaction with biblical texts, especially in Samuel and Kings, which deserves more serious attention than this review allows. There are three indices: texts, persons/authors from antiquity, and modern authors. Also, each chapter has a bibliography. The book also contains a list of the original location of the publication of the articles in the book as well as a complete list of all of Kreuzer's publications from 2005 to 2015. It is unfortunate that there are several distracting grammatical irregularities and misspellings in the first few chapters.

Kreuzer's main thesis in part 2 that the Antiochene/Lucianic text, especially in the older historical books, represents the original Greek with some corruptions has been challenged on several fronts, and probably most Septuagint scholars will not accept it. (See, for example, T. M. Law and T. Kauhanen, "Methodological Remarks on the Textual History of Reigns: A Response to Siegfried Kreuzer," *BIOSCS* 43 [2010]: 73–88.) However, the Antiochene text is one of the most complicated issues in Septuagint studies, and there is no consensus concerning it. This collection of essays provides not only a helpful compilation of Kreuzer's work on the Antiochene and kaige texts in the older historical books but also contains many other helpful articles on other aspects of Septuagint studies. In those regards it is an important contribution to the discipline, and Septuagint scholars and students more generally will profit from it.

Septuaginta: Paralipomenon liber II, edited by Robert Hanhart. Septuaginta Vetus Testamentum Graecum. Göttingen: Vandenhoeck & Ruprecht, 2014. Pp. 430. Cloth. €200.00. ISBN 9783525534496.

Roger Good, Anaheim, California

After a long hiatus in the publication of volumes in the Göttingen Septuagint series, we have the welcome addition of Robert Hanhart's edition of Paralipomenon II (meaning literally "of the things left over" or "of the things left out," the Greek translation of the book of 2 Chronicles). Hanhart has been a major contributor to this series beginning with his work on 3 Maccabees in 1960 and continuing with the later history and apocryphal books, Esther (1966), 1 Ezra (1 Esdras, 1974), completing 2 Maccabees (1976), Judith (1979), Tobit (1983), and Ezra-Nehemiah (2 Esdras, 1990). Hanhart spent much of the intervening time between the publication of 2 Esdras and Paralipomenon II revising Rahlfs's *Septuaginta*, which was published in 2006. This Göttingen volume is the first-ever critical edition of the volume Paralipomenon II and represents a major step in the continued publication of the oldest Septuagint text available.

Following other volumes in the series, Hanhart divides his work into four main parts (A–D), the textual witnesses, the layout of the apparatus, grammatical features, and a key to symbols and abbreviations, before the bulk of the book, which contains the text of Paralipomenon II.

Part A introduces the textual witnesses beginning with the Greek witnesses of both books of Paralipomenon: uncial manuscripts (A, B, V, but which is not present in ℵ), over forty miniscule manuscripts, and four papyri fragments. Next are the Syrohexapla (preserved in three main texts) and other translations, including the Old Latin translation (preserved in four main texts), the Ethiopic (preserved in nine main texts), the Armenian, and Coptic translations, which were made from the Greek text rather than the Hebrew text. In the third section we have the indirect tradition of Josephus and the Greek and Latin church writings that quoted Paralipomenon in their writings. These latter witnesses need to be taken with caution, since they cite the text perhaps from memory and sometimes freely. Finally, Hanhart lists the printed Greek texts, beginning with the Complutensian Polyglot, the Sixtine, Holmes-Parsons, Lagarde, Tischendorf, Swete, and Brooke-McLean, to Rahlfs. In this section he lists almost three pages of corrections to the Brooke-McLean text. He also mentions other texts, such as the Antiochian text of Fernandez Marcos and Busto Saiz, the revised Rahlfs text of 2006 that he edited, and the Lucianic text published by Fernandez Marcos as indicated in MSS 19, 93, 108 121 and cited in the Antiochian church father Theodoret and in the Old Latin and Armenian translations. Hanhart also mentions the witnesses to Paralipomenon in the parallel texts of 1–4 Reigns as indicated in Brooke-McLean and Rahlfs.

Part B deals with the layout and content of the apparatus. The Göttingen Septuagint features two apparatuses: the first containing LXX/OG textual evidence; the second with the so-called hexaplaric evidence of the later translations/ revisions of the translated LXX/OG (Theodotion, Aquila, and Symmachus), preserved largely through the work of Origen in his Hexapla. Almost all of the apparatus for Paralipomenon deals with the first apparatus of LXX/OG textual evidence. Hanhart presents and evaluates the witnesses to the text of Paralipomenon II beginning with the witnesses to the Hebrew tradition (important in order to try to establish the *Vorlage*, or the Hebrew text that was before the Greek translator of Chronicles). The most important witness is the Masoretic Text along with a few Qumran fragments, then translations directly from the Hebrew, the Aramaic Peshitta and Targums, and Jerome's Latin Vulgate. Also important are the parallel Hebrew texts found in the books of Kings and hexaplaric notes. The second section explains the arrangement and grouping of the textual witnesses in the apparatus. They begin with the lemma followed by its variations and notations used to reference these. Following this Hanhart explains in more detail and evaluates the Greek text witnesses, the secondary translations, and the indirect witnesses mentioned above.

Part C, "Grammatica," consists of almost forty pages and lists variants that did not make it in the apparatus, as they do not affect the meaning. They include paleography (confusion of similar-looking letters), orthography (especially itacisms), morphology, and syntax.

Part D contains twelve pages of symbols and abbreviations. One kind of abbreviation that was missing from these pages and the folded enclosed green abbreviation sheet was 1°, 2°, and 3° for the first, second, and third occurrence of a form in a verse.

One of the features of the Göttingen Septuagint is that all these introductory chapters are in German, often in long, complicated sentences. Perhaps the Göttingen Septuagint could follow the German Bible Society publications and also give

English translations of these pages in future editions to make them more accessible to a wider readership, although this would increase the number of pages by a fifth.

The bulk of the book, containing the text of Paralipomenon II, has four components. First is the critical text itself, which usually occupies less than a quarter of the page. Second is a line containing abbreviations of the manuscript source list for this portion of text as reconstructed on the page. Third is the LXX/OG textual evidence for portions of each verse, occupying almost three quarters of the page. Finally, occasionally below a ruling line, there are readings from the three (Theodotion, Aquila, and Symmachus) as found in hexaplaric witnesses, which are present on less than 10 percent of the pages and occupy one line or a few lines at most.

Following the other review of this book in *RBL* by Theo van der Louw, I continue his list of deviations from Rahlfs's edition (which is the most widely available Greek text both in print and digitally) with a list of about 170 differences for chapters 11–36 (Rahlfs's text follows the square bracket): 11:1 ἑαυτῷ] τῷ Ροβοαμ 11:4 ἀποστράφητε] ἀποστρέφετε 11:5 ἐν] εἰς 11:14 μὴ λειτουργεῖν] τοῦ μὴ λειτουργεῖν 11:17 κατίσχυσεν Ροβοαμ ὁ] κατίσχυσαν Ροβοαμ τὸν 11:19 Ζαάμ] Ροολλαμ 11:20 Σαλημώθ] Εμμωθ 11:23 ἔδωκεν ἐν αὐταῖς] om. ἐν 12:4 ἦλθον] ἦλθεν 12:6 Ἰούδα] Ισραηλ 12:7 ἐπὶ] ἐν 12:12 τῷ Ἰούδα] om. τῷ 12:15 αἱ πράξεις] om. αἱ 12:16 ἐν πόλει] καὶ ἐτάφη ἐν πόλει 13:2 τρία ἔτη] ἔτη τρία 13:3 δυνατῶν πολεμιστῶν] δυνατοὶ πολεμισταὶ 13:7 υἱὸν Σαλωμων] τὸν τοῦ Σαλωμων 13:12 καί, οἱ υἱοὶ τοῦ Ἰσραὴλ, μὴ πολεμήσητε] οἱ υἱοὶ τοῦ Ισραηλ πολεμήσετε 13:13 αὐτῷ] αὐτῶν 13:14 ὁ πόλεμος αὐτοῖς] αὐτοῖς ὁ πόλεμος 13:19 Ἰεσανὰ] Ισανα 14:6 κυριευόμεν] κυριεύσομεν 14:10 ἤλθομεν] ἤλθαμεν 15:1 Ἀδάδ] Ωδηδ 15:4 ἐπιστρέψει αὐτούς] ἐπιστρέψει 15:5 τῷ εἰσπορευομένῳ καὶ τῷ ἐκπορευομένῳ] τῷ ἐκπορευομένῳ καὶ τῷ εἰσπορευομένῳ | χώρας] τὰς χώρας 15:8 Ἀζαρίου] Αδαδ 15:17 ἐξῆρεν] ἀπέστησαν 16:4 Ἀϊὼν] Ιων | 16:4; 34:6 Νεφθαλὶμ] Νεφθαλι 16:6 Γάβεε] Γαβαε 17:5; 32:30 κατεύθυνεν] κατηύθυνεν 17:8 Τωβαδωνιὰ Λευῖται] Τωβιας οἱ Λευῖται 17:9 βίβλος] βύβλος 17:11 καὶ τράγους ἑπτακισχιλίους ἑπτακοσίους] om. 17:14 καὶ τῷ Ιουδα] om. καὶ 17:16 Μασαίας] Αμασιας 18:16 διεσπαρμένους τὸν Ἰσραὴλ] τὸν Ισραηλ διεσπαρμένους 18:25 Ἐμμὴρ] Εμηρ | τὸν ἄρχοντα] om. τὸν 18:26 ἐρεῖτε] ἐρεῖς 18:29 κατακαλύψόν] κατακαλύψομαι 19:1 ἐπέστρεψεν] ἀπέστρεψεν 19:2; 20:34; 22:7, 8, 9; 25:17 Ἰηοὺ] Ιου 19:3 εὑρέθησαν] ηὑρέθησαν 20:10, 22, 23 (2); 25:11, 14 Σηείρ] Σηιρ 20:16 Ἀσσίς] Ασας 20:26; 30:27; 31:8 εὐλόγησαν] ηὐλόγησαν 20:36, 37 Θαρσείς] Θαρσις 21:2; 26:11; 29:13, 14; 31:13; 35:8, 9 Ἰεϊὴλ] Ιηλ 21:5 ὧν αὐτὸς] ὄντος αὐτοῦ 21:10 Ἐδὼμ ἀπὸ χειρὸς Ἰούδα] ἀπὸ Ιουδα Εδωμ | Λοβνὰ] Λομνα 21:12 ἐν γραφῇ] ἐγγραφὴ 21:13 Ἰερουσαλημ] ἐν Ιερουσαλημ 22:5 Ραμαώθ] Ραμα 23:1 Ἀμασαίαν] Μαασαιαν | μετ' ἑαυτοῦ εἰς οἶκον κυρίου] μετ' αὐτοῦ εἰς οἶκον 23:9 Ἰωδᾶε ὁ ἱερεύς τοῖς ἑκατοντάρχοις τεταγμένοις] om. 23:13 καὶ οἱ ἄρχοντες] om. | 13, 21 εὐφράνθη] ηὐφράνθη 23:14 ἐνετείλατο] ἐνετείλατο Ιωδαε ὁ ἱερεύς 24:1 Ἀβιὰ] Σαβια 24:3 ἑαυτῷ] αὐτῷ 24:26 Σαμαρὶθ] Σομαρωθ 25:22 τὸ σκήνωμα αὐτοῦ] om. αὐτοῦ 26:3 Ἰεχελιὰ] Χαλια 26:18 τοῖς ἱερεῦσιν τοῖς υἱοῖς] τοῖς ἱερεῦσιν υἱοῖς 26:22 Ἡσαίου] Ιεσσιου 27:8 υἱὸς εἴκοσι καὶ πέντε ἐτῶν ἦν βασιλεύσας καὶ ἓξ καὶ δέκα ἔτη ἐβασίλευσεν ἐν Ιερουσαλημ] om. 28:1 ἦν Αχαζ] om. ἦν 28:3 ἔθυεν] καὶ ἔθυεν | γῆ βενεννὸμ] Γαιβενενομ | διήγαγεν] διῆγεν 28:5 καὶ εἰς τὰς χεῖρας] καὶ γὰρ εἰς τὰς χεῖρας 28:7 Ζεχρὶ] Εζεχρι | Μαασίαν]

Μαασαιαν | Εζρικαμ] Εσδρικαμ 28:9 τῶν πατέρων ἡμῶν] τῶν πατέρων ὑμῶν 28:10 κατακτήσασθαι] κατακτήσεσθαι 28:12 Ἀζαρίας] Ουδια | ὁ τοῦ Ἰωανὰν] ὁ τοῦ Ιωανου 28:16 ὁ βασιλεὺς Ἀχὰζ] om. ὁ βασιλεὺς 28:17 ἠχμαλώτευσαν] ἠχμαλώτισαν 28:18 Αἰαλὼν] Αιλων | Γαμεζαὶ] Γαμζω 28:20 Θαγλαθφαλνάσαρ] Θαγλαθφελλασαρ 28:21 οὐκ εἰς βοήθειαν αὐτῷ ἦν] om. ἦν 29:1 Ἀββαουθ] Αββα 29:7 τῷ ἁγίῳ] ἐν τῷ ἁγίῳ 29:12 Μάεθ] Μααθ | Ζαχαρίου] Αζαριου | Ἰωαὰ] Ιωα | Ἰωαδὰν] Ιωδαν 29:14 Ἰδιθούμ Σαμεΐας] Ιδιθων Σαμαιας 29:22 προσέχεαν bis] προσέχεον | περιέχεαν] περιέχεον 29:34 ἠγνίσθησαν προθύμως] προθύμως ἠγνίσθησαν 30:3 ποιῆσαι αὐτὸ] αὐτὸ ποιῆσαι 30:6 Ἰακώβ] Ισραηλ 30:8 ὡς οἱ πατέρες ὑμῶν] om. 30:9 ἐναντίον] ἔναντι 30:10 καὶ οἱ τρέχοντες ἦσαν] καὶ ἦσαν οἱ τρέχοντες 30:12 εἰς Ἰούδαν καὶ ἐγένετο] καὶ ἐν Ιουδα ἐγένετο 30:14 ἐθύμιων] ἐθυμιῶσαν 30:19 τῶν πατέρων αὐτοῦ] τῶν πατέρων αὐτῶν 30:27 οἱ ἱερεῖς καὶ οἱ Λευῖται] om. καὶ 31:5 ἤνεγκαν εἰς πλῆθος] εἰς πλῆθος ἤνεγκαν 31:10 plus καὶ εἶπεν | εὐλόγησεν] ηὐλόγησεν 31:15 Ἰησοῦ] Ἰησοῦς | Μαρίας] Αμαριας 32:9 Λαχείς] Λαχις 32:10 καθῆσθαι] κάθησθε 32:15 οὐ μὴ σώσῃ] οὐ μὴ σώσει 32:18 κατασπεῦσαι] κατασπάσαι 32:22 Ἰερουσαλήμ] ἐν Ιερουσαλημ 32:25 ἐπὶ Ἰούδαν καὶ ἐπὶ Ἰερουσαλήμ] ἐπὶ Ιουδαν καὶ Ιερουσαλημ 32:27 λίθου τιμίου] τοῦ λίθου τοῦ τιμίου 32:29 ἑαυτῷ] αὐτῷ 32:32 λοιπὰ] κατάλοιπα 33:6 διῆγεν] διήγαγεν | γῇ βενεννόμ] Γαι-βαναι-εννομ 33:14 κατὰ νότον] κατὰ Γιων 33:22, 23, 25 Ἀμὼς] Αμων 34:4 κατέσπαψεν] κατέσπασεν 34:7 κατέκοψεν] ἔκοψεν 34:8 ὅτε συνετέλεσεν] om. | Σελιὰ] Εσελια | Ιουαχ] Ἰωὰς 34:12 πᾶς Λευίτης συνίων] πᾶς Λευίτης πᾶς συνίων 34:22 Ἐσερή] Χελλης 35:12 ἐν βιβλίῳ νόμου] om. νόμου 35:15 Ἰδιθούμ] Ιδιθων 35:19 ἐποιήθη τὸ φάσεχ τοῦτο μετὰ ταῦτα πάντα, ἃ ἤδρασεν Ιωσίας ἐν τῷ οἴκῳ] om. 35:19a θεραφὶν] θαραφιν | καρεσίμ] καρασιμ | ἐν τῇ γῇ] om. τῇ | Ἰερουσαλήμ] ἐν Ιερουσαλημ 36:1 Λοβνά] Λοβενα 36:2c Αἵμὰθ] Εμαθ 36:5 Ζεχχωρὰ] Ζεχωρα 36:14 βδελύγματα τῶν ἐθνῶν] βδελυγμάτων ἐθνῶν 36:16 ἐξουθενοῦντες] ἐξουδενοῦντες

Such a list is instructive as to why a reading is preferred over Rahlfs's Greek text (which was based mostly on the B, S, and A uncial manuscripts). Aside from obvious scribal errors, mostly eliminated in Rahlfs's edition, differences in readings can be divided into readings deemed to make more sense from the context, readings that bring the Greek text closer to the Masoretic Text (the Hebrew *Vorlage*?), and inner-Greek readings that reflect a particular Greek style, such as the use of articles, genitive absolutes, more appropriate case endings on non-Greek names, particular spelling of words, or phonological changes to the language (e.g., the characteristic –α of the first aorist endings intruding into second aorist endings, and lack of augments with verbs beginning with certain diphthongs). Some readings may also be influenced by those found in parallel passages in Reigns. A large number of readings (over fifty) reflect different spelling of non-Greek proper names or the reading of a completely different name.

Of particular interest to me were three places where Hanhart preferred different verb tenses to Rahlfs, alternating between aorist and imperfect forms, and this may also illustrate how decisions are made in producing a critical Greek text. According to my studies on the translation of verbs in Chronicles, the translator sometimes varied the tenses between aorist and imperfect forms to indicate contrast between different Hebrew verb forms in the *Vorlage* or maybe for discourse pragmatic reasons. In three examples below, it seems Hanhart at least took into account the first consideration (mapping contrasting Hebrew verb forms) but not so much the second (discourse pragmatic considerations). In 28:3 Hanhart prefers an aorist διήγαγεν (the standard translation equivalent for the *wayyiqtol* form of the MT in Chronicles) to Rahlfs and almost all of the textual witnesses, which have an imperfect διῆγεν (which agrees with parallel passage 4 Reigns 16:3, in which the MT has a *qatal* form). Conversely, in 33:6 Hanhart prefers an imperfect διῆγεν (for a *qatal* form in the MT of Chronicles, which agrees with the parallel passage in 4 Reigns 21:6) to the aorist διήγαγεν of Rahlfs and most textual witnesses (which perhaps contrast the *qatal* form with the following *weqatal* forms, which are translated by imperfects). In the third example, in 29:22 Hanhart prefers three aorists προσέχεαν twice and περιέχεαν for the MT *wayyiqtol* forms rather than the imperfects προσέχεον and περιέχεον found in Rahlfs and in many textual witnesses, which may indicate a discourse pragmatic semantic contrast between the verb "sacrifice" (translated by an aorist) to the verbs "pour out" (translated by imperfects). However, Hanhart also considers the forms ending in -ον προσέχεον and περιέχεον second aorists rather than imperfects, citing contextual considerations that they are preceded by aorist forms ἔθυσαν and ἐδέξαντο (for *wayyiqtol* forms in the MT, 105).

Whether one agrees with Hanhart in all his decisions in trying to recover the Old Greek text, the Göttingen Septuagint is an invaluable resource making accessible thousands of variants for readers to carry out their own text criticism. Hanhart is to be commended for his fine and careful work in the latest edition of the Göttingen Septuagint, especially at this late stage of his life. Septuagint scholarship is indebted to him for his lifetime of labor on the Greek text.

HEBREW BIBLE/OLD TESTAMENT THEOLOGY

Is There Theology in the Hebrew Bible?, by Konrad Schmid. Translated by Peter Altmann. Critical Studies in the Hebrew Bible 4. Winona Lake, IN: Eisenbrauns, 2015. Pp. vii + 155. Paper. $26.96. ISBN 9781575063515.

John J. Collins, Yale Divinity School

Konrad Schmid's slim volume has two main parts, framed by brief introductory and concluding chapters. The first main part outlines "the emergence and history of the concept of theology with regard to the Bible." The concept of theology, we are told, originates from philosophical discourse. Plato used the noun *theologia* to denote the critically evaluated myths. Aristotle uses it for one of the three "theoretical philosophies," together with mathematics and physics. The term is found in Philo and Josephus but not in the Septuagint or New Testament. The concept of theology did not figure prominently in the first centuries of Christianity but attained a preeminent status from late antiquity to the Middle Ages. The adoption of a philosophical concept of God, from the second century onward, was an important factor in this development. Theology was developed as an academic subject by the medieval scholastics. "Theology became a process involving reason and systematic reflection.... It thereby pertains to a meta level of lived religion" (8). The Reformation modified this concept, defining theology as the doctrine of faith rather than the doctrine of God. The Bible was read as a record of faith experiences. Schmid sees here the root of the later difficulty in distinguishing between biblical theology and biblical religion.

Schmid proceeds to trace the development of Protestant biblical theology, especially in Germany. J.-P. Gabler, who is usually credited with inaugurating biblical theology as a distinct discipline, was building on the work of others. The Romantic movement led to a devaluation of theology in favor of religious consciousness. Bernhard Duhm saw his task as examining religion in the stage before it was dominated by theology. Hermann Gunkel argued that both the words *biblical* and *theology* were misleading: "especially for the O.T. it is clear that the living religion of the heart was quite prominent, while reflection on religion plays a comparatively minor role" (28). This comparative evaluation of religion and theology was reversed in dialectical theology between the two World Wars, and biblical theology again rose to prominence. Among the biblical theologians of the last century, Schmid pays special attention to von Rad and the notion of diverse theologies within the Bible, which broke with the view of theology as systematization. The proposal of Rainer Albertz, that history of Israelite religion is a more meaningful way of treating the Hebrew Bible than biblical theology, is viewed as an extension of von Rad's approach, but Schmid notes that Albertz's history of religion still relies primarily on the biblical texts and argues that it cannot adequately replace biblical theology.

Schmid pays only glancing attention to the discussion of biblical theology in the English-speaking world. He makes the rather infelicitous statement that "especially under the influence of the publications of Brevard S. Childs, the Biblical Theology Movement developed a strong working interest in the 'canonical approach'" (39). It is as if one were to say that liberal theology developed an interest in transcendence and dialectical theology under the influence of Karl Barth. Schmid acknowledges in a footnote that Childs only identified himself with criticism of the Biblical Theology Movement. In fact, his whole program was a frontal attack on it. Other North American biblical theologians, such as Walter Brueggemann or James Sanders, do not appear here at all. Nonetheless, Schmid's sketch of the development of biblical theology is valuable for its concise formulation of some fundamental issues.

The second main part of the book is entitled "The Emergence of Theology in the Hebrew Bible and Ancient Jewish Tradition as a Religious-Historical Inquiry." Schmid starts by distinguishing between explicit and implicit theology. He claims only the latter for the Hebrew Bible. He argues that "the Hebrew Bible should, to a large degree, be viewed as reflective interpretation of preexisting religious texts. It therefore fulfills—at least with regard to those texts containing reflective interpretations—a basic requirement of 'theology,' when understood as the reflective examination and interpretation of religious phenomena" (49). Schmid's discussion of biblical theology builds on his work on the literary history of the biblical corpus. The reflective interpretation of earlier tradition can be found not only in redactional additions but also in independent works, such as Deuteronomy, the Priestly Document, Second Isaiah, and Chronicles. Biblical prophecy, as we have it, has a scribal character, marked by writing down and further interpretation. Schmid sees this as a theological process, in the sense that it draws reflectively on preexisting experience and tradition and attempts to find an overarching meaning behind the older oracles. Also theological is the process by which Isaiah becomes a prophet of world history through the redaction of the book that bears his name. In the Pentateuch, Schmid singles out the theme of the promise, seen as a late redactional element. The conception of God in the Genesis stories is described as "integrative monotheism," as older conceptions of divinity are integrated into one. The formulation of law as divine is not found in Exod 21–23 but arises in reaction to the Neo-Assyrian vassal treaties. In the Deuteronomistic History, this conception is extended to political history. "As a result, history becomes readable as a text; it becomes a narrative whose meaning can be sought out" (83). Schmid entertains the idea of Persian authorization of the Torah, while admitting that it cannot be proved. The Pentateuch is a compromise document, produced under some external pressure. The redaction of the Torah, however, has a distinct theological perspective that reflects a Pentateuch-wide horizon and construes the whole Pentateuch as Torah. Torah theology is also evident in the redaction of the Psalter. Schmid also finds a theologizing process in the formation of the canon. References to the Torah of Moses in Joshua and again at the end of Malachi are deemed to subordinate the whole canonical section of the Nevi'im to the Torah. Schmid also construes the Writings as interpretation of the Law and the Prophets. So "the wisdom texts of the Ketuvim can be understood as exemplary instructions for a Torah-oriented life. Psalms, Proverbs, Job, Qoheleth, etc. show—when read canonically—how the pious should behave" (104).

The last quotation highlights the affinity of Schmid's approach to the "canonical approach" of Brevard Childs. Only from a canonical perspective can Proverbs, Job, and Qoheleth, which only acknowledge the Torah indirectly in the epilogue to Qoheleth, be read as instructions for a Torah-oriented life. Like Childs, Schmid attaches primary theological importance to the redactional elements in the text. This is perhaps an understandable reaction to the emphasis of earlier scholarship on the originating events and the devaluation of the redactional as secondary, but it is nonetheless one-sided. Schmid differs from Childs insofar as he sees the same process at work in postbiblical texts such as Jubilees and argues that the boundaries of the canon do not make a qualitative difference (53).

What remains unclear is whether Schmid attaches any normative significance to the views of those who shaped the canonical text, as Childs emphatically did. Schmid, if I understand him correctly, remains on the descriptive level. Of course, any biblical theology that wants to draw out the implications of the text for the modern world presupposes an understanding of how the text works. The kind of descriptive work that Schmid sketches here, and has done at great length else-where, remains fundamental. Conversely, the whole enterprise depends on the accuracy of the descriptive account, and this can surely be contested. To say that "the Hebrew Bible should, to a large degree, be viewed as reflective interpretation of preexisting religious texts" seems to this reviewer a considerable overstatement. Granted that reflection on older traditions was a significant factor in the composi-tion of these texts, they were also responses to the social and historical situations in which the authors found themselves. Reflection on older traditions is not the only theologically significant element in the biblical texts.

This volume is by no means intended to be a full theology of the Hebrew Bible. It is rather a suggestive preliminary sketch. It is encouraging and exciting to see a major European scholar engage again with biblical theology. It is to be hoped that he will develop his thoughts on the subject more fully in the years to come.

The Role of Old Testament Theology in Old Testament Interpretation: And Other Essays, by Walter Brueggemann; edited by K. C. Hanson. Eugene, OR: Cascade, 2015. Pp. xiv + 190. Paper. $23.00. ISBN 9781498206389.

Ben C. Ollenburger, Anabaptist Mennonite Biblical Seminary

The volume here under review, edited by K. C. Hanson, collects nine of Walter Brueggeman's essays published in books intended to honor other scholars, published in Festschriften, that is, between 1978 and 2003. The scholars to whom Brueggemann and his colleagues paid homage in these volumes include the likes of Samuel Terrien, Gene Tucker, James Crenshaw and, yes, Walter Brueggemann. The book's concluding chapter is Brueggemann's retrospective assessment of his own *Theology of the Old Testament* (Minneapolis: Fortress, 1997), from a 1998 volume in his honor. I should acknowledge being one of the editors of a Fest-schrift whose contribution by Brueggemann is included in this book.

In his foreword to the book K. C. Hanson writes (xi) that all of its chapters may be seen as "leading up to" or "flowing out of" Brueggemann's *Theology of the Old Testament*. This is undeniably the case, and it could be said of virtually every-thing that Brueggeman has published before or after his *Theology*—and he has published quite a lot. What lends this volume its coherence, though, is Bruegge-mann. Anyone familiar with his *Theology* will find connections, trajectories, or effluences here—and a voice, a tone, a settled direction relatively consistent since 1978. In that year he published "The Epistemological Crisis of Israel's two His-tories (Jer 9:22–23)," chapter 7 in the current book. Here Brueggemann pits the "Mosaic-covenantal tradition" against the "royal (sapiential) tradition" (118) and forcefully promotes the former. The essay is typically wide-ranging and provoca-tive, concluding with the suggestion of a theology of the cross. It may not be out of place to say that the essay charts the course toward *Theology of the Old Tes-tament*. Brueggemann's spirited critique of the wisdom and royal traditions, by way of Jeremiah, is remarkable for appearing first in a book on Israelite wisdom honoring Samuel Terrien, himself an able interpreter and champion of wisdom literature. It is even more remarkable for its critique of royal and wisdom traditions promoted so strongly by Brueggemann himself earlier in the same decade.[1]

The position Brueggemann took in the early 1970s, and the quite different one that he expressed a short time later, both grew out of his focused attention on the Old Testament and his listening in on work in other disciplines, as well as his attention to the culture in which he was writing. His ability to draw from work in other academic disciplines to clarify and expand the reach of his textual studies into broader theological and cultural contexts has long been in evidence. It is evident as well in this book's lead and titular essay, "The Role of Old Testament Theology in Old Testament Interpretation" (1999, for Ronald Clements), in which Brueggemann draws on or adverts to figures as diverse as Wesley Kort and Emmanuel Levinas. Among Brueggemann's principal points in the essay, as in *Theology of the Old Testament*, is the polyvalent (polyphonic) character of the Old Testament and its—and definitely Brueggemann's—resistance to closure or "interpretive domestication" (15) of the Old Testament. This means, for him, that the Hebrew Bible/Old Testament should not be related exclusively either to the New Testament or to rabbinic Judaism—"the Talmud" (15). In other words, Brueggemann disputes the claim of both Brevard Childs and Jon Levenson that Jews and Christians read different Bibles.

Chapter 2, "The Travail of Pardon: Reflections on *slḥ*" (2003, for Patrick D. Miller), surveys the diverse uses of the term for pardon (*slḥ*) in the Old Testament, from the rejection of pardon in Deut 29:20 to complete pardon in Jer 31:31–34; 33:8; 50:20. Brueggemann's reflections in these pages is particularly rich, imagining the dynamic of pardon in light of Israel's/Judah's destruction, God's covenant with Israel, and God's determination.

Chapter 3, "A Defining Utterance on the Lips of the Tishbite: Pondering 'The Centrality of the Word'" (2001, for Frederick R. Trost), begins with Karl Barth's reference to the threefold Word of God—as preached, written, and revealed (in Barth, the order is reversed)—to present Elijah as an utterer of the Word. Brueggemann examines several texts from the Elijah cycle in the context of 1 and 2 Kings and Elijah's legacy in the New Testament. He returns in conclusion to reflections about the threefold Word of God.

In "Texts That Linger, Not Yet Overcome" (2000, for James Crenshaw), Brueggemann again engages Brevard Childs. The issue under discussion is God's "abandoning absence," which the Bible variously affirms or laments. Brueggemann surveys unsuccessful attempts to deal with God's abandonment, including ones that offer God—God "out there" as he puts it—as a criterion by which to criticize, ameliorate, or eliminate offensive biblical texts. He instead proposes a seriously rhetorical approach in which "rhetoric constitutes the character of"

---

1. Brueggemann, "The Triumphalist Tendency in Exegetical History," *JAAR* 38 (1970): 367–80; *In Man we Trust: The Neglected Side of Biblical Faith* (Richmond, VA: John Knox, 1972).

Yhwh. (62). Childs, on the other hand, according to Brueggemann, subjects the text to doctrinal categories, so that God would be known apart from the details and nuances of the text. On Brueggemann's view, unsettling texts or offensive ones remain in the inventory (or library?) of God's rhetorically scripted character, even if God does not—usually—operate those parts of the script.

Chapters 5 and 6, "A 'Characteristic' Reflection on What Comes Next (Jer 32:16–44)" (1996, for Gene M. Tucker) and "A Shattered Transcendence? Exile and Restoration" (1995, for J. Christiaan Beker), accompany and prepare for Brueggemann's *Theology*. The first considers Jeremiah's prayer and God's response under the thesis that the text (Jer 32:16–44) may suggest what is characteristic of Israel's "faith-rhetoric" (72). Chapter 6 treats Deut 4:21–23; Isa 54:7–10; and Jer 31:35–37 as representative of the theological reflection that destruction and exile evoked.

Chapter 8, "'Exodus' in the Plural (Amos 9:7)" (1998, for Shirley Guthrie), analyzes the text "Are you not like the Ethiopians to me, O people of Israel?" (NRSV) as a critique of Israel's "mono-theology" (157) and of American Christian exceptionalism or election. Brueggemann says—and writes that Amos 9:7 says— yes to pluralism, but he cautions against both an ideological yes and an ideological no, drawing for this on Karl Barth as preceded by Amos of Tekoa.

The final essay, "Theology of the Old Testament: A Prompt Retrospect" (1998), as mentioned earlier, is Brueggemann's remarkably prompt retrospective on his *Theology of the Old Testament*, in a book honoring him. One sentence captures the sense of the essay, of the *Theology* to which it refers, and of this volume: "I have increasingly found thematic approaches to biblical theology wanting, not only because they are inescapably reductionist, but because they are characteristically boring and fail to communicate the open-ended vitality of the text" (166).

The open-ended vitality of the text could serve as the hermeneutical rule guiding Brueggemann's reading of the Hebrew text and deriving from it, analogous—at a distance—to the rule of faith to which Childs appealed. In any event, it is evident that Brueggemann opposes reductionist approaches (166), Cartesian reductionism (170), reductionist "canonical" proposals (172) and reductionist biblical-theological projects (175). To be sure, all but one of these antireductionist comments are directed against Childs. They reflect a long argument between colleagues that appears especially conflictual, to use a Brueggemannian term, because the conflict was between theological, hermeneutical, scholarly siblings.

Brueggemannian vocabulary (how many times "utterance"?) abounds in the book, and at points the rhetorical excess suggests preacherly caricature, as in his doubly redundant reference to the contrasting errors of a "credulous fideism" and a "suspicious skepticism" (17). But these do not much matter, and even the several irritating typographical glitches (as on 59, 113, 115, 159), do not ruin the book, though its author and its readers do deserve better.

Reading these essays, these chapters, again, I was impressed and challenged by Walter Brueggemann's consistently vigorous engagement with the text, the biblical text, and by the wisdom that attends and issues from that engagement. If he has been mistaken on some points, it has been in a productive, nonreductive way.

JUDAISM: GENERAL

The Status of Women in Jewish Tradition, by Isaac S. D. Sassoon. Cambridge: Cambridge University Press, 2011. Pp. xxix + 200. Hardcover. $85.00. ISBN 9781107001749.

Sarah Shectman, San Francisco, California

The flyleaf of this volume claims, "Impelled by the gnawing question of whether the inferiority of women is integral to the Torah's vision, Isaac Sassoon sets out to determine where the Bible, the Talmud, and related literature, especially the Dead Sea Scrolls, sit on [the] continuum of patriarchal condescension [toward women]." Though his topic is ostensibly women, Sassoon seems more concerned with illustrating the multivocality of Jewish tradition than with women's status per se. He sets the tone by noting early on that a "particularly lugubrious myth is that of a Judaism undifferentiated and synchronic and possessed of a monolithic set of foundational texts" (ix). Women are thus a vehicle for an exploration not of what halakah says about women but of what assumptions lie behind its authors' statements (xi–xii).

The book is divided into three parts, entitled "Monogamy," "Commandments (Miṣvot)," and "Intrinsic Equality," each of which is divided into several short chapters. Sassoon opens the first part with a brief discussion of the varieties of marriage found in the Bible, focusing on monogamy and polygyny and arguing that Gen 1 implies a standard of monogamy and "a playing field for spouses that is as level as any in the Bible" (1). His premise is that monogamy is a positive indicator for women's social status. He then develops an argument about polygyny based on the prohibition of it in the Damascus Covenant (CD). CD's prohibition is based on Lev 18:18, which is normally taken to be a prohibition of a type of incest involving marriage to two sisters simultaneously, but Sassoon argues that CD's reading is in fact the more authentic. The key phrase in Lev 18:18, *ishah el ahotah*, is used elsewhere in the metaphorical sense of "one with the other." As Sassoon notes, neither the *ishah* nor the *ahotah* in these other examples are people, leading him to argue that the usage in Lev 18:18 is metaphorical as well.

Sassoon then provides a longer discussion of the term *be-hayyehah*, which he sees as anomalous in that no other laws in Lev 18 dissolve a kinship problem with the death of the intervening relative (e.g., a father's sister is forbidden even if the father is dead). Sassoon uses this anomaly to argue that the issue in Lev 18:18 is not one of incest. Rather, the term *be-hayyehah* prohibits a divorced man from remarrying while his ex-wife is alive, effectively prohibiting divorce, even though elsewhere P seems to allow it—just as divorce elsewhere in the Dead Sea Scrolls does not seem to have been a problem for the authors of the CD passage. Sassoon argues that P's prohibition of divorce is related to the fact that it does not care about proliferation alone; the quality of the "seed" is important as well—and what better way to maintain it than through monogamy (and, apparently, disallowing divorce)? In the last chapter of this section, Sassoon returns to Gen 1:27–29, P's clarion call for monogamy. Although the rabbis of the Mishnah and Talmud do not mention this text in reference to monogamy or equality, this is a result of their focus on the subservience of women to men.

In part 2 Sassoon explores requirements that women observe certain *miṣvot*. The classic understanding of the issue follows the Mishnah (Qid 1:7), which exempts women from positive, time-bound commandments. However, Sassoon notes the divergence of opinion on this matter and the development of the tradition over time, with Maimonides noting that which commandments women have to observe is a matter of tradition, not a rule. Sassoon takes this as a launching point to explore the Mishnah's descriptions of gender roles, which he argues are not strictly necessary and therefore represent active choices in depicting both men and women according to these roles—thus attesting to a desire to perpetuate such roles. Nevertheless, when they are discussing gender roles within marriage, the rabbis never cite Gen 3:16 as the source of a husband's authority over his wife. Sassoon astutely notes that curses are not the same as normative law: Gen 3:16 is not prescriptive but descriptive.

Sassoon turns to the biblical evidence in the second half of this section, arguing that Deuteronomy "comes closest to miṣvah proportionality for all" (68), likely as a result of its lack of concern with ritual details. In contrast, P restricts women's roles in various aspects of the cult, including women's exclusion from eating food deemed holy of holies. Sassoon concludes that P also has a double standard around bodily impurity, making it more severe for women. Nevertheless, he offers a defense of the prohibition in Exod 19:15 of approaching a woman, in preparation for the revelation at Sinai. Sassoon draws an analogy to the deeply monotheistic D's use of plurals in reference to God to conclude that Exod 19:15's "do not go near a woman" is a "wonky idiom" (92) and not a statement about who is considered an Israelite person. "Less straightforward," Sassoon notes, "is the nexus between P's purity program and women getting the thumbs down" (97), namely, being banned from the holy of holies (the location and the food).

From here Sassoon moves to the related topic of Torah study, from which Jewish women have also traditionally been excluded. Maimonides is responsible for codifying the idea that it is largely pointless for women to study Torah, in contrast to the Talmud's fairly consistent opinion that women are required to study Torah. Sassoon traces the shift to the aftermath of the Bar Kokhba revolt, when Jewish men could no longer be warriors and so had to become Torah "warriors" instead. As a result, women had to be stripped of participation in Torah study, men's "last bastion" of maleness. Even the stipulation in Deut 31:11–12, which says everyone, including women, is to come annually and learn Torah, falls to rabbinic interpretation, which concludes that women "hear" but only men "learn."

Sassoon opens the third part of his book with a citation from Mekilta on inclusivity as a principle operative before chosenness, arguing for the original inclusion of women in Torah. He looks to various rabbinic and biblical texts that seems to attach value to women as people. He notes that the Talmud never suggests that women do not have souls whereas men do, nor does it value a woman's life less than a man's. At issue are the *qatlanit* (the "killer wife") laws, which Sassoon argues are only about women because the woman's string of dead husbands is seen as a result of something in the women's "source/well" (internal). Her luck causes her to marry men who die; it is not because of her innate value as a woman. Likewise, Mishnaic stipulations about who should be first to receive aid (*le-haḥayot*) have to do with providing food, not with decisions over life and death—and therefore they do not value women less than men as humans when they rank women below men. Though the rabbis do mark character distinctions between men and women, Sassoon explains these as a product of the time and the rabbis' lack of understanding of such things, as they did not have the same scientific means of understanding behavior that we do. Sassoon seems to be suggesting that we keep historical context in mind in reading and evaluating tradition on such matters, though he stops short of making this suggestion explicit.

A clear stumbling block for equal inclusion of women in Torah and covenant is the rite of circumcision. Here Sassoon notes that the Bible includes other covenants that do not have a sign, in addition to passages that reflect a metaphorical rather than a literal understanding of circumcision. Once again, it is only in the (later) P material that the physical type of circumcision is ritualized and required for the covenant, becoming hugely important and prevalent in the time between P and the rabbis. When P made circumcision part of Torah, it made covenant something for men only. Some scholars emphasize genealogy and patrilineality in P, but Sassoon argues that these play "second fiddle to corporeal purity and holiness" (152), which carry serious consequences in P. He follows Daniel Boyarin in noting that for P bodies define human beings, and thus distinctions between bodies—sex and gender—are paramount. This focus on body leads to gender hierarchy. Though many think of religion as being concerned with the soul, P is very much concerned with the body. The emphasis on body brings gender to the fore, but "it does not follow that women have to wind up a caste apart" (161). The Priestly writings existed alongside others, such as the prophets, that emphasize things such as volition and choice and the spiritual over the physical. The rabbis, too, emphasize the metaphysical alongside the physical, allowing more opportunities for women to have equal footing.

Sassoon concludes this volume with the observation that Jewish traditions about women are complex but that complexity and even contradiction do not have to be harmonized away. Jewish tradition allows for variant views to coexist. Here he comes to his heretofore unstated purpose in this volume: "where standardizaton and continuity are enthroned, halakhah turns into politico-halakhism whose primary goal is no longer the ongoing search for the divine will as revealed in Bible and Talmud. … Once conformity becomes a virtue, obscuring tradition's versatility tends to take on the aura of piety" (177). This conclusion, however, says almost nothing about women in Jewish tradition. It is less a synthesis of his discussion than an implicit claim that observant Jews should recognize the ambiguity and contradictions in Jewish tradition and follow (or at least acknowledge) the more positive aspects of Jewish tradition where women are concerned.

Though this concluding argument is commendable, and one with which I would not argue, there are some problems with Sassoon's path to it. The primary issue is that he does not adequately set out his purpose or his method; there is no larger framework that makes the development of his argument clear. He does not adequately define what he means by the titular "Jewish tradition," his selection of material being fairly broad in range but also leaving the reader with the feeling that it is selective without an explanation why. He begins with CD, goes back to some biblical texts, moves on to the rabbis, and then shifts back and forth between these last two. His argument about monogamy, for example, is focused almost entirely on one passage from CD and one from Lev 18, with brief mention of a couple of verses from Genesis. Though he occasionally mentions things such as the levirate marriage, there is no careful discussion of monogamy and polygamy in ancient Israel—a topic for which the corpus of biblical material is ample. He does not examine what these institutions might have looked like, and, more important, he does not justify his use of monogamy as a starting point for his study or explain how monogamy is an indicator of women's status. The latter is an important methodological claim, one that he does not address until nearly halfway through the volume, and then only in the vague parenthetical comment that monogamy was "presumably congenial to the individual woman" (72). On the whole, this is a very selective discussion of women in "Jewish tradition."

Sassoon's treatment of the source material does incorporate the work of numerous scholars, though some are notably missing, especially some of the more recent ones. In particular he does not cite important feminist scholars such as Phyllis Bird, Carolyn Pressler, or Naomi Steinberg on women in Gen 1–3 and in Deuteronomy. His treatment of the relationship between D and P/H is cursory and largely stops after the ideas of Yehezkel Kaufmann (with a nod to Jacob Milgrom), leaving out the more recent work of scholars such as Bernard Levinson, Jeffrey Stackert, and Christophe Nihan, among others. In addition, his argument about access to the holy or holy of holies, which is denied to women, does not directly note that the issue is priests versus laypeople, and women cannot be priests—which is an issue, to be sure, but not the issue here. Moreover, women in Levite and priestly families can eat holy things, which laypeople—both men and women—cannot. There are hierarchies at work here that Sassoon does not address.

As for the form of the volume itself, it has both strengths and weaknesses. There is a useful glossary at the front, along with a list of abbreviations, though the latter does not seem comprehensive (and the author appears to refer to BDB as D.B.D.). Though the division of the volume into three parts is helpful, the further division of those parts into so many short chapters is disruptive and masks the coherence of each part. Headings and subheadings within fewer, larger chapters would have been much more useful. Sassoon's conventions for punctuation in translations of primary texts seem idiosyncratic—the general lack of anything other than periods, presumably to mark the use of *sof pasuq*, makes the texts difficult to read at times, though this seems likely to be the author's acknowledgment that punctuation was not a part of the composition of these texts. Finally, the author seems partial to old-fashioned and at times amusing language. Examples include *epigones, doggo, pooh-pooh, umpteen, distaff* and *spear* (as a pair), *whilom, succedanea, booby prizes*, and my personal favorite, *cocking a snoop.*

Judeans and Jews: Four Faces of Dichotomy in Ancient Jewish History, by Daniel R. Schwartz. The Kenneth Michael Tanenbaum Series in Jewish Studies. Toronto: University of Toronto Press, 2014. Pp. xvii + 173. Cloth. $35.00. ISBN 9781442648395.

Lester L. Grabbe, University of Hull

The author of this excellent study is well known to those in Second Temple studies. Although it contains several essays that can be read independently, the volume focuses on the current question of what terminology to use for the people in Second Temple studies. Some have argued that *Jews* should be abandoned and *Judeans* used instead, while a number maintain that *Judaism* for this period is an anachronistic concept. As one of those working on volumes in the Josephus translation and commentary for Brill, Schwartz has had to face the question of what terminology to use when translating the frequent term *ioudaios/ioudaioi* in Josephus's writings.

Each of his chapters is on a dichotomy that helps to illustrate and deal with the issue at hand. The first chapter compares the books of 1 and 2 Maccabees and notes a number of dichotomies. One of the most important of these is that 1 Maccabees is a Judean work, that is, a work written in Judah that focuses on issues that have to do with the Jewish community in Palestine. On the other hand, 2 Maccabees is a work of the diaspora and reflects the interests and attitudes of an author living among Greeks and other Gentiles rather than in Judah. Although the temple is presupposed and honored, there is a surprising lack of interest in the temple cult in 2 Maccabees. But the real difference between 1 and 2 Maccabees lies in their views of divine providence: 1 Maccabees basically rejects it (an important contrast to the biblical perspective), whereas it is central to 2 Maccabees. This makes 1 Maccabees a Judean book and 2 Maccabees a Jewish one.

Chapter 2 is on priestly religion versus rabbinic Judaism (Qumran is grouped with priestly religion). Schwartz notes the obvious differences (e.g., priests are born, whereas rabbis are made), finally characterizing the priestly position as "realism" but the rabbinic as "nominalism." His most important distinction, however, is that rabbinic religion is diasporan in perspective. This last dichotomy might seem surprising, since we are not sure there were any Pharisees in the diaspora, but the point is the outlook rather than the location. Here Schwartz argues that priestly religion represents a *Judean* viewpoint, while rabbinic religion is *Jewish*.

The third chapter discusses Josephus, with the question of Josephus's movement from being a military commander in Judea, a member of the aristocracy, and of priestly descent to living in the diaspora in Rome as an adopted son of Vespasian. This change of perspective is reflected in differences between the *War* and the *Antiquities* where they are parallel. The *War* is more truthful about the prewar situation, in which major religious figures were involved in the affairs of state and played a central role in the rebellion against Rome. When he wrote the *Antiquities* two decades later, Josephus had learned a basic principle for Jews to survive in the diaspora: Jews must not represent a threat to Roman rule. Thus, his description of events distances the rebels and "brigands" from the rest of the Jewish people—at times, he even implies they were not Jewish. Thus, the *War* normally talks about *Judeans* whereas the *Antiquities* refers to *Jews*.

The last chapter is on Heinrich Graetz's *Geschichte der Juden*, noting how volume 3 (of the German edition), which covers the biblical period down to 160 BCE, changed its volume title over time. It was an important volume to the reading public and went through several editions (in contrast to the volumes on the later history, after 70 CE). Graetz had initially proposed that *Juden* was the proper nomenclature. However, over several decades he experienced a number of influences that changed his approach, including a visit to Palestine and an anti-Semitic attack by Heinrich von Treitschke. Whereas volume 3 bore the title *Geschichte der Juden...* in the 1856 (first) edition, this changed to *Geschichte der Judäer...* in the 1878 (third) edition. (Note that the overall title of the history, *Geschichte der Juden*, did not change, only that of volume 3.) Graetz's original tripartite division of Judaic history also seems not to have been followed. It is clear from the revision of his introduction to the volume from edition to edition that he was having difficulty reconciling such issues, and the introduction was dropped in the last edition (1888).

A useful conclusion rounds off the main text. There is also an appendix that is a detailed critique of Steve Mason's "Jews, Judaeans, Judaizing, Judaism: Problems of Categorization in Ancient History," *JSJ* 38 (2007): 457–512. Schwartz especially takes up the question of whether *Judaism* and even *religion* can be appropriate terms in discussion relating to the Second Temple period. He concludes that they both can be in some instances. I think his point is well made and that he is quite correct in his conclusions that one can talk of *Judaism* in various passages and of Jewish *religion* at this time.

In sum, Schwartz's basic conclusion is that *Judean* is an appropriate term to use when the reference is to a person's geographical situation in Judah and the ethnic identification with the Jewish people. However, *Jew* is a better translation where the person is located in the diaspora and the identity focuses on the person's religion. Schwartz also argues—quite rightly, in my opinion—that *Judaism* as a religion is explicitly presupposed in a number of literary passages.

As noted above, the central issue of this volume is use of the terms *Judean* versus *Jew* in contemporary scholarly literature. In some ways, one could regard it as a tail-that-wags-the-dog question: Is it really worth all the fuss that has been made (in a few narrow circles)? Yet as scholars we often find the need to resolve such conundra. I believe Schwartz is correct overall, though I would perhaps put the matter slightly differently. To begin with, there are several points that I think we all agree on. There is only one word in the relevant languages (Hebrew/

Aramaic *yehudi*; Greek *ioudaios*), though it of course occurs in the feminine and the respective plurals. Until recent times the main—almost universal—translation was "Jew," as far as I am aware (though see Schwartz's quite acute analysis of Graetz). Thus, the question of translating by "Judean" is mainly a recent scholarly practice. Scholars sometimes have a tendency to concoct new terminology over a somewhat specious argument that it is *better* or *more exact*, without really advancing understanding, clarity, or scholarship.

The word *Yehudi* originally implied an association with a place, the area (or nation) of Judah. This would have been the usage during the Judean monarchy (and thus many of the occurrences in the Hebrew Bible). I agree that the translation "Judean" is probably a better choice, at least in scholarly works. Even in the Babylonian and Persian periods most of those labeled *Yehudim/Yehudin* were connected with Judah in some way, usually being a sort of colony of people of Judah. "Judean" would not be an inappropriate term even for those in Elephantine and Babylonia, though I would see no reason why "Jew" could not also be used.

But some argue that *Jew* is a religious term. I would completely disagree. It may well imply a religion, but it is definitely an ethnic term in the Greco-Roman world. Even today *Jew* has both ethnic and religious connotations; how can one say it is purely religious when anyone born of a Jewish mother is Jewish, regardless of belief or practice? The fact is that throughout most of history *Jew* was a self-designation. In only a few instances that I am aware of did individuals in antiquity attempt to repudiate their Jewish identity. Since in no case do we have the person's own thoughts on the matter, we are left to guess from the declaration of an outsider. For example, did Tiberius Alexander regard himself as Jewish or not (see Josephus, *Ant.* 20.5.2 §100)? Further, most of us know people who are happy with the designation *Jew* yet are nonreligious or even self-declared atheists.

But mainly I would argue that being a *Ioudaios* in antiquity was a matter of birth to the overwhelming majority of those in question. Conversion took place only occasionally (even if more frequently in the Roman period)—and when it did, it was primarily a matter of taking on the religious practices of Judaism. While circumcision and avoiding pork could well be ethnic and cultural customs in some contexts, they were justified by Jewish religious law. Thus, becoming a member of the Jewish community involved something religious for converts. It is difficult to imagine one becoming a *Ioudaios* as a purely cultural transition (in antiquity as well as now).

Like Schwartz, the question of usage is one I face, primarily in my history of the Second Temple period. I have generally chosen to use the term *Jew* and *Judaism* for the period after the monarchy (though after reading Schwartz's book the Persian period presents me with a bit of a dilemma). But I would not feel bound to refer to those in Judea as *Judeans* (certainly after the Persian period) because I see both a religious and an ethnic component in the term *Jew*, including the fact that most individuals were born Jews and did not choose either their religious practice or their ethnicity. All these arguments appear somewhere in Schwartz's study, though with perhaps a little difference of emphasis.

I have only one criticism, and this has to do with the format of the printed edition, not its content. First, there are endnotes rather than footnotes. This is conventional for a popular book, but I thought we were past this unfortunate arrangement for scholarly works. Surely the University of Toronto Press is capable of printing footnotes. Second, there is no overall bibliography but only a listing of bibliographical items in the notes, using short titles after the first reference to an item. This can be done in an individual article, but it is very awkward for a book with several chapters in which the footnote numbering starts afresh with each chapter. For example, the appendix is a stand-alone essay that could (and should!) be read by many who do not read the entire book. As indicated above, the main item critiqued in the appendix is an article by Mason. Yet the reference to this article is not given in the text but in an endnote on page 198, but this has only a partial title rather than full information. This means that the reader has to wade through all the endnotes until he or she finally finds it in note 17 on page 117, many pages earlier. Such an arrangement for bibliographical references (of which there are many—and very helpful they are) is unsatisfactory. Readers need to be able to find references quickly and easily. Authors should insist that publishers use proper footnotes, and monographs should normally have a complete bibliography.

This is a commendable volume addressing a current issue of debate about scholarly usage. Schwartz has made his point well, and this should have a significant influence on future discussion. I recommend it as essential reading for all those interested in terminology being used in Second Temple studies.

Ancient Jewish Sciences and the History of Knowledge in Second Temple Literature, edited by Jonathan Ben-Dov and Seth Sanders. New York: New York University Press/Institute for the Study of the Ancient World, 2014. Pp. 275. Cloth. $55.00. ISBN 9781479823048.

John J. Collins, Yale Divinity School

This volume originated in a one-day conference in 2011 at the Institute for the Study of the Ancient World at New York University. One essay is included that was not presented at the conference: Philip Alexander's "Enoch and the Beginnings of Jewish Interest in Natural Science," from 2002. Four essays, those of Alexander, James VanderKam, Seth Sanders, and Loren Stuckenbruck, deal with the Astronomical Book of Enoch. Jonathan Ben Dov discusses ideals of science in the apocalyptic literature and in the Yahad. Mladen Popovic considers the network of scholars that enabled the transmission of astronomy and astrology between Babylonians, Greeks, and Jews. Finally, Annette Yoshiko Reed suggests possible continuities between scientific pseudepigrapha in the early Middle Ages (Asaf ha-Rofe, Sefer Yetzira) and the earlier material discussed in this volume.

The recurring question throughout the volume is whether the material in question should be considered science. The editors insist in their introduction that *science* cannot be rigorously defined and cite historians of science to this effect. This position begs the question how the editors decided what material was appropriate for inclusion in this book. In fact, several of the contributors are more forthcoming on the subject. Philip Alexander argues that we can identify science wherever we find a strong interest in understanding how the physical world works, together with an assumption that the world is regular, an attempt to reduce phenomena to underlying principles, and some use of direct observation. Even Seth Sanders, who argues at length that science cannot be defined, adopts a provisional heuristic definition: "a system of exact knowledge of the physical world" (79). The prominence of astronomical concerns in several of the articles shows that there is a de facto understanding of what constitutes science, so the insistence on the undefinability of science in the introduction is both unhelpful and misleading.

Philip Alexander highlights the role of Enoch as the patron of Second Temple Jewish science and notes that "there is something anti-Mosaic in the Enochic literature" (38). He argues that the authors of the early Enoch material "were consciously attempting to domesticate within Jewish tradition a body of alien wisdom" (37). He characterizes the group that stands behind the early Enoch material as "in a sense, modernists" (38)—intellectuals who had access to foreign ideas and were open to the scientific thought of their day. Nonetheless, they were extremely conservative vis-à-vis the technological innovations introduced by the watchers. In fact the "modernism" of this literature must be qualified. Other studies have argued that Enochic astronomy was out of date in the Hellenistic period. The authors did not keep up with the scientific thought of their day. Nonetheless, the fact that they grappled with scientific thought at all is noteworthy. Alexander locates the beginning of the tradition in the Persian era, when the westward spread of Babylonian ideas was facilitated by the Persian Empire, and he sees an analogous development in the philosophers of Ionia in the same period.

VanderKam's essay is primarily a careful presentation of Astronomical Enoch. He notes that it combines observation of natural phenomena with the use of earlier scientific corpora, especially the more primitive kind of astronomy in Mul.Apin and Enuma Anu Enlil 14, and infers that this suggests an origin in the eastern diaspora. He suggests that this was likely the work of priests, who need astronomical information for calendrical purposes, although he admits that the book is not concerned with festivals. If it was the work of priests, they can hardly have been the priests who functioned in the Jerusalem temple.

Seth Sanders also relates Astronomical Enoch to priestly circles. He notes the minute observation of physical details in the purity laws in Leviticus. More specifically, he argues that the Aramaic passive of the verb "to see" in 1 Enoch is a calque from the Priestly tabernacle vision. From this he infers that "the creators of the early literature drew more heavily on the language and imagery of the Pentateuch than has previously been acknowledged" (93). The argument hangs by a narrow thread that cannot bear the weight. Without further correspondences between the Priestly source and Astronomical Enoch, the grammatical similarity must be regarded as coincidence.

Loren Stuckenbruck's contribution is designed as a response to the articles of Sanders and VanderKam. Stuckenbruck rather surprisingly accepts Sanders's linguistic argument, although he notes that Enoch is not just a passive recipient of revelation but also an active mediator. He also wonders why Sanders persists in using the term *science* in view of the problems with its use in an ancient context.

Jonathan Ben-Dov does not provide a definition of science in his essay, but he lists examples of writings from the Dead Sea Scrolls that he regards as scientific: Astronomical Enoch, the corpus of calendars and *mishmarot*, some texts that combine astrology and physiognomy, and possibly medical texts. He argues that the Yahad not only continues a preceding scientific tradition but introduces some novel concepts. Chief among these is the diagnostic use of astrology and physiognomy to determine the share of members in the lot of light. In contrast, the interest in nature in the Enoch tradition was dependent on a one-time revelation to an ancient patriarch, and this did not encourage creative scientific work. Ben-Dov admits that the kind of science in question may seem odd to modern eyes. The degree of creativity also requires some qualification. While the sectarians seem to have improvised new diagnostic methods, the Yahad was hardly a hive of scientific innovation.

Mladen Popovic tackles the question of how anyone in Judea learned of Babylonian astronomy in any form. He denies that Jewish scholars had access to Babylonian centers of higher learning and objects to speaking of a disembodied Babylonian stream of tradition. Appropriation of literary motifs, legal formulae, and astronomical lore should not be lumped together. Each would have its own context. There is evidence of high-level contact between Greek and Babylonian scholars, but Jewish scholars were not part of the same high-level network. Contacts must be explained through indirect channels, with various intermediaries.

In the concluding essay, Reed argues that recent work on ancient Jewish sciences has much to teach us about how much is lost when the history of Jewish thought is reduced to religion. She also notes that the distinction between science and religion is not really applicable to ancient Judaism, but that the "scientific" element, the concern with the workings of nature, has too often been overlooked.

The editors claim in the introduction that this volume marks the first public discussion of a new frontier in the history of science and of Judaism. This in itself is no small achievement. If questions remain about some of the essays, this is only to be expected in a pioneering venture. The contributors have shone a spotlight on an aspect of ancient Judaism that has received minimal attention to date. Their work should serve as a stimulus to further exploration.

Revelation and Authority: Sinai in Jewish Scripture and Tradition, by Benjamin D. Sommer. Anchor Yale Bible Reference Library. New Haven: Yale University Press, 2015. Pp. 440. Cloth. $50.00. ISBN 9780300158731.

Paul Sanders, Protestant Theological University

When I received this volume, I did not expect that I would read it in one shot, but having started with the introduction I decided to put aside my other tasks temporarily. The book appeared to address fundamental issues that are relevant to Judaism as well as Christianity, and its comprehensive approach seemed to be quite inspiring.

The book contains original insights expressed in clear terms that will help readers from both religious backgrounds to develop a more balanced view on the authority of the Bible. The author is professor at The Jewish Theological Seminary of America. Although he has Jewish readers in mind, he takes the work of Christian biblical theologians seriously. I appreciate the honest way in which Sommer confronts the issues concerning the status of Scripture. He does not take commonplaces for granted but discusses them critically. Also, he treats possible objections to his own approach with sincerity. Having read the whole book, I am critical of several conclusions, but I still appreciate the innovative way in which it addresses questions that are tacitly bypassed by most biblical theologians.

Sommer regards Scripture as a translation, the product of human efforts to describe God's self-revelation. Therefore, it contains not only divine but also human elements. Sommer hopes that this approach to revelation and Scripture will enable contemporary communities to rejuvenate Jewish law and to render it more compatible with their modern worldview, while maintaining their loyalty to God. Sommer evaluates postbiblical innovations remarkably positively. He argues that Jewish theology cannot construct teachings concerning God and his will primarily on the basis of Scripture but will always read Scripture along later Jewish writings that are no less sacred than Scripture itself.

Chapter 1 describes two fundamentally different approaches to the Bible. Religious Jews and Christians expect Scripture to disclose insights on an existential level, due to its supposed connection to a divine source. Biblical critics, however, treat it as an artefact that does not differ essentially from other ancient writings. Many of them believe that it was composed of different sources and that it contains imperfections and contradictory details. Also, they are quite critical of the classical Jewish and Christian interpretations of the biblical texts and wish to recover what these texts intended to disclose to their first audiences. Although Jews and Christians may experience such an academic approach as a threat, Sommer is convinced that they do not need to reject the methods of modern scholarship if they want to continue reading the Bible as Scripture. Pointing out that Jewish theologizing is characterized by dialogue and debate, Sommer stresses that seeing the Bible as sacred does not require feigned naïveté and turning off one's critical attitude.

Chapter 2, by far the lengthiest of the book, discusses the question of how the revelation of God and his will took place at Mount Sinai. Right at the beginning Sommer describes his personal unease with the idea that the Pentateuch is sacred, for instance, when it appears to be highly patriarchal or when it describes God as sweeping away the innocent together with the guilty or when it seems to condemn homosexuality. Such aspects make it difficult to believe that the Pentateuch is divine in its entirety.

In Sommer's view, the "stenographic" theory of revelation, which implies that the Pentateuch records God's utterances word for word, is not as biblical as many traditional Jews and Christians believe. The many inconsistences establish the Pentateuch to be the product of multiple human authors. Remarkably, some of the most apparent contradictions are found in the highly relevant section Exod 19–24. Sommer expresses some doubt with regard to the classical Documentary Hypothesis (16, 46, 50), which claims that the Pentateuch was composed of the sources J, E, D, and P. Sommer is well aware of the innovative approaches of David Carr and others, but still he decides to base his discussion of the biblical evidence on the recent version of the four-sources theory as propounded by Baruch Schwarz.

Especially in the passages ascribed to the E source, Sommer finds ambiguity with regard to the question of what the Israelites heard and saw at Sinai. The source suggests that Israel's knowledge of God and the law did not come directly from heaven but resulted partially from human interpretation. According to E, God's קול played a decisive role during revelation, but this Hebrew word may relate not only to a human voice providing specific information but also to an overwhelming noise. Also, it is dubious whether the people heard the Decalogue directly from God's mouth: the refusal of the terrified people to listen to God's voice (Exod 20:18–22) is possibly supposed to have occurred at the beginning of the Decalogue's proclamation, not after it (see participle ראים in 20:18). Remarkably, the introduction to the Decalogue in Exod 20:1 does not reveal to whom God spoke the text of the Decalogue. Finally, the remark that the people "saw" God's קולות "voices/thunders" suggests that the way in which God communicated was extraordinary, not similar to communication between humans. Comparable ambiguity is found with regard to the writing on the tablets. No one but Moses saw what was written on the first tablets, and it is unclear whether God actually wrote the text on the new ones (34:1) or whether the writing was done by Moses (34:28).

Despite the uncertainties regarding the precise delimitation of the E source, Sommer concludes that E deliberately encourages its audience to wonder how God revealed the law, either directly and stenographically or by human mediation. In his view, the second option comes close to the "participatory" theory of revelation developed by Franz Rosenzweig and Abraham Joshua Heschel. These Jewish thinkers regarded the Bible as a human response to God's act of revelation but believed that, despite its human wording, it is possible to sense the divine in what is humanly written. This line of thinking implies that the authority behind the law remains fully divine but that the specifics of any given rule are due to a human translation of the revelation into language. Just as a translation from one language to another never matches the original precisely, Scripture reflects revelation but also contains flaws and imperfections.

Having shown that P and J suppose that all lawgiving was mediated through Moses, Sommer argues that D intends to answer the questions regarding the character of revelation raised by the text of Exodus. In Deut 4–5, it is clear that at Sinai God's "voice" (קול) transmitted words (4:12) and that the Israelites heard the Decalogue directly from the mouth of God. (Sommer regards the reference to mediation in 5:5 as secondary.) Only after the proclamation of the Decalogue do the Israelites ask Moses to mediate (5:25). Sommer describes E's approach to revelation as "minimalist" and D's approach as "maximalist."

Jewish views on the revelation of the laws appear to diverge. Some sages argued that God revealed the entire Decalogue directly to the people, but others stated that the people heard only the first two commandments from God's mouth. Maimonides argued that God's "voice" differs fundamentally from human voices and that Moses did not hear specific laws from the mouth of God. In Sommer's words: "He apprehended something divine that no other human had apprehended, and on the basis of that apprehension Moses composed the law" (84). Sommer admits that it may seem unjustified to posit a connection between the theology of E and Maimonides's rejection of the idea that God spoke as humans speak, as the latter reflects Neoplatonic and Aristotelian thinking. Still, he suggests that the undeveloped ideas of E recur in full flower with Maimonides, Rosenzweig, Heschel, and other Jewish thinkers. In any case, there appears to be a discrepancy between D's description of revelation, which is so dominant in the Pentateuch, and Maimonides's emphasis on Moses's intermediary role.

Chapter 3 goes on to describe the "participatory theology of revelation" as it took shape in Jewish tradition. Sommer stresses that, according to this approach, the biblical revelations were nonverbal but definitely not devoid of content. According to Rosenzweig, God's nonverbal revelation included two fundamental elements, God's self-identification "I am YHWH" and his command "Love me." Israel concretized the abstract demand (*Gebot*) by creating the laws (*Gesetze*) of the torah. Although Heschel's position on the issue is more ambivalent, he suggested that revelation always takes place in dialogue, with each side influencing and being influenced.

Sommer is inspired by Rosenzweig and Heschel but also by the earlier sage Maimonides when arguing that Moses was not a stenographer who received precise words from heaven. He argues that the human authors of the sources of the Pentateuch attributed their own insights to Moses, which reflects humility instead of mendacity: these authors were convinced that something extraordinary had happened at Sinai and sincerely believed that their own ideas ultimately resulted from God's revelation to Moses.

Despite its assumed divine origin, Sommer claims that putting aside part of the legislation is inevitable in view of its contradictions. Exodus 12:8–9, for instance, directs the Israelites to roast the Passover offering, but Deut 16:6–7 requires that the offering be boiled. Such tensions can be explained by Rosenzweig's distinction between *Gebot* and *Gesetze*, but also by Heschel's distinction between the heavenly torah and the earthly torah, the earthly torah being no more and no less than an approximation to the heavenly torah. Even the Talmud implicitly admits that the Pentateuch is not fully divine when it forbids applying certain parts of the biblical legislation, such as the command to execute a rebellious son (Deut 21:18–21).

Sommer admits that his own ideas go some steps further than those of Heschel and Rosenzweig and that they would be troubled by the downgrading of the Bible that he proposes. In Heschel's thinking, robust notions of obligation and dedication play a decisive role. In the case of Rosenzweig, this may at first seem to be different because of his emphasis on autonomy and personal choice, but this emphasis reflects Rosenzweig's ideal of truly free acceptance of God's sovereignty, without external compulsion, certainly not a rejection of obedience as such.

In chapter 4 Sommer argues that the classical Jewish distinction between Scripture, known as the Written Torah, and the later rabbinic traditions, the so-called Oral Torah, is misleading. Religious Jews assume that both stem from revelation at Sinai but commonly regard the Written Torah as having been revealed in its entirety and, therefore, as more authoritative than the Oral Torah. Sommer, however, shows that several passages in rabbinic literature break down the boundary between the two. Some sayings express the primacy of the Written Torah, always without denying the importance of the Oral Torah, but surprisingly others accord greater priority to the Oral Torah. Sommer goes a step further than classical Judaism by subverting the distinction between Scripture and tradition completely, denoting Written Torah as part of the larger entity, Oral Torah. According to Sommer, the boundary between Bible and tradition is blurred not only in rabbinic texts but also in Scripture itself. The formulations of Scripture are no less human and tentative than those of the Oral Torah, and, just like the Oral Torah, Scripture contains voices that supplement, criticize, and contradict other voices within the same textual corpus. Like many later works of rabbinic Judaism, the Bible offers a mix of revelation, reflection, and discussion. Thus it constitutes a formative instead of a normative canon, an anthology worthy of study and contemplation, just like rabbinic traditions.

Chapter 5 addresses the question of whether revelation is ongoing throughout Jewish history. In Judaism it is not uncommon to assume that Oral Torah continues to develop, but the idea that postbiblical tradition is divinely inspired is expressed only rarely and with great caution. Heschel and Rosenzweig, for instance, can say that the "today" of the revelation at Sinai must be experienced as "today" by Jews of all generations, but they reject the idea of continuous revelation and tend to deny the legitimacy of innovation. In his discussion of the biblical evidence, Sommer shows that, while P describes lawgiving as a durative process, D limits revelation to the days of Moses: God spoke only at Sinai, and nothing may be added to the words that Moses spoke in his name (Deut 4:2; 13:1). Although this suggests that the law cannot be improved over time, Sommer points out that D's own revisions of older biblical laws implicitly legitimizes the idea of innovation, thereby suggesting that a flexible approach may also be assumed in later times.

In the crucial chapter 6 Sommer describes his "modern" Jewish approach to Scripture. He regards the Bible as the first rabbinic work, distinguishing contradictory biblical voices that can be associated with similar voices of later Jewish sages. A difference from later rabbinic works is that the Bible does not identify the voices that it contains, but modern biblical scholarship is able to describe the schools of thought that were behind them.

Sommer demonstrates that in Jewish biblical exegesis centrifugal approaches were prominent. Small units consisting of no more than three successive verses, not the larger literary units, were regarded as the main unit of expression. On the other hand, there were also unity-seeking forces trying to harmonize contradictory verses, but these were less widespread than the atomizing form of reading. Scripture also manifests centrifugal trends, with most of the Pentateuch giving no indication that laws needed to be reconciled, and centripetal tendencies in Chronicles and Ezra-Nehemiah, which seek to harmonize the contradictory laws of the Pentateuch.

Rosenzweig and the Protestant Biblical theologian Brevard Childs regard Scripture as a literary unity and focus on the final form of the text. They do not deny the intellectual legitimacy of biblical criticism but focus on the work of the redactors instead of the sources they incorporated. Sommer objects that "there is no reason to see the anthologizer as more sacred, more authoritative, or even more interesting than the anthologized" (231). He believes that the scholarly approach of Julius Wellhausen and Baruch Schwartz is closer to the atomistic biblical interpretation of midrash than the canonical approach of Rosenzweig and Childs.

The last chapter shows that in Judaism something has always remained unaffected, despite the disputes and innovations: all biblical and later Jewish texts affirm that Israel owes covenantal loyalty to a single deity, the God who elected it, and that this loyalty implies the observance of a law. Antinomian thinkers such as Paul were written out of Jewish tradition, which shows that the notion of legal obligation is indispensable to any Jewish theology. This continuity encourages Jewish communities to find ways to obey God in their contemporaneous contexts. Innovation is required, and the classical halakic system of the rabbis may become obsolete, but the traditions must be taken seriously, knowing that in the end new readings may turn out to be improvements but may also prove to be misreadings.

Not being an expert in Jewish theology, I will limit my reaction to the issue of Scripture's authority. I share Sommer's observation that the Bible expresses ideas that we can no longer accept. Even for conservative theologians the Bible has aspects that are irreconcilable with their own thinking. It is important to admit this and to reflect on it rather than to sweep it under the carpet. As Sommer clearly shows, we should not feel obliged to brainwash ourselves in order to embrace biblical truths. We do not need to repeat naïvely what offensive biblical passages suggest with regard to the character of God or the position of women or the punishment of rebellious sons.

However, this raises the central issue of authority. When we reject aspects of biblical thinking, on what basis do we do this? Where does our conviction that an offensive biblical text cannot be divine originate? How was the new criterion "revealed" to us? Do we reject biblical ideas on the authority of talmudic or other Jewish sages? Do we reject them on the basis of the New Testament writings? Is our rejection due to progressive insight or to the Enlightenment? I do not reproach Sommer for not having answered these questions, because these are questions that I cannot easily answer myself, but the issue of the provenance of our criteria deserves attention in our future reflection.

Further, the occurrence of biblical ideas that we regard as obsolete or even offensive requires an explanation. Nowadays we know so much more about the ancient Near Eastern context in which the biblical texts were composed. Biblical narratives and laws have clear counterparts in other ancient Near Eastern texts. For instance, the incorporation of laws from Codex Hammurabi into Exod 21:1–22:16 shows that the authors of the biblical texts were children of their time. Sommer mentions such correspondences only in passing. However, many aspects of biblical thinking that are incomprehensible to present-day readers can be explained against an ancient Near Eastern background.

Sommer does not pay much attention to the theory of divine accommodation, although it played a significant role in Maimonides's thinking, for instance in his discussion of sacrifices (*Guide of the Perplexed* 3:32). This ancient theory, which can already be found with several church fathers, intends to clarify why God in Scripture did not always adequately reveal his true nature or give laws that do not reflect his ultimate will, such as the sacrificial laws, which according to Maimonides were a concession to ancient Israel's expectations but later became obsolete. In view of the correspondences between Scripture and other ancient texts, it may be apt to consider whether the theory of divine accommodation can be rejuvenated. Further, is it justifiable to suggest that the divine shines through, especially where the biblical texts break away from the usual ancient Near Eastern conceptions?

In Sommer's discussion of the authority of Scripture, the problem of its imperfections and contradictions stands out, but it remains unclear whether the Written Torah has advantages over the later Oral Torah. Sommer does refer to the lasting significance of Scripture, especially the idea of God's love for Israel and Israel's obligation to be loyal to God, but he does not clearly indicate when the later Jewish and Christian traditions run the risk of narrowing down the rich variety of biblical voices. The wish to avoid elements that cannot be integrated easily or that provoke self-criticism may result in inflexibility. In order to recover Scripture's surprises and inspiratory aspects, it is necessary to reread Scripture with new eyes and to put the rooted interpretations aside.

In my view, it is highly important to maintain the distinction between Scripture and tradition, not only in religious communities but also in biblical scholarship. Within Christianity, the Old and New Testaments may not only be read as two parts of the same canon but should also be studied separately, thereby demonstrating that the New Testament does not seamlessly complement the Old Testament. In the case of Judaism, the Written Torah should not be put on a par with the Oral Torah. Of course, it is interesting to point to unexpected interpretations of biblical texts. Sommer mentions the example of Deut 5:22, which in several targums—contrary to the Hebrew text—implies that God did not stop speaking after pronouncing the Decalogue. Sommer recognizes wholeheartedly that the interpretation of the targums is secondary and does not reflect the intention of the Hebrew text (199, 202, 204–5). In general, however, I wonder whether biblical texts can still speak in their own voice when we blur the distinction with their classical, but sometimes obscuring, interpretations.

Therefore, to a certain extent the approaches of Jewish Karaism and Christian Protestantism are cogent. Even if we believe in the authoritative status of tradition, regrettably we must admit that tradition may impose its own values on the sacred writings. Instead, close reading of the biblical texts may enable Scripture to speak for itself. It may show that the redactors incorporated the older sources quite consciously into the transmitted text. If we, with Rosenzweig, Childs, and others (229), concentrate on the transmitted text, it will show unity as well as diversity. That may be confusing, but in the end Scripture will undoubtedly surprise and inspire us more than before.

Sommer's book is thought-provoking. It bridges the gap between the academic and the religious approaches to Scripture. The relevant questions that it raises are all too often bypassed in Jewish and Christian theology, which is strange in view of the prominent role that they played in the thinking of Maimonides, Heschel, and Rosenzweig as well as several Christian thinkers. Therefore, this book deserves to be taken seriously. I am grateful to the author for making me familiar with his creative thinking.

JUDAISM: DEAD SEA SCROLLS

The Dead Sea Scrolls Reader, Second Edition, Revised and Expanded, edited by Donald W. Parry and Emanuel Tov. Leiden: Brill, 2013. 2 vols.: xxx + 1102, xxxiv + 1150. $199.00, $199.00; set: $349.00. ISBN 9789004264618, 9789004264625; set: 9789004264687.

Peter Porzig, Georg-August-Universität

The two renowned main editors, Donald W. Parry and Emanuel Tov, who certainly do not need to be introduced here, describe their revised and expanded version of *The Dead Sea Scrolls Reader* (hereafter *DSSR* 1 or 2, depending on the edition in view) as follows:

> The purpose of *The Dead Sea Scrolls Reader* [is] to enhance the research facilities of the individual texts within their respective genres. The nature of the Dead Sea Scrolls publication project was such that texts belonging to the same liter-

ary genre were published in different volumes in the *Discoveries in the Judaean Desert (DJD)* series, although those from cave 4 were often published by subject. The dispersion of these texts in several different volumes complicated their analysis, a problem that is now overcome in DSSR. (xiii)

One might probably add that many users of the first, six-volume edition faced similar problems with *DSSR* 1. The most apparent difference with the first edition, therefore—the publication of six volumes in two, the first comprising the material of *DSSR* 1 volumes 1–3, the second volumes 4–7—is presumably one of the most welcome features of this new edition. As it now stands *DSSR* 2 competes with the *Dead Sea Scrolls Study Edition (DSSE)* by Florentino García Martínez and Eibert J. C. Tigchelaar, available in paperback since 1999 from the same publisher. Both editions, however, differ in character as well as in presentation: while *DSSE* is a stand-alone edition of the texts produced by García Martínez and Tigchelaar, *DSSR* attempts to collect and present the most authoritative publications of these texts. To a very high degree this collection resembles the texts as they can be found in the DJD volumes (note the designation *reader* rather than *edition*, yet compare the classification in the introduction as "*editio minor*" [xix]).

In contrast to *DSSR* 1, *DSSR* 2 is no longer forced to use preliminary editions of many texts but can provide published editions, "fine-tuned," as announced in the introduction. Most welcome are the transcriptions of Émile Puech's DJD XXXVII volume (with English translations of his original French translation) and the reconstructed Hodayot Scroll from DJD XL by Hartmut Stegemann, Eileen Schuller, with Carol Newsom's translation. Some of the preliminary editions have been replaced with their printed counterparts in what is now commonly abbreviated as *PTSDSSP (Princeton Theological Seminary Dead Sea Scrolls Project)*, that is, the volumes edited under the aegis of James H. Charlesworth (mostly DJD V material). *DSSR* 2 presents "improved and revised texts" (among them 4Q169 = 4QpNah [in Shani Berrin/Tzoref's edition], 4Q184 "Wiles of the Wicked Women," and 4QMMT [no longer from DJD X but from the *DSSE*, thus unfortunately, yet surely for good reasons, no longer presenting the often used "composite text"]). It further contains some texts that were not included in *DSSR* 1 (again some from DJD XXXVII and many unclassified texts). This update and improvement is extremely helpful for many purposes. On the other hand, it forces a user to always keep in mind which underlying edition one is currently using and to have other editions, such as the corresponding DJD volume, at hand when quoting from a certain passage.

Some very small fragments that are unimportant for scholarly textual discussion were righly deleted, while texts that were segmented in the first edition (Serekh Hayahad [1QS], Temple Scroll [1Q20]) were reassembled for good reasons. In some cases the names of the compositions were updated, though in a bit of an inconsistent fashion (e.g., 4Q180–181 = "AgesCreat A and B" are now "4QWicked and Holy"). Quotations in the translations of the pesharim and commentaries are now highlighted in italics, yet this is also true for works such as the Damascus Document (Cairo Genizah manuscripts in Martin Abegg's edition with Edward Cook's translation). Even though these changes might undoubtedly be viewed as methodologically sound and convenient decisions, such a procedure always bears the risk of producing a slightly distorted picture when these texts are to be compared with other passages and works.

Two questions are addressed only *en passant* by the editors but have an important impact on the form and use of *DSSR 2*. The first is the order of the manuscripts by *genre*. In most cases they rely on the classification by Ute Mittmann-Richert and Armin Lange in DJD XXXIX. When the first edition was published, doing so was undoubtedly on top of the list. Yet already then, in their introduction to the first edition (2005), the editors admit that the "subjective nature of each classification proves to be problematic" (1:xvii). Since then classifications such as these have become more problematic to many researchers, as the latest discussion shows (e.g., Eibert J. C. Tigchelaar, "Classifications of the Collection of Dead Sea Scrolls and the Case of Apocryphon of Jeremiah C," *JSJ* 43 [2012]: 519–50, or Tigchelaar and Hindy Najman, "A Preparatory Study of Nomenclature and Text Designation in the Dead Sea Scrolls," *RQ* 103/26 [2014]: 305–26). In a way, the greatest advantage of the *DSSR* is at the same time not its strongest point. Is, for example, the Temple Scroll a "text concerned with religious law," an "exegetical text," or a "parabiblical text"? Every classification will inevitably produce cases that are either less or more doubtful or fitting, but one wonders if genre really is a category that still suits the Qumran texts. For practical uses, it might still be helpful here and there, but for an exhaustive text edition it seems almost a bit outdated, an order by cave and number might perhaps have been more "honest," as scholarship has not yet found a fitting method of classifying these manuscripts.

The second point to be mentioned here is the selection of the underlying editions. The editors have good reasons for switching to editions other than DJD in some cases (DJD V [John M. Allegro], X [Elisha Qimron with John Strugnell]). Every reader of *DSSR 2* should be thankful that the best published text available is reprinted here. In case of DJD texts, even improvements and spelling errors are noted. On the other hand, in cases where one would like to quote from a certain text that is not presented as in the series, one still needs to go to the DJD shelf, pick the right volume, and look it up there. Perhaps a juxtaposition of the DJD text and newer edition(s) would have been helpful in such cases. Of course, such a procedure would evidently have expanded the volumes even more. This question is also a result of the *concept* of the *DSSR*—being a collection of reprinted editions and thus not an edition on its own—rather than of its realization.

Regarding the usability of *DSSR* 2, the two volumes are now much easier to handle. Furthermore, the quality of the bindings is better, and the books stay open at the desired pages. On the downside, each volume weighs no less than roughly 4.5 lbs. or 2 kg (i.e., roughly twice the weight of *DSSE*). As the same proportion applies for the prices of *DSSR* 2 compared to *DSSE*, students will probably think twice when deciding whether the advantages outweigh the price, especially with regard to their own purposes. Unfortunately, one major disadvantage of *DSSR*

2 that could easily have been eliminated remains: when searching for a certain manuscript, the index at the end of both volumes (by cave and number) only points the reader to the number of the volume where it is found (in this case, vol. 1 or 2). Because the index lacks page numbers, it is still necessary to take a second step and search the (rather detailed) table of contents of the respective volume, where the texts are naturally sorted by genre, subgenre, and the name of the composition.

My sincere apologies to the editors and their team for the following (theoretical) example: Looking for the main manuscript of, for example, the Temple Scroll, one must first know its cave and manuscript number. In this case, this is admittedly easy: according to the index, 11Q19 is found in volume 1. Where in volume 1? In part 1, "Texts concerned with Religious Law," as the Temple Scroll mainly comprises law material? No. In part 2, "Exegetical Texts," since it treats long passages of Deuteronomy and other "biblical" books? No. In part 3, "Parabiblical Texts"? Yes, in "A. Rewritten Bible," subcategory "Temple," page 632. If there were an alphabetical index with page numbers, the whole procedure would be much easier, as we would only have to look for "Temple Scroll," volume 1, page 632.

In the eyes of old-fashioned readers—and the author of this review counts himself among these people—who like to have a book in their hands instead of an electronic concordance on their computer screen (which is, of course, useful in many other ways), the *Dead Sea Scrolls Study Edition* found a strong competitor, if not a more or less up-to-date replacement with the new *DSSR 2*—at least, until a revised and updated edition of the former sees the light of day and will open the next "round."

As a matter of course, all the above observations are of minor importance and must in no way diminish the editors' and their assistants' achievements. Parry and Tov are to be praised once more for this highly comprehensive and most up-to-date collection of texts and for a most valuable and useful tool for everyone who wants to delve into the world of the Dead Sea Scrolls.

The Qumran Paradigm: Critical Evaluation of Some Foundational Hypotheses in the Construction of the Qumran Sect, by Gwynned de Looijer. Early Judaism and Its Literature 43. Atlanta: SBL Press, 2015. Pp. xviii + 297. Paper. $37.95. ISBN 9780884140719. Hardcover. $52.95. ISBN 9780884140733.

Jutta Leonhardt-Balzer, University of Aberdeen

The revised Durham PhD thesis critically examines some "foundational hypotheses" of what the author calls the "Qumran paradigm" (253), the idea that the Dead Sea Scrolls found in the caves form a coherent library reflecting the ideas of a community settled on the archaeological site in Qumran.

The introductory chapter summarizes the theories around the Qumran community: the Essene, Groningen, and Collins's "multicommunity (Essene) hypothesis" (10), as well as Schiffman's Sadducean hypothesis. The theory of a

Qumran library is addressed based on Dimant's criteria for classifying sectarian texts and criticized using García Martínez's divergent system, which abandons the differentiation in sectarian and nonsectarian. De Looijer rejects the concept of sect due to its imprecise definition and suggests viewing the Qumran texts in the context of the Jewish situation in postexilic, Maccabean, Hasmonean, and Roman times. She then questions the basis of "Qumran paradigm," the identification of the archaeological site with the scrolls, the identification of the texts with the Essenes, the relationship between 1QS and CD, the coherence of the scrolls as a library, and the use of the sociological model of sect. The subsequent chapters address prominent theories for these bases, using two important texts, 4QMMT and the Treatise on the Two Spirits (1QS III, 13–IV, 26), as test cases. De Looijer's aim is not to provide an exegetical study but to focus on methodology.

Chapter 2 addresses the theory of a library, based on Dimant's classification of texts in biblical, sectarian, and nonsectarian as well García Martínez's into pre-sectarian and sectarian texts. Dimant's classification is seen as too imprecise, as one needs to include an "in-between" category to fit the texts that do not precisely fit with the basic criteria. While Dimant distinguishes between texts synchronically, García Martínez and the Groningen hypothesis provide a diachronic pattern by classifying the nonbiblical texts into those belonging to the pre-Essene "apocalyptic tradition," Essene works, works belonging to the pre-Qumranic "formative period" before the break from the Essenes, and, finally, the sectarian texts (63). De Looijer sees the concept of a "formative period" as another attempt to fit in texts that do not match the other categories. The difficulties of both positions with classifying all texts makes de Looijer question the idea of a coherent library. She seems to assume that the term *sectarian* does not allow for influence of concepts from outside the sect (61, 79) and that a library must not show contradictions, growth, or variety.

Chapter 3 studies 4QMMT in its relevance for the classification of the scrolls. De Looijer does not produce an exegesis herself but lists instances in which scholarship questions the reconstruction of the text and its interpretation as a foundational document in the sectarian separation from its mother group. De Looijer criticizes the theories about "mild polemics" in the text and follows those who read the text on a purely literary level and therefore assign a rhetorical function to any distinction between the author with the readers and others. The difficulties in reconstructing the text and divergent theories about its interpretation suffice for de Looijer to dispute the whole theory about the separation of the Yaḥad.

Chapter 4 addresses the theory of dualism as an example of the idea of the theological coherence of the scrolls. De Looijer summarizes the history of research on dualism in Qumran, from Peter von der Osten-Sacken with a linear theory of dualistic development, via his criticism by Jean Duhaime, to the dualistic categories of James C. Charlesworth. She ultimately focuses on the patterns of dualism as described by Jörg Frey, who distinguishes ten different types of dualism, three of which he finds in the Qumran texts, and finds dualistic thoughts only in few texts and in differing versions. Thus he sees the Treatise on the Two Spirits as presectarian wisdom tradition containing a complex web of cosmic, ethical, and psychological dualism, which is taken up in some sectarian texts, but only in a simplified way. By contrast, the (also presectarian) nationalistic tradition of 1QM contains only a cosmic war dualism influenced by Daniel and possibly by Zoroastrian thought. There is also evidence of a cosmic dualism in the shape of demonology in 11QApPs[a] (11Q11), Jubilees, and 4Q390. Based on the age of these traditions, Frey observes a radicalization in the dualistic thought of the Yaḥad. Against this theory, de Looijer lists Eric M. Meyers's reconstruction of dualism as a part of apocalyptic thought and argues for apocalyptic as a more comprehensive category to interpret the texts than dualism. At times de Looijer creates artificial opponents, thus when she criticizes the view that "the concept of dualism is seen as simply or exclusively Qumranic" (161), for which there is no evidence. The problem with de Looijer's substitution of dualism with apocalyptic is that apocalyptic, like dualism, is an anachronistic concept that derives from our understanding of the texts and serves only to interpret them. The usefulness of each term depends on its definition, and both definitions are debated. De Looijer chooses Bianchi's definition of dualism, which is not derived from Jewish texts, as a "duality or polarity of causal principles" (170), against Frey's classification of dualisms. Consequently, she concludes that dualism is neither an "independent ideological concept" (187), nor does it exist in its strict definition in the Qumran texts.

To prove this claim, chapter 5 focusses on the dualism of the Treatise on the Two Spirits. De Looijer emphasizes that the Treatise needs to be seen as a nonsectarian text but that it is not possible to reconstruct its original shape. What has been described as dualism in the Treatise is interpreted as merely the psychological struggle of good and bad intentions in the elect, as already argued in 1961 by P. Wernberg-Møller's psychological interpretation of the spirits. De Looijer does not consider the fact that the text also speaks about the "sons of deceit" who exclusively follow the "angel of darkness," which indicates that there is a cosmic division of two external influences and their followers. She argues against Frey's wisdom attribution of the Treatise based on the fact that the Two Ways tradition of Ben Sira and the Epistle of Enoch are nondualistic, without considering that traditions are never taken over without adaptation and change. Furthermore, even if the Treatise of the Two Spirits originated in a nonsectarian context, the fact of the matter is that it now can be found only in 1QS. Therefore, it needs to be interpreted not only as an independent text but also in the context of the Community Rule.

De Looijer concludes that the sociological conclusions drawn from the scrolls are based on a circular argument, on the assumption of the existence of a sect. After all these questions, de Looijer ultimately does not seem to aim at doing away with the Qumran paradigm but ends by suggesting that "for a certain number of texts" scholarship needs to step away from the paradigm to do them justice (269). She asks some necessary questions about the way in which the assumption of a coherent sectarian library influences the reading of the texts. However, she does not consider the genre of some of the texts, which are rules and rituals aimed at being executed. Her merely literary approach that refuses to consider the social realities behind the texts does not do justice to their intention. Her warning against reading the texts together is an important cautionary point, but it does not exempt the reader from developing a view on why a text was found in this accumulation of texts in these caves located in a comparatively small area and what kind of a collection this is. Not seeing the scrolls as a library is just as much a preconception as the opposite.

The book is a thorough, beautifully summarized account of the positions on which it focusses. However, these positions alone do not suffice to dispute the Qumran paradigm, thus no concept of the Yaḥad's ideology is based on dualism alone. A peculiar feature of de Looijer's approach is not to argue herself but to produce other scholars who disagree with the proposed argument. Likewise, the mere existence of a divergent definition does not disprove a definition. Her approach assumes that the mere existence of a question questions the whole theory. The problem is that "it ain't necessarily so" is not a valid academic argument. To disprove a theory, one must engage with its sources, and this de Looijer's study does only in a very limited way. Fundamentally, de Looijer refuses to acknowledge that some texts have parallels and some even describe a community—of whichever shape—and that not only their differences but also their similarities need to be explained.

The book provides a valuable overview of scholarship and is useful in that it challenges certain common assumptions, but ultimately it demonstrates that it is not methodologically possible to criticize theories without detailed recourse to the material on which they are based.

JUDAISM: RABBINIC AND MEDIEVAL

The Dynasty of the Jewish Patriarchs, by Alan Appelbaum. Texts and Studies in Ancient Judaism 156. Tübingen: Mohr Siebeck, 2013. Pp. xii + 246. Cloth. $152.00. ISBN 9783161529641.

Joshua Schwartz, Bar-Ilan University

Most scholars seeking a new topic on which to spend years of research in order to publish a book would not choose to study once again the Jewish patriarchs or the Patriarchate in late antique Palestine. So much has been written, and much of this relatively so recently, that it would hardly seem worthwhile or wise to study the same patriarch and Patriarchate sources yet another time to try and come up with new and different (and, one hopes, correct) interpretations.[1] It was,

---

1. The author is, of course, aware of all this and he provides a rather comprehensive list in the footnotes of his introduction.

after all, Mohr Siebeck, the publisher of the present volume, that published one of the classic works on the Patriarchate some twenty years ago, the study of Martin Jacobs, *Die Institution des jüdischen Patriarchen: Eine quellen-und traditionskritische Studie zur Geschichte der Juden in der Spätantike* (1995). Jacobs showed, *inter alia*, how historically problematical the Patriarchate sources were regarding the institution in general and individual patriarchs in particular. Could one or should one indeed attempt to write the history of the Patriarchate?

Yet, author Alan Appelbaum claims to have found a new unexplored aspect of the Patriarchate. Building on the fact almost all scholarship agrees that the Patriarchate was a "family affair," with individual patriarchs being succeeded by their heirs, whether the son or the oldest son of the previous patriarch, Appelbaum seeks to redefine the societal structure in which all this took place: it is no longer just a family affair but rather a dynastic one, and it is this new aspect which serves as the purpose for the new study.

The first impression of the reader, of both the book and probably of this review, is that family and dynasty are the same or so close that the difference does not warrant a book-length study. This might be true in terms of modern usage of the two terms, so the first thing that Appelbaum does is to define dynasty as a "social arrangement in which office or function is transmitted over the generations of a family to one and only one successor at a time, by default a son and probably an eldest son." Appelbaum uses the word "family" in its wider context. To be honest, this clarification is not entirely satisfactory during the course of the work, and only at the end does it really become clear.

The goals of this work are many. Appelbaum first determines when and how the role of the patriarchs began in order to uncover the origins of dynastic features. Then he studies the various members of the dynasty within the framework of how dynasties work. He seeks to uncover actual history in his analysis, knowing that the attempt, even the suggestion, might arouse antagonism in the scholarly world, which tends not to see any real, tangible history in rabbinic sources, including those on the patriarchs and the Patriarchate.[2] Finally, he compares the Patriarchate dynasty with other real or supposed dynasties in the hope of locating it among the various family arrangements of its period that are often called dynasties.

The work has an introduction and eight chapters. The introduction briefly recounts the history of research, explains the need for a new study within the framework of patriarchal dynasties, and then maps out the work. Chapter 1 ("Before the Patriarchate") examines the rabbinic traditions positing the early existence of the Patriarchate; Appelbaum negates them one by one. The "Pairs" mentioned in Tractate Avot, Hillel, Rabban Gamaliel of Second Temple times, and Rabban Shimon ben Gamaliel of Second Temple times were not patriarchs. The same is true regarding candidates for the Patriarchate after the destruction of the

---

2. E.g., the rather blistering review of Catherine Hezser of this volume in *Theologische Literaturzeitung* 139.7/8 (2014): 859–61.

temple. Rabban Yohanan ben Zakkai, Rabban Gamaliel of Yavneh, and Rabban Shimon ben Gamaliel were also not patriarchs. They might have been members, founders, or continuators of an important family with "dynastic tendencies," but they were not the founders of the patriarchal dynasty nor patriarchs. The chapter ends with Appelbaum's suggestion that the Patriarchate was established by the figure known in rabbinic literature as Rabbi Judah the Patriarch (*nasi*, also translated as "the Prince").

Chapter 2 ("The First Patriarch"), makes the case for Rabbi Judah the Patriarch as the first (official) patriarch and founder of the dynasty. Was he related to or part of the Gamaliel or Shimon ben Gamaliel family, his supposed patriarchal forbearers according to the rabbis? Appelbaum leans toward the view of Sacha Stern that Judah the Patriarch was a member of a wealthy Galilean family who joined the rabbinic movement and superimposed on it the concept of patriarch that already existed in the Galilee.[3] Applebaum stops short of actually accepting Stern's view, since his purpose, as he states, was to identify the origins of the Patriarchate and not the family background of the first patriarch. Be all this as it may, Rabbi Judah the Patriarch, whoever his ancestors were, was indeed a patriarch.

Chapter 3 ("The Dynasty: How Dynasties Work") discusses patriarchal powers, status, and activities from the death of Rabbi Judah the Patriarch to the end of the Patriarchate in the chronological sequence of patriarchs. Applebaum's discussion is based on the view of Seth Schwartz that individual patriarchs were powerful not because they occupied the office of patriarch but because as individuals they acquired power.[4] Claiming to "refine" and modify somewhat Schwartz's views, Appelbaum sees the power that they acquired as an outgrowth of the dynasty that they established. The ideal of this dynasty was primogeniture, but from time to time it was necessary to deviate from this ideal to preserve the dynasty. Thus, in accordance with dynastic needs, the successor might have been a younger son or brothers or other relatives.

Chapter 4 ("The Dynasty in the Early Third Century") deals with Gamaliel "III," or Gamaliel be-Rabbi, that is, the son of Rabbi Judah the Patriarch, whose succession established the continuation of the dynasty. This chapter provides some good examples of Applebaum's willingness to learn history from rabbinic sources. Bavli Ketubot 103b, "Rabbi's (= Rabbi Judah the Patriarch) will," contains early strata likely to be historical, claims Applebaum. Yerushalmi Shabbat 6:3, 8a relating the tradition of Rabban Gamaliel's Shabbat stroll while carrying a golden key, provides biographical information. It is hard to understand why Applebaum is so insistent on establishing this potential historical veracity. He could have gotten to where he wanted to be in terms of the social dynastic background within the

---

3. Sacha Stern, "Rabbi and the Origins of the Patriarchate," *Journal of Jewish Studies* 54 (2003): 193–215.

4. Seth Schwartz, "The Patriarch and the Diaspora," *Journal of Jewish Studies* 50 (1999): 208–22.

framework (and there are many possibilities) of accepted methodologies. The biographical information does not necessarily help. Appelbaum also tends to accept the nonrabbinic sources as containing historical material and thus accepts Origin on the "forgotten" patriarch Ioullas (Hillel).

Chapter 5 ("R. Judah Nesiah") deals with Rabbi Judah Nesiah, for the rabbis the model of what a patriarch should be. Only he and his grandfather Rabbi Judah the Patriarch, Ha-nasi, had their title become part of their name. His grandfather, however, sometimes might have been known just as "Rabbi," but Nesiah, based on *nasi*, was never omitted from the grandson's name. In this chapter as well Appelbaum claims that it is possible to extract from the sources biographical and historical material on the career of Rabbi Judah Nesiah. These sources show him boldly and confidently displaying initiative and energy, raising substantial amounts of money, initiating contacts with the imperial government, beginning the supervision of teachers in nonrabbinic Palestine, trying to make Jewish courts the equal of Roman courts for Roman-law purposes, and more. The raising of funds was extremely significant. Rabbi Judah Nesiah firmly established the *aurum coronarium*, the collection of funds for the patriarchs from the Jews of the Diaspora. This was the basis for the great wealth of the dynasty as well as probably its imperial and social standing. Its prestige to a great extent was dependent on this.

Chapter 6 ("The Patriarchal Dynasty: During the Dynasty of Constantine the Great") discusses Gamaliel IV, the successor to Rabbi Judah Nesiah and his oldest living son, according to Appelbaum, and then Hillel II, who was the first "fully empowered" patriarch whose name we know. Evidence from Jewish, Roman, and patristic sources of the period shows a patriarch recognized by the emperor as the leader of the Jews of the empire, exercising empire-wide power over Jewish practice, appointing Jewish civic officials, and making a claim to Davidic ancestry. Chapter 7 ("The Culmination, and the End, of the Dynasty: Identifying the Last Patriarchs") takes the story of the Patriarchate to the last patriarch, Gamaliel VI. This represents the end of a period in Jewish history. The Jews were no longer represented before the imperial government by a powerful leader and advocate. Jewish society became more and more decentralized with an increasing emphasis on the synagogue as the center of Jewish life as well as on what was left of the rabbinic movement.

Up until now the dynastic element has always been there in Appelbaum's presentation, but somewhat in the background. In chapter 8 ("Other Dynasties and Other 'Dynasties'") he finally highlights the issue and elaborates on the functions of a dynasty. The patriarchal dynasty was grounded within the framework of hereditary Davidic kingship and dynasties of Jewish priests and high priests. Patriarchal prestige was founded on the money of the *aurum coronarium*, as mentioned above, but also dependent on the dynastic myths that the patriarchs established and fostered seeking to compare them with former regal and priestly dynasties. The patriarchs also cemented their standing within the "dynastic culture" of the rabbis. The Patriarchate then was accepted as a true dynasty and not as a "family business."

Reading this volume was often like taking a walk down memory lane in terms of much of the methodology. The search for the "historical" or early kernel in rabbinic literature was, after all, the methodology in which this reviewer received his academic training decades ago. Applebaum, as pointed out, was certainly aware of the pitfalls of his positivistic and somewhat harmonistic methodology in the face of more accepted "critical" methodologies popular today. However, this does not negate the contribution of the volume. It is certainly the best up-to-date summary that I know on the Patriarchate, and Applebaum's readings on the "historical" sources and many of the other ones provide interesting insights. More importantly, the dynastic element is new. It is not family but something else, as becomes clear at the end. It might have been better, though, if some of the elements expanded upon in the final chapter had been discussed earlier in order to more actively highlight the issue of dynasty.

It is in the nature of scholarship that whenever we think that the final word on a topic has been said, a new study appears, sometimes providing new approaches to old issues or new readings or understandings or arousing new interests in a topic that seemed to have been played out. This is the case regarding *The Dynasty of the Jewish Patriarchs*. Patriarchal dynasty is indeed new and innovative; Applebaum's approach, though, is somewhat less new and innovative, but the work makes an important contribution to scholarship and well worth reading for anyone interested in late antique Palestine.

The Targums in the Light of Traditions of the Second Temple Period, edited by Thierry Legrand and Jan Joosten. Supplements to the Journal for the Study of Judaism 167. Leiden: Brill, 2014. Pp. xiii + 259. Cloth. €110.00. ISBN 9789004269545.

Simon Lasair, Saskatoon, Saskatchewan, Canada

In recent years the nature and character of targumic literature has received intense discussion. This has occurred across the spectrum of targum scholarship. Linguists are attempting to establish the precise dialectology of the Aramaic used by Targums Onqelos and Jonathan, as well as by the other Pentateuch Targums, philologists are attempting to establish tradition histories for the various literary expansions in the targums, and literary scholars are searching for adequate concepts to describe the defining characteristics of the targumic genre. Yet part of the challenge for all such research is that little is known of the origins of the written targums, what their roles and positions were within early Jewish liturgical and devotional life, as well as what might possibly have been their relationship to rabbinic Judaism. Matters are increasingly complicated when considering the documents resembling targums in the Qumran corpus, the Samaritan targums, in addition to the Syriac Peshitta literature, precisely because of their seeming relatedness to the Aramaic targums.

The volume reviewed here sheds some light on almost all these critical issues, with particular focus on the Aramaic targums of the rabbinic period, specifically examining their literary, linguistic, and exegetical traditions connected to Second Temple literature. The volume is divided into three sections: "Targumim and Targumisms"; "Comparative Approaches"; and "Thematic Issues." The volume also includes an introduction and an index. The majority of essays contained herein are written in French; three are in English, and one is in German. The volume thus displays the international nature of targum scholarship, although the absence of Israeli and North American voices in this volume is somewhat regrettable.

In the first section, "Targumim and Targumisms," Ingo Kottsieper's contribution gives an overview of the current state of linguistic research into the language of Targums Onqelos and Jonathan. Citing some of the difficulties in clearly fitting Onqelos and Jonathan's language into the category of Jewish Literary Aramaic, Kottsieper's essay follows Edward Cook's theory of an Aramaic that emerged somewhere between Babylonia and Palestine, this being the Aramaic used by Onqelos and Jonathan. Perhaps most useful in pursuing this argument is Kottsieper's examination of the migrations of Aramaic speakers that might have facilitated the emergence of such a hybrid Aramaic dialect.

Jan Joosten's contribution examines something of the relationship between targumic translation techniques and those utilized in the LXX. Noting several similar renderings of problematic phrases, and the occasional use of Aramaic calque terms in the LXX, Joosten explores the question of dependence between Aramaic targums and the LXX. He concludes that, although the similarities between the targums and the LXX are striking, it would be highly premature at the current stage of research to argue strongly in defense of a specific direction for the dependence or even how it might be possible to account historically for the similarities in translation.

Beate Ego explores the relationship between Targum Sheni Esther and other versions of Esther from the Second Temple period, focusing particularly on the LXX. Engaging in a broad survey of Targum Sheni Esther's representation of the Esther narrative, Ego argues that the targum not only interprets Esther but that it also interprets interpretations of Esther, thus drawing together a number of different literary and exegetical traditions.

The first section is completed with a brief contribution from Christophe Bonnard, who brings the Samaritan Targums into conversation with Second Temple traditions. Examining such issues as toponyms, the motif of the three books of creation, and interpretations of Num 24:17, Bonnard concludes that the Samaritan Targums, Qumran literature, and the Aramaic Targums preserve many traditions from the Second Temple period, carrying these traditions forward into the medieval era.

The second section, "Comparative Approaches," opens with a lengthy contribution by Robert Hayward in which the author examines the motif of God as father in targumic literature. Drawing upon material across the targumic corpus, in addition to the Qumran corpus, the pseudepigrapha, and rabbinic midrashim, Hayward argues that, when presented as father in the targums, God is figured as something like a *paterfamilias* who can be approached in times of need and who will attend to his children.

Next comes a contribution by Claude Tassin, who seeks to examine the characterizations of Zebulun and Naphtali in the targums. This is to establish whether the Aramaic presentations of these characters and tribes might have some bearing on how scholars understand Matt 4:13–16, which quotes from Isaiah (mentioning the territories of Zebulun and Naphtali) to characterize Jesus's early ministry. Despite Tassin's targumic information offering some interesting possibilities concerning how the Matthew passage might have been understood in a Jewish context, he states that the targumic material cannot be considered reliable enough for providing solid contextual information, due primarily to difficulties in dating the traditions contained in the targums. Nevertheless, because the targumic material is so striking, Tassin believes such material might present opportunities to explore what methodological steps need be taken to render a comparative approach credible.

In the following essay Willem F. Smelik seeks to assess the methodological feasibility of comparing targumic material with Second Temple literature, using the narration of Moses's death in Deut 34:5–6 as a test case. There are several interpretive motifs pursued by Smelik, such as the location of Moses's tomb, the notion that Moses wrote about his own death, and Moses's departure for paradise. Throughout Smelik argues that the targumic material might signal transitions in the development of these specific literary traditions. However, overall the contents of the targumic renderings bear more similarity to rabbinic exegetical literature, in contrast to their Second Temple antecedents. Smelik does not discuss extensively what methodological bearing his findings might have on the ongoing study of targumic literature.

Innocent Himbaza's contribution completes the second section. There are two general areas Himbaza examines: sacrificial practices in Pseudo-Jonathan; and Moses's time in Egypt in the same targum. Of particular relevance to Himbaza's discussion are Jubilees and the Temple Scroll. Overall, Himbaza concludes that Pseudo-Jonathan represents a development of Second Temple traditions and can therefore be viewed as an important source representing one example of Jewish diversity and evolution in times subsequent to the Second Temple period.

The final section, "Thematic Issues," begins with Michael Langlois's essay concerning the targums and the critique of power in the Second Temple period. Of particular interest to Langlois are targumic passages that intensify negative biblical presentations of power or royalty. Drawing mainly from the Former and Latter Prophets, Langlois demonstrates that targumic narrative and poetic expansions will often explicitly identify monarchs or nations that are criticized anonymously in the Bible. The targums will also often use more disparaging language than the Bible to heighten the critiques of these monarchs and nations. To explain this trend, Langlois demonstrates that many of the monarchs and powers mentioned by the targums were similarly named and negatively constructed by Second Temple sources. He therefore suggests that Second Temple sources might offer some insight as to why powers and nations whose influence had long diminished by the targums' times remained objects of disdain in targumic literature. In short, Langlois believes the targums directly advanced Second Temple motifs and ideology.

Finally, Thierry Legrand's essay about miracles and spectacular events in Targum Pseudo-Jonathan ends both this section and the book. Legrand focuses on how the merits of Moses, and others like him, brought benefit for all Israel in Pseudo-Jonathan. Drawing this motif into dialogue with Second Temple sources, Legrand demonstrates that many of Pseudo-Jonathan's motifs can be seen also in Jubilees, Biblical Antiquities, the Genesis Apocryphon, and the Testament of the Twelve Patriarchs. Acknowledging that pinpointing the specific source of a particular tradition is difficult, Legrand does suggest that all these traditions might have been circulating within the *beth hamidrash* in the rabbinic period, thus providing opportunities for Pseudo-Jonathan's framers to incorporate them into their targum.

As should be evident, this volume presents a variety of approaches for discussing the relationships between the Aramaic targums and Second Temple literature. There are three questions that could be raised from reading these essays: (1) If comparisons between two distinct yet related literary corpora, such as Second Temple literature and the Aramaic Targums, are going to be feasible, how do we account for the many literary, linguistic, and ideological resemblances and differences found in such comparisons within a sweeping, yet robustly articulated, historical narrative? (2) What are the methodological and philosophical principles that make such comparative work feasible in terms of offering potential epistemological frameworks for the kind of research undertaken in this volume? (3) How do the smaller studies in this volume fit in emerging understandings and models of Jewish social and religious evolution and identity formation within the historical periods under discussion? To date there have been few attempts to answer questions such as these and others of their ilk with particular focus on targumic literature. However, this volume does make an important contribution to exploring such broader methodological and historical questions, precisely because of its detailed focus on targumic literary, linguistic, and exegetical data.

The essays contained in this volume thus represent some of the best trends in current European targum scholarship. The problems explored and issues raised by each contributor point to the many directions that targum scholarship could go in terms of developing a greater understanding of the nature and character of targumic literature. The questions I have raised offer some broader issues to consider in response to these essays. The volume adds an important collection of voices to the ongoing enterprise of understanding and describing the content and structures of targumic literature. Moreover, because of its detailed engagement with all its subject material, this book offers a significant body of concrete data that can be incorporated into broader historical, methodological, and social accounts of early and rabbinic Judaism. Accordingly, this book is essential reading for anyone interested in Jewish translation literature, Second Temple literature, targumic literature, and methodological and historical questions pertaining to the literary motifs and traditions circulating during the Second Temple and rabbinic periods.

Migrating Tales: The Talmud's Narratives and Their Historical Context, by Richard Kalmin. Oakland: University of California Press, 2014. Pp. xxii + 282. Hardcover. $65.00. ISBN 9780520277250.

Rivka Ulmer, Bucknell University

The study of the Babylonian Talmud has progressed far over the last twenty years by considering cultural influences and cultural connections. Richard Kalmin's book is part of the current trend of culture-based scholarship in many fields, including the analysis of rabbinic literature. Kalmin suggests that the Christianity of Eastern provincial Rome should be a significant factor in understanding the Babylonian Talmud, whereas the influence of Persia should be assigned a place among many cultural factors. If commonalities between cultures—rabbinic and Christian texts—are specific, one may make the case for an actual historical connection. Kalmin finds that the cultures discussed—Babylonian rabbinic texts and Eastern Roman Christian texts—share specific motifs, narratives, and sources. The focus on specificity and a similar time in history is of great importance to Kalmin's argument; he is to be applauded for avoiding the pitfalls of comparing everything with everything. One may add that the application of coherence theories, in addition to cultural theories, would have even further supported Kalmin's fine arguments. The observation of specific terms leads to Kalmin's major argument that there must have been a historical connection between these cultures. Thus in this book there is sound methodology that goes beyond loose connections and comparisons.

Migrating Tales comprises the following chapters: (1) "'Manasseh Sawed Isaiah with a Saw of Wood': An Ancient Legend in Jewish, Christian, Muslim, and Persian Sources"; (2) "R. Shimon bar Yohai Meets St. Bartholomew: Peripatetic Traditions in Late Antique Judaism and Christianity East of Syria"; (3) "The Miracle of the Septuagint in Ancient Rabbinic and Christian Literature"; (4) "The Demons in Solomon's Temple"; (5) "Zechariah and the Bubbling Blood: An Ancient Tradition in Jewish, Christian, and Muslim Literature"; (6) "Pharisees"; (7) "Astrology"; and (8) "The Alexander Romance."

Several chapters of the book are based on Kalmin's previously published articles, which he rewrote by utilizing his new lens of comparing Judaism in Sasanian Babylonia to an Eastern Roman context and which he weaves into a coherent presentation of his argument. Kalmin presents the reader with close readings of the texts he discusses; this includes informed new translations of the talmudic passages and other materials by incorporating relevant differences in the manuscripts. This procedure renders new information regarding the diverse source materials of the Babylonian Talmud and its formation; this approach accentuates Kalmin's notion that many sources are derived from the Roman East rather than from Christian or pagan Mesopotamia. In his discussion of previous scholarship, Kalmin mentions the sweeping claims by some scholars (e.g., Peter Schäfer) that Babylonian Jews gained knowledge of the New Testament from the Diatessaron via their knowledge of Aramaic. Kalmin argues very convincingly that it is preferable to collect examples of cultural connections than to make sweeping claims. This is exactly what Kalmin does, and he proposes that it is more likely that the rabbis reacted to the type of Christianity in the Eastern parts of the Roman Empire.

In the first chapter Kalmin compares the execution of the prophet Isaiah in the (Christian) Ascension of Isaiah with a text in the Babylonian Talmud, Yevamot 49–54a, in which Isaiah is swallowed by a cedar tree that is sawed into pieces until Isaiah is killed. In the Ascension of Isaiah the prophet is cut in half. Kalmin prudently acknowledges the difference between the texts; in the Babylonian Talmud the scriptural passage in 2 Kgs 21:16 is read as King Manasseh filling Jerusalem with the innocent blood of Isaiah, whereas in the Christian text Isaiah becomes a martyr. Additionally, Kalmin also consults Persian texts that contain similar events. He notices that execution by sawing in literary accounts is infrequent, an exception being Bereshit Rabbah 65:22, which ascribes the sawing of Yosi Mishita to the Romans. Kalmin concludes that, based on chronological and geographical reasons, the tradition concerning the sawing of Isaiah is earlier in the Roman East than in Mesopotamia and Persia.

Chapter 2 pushes the argument even further and perhaps moves onto shaky ground, when Kalmin attributes the Babylonian Talmud's response to a story from Armenia and refers to "overheard conversations in the marketplace or Christian preachers on the street" (53). In comparative studies of rabbinic texts, it is often difficult to pinpoint the exact peregrination of a tradition. Babylonian Talmud, Me'ilah 17a–b, a composite text, has a tradition concerning R. Shimon ben Yohai and Ben Thalamion (St. Bartholomew); this narrative, according to Kalmin, is not a polemic against Christianity; rather, it represents a way for the rabbis to engage in self-reflection.

Chapter 3 continues Kalmin's approach to read the Babylonian Talmud in comparison to multiple cultural contexts. In my opinion, Kalmin's methodology constitutes enormous progress in talmudic studies that often were obsessed with a discussion of the *stammaim* (an editorial level of the text) or applying infantile literary theories without sophisticated and complicated meta-textual analysis. Pushing talmudic analysis beyond simplistic comparisons is a great achievement, since it provides important insights into the formation and the purpose of the Talmud that was a crucible of the cultural transformation of the Jewish people. Kalmin analyzes a famous baraita about King Ptolemy and the Greek Bible translation. The story is also found in nonrabbinic sources from the eastern Roman provinces. According to Kalmin, it is necessary to reduce the versions found throughout rabbinic literature and elsewhere in order to draw conclusions based upon ancient versions (e.g., Talmud Yerushalmi, Mekhilta, Babylonian Talmud). Like Philo, *De vita Mosis*, the Babylonian Talmud mentions the divinely inspired agreement between the translators of the Hebrew Bible into Greek. Kalmin finds convincing evidence that a part of the narrative derived from Christian Mesopotamia based on a Syriac text whose author, Eustathius of Tarihan, had knowledge of *Cohortatio ad Graecos*.

Chapter 4 is dedicated to the exploration of the demons in Solomon's temple. Babylonian Talmud, Gittin 68a–b, contains a narrative about King Solomon and Ashmedai, king of demons, which is analyzed within its Eastern provincial Roman and Persian contexts. There are specific parallels between the Testament of Solomon and the Talmud, although a direct knowledge seems unlikely. The story claims that only rabbis due to their superior understanding of the Bible were able to purge demons from the human body and other locations of demons. Furthermore, Ashmedai is depicted as a thoroughly "rabbinized" holy man. Both Gittin and the Testament of Solomon claim that Solomon forced the demons to assist him in the construction of the temple and to reveal the locations of other demons as well as to divulge secrets.

Chapter 5 focuses on the murder in the temple of a priest named Zechariah ben Jehoida and the murder of Zechariah, the father of John the Baptist. The texts mention the "bubbling blood" of Zechariah. The rabbinic version is an adaptation of a Christian story; the Christian version claims that God abandoned the Israelites, whereas the rabbinic version (b. Sanhedrin 96b) claims that God bestowed compassion on the Israelites despite the murder.

In two shorter chapters (6 and 7) Kalmin continues similar explorations of Christian and other literature in regard to the Pharisees and the topic of astrology. The term *Pharisees* is quite problematic; the Hebrew *perushim* as used in rabbinic literature sometimes referred to a Jewish group in the Second Temple period but mostly indicates something else. For example, viewing the Pharisees as hypocrites in the Babylonian Talmud is based on such views as found in the Roman East. A sentence usually rendered as "Astrology has *no* power over Israel" must be corrected, according to Kalmin, to read as "Astrology has power over Israel." Astrological influence is counteracted by the performance of religious obligations. Kalmin maintains that the Babylonian Talmud to a greater extent than the rabbinic sources from the Land of Israel echoes the Roman concept that the constellation of planets on the day of birth of a person influences one's fate. This astrological belief may be traced back to an East Roman source, the second-century Christian writer Bardaison of Edessa.

The difficult Alexander Romance is discussed in chapter 8; mainly, Alexander is depicted as having dialogues with the Elders of the Negev (b. Tamid 31b–32b), whereas parallel accounts mention the dialogue with the gymnosophists of India, as in the Syriac version of Pseudo-Callisthenes. Although most of the compositional and topical units of the Alexander Romance are found in Jewish literature, the journey of Alexander the Great to find the waters of life is parallel in sixth-century Syriac sources and in the Alexander Romance.

Kalmin repeatedly points to the alternating use of Hebrew and Aramaic in single talmudic units of discourse. This type of "code-switching" (a term in sociolinguistics and bilingualism) has important implications regarding the narratives that are analyzed. Kalmin acknowledges that this alternating use of languages serves the narrative and that it is an indication of additions by editors. Furthermore, these additions may derive from different sources. One example from the Babylonian Talmud, Gittin 58, superbly demonstrates Kalmin's contentions. The narrative is about an evil apprentice and the wife of his master who becomes sexually involved with the apprentice, while the master becomes the apprentice to his former apprentice. Beyond the "story" level, the underlying message of the narrative is the interactions between people in an upside-down world, as experienced by Jews in the presence of Christianity.

This wonderful book is a source of knowledge for scholars, and it may appeal to nonscholars as well. Kalmin sets the stage in the preface in which he explains in simple but elegant language the major genres of rabbinic literature, the ways that rabbinic literature works (e.g., what is an editor), and terms such as *rabbi* and *rav* as well as abbreviations (R. for Rabbi, y for Talmud Yerushalmi, etc.) used by scholars who usually do not see a need to explain them.

In sum, Kalmin convincingly argues that literature from Eastern provincial Rome played a decisive role in the formation of the Babylonian Talmud and that the creators of this document were culturally "literate" to a greater extent than previously thought. The book contains a vast bibliography and indices. This book is highly recommended for its thorough research, elegant translations, and readable style. It is a significant addition to talmudic scholarship.

Tradition and the Formation of the Talmud, by Moulie Vidas. Princeton: Princeton University Press, 2014. Pp. 239, Hardcover, $35.00, ISBN 9780691154862.

Joshua Schwartz, Bar-Ilan University

Moulie Vidas never set foot in a yeshiva as a youth, yet as a secular undergraduate in Tel-Aviv University he chose to study in the Talmud department, a department that at that time had only two students, including him. He wanted to know "what the other side thinks." The irony is that many on the "other side," especially among the more modern observant, are happy to go through life giving minimal lip service to the study of Talmud, and many were totally turned off by their Talmud-study experience during their (yeshiva) high-school studies. It is a good thing that Vidas did not ask them but decided to try it out on his own: "When I got to actually study these texts, the brilliance of the Talmud, the great erudition, attracted me to it."[1]

---

1. The quote is from an article by Dan Pine, "U.C. Davis Snags Dynamic, Young Scholar," *J. The Jewish News Weekly of Northern California* (14 January 2010), http://www.jweekly.com/article/full/41066/u.c.-davis-snags-dynamic-young-talmud-scholar/)

Obviously, though, he could not continue graduate Talmud studies in Tel-Aviv, since the department was not viable and eventually closed as an independent department; what was left combined into a catch-all Jewish studies department. He did not choose to continue in other Talmud departments in Israeli universities, which for the most part still stress philology as well as the academic methodologies formulated during the last few decades by the Israeli giants in the field. Rather, Vidas chose a different approach, studying Talmud in Princeton under Peter Schäfer in the Religious Studies Department in a milieu that stressed placing the study of Talmud within the cultural and religious framework of late antiquity. This makes sense, as the Talmud is, after all, the largest single document from the period. After completing his doctorate, Vidas spent a brief period at UC Davis and in 2012 returned to Princeton.

At first glance, one might wonder why there is a need for another book on the formation of the Talmud and whether a beginning scholar is the one to write such a book. The major questions have been studied often in academic talmudics, and recent scholarship on formation seems to be nothing more than working out the details or building upon this or that school of thought. From the second half of the twentieth century, scholarship has focused on the literary creation of the redactors of the Talmud. Various forms of literary activity were attributed to sages living toward the end of the talmudic period. These sages might have been Amoraim, Savora'im, or Stammaim, depending on the view of the scholar. They adapted and transformed earlier sources of the Tannaim, formed the interpretive layer of the Talmud, and shaped the *sugyot*, or discourses. Scholars such as David Weiss Halivni, Shamma Friedman, Yaakov Sussman, Jacob Neusner, Jeffrey Rubenstein, Daniel Boyarin, and many others developed and fine-tuned various aspects of the general thesis, although there were certainly many points of divergence and disagreement between these and other scholars, all of which Vidas is well aware. To come up with a brand new idea, albeit in relation to certain aspects of previous work and theory, would seem to be a rather daunting challenge for a beginning scholar.

Vidas begins by explaining how tradition, the "tradition" in the title of his book, can be used to invoke discontinuity rather than the more commonly assumed opposite. Tradition is contrasted with the contemporary; there is a gap between us and tradition. The creators of the Talmud employ a variety of techniques to create a distance between themselves and the traditions they cite. The traditions remain binding, but this distance also undermines their validity; they are fossilized and contained in the past. The creators see themselves as having a subversive role. Moreover, they also defined themselves as being in opposition to those who focused on transmission of traditions. Thus, their literary activities were grounded in tension: tension between themselves and tradition and tension between themselves and those who transmitted tradition. All this tension and attendant creativity remained undetected for centuries.

The book begins with an introduction that provides a history of research on the Talmud's authorship and a general description of the points of departure from those views that will occupy the author. Part 1 of the work explores the Talmud's literary practice through a close analysis and reading of selected passages, or *sugyot*. The readings are meticulous, creative, and erudite, but the number of selected passages is rather small.[2] Vidas is of course aware of this and admits that the *sugyot* chosen are not more representative than those that have informed previous theories. Rather, these *sugyot*, or at least his readings, problematize the conclusions reached through the analysis of different *sugyot* by other scholars, and the traditions he analyzes also make explicit and visible certain features of talmudic compositions that everyone else seems to have missed. Obviously, though, other scholars might say the exact same thing about the sources that they have chosen in relation to the views of Vidas, while their selection of sources was usually much larger.

Part 1 has three chapters. The first, "The Alterity of Tradition," emphasizes the distance between the approach expressed by the *stam* (the creator's anonymous layer) and the approach expressed by the Amoraic dictum that it cites. The authors of the *stam* do not "hide" behind tradition, revising or reinterpreting this dictum, but create a literary structure that contrasts their own reasoning with the implications of the earlier tradition. Chapter 2, "The Division into Layers," reevaluates much of the current thought regarding the layers of the Talmud. The apparent divisions into layers, between cited and anonymous layers, are not a matter of different dating or provenance but rather the Bavli reorganizing the *sugya* to reflect a difference in function between the narrating, interpretive, discursive anonymous layers and the shorter, nondiscursive, attributed rulings. The gap between the layers is a compositional strategy of the Talmud's creators. The last chapter in part 1, "Composition as Critique," focuses on a thematic series of *sugyot* that concern the genealogical division of the Jewish people and argues that the Bavli trains its readers to view this genealogical knowledge and the traditions that transmit it as manipulated and personally motivated. Readers are supposed to become suspicious of these traditions on juxtaposition and arrangement, in this case not because of any division between layers. The lack of revision and redaction create the distance and the tension. One wonders, however, how much of the Talmud's ancient audience was actually up to this type of critical sophisticated reading.

Part 2 deals with the rhetoric of self-presentation and self-definition of the Talmud's creators, who seemed to have placed a higher value on dialectic and analysis than on tradition and memorization. The first of the three chapters in this part, chapter 4, "Scholars, Transmitters, and the Making of *Talmud*," examines a number of passages to demonstrate this preference as well as to situate it within a polemical conversation of Jews in Mesopotamia. This polemic relates

---

2. Previous reviews have already pointed this out, but it is impossible not to mention again what is certainly a weak link in the chain. See the review, e.g. by Raphael Magarik in MAKE (19 August, 2014), http:// makemag.com/review-tradition-and-the-formation-of-the-talmud-by-moulie-vidas.

to the tension between "sages" and "reciters," between "masters of *Talmud*" and "masters of *mishnah*," between "living books" and halakic authorities. Vidas also devotes a good deal of attention to trying to understand what exactly the reciters did. Apparently, they were not simply unintellectual "bags full of bugs" but represented the ritual of recitation that developed independently and functioned parallel to world of the sages.

Chapter 5, "The Debate about Recitation," examines the discourses about recitation in Zoroastrian and Christian literature. Vidas discusses a Zoroastrian distinction similar to the one that the Talmud makes regarding reciter and scholar. Both the Jews and the Christians represented Zoroastrian recitation in a negative manner, and this was not just a comment on cultural practice but part of a polemic against Zoroastrianism and the drawing of a boundary between Jewish and Zoroastrian practice and between Jewish and Christian practice, respectively. This was also part of the internal polemics in both the Jewish and Christian worlds in the battle of the sages against the reciters.

Chapter 6, "Tradition and Vision," continues to explore the development in the tension between sages and reciters at the background of the encounter with Zoroastrian culture in which recitation took on a central role in ritual. There was a conversation between these two groups, but for the most part it is assumed that we have only the Talmud's side of the debates and that it was pointedly polemical. Vidas argues that the opposing side of the reciters might be preserved in a few texts in the tradition of the *hekhalot* literature. Thus, the Sar Hatorah narrative, according to the author, might present a parody of the ethos of the Babylonian academies that stressed "academic" torah study as opposed to torah study that emphasizes retention, recitation, and memorization.

This is a brilliant book with numerous new readings of traditions and new ideas. It is, however, not an easy book to read. Part 1 is especially difficult. The lack of texts in the original language, together with the heavy use of jargon makes it extremely difficult to follow the *sugyot* and subsequently the discussion. Part 2 is a much easier read; even though there are many sources, there is a lot less theory and jargon.[3] Is Vidas convincing? Does he make his case? Here, too, there seems to be a difference between part 1 and part 1. With respect to part 1, if Vidas is correct, the creators of the Talmud did such a successful job in their subversive creativity that this creativity remained undetected for centuries. The creators' success was seemingly, then, their failure and downfall. Whatever they wanted to show, we, and that "we" is countless generations of Talmud readers and students, did not detect it. Those who do not agree with Vidas would argue that this is so for good reason, because this is not what the creators were doing. This is, of course,

---

3. The lack of texts in the original has already been pointed out by Magarik in his review (see n. 2). For additional reviews, see also Itay Marienberg-Milikowsky in The Talmud Blog (https://thetalmudblog.wordpress.com/2014/11/06) and Catherine Hezser in *Journal of Jewish Studies* 66 (2015): 219–22.

not something that can be proven either way. Vidas, though, does make a good case, and the presentation along the way is extremely sharp.

Part 2 is much easier to accept. Internal tensions and polemics and turning these outward are common phenomena. The Talmud itself sets up the mechanism for the polemics between sage and reciter. Similar tensions exist in other societies and religions. Is Vidas convincing that parts of the *hekhalot* literature reflect this tension between the academies of the sages and an alternative religious experience? Possibly, but his including the study of mystical tradition within the purview of the formation of the Talmud, or at least as a reaction to it, is intriguing and warrants further thought.

As a final note in relation to the tension between sages and reciters, I should like to point out personal impressions from a more modern-day phenomenon that seems to reflect tension of a sort similar to that which Vidas describes. On Rosh Hashanah 1923, the Daf Yomi project envisioned by Rabbi Meir Shapira of Lublin began its first cycle. The idea was that throughout the Jewish world everyone should "study" the same page of Talmud on the same day. However, anyone who has studied Talmud knows that it is for the most part impossible to "study" a page of Talmud every day. Those who participate often find themselves reciting and not studying or listening to someone else recite at break-neck speed while they hope to absorb by osmosis. Daf Yomi is usually for *baale batim*, lay persons, neither for yeshiva students nor for academic Talmudists who seek more depth than the hurried pace allows. Often, the recitation becomes almost like prayer. Is there tension between Daf Yomi and the yeshiva world? Some object to the seeming superficiality of the study and lack of repetition. This, of course, represents a different framework from that which Vidas describes, as Daf Yomi has no connection to mystical literature, but there could certainly be more than one manifestation of tension between sage and reciter, and that might have been the case also in the past.

Vidas has produced a magnificent work. This is, of course, a first step or preliminary presentation, but he has provided much that will occupy scholars for a good deal of time and has provided for himself a springboard for his future studies. Anybody studying Talmud or Jewish studies will benefit from a close reading of this book.

The Jewish-Greek Tradition in Antiquity and the Byzantine Empire, edited by James Aitken and James Paget. New York: Cambridge University Press, 2014. Pp. xxii + 359, Hardcover, £65.00, ISBN 9781107001633.

Jonathan M. Potter, Emory University

Introduction

Jewish engagement with Greek language and culture is universally recognized from the last three centuries BCE through the first century CE. The debate over "Judaism and Hellenism" has generated an enormous amount of scholarship and continues today. Yet one often encounters the impression that such Jewish-Greek interaction died off quickly after the first century CE, amid the rise of Christianity and rabbinic Judaism. The terms *Hellenistic Judaism* and *Hellenistic Jewish* are usually defined by an endpoint of around 100 CE, with the exception of the second-century Greek Bible translations by Aquila, Theodotion, and Symmachus. It is not as if the academy is unaware of the implications of Origen's interaction with Jewish scholars or the references to Greek language in rabbinic literature. No one claims that Jewish usage of Greek completely ceased. Rather, the apparent dearth of direct evidence creates an impression of a sudden demise of Hellenistic Judaism—or whatever one chooses to call it (and terms are part of the problem). But thanks especially to the honoree of this volume, Nicholas de Lange, more and more evidence of ongoing Jewish-Greek interaction over the past two thousand years is being discovered and published. To be sure, there is still no sign of Jewish Greek literature on the scale of a Philo or Josephus after the first-century CE, but there is plentiful evidence, much of it surveyed in this volume, for continuous and varied engagement with Greek language and culture all the way through the Byzantine Empire (which ended in 1453) and beyond.

This volume in honor of Nicholas de Lange is a collection of essays covering many aspects of "Jewish-Greek tradition" from its beginnings until early modernity. But more than many such Festschriften, it strives to be a handbook of sorts (the book description on i suggests this). About half the chapters succeed in providing the kind of topical overview one expects from such a handbook, while the other half are rather more technical and specific (which is not to say less interesting). Before going further, it may be worth asking what exactly "Jewish-Greek tradition" means. The volume's editors and contributors never directly address this question, although the book's description comes closest to a definition: "The Jewish–Greek tradition represents an arguably distinctive strand of Judaism characterized by use of the Greek language and interest in Hellenism" (i and back cover). This is an extremely rare phrase within the field, and within the volume itself it is used inconsistently. Even the combination "Jewish-Greek" is fairly rare. Why use this term rather than another? Yet as soon as one tries to think of another suitable and concise term for the entire range of Jewish participation in Greek language and culture, the reason for this new term emerges. Language of "Hellenism" is problematic even for the circumscribed historical period it usually denotes (and even that cannot be agreed upon); it would be even less appropriate for the broad historical and thematic array covered in this volume. Thus "Jewish-Greek tradition" seems a useful term. The question that remains is what "tradition" implies—does the material surveyed in this volume support the implication of a singular, cohesive tradition? I will return to this question after an overview of the individual chapters.

SURVEY OF CONTENTS

The introduction of the volume helpfully reviews de Lange's contributions, highlighting the wide range of this impressive scholar. It then gives a summary of the remaining chapters, which are divided into four topical parts: history, historiography, Greek Bible and language, and culture.

Part 1 opens with Günter Stemberger's overview of "Jews and Graeco-Roman Culture: From Alexander to Theodosius II." Despite the references to Theodosius II in the chapter title and to the Theodosian Code in the second section title (29), neither is mentioned anywhere in the chapter. This calls into question the appropriateness of these titles and the rationale for the chapter's chronological scope. It would be helpful if the appropriate dates were at least mentioned (Theodosius II: Roman emperor 408–450; Theodosian Code: 438). This stems, perhaps, from the purpose of this chapter as a survey of cultural interaction rather than a historical summary. Whatever the case, Stemberger helpfully reviews the topics typically treated under the rubric of "Judaism and Hellenism," discussing major aspects of Jewish engagement with Greco-Roman culture (but mostly Hellenism) in Palestine and the diaspora. He also covers the main contours of scholarship on the subject (e.g., Bickerman, Hengel, Feldman). Use of archaeological and epigraphical evidence is well-integrated. Stemberger also brings his rabbinic expertise to bear with numerous poignant examples. On a whole, Stemberger adopts a position similar to that of Erich Gruen by seeing Judaism as largely compatible and overlapping with Graeco-Roman culture (see esp. 34–36).

In "The Jewish Experience in Byzantium," Steven Bowman picks up where Stemberger left off and continues the historical discussion down to the fall of Byzantium in 1453. The chapter consists of two distinct parts. The first (longer) section concerns the periodization of Byzantine Judaism. Here Bowman first presents the "received" chronological scheme, which ties Jewish experience to the political events of the Byzantine Empire. After describing the major elements and evidence of Byzantine Jewish life, he suggests a twofold division based on "the internal Jewish story" (44). In this alternate schema, a long first period of "increasing degradation and persecution" (44) until the mid-tenth century gives way to a period of greater tolerance under the restored empire, with the Crusader occupation of Byzantium acting as the hinge between the two. The second part of the chapter focuses on three types of evidence that Greek was the primary language of Byzantine Jewry: (1) references in Justinian's Novella 146 (553 CE) to some Greek-speaking Jews' complaints concerning other Jews demanding that only Hebrew be read in the synagogue; (2) a bilingual (Greek and Hebrew) fragment of a Mishnaic glossary, along with Judaeo-Greek biblical commentaries from the Cairo Genizah; and (3) "Greek lexeis in the Hebrew commentaries and philosophical texts" of Byzantium (49).

Alexander Panayotov completes the history part of the volume with a survey of "Jews and Jewish Communities in the Balkans and the Aegean until the Twelfth Century" (ch. 4). Rather than a continuous narrative, this chapter gives a concise listing of evidence for the presence of Jews throughout the Balkans, the Aegean, and Cyprus. For each region (e.g., Dalmatia, Thrace, Macedonia), Panayotov lists the following (when relevant): locations (specific towns and cities), bibliography (both primary sources and scholarly discussions), archaeological data, inscriptions, literary sources (including documentary evidence), Jewish names (or rather, names of Jews, including some that are not self-evidently Jewish, such as Aurelius Dionysius), and occupations. Overall, this impressive collection of evidence demonstrates the breadth and depth of Jewish experience in the ancient and medieval Mediterranean world.

The next part of the book, on historiography, focuses on the modern inquiry into the Jewish-Greek tradition. First, in "Origen and the Jews: Jewish-Greek and Jewish-Christian Relations," William Horbury reengages Nicholas de Lange's career-defining first book, *Origen and the Jews*, showing its lasting significance and where the discussion has gone more recently. Horbury reasserts the usefulness of consulting early Christian writers for reconstructing Jewish Greek tradition in late antiquity, when it is properly balanced by other sources.

Giuseppe Veltri then peels away further historiographical layers by tracing the emergence of the subdiscipline in "Jewish–Greek Studies in Nineteenth- and Early Twentieth-Century Germany: A Brief Overview" (ch. 6). Veltri first reminds readers that Christian scholarship of this period was mainly concerned with Judaism as a background to Jesus. There was thus little interest in the shape of Judaism after Jesus (second century CE onward). The root of the contemporary interest in the full spectrum of Jewish-Greek tradition thus lies in the *Wissenschaft des Judentums*, represented by such Jewish scholars as Leopold Zunz, Zacharias Frankel, Heinrich Graetz, Abraham Geiger, and Samuel Krauss.

Part 3 centers on the topic most closely associated with Jewish usge of Greek: Bible translation. In "The Origins of the Septuagint," James Carleton Paget summarizes the major theories of the Septuagint's origin, assessing the strengths and weaknesses of each. Carleton Paget remains unconvinced by theories that are merely plausible but lack confirmatory evidence. In the end, he supports a Jewish-oriented translation project, but with some kind of support or patronage, although not necessarily of the Ptolemaic monarch. This is one of the essays that would be useful for a broader readership, since it introduces the main theories of Septuagint origins.

Continuing on the same theme, James Aitken develops a more specific and forceful argument concerning "The Language of the Septuagint and Jewish-Greek Identity." Aitken examines brief texts from the LXX and Egyptian documentary papyri in support of his thesis of a Ptolemaic Egyptian scribal origin for the LXX. His examples suggest that the translators were educated but not literarily sophisticated.

Cameron Boyd-Taylor moves the discussion away from origins to "Afterlives of the Septuagint: A Christian Witness to the Greek Bible in Byzantine Judaism." Contrary to earlier opinion, current evidence proves that Greek Bible translations of the Bible did not fall out of Jewish use after the second century CE. Boyd-Taylor traces some of the nitty-gritty evidence in the marginalia of Codex Ambrosianus (F[b]). What the manuscript evidence suggests is that Byzantine Jews were still engaged in translating Hebrew to Greek, as attested by "unique variants" of probable Jewish provenance (e.g., reflecting identifiably Jewish exegetical background) that are unattested in LXX or "the Three" (the later Jewish Greek Bible translations of Aquila, Symmachus, and Theodotion).

Julia G. Krivoruchko also examines later translations in "Medieval and Early Modern Judaeo-Greek Biblical Translations: A Linguistic Perspective." Krivoruchko aims at a linguistic description of the Judaeo-Greek language used in biblical translations that survive in medieval and early modern manuscript fragments and the printed Constantinopolitan Pentateuch of 1547. (Judaeo-Greek is Greek language written in Hebrew characters; after the fifth century CE, evidence for Jewish writing of Greek letters is scarce; see 138 n. 22.). Krivoruchko calls this "Biblical Judaeo-Greek" (BJG) and argues that it should be regarded as a "calque language variety" and thus not a representation of colloquial, spoken Judaeo-Greek. BJG was "nobody's mother tongue" (169). Rather, these biblical translations functioned as liturgical and didactic aids for understanding the Hebrew Bible.

The final part of the volume concerns culture broadly construed, although some of the essays are just as concerned with language as the previous section. First, Tessa Rajak revisits an old question in "Philo's Knowledge of Hebrew: The Meaning of the Etymologies." Rajak does not offer a positive argument that Philo knew Hebrew. Rather, she demonstrates the weaknesses of some arguments that he did not know Hebrew, taking aim especially at Lester Grabbe's *Etymology in Early Jewish Interpretation: The Hebrew Names in Philo* (1988). Rajak offers alternate explanations for many of the etymologies that Grabbe asserted betrayed Philo's ignorance of Hebrew. She essentially shifts the burden of proof back onto those who would deny Philo's knowledge of Hebrew.

In "The Plain and Laughter: The Hermeneutical Function of the Sign in Philo of Alexandria," Francis Schmidt examines the formal usage of the term *semeion* in Philo. His starting point is a pair of instances where Philo labels something in the biblical text as a manifest sign of hidden reality: the plain in Gen 4:8 and Sarah's laughter in 21:6. Schmidt argues that a similar hermeneutical function is at work in other cases where Philo uses *semeion*.

David Noy offers one of the best chapters of the volume in his discussion of "Jewish Archaeology and Art in Antiquity." Noy interrogates the difficult question of how to identify Jewish art and architecture in antiquity. He focuses on four problematic archaeological sites that have been identified as synagogues by at least some scholars: Delos, Ostia, Apamea, and Mopsuestia. Rather than offering a "solution" to the problem, he highlights the fact that "Jewishness" did not necessarily leave an archaeological footprint. The earlier one goes, the less one can expect Jewish markers. The accidents of preservation are often what allow us to identify a site as distinctly Jewish.

In "Jewish-Greek Epigraphy in Antiquity," Pieter van der Horst practically celebrates the numerous ways inscriptions enhance our understanding of Jewish culture and society in antiquity, all the more so Jewish-Greek tradition in particular, since the majority of Jewish inscriptions are in Greek. This chapter is an excellent introduction to the subject, especially since it surveys all the major editions and collections of Jewish-Greek inscriptions. One of the most promising aspects of the epigraphical sources is their potential to illuminate a vast "Greek-speaking diaspora in the west, not dominated by the rabbis, with a flourishing culture" (228), that is, a Jewish-Greek tradition with an otherwise shadowy existence in the literary sources of late antiquity.

Returning to issues of translation, Philip Alexander considers the relationship of "The Rabbis, the Greek Bible and Hellenism." Alexander's main point is that rabbinic views of the Greek Bible (about which explicit rabbinic remarks are ambivalent) need to be situated within the broader rabbinic dialogue concerning interpretation and translation (as in discussions of Aramaic targums). Opposition to Greek translations may have more to do with the particular characteristics of a specific Greek translation (i.e., whether it interprets the text "correctly" from that rabbis' standpoint) than to overall objections to translation itself. But views exist on a spectrum between considering translations themselves as holy writings and withholding any such status. Alexander finds no significant geographic difference of opinion between Palestine and Babylonia, but he does see an increasingly negative stance toward Greek translations from the second century CE onward, coinciding with the rise of Christianity.

Gideon Bohak discusses "Greek-Hebrew Linguistic Contacts in Late Antique and Medieval Magical Texts." This is a detailed examination of a range of multilingual magical texts. One of Bohak's chief concerns is to demonstrate the potential these texts have for "non-magical" questions, and he succeeds. The diverse usage in these magical texts of Hebrew, Aramaic, and Greek, including transliterations in both directions, well illustrates the dynamic language environment of Jews in late antiquity and the Middle Ages. Such "ground-level" sources are an especially useful complement to the literary and epigraphical sources, which mainly tell us about the language(s) of the elite.

In "Jewish and Christian Hymnody in the Early Byzantine Period," Wout van Bekkum focuses on *piyyutim* (Jewish liturgical poems) from late antiquity and the Byzantine period. This chapter moves from a general discussion of Byzantine hymnody to a closer examination of one particular *piyyut* by Yehudah. Surprisingly for this volume, however, van Bekkum does not significantly engage the question of contact between (Hebrew) Jewish and (Greek) Christianity hymnody beyond noting the prevalence of scriptural motifs in both traditions and the probable Greek origins of the word *piyyut* itself (from the Greek *poietes* or *poiesis*; 262). While van Bekkum suggests that there are "Byzantine allusions" in Yehudah's *piyyut* (270), he does not discuss or even identify them. Perhaps the best feature of this chapter is the full translation (almost six pages) of this *piyyut*, illustrating the fascinating intertextual and even midrashic nature of this literature.

The volume then ends with Judith Olszowy-Schlanger's careful analysis of "The Hebrew Script of the Greek–Hebrew Palimpsests from the Cairo Genizah." She analyzes the Hebrew script of one group of Jewish-Greek texts from the Cairo Genizah—Hebrew palimpsests written over earlier Greek texts—and shows that all fourteen fragments, representing nine codices, exhibit a distinct subtype of Oriental Hebrew square script. Olszowy-Schlanger identifies features that distinguish this script from the classical Oriental Hebrew square script of the tenth-century Babylonian and Tiberian biblical codices: (1) clearly differentiated shapes for similar letters (e.g., *beth* and *kaph*); (2) slanted bases; (3) "spiky" aspect; (4) short and decorative descenders; (5) *gimel*, *'ayin*, and *pe* going below the baseline; (6) short downstrokes; (7) decorative heads; (8) particular shapes of *aleph* and *pe*. The author also highlights some broader implications of these texts, such as the ready availability of high-quality Greek texts to be overwritten with Hebrew.

CONCLUSION

As there is no shortage of books covering what is typically referred to as the "Hellenistic Judaism" of the Second Temple period, the most distinctive contribution of the volume is the many chapters on the Jewish-Greek tradition as it existed in the aftermath of three major violent conflicts that shook the Jewish world in the first and second centuries CE: the Judean revolt of 66–70, ending in the destruction of the temple; the "diaspora" revolt of 115–116, resulting in the end of the Jewish community of Alexandria; and the Bar Kokhba revolt of 135. But since the Jewish-Greek tradition from the second century onward is bound to what came before, the essays on the earlier period are also important.

The question that remains is whether one can speak of a single Jewish-Greek tradition and, if so, how to define it. Even usage of Greek language—the lowest common denominator— fails to identify a single, cohesive tradition. As the chapters of this volume demonstrate along with the scholarship of many others before, Jewish usage of Greek language varies on a spectrum from nearly exclusive use (e.g., Philo) to the occasional use of Greek loanwords by those for whom the language is otherwise unknown (much of the rabbinic tradition). In between lies a range of multilingual configurations. When we look beyond language to culture or ideas, it becomes even harder to speak of a single tradition. Thus if the evidence covered by this volume characterizes a Jewish-Greek tradition, that "tradition" must be understood as designating a diverse range of Jewish interactions with Greek language and culture—and in that sense, this volume provides an excellent entrée into the Jewish-Greek tradition.

JUDAISM AND CHRISTIANITY

The Making of the Abrahamic Religions in Late Antiquity, by Guy G. Stroumsa. Oxford Studies in the Abrahamic Religions. Oxford: Oxford University Press, 2015. Pp. xii + 225. Hardcover. $110.00. ISBN 9780198738862.

Brent Nongbri, Macquarie University

This is a book on the formation of Abrahamic religions, in a series named Studies in the Abrahamic Religions, written by the former Professor of the Study of Abrahamic Religions at Oxford. I detect a theme.

The speed with which the notion of "Abrahamic religions" has permeated scholarly and popular discourse in the last two decades is remarkable. Although the terminology has existed for centuries, the years since the World Trade Center attacks have seen a considerable growth of interest in the concept of Abrahamic religions, in the form of book titles, conferences, professorships, university course catalogs, and, of course, media outlets.[1] The usefulness of the concept for historical study, however, remains an open question. In a recent book entitled *Abrahamic Religions: On the Uses and Abuses of History* (Oxford University Press, 2012), Aaron W. Hughes subjected the concept to a stringent examination. Hughes argued at length that *Abrahamic religions* is a vacuous term more at home in interfaith dialogue than academic inquiry. The critique leveled by Hughes claims that Abrahamic religions are "a modern projection that we then transcribe onto the historical record" (3). For Hughes, if we wish to study the lives of Christians, Jews, and Muslims in an academically responsible way, a great deal of rethinking must occur:

> Our employment of "Abrahamic religions" is not simply a terminological mistake, but primarily a categorical one. Rethinking both the term and category must take the form of developing a new conceptual language that avoids positing discrete religious traditions interacting with and borrowing from one another, and that instead envisages complexity and porosity between manifold and overlapping subgroups within and among "religions." (3)

This is a demanding agenda indeed. But, in fact, it would be a fitting description of Stroumsa's new volume. *The Making of the Abrahamic Religions in Late Antiquity* collects and revises material from eleven essays, most of which were published between 2007 and 2015. The resulting book has less in common with the growing literature on Abrahamic religions and seems more a part of a different, though related, scholarly growth industry, namely, the push to view early Islam as a part of the late antique world.[2] The introduction, aptly titled "From Qumran to Qur'an," captures the temporal and conceptual spread of the essays gathered here. Stroumsa begins by challenging the traditional view that, over this time period, there was a neat division between monotheism and polytheism. He both surveys recent work on "pagan monotheism" and questions the supposed monotheism of Christians, quoting Origen's *Dialogue with Heraclides* as "the best

---

1. See Mark Silk, "The Abrahamic Religions as a Modern Concept," published in a volume that itself shows the newly achieved normative status of the discourse in the current academic climate: Adam Silverstein and Guy G. Stroumsa, eds., *The Oxford Handbook of the Abrahamic Religions* (Oxford: Oxford University Press, 2015), 71–87.

2. See, for example, the recent book by Garth Fowden (who, it should probably be pointed out in this context, is the Sultan Qaboos Professor of Abrahamic Faiths at Cambridge), *Before and after Muhammad: The First Millennium Refocused* (Princeton: Princeton University Press, 2014).

proof text in all of Patristic literature showing that the doctrine of the Trinity is inescapably polytheistic" (14). Against this backdrop, Stroumsa suggests (following several scholars of Islam) that the Qur'an's *mushrikūn*, generally thought to be polytheists, may well have included what we would call monotheists as well.

The body of the book is divided into four parts. Part 1, "Transformations of Religion in Late Antiquity," consists of two chapters. The first, "The End of Sacrifice," borrows its title from Stroumsa's important 2005 book, but the contents of the chapter constitute a focused critique of Karl Jaspers's notion of the Axial Age as it is employed in Robert Bellah's monumental *Religion in Human Evolution* (Belknap, 2011). Stroumsa notes that periods aside from the middle of the first millennium BCE also witnessed widespread transformations in human life. He points to the cessation of animal sacrifice and the rise in importance of codified "scriptures" across cultures in the late antique Mediterranean as one such period of profound change. From here, Stroumsa moves on to explore "Patterns of Rationalization," by which he means a broad set of innovations and transformations, ranging from the dualism embraced by gnostic and Manichaean groups as a response to the philosophical problem of evil presented by monotheism, to the establishment of rules of biblical interpretation in the talmudic tractates, and the intellectual efforts of patristic authors to hold together elements of their tradition that appear contradictory.

Part 2, "The True Prophet," includes three chapters. The first, "False Prophets of Early Christianity," frames the early Christian reception of Muhammad as a heretic and false prophet in terms of the history of polemic against false prophets, beginning with Deuteronomy and ranging through early Christian literature, but focusing on the Ebionites and Elchasaites, especially that renegade Elchasite, Mani. The next chapter, "False Prophet and False Messiah," draws out this story further, first by arguing for the continued existence and importance of communities of "Jewish Christians" into the seventh century, then by investigating how the rise of Muhammad fit into various strains of Jewish and Christian eschatological thought. The final chapter in this section, a chronological outlier first published in 1986, is a valuable exploration of the prehistory of the "Seal of the Prophets." While the designation is most generally associated with its occurrence in the Qur'an and interpreted as meaning that Muhammad was the last in the line of prophets sent by Allah, Arabic sources also describe Mani as the "Seal of the Prophets." Stroumsa traces changing uses of the term *seal* in the Hebrew Bible, early Christian literature, Mandaean sources, and Manichaean texts.

Two chapters make up part 3, "Religious Communities and God's Law." In "Religious Dynamics between Jews and Christians," Stroumsa begins with the observation that "it was sometimes difficult to distinguish a Christian from a Jew in the late ancient Near East" (103). With that caveat in mind, he goes on to narrate the changing fortunes of Jewish and Christian communities under the shifting imperial structures of the Roman (and later Christian) Empire in the West and the Sassanian (and later Muslim) Empire in the East. The next essay,

"God's Rule in Late Antiquity," continues this train of thought by problematizing the idea of "theocracy" in Jewish, Christian, and Muslim sources.

Part 4, "The Way to Mecca," consists of three chapters. In "Jewish-Christians and Islamic Origins," Stroumsa provides a history of scholarship on the notion of Jewish-Christians and a *status quaestionis* on the question of Jewish and/or Christian influences in the emergence of Islam. The next chapter, "Christian Memories and Dreams of Jerusalem," focuses on the Temple Mount as a locus for the eschatological hopes of different groups of Christians and Jews. Amidst these competing visions, the Temple Mount becomes, in Stroumsa's words, "a *Rashomon* of sorts: to each community, it tells its own story" (173). The final chapter in this section, "Barbarians or Heretics?" investigates perceptions of Jews and Arabs through the complicated lenses of Byzantine identity. The Byzantines were not only both the true Christians and the true Romans; they were also the true Hebrews (*verus Israel*) as well as being linguistically Greek. They thus inherited a variety of "toolkits" for understanding those perceived as "others." It should not be surprising, then, that in Byzantine eyes "Jews and Arabs retained an unstable status, at once barbarians and heretics, ever on the lines" (188).

The book concludes with a short coda "Envoi: Athens, Jerusalem, Mecca: *Praeparatio coranica*," in which Stroumsa explicitly deals with late antique debates over who were the true heirs of Abraham. This "Abrahamic moment" was contentious, though less a clash of civilizations than a conflict of interpretations, to use a phrase Stroumsa deploys elsewhere in the work. In additoin, the contentiousness of the Abrahamic moment provided its generative power as *praeparatio coranica*: "The Abrahamic moment did less to promote ecumenism than to enhance the rise of heretical movements, each claiming that its own vision was the only correct one" (198).

The book is a pleasure to read. We are able to witness an excellent historian overturn a number of truisms by means of careful examination of a wide array of ancient evidence. Yet, even more old notions could be overturned. For instance, Stroumsa sets the stage for his discussion by offering the apostle Paul as a foil to followers of Jesus who maintained Jewish practices: Paul "gave up ... on the traditional Jewish patterns of behavior" (5). A growing body of scholarship has greatly complicated, if not completely upended, such a view of the apostle.[3] Similarly, the discussion of conversion (109) that makes a singular reference to Arthur Darby Nock's classic 1933 book could be enriched by more recent studies that have challenged Nock's premises.[4] But these are rather small matters; what of the larger concerns expressed by Hughes? Does the study of this material under

---

3. See, for example, Paula Fredriksen, "Judaizing the Nations: The Ritual Demands of Paul's Gospel," NTS 56 (2010): 232–52; and Stanley K. Stowers, *A Rereading of Romans: Justice, Jews, and Gentiles* (New Haven: Yale University Press, 1994).

4. See Zeba A. Crook, *Reconceptualising Conversion: Patronage, Loyalty, and Conversion in the Religions of the Ancient Mediterranean* (Berlin: de Gruyter, 2004).

the overarching rubric of Abrahamic religions tend to reduce Islam, Judaism, and Christianity to monolithic wholes? There are some passages in the book that appear liable to that criticism (e.g., 123–24), but such a reading of Stroumsa's work would be uncharitable. Time and again the book undercuts and complicates those sorts of broad comparisons, and the points where Stroumsa explicitly articulates his theoretical orientation are worth noting. In the course of challenging some of Daniel Boyarin's claims about Jewish-Christians, Stroumsa offers a statement on methodology:

> Suffice it here to say that, in any domain, research demands an intellectual effort to identify common denominators of various phenomena (for instance, multiple religious sects and groups). Such common denominators allow us to retrace central trends underlying the complexity of observable reality. One cannot fulfill this task without creating categories, the primary justification of which is their heuristic usefulness. Gnosticism and Jewish-Christianity are examples of such categories, which cannot be abandoned, although they must be used with care, without forgetting what they are not: a truthful representation of historical reality. (141)

This approach to history seems to me to be the sort of study that Hughes envisions (though I suspect it is also a statement with which Boyarin would agree). The key point is that self-consciousness represented by the words *without forgetting*. It is a reflexivity toward which to strive, even if we all (both as authors and readers) will inevitably fall short.

Early Christian Monastic Literature and the Babylonian Talmud, by Michal Bar-Asher Siegal. New York: Cambridge University Press, 2014. Pp. viii + 236. Hardcover. £60.00. ISBN 9781107023017.

Joshua Schwartz, Bar-Ilan University

Few first books of a scholar based on a doctoral dissertation can be described as both pioneering and outstanding. While it might be an exaggeration to state that Michal Bar-Asher Siegal has established a brand new cutting-edge field in talmudics, she has come close. Scholars have long studied the relationship between the writings of the church fathers and rabbinic literature as well as the historical relationship between Jews and Christians in the ancient world, but few have touched upon the relationship between the writings emanating from early monastic communities, whose heroes are the holy men of late antiquity, and rabbinic literature or Jewish-Christian relations. Bar-Asher Siegal not only set out to do so but established a methodology for the further study of the comparisons between monastic and rabbinic literature. The methodology is extremely important because the author does not and cannot provide an exhaustive treatment of the subject, a lifetime's work. Thus the book represents the beginnings of a process, and the author's methodology enables the continuation of that process in the future.

The book has six chapters. The first two ("Christianity in the Babylonian Talmud: An Introductory Discussion" and "Monasticism in the Persian Empire") offer a survey of the Sassanian Persian Empire during the time in which the Babylonian Talmud was produced, with a focus on the Eastern church and the monastic community. The most important monastic text for the author is the *Apophthegmata patrum*, the Sayings of the Desert Fathers, a collection of stories about Coptic Skete monks of Egypt that were translated and became popular throughout the world of Christendom, including among Christians in the Sasanian Empire. The next two chapters ("The *Apophthegmata Patrum* and Rabbinic Literature: Form, Style, and Common Themes" and "The *Apophthegmata Patrum* and Rabbinic Literature: Narrative") present the rabbinic and monastic corpora in broad brush strokes to demonstrate affinities in style, form, and themes. These chapters do not focus on the Babylonian Talmud but on rabbinic literature as a whole. They also do not reach historical conclusions but rather make a case for the entire enterprise by showing that the comparison between the monastic and rabbinic communities is worth exploring and that it is possible to choose sets of texts that can be compared and read in light of one another. The final two chapters ("The Making of a Monk-Rabbi: The Stories of R. Shimon bar Yoḥai in the Cave" and "Repentant Whore, Repentant Rabbi: The Story of Eleazar b. Dordya") provide an in-depth analysis of two examples from the Babylonian Talmud that find literary analogues in the monastic texts. These examples open the door for further study of additional examples as well as for a reconsideration of the nature of the relationship between Jews and Christians in the ancient world in general, with possible differences in this between the Palestinian and Babylonian Jewish communities and their Christian neighbors affecting when the "parting of the ways" might have taken place. In Babylonia, in particular, that relationship between Jewish and Christian communities need not be only polemical but might include the possibility of conversation with one another, allowing for analogies and literary borrowing between the communities and parallel development.

The author had somewhat of an up-hill battle. Until recently, scholars minimized the possible significance of Christian materials for the formation of the Babylonian Talmud, based on a famous passage in the Babylonian Talmud (Avodah Zarah 4a) that describes a Babylonian rabbi who came to Palestine and was not learned in the polemical use of scripture to answer questions from *minim*, probably early Christians, precisely because he came from Babylonia, an area in which there was seemingly no need for such knowledge. Bar-Asher Siegal, in line with other recent studies, claims that this is not the whole story and that rabbinic texts do indeed reveal interactions between the rabbis and their monastic neighbors. She leads up to this by showing first that a connection between the two religious populations was not only possible but indeed expected. She then shows how it makes absolute sense to assume connections between any religious group and its surroundings and how the texts themselves reveal such connections.

In order to make her case for connections between rabbinic and monastic sources, Bar-Asher Siegal explores a number of stylistic and thematic motifs found in both literatures that strongly suggest a common worldview. She is aware of the dangers of generalization and "parallelomania." As it is often difficult if not impossible to prove actual cases of borrowing, she presents a vast array of examples of similarity between the monastic writings and rabbinic literature. The literary similarities between the two literatures that Bar-Asher Siegal examines are in relation to style and form. In terms of content, she examines pious life, prayer, fear of mundane conversation, anger and laughter, asking forgiveness, and scripture. An analysis of the sources and analogous passages is suggestive of mutual worldviews. The comparison in broad strokes shows that monks and rabbis often thought alike. This provides a strong foundation for detailed analysis to come later in the work.

Another foundation is built upon an examination of imagery and narrative found in both corpora of texts that express a shared cultural world and a shared literary language. The first image Bar-Asher Siegal studies is water, such as the word of God as the saving water of life. The next image studied is that of educational imagery, particularly in connection with the training and education of the next generation. From there Bar-Asher Siegal moves on to relatively detailed examples and analyses of the ignorant youth or the forty-year-old shepherd, the virtuous commoner, talking to the dead, rain and the Resh Lakish narratives (i.e., the repentant robber), crossing rivers, losing power, and the affected sister. While these examples are meant to be more of statistics than detailed analysis, and while they relate to rabbinic literature in general and not just to the Babylonian Talmud, they do reveal the author's methodology in comparative analysis. Since Bar-Asher Siegal's treatment of the rather famous and well-studied Resh Lakish story has been ably scrutinized by Daniel Boyarin in his extensive review of this book,[1] I should like to comment on a different set of stories: the rain motifs.

The author cites a number traditions from the Babylonian Talmud regarding the ability and power of the holy man to bring rain through prayer (b. Mo'ed Katan 28a; b. Ta'anit 24b; b. Yoma 53b). She then makes reference to the earlier rain-making traditions, those of Ḥoni HaM'agel (m. Ta'anit 3:8; cf. Josephus, Ant. 14.2.1 21 [known here as Onias]) and to the Babylonian Talmud's reworked version of this (b. Ta'anit 23a). Earlier traditions had stressed Ḥoni's power, on the one hand, but discomfort at his somewhat abrasive manner toward God, reflecting tension between the rabbis and charismatics. The Babylonian Talmud's reworked version portrays Ḥoni more favorably and plays down the tension between rabbi and charismatic. The desert fathers are, of course, also capable of bringing rain through prayer, but, like the charismatics, they, too, were not averse to strong-arm tactics to get God to do their bidding. The similarities are apparent;

---

1. "The Talmud and the Desert Fathers," *Marginalia*, 9 June 2015, http://marginalia.lareviewofbooks.org/ the-talmud-and-the-desert-fathers-by-daniel-boyarin/. See also Holger Zellentin's review in *Studies in Christian Jewish Relations* 10 (2015), https://ejournals.bc.edu/ojs/index.php/scjr/article/viewFile/8700/ 7818.

the difference is that the monastic tales do not contain any reproach toward the impertinent prayer, as opposed to the rabbis who found fault in this approach by the charismatics.

Bar-Asher Siegal, of course, is interested in comparing narratives, not in the realia surrounding them. Her one comment on this comes at the beginning of her discussion on rain when she states that the similarities between rabbinic and monastic holy man rain traditions may derive from the fact that the Egyptian monks were sensitive to rain because they lived in desert regions far from the Nile and were dependent therefore on rain; "a similar desert climate in the land of Israel" would have influenced the rabbis. It is hard to imagine what she means by a "similar desert climate" in the Land of Israel. Perhaps in the regions inhabited by Palestinian monks but certainly not in those inhabited by and frequented by rabbis. But the more interesting use of realia would have been to understand the rain and water situation in Babylonia, as this may have had more bearing on the Babylonian Talmud.[2]

Babylonia did not get a lot of rain, but this did not prevent parts of the country from being fertile or harm the Jews there, many of whom were farmers. The water issues of Babylonia were connected to its two major rivers, the Euphrates and the Tigris, and the systems of canals that helped irrigate the land. Thus it was possible to cultivate and harvest wheat even without any rain (b. Ta'anit 10a). The seeming lack of dependence on rain was what differentiated Babylonia and Egypt from the land of Israel (Sifre Deut. 38, p. 73 ed. Finkelstein; cf. b. Bava Mezi'a' 107a). In fact, in Babylonia there was a danger of too much rain, as this might result in the rivers and canals flooding and causing great damage (b. Ta'anit 22b; b. Eruvin 21a), as was the case in b. Ta'anit 24b, cited by Bar-Asher Siegal, when Rabba made it rain in the summer and it rained so much that the gutters overflew and emptied into the Tigris. Bar-Asher Siegal stresses the power of Rabba but seems to miss the fine points of climate that impact on the story. There was, of course, a danger of drought in Babylonia, but this was more of a concern regarding the effects on the rivers and the damage to irrigation. All of the above does not necessarily refute Bar-Asher Siegal's interpretation of the Babylonian rain traditions. Just the opposite; had she placed them within their context, the difference between them and the Palestinian traditions might have been sharpened and the similarities between Egypt in general and Babylonia might have helped with the monastic literature.

The *pièce de résistance* of Bar-Asher Siegal's work is her analysis of the R. Shimon bar Yoḥai traditions, particularly comparing the version of the Palestinian Talmud Sheviæit 9:1, 38d and the Babylonian Talmud Shabbat 33b. Building on an off-the-cuff suggestion of Ben Zion Rosenfeld years ago that the version in the Babylonian Talmud and the depiction of R. Shimon there should be seen in light of

---

2. See, in general, Moshe Beer, *The Babylonian Amoraim: Aspects of Economic Life* [Hebrew] (Ramat-Gan: Bar-Ilan, 1974), 24–35.

the Christian tendency to promote its own saints and holy men,[3] Bar-Asher Siegal takes up the challenge and finds that there are marked parallels in monastic literature to numerous aspects in the R. Shimon story that appear in the Babylonian Talmud but not in the Palestinian one. These parallels indicate the familiarity of the rabbinic authors with Christian holy men traditions, through the Syriac translations, and as a result R. Shimon in the Babylonian tradition looks very much like an early desert father of the fourth and fifth centuries CE and not like a second-century CE Palestinian rabbi. This chapter was published in Hebrew a number of years ago, and I have taught it both in academic and nonacademic settings.[4] Bar-Asher Siegal's presentation has always been thoroughly convincing, albeit some eyebrows being raised and a good deal of surprise at the rabbi-monk comparison.

Bar-Asher Siegal's groundbreaking work sheds light not only on talmudics and rabbinic literature but also on the understanding of the history of Jew and Christian and their religions in the ancient world and the relationships between them. I look forward to her future work as well as of those who will also continue the study of the cultural and historical phenomena that she began.

GRECO-ROMAN WORLD AND HELLENISM

Language and Literacy in Roman Judaea: A Study of the Bar Kokhba Documents, by Michael Owen Wise. Anchor Yale Bible Reference Library. New Haven: Yale University Press, 2015. Pp. xii + 523. Cloth. $85.00. ISBN 9780300204537.

Pieter W. van der Horst, Universiteit Utrecht

Ever since Gustav Dalman, the linguistic milieu of Roman Palestine has been an area of much debate, if only because New Testament scholars were eager to know which language(s) Jesus knew and spoke. In this well-researched book, Wise attempts to bring the debate a step forward by means of a meticulous and thorough analysis of the many papyri from the period of the Bar Kokhba revolt (132–135 CE). It is one of the very best books about this knotty problem that I have read in the last half century. In a long introductory chapter, Wise presents a lucid survey of the history of research in which he shows, *inter multa alia*, how the discovery (in the early 1960s) and publication of these documents brought about a gradual shift in the debate because the fact that so many letters among these finds were written in Hebrew and Greek made scholars rethink their opinions about the position of these languages in the linguistic landscape of Judea in the early Roman period (63 BCE–135 CE). Here Wise also briefly discusses the evidence

---

3. Ben Zion Rosenfeld, "R. Simeon b. Yohai—Wonder Worker and Magician Scholar, 'Saddiq' and 'Hasid,'" *Revue des Études Juives*, 158 (1999): 351–86.

4. Michal Bar-Asher Siegal, "The Making of a Monk-Rabbi: The Background for the Creation of the Stories of R. Shimon bar Yohai in the Cave" [Hebrew], *Zion* 76 (2011): 279–304.

from epigraphy. Next he informs the reader about the scholarly debate on ancient literacy in the last three decades and presents a trenchant critique of Catherine Hezser's *Jewish Literacy in Roman Palestine* (2001). In the rest of this chapter Wise sets out his own approach in the present study. He will analyze 145 documents (118 contracts and 27 letters) in Hebrew, Aramaic, Greek, and Nabataean from the Roman province Judea (which comprises also Galilee, Samaria, and Perea). The focus will be on the language and writing skills of some 400 signatories (witnesses and other subscribers), *signature literacy* being the key term here.

In chapter 2 Wise deals with the Murabba'at evidence. After a sketch of the history of the finds, he argues at length that at least eighteen Murabba'at documents are from the period of the First (not the Second) Revolt (66–74 CE) and form the archives of three intertwined families from Jerusalem. He ingeniously reconstructs the genealogical trees of these families, which in some cases reach back to circa 30 BCE. Much of this is very tentative (and Wise is well aware of the speculative nature of these reconstructions), but it opens potentially important perspectives. Hereafter Wise turns to the Greek documents from Murabba'at; from these very few scraps of text he is able to conclude that in the first century CE there were some Jerusalem families with a modest library of Greek literature. The documents from the Second Revolt are, in Wise's view, mainly the personal archive of the Galgula family plus the state documents that Jesus ben Galgula had amassed in his role as chief administrator of Bar Kokhba. Most of these documents are in Greek, since Bar Kokhba "had retained the mechanism Rome had put in place over the previous century" and "the language of formal administration in the Roman East was Greek" (114). Finally, Wise uses the cache of documents from a cave near Jericho to prove that "well before the First Revolt, Hebrew was a language used in Jericho and its environs to inscribe documents of various sorts" (131), against the expectations of many scholars.

Chapter 3 begins with a detailed description of the complicated history of the manuscript discoveries in caves near and to the south of En Gedi and attempts to establish which texts came from which cave (the results being very different from the disinformation spread by the bedouin). The next fifty pages deal with the archives of the Cave of the Letters, their scripts, languages, and the family relations of the persons mentioned in these documents. This is a rather technical chapter, the main results being that "it is possible to discern a total of six [not four!] archives among the deposits in the Cave of Letters" (154), of which that of Babatha is of course the most well-known, and that the documents belonged to a group of intermarried extended families, "powerful members of the elite" in their respective villages (179). By ferreting out information from the minutest details, Wise is able to offer some dazzling reconstructions of family ties that, even though often hypothetical, do make a lot of sense.

Chapter 4, titled "Epistolary Culture in Roman Judaea," argues that "a well-attested Mediterranean *koine* governing fundamental practices of letter writing had taken root" among Judeans and that "Roman Judaea was an epistolary culture" (213). Wise demonstrates this by studying in the Bar Kokhba letters typically

Greco-Roman techniques such as the variety of activities of secretaries, the ways of folding written papyrus, and the use of Greek tachygraphy. "Judaeans wrote to other Judaeans in Greek," and in this respect "Judaea was integral with the larger Mediterranean world" (222). That Greek was a language used also by nonelite Judeans is further supported by Wise in his brilliant defense of the Jewish (not Nabatean) origin of the famous P.Yadin 52. "No nationalist animus was aimed at Greek" (251). Next Wise demonstrates clearly that the Hebrew used in the Bar Kokhba documents differs markedly from Biblical Hebrew and contains many elements "best explained as of colloquial origin" (272), which implies that it was a language still spoken (but with Aramaic influences). The Aramaic, too, was mostly colloquial (but with Hebrew influences).

In the final chapter Wise draws the conclusions from his painstaking analyses. In the two centuries between Pompey and Hadrian, Judea was a trilingual society. Hebrew was used, in a variety of forms and on different levels, as both a spoken and a literary language by no less than 65–80 percent of the Judeans across all sectors of society (but only a small percentage of them was able to read classical Biblical Hebrew). For the majority of the ordinary Judeans, however, Aramaic was the vernacular. But "Aramaic literature was the preserve of an elite guild of scholars" (330; perhaps an overstatement?), and a considerable portion of the Judeans, perhaps some 30 percent, could speak and read Greek as well, at one level or another. As to literacy, some 65 percent of the elite males were literate at one level or another, but probably only some 7–8 percent of these were "literary literate" (able to read books). As to the population of Roman Judea as a whole, no more than 2–5 percent were literate. Almost 100 percent of the females were illiterate.

The book has two very useful appendices (357–91): one of the signatories and writers of the significant Bar Kokhba documents listed in chronological order with the languages used and writing level indicated, and one of the same people listed alphabetically by name with similar relevant information added. The book concludes with indices of subjects, modern authors (almost three hundred), and ancient sources. Regrettably, there is no bibliography.

In this short review it is, alas, impossible to do justice to the richness and complexities of this fascinating book and to show how each chapter carefully builds upon the results of the previous one(s). The reader can be assured, however, that Wise's study is very well argued, even though much of his reasoning is bound to be tentative and speculative, and hence uncertain, due to the paucity and fragmentary state of the evidence, but Wise is the first to admit this. Wise's scholarship is very wide-ranging: he is at home in classical and Semitic languages and literature, ancient history, biblical studies, Judaic studies, general linguistics, statistics, and more. His book is written in an elegant, sometimes flowery, style, albeit at times somewhat verbose. *Sed caveat lector*: this book is not an easy read, and that is not only due to the often very technical nature of the subject matter, but also to the fact that the reader is supposed to be able to read (apart from English) also French, German, Greek, Latin, Hebrew, and Aramaic (even though ancient quotes are often provided with translation).

In such a comprehensive book there are of course always matters on which one can disagree. Let me take just one example. Wise seems to me not to take seriously enough the epigraphic evidence and hence to belittle the fact that some 40 percent of the hundreds of inscribed ossuaries from Judea have Greek epitaphs. To mention only one of his arguments, he states that here the use of Greek does not reflect actual usage, for it is an element of display: "The money and time spent to produce it argue that people outside the family were the audience. Otherwise a careless cursive scrawled across the bone-box by a family member would have served equally well" (16). I think that the spending of money and time is a sign of piety toward the deceased rather than of ostentation. Moreover, there *are* carelessly scribbled inscriptions in Greek on Judean ossuaries, and very many Greek epitaphs mention only the name of the deceased, without any element of display. I do not imply that this evidence proves that 40 percent of the Judean population spoke Greek, but this high percentage cannot that easily be ignored. Further, does an elegantly written signature *always*, by definition, imply literary literacy, and does a carelessly executed signature *necessarily* imply a low level of literacy? Moreover, on matters of phonology and morphology in Hellenistic Greek (discussed several times by Wise) F. Gignac's *Grammar of the Greek Papyri of the Roman and Byzantine Periods* (2 vols., 1975–1981) is the standard work. Finally, the chapter on epistolography could have profited much from L. Doering's magisterial *Ancient Jewish Letters and the Beginnings of Christian Epistolography* (2012); perhaps that book appeared too late to be taken into account. But all in all, these minor quibbles do not detract from the great value and significance of this immensely learned and "wise" book.

Inside Roman Libraries: Book Collections and Their Management in Antiquity, by George W. Houston. Studies in the History of Greece and Rome. Chapel Hill: University of North Carolina Press, 2014. Pp. xvi+ 327. Hardcover. $59.95. ISBN 9781469617800.

H. Gregory Snyder, Davidson College

"Our subject," says the author, "is everything that one might find in a Roman Library." By *Roman*, the author means *Roman Empire*, so evidence from around the Mediterranean that can be categorized as Greek or Roman is in view (the Qumran texts are thereby excluded, as are the Nag Hammadi documents). The time frame runs from Cicero to Constantine. One of Houston's goals is to acquire a more nuanced understanding of the term *library* and what this might mean. Modern ideas about libraries, whether public or private, do not map so well over the ancient world, and Houston intends to redraw these lines. But even more deeply, Houston is trying to understand the way that knowledge is arranged: What were the mental habits and contours of ancient people when it came to organizing collections of texts? Were works of prose and poetry kept separate? medical and philosophical works? Were Greek and Latin texts kept separate? Were works arranged chronologically? alphabetically? by philosophical school? In the same way that someone might look at a digital music collection and make inferences about its owner, based on the items in the collection or the titles of playlists, Houston is trying to get at the "intellectual personality" of ancient book collectors.

The volume begins with a brief introduction on the mechanics of Roman bookrolls and certain aspects of use, such as the practice of annotating. The codex format, interestingly, receives no treatment at all. We are left to infer that texts in this format were not present in Roman libraries.

In the first chapter, "Assembling a Collection," Houston discusses the ways in which Roman collectors acquired their texts. Exemplars could be borrowed from friends, other libraries, or bookshops and copies produced, written either by the collectors themselves or professional scribes. Collections might be bought, inherited, or captured in war. The book is richly furnished with up-to-date evidence drawn from sources such as Galen's recently discovered *De indolentia*.

The second chapter treats "Lists of Books Preserved on Papyrus." These lists have been compiled and discussed (Puglia 1998; Otranto 2000) but have not received detailed treatment in English or been as thoroughly queried as they might. In particular, Houston translates five lists and discusses three more. After a discussion of individual lists, he makes inferences about the processes of producing and acquiring texts, the "personalities" of the collections, the size of collections, and possible ways of arranging them. None of these lists is complete, and several are quite fragmentary. Most collections are small—a few dozen volumes—although a few others are larger. List 4 is among the most complete, mentioning 296 rolls (142 of which are philosophers, with 13 medical writers represented), and 59 others, for a total of 355—a large collection. List 5, which lists writers of old comedy, would, if complete, number several thousand items. It is difficult to know whether this describes an actual collection or simply a comprehensive list of authors.

Chapter 3 treats the library at the Villa of the Papyri in Herculaneum. Only a small fraction of that site has been excavated, with book rolls found in four separate rooms. It seems likely that further excavations on the unexplored levels of the villa will yield more finds, so it is impossible to determine the full extent of the collections at present. At a minimum, it contained hundreds of volumes, perhaps as many as one to two thousand, by some estimates. The character of the collection is quite philosophical, favoring Epicurean works, those by Philodemus in particular. There may be other rooms, however, where poetic texts were stored or more manuscripts in Latin, so not only the number of volumes but its general contours cannot be fully described. But it is possible, based on the many texts that do survive, to observe patterns of use. Few of the volumes, for example, feature any interventions by readers—annotations, marginalia, and the like—perhaps not too surprising if volumes were not directly handled by readers with pen in hand but voiced by readers. It is possible to date many of the rolls, and based on this the useful life of a papyrus manuscript seems to have been, on average, around two hundred years (121). A good deal of the basic work on the collection is done by other writers (e.g., Cavallo 1983 on the growth of the Herculaneum collection), and Houston passes along their results with updates, comments, and qualifications. It is less clear than once believed that the Villa of the Papyri belonged to L. Calpurnius Piso or that Philodemus himself resided and worked there. The quality and elegance of the collection, when judged overall, is somewhat less lofty than one might expect for a library found in such a deluxe environment.

An examination of the book collections of Oxyrhynchus forms the fourth chapter. Three clusters of discarded papyri turned up in the investigations of Grenfell and Hunt; two others were identified later. Examining these collections poses particular challenges, as these "collections" were manifestly thrown out. As such, they cannot tell us about the overall shape of the library from which they originated. But with the proper circumspection, these collections can still convey important information about ancient libraries. Grenfell and Hunt's second collection is noteworthy for the amount of annotations that it includes: roughly half of these texts have marginalia, some of it quite extensive. In some cases it seems to have been added later, as much as two hundred years after the manuscript was first created. In other cases the marginalia was copied by the scribe at the same time as the main text. Based on the number of scribes involved in the different collections, Houston believes that book collectors tended to purchase ready-made bookrolls from professional scribes or have them commissioned with such scribes rather than having them produced by in-house slaves (176).

Chapter 5 treats the physical aspect of Roman libraries: facilities for storage (*capsae, scrinia, armaria*) along with other furnishings designed to hold book rolls, as well as chairs and statuary. Ground plans for two libraries, that of Celsus at Ephesus and the library at Timgad, are provided and discussed.

The sixth chapter discusses the people who used and worked in these settings: the staff who organized and maintained the collections (*librarioli, glutinatores*). The business of acquiring papyrus, copying, correcting, and repairing rolls is dealt with in summary fashion. Houston discusses the ways library patrons would have been served, concluding that library personnel were probably responsible for retrieving volumes and bringing them to readers. Libraries belonging to emperors form a special case: we know the names of six commissioners of libraries (Suetonius among them), and some treatment of their careers is provided. Houston infers that these libraries "were intended not so much for the use of people in general as for the internal working of the administration" (238). The chapter concludes with a section titled "Troubles in the Libraries," which treats issues ranging from the misshelving of books, damage due to failures on the part of staff to guard against dampness and mildew, thefts, and destruction by fire.

A concluding chapter summarizes and restates the most important results. Three appendices follow: the first being a list of the book collections on papyrus discussed in chapter 2, with critical additions of the Greek and English translation; a checklist of books found so far in the Villa of the Papyri; and a catalogue of manuscripts in one of the Oxyrhynchus collections discussed in chapter 4.

The book is full of small yet interesting observations on the nature of literary collections and how the shape and character of the texts can inform us about patterns of usage. Its chief value lies in its detailed description, not in any new or novel claims about the organization of knowledge in antiquity.

Readers of *RBL* will naturally wonder what account Houston takes of matters such as the transition from roll to codex or the use and collection of books by the likes of Origen or the library of Pamphilius at Caesarea Maritima. The surprising answer is: none at all. The term *codex* is listed only once in the index (74, though it crops up on 2, 105, 132, and 172). Apart from a passing comment on page 2, one would hardly know that the religions of Judaism or Christianity even existed, let alone that texts were crucially important to them. Neither the text nor the bibliography contains any mention of books such as Gamble's *Books and Readers in the Early Church, Christianity and the Transformation of the Book* by Williams and Grafton, James O'Donnell's *Avatars of the Word*, or, remarkably, any book by Bart Ehrman, a colleague of Houston's at Chapel Hill. Thus, while the author attends to the ways that knowledge was bounded and organized in the ancient world, the arrangement of knowledge in the modern academy receives no such scrutiny: a disciplinary chasm dividing the study of ancient religion from that of classics is simply assumed. On the upside, scholars coming at this work from the precincts of early Christianity will find that Houston introduces them to many important items from the field of classics and papyrology, and that is a great benefit.

But books, like book collections, are strong in some areas, less so in others. Houston has given his readers an engaging and enlightening account of ancient libraries that should itself find a place in the *armaria* of anyone interested in ancient books and reading practices.

Depicting the Dead: Self-Representation and Commemoration on Roman Sarcophagi with Portraits, by Stine Birk. Aarhus Studies in Mediterranean Antiquity 11. Aarhus: Aarhus University Press, 2013. Pp. 333. Hardcover. €54.56. ISBN 9788771240184.

Eric C. Smith, Iliff School of Theology

Stine Birk's *Depicting the Dead: Self-Representation and Commemoration on Roman Sarcophagi with Portraits* would seem, at first glance, not to be of much interest to biblical scholars and others working on Second Temple Judaism or early Christianity. The book is, after all, only incidentally related to Christianity, and Judaism makes no appearance whatsoever. The volume belongs most naturally to the work of classicists and art historians, and the SBL crowd could be forgiven for passing over it. To do so, however, would be a mistake; Birk has produced a fine (and handsomely executed) work that exemplifies the virtues of viewing the macrocosm through the microcosm. From her starting point of Roman sarcophagi that include portrait figures, Birk opens up a world of inquiry into gender, family, social and public life, and construction and negotiation of identity that will inform and benefit anyone studying the early centuries of the Common Era.

The book functions on two levels, both useful. First, it is a primer for those who want to know how to "read" sarcophagi, and the introduction and first chapter are devoted to this task. Second and more significantly, the book follows Birk's own analysis of this particular class of sarcophagi, which is deeply attentive to the construals of identity that are expressed in the stone. The balance of the book is devoted to this analysis, and it is the most compelling part of the work.

The introduction, titled "Negotiating Identity on Sarcophagi," sets out a kind of interpretive scheme for the later chapters. Birk declares her intention to interrogate gender in the course of the volume, and she articulates what turns out to be a major guiding principle. Sarcophagi, she argues, ought to be viewed not only as private expressions of mourning and loss but also as public expressions of virtue, constructing and negotiating the identities of the deceased, the mourners, and the patrons who have paid for the whole endeavor (and who are sometimes identical with the first two categories). Sarcophagi are public documents, designed and used to assert identity for the living and the dead.

Chapter 1, "Images for Contemplation," is by Birk's own admission most useful for those with no experience in interpreting sarcophagi, as it describes the production, decoration, use, and interpretation of the objects. For this reason it is commended to anyone with an interest in learning the visual language of sarcophagi. But this chapter is more than a simple handbook; it contains in it the seeds of Birk's later analysis and sinks roots in questions of patronage and production that produce growth later in the volume.

Chapter 2, "*Exempla Virtutis*: Portraits and Self-Representation on Sarcophagi," begins Birk's analysis proper. In this chapter she examines some of the major visual programs found on sarcophagi. At times she does this with the deft eye of an attentive viewer, giving rich descriptions that complement the plentiful and high-quality images. At other times Birk collates data in useful ways, demonstrating in several effective charts and graphs the commonalities and differences among extant sarcophagi. The combined effect of these efforts is that the reader understands not only how certain motifs function on sarcophagi but also how particular instances of those motifs play within the viewer's expectations. This chapter is particularly helpful in banishing the old scapegoat of production; Birk allows for the existence of "blank" or "stock" sarcophagi bought off the shelf but still succeeds in demonstrating the ways identity is nevertheless embedded and negotiated in those items.

"Visualizing Gender" (ch. 3) is the heart of the argument. It begins with a challenge to interpretive laziness: we cannot, Birk argues, assume that sex and gender were always (or even usually) coextensive and coterminous in antiquity and that they can be plainly read on sarcophagi. Depictions on sarcophagi could be extraordinarily playful with both sex and gender. Gender roles for men and women were depicted only to be reversed. Feminine ideals of beauty were applied to men and masculine roles assigned to women. Mythological scenes seemed especially prone to provoke cross-gendered substitution. Gender hierarchies were inverted (except, interestingly, when marriage was depicted). In general, a libertine ethos prevailed, but then there were striking instances of conservatism (or sex-gender conformity): nudity was not as forbidden as one think (given the funerary context), but a couple was never depicted naked together. When a man and a woman were depicted together with a scroll, the man held the scroll, and, as noted above, depictions of married couples seemed impervious to alteration of gender roles. Birk's argumentation in this chapter, always making careful recourse to the images themselves, is illuminating of the ways modern interpreters import interpretative schemes into antiquity, often without realizing it. She cautions readers at every turn to question our assumptions, then demonstrates the ways our interpretations have been improved by the effort.

The fourth chapter, "*Filiae Innocentissimae, Filio Dulcissimo:* Commemorating Children," is similarly absorbing. This chapter, which fills the reader with pathos at the litany of children's sarcophagi, reiterates a recurring theme of the book, that in sarcophagus decorations accuracy of likeness was never the intention of either the artist or the patron. Decorative programs on sarcophagi were always identity claims, and this is nowhere so apparent as on the sarcophagi of children. In a way parallel to the gender-shifting she discussed in the third chapter, Birk in the fourth chapter describes the ways children's sarcophagi could depict the deceased child as an adult, as a person of the opposite sex, or as having unrealistic identities (poet, philosopher) in the interest of constructing identity for the child and, significantly, the parents. Picking up on a notion she uses elsewhere in the book, "ideal life course," Birk demonstrates that depictions of children say less about the child's life and more about the child's lost potential and the parents' virtuous child-rearing. Memorializations of children were at pains to describe the arc of their lives in adult terms, always on the grounds of an uncompleted trajectory.

A short section titled "Retrospect" functions as a conclusion for the work as well as a prospectus for further work. Some of this work could well be undertaken by scholars of Christian origins; Birk claims provocatively at one point that the depictions of women on Christian sarcophagi might signal a greater role for women in Christianity in the city of Rome than we have usually thought. More generally, she points the way forward to understanding the construction and negotiation of identity through material culture, which will be of interest to many.

At the back of the book Birk includes a substantial catalog that ought to be considered a contribution in its own right. The catalog is organized by motif and categories of age and sex, and it is therefore a crucial resource for anyone undertaking work in this area. Brief descriptions are included for hundreds of portrait sarcophagi, along with locations and bibliographical information. This will be invaluable to future researchers.

The difficulty with a book like this is that it is an act of interpretation. Material is subject to interpretation in the same way that texts are, and meaning is no more or less self-evident on a sarcophagus than it is on a papyrus fragment. Birk's interpretations are convincing, but they remain interpretations, and they will therefore fail to satisfy everyone. This is a criticism that can hardly be avoided, but it goes to the heart of the book. In the third chapter, for example, much of the argument depends on identifying which persons are depicted in which scenes. But this is necessarily a messy business; there are, after all, no captions on the images on sarcophagi. So when, to choose but one mostly random example, Birk describes a sarcophagus fragment (her fig. 84) as depicting a couple, she has to make several judgment calls that put her conclusions on shaky footing. The person on the left is female because she has an exposed shoulder, but the head has not been carved with any sex-identifying features (or at least none that have survived). The figure on the right, meanwhile, is taken to be a male based on its position relative to the other figure and the scroll it holds in its hand … *despite* the figure's clear female features. This, argues Birk, is evidence that the "woman commemorated on this sarcophagus has specifically chosen to be carved onto the figure of a learned person," in contravention to gender and iconographic norms (154). This may well be so, and, it bears repeating, Birk is convincing, particularly on the accumulated weight of her observations. But this interpretation is hardly obvious, even on Birk's own terms. The same could be said for many if not most of the sarcophagi in the book, of which a great number display counterintuitive images—evidence, no doubt, of the kind of identity negotiation Birk is describing. Adding to the difficulty is Birk's insistence that portraits are idealized and not meant to depict specific traits of the person depicted; if this is true, then gender and gender roles must always exist under a cloud of doubt. All of this messiness of the evidence leaves room for alternative explanations—such as stock, blank panels bought off the shelf or reused sarcophagi—that Birk considers but mostly rejects.

This broad (and unavoidable) criticism aside, this volume is a treasure for those interested in sarcophagi specifically, in material culture generally, or in the whole universe of identity formation and contestation in antiquity. The recent concern for identity within our guild will benefit from attention to this book, which considers the subject with a different set of evidence than what biblical scholars and scholars of Christian origins are used to considering. Our own conversations can only be enriched by contact with Birk's analysis.

The Gods, the State, and the Individual: Reflections on Civic Religion in Rome, by John Scheid. Translated by Clifford Ando. Philadelphia: University of Pennsylvania Press, 2016. Pp. 200. Cloth. $55.00. ISBN 9780812247664.

Jeffrey Brodd, California State University, Sacramento

John Scheid has long been a major contributor to scholarship on Roman religion. Relatively few of his writings have been translated into English, so this publication is especially welcomed. The book was originally published as *Les Dieux, l'État et l'individu: Réflexions sur la religion civique à Rome* (2013); Clifford Ando has produced a lucid translation. Scheid presents a spirited defense of the "civic religion model" that he has played a large role in developing.

Ando's translator's foreword deftly contextualizes Scheid's book within the scholarly debate that has persisted for some four decades over the efficacy of the civic religion model. Its opponents have tended to insist in one way or another on the primacy of the concerns and choices of individuals as having determined the nature of Roman religion. The foreword enhances the book's accessibility for readers not familiar with the debate.

Scheid's preface focuses on methodology, making clear his insistence on the "well-known principle of secularism, which is to say, of religiously disinterested research" (xx). In the introduction Scheid becomes more explicit and specific with regard to methodological shortcomings of the civic religion model's detractors. The approach in Germany, he asserts, violates the principle of secularism by being beholden to Protestant theology, along with Romantic philosophy. In England, methodological failings have included "the influence of British liberal thought" and deconstructionism. Whatever the root cause and wherever the critics call home, they all errantly challenge the civic religion (or "*polis*-religion") model for not taking "account of the religion of the individual, of religiosity viewed as a universal phenomenon, everywhere and always identical and present" (1).

Chapter 1, "The Critique of *Polis*-Religion," begins by establishing the historical foundations of the scholarly debate, noting the enormous influence of Hegelian dialectic on nineteenth-century scholarship, then detailing the vital contributions of Georg Wissowa and his ground-breaking book, *Religion und Kultus der Römer* (1902). Wissowa is heralded as an early champion of what for Scheid is the fundamental methodological principle of alterity: "the obligation to take the otherness of the ancients as a point of departure" (6). Adherence to this principle stands in stark contrast to "reduction of all religion to a precocious manifestation of some religiosity approaching Christianity" (5). Scheid asserts that this contrast has characterized the debate between advocates of the civil religion model and its critics to this day. Chapter 1 proceeds by presenting the inventory of objections raised by the critics. Scheid takes up these objections in turn throughout the rest of the book, defending the civic religion model at every turn, often with extraordinarily concise yet substantive explications of aspects of Roman religion. Chapter 1 concludes with a focused analysis of "religiosity," the notion that Scheid believes lies "behind all these separate criticisms" (16).

Chapter 2, "*Polis* and Republic," explores the first of what Scheid perceives as three major problems with the perspective of the critics, that they have misunderstood the true nature of the Greek and Roman city. His main concern is to show that, contrary to common opinion, the city did not undergo serious decline and actually retained its vitality in the Roman imperial period. Chapter 3, "The Individual in the City," furthers the defense of the civic religion model by arguing that the role of the individual in this enduring ancient city is compatible with the model; this in response to the second major problem with the critics' perspective: "a poor comprehension of what one might call the individual in the ancient world" (4). Chapter 3 concludes with analysis of the categories *public* and *private*, emphasizing that the nature of the private sphere resulted in a conception of individuality in ancient Rome that was quite different from that of modern society.

Chapters 4–10 analyze the various implications of the third major problem: "a limited and distorted understanding of the religions of this world of city-states" (4). Chapter 4, "Civic Religion: A Discourse of the Elite?," refutes the common notion that the priesthoods and practices of Roman religion were manipulated by elites for sake of maintaining control. The "broader" problem of "the opposition between civic religion and the 'religiosity' of the individual" (44) is addressed in chapters 5, 6, and 7, "Civic Religion and Identity," "For Whom Were the Rituals Celebrated?," and "Religious Repression." In chapter 8, "Civic Religion, a Modality of Communal Religion," Scheid argues for the special significance of the civic religion model based on its being merely "one face" of "the dominant model of collective religion in the Roman world" (104). Chapter 9, "Emotion and Belief," takes up the critics' claim that emotion is a necessary element of true religion and that civic religion was devoid of emotion. Scheid includes analysis of ritualism and the relationship between religious practice and meaning, asserting: "It is this separation between religious practice and meaning, of religion and 'religiosity,' that is the preeminent characteristic of the religion of the ancient Greeks and Romans, much more than its civic and communal character" (123). Chapter 10, "Why Did Roman Religion Change?," challenges the common view that "individual religiosity" and a deepening thereof were primarily responsible for the introduction of healing cults and mystery religions.

Chapter 11, "The Gods, the State, and the Individual," reviews some of the book's main arguments while emphasizing further the need to be conscientious of the alterity of the Romans. By way of example, Scheid notes that "Roman gods were seen as *patroni*, as powerful persons who protected and helped their *clients*, according to a model of social relations shared by all Romans. The contradiction with the Christian way of seeing things is total" (139). Scheid concludes by asserting that the critics of the civic religion model reject "the very idea of the relative alterity of the ancients," a rejection that is "at the base, the result of a confessional approach to religious history" (140–41).

When attending to aspects of Roman religion, this book is a marvelous work of historical scholarship. Ando has it right when he comments in his translator's foreword that Scheid proceeds "with a profound respect for historical and philological detail" (xi). The approach yields much by way of substantive descriptions of Roman practices, for example, a highly informative account of the distribution and consumption of meat of animals sacrificed in Rome—this by way of countering the claim that the public did not participate in civic cult. Scheid's attention to the history and cultural context of scholarship on Roman religion is also helpful. The reader might wonder, however, as to the identity of "the critics" who, in anonymous fashion, are so frequently evoked, given that when Scheid is specific he often refers to just one critic, Stefan Krauter, whose book is cited in endnotes over twenty times. This is somewhat surprising in light of Ando's overview of the *variety* of critical responses to the civic religion model (xv). On a related note, the reader might indeed wonder how likely it is that *all* of those anonymously evoked critics could fall victim to *all* of the problems with their methodology and conclusions that Scheid attributes to them. This "blanket approach" seems most problematic with regard to the claim that the critics are engaged in Christian theology rather than religious history. There seems to be no direct evidence that would support this claim. In some respects, then, the spirited nature of Scheid's defense goes a bit too far—although at the same time this spirited nature is one of the book's many charms. Its publication provides English readers with an entry point into the debate concerning the civic religion model while at the same time furnishing a wealth of sound historical information from one of its founding figures.

NEW TESTAMENT: GENERAL

Kultmetaphorik und Christologie: Opfer- und Sühneterminologie im Neuen Testament, by Christian A. Eberhart. Wissenschaftliche Untersuchungen zum Neuen Testament 306. Tübingen: Mohr Siebeck, 2013. Pp. xv + 328. Cloth. €99. ISBN 9783161518829.

Jennifer W. Knust, Boston University

With *Kultmetaphorik und Christologie*, Christian Eberhart builds on over a decade of research into the sacrificial terminology used by the Hebrew Bible and New Testament. The result is a detailed, comprehensive analysis of the New Testament's reception of Israel's sacrificial system that reconsiders the multiple ways that Jesus's death was interpreted by his first followers. Jesus's life, not his crucifixion, was the primary focus of the cultic and sacrificial metaphors employed by the New Testament writers, Eberhart argues, and, when placed in an ancient context, even motifs such as the cleansing properties of Jesus's blood or comparisons between Jesus and the paschal lamb can be interpreted as referring above all to his holy life and only secondarily to his death. Such metaphors do assume the crucifixion, but they do not dwell on it. Instead, they expand Old Testament and early Jewish cultic terminology in order to invest this death with diverse meanings.

The idea that Jesus's death was required for the expiation of sin, Eberhart points out in his introductory chapter, is problematic, especially from a modern perspective. Nowadays sacrifice is often perceived to be a violent, bloody act; an emphasis on the atoning character of Jesus's death can therefore seem to imply that God brutally required the suffering of his own son. Yet such a teaching is not actually found in New Testament soteriology; this form of atonement theology glosses over the specificity of Old Testament cultic terminology, misrepresents the meanings of the ancient sacrificial cult, and fails to attend to the variety of ways in which cultic motifs were specifically employed by the New Testament writers. There are a range of christological and soteriological images in the New Testament, and individual writers evoked them in distinctive ways.

Chapter 2 begins by describing metaphors and their function: metaphors necessarily depend on strings of words, linked together in a unit, that are open to a variety of interpretations; they reciprocally transfer meaning from a contributing to a receiving image, such that both the referent and the contributing image are transformed in the process. Careful investigation into the terminology and linguistic contexts of the source image and the receptor is therefore required. In the case of New Testament literature, which depends heavily on images drawn from the Jerusalem temple cult, this means thoroughly studying Old Testament and early Jewish cultic terminology and practices first, before attempting to decide what a given New Testament metaphor can mean. These interpretive principles are applied in the next five chapters, which address New Testament vocabulary and images in turn, and place them within a detailed reconsideration of ancient Israel's sacrificial system, as described in the Old Testament (Hebrew Bible and LXX) as well as in early Jewish literature and practice.

Chapter 3 addresses the image of Jesus as a "fragrant offering" (εἰς ὀσμὴν εὐωδίας), a metaphor that links Lev 1–7 to Jesus's life. Ephesians 5:2, for example, claims that believers should "live in love, as Christ loved us and gave himself for us, a fragrant offering and sacrifice to God" (NRSV). This verse, Eberhart contends, draws on earlier Old Testament terminology to present Jesus's life as a model of "fragrant" living. "Sacrifice" (θυσία), a polyvalent term, refers in these examples to what is given; to "sacrifice" is therefore to engage in an act of reciprocal offering on behalf of others. Chapter 4 continues the analysis by reconsidering New Testament references to Jesus's blood. In the Hebrew Bible, Septuagint, and early Judaism, blood was associated with life and revered for its cleansing properties. Building on this tradition, New Testament writers also depicted Jesus's blood as a purifying and consecrating agent (e.g., in Rom 5:8–10; Col 1:19–20; 1 Pet 1:19). Jesus's actions at the Last Supper can be interpreted this way as well: the reference to the "blood of the covenant" (Mark 14:22–25 and parallels) evokes Exod 24:8; by associating the cultic consecration at Sinai with the act of partaking in Jesus's "blood." This act therefore symbolizes the transformation of believers into a holy and priestly community while also anticipating Jesus's impending death. It is only Hebrews, Eberhart shows in chapter 5, that actually places the death of Jesus at the center of soteriological thinking: at his death Christ entered the holy of holies and redeemed humankind. Yet in Hebrews as well Jesus's blood connotes the dialectic between life and death: by shedding his blood and offering himself as a sacrifice, Christ entered the heavenly sanctuary to dwell eternally with God; in this sanctuary he speaks on behalf of humankind in order to make transcendent life available. By mixing earlier sacrificial motifs, the writer of Hebrews asserts that Jesus's blood purifies Christians so that they, too, may readily approach God's presence.

Chapter 6 focuses on the lexeme ἱλάσκομαι, which has often been misleadingly translated. In the Old Testament (both the Hebrew Bible and LXX), this lexeme references the places where the blood of atonement was applied, not the slaughter of a sacrificial animal. Thus translations such as "sacrifice of atonement" for ἱλαστήριον (Rom 3:24; Heb 9:5) unnecessarily focus on sacrificial death;

tradition history suggests instead that this term conceives of Jesus himself as a place of atonement where humanity is reconciled with God. The lexeme is also used in 1 John (ἱλασμός at 2:2; 4:10), in this case to emphasize the reconciliation this purifying blood brings, a focus shared by Rom 8:3 and 2 Cor 5:21. Chapter 7 treats the lamb metaphor and other images drawn from the Passover feast. Reading such imagery in light of Exodus, Eberhart observes that the shedding of lamb's blood at the Passover was viewed an apotropaic rite, not as a sacrifice; the lamb metaphor therefore proposes that Jesus Christ obtained protection against powerful, threatening forces, a concept that was combined with the suffering servant tradition of Isa 52 to emphasize his silent acceptance of this role. Once again, Jesus's life, as symbolized in his blood, is the agent of this transformation, not his death on a cross.

The conclusions of the book are summarized and reiterated in chapter 8, which further underscores the importance of placing New Testament soteriology in a tradition-historical context. Ancient Israel's sacrificial system was much more complex than is commonly assumed; the sacrificial and cultic metaphors employed by New Testament writers are also characterized by diversity, not unanimity. With the exception of Hebrews, no New Testament writer emphasizes the saving quality of Jesus's death, focusing instead on the reconciling atonement brought by his life, as symbolized in images such as his cleansing blood, his role as lamb, the "fragrance" of his loving example, and his ability to protect believers from evil. By carefully reconsidering ancient sacrifice, which (contrary to popular belief) emphasized slaughter and death, and attending closely to the reception of biblical and early Jewish cultic terminology in the New Testament, *Kultmetaphorik und Christologie* challenges readers to reconsider the possible significance of sacrificial atonement. As such, the theological stakes of this volume are clear, if implicit: Eberhart is employing the latest developments in the study of ancient sacrifice to overturn doctrines such as the theory of substitutionary atonement. When read in their own tradition-historical context, the New Testament writers did not interpret Jesus's death as a violent sacrifice demanded by an angry God. They did, however, depend heavily on Israel's cultic motifs and early Jewish sacrificial terminology to reinterpret that death as a life-giving, redemptive act that enables believers to approach God and gain eternal life. Cultic metaphors are just that: metaphors. They are therefore open to creative and imaginative reception. Still, thoughtful interpreters would do well to situate these metaphors within their historical and linguistic contexts, or so this study suggests.

A Short History of the New Testament, by Halvor Moxnes. I.B. Tauris Short Histories. London: I.B. Tauris, 2014. Pp. 256. Paper. $15.95. ISBN 9781780766089.

Dieter T. Roth, Johannes Gutenberg-Universität Mainz

The opening sentence in Moxnes's preface to this recent volume in the I.B. Tauris Short Histories series entails the blunt admission, "It is, of course, impossible to write a 'short history of the New Testament'" (x). Nevertheless, Moxnes has provided a valiant and often quite successful effort at accomplishing the impossible. Though the book includes some discussion of elements found in traditional introductions to the New Testament, in three sections entitled "Beginnings," "Shaping History," and "Reading and Meaning-Making," the focus falls primarily upon the reception of the New Testament and its use and influence in history.

Part 1, "Beginnings," includes an opening section "From Jesus to the Gospels" and four chapters. The introductory pages provide an overview of information deemed trustworthy concerning the historical Jesus, including that he was a Jew living in Galilee, was at some point a disciple of John the Baptist, proclaimed the kingdom of God, and came into conflict with Jewish leaders and Roman authorities, the latter of whom ended up crucifying him. At the same time, the fact that the four canonical gospels are different from each other "shows that there must have been diversities and different emphases in the Jesus movement from its beginning" (7). Chapter 1, "Becoming Christians: Letter Writing as Community Formation," treats Paul and, though providing a brief discussion of his life and the chronology of his letter, focuses primarily on issues of community formation, identity, and relationships. In fact, Moxnes contends that a better candidate for the heart of Paul's theology than justification by faith or participation in Christ is to "avoid conflict, live in harmony and be of the same mind" (17). The comments on various letters of Paul always return to this theme as well as the manner in which Paul employed it to create an identity among the followers of Christ. The Pastoral Epistles are pseudonymous (Moxnes thinks the term *forgery* may be misplaced) and reveal "a wish to be integrated into Roman society and a mentality that is very different from Paul's message in an earlier generation" (33). The final pages of the chapter consider the Catholic Epistles as a further indication of diversity and conflicts in early Christianity. Chapter 2, "Memory and Identity: The Gospels as Jesus-Biographies," provides a narrative reading of the canonical gospels and Q, highlighting how "written preservations of once-spoken memories of Jesus would have the capacity to shape the identity of the audiences in particular directions and introduce community ideals" (38). Once again Moxnes emphasizes that there are five different pictures of Jesus found in the four canonical gospels and Q and that therefore diversity was not a later deviation from an initial unity: "diversity was there from the beginning" (63). Chapter 3, "Acts and Apocalypse: Ambivalent Living under the Roman Empire," considers the Acts and Revelation from a postcolonial perspective. Acts is not an apologetic text for a Roman audience but rather is addressed to followers of Christ negotiating Roman power. Though Revelation rejects the Roman Empire, it also reveals the extent to which "elements of imperial thinking had actually penetrated primitive Christian thought so that imperial ideology and terminology was combined with a theology of God the Father and Son" (73). Chapter 4, the final chapter in this section, considers canon questions and thus is entitled "Included or Excluded: When Was the New Testament Created?" Considering the significance of the

Gospel of Thomas, the Gospel of Mary, and the Proto-Gospel of James, Moxnes views the noncanonical gospels as "not as widespread as some would think, and they often served as supplements to the four (later canonical) gospels, rather than alternatives to them" (75). Particularly interesting are Moxnes's observations on the perpetuation of the canon-formation process, seen, for example, in Martin Luther's view of James and the manner in which canon questions are part of "a common human enterprise of imaginative community making and remaking" (91).

Part 2, "Shaping History," is more overtly devoted to the reception history of the New Testament (*Wirkungsgeschichte* and *Rezeptionsästhetik*); this section is introduced by "The Reception of the New Testament," followed by three further chapters. In chapter 5, "'Christianity goes to Press': The Communication History of the New Testament," Moxnes provides a helpful overview and discussion of the material production, translation, and modern critical editions of the New Testament. Here it is not only antiquity, the Middle Ages, the printing press, and textual criticism that is discussed but also the manner in which Bible translations were coupled with colonialism and the manner in which the digital age has (once again) ushered in a revolution in access to and interaction with the New Testament. "'Their Eyes Were Opened and They Recognized Him': Glimpses of Receptions of the Jesus Story" is the title of chapter 6, which turns away from the reception of the New Testament by "expert readers" and pursues "cases of reception among 'ordinary people'" (116). Here Moxnes considers the Eucharist in art, pilgrimages in various eras, the construction of churches, and the stained glass windows of Canterbury Cathedral. He concludes the chapter with two depictions of paintings by Roger Wagner (*Walking on Water* [2005] and *The Road to Emmaus* [2008]) in order to indicate the manner in which Wagner's art illustrates that "faith in Jesus lives hidden in the modern world" (132). "Race, Class and Gender 'in Christ'? The Ambiguous Reception History of Galatians 3:28" (ch. 7) is devoted, as would be expected, to Gal 3:28 and its history of interpretation. Using Charles Taylor's concept of "social imaginaries," Moxnes considers the manner in which this verse was interpreted in antiquity, the Reformation, and modernity, emphasizing the manner in which the "broader understandings of how people understand themselves in their social reality" (134) impacted the interpretation and use of this verse. Moxnes is rightly critical of anti-Jewish and anti-Semitic positions found in the history of Christianity and is hopeful that work such as the 2002 report from the Pontifical Biblical Commission, *The Jewish People and their Sacred Scriptures in the Christian Bible,* reflects an increasing awareness of Christian responsibility to address its presentation of Jews and Judaism post-Holocaust, even as the report still has shortcomings and there is still much work to be done. Moxnes here also considers feminist readings and points out that, among a variety of different feminist voices, including the differing perspectives of Elisabeth Schüssler Fiorenza and Lone Fatum, "they find that what Paul said still makes a difference in that it has the power to affect women's situations today, either as an oppressive force or as a potential for liberation" (155).

Part 3, "Reading and Meaning-Making," begins with "The History of How to Read the New Testament" and comprises two numbered chapters along with the conclusion. Chapter 8, "Historical Readings: How Modernity Shaped New Testament Scholarship," actually begins with premodern readings and then briefly considers the Renaissance, Reformation, and Enlightenment eras before devoting more attention to the manner in which historical criticism led to the quest for the historical Jesus , the question of sources (John or the Synoptics?), and methodologies such as form criticism and redaction criticism. Particularly helpful is Moxnes's observations about an often underemphasized element in historical Jesus studies: the influence of "Orientalism" on nineteenth-century interpretation. The final chapter before the conclusion, "'Reading from This Place': Paul in Recent Interpretations" (ch. 9), considers the way in which New Testament studies has changed since the 1960s by using interpretations of Paul as an example. With the challenge to the "norms" of *original* meaning and the *objective* reader … scholars from different parts of the world, women and men, presented interpretations of biblical texts from their particular social, racial, geographic and gender location" (185). Here Moxnes discusses the "linguistic turn," the new perspective on Paul, Paul and Hellenism, feminist readings, political and postcolonial readings, along with Paul as read by philosophers. The brief conclusion with the title "Where Is the Future of the New Testament?" sums up the manner in which "the history of the readings of the New Testament shows how they have been integrated into their contemporary cultural, political and religious contexts" (205) and emphasizes the manner in which this volume has sought "to enable readers to become active dialogue partners with the New Testament" (206).

Of course, in a volume such as this, much must be left out, and Moxnes says as much in his preface. Nevertheless, a few omissions are surprising, especially when Moxnes usually does a good job of helping his readers understand various issues in New Testament scholarship with which they may not be familiar. For instance, it could be somewhat confusing when Moxnes simply refers to the ending of Mark at 16:8 (44) with no mention of various additional endings and the fact that, even though there may be footnotes or brackets present, no modern Bible ends the Gospel of Mark with Mark 16:8. In addition, it is unfortunate that there is no reference at all to the staurogram when considering visual depictions and art in early Christianity. On occasion a few statements seem to have slipped through the editing process, such as when the reader finds on page 104 the observation that "it is uncertain if the original [Diatessaron] was composed in Greek or Syriac," having read in the previous chapter that, when Tatian returned to Syria, "he translated the *Diatessaron* into Syriac" (87). Such minor quibbles aside, if writing a short history of the New Testament is impossible, establishing a dialogue with the history of the New Testament is eminently possible, and Moxnes has done an admirable job of achieving this goal.

Apocalyptic Literature in the New Testament, by Greg Carey. Core Biblical Studies. Nashville: Abingdon, 2016. Pp. xv + 176. Paper. $29.99. ISBN 9781426771958.

David A. Sánchez, Loyola Marymount University

Greg Carey's contribution to Abingdon's Core Biblical Studies series is a reassessment and expansion of that material categorized as apocalyptic in the New Testament. The series, according to general editor Warren Carter, is "designed as a starting point for New Testament Studies" (xiii). Thus any assessment of the targeted reading audience should take due note. Other contributions to the series include: *The General Epistles* (Sharon Ringe), *God in the New Testament* (Warren Carter), *The Dead Sea Scrolls* (Peter W. Flint), and *The Apocrypha* (Louis Stulman and David Desilva).

The preface and chapter 1 introduce what may be the most important contribution of this work, an expansion of the list of texts categorically regarded as apocalyptic in the Christian canon. This expansion requires Carey to shift our focus from the classical literary apocalypse, Revelation (which is still regarded as apocalyptic in the new schema), to include texts he defines as apocalyptic discourses (a majority of the New Testament writings). Thus he sets in contrast *literary apocalypses* and what he terms *apocalyptic discourses*. Contemporary New Testament scholars will recognize literary apocalypses as those texts defined by John Collins and others (*Semeia* 14, 1979) as including literary forms such as "heavenly guide[s that] provide … instructions and explanations to the visionary, some focus on the resolution of history, while others emphasize 'tours' of heaven and hell and still others combine both features" (6). According to these criteria, only the book of Revelation is accepted as a literary apocalypse in the New Testament.

The expansion of the apocalyptic corpus in the Christian canon comes with the introduction of a new category that Carey calls *apocalyptic discourse*. In this classification Carey sites the following thematic tendencies: messianic character(s), resurrection, cosmological dualism, displacement of this present era with a new reality, an end-time scenario that is imminent (in most cases), God's decisive intervention, the return of Jesus, final judgment, and a blessed new age (14–15). This proposed shift from literary form (genre) to thematic elements (function) allows Carey to expand those texts deemed apocalyptic in the New Testament. This modification in grouping drives the remainder of the book, allowing Carey to reevaluate the Pauline epistles (ch. 3), the Synoptics (ch. 4), Q, Thomas, John, and Jesus (ch. 5), and Revelation (ch. 6) as apocalyptic discourses. The book concludes with a summation of his findings in the epilogue (ch. 7).

Chapter 2's primary assertion is that "Christian apocalyptic [should be assessed] within the contexts of Judaism and Jewish apocalyptic" (17). The chapter offers a background foundation squarely locating Christian apocalyptic discourse on a trajectory within Jewish literary productions and Judaism proper. Digressions on protoapocalyptic texts such as Isa 24–27 and Ezek 38–39 as well as early Jewish apocalypses, including 1 Enoch, Daniel, the Dead Sea Scrolls, Jubilees, and

The Testament of the Twelve Patriarchs, are employed to demonstrate Carey's background landscape.

Chapter 3 evaluates the Pauline corpus as apocalyptic discourse. It should be noted here that no Pauline or Deutero-Pauline letter has ever been labeled a *literary* apocalypse. Carey does note, however, that "a strong apocalyptic core animated [Paul's] message" that functioned rhetorically "to correct his opponents, support his own authority, comfort anxious believers, exhort communities to faithful discipleship, and admonish wayward members of his character" (70). A majority of the Pauline corpus is used to demonstrate this point. Carey goes on to note that Paul himself, as well as those letters recognized as Deutero-Pauline, later "shifted toward a more realized eschatology (Ephesians and Colossians) and by adding a detailed scenario of apostasy and crisis prior to Jesus' return (2 Thessalonians and the Pastorals)" (70). This is an important observation. Apocalyptic discourse, according to Carey, is not a static category and may in fact be influenced by perceived delay(s) of the parousia, prompting some New Testament authors, including Paul and the Pauline school, to shift to less dramatic (i.e., imminent) forms of eschatological speculation (e.g., reserved and realized eschatologies).

Chapter 4 argues that Mark demonstrates a thoroughly apocalyptic worldview based on his utilization of apocalyptic discourse themes. He cites Jesus's relationship with John the Baptist, the absence of any birth narrative, the apocalyptic vision (1:10), the imminent contestation and temptation with Satan (1:12), Jesus's pronouncement of the imminence of God's kingdom (1:15), encounters with demons (John 1, 3, 5), Jesus's messianic identity (e.g., proclaimed by the narrator in 1:1 and Peter in 8:29), the mini-apocalypse (John 13), the adoption of Daniel's Son of Man terminology (e.g., John 2), the resurrection of Jesus (John 16), and the implied return of Jesus as the Son of Man (John 13)—all thematic features, according to Carey, of apocalyptic discourse. Mark's incorporation of these elements leads Carey to conclude that Mark is "thoroughly apocalyptic" (94). Matthew, we are instructed, "tends to soften Mark's stress upon the nearness of Jesus' return, but ... intensifies the theme of a final judgment" (94). Luke and Acts, on the other hand, focus "not with the end of history but with the spreading of the Gospel in the here and now" (94). See, for example, the slight nod toward realized eschatology in Luke 17:20–21. So, similar to the Pauline corpus, the Synoptics also demonstrate an apocalyptic fluidity when faced with Jesus's delayed return while simultaneously retaining several core elements of apocalyptic discourse proper.

Chapter 5 turns its attention to Q and the Gospels of Thomas and John. Carey recognizes that there are indeed elements of apocalyptic discourse in the Sayings Gospel Q but also considers the layering theory proposed by John Kloppenborg (*The Formation of Q*, 1987). This theory argues that Q came together in three separate acts: Q1, a sapiential collection of Jesus pronouncements; Q2, an apocalyptic layer added on after the Q community was rejected as a legitimate social movement; and Q3, the attempt of the Q community to introduce a custodial element to the movement. Thus Q is quite the challenge for the evaluation of its apocalyptic tendencies at a specific point in history. Was the apocalyptic layer early and foundational or a later addition to the tradition? The Gospel of Thomas, another collection of Jesus sayings, "totally rejects apocalyptic questions and categories" (104), thereby standing in stark contrast to the earliest recollections of Jesus's apocalyptic representation promoted by both Paul and the Synoptics. Thomas also heightens the stakes on how we categorize Q. Does Thomas stand alone as an anomaly that has no features of apocalyptic discourse, or does Thomas fall within a minority category of texts that recollect a Jesus with no apocalyptic characteristics (with Q1 and perhaps the Epistle of James)? The Gospel of John, according to Carey, offers a unique "distinctiveness from the Synoptic tradition, [but] John affirms quite a few of the distinctively apocalyptic motifs we find in the other canonical Gospels" (102). A very instructive comparison between the outstanding features of John and the Synoptics is included (see 109–10). The chapter concludes with an insightful section entitled "What About Jesus?" Here Carey notes the saturation of apocalyptic discourse in the New Testament according to his proposed schema. He also recognizes that a majority of "scholars, though clearly not all, see Jesus as an apocalyptic figure" (111). He thus concludes, "If it [i.e., the narrative arc of an apocalyptic Jesus] is inaccurate, we know very little about Jesus. If it is accurate, we know quite a bit" (111.) If I read Carey correctly, he situates himself in the latter camp.

Chapter 6 is titled "The Big Show: Revelation." The book of Revelation stands alone as the only literary apocalypse in the New Testament. Here Carey's task is not to argue for the validity of Revelation as an apocalyptic discourse (we assume that all literary apocalypses are apocalyptic discourses but not all apocalyptic discourses are literary apocalypses); rather, the reader is subtly coaxed to parse Revelation's ongoing influence on our apocalyptically saturated (contemporary) world (114). The remainder of the chapter reflects on long-standing conversations about Revelation's writing circumstance, aims, and eclectic cast of characters.

The epilogue (ch. 7) restates many of the main points identified above (the ubiquity of apocalyptic discourse in the New Testament, the Jewish literary background of apocalyptic discourse, the rhetorical flexibility of apocalyptic discourse, the connection of apocalyptic discourse and politics) and prompts the reader to consider the relevance of the study of apocalyptic in the modern world. Carey also attends to the practical nature of apocalyptic discourse when he notes, "one remarkable quality literature is that while it seems otherworldly, it often inspires daily action on a very practical basis" (151).

The value of Carey's work cannot be overstated. It is an invitation to transgress former categories of apocalyptic literature that have for too long have been assessed in a cultural vacuum apart from authorial *Sitz im Leben*. (Carey makes a brief attempt at illuminating this omission in his consideration of the two Jewish revolts as catalysts for apocalyptic writing. See, e.g., the box entry on 8.) Perhaps the subversive nature of apocalyptic worldviews is too critical of empire, both ancient and modern, to render this an easy task for the contemporary biblical guild. In *Apocalyptic Literature in the New Testament*, Carey unshackles the breadth of apocalyptic discourse(s) embedded in the Christian canon. The New

Testament, Carey contests, is saturated with apocalyptic overtures, and Carey illuminates it. Thus his invitation to think outside the literary box coaxes moderns to recognize the omnipresence of apocalyptic discourse in the New Testament *and* our world today. No longer can we hold Revelation solely culpable as the lone apocalyptic influence on modern society. Apocalyptic residue is too ubiquitous, too embedded in our culture, to limit our indictment to the New Testament's only literary apocalypse. With the introduction of the concept of apocalyptic discourse, Carey is able to demonstrate that the roots of our Christian apocalyptic heritage are deeper than previously assessed. This observation, in my estimation, is the greatest contribution of Carey's project.

My primary critique is that I find some level of "serious definition or analytical precision" important for guiding this project, which Carey rejects early on (7). It may be that at this early stage of deconstruction of the category *literary apocalypse* a certain level of nomenclature fluidity was essential, but I urge Carey and subsequent scholars taking up this project to provide definitive terminological categories from which to contrast older forms.

Information boxes found in each chapter and brief glossary are informative. Even though presented as a starting point for New Testament studies, I recommended this volume for undergraduates and graduate students of Bible, seminary students, pastors, and religious educators. Seasoned scholars are also likely to benefit from the provocative thesis Carey presents.

JESUS

Jesus Monotheism, Volume 1: Christological Origins: The Emerging Consensus and Beyond, by Crispin Fletcher-Louis. Eugene, OR: Cascade, 2015. Pp. xx + 368. Paper. $43.00. ISBN 9781620328897.

Larry W. Hurtado, University of Edinburgh

This book is the first of a promised four-volume project in which Fletcher-Louis will lay out his own "new paradigm" of why and how what he calls "Christological monotheism" arose, that is, how Jesus came to be treated as sharing in divine status and honor with God. In this initial volume, Fletcher-Louis's two aims are to review "the convincing arguments … for an early high Christology," which he calls the "emerging consensus," and also to explore what he regards as weaknesses in that work thus far that make it "unable to account satisfactorily for some of the hard data of the primary sources" and that justify "a new approach" (xv).

In roughly the first half of the present volume Fletcher-Louis describes appreciatively, and defends against key detractors, the emerging consensus (that treatment of Jesus as sharing in divine honor erupted quickly and early and initially among circles of Jewish Jesus-followers) and also lodges his own critique as grounds for the new and programmatic proposal that he will explicate more fully in the future volumes. Chapter 1 is an affirming introduction to the "New

Emerging Consensus," focusing on the contributions of Martin Hengel, Richard Bauckham, and myself. Fletcher-Louis includes in this chapter an initial discussion of 1 Cor 8:3–6, which he regards as "an interpretative key to all his [Paul's] other Christological statements" (8). He specifically supports the view that this text reflects a "reworking of the Shema in which the identity of the one God is split in two," with the result that "*Yhwh* is now somehow identified with Jesus Christ" (10). He also supports the emphasis on the significance of the devotional practices reflected already in Paul's letters in which Jesus is reverenced in ways that link him uniquely with God, but Fletcher-Louis really gives primacy to christological *beliefs*. Indeed, he sees Paul's letters as reflecting the view that "the one unique God—*Yhwh-Kyrios*—had climactically, at the end of Israel's history, appeared in fully human and a highly personal form" (22). (The phrase "the end of Israel's history" raises questions that I cannot pursue here.)

Chapter 2 treats "Unconvincing Objections" to the emerging consensus and offers Fletcher-Louis's own "fresh support" for it against critics such as Maurice Casey, Adela Yarbro Collins, James McGrath, and James Dunn. In this chapter Fletcher-Louis returns to 1 Cor 8:3–6 for further attention, designating the text as "historically and theologically load-bearing for key parts of the new paradigm" that he will lay out in subsequent volumes. Here he introduces and applies what he calls "numerical criticism" (39–49), observing that the twenty-six Greek words in the Nestle-Aland text of 1 Cor 8:6 (minus the initial ἀλλ') correspond to the numerical value of the Hebrew יהוה. Dismissing any suggestion of coincidence, he contends that this further confirms that the two-part confessional statement places Jesus "inside a split Shema" (47) and also that this numerical correspondence suggests a "Greek-and-Hebrew-speaking" provenance of the confession that now constitutes 1 Cor. 8:6 confirming that this dyadic belief-pattern is very early. It remains to be seen whether others will be as taken with this argument as he obviously is.

Then, in chapters 3–4 Fletcher-Louis probes further what he regards as questions not satisfactorily dealt with in the emerging consensus in order to "prepare the ground for [his] new paradigm." Again he concentrates on the work of Bauckham and myself. It would be inappropriate and tedious here to respond to the various individual points where I find Fletcher-Louis's critical characterization of my views unsatisfactory. Instead, I will engage briefly one major emphasis.

The main direction of his sustained critique of my work is expressed in his allegation of "a gaping incarnation-shaped hole at the center of the Hurtado model of Christological origins" (83). Specifically, I have proposed that treatment of Jesus as sharing divine glory and as worthy of worship was initiated in the post-Easter experiences of the risen and exalted Jesus and that beliefs about Jesus's *preexistence* then quickly emerged on the same basis. Fletcher-Louis contends, by contrast, that prior beliefs about Jesus's preexistence and incarnation stemming from the historical Jesus were the bases for worshiping him (e.g., 78–79). We will have to wait for his full defense of his claims about the historical Jesus, but I make one observation at this point.

It seems to me that in his handling of various New Testament texts Fletcher-Louis confuses the *contents* of the praise/worship of Jesus with the *historical bases/impetus* for it. I heartily agree that there are New Testament texts that laud Jesus as preexistent and "incarnate" (e.g., Phil 2:6–8; John 1:1–18; Col 1:15–16), but this *content* of the praise given does not constitute the historical *basis* for the praise. Instead, I remain persuaded that New Testament texts typically posit God's exaltation of Jesus as the decisive basis and justification for devotion to him as vindicated "Son" and designated *Kyrios* (e.g., Phil 2:9–11; Rom 1:3–4). That is, I see these various texts as basing the reverence of Jesus on the actions (and will) of God, the convictions about God's actions conveyed via powerful religious experiences. Fletcher-Louis, however, seems to demur from this and prefers to take Jesus's forthright self-declarations of preexistence in the Gospel of John as direct indications of the kind of statements that the historical Jesus made about himself, a stance that many will likely judge as requiring considerably more justification.

In his discussion of Bauckham's views in chapter 3, Fletcher-Louis agrees that Jesus can be thought of as included with "the divine identity." But his critique of Bauckham (88–101) focuses on his alleged failure to do justice to the *distinct* identify of Jesus as divine *Son,* in relation to God. Specifically, Fletcher-Louis emphasizes that Jesus is also tightly identified with those who are redeemed through him and that Jesus's identify as a *human* included within "the divine identity" is crucial, prefiguring "some sense of *theosis*" that is to be involved in the ultimate salvation of the redeemed (92).

In the remainder of chapter 3 (101–27) Fletcher-Louis focuses on the *son of man* expression, laying out a case for the view that it is a title that "ascribes to Jesus a transcendence well beyond … an ordinary human messiah." Indeed, Fletcher-Louis sees the expression as "the title that defines the *shape* of the Christology of the Gospels" (104). In making his case, he again offers a critique of my view that the expression does not function as a title in the gospels. He grants that the expression was not a *title* but urges that it had *titular force* and that there was a son of man *figure* well-known in ancient Jewish hopes. Again, there are a few interesting points at which I could offer some correction or counterargument, but I should not do so here. Perhaps, however, one protest. Contra his assumption, my view that the messianic figure of the Similitudes of Enoch is not the crucial datum for the use of the expression "son of man" in the gospels does not arise from a lack of attention to the Similitudes but from a judgment about what that material tells us, based precisely on careful consideration of the texts in question.

In chapter 4 Fletcher-Louis continues his critique of the emerging consensus, contending that it fails to account adequately for the origins of "christological monotheism." First, granting that "the complete pattern" of Jesus-devotion reflected in the New Testament is "unique and unprecedented," he nevertheless posits that there is "far more continuity" with "Jewish and biblical theological categories and devotional patterns" than Bauckham and I, for example, recognize. He accuses us of "idiosyncratic" handling of relevant evidence and thinks that I demand too much of the pre-Christian Jewish material, thereby failing to see "that there are precedents here and there to parts, if not the whole" of Jesus-devotion (131). I find this just a bit puzzling, however, given that my 1988 book, *One God, One Lord: Early Christian Devotion and Ancient Jewish Monotheism* (3rd ed., 2015) specifically urged that Second Temple Jewish tradition provided key conceptual resources drawn on and adapted creatively by earliest believers in accommodating the exalted Jesus next to God.

As another argument against the view that early Jesus-devotion was a remarkable innovation, Fletcher-Louis also alleges a lack of Jewish opposition to Jesus-devotion (on this topic, curiously, agreeing with Casey, Dunn, and McGrath). I can only say here that his discussion of this matter seems to me a resolute minimizing of the argumentation and analysis that I have offered. He then lodges a critique of the view (of Bauckham and others) that Ps 110:1 was crucial in generating the high view of Jesus reflected already in Paul, Fletcher-Louis judging that the text instead played only an "incidental" role (141). Thereafter, he briefly posits inadequacies in attempts to account for the origin of the belief about Jesus's role as agent of creation (141–47). The remainder of the chapter is given to further critique of my proposals about the origin of "the Christ cult" (147–57), focusing particularly on my suggestion that powerful revelatory experiences were crucial. I can only say that, whereas he finds my proposals unconvincing, I find his critique ineffective.

In an appendix to chapter 3, Fletcher-Louis turns from historical analysis to "theological problems posed by the emerging consensus," again focusing particularly on my work. I must lodge surprise at his claim that "an implicit purpose" of my work "seems to be to provide a secure historical basis for an orthodox Christology" (159). Though some have made use of my work to that end, others of such an orientation (including Fletcher-Louis!) find it uncomfortable theologically. Indeed, in this appendix Fletcher-Louis actually characterizes my proposals as incompatible with what he sees as a "healthy" theological stance and as effectively portraying Jesus-devotion as "idolatrous." In any case, as stated rather clearly in my publications over the years, my own aim has been simply to offer a historical analysis, to be assessed as such, irrespective of readers' religious stance.

In the remaining chapters Fletcher-Louis discusses what he regards as the key Jewish traditions and texts that provide some "categories and expectations" that prepared for the emergence of Jesus-devotion. Though he grants that none "provides a straightforward line" of connection or direct parallel to Jesus-devotion and that earliest christological convictions "cannot be explained as a simple outgrowth of pre-Christian Jewish traditions," he contends, nevertheless, that there are important points of continuity.

First, in chapter 5 he urges that the Similitudes of Enoch and "related texts" reflect "a pre-Christian Son of Man expectation that prepared the way for a high and fully divine Christology" (172). Indeed, Fletcher-Louis characterizes the Similitudes as providing "a golden key to unlock the puzzle that is the origins of Christ devotion" (180) and argues that "it was specifically *as the Son of Man* that Jesus was first identified with *Yhwh-Kyrios*" (188). Moreover, Fletcher-Louis urges that "the historical Jesus claimed he was 'the Son of Man' ... now attested in the *Similitudes* and *4 Ezra*" and that in doing so "he also claimed an identification with *Yhwh-Kyrios*." Fletcher-Louis further claims that Paul and other early believers took "that *Yhwh-Kyrios*-Son of Man Christology for granted" and "worshipped Jesus precisely because they came to believe that Jesus was, indeed, the Son of Man figure of contemporary Jewish hope" (188–89).

Then, in chapter 6 Fletcher-Louis turns to consider proposals about the relevance of messianism and ruler cult, with particular attention to William Horbury's proposals. After repeatedly (and misleadingly) alleging that "the emerging consensus" presumes "a Palestinian Jewish context hermetically sealed off" from the wider Roman-era religious environment (206, 207, 210), he then considers Horbury's arguments that Greco-Roman ruler-cult influences had effects upon Second Temple Judaism that "prepared the way for the worship of Jesus as Israel's messiah" (207). Fletcher-Louis affirms much of Horbury's case as comprising "a small, but vital, contribution" to his own "new paradigm" (213). Then, however, he lodges some criticisms, the main drift of which is to question the particular significance of *royal/ruler-cult* influences, Fletcher-Louis urging in a final large section of the chapter (219–49), instead, that Jewish priestly traditions are more relevant.

Chapter 7 lays out the case for the importance of traditions of "a 'divine' and glorious Adam" as recipient of worship. Fletcher-Louis here invokes various texts from Qumran, the Life of Adam and Eve (to which he devotes extended treatment, 253–85), and Daniel to contend that the worship of Adam was "theologically unproblematic for biblically faithful Jews" (290). Indeed, in Fletcher-Louis's view, earliest worship of Jesus was predicated on seeing him as "a true Adam who recapitulated humanity's pre-fall identity" (255). That is, Fletcher-Louis urges that the worship of Jesus had its basis in a putative tradition of the worship of the "prelapsarian" Adam. Nevertheless, he grants that the various texts and traditions surveyed in this and preceding chapters "*do not in themselves satisfactorily explain either the origin or the shape of the distinctive 'Christological monotheism*'" attested in the New Testament (292, emphasis original; similarly 294).

A final appendix addresses "the theological issues" raised in the preceding chapters, particularly focusing on questions about the distinction between God and created reality. The main dialogue partner in this material is Bauckham (esp. 305–9). In the final pages Fletcher-Louis sketches "a new model of 'exclusive inclusive monotheism'" in which we probably glimpse the shape of the larger theological standpoint from which Fletcher-Louis works. In particular, he urges that from Genesis onward there is the notion that the one God was both transcendent and also "would take *on* and take *up* materiality—even into his own life" (315).

This book reflects impressive acquaintance with a large body of primary data and a wide swath of scholarly literature and prolonged and energetic engagement with the issues discussed. With only occasional lapses, his engagement with the scholarly work of others (especially those whom he credits with shaping the

emerging consensus) combines an irenic and careful description with his criticisms. The book is also the first installment on a remarkable big-idea project. This
book deserves (and will require) careful study and will surely create interest in
the projected volumes in which Fletcher-Louis will explicate fully his own "new
paradigm" of how the remarkable devotion to Jesus reflected in the New Testament first emerged.

The Jesus Movement and Its Expansion: Meaning and Mission, by Sean Freyne.
Grand Rapids: Eerdmans, 2014. Pp. xii + 383. Paper. $35.00. ISBN 9780802867865.

Richard Horsley, University of Massachusetts Boston

I was deeply saddened to learn of the death, in 2013, of long-time colleague
and dear friend Sean Freyne. Specially poignant are the memories of intense
discussions and good fun we enjoyed as the two principal *Galilaioi* among the
assembled colleagues at several conferences. This book, completed shortly before
his death, is the fruit of his lifelong study of Galilee and the gospels and their
relationship.

In this book Freyne expanded his scope into exploration of some of the
branches of "early Christianity." In chapters 5–7 he focuses on the interrelated
branches of "the Jesus movement" based in Jerusalem and Syria/Galilee, as discerned in the book of Acts, the "sayings sources," and the Gospels of Mark and
Matthew. He devotes chapters 1–3 to the historical matrix of the movement(s),
sketches the "public ministry" of Jesus in which the movement(s) were generated
(ch. 4), then attends to topics in "Christianity" of the second century in chapter 8.

Like most other interpreters of the gospels and Jesus, Freyne has remained
faithful to the fundamental assumptions, conceptual apparatus, and interpretive
schemes long standard in the field of New Testament studies as a branch of theology. Most fundamental in the field, and evident at many points in this book, is
the broad theological scheme of Christian origins and its component constructs:
originating from Judaism, which was a more parochial religion, Christianity
developed into a more universal religion as it expanded among the gentiles in the
Hellenistic world. In another example, Freyne still applies the synthetic scholarly
concept of "the Zealots" as a long-standing party of armed revolt (59, 69–71, 80,
118, 184, 187, 288, 290), while also citing those of us who have deconstructed it.

Freyne's principal concern (1, restated 242–43, 273–74), is to counter the
scholarly construction of a "Galilean Christianity" that he sees resulting from
the recent scholarly tendency to view Roman Galilee as culturally different
from Jerusalem/ Judea. He is thus further stirring up a conceptual muddle that
is fundamental in the field of New Testament studies in general and in study of
Jesus and the gospels in particular. Some have attempted to reduce the density
and distortion of this muddle, for example, by focusing on "formative Judaism"
as it developed toward what became rabbinic Judaism in late antiquity. Others
have closely examined the use of terms such as *ioudaios/oi* in our sources, which

has made it possible to discuss people in more precise historical terms of location, position, and social identity. As Freyne himself discussed some time ago, the Judean historian Josephus is relatively consistent in distinguishing *ioudaioi*, *samaritai*, and *galilaioi* by geographical area of residence or origin, all descended from and sharing Israelite heritage.

Freyne, however, not only sticks with the standard synthetic concepts of "Judaism" and "the Jews" but insists that "the vast majority of the population of Roman Galilee" were ethnically and religiously Judeans (273). His interpretation of texts and history in the rest of the book depends on this claim. Given the extremely limited and fragmentary information available, however, it is difficult to discern who the people were that our sources (such as Josephus and the Gospel of John) refer to as "Galileans." Judea, Samaria, and Galilee had been separate for centuries, under different client rulers or a separate branch of imperial administration. The Hasmonean high priests conquered Idumea, then Samaria, destroying its temple, and finally took over Galilee as well in 104 BCE (Josephus, *Ant.* 13.254–258, 318–319). Freyne speculates that immigrant Judeans then colonized a relatively depopulated Galilee, inspired by the belief that Galilee and the lands beyond were part of their inheritance prophesied in Ezekiel's vision of an ideal temple and its lands and a few other passages in the Hebrew Bible.

Freyne offers mainly archaeological support for his argument (18–20). While admitting that surface surveys can be unreliable, he appeals to "identity markers" such as stone vessels and stepped pools found in archaeological digs that suggest that the "immigrants" in various sites shared certain features of culture with Judeans. Critical archaeologists point out that, while such material items may indicate a common cultural heritage, they cannot indicate loyalty to Jerusalem or devotion to the temple (something Freyne seems to forget later, 273). It is surely significant, however, that these "identity markers" were found mainly at what were Hasmonean and Herodian fortresses and/or administrative sites, such as Sepphoris, Yodfat, and Gamla. In the wake of the Hasmonean takeover and continuing Jerusalem rule under Herod, there were surely Judeans in Galilee, at least in those fortress and administrative sites. But where is the evidence for a flood of Judeans migrating north? Whatever their provenance, there was a sharp division between the villagers whom Josephus calls "the Galileans" (Freyne's immigrant Judeans) and the Herodian fortress towns and later (pro-Roman) cities such as Sepphoris that they attacked in 4 BCE and again in 66 CE.

Later Freyne claims that the immigrant Judeans who became "the older peasant residents of the region" resisted "Herodian values" by drawing on "the older Hasmonean values of their right to the ancestral land" (which they had colonized only a few generations before) "while supporting the temple in Jerusalem as the central symbol of their belief system" (242). He asserts, further, that "the holy city" had a "central role in all branches of Jewish restoration hopes" (242). I should point out, however, that "apocalyptic" texts prior to the time of Jesus, such as Dan 7, 10–12 and the Animal Vision in 1 En. 85–90 do not include the temple in their visions of renewal.

Freyne's emphasis throughout chapters 1 and 2 on the Hellenistic and Roman "presence" is on the cultural dimension of the conflict. As is increasingly recognized, however, culture/religion was inseparable from political-economy in antiquity. The conflict in which Jesus's mission and the Jesus movement(s) emerged (along with the many other movements of resistance and renewal) really begins to become clear in Freyne's historical survey of the structural polit-ical-economic(-religious/cultural) conflict in chapter 3. Unusual for biblical and classical scholars, Freyne recognizes that the economy was political-economy and that in an agrarian society access to and control over land and its produce was key (94, 120; although he sometimes slips back into the old assumption that the Hellenistic-Roman economy was commercial).

What leads Freyne to discern the structural political-economic conflict are some poignant questions. What was the source of the wealth piled up in the temple that the Hellenizing high priests Jason and Menelaus used to maneuver for position with the Seleucid imperial regime? "How much of it was the fruit of Judean peasant labor?" (97). How could the Hasmoneans hire the mercenary troops they used in their conquests? What was the source of Herod's amazing wealth with which he funded his massive building programs, his lavish court, and his extraordinary benefactions to the imperial family and cities of the empire (111–19)? Freyne recognizes candidly that the only way the Hasmoneans could have hired all those mercenaries was to combine their income from the temple with the state taxes they commanded as "kings" and the revenues from the royal lands of previous (Hellenistic) rulers that they took over (100–101). Herod took over all these revenues and more. Freyne recognizes that the rulers' tax base was mainly the peasant small-holders and, in passing comments, that they were operating at subsistence level (102–3), given the "drain" on their produce for taxes, tithes, and offerings (114). The point is that the same fundamental overall political-economic(-religious) structure prevailed in Palestine, whether headed and enforced militarily by the Seleucids, the Hasmoneans, or the Romans. The imperial regimes ruled through client rulers, whether the high priests of the tem-ple-state or Herodian kings. It is curious that Freyne does not include a section on Herod's expanded high-priestly aristocracy who became the Roman client rulers in the first century CE and collected the tribute as well as their own temple and priestly revenues (cf. 70, 76).

A more comprehensive understanding of the overt conflicts that erupted in Roman Palestine could emerge by combining Freyne's discussion of the cultural dimension with his discussion of the political-economic dimension of the divide between the people and their rulers. The protests and movements and revolts of Judeans *in Judea* from Herod's death to the great revolt (in Josephus's accounts) were not just against the Romans but also against the high-priestly heads of the temple who were representatives of Roman rule. This was more than simply a clash between "opposing worldviews" (54). The Roman demand of tribute, its col-lection by the high priests, and the resistance to its payment is a vivid illustration of the fundamental conflict. The second commandment was far more than just

the root of a "strong aniconic tradition" (54). It was also a prohibition of the concrete political-economic "bowing down and serving other gods" with tribute, and
that is what motivated the resistance to paying the tribute to Caesar as lord and
master by the "fourth philosophy," according to both of Josephus's accounts (*Ant.*
18.23–24; *War* 2.118). After sixty years of high-priestly rule, the first actions of the
rebels in 66 CE was to burn the archival records of debts and to attack the man-
sion of the high priest Ananias (*War* 2.426–427).

The same fundamental political-economic and cultural divide continued
under Antipas and his successors in Galilee. It is good to find my fellow *Galilaios*
recognizing how disruptive the cities built by Antipas were for Galilean villagers
(64–66, 126–27). His summary of some recent constructions of Galilean society
and economy, however, is not very clear or accurate. He does not appreciate the
difference between others' construction and application of a model of social stratification (*Lenski,* not "Lynski") and my analysis of the political-economic relation
between the rulers and the villagers based on evidence from Josephus, rabbinic
traditions, and archaeological explorations. Yet Freyne makes several sound critical judgments (that largely confirm points in my books on Galilee of twenty years
ago). In contrast with previously standard assumptions based on Jesus's parables
and recent suggestions by some archaeologists, land tenure in much of Galilee
consisted of small plots farmed by local villagers (121). While many of those
addressed in Jesus's teachings appear to have been impoverished, Galileans do not
appear to be landless in Josephus's histories or in the gospel narratives. The extent
of "urbanization" in Galilee at the time of Jesus was overblown by archaeologists
in the 1980s. Freyne is appropriately skeptical of archaeologists who argue that
villagers derived mutual benefit from "exchange" with the cities (129). "The use
of archaeological evidence alone to determine the economic realities cannot be
decisive" (131).

Chapter 4 ("not substantially different from *Jesus, a Jewish Galilean,* 2005")
offers a discussion of Jesus's "public ministry" that is more balanced than many
recent Jesus books. Freyne takes Jesus's healing, especially his exorcisms (150–56),
as seriously as his teaching (156–64). Absent a critical discussion of the gospel
sources, however, his own agenda seems to determine his choice of sayings and
stories for discussion. It is difficult to know, for example, what to make of his contention that Jesus may have been pursuing a vision of the restoration of "greater
Israel" beyond Galilee to the north (140–44) that he bases on statements in Mark
about Jesus's travel.

In treatment of Jesus's teaching, Freyne opposes the dichotomy of apocalyptic
and wisdom as different worldviews (prominent in North American Q scholarship and liberals' interpretation of Jesus), joining those of us who have been
arguing against it for twenty years. Like most Jesus interpreters, however, Freyne
still assumes the dominance of "the apocalyptic worldview" among Judeans in
Palestinine (151, 165–76). The modern scholarly construction of this supposedly
widespread "end-time expectation" (the "apocalyptic scenario") became standardized over a century ago. Freyne follows the neo-Schweitzerian revival of the view

that Jesus not only shared this scenario but also had a sense of extreme urgency about his own central role in it (167–68; like Schweitzer, focusing on Matt 10:23 as the key text).

In the concluding section of the chapter, Freyne reaches a conclusion very different from most recent interpretations of Jesus (and similar to what I have been arguing for thirty years): that Jesus was leading a movement of the renewal of Israel in the villages of Galilee opposed to the ruling house of the Jerusalem temple (176–83). He focuses in particular on Jesus's prophetic lamentation over the imminent destruction of the Jerusalem ruling house (Q/Luke 13:34–35) and his prophetic demonstration of God's judgment of the Jerusalem temple (Mark 11:15–18).

While Freyne recognizes that the narrative in Acts is idealized and at points misleading (187–90), he argues in chapter 5 that the community formed early in Jerusalem became the center of the Jesus movement. To explain why, he reverts to a broad (biblical-) theological synthesis of the resurrection faith, Jesus as the Davidic Messiah, and "the Zion tradition" as the explanation for the Jesus loyalists locating in Jerusalem (201–5). This composite picture includes the standard older reading that the Jesus loyalists were "attending (the) temple." Acts, rather, portrays Peter and other leaders as using the public area of the temple complex to recruit people into the movement (2:46; 3:11–26; 4:1–4; 5:12–16, 25–26). They consistently challenge the Jerusalem priestly rulers, who have them arrested, in a conflict that continued for decades, through the execution of James the brother of Jesus by the high priest Ananus (*Ant.* 20.200). It seems highly doubtful that the Jerusalem community of the Jesus movement was loyal to the temple.

At the beginning of chapters 6 and 7 Freyne repeats his concern to counter the construction of "Galilean culture" and "Galilean Christianity" as different from Jerusalem/Judean religion and the Jesus movement located in Jerusalem, insisting again that the inhabitants of Galilee were immigrant Judeans and loyal to the Jerusalem temple. He focuses his discussion of gospel texts whose origin has been located in Galilee or Syria on three key (theologically derived) issues that he brings to the texts.

On the inclusion of "the gentiles," he recognizes that the sayings source Q, focused on the renewal of Israel, gives no indication of this (264–66). He claims that a "universal mission" to gentiles must be inferred from the Markan narrative as a whole (291–94), perhaps realizing that Mark, focused as it (also) is on the renewal of Israel, includes no clear indications of any "gentile mission," as some recent studies have pointed out. He argues that Jesus's charge to "make disciples of all peoples" at the end of Matthew is a "universal mission," in the gospel that represents a movement that still identifies itself as a branch (fulfilment) of Israel (306–10).

To ask about "relations with parent Judaism" is a Christian theological issue that seems inappropriate to any of these texts that lack the concept. Like Q, Mark and Matthew are about Jesus generating the renewal of Israel in the villages of Galilee and nearby areas and then confronting and prophesying judgment against the high-priestly rulers and their representatives in Jerusalem. Having discussed the lament over (God's) impending destruction of the Jerusalem ruling house (Q/Lk 13:34–35) as attesting Jesus's own prophetic pronouncement (in ch. 4), Freyne attempts to soften its impact at the Q level (259–60). He similarly attempts to soften the sharp judgment against the Pharisees and scribes (Q/Luke 11:39–52; 261–64). What he, with most others, sees as the deepest division between Jesus and "the Jewish establishment" in Mark, over the torah, he explains as resulting from the scribes and Pharisees being the only guardians of "the symbol system" that survived the Roman destruction of Jerusalem (289–91). Freyne follows the tendency among interpreters to take the woes against the scribes and Pharisees in Matthew as rejection of the alternative leadership of a rival branch of post-70 "Judaism" (300–305).

What about the Jerusalem temple, to which Freyne insists the immigrant Judeans in Galilee were loyal? He suggests that Mark paints an almost nostalgic picture of Jesus walking and teaching in the temple courts (288), but this ignores the prophetic demonstration against the temple that he cited as a source for a key actions of Jesus in chapter 4. He does take note of the rending of the temple veil, a "radical symbolic statement" (289), but then takes no notice of the prophecies against the temple and high priests in Matthew. By the end of chapters 6 and 7 it is unclear how Freyne's survey of these gospel texts that originated in Galilee or Syria mitigate his principal concern, how the restoration hopes behind these movements included "a central role" for the holy city. Q, Mark, and Matthew all have Jesus engaged in the renewal of Israel, mainly in Galilean villages. These texts do not yet know any "split" between their respective Jesus movements and Israel. But all of them include prophetic pronouncements of God's condemnation of the temple and its Roman-appointed high-priestly heads.

In chapter 4 Freyne offers some analysis of the structural political-economic division in Hasmonean and Roman Judea and Galilee that is unusual in the field. He is also skeptical of constructions by archaeologists who seem to ignore textual evidence of this division. When he comes to the gospels and Acts as sources for the Jesus movement, however, he seems to forget the results of his political-economic analysis and reverts to standard theological concepts and schemes in the New Testament field, as he argues his own earlier construction of a Galilee colonized by Judeans who were loyal to the Jerusalem temple.

The Nonviolent Messiah: Jesus, Q, and the Enochic Tradition, by Simon J. Joseph. Minneapolis: Fortress, 2014. Pp. xvi + 352. Paper. $39.00. ISBN 9781451472196.

Blake A. Jurgens, Florida State University

As the title suggests, this monograph authored by Simon Joseph proposes that the messianic identity of the historical Jesus was characterized by a commitment to nonviolence. Joseph sees the earliest elements of Jesus's message standing in stark tension to the prevailing traditions of other Second Temple messianic figures typified as political or military leaders ushering in a period of violent eschatological judgment. In this manner, *The Nonviolent Messiah* attempts to fill a perceived neglect in Jesus scholarship regarding the importance of Jesus's apparent emphasis upon nonviolence in Q for a more acute understanding of the historical Jesus and his relationship to the messianic views of his time.

This volume is divided into three portions. Part 1 (chs. 1–4) attempts to lay the initial groundwork for Joseph's presentation of Jesus as a nonviolent messiah. Chapter 1 offers a short yet detailed survey of scholarly perspectives on Jesus's place within first-century Judaism as well as Q and its place in the study of the historical Jesus. For Joseph, Q is "an ethnically and geographically Palestinian Judean text" (15) that offers a composite collection of information regarding the earliest Jesus traditions. In chapter 2 Joseph addresses certain episodes in Q that potentially portray Jesus as violent. After defining what he means by *nonviolence*, Joseph explores three episodes: Jesus's claim not to bring peace but a sword (Matt 10:34); the "give to Caesar what is Caesar's" dialogue (Mark 12:13–18 // Matt 22:15–22 // Luke 20:20–26); and Jesus's supposed role as revolutionary, including the temple incident, and his association with Zealots. While these episodes at first glance suggest that Jesus advocated political or military violence, Joseph states that none can be held as "unambiguous evidence" positively associating Jesus with violence toward humans (or animals) (38). Joseph then proceeds to criticize the inability of past scholarship sufficiently to integrate nonviolence into their studies of the historical Jesus, asserting that Jesus's opposition to violence should function as a "criterion of authenticity" and "a key to authenticating Jesus traditions" (50). Concluding this section, chapters 3 and 4 respectively explore divine violence in biblical literature and seek to navigate what Joseph perceives as a fairly tenuous relationship between the divine violence of the Old Testament and Jesus's own stance toward violence.

Part II (chs. 5–9) attempts to locate more precisely the nonviolent messianic identity of Jesus within messianic traditions extant during the first century CE. After expressly noting the complexity of messianic roles and functions in historical and literary traditions, chapter 5 assesses the terms *māšîaḥ/Christos* and their conceptual fluidity, ultimately concluding that many politico-military elements of Davidic messianic expectations were unfulfilled in Jesus despite his crucifixion as a political messiah. Having acknowledged this dissonance, chapter 6 argues that Jesus's actions and message in Q subvert many of these traditional messianic politico-military claims, thereby constructing Jesus as a much different sort of messiah (see 117, 123). This does not mean, however, that Q contains a monolithic, nonviolent portrait of Jesus. This becomes most clear in chapter 7, where Joseph contends that the presentation of the Son of Man found in Q and its overtones of hostility and apocalyptic judgment reflect a later shift among the Q community, who, having experienced perceived rejection and opposition, utilized "rhetorical violence" (not "*physical* violence") in order to criticize and condemn their opponents (141–42). It follows, therefore, that Joseph sees Q as consisting of two traditional strands: one that contains a nonviolent Jesus advocating the way of the kingdom and another that portrays Jesus as an eschatological heavenly judge (144).

Chapters 8 and 9 conclude part 2 and endeavor to contextualize Jesus's messianic claims in Q in light of Enochic traditions. Chapter 8 analyzes the depiction of the messianic Son of Man in the Book of Parables of 1 Enoch and his role as an apocalyptic judge. Noting how the Parables conflates Davidic messianic tropes with the Son of Man of Dan 7:13 and the Suffering Servant of Isaiah, Joseph views the Parables as the "missing link" to understanding "early Jewish Christology" (160) both in Q and in other sources (e.g., Paul, Matthew), going as far as to claim that Q was influenced by the Parables. Chapter 9 finishes the section by exploring the messianic figure of the white bull in 1 Enoch's Animal Apocalypse. More specifically, Joseph argues that the white bull in 1 En. 90 should be identified as the Adamic messiah who brings the restoration of creation without being a "warrior-king defeating Israel's enemies" (174). Joseph concludes that the Son of Man of the Parables and the Adamic messiah of the Animal Apocalypse represent "the two most relevant messianic models or templates for Jesus research" (xiii).

Lastly, part 3 (ch. 10 and the conclusion) seeks to show how these two strands of Enochic messianism—the restorative Adamic messiah and Son of Man of the Parables—correspond to the two messianic portraits extant in Q and reflect the changing social situation of the Q community integrated with material recording the life and teachings of the historical Jesus (231). Thus Q contains "two different Christological orientations" (225), which, in its final form, concurrently holds Jesus as the "the end-time judge and the transforming Adamic messiah" (226).

As a whole, Joseph's project is without question highly motivated and well-researched, a fact indicated by the over eighty-page bibliography in the back of the volume. Likewise, Joseph consistently provides insightful and helpful summaries of major academic perspectives, making this volume accessible to scholars and theologians whose expertise lies outside the scope of his focus. In addition, Joseph's overall thesis does provide an intriguing and at times compelling argument that ventures upon fairly new territory in the study of the historical Jesus. At a minimum, Joseph's insistence that the nonviolence of Jesus has not received a fair shake in academic dialogue certainly hits the mark and deserves further attention.

This being said, *The Nonviolent Messiah* contains several points worthy of critique. To start, as Joseph himself notes, chapters 6–10 contain various amounts of previously published material. Because of this, at times Joseph neglects openly or lucidly to chart the trajectory of his argument throughout these chapters. For example, chapters 8 and 9 rarely explicitly engage the issue of nonviolence, and while these chapters certainly do contribute to Joseph's overall thesis, some more tangible and concrete connections to his primary argument would have made Joseph's point much clearer. It is also somewhat surprising to note that, despite Joseph's intense focus upon Jesus's messianic identity, texts such as 2 Baruch or Pss. Sol. 17, both of which bear important implications for the discussion of Jewish messianism, are only treated sporadically in footnotes. Relegating these texts to the periphery could simply be the result of Joseph's concentration on the integral and influential role Enochic messianism plays in the composition of Q and the gospels, although this did not hinder Joseph from engaging with other texts, such as the Dead Sea Scrolls, with a fair amount of diligence. One additional issue that is sure to catch the eye of other scholars is Joseph's interpretation of the white bull of 1 En. 90 as Adam. While Adam is certainly a possibility, the symbolic identity of the final white bull in the Animal Apocalypse is fairly vague and could connote Abraham, Jacob, or another figure. While Joseph's equation of the white bull with Adam is not totally farfetched, it would have benefited him to offer a more plausible evidence for the Adamic identification in order to buttress his proposal here, especially considering its pivotal place in Joseph's overall argument.

Finally, in terms of his treatment of nonviolence, additional questions arise when reading this work. First, in portions of his book, Joseph distinguishes between physical violence intended to commit harm and rhetorical violence intended to construct social boundaries as well as to criticize or attack opponents without recourse to physical harm (e.g., 142; see also 72). However, since Joseph is dealing almost exclusively with texts and their language and rhetoric, a question follows: What distinguishes actual and concrete calls to physical violence from the use of violent imagery and symbolic devices as forms of legitimization, delegitimization, or the construction of new social spheres? In turn, if physical violence is the true antithesis of nonviolence, does it follow that other texts that could be said to use rhetorical forms of violence (e.g., the War Scroll, the Epistle of Jude) are nonviolent? Likewise, if a text promotes violence in the form of eschatological divine judgment, but no evidence exists proving that said authors actually engaged in violent acts, can we really call such a text violent if violence is, by definition, causing *physical* harm?

Questions aside, Joseph's volume is a well-thought and perspicacious work that pushes the boundaries on the topic of Jesus's messianic identity while presenting a fairly nuanced approach to some major scholarly discussions in the study of historical Jesus that most certainly will motivate at least some future dialogue.

SYNOPTIC GOSPELS

The Oral Ethos of the Early Church: Speaking, Writing, and the Gospel of Mark, by Joanna Dewey. Biblical Performance Criticism. Eugene, OR: Wipf & Stock, 2013. Pp. xviii + 204. Cloth. $24.00. ISBN 9781606088524.

Werner H. Kelber, Rice University

Joanna Dewey's book is volume 8 of the Biblical Performance Criticism series, and it adds significantly to the growing prestige of the series that studies biblical traditions in the context of heavily oral and marginally literate societies. Ten of its essays appeared between 1989 and 2009, and the last, "Our Text of Mark," is presented here for the first time. All are organized not in the chronological order of their composition/publication but thematically divided into three major parts.

In its initial stage, Christianity was a mixed oral-written media phenomenon where oral recitation predominated and texts were for the most part composed as aids to memorization and performance. Literacy was largely limited to the political elite and its retainers. Given this situation, the New Testament writings embody a rather restricted representation of the total media reality. Historical-critical scholarship that operates on a fundamentally documentary model is for that reason disposed to treat oral tradition and dynamics as an epiphenomenon, to marginalize the speaking majority, and to show partiality toward the relatively few who were literate. This, in a nutshell, is the core of Dewey's thesis.

Part 1, "The Oral-Written Media World," surveys the uses of literacy and oral communication in the first- and second-century Mediterranean culture. Citing William Harris's *Ancient Literacy*, Dewey agrees that literacy was very low across most parts of the ancient world, with the early Christians generally belonging to the "nonliterate" majority of people. Literacy rates were lower among women than among men, but women were more closely associated with the oral practice of storytelling. Textuality was perhaps more central to Jewish culture, but the ability to read the sacred texts was by no means a prerequisite for Jewish identity.

Paul and his communities were "fundamentally dependent on the oral medium and oral authority" (25). Among the gifts of leadership, for example, the apostle does not mention reading and interpretation of Scripture, practices that appear not to have occurred at all. As for the continuation of the Pauline tradition into the second century, documents such as the Acts of the Apostles, the apocryphal Acts of Paul, and the Pastoral Epistles make no reference to Paul's identity as a letter writer and largely ignore his thought. The reason, Dewey argues, is that it was "not the textual Paul of the letters, but the oral Paul of Christian memory" (24) that governed the early tradition.

Part 2, "Oral Patterning in Mark and Implications for Interpretation of Mark," discusses the gospel's oral narrative techniques and performative stance. As Dewey realizes herself, her work reflects a shift from an initial literary approach toward an oral hermeneutics. Following a 1973 article that described the chiastic arrangement of the five controversy stories in Mark 2:1–3:6 as "a tightly constructed literary unit" (59) and Mark as "a writer of considerable literary skill" (62), by 1989 she had come to understand the passage as an instance of Markan ring compositions that operate on acoustic principles and verbal echoes (86–88). Henceforth her interpretation of the gospel steadily moved toward an apprehension of its oral style and performative impact. Disavowing the form-critical model of Mark's compositional history, she makes the case for a coherent oral narrative underlying both Mark and John, citing approvingly Albert Lord's thesis of the gospels as oral traditional literature (162, 179). As for the gospel's narrative plot, Dewey dissociates herself from the widely accepted model of a climactic linear structure and favors "interwoven tapestry" or "fugue" (78), suggesting a succession of anticipations of what is to come and echoes of what has come before, a pattern, she argues, that is suited to assist a listening audience (78–79). Drawing principally on Havelock and Ong, she interprets the gospel as a series of happenings, visually imaginable episodes, and pluralized events, rather than a causally coherent narrative. The gospel "is made up of the many; it does not subordinate the many to the one" (86); it invites participation rather than giving information on Jesus or the Markan community. In a lengthy argument, finally, Dewey challenges some of my core theses developed in *The Oral and the Written Gospel*, among them the role of the disciples, Jesus's family, and the false Christs—Markan characters, she argues, who are presented negatively for their own intrinsic narrative reasons, none of which having anything to do with their function as authorities of oral tradition, as I claimed.

In the concluding part 3, "Wider Implications of the Oral Media World," Dewey integrates feminist scholarship and recent developments in text criticism. What distinguishes the oral medium and oral authority, she writes, is its democratic and egalitarian nature: "Everyone had some access to oral authority, regardless of race, class, or gender" (138). This insight in turn illuminates how far removed ancient writings are from a genuinely democratic communication. Those few who mastered the chirographic medium or had the means to employ scribal experts constituted an initially small and increasingly larger elite of males. Just as in our time those who own and manage the television medium hold power over the rest of us, so did in the ancient world those who had assimilated chirographic technology, or had acquired privileged access to it, command authority over the vast majority of nonliterates (138–40). As may be expected, the products of the chirographic medium came to reflect the interests and mindset of males who exercised control over it. Given this interrelationship of power, media, and gender, the representation of women in early Christian and most other ancient writings was filtered through an androgenic lens, which had the effect of marginalizing, distorting, and suppressing the role and identity of women.

As for text criticism, Dewey draws implications from the recent emphasis on the variability and multiformity in the early Jesus tradition. Focusing again on Mark, she points out that the gospel exhibited the lowest count of variant-free readings among all New Testament texts. This, she explains, was due to the realities of an active oral performance environment. As far as sayings, stories, and gospel were concerned, none of them existed as one archetypal text, and all were heard in a variety of versions. Dewey agrees with my premise "that we should not speak of original Jesus sayings" and adds that "perhaps we should not speak of the original Gospel of Mark, either" (127). To be sure, manuscripts were bound to bring about a measure of stability, yet they were far from being frozen in unalterable fixity. Due to the continuous interface of manuscripts with oral performance, no two manuscripts were ever identical.

Dewey's book makes a convincing case for the urgent relevance of media and performance studies. It succeeds as a reliable guide for those uninformed about oral hermeneutics, and it offers new challenges to those who are already proficient in the oral-scribal-memorial culture of antiquity. The book develops a striking communicative ecosystem made up of living species in which oral-scribal variability—not textual originality—was the rule, knowledge was transmitted less geometrically according to form and more dynamically via the force of voice, repetition was a symptom and not a disease, and media fluency, which had priority over textual fixity, entailed a myriad of interactive dynamics. As Dewey has rightly pointed out, there are a host of substantial agreements between her work and my own as far as the interpretation of Mark, oral epistemology, and media studies generally are concerned, and I am grateful for her thoughtful and empathetic assessment of my work. Three critical observations are intended to foster a continuing discourse.

Dewey perceptively points out that "even for the elite, literacy was not a defining characteristic of what it meant to be a proper human being" (32). All the more reason, therefore, to abstain from the designation of "nonliterates." Historically, the vast majority of ancients were not deficient in communication skills, except when measured by our modern alphabetic and literary competence. People did not lack something that we have but they were proficient in their own ways. There is, second, the exceedingly difficult issue about the relationship between oral tradition and gospel textuality. Principally, Dewey argues for the oral compositional nature of Mark. Hence her affirmation that a coherently developed oral narrative was textualized "in entirely oral form" (43). But elsewhere she appears to be unsure whether Mark was composed orally because "there also seem to be indications of writing" (78), and she concurs with my thesis that "Mark is reshaping the tradition to deal with the Roman-Jewish War and the destruction of the temple" (120). Writing, I have long maintained, makes a difference. Ask any ethnographer who is struggling with the transcription of his or her oral, performative fieldwork onto the linearized, voiceless page. Even Albert Lord had to concede that "it is impossible to believe" that the texts of the *Iliad* and *Odyssey* represent the songs as they were actually performed; "some reliance on writing" must be assumed (*Epic Singers and Oral Tradition*, 1991, 45). A third point concerns the ending of Mark's Gospel. Dewey challenges my reading of the lack of a resurrection appearance story in terms of Jesus's absence. In her view, it is in the immediacy of oral storytelling that "the gospel implicitly exhorts the audience to continue following Jesus" (125). But it is worth noting that in oral tradition texts by themselves do not carry the full meaning. Word-power emerges from the interface of textual performance and the informing but ever-changing context. Mark's ending is bound to be heard differently—in the past as much as in the present. If textual hermeneutics insists on a single reading, the challenge of oral hermeneutics is to remain open to many and various hearings.

Mark 1–8: A Handbook on the Greek Text, by Rodney J. Decker. Baylor Handbook on the Greek New Testament. Waco, TX: Baylor University Press, 2014. Pp. xxxii + 334. Paper. $34.95. ISBN 9781481302388.

J. Andrew Doole, University of Innsbruck

I never had the opportunity to meet Rodney Decker, but I am in no doubt that I would have both liked and respected him. In this, the first of his two handbooks on the Greek text of Mark in the BHGNT series, his personality shines through. One is left with an impression of both what is increasingly rare, erudition, and even rarer, common sense. His analysis of the text of Mark is a fine academic legacy.

The author's introduction stresses the importance and oft-overlooked complexity of Mark. There follows a brief summary of other works on the textual analysis of Mark and Decker's indebtedness to these, especially Gundry, *Mark: A Commentary on His Apology for the Cross* (xxii–xxiii). Reference will be made repeatedly to Gundry throughout the handbook, but one will no doubt notice the difference in both style and goal between the two. Decker's respectful handling of Gundry's commentary should not distract us from the fact that the two often disagree, and where they do (I feel) it is Decker whose view appears the more grounded, sensible, and viable. The introduction proceeds to explain the role of linguistics in the analysis, though Decker will seek to avoid the unnecessary specialist terminology of which he himself is no doubt master: "I am writing primarily for those who are not professional grammarians, linguists or theoreticians." (xxiii) He may, however, have forgotten himself in cases such as τοῦτο in Mark 1:27 (29), where he writes, "Where there are two nominative pronouns with a linking verb, the demonstrative takes precedence over an interrogative pronoun as the subject since the demonstrative refers to a known quantity whereas the interrogative is only anticipatory." One notices immediately at least that he knows what he is talking about.

The introduction concludes with discussion of several important linguistic aspects in Mark: indefinite plurals, the use of καί and δέ, the verbal aspect (and *Aktionsart*), voice, periphrastics (as Aramaisms), prepositions with verbs of movement, and the imperfect tense. Decker shows himself to be both consistent and sensible (and argues quite convincingly that Mark, too, is consistent and sensible, e.g., in his use of the imperfect or narrative present and in his choice of καί or δέ!), and his verdict on each of these aspects is always explained individually when they appear in the text.

The handbook itself follows, with the general format of the rest of the series. A pericope (or less) is given in English translation (Decker's English renditions are helpfully representative of Mark's Greek but nonetheless *good* English, a difficult balance to strike), then a verse-by-verse analysis of the Greek in which verbs and nouns are parsed and issues of meaning and interpretation are addressed (the distance from the translation to the analysis is often a couple of pages, which means one has to make good use of one's opposable thumbs, but this is by design of the series). A fine example are his various translations of καὶ εὐθύς: "then" (23), "now" (23), "so" (31), and, alas, "immediately" (38). Mark's style is closely analyzed for Semitisms (although these are not always cited where they might have been), Septuagintisms, Markan idiolect, and the readings of Matthew and Luke (and John).

The analysis includes many comments on the frequency, rarity, or uniqueness of terms or styles in the gospel or elsewhere in the New Testament, such as "Jesus Christ" (2), the triple negative (117), Jesus "marvels" (147), αὐτός (154), "baptizer" (162), and metaphorical περιτέω (184). Within the text of the analysis, not demarcated, is also a pseudo-excursus on a certain issue has just now cropped up, including κύριος (4–5, 66–67), ὅτι (18), double negatives (41), Jerusalem (72–73), ὅ ἐστιν (78–79), Latinisms (102–3), the name of Herod's dancing girl (158–59), εἰ (210–11), and οὐ μή (227–228). At times the analysis of the elements is succinct: "πᾶσα. Hyperbole" (7), "εἰς τὸ πνεῦμα τὸ ἅγιον. Disadvantage" (86), and the final words of the book "ἐν δυνάμει. Manner" (228). Mark 6:28 is simply parsed without further comment (163). Decker is also keen to stress the need to contain overexcited exegesis, for example, with reference to baptism in water or spirit, "The grammar, however, must not be pressed too far in defense of theological nuances" (11). Likewise with reference to claims of μετά + genitive indicating Jesus's living "peacefully" with the wild animals in the wilderness: "The diversity of explanations in the commentaries suggests that caution is warranted." (15) This sensible reluctance continues throughout.

There are, however, many instances where Decker's suitably creative grammatical analysis of the text leads to wonderful observations and forewarns of any overinterpretation.

> Mark 3:26: "The wording plays off verse 22: rather than Jesus 'having Beelzeboul' (Βεελζεβοὺλ ἔχει), Beelzeboul 'has an end' (τέλος ἔχει)." (84)

> Mark 4:4: "Jesus speaks 'better', more formal Greek than is spoken by those around him and used by Mark in the narrative." (92)

> Mark 4:34: "The combination of κατ' ἰδίαν, the constrastive conjunction δέ, and τοῖς ἰδίοις μαθηταῖς presents a sharp contrast between Jesus' disciples and the crowds." (111)

> Mark 5:15: "Although the lexical form of this word [λεγιών] is feminine, the form in the text is clearly masculine (note the article) ... but speculating on the sexual orientation of a demonic being based on morphology is precarious." (125)

> Mark 6:32: "ἐν τῷ πλοίῳ. Locative. The article is interesting, perhaps suggesting that this was their usual boat." (165)

> Mark 7:32: "μογιλάλος can refer to a speech impediment or the complete inability to speak ('mute'), The comment in verse 35 that after Jesus healed him he was able to speak ὀρθῶς ('correctly, normally') would suggest an impediment rather than muteness." (200)

Decker also refers to an e-mail correspondence with Carl Conrad, who suggests a series of bewildered questions from the disciples that might explain the roughness of Πόθεν τούτους δυνήσεταί τις ὧδε χορτάσαι ἄρτων ἐπ' ἐρημίας; (Mk 8:4): "'From what?' 'These people?' 'Will anyone have the ability?' 'Here?' 'Supply enough loaves to satisfy?' In the wilds?'" (206–7)—further evidence of the down-to-earth yet detailed approach of the book. (I remain unsure as to whether he is writing tongue-in-cheek when he explains, with reference to Louw and Nida's *Greek-English Lexicon*, "In this context βλέπω means 'to be ready to learn about future dangers or needs, with the implication of preparedness to respond appropriately'" [212].)

The works on which he has drawn include secondary literature from 1896 to 2008 (xxiv) and mostly BDAG on lexical issues (e.g., "See BDAG ([page]) and the commentaries for various views" twice on page 79, which disappoints in that no views are mentioned or preference given). BDAG is listed in the author index, and one quickly sees that hardly a page has gone by on which reference has not been made (265–66). Decker also shows a great awareness of the various solutions of modern English translations of Mark.

The book contains a glossary (229–36) that applies to both volumes and provides a helpful list of linguistic terms employed, such as "Apollonius' Canon" (19), "a third-class condition" (82), "a first-class condition" (83), and "attraction" (189). The book concludes with a bibliography, grammar index and author index.

Decker hopes that the handbook will be used. From the outset he writes, "As a grammatical handbook it forms the first step that ought to be taken before anyone sits down at the keyboard to write a commentary or who prepares to expound the message of Mark to a congregation. I suspect that both tasks are too often undertaken without this first step" (xxi). As a reference book it does provide a detailed explanation of the meaning of the Markan text (with generous use of cross-references to avoid needless repetition). It is also to be used in conjunction with the second volume and indeed with others in the BHGNT series. This is raises two issues that apply to the whole project:

Who still reads the New Testament in Greek? It is the express hope of the editor that these handbooks will encourage engagement with the Greek texts of the New Testament. This is surely to be applauded in a new century in which biblical languages are no longer seen as compulsory. It was surely also the hope of Rodney Decker, whose ability and enthusiasm for Greek must inspire others. Let us hope.

Who will buy these books? In comparison to the real "hand"-books of grammatical analysis of the New Testament (e.g., Zerwick/Grosvenor in English, Rienecker in German), we now have much richer and detailed editions (Haubeck and Siebenthal's *Neuer Sprachlicher Schlüssel* in two volumes and the Baylor handbooks as a series). While such growth is naturally beneficial to the study of the texts, it impacts upon both the viability of purchase and ability to carry them about. We may have to rely on libraries to provide us with these reference works, where before we might have decided to shell out for a grammatical "hand"-book on the Greek New Testament.

None of this, however, should detract from the erudite analysis of Mark that Decker has left us. Clichés and presumptions about this first gospel are obliterated, as once again Mark proves its lasting status as the enigmatic and elusive story of Jesus. Decker brings us closer to Mark, so that we realize how little we saw. "Mark has a reputation of being a simple book. I am not so sure that status is deserved. … This is a Gospel that, if read seriously and attentively, will challenge any reader" (xxi).

The Homeless Jesus in the Gospel of Matthew, by Robert J. Myles. Social World of Biblical Antiquity 2/10. Sheffield: Sheffield Phoenix, 2014. Pp. xiii + 220. Paper. $95.00. ISBN 9781909697386.

Warren Carter, Brite Divinity School at TCU

This stimulating ideological study was originally a PhD dissertation at the University of Auckland, New Zealand, under the direction of Elaine Wainwright and Tracey McIntosh. Myles locates his study of Jesus's homelessness in Matthew's Gospel over against those who, influenced by neoliberalism, have noticed but idealized Jesus's homelessness without attending to the destitution, desperation, and lack of agency that constitute its displacement. Shaped by a Marxist critique of the neoliberalism that pervades contemporary New Testament scholarship, Myles sees Jesus's homelessness not as freely chosen in response to his divine mission to save from sins (1:21) but as the by-product of wider economic, social, and political forces. He employs Žižek's theory that ideologies refer to extrapolitical *sublime objects*; that is, material objects are elevated to positions of inexplicable importance so that they stand out from or above the reality of ordinary things. He argues that Jesus's homelessness is such a sublime object in biblical scholarship whereby homelessness is idealized and attention is diverted from crucial questions concerning why people become homeless and what role the wider socioeconomic and ideological-political systems play in the production of homelessness.

Chapter 1, "Homelessness and Ideology," elaborates the rich theoretical foundations for the study. It locates Matthew's Gospel in Antioch in Syria and declares its concern with the Matthean Jesus. Myles rejects so-called objective historical criticism, locating his discussion in ideological biblical criticism and particularly in a Marxist framework concerned with class struggle. Myles understands ideological criticism as an approach concerned to connect biblical scholarship with the structures of power and power relations in the wider society. In a helpful discussion of definitions and causes of contemporary homelessness, he sees "displacement" or "placelessness" as central to homelessness. He rejects individualist (homelessness is a choice) and structuralist (failed government policies) approaches and favors a *symptomatic* understanding that sees homelessness as a symptom of well-functioning societal power structures. He claims that inadequate understandings (homelessness is a lifestyle choice) shape interpretations of Matthew's Gospel. His alternative framework for reading the Matthean Jesus's homelessness emphasizes that it emerges as a symptom of the societal arrangement of power where displacement, deviancy, social class, and objective violence are dynamics of the normal and smooth functioning of the sociopolitical and economic order. Finally he introduces Vernon Robbins's sociorhetorical approach with its five textures (ideological, inner, social and cultural, intertexture, sacred) as the framework for investigating selected Matthean texts.

Chapter 2, "Displacement," focuses on Matt 1–2 as the gospel's supreme example of homelessness and displacement. Throughout Myles rejects scholarship that has romanticized and/or spiritualized the chapters and neglected the significant displacement of the narrative. Myles observes that "of the forty names mentioned in the genealogy at least fifteen can be connected to episodes of forced displacement, itinerancy and/or homelessness" (58). The displacement of Jesus, Joseph, and Mary (2:13–23) initiates themes that will recur through the gospel. Myles's discussion of the flight to Egypt sets aside previous scholarly concerns with intertextual evoking of Moses and scriptural fulfillments to attend to the geographical and social uprooting and displacement experienced by Jesus and his parents. The chapter links this forced displacement with a marginal self-identity that conflicts with the status quo cultural and political institutions.

Chapter 3, "Reaction," critically rereads the beginning of Jesus's itinerant mission and calling of the first disciples (4:12–25). The target comprises dominant ideologies of homelessness that foreground agency or choice. John the Baptist is "an archetypal homeless prophet" (84) whose food and existence in the wilderness denote outsider status. He is a forerunner for Jesus and for the first disciples. The latter respond to Jesus's proclamation of the kingdom of heaven as an alternative kingdom that disrupts dominant arrangements of power and embraces the homeless. Accordingly, they leave their livelihoods and households to form an alternative community. He critiques readings of these scenes that reinscribe neoliberal discourse focusing on individualism and free choice without regard for structural and systemic factors.

Chapter 4, "Destitution," takes up 8:20 ("foxes have holes and birds of the air have nests, but the Son of Man has nowhere to lay his head"). Myles reads Jesus's saying as a lament of homelessness that expresses "the destitution, desperation and offensiveness that accompany Jesus' homeless existence" (113) and against readings that romanticize homelessness. The discussion of the rejecting scribe and the grieving disciple plays down individual choice or agency to highlight cultural norms that indicate the offensiveness of an itinerant existence.

Chapter 5, "Rejection," examines Jesus's return to his hometown (13:53–58), where he is met with disdain and rejection. Central to the reading is Myles's construction of Jesus's status as an expendable outsider who struggles to be recognized with honor in his hometown. In this dishonoring and disdain are tensions with Jesus's kinfolk. A focus on differentiations of power in this hometown rejection scene highlights Jesus's marginalization from normalized society. The irony that Jesus has a "hometown" seems to be missing from the argument.

Chapter 6, "Extermination," attends to the arrest and execution of Jesus as a homeless deviant who threatens the security and stability of everyday life. Extermination and systemic violence are the dominant perspectives in the discussion of Jesus's arrest (26:47–56) and death on the cross (27:38–50). Jesus's homelessness and deviant behavior are understood by the ruling powers as a criminal threat that has to be removed in order to preserve normal functioning.

Myles offers a rich and provocative study that is a welcome addition to the studies of Matthew that take seriously the socioeconomic and political factors shaping the gospel's production and the homelessness it reinscribes. One disappointment is that this well-written and engaging study focuses on a limited sample of six text segments (though with some discussion of literary context). Can the argument be sustained throughout the whole gospel? How does Myles's thesis, for example, cope with the alternative household code of Matt 19–20?

Problematic are the references to Jesus's "own city" (9:1) and "the house" that seems to belong to Jesus (9:10, 28; 12:46 [?]; 13:1, 36, 57; 17:25). Myles acknowledges these "house" texts (e.g., 5, 37, 123–25) but in my view does not deal adequately with them. His distinction between "house and home" (123–25) is not adequate. Here he argues the issue in terms of "literal or metaphorical" homelessness, a distinction proposed by some previous interpreters but one that he has convincingly dismantled in showing that Jesus is literally displaced/homeless for sustained periods of time. Rather, the issue that needs address comprises Myles's insistence that Jesus's homelessness is not a matter of individual choice but is a symptom of the socioeconomic and political forces of a well-functioning system. The binary seems unnecessarily restrictive. Of course, individual choice is never "pure" or isolated from systemic shaping. But individuals can contest societal power, so why deny any role for choice in favor of systems? In a textual analysis of Matthew the two might more usefully be held together in tensive relationship.

For example, various texts seem to recognize that Matthew's Jesus exercises some choice in favor of his challenging, divinely sanctioned task that creates his homelessness. Myles rushes over 4:23, when Jesus begins his homeless travels around "all Galilee." This is a crucial text for his consistent rejection of Jesus's homelessness as a chosen consequence of his divine mission and his advocacy for homelessness as symptomatic of sociopolitical and economic forces. Myles argues that the sociopolitical arrest of John the Baptist (88–90, 110) forces Jesus and his followers into homelessness at this point. But against this claim it must be noted that in 4:12 Jesus's "withdrawal" to Galilee is to *dwell* there (4:13). Homelessness follows later in 4:23, when he undertakes his tasks of "preaching the gospel of the kingdom/empire" and "healing." As much as John's death has forced him to dwell in Capernaum, it is by no means clear that it launches his public activity.

The commencement of this activity has more to do narratively with the force of his commissioning of 1:21–23 that he embraced in his baptism (3:15) and temptation as God's agent (4:1–11). Yet imperial structures are not absent from this commissioning. This preaching and healing activity contests imperial power, though Myles fails to recognize any link between sickness and imperial power. Further, narratively, the house texts indicate periods of time when Matthew's Jesus chooses not to be homeless. Concerning disciples, is their homelessness chosen or symptomatic of socioeconomic and political factors or both (4:18–23)? Another troubling text, 19:29 ("everyone who has left … houses … for my sake"), receives little attention (mentioned once in the index) in relation to the binary. This element of a chosen mission belongs, in my view, with but does not negate Myles's welcome attention to sociopolitical and economic factors. Perhaps, like many binaries, there is some truth in the either/or, agency/choice, or symptom/system options but more truth in a both–and approach. I do not find the text to be as sharply contrastive as his argument draws it. The forced homelessness of 2:1–23, the chosen homelessness of 4:23; the lament of 8:20, the house texts, 19:29 ("for my sake"), the decision to go to Jerusalem, and so on seem to hold choice/agency and symptom/system together more than this study's argument recognizes.

That being said, Myles offers an important study that draws attention to an often-neglected dimension of Matthew's Gospel.

The Turning Point in the Gospel of Mark: A Study in Markan Christology, by Gregg S. Morrison. Eugene, OR: Pickwick, 2014. Pp. xiii + 268. Paper. $25.60. ISBN 9781610977609.

Elizabeth Struthers Malbon, Virginia Tech

Morrison's book represents a revision of his 2007 doctoral dissertation for The Catholic University of America, under the direction of Francis J. Moloney, SDB, who has contributed a gracious foreword to the published version. Moloney praises the revision for manifesting "two dimensions that a 'passion' for the Word of God must address" for those "who seek to interpret the New Testament within the Christian church": "a scholarly passion to ensure that every textual, historical, literary, and theological possibility is discussed and evaluated, no matter how significant or insignificant any single one of them may or may not be," and "a passion to make a critical analysis of the Word of God 'relevant'" (vi). It does seem that Morrison's book seeks to reach both a scholarly audience and a more general audience, as challenging as that might be.

Morrison's work is presented in six chapters, including a full introduction and brief conclusion. Each chapter is made easy to follow by frequent headings and subheadings and a succinct summary conclusion. In addition to Moloney's foreword, the book includes an author's preface, a list of its ten tables distributed throughout the text, three appendices (a graphic chart of The Narrative Flow of the Gospel of Mark, a Summary of Major Commentators and Mark's "Turning Point," and a highlighted version of the Greek text of Mark 8:27–38; 9:1; 9:2–13), and a twenty-four-page page bibliography (Moloney calls Morrison "a *passionate* bibliophile"). There are no indexes.

Although Morrison's starting question is whether there is a "turning point" in Mark, he opens his introductory chapter with a broader question: What is the structure of Mark's Gospel? He answers by reviewing scholarly suggestions about the "outline" of Mark in several categories: topographical, thematic, topical, literary and rhetorical, and "alternatives"—basically those who argue that the search for a single outline of Mark is misguided. After reading this extensive review, I was somewhat surprised that Morrison seems to concur with Joanna Dewey's image of Mark as "an interwoven tapestry" rather than arguing for *the* outline of Mark. But the second section of the introduction, "Turning Points and the Genre of Mark," opens with this declaration: "Outlines and turning points, however, are two different things" (26), confirming what the book's title had already suggested in *the* turning point. In a thorough manner Morrison discusses the nature of the literary term *turning point* (from Aristotle's *Poetics* to "Freytag's Pyramid") and its meaning within various genres: Greek tragedy, Hellenistic novel, apologetic tract, Jewish midrash, and Greco-Roman biography. Based on these summaries of scholarship, Morrison concludes that "the common thread that ties disparate type[s] of literature together is the notion of plot" (34). Noting general scholarly agreement that there is a turning point in Mark's central section (8:22–10:52), Morrison's task is to determine *the* turning point.

Thus chapter 2 surveys possible turning points. Here we see that, unlike the archetypical dissertation with its "literature review" chapter, Morrison's work will continue to review and summarize an array of scholarly studies throughout the work as he builds his argument. Chapter 2 opens with a review of the history of turning-point language—from its early uses in historical criticism (turning point in Jesus's ministry) to its later uses in literary criticism (turning point in Mark's narrative), which will be Morrison's concern. Second, Morrison presents an overview of Mark's central section, defining its limits and summarizing its content in six sections. Finally, Morrison surveys scholars who say there is no single turning point, (in detail) those who argue for one of five options for a single turning point, and those who suggest more than one turning point. This sets up chapter 3.

In chapter 3 Morrison presents an overview of his own argument that Mark's turning point rests in two "twin" pericopes, Peter's confession and the transfiguration. Morrison introduces the Roman mythological character with two faces, Janus, as a heuristic device for calling attention to the fact that these two pericopes in the middle look both backward to the narrative's beginning and forward to the narrative's ending, something other scholars (such as Dewey) have called attention to as echoes and foreshadowings. Morrison bases his argument about the two pericopes on shared vocabulary and syntactical constructions, thematic similarities, and their presentation of shared significant christological titles.

Chapter 4 presents this argument in great detail, necessitating some duplication. It lists thirteen specific grammatical links (not all of which are equally distinctive, as Morrison readily admits) and an array of "thematic links": (1) the characters other than Jesus—Peter, the disciples, John the Baptist, Elijah, and a Prophet (Moses), (2) Jesus as a main character, including Jesus's identity, charge to secrecy, passion/resurrection, and (3) discipleship, especially its costs (8:34–38) and benefits (9:1, an interpretation I find inviting but not quite convincing) of following Jesus. Next Morrison argues that reading the two scenes together is supported by the fact that "neither Matthew nor Luke tinkered with the order of presentation in these two scenes" (144). Finally, Morrison summarizes four significant "recent" (2000–2006) works that have a bearing on this reading of the two pericopes: books by John Paul Heil, Dorothy Lee, and Marie Noonan Sabin, and an article by C. Clifton Black that is particularly influential for Morrison. In all this, Morrison identifies his methodological approach as threefold: narrative criticism, rhetorical criticism, and redaction criticism, with its focus on identifying Mark's theology, or in this case, primarily Christology.

It is this redaction-critical focus on theology that is clear in the final substantive chapter, chapter 5: "Converging Lines in Markan Christology." Again, Morrison supplies the reader with an overview of scholarship, here a vast sweep of Markan christology since 1900, much of which has already been touched on earlier. The first two categories summarized are "Messiah and Messianic Secret" and "Divine Man," with a discussion of "corrective christology." Next "Son of God" is discussed in detail that requires its own subcategories: "Hellenistic vs. Jewish Theories of Son of God," "Son of God as Royal Messiah," "Son of God as Suffering Servant," and "Son of God as Eschatological Prophet." This is followed by summaries of Markan scholars who focus on Son of Man or on Christologies based on structure or on Jesus as Teacher or Prophet, with brief mentions of Jesus as Shepherd or Son of David. Clearly there is a tendency here to organize—and to think—in terms of traditional christological titles. Then a "Methodological Interlude" on "The Move from Redaction to Narrative Criticism" introduces a review of eight scholars' work under the category "Narrative Christologies of Mark's Gospel." The scholars include Tannehill, Kingsbury, Malbon, Broadhead, Naluparayil, Matera, Marshall, and Hooker. Morrison seems closest to Matera and Hooker here. Summaries, of course, risk flattening out contributors' unique emphases, but Morrison's readers are enabled to see a panorama of modern Markan scholarship. (There are lacunae in this overview: reader-response criticism and orality studies receive only mentions, and deconstruction or anything significantly postmodern in orientation, even if that might be implied in some of the work reviewed, is simply absent.) What converges for Morrison in the twin pericopes that define *the* turning point are Jesus as Messiah, Son of God, and Son of Man in Mark's Gospel, emphases that occur in the beginning, middle (turning point), and end of the narrative.

Chapter 6, a brief summary conclusion, offers four theses that reiterate Morrison's main points, which should be quite obvious to the reader at this point because Morrison's presentation is clear and direct throughout. The two theses that I have not yet stressed in this review, and that receive less emphasis in the book, note that references to "the kingdom of God' also converge with the three stressed christological titles, connecting message and messenger, and that "there remains something elusive about Jesus, the kingdom, and God." In fact, "elusive" is Morrison's own last word and the book's last word, which he gives (as he thinks "perhaps" he "should") to Clifton Black.

Overall, my response to Morrison's carefully crafted book is paradoxical, probably not because both author and reviewer are steeped in the paradoxes of Mark's Gospel but perhaps because of the paradoxical passions Moloney mentions in his foreword: a passion for detail and a passion for relevance, or the challenge of trying to reach both Markan scholars and a broader audience. As a scholar I have experienced several difficulties with Morrison's book, from the larger ones of reading too many summaries and not finding enough new insight into the Markan narrative and wondering about the absence of the implied author from the narrative-critical discussions, to the smaller ones of incomplete footnotes (without full publication data at the first mention of a work) and proofing errors and grammatical anomalies. Although some of the summaries of research seem ideal for a broader (although generally educated and interested) audience, the frequent untranslated and untransliterated Greek would seem to be a formidable hurdle. But both passions are present in Morrison's book, with clarity enough to give both audiences encouragement.

Discovering Matthew: Content, Interpretation, Reception, by Ian Boxall. Discovering Biblical Texts. Grand Rapids: Eerdmans, 2014. Pp. 216. Paper. $22.00. ISBN 9780802872388.

Jeannine K. Brown, Bethel Seminary, San Diego

Discovering Matthew is the first of the series Discovering Biblical Texts. Ian Boxall's book is an exemplar for the series, which provides "comprehensive, up-to-date and student-friendly introductions to the books of the Bible: their structure, content, theological concerns, key interpretive debates and historical reception" (ii).

In his introductory chapter Boxall provides a review of the church's historical preference for Matthew as the first gospel, before discussing the nineteenth-century shift toward Markan priority. In this introduction, the author sets a trajectory: a careful and coherent analysis of Matthew illuminated by its history of reception. He then highlights various points of tension within Matthew (e.g., particularist or universalist mission), concluding with an extended summary of the gospel.

Chapter 2 introduces various historical and contemporary approaches under the rubrics of author-, text-, and reader-focused interpretation. Boxall addresses early church precritical exegesis, including allegorical and figurative readings, elucidating the ways in which these may differ but also converge with modern approaches. For example, Bornkamm's seminal essay on the stilling of the storm (Matt 8), with its reference to "the little ship of the church," is not so far afield from Jerome's figurative readings. Boxall also explores modern approaches, explaining historical criticism, social-scientific approaches, narrative criticism, feminist criticism, postcolonial interpretation, and *Wirkungsgeschichte* (history of effects).

Chapter 3 covers introductory topics of authorship, composition, dating, structure, and establishing the text. For each, Boxall incorporates ancient as well as modern sensibilities. In discussion of the Greek text, he notes the recent turn to valuing variants as early interpretations. For example, a scribal expansion of 4:10 ("Depart, Satan!") in some manuscripts to cohere with 16:23 ("Get behind me, Satan") highlights connections between these passages, as temptation to abandon God's will is tied to Jesus's impending death.

"Characters and Places in Matthew's Story" (ch. 4) considers the Matthean characters of God, Jesus, angels and demons, political and religious leaders, John the Baptist, the disciples, and the crowds and minor characters. Although brief, these discussions are generally narratively insightful. For instance, while recognizing a typical portrait for the crowds, Boxall is unwilling to lump together all "crowd" groups across Matthew, especially in the passion narrative, where the stakes are high regarding a monolithic, composite reading of *ochloi* and *laos*. Boxall also rightly distinguishes the crowds—generally positively disposed to Jesus—from the antagonistic Jewish leadership. A point of confusion regarding Pilate's portrayal comes in Boxall's suggestion that Pilate affirms Jesus's innocence (27:24 [52, 84, 161]). While a textual variant at 27:24 describes Jesus as *dikaios*, it is likely secondary, given scribal tendencies to augment Christology. Few modern translations (including Boxall's preferred NRSV) follow this reading. Either way, Boxall does not comment on the text-critical issue, leaving the reader to discern how Pilate's claim of his own innocence translates to a claim about Jesus. The chapter concludes with a discussion of key Matthean settings, including geographic and more symbolic settings (e.g., mountains).

Chapter 5 surveys perspectives on Matthew's social location vis-à-vis Judaism as well as Rome, concluding with a discussion of Matthew's provenance. Boxall focuses attention on whether Matthew's community/communities are still participating in synagogue life or have already disengaged (or been ousted) from it. Boxall draws on literary and historical evidence to suggest that it is possible "for post–70 Jewish followers of Jesus to regard themselves as still part of the wider community of Israel while not frequenting, or being prevented from frequenting, the Synagogue or at least specific synagogues" (68).

In chapters 6–12 Boxall provides a coherent reading of Matthew, while also attending to interpretive voices, both ancient and modern. He makes an advantageous choice to emphasize Matthew's beginning and ending, where key themes arise; chapter 6 explores the infancy narratives, and chapters 11 and 12 are devoted to Jesus's passion and resurrection. In these chapters Boxall attends to literary features such as genre (e.g., genealogy, apocalyptic), portrayals and functions of key characters, and the significant number of Old Testament intertexts used.

The intervening chapters deal with key facets of Matthew's Christology (chs. 7–8), his fulfillment theme (ch. 9), and his ecclesiology (ch. 10). "Jesus as Teacher" (ch. 7) demonstrates how Matthew heightens this theme (from Mark) and notes the transparency of the five teaching discourses that draws the reader to learn from Jesus.

The chapter concentrates on the Sermon on the Mount, Jesus's use of parables, and his teachings on final judgment within Matthew's apocalyptic framework. A minor criticism attends Boxall's discussion of *dikaiosynē*. He assumes that Matthew uses the term uniformly to refer to human activity (98), yet recent discussions move beyond Przybylski (1980) to argue that some instances of *dikaiosynē* refer to divine activity (3:15; 6:33; Hagner, *Matthew*). "Jesus as Healer and Exorcist" (ch. 8) examines the gospel healing traditions and certain emphases in Matthew's healing accounts, concluding that the evangelist heightens their christological focus. Boxall finds the backdrop for Matthew's connection between Jesus as Son of David and his healing ministry in the Davidic shepherd motif. The chapter concludes with discussion of interpretive frames for Matt 8–9, including a symbolic interpretation of Jesus's miracles.

Chapter 9 contemplates the complexities of Matthew's fulfillment motif, including the distinctive fulfillment quotations—their function, text forms, and origins. In addition to prophetic fulfillment, Matthew also highlights Jesus as one who accomplishes the law. Boxall examines the so-called antitheses and argues for Jesus's "radicalizing" of torah. He explores various interpretations of fulfillment in Matthew, from the view that the Mosaic law is still in force for Christians to the perspective that Jesus's teachings substitute for torah (28:19).

Chapter 10 explores Matthew's ecclesiology. Boxall examines the relationship of church to Israel in Matthew and concludes that the former does not replace the latter; rather, Jesus and his followers replace the present shepherds of Israel— the Jewish leadership. Boxall then discusses Peter's role (16:13–20) and his mixed portrayal in Matthew, shedding light on differing historical interpretive options. Boxall concludes the chapter by surveying the theme of gentile inclusion in relation to the historical primacy of Israel (e.g., 15:24) and reviewing the role of Matt 18 for ecclesial life.

The final chapter suggests areas for further reflection: (1) Matthew's multivalence, in which authorial intention is only one dimension of textual meaning; (2) the resulting importance of a variety of methods for interpreting Matthew; (3) the reality that texts and their interpretations have consequences; and (4) a commendation of participatory methods that invite readers into identification and action.

Boxall's expressed goals are to "open up some of the questions posed by, and to, this multifaceted text, and some of the different strategies interpreters have used to provide some answers" (175). Boxall achieves these goals and does so in a lucid and engaging style. Throughout the book he demonstrates a keen understanding of Matthean studies: its seminal works, key contextual debates, and central cruxes of interpretation. He provides succinct explanations of wide-ranging scholarly debates (e.g., Matthew's structure). Boxall's work is well documented; he attends to both recent and seminal works as well as to ancient voices.

Another strength of the book is the coherent reading of Matthew that Boxall provides. This is particularly commendable, since his task of addressing Matthew's history of reception could have easily devolved into inventory. Instead, he has produced a more cohesive reading by incorporating various interpretive insights while clearly communicating his own perspective. For example, he consistently maintains a narrative distinction between the Jewish crowds and their leadership, highlighting historical questions raised by the latter and the detrimental historical effects of not distinguishing the two portrayals. Part of the reading coherence derives from Boxall's well-honed narrative sensibilities. Methodologically, he helpfully distinguishes between the story and discourse levels of a narrative. Examples of careful narrative reading include Boxall's exploration of key connections between Matt 2 and the passion narrative (149), his insightful work across Matthew's narrative arc on the shepherding motif (136–37, 153), and his skill in intertextuality, specifically his sensitivity to potential allusions contributing to the messages of Matthew.

A key contribution of this book is its attention to reception history. Boxall's historical examples are well chosen and far-reaching. He often employs ancient voices at the beginning of a chapter to pique the reader's interest and to set a tone for what follows. His explicit goal—executed well—is to "explore the strengths as well as the weaknesses of alternative interpretations across the centuries" (175). A notable example of this reception focus is his discussion of the Sermon on the Mount (96–98). Additionally, Boxall does not limit himself to reception in texts; he draws upon art (118) and music (151) to illustrate textual effects. Across the book, his attention to Matthew's reception history is substantive and not merely ornamental.

Discovering Matthew illuminates reflections on the First Gospel from recent scholarship and from reception history in ways that are compelling and clarifying. I am appreciative of Boxall's work and highly recommend it to students new to Matthew as well as to its seasoned readers.

Kingdom of Bureaucracy: The Political Theology of Village Scribes in the Sayings Gospel Q, by Giovanni B. Bazzana. Bibliotheca Ephemeridum Theologicarum Lovaniensium 274. Leuven: Peeters, 2015. Pp. xii + 383. Paper. €85.00. ISBN 9789042931787.

Sarah E. Rollens, Rhodes College

Kingdom of Bureaucracy is one of the most significant recent efforts to explain the origin of the Sayings Gospel Q. Giovanni B. Bazzana draws together his long-standing interest in the Synoptic Gospels and his extensive familiarity with ancient documentary papyri to produce a remarkable study that is required reading for all those interested in Q, as well as for those more broadly fascinated with the emergence of the earliest Jesus movement.

The book has two goals: to think in a historically and sociologically disciplined manner about the group of people most likely responsible for writing Q, and to probe Q for clear evidence to confirm that the text does indeed stem from such a group and to make sense of it on those terms. To this end, Bazzana focuses on "subelites" known as village scribes (or, more generally, village administrators) as the best candidates for Q's authors. This project thus builds on the previous proposals and explorations undertaken by John S. Kloppenborg and William E. Arnal regarding Q's authors as village scribes.

To access the social location of village scribes responsible for Q, Bazzana engages in careful readings of documentary papyri, which although dealing with mundane legal and administrative affairs often preserve the unique worldview of these subelites and the particular assumptions they held about proper governance, civic order, and social exchange—in other words, their distinct political ideology. His use of this papyrological data is crucially important to note, because this sort of evidence has rarely been attended to by biblical scholars. Indeed, documentary papyri represent a cache of historical data that many are either unskilled in using or simply unaware of altogether. Furthermore, even though much of this papyrological evidence stems from Egypt, recent studies have suggested that the Egyptian evidence is "much less exceptional" (11) in the Roman Empire than was once thought, which allows for a productive comparison between its language and ideas with those in Q. Bazzana's analysis is guided by uncovering the "ideological work" (6) that Q engages in, on the assumption that, were we to identify the ideological goals and unstated assumptions of such a text, then we could reasonably conclude something about the people responsible for them. More precisely, by analyzing the ideological framework of Q, the author proposes that we can learn about its "political theology," a term that transcends modern (and problematic) binaries between religious and political discourse.

Chapter 1 profiles the social and cultural dynamics of village scribes in the Greco-Roman world. By carefully assessing the Egyptian papyrological evidence and some key passages from Josephus, Bazzana concludes that a village-based organizational structure with low-level administrators playing key bureaucratic roles (such as overseeing taxation, receiving legal petitions, and registering accounting documents) would have existed in Galilee and Judea in the Herodian period. In fact, judging by the Egyptian evidence, village scribes were responsible for such indispensable aspects of social and economic administration that Bazzana claims they inhabited "the very heart of the entire village's economic and social life, with remarkable power conferred on [them] by virtue of his privileged position vis-à-vis the authorities of the nome" (41). He draws on Anthony Giddens's notion of distanciation (the generation of power through the restriction and control of limited material resources, as well as more abstract resources, such as time and space) to understand village scribes' bureaucratic activities in the context of imperial policies. By such activities as regulating social exchange, documenting economic production, and handing down administrative demands from higher up the chain of command, village scribes were vital components of the imperial bureaucracy. Their tasks ensured that power and privilege were restricted to a small group, which could then control the majority of the population.

While we have no clear evidence for the salary and duration of the post of village scribe, they do emerge from the sources with a curious sociological profile. Though most were likely educated, ancient sources evince a clear "elite bias" (33) against them, suggesting that these scribes occupied a rather precarious "middle position" (34) in the wider social landscape. Bazzana also uncovers evidence of multiple cultural personas (e.g., Egyptian, Greek, or Jewish) that scribes could inhabit and perform in different settings, depending on which was most advantageous in a particular situation. Cultural flexibility, literacy, and accounting skills could be politically advantageous, which rendered them reasonably powerful despite the relatively low social clout of their positions.

Chapter 2 examines three instances in Q where the language reflects precisely the "bureaucratic jargon" (86) that Bazzana encountered in his perusal of documentary papyri. While the Greek terms and cognates he examines are not uncommon, the distinctive uses to which Q puts them suggest a familiarity with the compositional techniques and ideological bents that village scribes were known for elsewhere. The first example is ἐκβάλλω ("send out"), which Q employs in a manner that relies on its connotations of compulsory labor in rural settings—a meaning most strongly attested in documents dealing with agricultural administration. The second example is οἰκετεία, which occurs less frequently in ancient sources than ἐκβάλλω, and is often translated with the unremarkable term "household." A comparison with documentary papyri, however, reveals that "servitude" is a more precise translation, for the term most often signals a group of servants tied to a household. This means that Q 12:42 does not imagine a servant being given power over the *entire household* but only over a specific *group of subordinates*—exactly the imagined scenario one would expect from villages scribes occupying a middle social location between elites and lower classes. The final example is θησαυρός. Q uses this term and its cognates as a set of metaphors about storing up agricultural produce. Thus the metaphorical currency of these notions once again depends on the specific use to which these terms are put in a particular body of texts: documentary papyri.

Chapter 3 looks more closely at the situation that village scribes would have experienced in first-century Galilee. Village scribes functioned as the intermediaries and facilitators for Roman administration, serving as bilingual hinge points between the urban elites and the rural countryside. Bazzana surmises that Greek language training and education must have been available in Galilee from the Ptolemaic period through the Herodian period; Greek language skills especially would have been virtually required for administrative management in the region. The education necessary for such activities was likely rather extensive; Bazzana supposes that village scribes "at best" were acquainted with Homer, Euripides, Menander, and perhaps Isocrates (137). This results in a situation in which village scribes were sometimes drawn from the local population, were educated into the ideological values of the elite rulers, and yet also wielded multiple cultural identities and language competencies—all of these experiences amounting to a resourceful but precarious social identity. This matrix of social factors, in turn, gives us the framework to decode the "perceived problem" (159) that Q's authors thought they faced that inspired them to pen the document. Such an exploration is more responsible, Bazzana argues, than trying to identify an objective "crisis" in Galilee to which the authors reacted. In particular, changes in Herodian administration in the early first century (not an objective crisis by any means) created a scenario in which the village scribes responsible for Q became anxious about the bureaucratic hierarchy in which they had, until recently, rather comfortably fit. It is no wonder, then, that Q is so concerned with "loyalty and hierarchical trustworthiness" (161), for they are hallmarks of a well-regulated bureaucratic system.

Chapters 4 and 5 analyze the infamous phrase βασιλεία τοῦ θεοῦ (usually rendered "kingdom of God") with which biblical scholars have been preoccupied for centuries. Instead of using Q's references to the βασιλεία as a window onto particular beliefs or practices of the Q people, Bazzana proposes that a more fruitful method is to attend to "the cultural and political agendas that led the Q people to deploy the language of βασιλεία" (265) in the varied ways that they did. Moreover, a close comparison of the concept βασιλεία τοῦ θεοῦ with related terms in documentary papyri suggests that "kingdom of God" is a misleading translation, clarifying why it continues to be an interpretive "stumbling block" (203) for scholars. In his analysis, the author prefers a translation more akin to "sovereignty" but often simply leaves βασιλεία untranslated, since the semantic domain is rather more complex.

The language in the Lord's Prayer, for instance, assumes a multifaceted political ideology as part of the βασιλεία, including the presumption of a beneficent ruler who will provide concrete subsistence needs to his subjects and will forgive financial debts periodically. Such language of debt relief and providential care (including "food-benefaction" [188]) is also found in rulers' amnesty decrees, which are meant to communicate the beneficence of Greek and Roman rulers to their subjects. In Bazzana's sketch of the mediating role of village scribes, these administrators act as the transmitters of this political ideology of the people, explaining why they can easily view themselves as envoys of divine kingship in the Sayings Gospel. Q 11:20 similarly "evokes an image of God's rule that is close to the models of Greco-Roman sovereignty" (210); it builds on the notion of kingship that impacts subjects by bringing them tangible benefits of the munificent rulers. All this is to suggest that the village scribes responsible for Q were familiar with a particular set of metaphors and terms to describe how rulers' sovereignty translated into the lives of their subjects, and thus when it came time to compose a similar set of statements about God's rule in Q, they drew upon the language and ideas with which they were most familiar. Importantly, this analysis must be situated within political developments in the Roman Empire in this time period, especially Augustus's aversion to using the term βασιλεία in official documents, which was likely a strategy aimed at "maintain[ing] the fiction that the new regime remained a republic" (238). For Q to continue to use the discourse of βασιλεία becomes a way of negotiating and asserting local power in such a political climate.

Chapter 6 ties the preceding discussions together by asking: What precisely is the political theology promoted by the village scribes responsible for Q? *Political theology* is a term borrowed from Giorgio Agamben and then developed by Bazzana in order to attune us to the text's nexus of ideas about divine sovereignty and the bureaucratic-like structure that was understood to maintain it. Q's βασιλεία, embodying divine providence, debt relief, and other aspects of royal welfare, is presented as something that is both mediated and established by humans, not God. It is *human* agency (via preaching, healing, and other activities) that Q imagines to generate the βασιλεία. In fact, focusing on human agency is a clever strategy, Bazzana suggests, to dissociate God from specific claims to kingship, perhaps a strategy for political protection. Within the text, moreover, Q's authors retain their function as mediating bureaucrats, but instead of mediating royal ideology on earth, they write themselves into divine scenario to mediate God's sovereignty in the βασιλεία, helping to bring divine providence, healings, miracles, and other benefits to the subjects of the Father. They become critical cogs in "the divine governmental machine" (307).

Through Bazzana's impressive comparison of Q's language to documentary papyri, Q emerges as a text with a "hybrid mixture of literary and ideological features" (16) drawing on multiple linguistic and cultural domains, as well as a variety of social and economic experiences. Moreover, Q's notions of the βασιλεία and God's sovereignty, which recast the authors as critical envoys and mediators in the divine bureaucracy, become "a representative instance of how these rural social groups coped, at a cultural and literary level, with the arrival of Roman hegemony" (26). Though it is difficult to identify precisely any practices associated with Q, it likely "circulated as a 'private' document, copied in informal and relatively unskilled ways by the sub-elites who had an interest in it" (4). In other words, Q's focus and interests are highly *local*.

This exciting study shows that *serious* work with wide-ranging implications can be done on Q on the basis of its literary and sociocultural profile—despite its "hypothetical" nature. Q might only be a hypothesis, but *Kingdom of Bureaucracy* only further attests to what a compelling hypothesis it is.

Silent Statements: Narrative Representations of Speech and Silence in the Gospel of Luke, by Michal Beth Dinkler. Beihefte zur Zeitschrift für die neutestamentliche Wissenschaft 191. Berlin: de Gruyter, 2013. Pp. xi + 261. Hardcover. €99.95. ISBN 9783110331042.

Mikeal C. Parsons, Baylor University

Silent Statements by Michal Beth Dinkler is a revised version of a 2012 Harvard dissertation, the last one directed by the late François Bovon. As such, in addition to establishing Dinkler as an important contributor to the literary analysis of the Lukan corpus, this book is a remarkable testimony to the brilliant breadth of Bovon's erudition, which in his later years expanded beyond traditional methods of historical criticism to include interest and expertise in newer literary methods. Lukan speeches, of course, have been the topic of many studies (e.g., Dibelius, Cadbury, Soards), so in this book Dinkler now Assistant Professor of New Testament at Yale Divinity School, explores the complementary but understudied literary device of silence employed by the author of Luke to enhance and at points complicate or even challenge speech. Along the way, she addresses a number of *cruces interpretum* in Lukan scholarship in a thoughtful and refreshing way.

The book consists of an introduction, four major chapters that follow the sequence of the Third Gospel and focus on issues of silence and speech, and a conclusion. In the introduction Dinkler demonstrates her command over previous scholarship produced by secular literary theorists, classicists, and (some few) New Testament scholars, revealing that silence is multivalent, contextually determined, and rhetorically powerful (8–13). She situates her own analysis within the narrative-critical approach to biblical narrative, noting both its "promises and perils" (19–21). She is concerned to consider "silence as it relates to speech" in Luke's Gospel (43). These silences may be on the part of the narrator, Jesus, or other characters in the narrative and include, among other things, rhetorical questions that presume no response on the part of the interlocutor. In all this, Dinkler proves herself a sure-footed guide through the maze of secondary literature.

Chapter 1 considers the "Prologue and Narrative Beginnings (Luke 1:1–4:13)." Dinkler acknowledges that many commentators consider Luke 1–2 to be the proper beginning of the Third Gospel, but she opts to extend the introduction to include material up through the baptism and temptation narrative (Luke 4:1–13), following the lead of Charles Talbert (*Reading Luke*) and Bovon. She also mentions at this point (47 n. 235) the work of Fearghus O'Fearghail (*The Introduction to Luke-Acts: A Study of the Role of Lk 1,1–4,44 in the Composition of Luke's Two-Volume Work*, AB 126 [Rome: Pontifical Biblical Institute, 1991]) who in my opinion gives the most convincing argument for including the material in 3:1–4:13 (if not through 4:44) as part of an extended comparison, or rhetorical *synkrisis*, between John the Baptist and Jesus. O'Fearghail's work would have supported Dinkler's later point (in agreement with Karl Kuhn, *NTS* 47 [2001]: 38–49) that Luke's work is not "apologetic," that is, not intending to argue for the inferiority of John the Baptist. By placing Jesus in a (presumably encomiastic) *synkrisis* with John the Baptist, Luke is presenting Jesus as one who is superior to one who is good (John the Baptist is, after all, a pivotal figure in the Lukan history of salvation, Luke 16:16). By extending the introduction to 4:13, Dinkler highlights the "narratorial silence" between 2:52 and 3:1 in redirecting readerly attention to Jesus, the main protagonist of the narrative. Her analysis of Zechariah's speech and silence in this chapter provide a more complex, and therefore more satisfying, explanation; that is, Zechariah's silence is, *inter alia*, punitive *and* an opportunity for Luke to underscore the "tension between divine providential guidance and human response" (84).

Chapter 2 analyzes Jesus's Galilean ministry (Luke 4:14–9:50). Instances of silence between narrator and reader, as well as between Jesus and the religious authorities and the disciples, lead Dinkler to conclude that Luke "uses instances of speech and silence to depict divine providence" (88). Beyond hearing and doing, Jesus's words and actions (miracles) involve speech. Jesus commands miracles to occur, refuses to allow demons to continue silencing their victims, and controls the speech of others. Regarding Jesus's speech in this section, Dinkler concludes: "Jesus' speech-related teachings align his words with God's words ... and create an evaluative framework by which readers can judge various characters" (131). The subject of an excursus in this chapter on "The Literary Technique of Internal Monologues" is taken up again by Dinkler in an excellent article, "'The Thoughts

of Many Hearts Shall Be Revealed': Listening in on Lukan Interior Monologues,"
JBL 132 (2015): 373–99.

Chapters 3 ("Speech and Silence in the Central Section (Luke 9:5–19:44") and
4 ("The Passion and Post-Resurrection Narratives [Luke 19:45–24:53]") follow
the same pattern, though not rigidly so. Dinkler allows the narrative's particular
shape and the specific uses of speech and silence in each section to determine
the way in which the analysis is framed. In chapter 3, then, Dinkler attends to
the speech of the parables, noting the "open-endedness" (another form of narratorial silence) in several of those tales. The silences of religious authorities and
disciples contribute both to their own characterization as well as to Jesus's. Dinkler argues that "the narrator's silences like ambiguities and delays engage readers
by increasing suspense, maintaining attention, engendering surprise, and subverting conventional expectations" (163). Chapter 4 follows the sequence of the
passion/resurrection narratives (with special attention to the pericope of Jesus's
trial before Herod in Luke 23:6–12). She finds that "speech and silence militate
against a sense of closure at the of Luke's Gospel insofar as unfulfilled prophecies
create unfinished business for Luke's readers" (204). In the conclusion to the book,
Dinkler showcases what analyses of speech and silence teach us about plot and
characterization in the Third Gospel. She also includes a section on the implications of speech and silence for disclosing Lukan theological themes, an aspect to
which she has attended throughout the study and for which I, for one, am grateful.
A closing note that (appropriately) leaves open the door for future work on speech
and silence finishes off the book.

Every great book—and *Silent Statements* is a great book—provokes other kinds
of questions on related topics or invites reflection on how different approaches
might affect the same problem. In light of the recent exchange between Kelly Iver-
son and Larry Hurtado (*NTS* 62 [2016]: 183–200, 201–6), one wonders how the
orality/aurality issue might affect our understanding of speech and silence in the
Third Gospel. Dinkler is not unaware of the issue; she mentions it (3–4 n. 9), but
I wonder if her equation of "reader" with "hearers" ("I refer to the Lukan 'reader'
throughout the work, but my observations apply to 'hearers' as well"; 4 n. 9) is
not too facile. Imagining how a lector/reader's pause or silence in oral reading/
performance would affect a communal, listening audience would complicate the
"narrator/implied reader" model. For example, with regard to the parables, Dinkler quotes Bovon: "Luke *writes* what Jesus *says*" (146 n. 50). To complete the
circle, we might rephrase: "Lectors/readers *say* what Luke *writes* that Jesus *says*."
If we want to know how ancient listening audiences experienced both the speech
and silent statements of Luke, such disciplined historical imagination would be
well worth the effort. One wonders, too, if the textual evidence of intentional
additions/omissions left by scribes might reinforce the early reception (rejection?)
of gaps or silences between narrator and reader in Luke as the manuscript seems
to suggest for Acts (cf., e.g., Kathy Maxwell's discussion of the Western expansion of Acts 24:8 as a way to "fix" the missing proof in Tertullus's speech; *Hearing
between the Lines* [New York: T&T Clark, 20110], 166–67). These musings are not

meant as criticisms of what Dinkler has accomplished, but are rather intended to compliment and complement a work that stimulates further reflection.

There are a few peccadillos in this very fine study. For example, *Let the Reader Understand* is misattributed to Richard (rather than Robert) Fowler, and that source is missing altogether in both the bibliography and author index. Footnote references 223 and 224 appear in the text on page 44, but the footnote themselves follow on page 45 (surely the publisher bears as much responsibility for this as does the author). But such problems are few and far between in a book that is well-written and a pleasure to read, with such sentences as: "The Transfiguration is ineffable, the narrator's subsequent pithy explanation renders Peter's speech almost laughable" (104).

The importance of silence has long been recognized in other fields. "The pauses between the notes—Ah, that is where the art resides!" (Artur Schnabel). "The right word may be effective, but no word was ever as effective as a rightly timed pause" (Mark Twain). "I prefer silence to sound, and the image produced by words occurs in the silence. That is, the thunder and the music of the prose take place in silence" (William Falulkner). With *Silent Statements*, Michal Beth Dinkler has underscored the significance of silence (in relation to speech) for the literary and theological artistry of the Third Gospel, and she has issued her own, not-so-quiet declaration that there is another new and formidable Lukan interpreter whose voice, especially regarding silence (!), deserves to be heard.

Reading the Gospel of Mark as a Novel, by Geert van Oyen. Translated by Leslie Robert Keylock. Eugene, OR: Cascade, 2014. Pp. x + 143. Paper. $15.20. ISBN 9781625644381.

Gregg S. Morrison, Birmingham, Alabama

Geert van Oyen, Professor of New Testament at the Faculty of Theology at the Catholic University of Leuven, has written a delightful book that seeks to introduce nonspecialists to the narrative method of biblical exegesis using the Gospel of Mark as a guide. In so doing, he explores the dynamics involved in the interaction between an ancient text and a contemporary reader—an interaction that he hopes will lead to a lifelong dialogue with the text. After a short preface, the work is divided into two parts. In the first part (chs. 1–3), entitled "Reading the Bible Today," he explores several hermeneutical questions involving narrative criticism, the concept of meaning, and introductory questions about Mark's Gospel, to name a few. Part 2 of the book (chs. 4–9) focuses more on Mark's Gospel and combines a discussion of the narrative of the gospel with several thematic and theological issues. Annotated bibliographical entries (which include works in English, German, and French) conclude each chapter for the reader who wishes to explore further. There are no indices.

In chapter 1, "Mark: An Enigmatic Gospel," van Oyen suggests that Mark may have been "telling his story" with two levels of meaning in mind: one in which the story of Jesus could be understood by everyone; the other a more subtle message to a small number of initiates (i.e., the Twelve)—it is to this latter group that the notion of secrecy prevails (4:10–12). Regardless, in the end this mystery is not something that is beyond the reach of an audience or reader. Rather, each reader is able to discover its message and, thus, in this sense the message of the gospel is "an open secret" (7). The open secret, van Oyen contends, is about Jesus, who is both Messiah and Son of God. In Jesus, readers are presented with a person whose words and actions demonstrate the way one should conduct onself toward other people and toward God. Readers are encouraged to model themselves after the pattern of Jesus.

Chapter 2, "An Antivirus Program for the Bible," offers a narratological approach as an "antivirus program," which van Oyen hopes can be used to reverse the trend that the Bible has become "no more than a great unknown" (13) to contemporary readers. Van Oyen's narrative approach entails dealing with the biblical text with its attendant notion of authorial intent, but it also includes approaching the text from the perspective of today's reader, which for him means that readers will bring their own questions to the text and will resist the notion of an exclusive meaning of a text. Van Oyen acknowledges that, when presenting narrative criticism this way—with the tension inherent between ancient text/author and contemporary reader—there becomes a need for an "ethic of reading," a phrase he borrows from David Rhoads in *Reading Mark: Engaging the Gospel*.

Part 1 concludes with chapter 3, "Before Reading: Eliminate the Misunderstandings," in which van Oyen suggests that the final step before approaching a text should be to eliminate the misunderstandings. Admittedly, this chapter is aimed at readers "who do not spontaneously choose a book on the Bible for their personal libraries" (27). The focus of this chapter is on three topics in which misunderstanding is common: (1) the truth of the Bible, (2) the Bible as a book for believers only, and (3) the true meaning of religious texts being hidden. He suggests the Bible should be "an open book" in which all those engaged in the public square can benefit, regardless of social location and/or religious background.

The conclusion to chapter 3 (36–39) presents van Oyen's structural outline for the gospel, one that includes three major parts (1:14–8:26; 8:31–10:52; 11:1–15:47) centered around four important themes in the gospel: the relation between Jesus and the disciples, the lack of understanding of the disciples, the opposition to Jesus, and Jesus's passion.

Chapters 5 and 6 ("How Does the Evangelist Narrate?" and "Jesus with a Question Mark," respectively) include nontechnical presentations of narrative and rhetorical criticism, including short discussions on the narrator (whom van Oyen considers omniscient), the concepts of space (both geographical and cosmic) and time (*chronos* versus *kairos*), plot (particularly the promise-fulfillment motif), doublets or repetition (including the so-called "Markan sandwich"), Mark's use of the Old Testament, and implied versus real authors/readers. Real readers, when confronted with the gospel for the first time, notice that "Jesus is someone who arouses questions in his wake" (71). Moreover, the questions the narrator puts on the lips of Jesus (2:19, 25; 3:4; 8:12; 11:29–30; and esp. 8:29) become central in Mark's presentation. For van Oyen, the question of Jesus to the disciples in 8:29 "rises above the centuries" (84) and takes primary place: "But for you, who am I?" This is the question to which every reader must give a personal answer.

Mention of the identity of Jesus leads van Oyen to consider in chapter 6, "The Burden of Honorary Titles," the titles of Jesus that Mark employs. Van Oyen notes that Mark is only concerned with five titles: "Son of God," "Messiah" or "Christ," "Son of man," "Son of David," and "Lord." The last two are of no real importance to the evangelist, van Oyen acknowledges. *Christ* has the "highest christological tenor" other than *Son of God*, but van Oyen observes that "the earliest evangelist rarely refers to Jesus as the Christ and … the few times he does, he hastens to correct by a reference to the Son of man" (96). *Son of man* conveys the notion that Jesus will suffer and be vindicated by God. Since Jesus uses this title exclusively, readers must come to terms with this "title" despite what they may think about the other titles. The final title, *Son of God*, receives the most attention in this chapter. After highlighting the various uses of *Son of God* in Mark (1:1, 11; 3:11–12; 5:7; 9:7; 14:61–62; 15:39), van Oyen concludes:

> At first sight there cannot be a misunderstanding. Jesus is the Son of God. However, in attentively analyzing the passages concerned and placing them in their context, we notice that, apparent from the first verse, there exists in the head of the narrative like a strange hesitation to be fully involved with this term. It would rather seem that the evangelist retains and does not strongly affirm Jesus' identity by means of this honorary title. (89)

Chapter 7 traces the disciples' relationship to Jesus. The disciples misunderstand Jesus's teachings and fail to understand the true nature of the kingdom of God: they are unable to grasp the notions of suffering (8:31) and servanthood. Passages such as 8:34–7, 9:35, and 10:42–5 contain what van Oyen calls "the standards of judgment" that permit readers to judge whether disciples have responded appropriately to Jesus and his message (117). The penultimate chapter, "The Strength of the Powerless," presents van Oyen's "hermeneutic of Golgotha" (borrowed from Leander Keck), which brings this gospel's message to its undeniable point: giving of one's life in order to gain it. The final chapter asks the question "Where Is Jesus?" In addition to the obvious answer ("He has been raised; he is not here."), van Oyen believes the evangelist leaves readers with an "open ending." Readers are supposed to continue to "write" the gospel (133). What should readers write? Van Oyen offers "two paradoxical dyads" for consideration as the summation of the message of Jesus's identity. Jesus is, on the one hand, the crucified and risen one; on the other hand, he is the absent yet present one (137).

It is incumbent on a reviewer to review a book on its own terms. Van Oyen set out to write a book that would engage nonspecialists "to rediscover … the freshness and the energy of the originals" with the hopes of them beginning a dialogue with the Gospel of Mark. Has he been successful in this cause? I believe he has. Furthermore, I think he has done so in a way that has been faithful to the text of Mark's Gospel and to current biblical scholarship on the gospel. He engages the "postmodern" (or perhaps "post-Christian") reader through a hybrid of narrative-critical and reader-response methodology. He paves the way for this construction by setting forth the reasons why these approaches should lead toward an eventual "dialogue" with the ancient texts. He argues that this approach should be welcomed in the "public square," since the reader controls the definition of meaning and therefore all views should be welcomed. In short, would this book be helpful to a person outside the scholarly guild wishing to engage the Gospel of Mark? I think so.

Having said that, will the New Testament specialist find matters of concern in this work? Yes. Not all scholars will embrace van Oyen's methodological approach, and many narrative critics might think he has leaned a little too far in the direction of reader-response criticism. Others will think he has overstated Mark's hesitation to be "fully involved" with the title Son of God. Some may argue with what he sees as the purpose of Mark's narrative (declaring the identity of Jesus) or the manner in which he structures the gospel (three main parts centered on four major themes). Nevertheless, I think the New Testament scholar would be pleased with van Oyen's objective: helping the nonspecialist begin a dialogue with the Gospel of Mark. The specialist would also approve, I believe, in the choices of Markan (and other) scholars on whose shoulders van Oyen has attempted to stand. That fact is evident in the bibliographical entries he offers, which include works from Wrede to the present from scholars on both sides of the Atlantic and beyond. Finally, I think specialists will be impressed with how often van Oyen drives his readers to the biblical text itself. The volume is saturated with passages from Mark that fit nicely van Oyen's own narrative flow. An attentive scholar will find a few typographical errors (50, 60), but generally this slim book is clearly laid out and easy to read. A word of commendation should go to its translator as well. This is a book that could work well with undergraduate or graduate courses in the gospels (in general), the Gospel of Mark (in particular), or biblical interpretation.

Matthean Posteriority: An Exploration of Matthew's Use of Mark and Luke as a Solution to the Synoptic Problem, by Robert MacEwen. Library of New Testament Studies 501. London: T&T Clark, 2015. Pp. xxiii + 309. Hardcover. $112.00. ISBN 9780567364340.

J. Andrew Doole, University of Innsbruck

In theorizing over the chronology of four canonical gospels, we must essentially choose one of twenty-four possible arrangements. If we set aside John as insufficiently synoptic, we have still the complicated issues of not only the order but the relationship between the remaining three. While Markan priority is by no means universally accepted, the most common proposals have simply to sort out what is going on with Matthew and Luke in order to reconstruct a family tree from an apparently incestuous love-triangle.

We all learned the Two Document Hypothesis (2DH) as students, and most have come into some sort of dialogue with the Farrer Hypothesis (FH) of Luke's familiarity with some form of the Gospel of Matthew, a view with—rightly— many fans and advocates among modern Biblical scholars. It is therefore not only the self-esteemed holy and apostolic Church of the Two-Sources, with its inviable doctrine of *Logienquellioque*, that MacEwen comes to challenge but also the not inconsiderable might of the Great Schism of Lukan Creativity, a war on two fronts that, whatever its outcome, will, one hopes, force both opposing camps to reexamine their doctrines.

The book is the published result of a 2010 dissertation at Dallas Theological Seminary. It is, as MacEwen states in the subtitle, an "exploration" of the idea not only that Matthew is the last of the three synoptic evangelists to write, but that the Matthean Posteriority Hypothesis (MPH) implies that Matthew knows and uses Luke.

This is indeed a neglected proposal in the study of gospel origins. Although the idea has been around for a while, it remains a fringe theory, rarely studied in detail and at length. Thus, MacEwen confesses, "At the initial stage of this investigation I was not committed to the MPH, but wished to explore and test it." (4)

The book begins with a fair overview of important MPH proponents in their various forms (3–4, 6–26). A neat observation is that "the MPH has remained in such obscurity that proponents of the theory have sometimes been unaware of their predecessors" (6–7). MacEwen provides a list of problems that may need to be overcome, including "early church tradition," "the apparent complexity of Matthew's procedures," the "very different versions of the same event or topic" in Matthew and Luke, Matthew's "failure to be influenced by meaningful Lukan redaction" in Triple Tradition (TT) material, Luke's "different settings" for Double Tradition (DT) material, apparently "alternating primitiveness" and "whether the MPH should allow for Matthew to have used additional, hypothetical sources" (26). All but the first and last of these (early tradition and additional sources) are handled in detail in what follows.

MacEwen then turns to supporting evidence in chapter 2 (entitled "*Further* Arguments" in light of the *Forschungsbericht* discussed) and demonstrates intelligent study of parallel passages to explain how Matthew might have read Luke, including TT, DT, and Lukan *Sondergut* (27–50); he then provides a wealth of statistical evidence of "Strings of Verbatim Agreement" (SVAs), with preliminary conclusions (50–73) drawn from tables appended to the monograph (197–280, explained on pages 52–53). It is at this point that the reader may be overwhelmed with figures and abbreviations.

The Two-Gospel ("Griesbach") Hypothesis (2GH) is generally found wanting. The 2DH also suffers, primarily due to (1) a third of minor agreements being outside possible Mark-Q overlaps, (2) DT being more detailed in parallel than TT and thus more likely to have been unmediated, and (3) the unusual nature of the idea that two writers would undertake word-for-word copying from a common source. The MPH is found the "least problematic," as Matthew can be seen to be consistent in his conservatism in taking over material from sources, against the portrayal of an inconsistent Luke under the FH (72–73).

Chapter 3 then concerns "Some Challenges for Matthean Posteriority" (75–187). These challenges come generally from the arguments in favor of the 2DH (but the FH and the 2GH are also consistently considered and evaluated) and comprise apparently alternating primitiveness, Matthew's (strange?) omission of Lukan *Sondergut*, differences in parallel traditions (infancy and resurrection narratives and an inaugural sermon), and reasonable procedure for first-century author-scribes. It is here that MacEwen best demonstrates his skill as an exegete and argues convincingly against each challenge to his proposal of Matthew reading Luke, not Q.

In at least one element of MacEwen's research he appears to have surprised even himself, discovering through his statistics that the International Q Project most often prefers Matthew's wording (92–99). Evidence of alternating primitiveness is thus so rare as to provide little support to the 2DH but may provide fodder for the proponents of the FH. However, the general observation of agreement between Matthew and Luke in the wording of dominical *logia* more than in narrative remains a strong argument for the case for a *Logienquelle*, despite valiant and impressive attempts to explain theological and creative traits in either Luke (FH) or Matthew (MPH).

There are many interesting areas for debate, such as the claim, for example, that it should surprise us that two evangelists independently decided to provide a birth narrative and a genealogy "against the grain of the church's standard κήρυγμα" (129), that is, with reference to Mark, John, Paul, and the mini-gospels of Acts. Further, there is evidence of an evangelist being creative with or despite his source (MacEwen calls these "discordant parallels") in Luke's treatment of Jesus visiting Nazareth, calling fishermen, and being anointed by a woman, which do not lead us to dismiss the idea that Luke knew Mark (164). There is also the question of Matthew's omission of many of Luke's parables, which means he must omit more material than Luke under the FH or than both Luke and himself under the 2DH. Is he avoiding doublets? Does he not like the idea of a good Samaritan? Does he not approve of parables that portray God as an unjust steward (Luke 16:1–9), a fickle judge (18:1–8), a sleepy and grumpy friend (11:5–8), or a foolish father (15:11–32)? Perhaps Matthew just really did not like stories (116)!

In all of this MacEwen faces the perhaps inevitable difficulty of considering and rejecting each alternative theory (2GH, 2DH, FH) while arguing for his own (MPH). He can suggest Matthew changing his mind midcomposition (45) and being so familiar with Luke as to recall certain logia from memory (163), even suggesting that it is possible to see Luke as a user of scrolls, while thoroughly modern Matthew opts for codices (178), the iPad of the first century. The arguments MacEwen brings are well presented and incisive, though it is often difficult to see Matthew and his Christian contemporaries as quite as logical and systematic as modern biblical scholars.

This begs the question as to what the Gospel of Matthew represents. Observations on a micro-level may help to explain why Matthew made the individual changes assigned to him under the MPH, resulting in what quickly became for the church the "culmination" of gospel tradition (37 n. 29), but we can still ask of the MPH: What on earth (and in heaven) was Matthew doing? The same question is posed of Luke under the FH and Mark under the 2GH. Each final evangelist's relationship to his sources must be explained; it is not enough simply to explain the details.

MacEwen provides us with a thorough and well-researched study of the *possibility* that Matthew knew not only the Gospel of Mark but also that of Luke. He is well-read on the most up-to-date contributions of scholars who support the MPH (from the famous to the obscure) and rival theories (especially, of course, the leading proponents of the 2GH, 2DH, and FH, respectively).

In New Testament gospel studies, of course, the 2DH remains the democratically elected head of state. The leader of the opposition has recently been a post held securely by the FH, and it is refreshing to have a new case for a peripheral candidate. MacEwen almost always comes down against the 2GH, whose position becomes all the more untenable. His criticism of his main rival, the FH, proves successful in many regards and should be taken seriously by anyone considering Lukan familiarity with the Gospel of Matthew. At times one wonders if the arguments against the established 2DH are directed too specifically to the International Q Project and the idea of a reconstruction of Q. Nevertheless, MacEwen is surely correct in concluding, following a desideratum of an MPH commentary on the Gospel of Matthew, that the theory of Matthew's familiarity with Luke "is worthy of more consideration than scholars have usually given it" (196). He has certainly convinced me.

Jesus and the Thoughts of Many Hearts: Implicit Christology and Jesus' Knowledge in the Gospel of Luke, by Collin Blake Bullard. Library of New Testament Studies 530. London: T&T Clark, 2015. Pp. xviii + 210. Hardcover. $112.00. ISBN 9780567660350.

Tyler Smith, University of Ottawa

This volume is a revised version of Collin Blake Bullard's 2013 dissertation, supervised by Simon Gathercole at Cambridge. Its subject is the Lukan motif of Jesus's privileged access to the "thoughts" of those he encounters in the Third Gospel, especially those with whom he comes into opposition. In a nutshell, the argument is that Luke's Jesus can bring the "thoughts of many hearts" to light, which is a special and notable characteristic of the Jewish God, with the consequence that Luke's Jesus is closer to sharing his identity with that God.

Bullard uses redaction and narrative criticism in his argument that Luke's Jesus possesses the ability to reveal thoughts by virtue of his identity as Lord. While the ability is apparently assumed of Jesus also in Mark and Matthew, Luke goes further than either of his synoptic counterparts in developing the motif. Furthermore, comparing Lukan and Matthean redaction in parallel passages shows how a common store of material could be developed differently to suit different agendas in Matthew and Luke. Bullard proposes that the Lukan agenda in this respect is set by the prophecy of Simeon at Luke 2:34–35, which speaks to Jesus's destiny: "This child is destined for the falling and rising of many in Israel, and to be a sign that will be opposed so that the inner thoughts [*dialogismoi*] of many will be revealed." Bullard indicates that studies of Simeon's prophecy have not satisfactorily connected its final line to subsequent narrative representations of inner thoughts revealed in the presence of the Lukan Jesus and that studies of the motif in Luke are generally limited to passing remarks connecting it to a handful of ancient texts and figures roughly contemporary with the activity of the gospel writers. These typically include figures such as the priest of Isis in Apuleius's *The Golden Ass*, anonymous magicians in the Greek Magical Papyri, and especially Apollonius of Tyana as represented in the third-century *Vita Apollonii* by Philostratus. What has been missing, and what Bullard provides, is an exhaustive account of the motif in Luke. With Simeon's prophecy as his anchor, Bullard traces a narrative-critical account of the motif through the Third Gospel, the upshot of which is that Luke implies (hence the "implied Christology" featured in the book's subtitle) that Jesus is *kyrios*.

The book is divided into three chapters prefaced by a substantive introduction and followed by a summary conclusion. The introduction collects and associates the passages in Luke that best illustrate the "knowledge of thoughts" phenomenon, surveys the history of scholarship on two topics (Jesus's knowledge of thoughts and Simeon's oracle), and previews the coming chapters. Chapter 1 is mainly concerned with the knowledge of thoughts motif in Greco-Roman sources, on the one hand, and Jewish sources, on the other. Against intimations in earlier scholarship that the motif in Luke is a "Hellenistic touch," Bullard argues that knowledge of thoughts is equivalent to "knowledge of hearts" and a special prerogative of the Jewish God (see Luke 1:51; 16:15) and so an integral feature of Luke's Christology.

Chapter 2 follows Luke Timothy Johnson in reading Simeon's oracle as "programmatic prophecy," that is, a prophecy that introduces a major theme. Here the theme is, of course, the opposition and conflict that would result from Jesus's ministry. The revelation of thoughts, Bullard contends, are thus positioned to function as a chief mechanism in bringing that opposition and conflict to light.

Chapter 3, constituting about half of the book by page count, offers close readings of six passages in the gospel in which the motif appears (the healing of the paralytic in 5:17–26; the man with the withered hand in 6:6–11; the exchange with Simon the Pharisee in 7:36–50; the disciples' question of who is the greatest in 9:46–48; the Beelzebul controversy in 11:14–32; and the "woes" against the Pharisees and scribes in 11:37–54) as well as shorter remarks on the Nazareth sermon (4:16–30), the parable of the good Samaritan (10:25–37), the parable of the rich farmer (12:16–20), Jesus dining with the Pharisees (14:1–6), God's knowledge of the heart (16:14–15), and taxes to Caesar (20:20–26). This sprawling chapter then moves into narrative-critical remarks about the introductions to speeches, remarks on the special Lukan parables, analyses of the appearance of Jesus to his disciples at the end of Luke (24:36–43) and the prayer of the disciples in Acts 1:24, then concludes with a section proposing that Luke's development of the motif was informed specifically by verse 11 of Ps 94 [93 LXX], where the Lord knows thoughts (*dialogismoi* in the LXX, as in Simeon's oracle of Jesus). Luke's presentation of Jesus as Lord will ipso facto have involved Jesus's knowledge of thoughts. The point, Bullard is careful to emphasize, is not that Luke set out to prove that Jesus in his capacity as Lord knows thoughts. Rather, "some of Luke's latent assumptions concerning Jesus' knowledge of thoughts are evident in the way in which Luke incorporated the theme into the Gospel narrative" (174). The short conclusion to the book summarizes its findings under four headings: "Ancient Context," "Jesus as Revealer," "Jesus as Judge," and "Jesus' Knowledge of Thoughts as a Divine Ability." The upshot of the first is that Luke has not integrated the motif as a "light Hellenistic touch" from a *theios anēr* typology; the second and third points connect knowledge of thoughts to revealing and judging as kyriotic functions attributed to the Lukan Jesus; and the fourth heading speaks for itself. Bullard's argument is that the revelation of thoughts is a divine quality in Luke, not a remarkable human ability and not (at least not primarily) a prophetic characteristic.

Bullard's well-organized study carefully identifies a research question that had been widely noted but never addressed in a monograph-length study. He collects and engages a broad range of secondary scholarship on Luke, much of it in French and German, and models the fruitful results of coordinated redaction- and narrative-critical scholarship. He schematizes possible ways making sense of the motif (a supernatural human ability? a prophetic ability? a divine ability?) and takes a clear and consistent stand on how best to account for the data (knowledge of thoughts is a divine ability). The book will be of interest to those working on the history of prophecy, on preliterary Jesus traditions, on the *theios anēr* question, and especially to those whose interest is Lukan Christology. The book is well footnoted, providing an extensive record of Bullard's journey of discovery and opportunities for the interested reader to carry on the investigation. Readers who are interested in Bullard's work should also be alerted to Michal Beth Dinkler's "'The Thoughts of Many Hearts Shall Be Revealed': Listening In on Lukan Interior Monologues" (*JBL* 134 [2015]: 373–99), which must have appeared just a little too late for Bullard to engage in his book.

Although Bullard does not make them the focus of his exegetical labors, some of his most potent insights have to do with Lukan passages that have troubled early scholarship because of apparent inconsistencies in what happens at the level of story (the things said and done by characters on the scene) and what Jesus says in response. Jesus's responses are shown to be made *not* to the things said or done but rather at exposing and confronting the unspoken thoughts and motives that lay behind the words and actions of his interlocutors. A banner example is in

Jesus's exchange with the lawyer who comes to test Jesus in Luke 10. Many have pointed out that Jesus's answer, with its so-called parable of the good Samaritan, does not answer the man's question, "Who is my neighbor?" (10:29b). What Jesus's response *does* answer is the man's unspoken motive—relayed by the narrator to the audience—"wishing to justify himself" (10:29a). When the parable is read as an answer to this unspoken motive—the "thought of the man's heart"—Jesus's parable becomes an exposé of the man's self-justifying machinations, aligning him with those in the parable who want to limit the scope of their obligation to love and establish their own righteousness in the process (142).

As might be expected in a monograph that is, by the author's own admission, designed to explore the title's subject ad nauseum (139), Bullard's reader must be prepared for a certain amount of repetition. Bullard is to be commended, though, for his conscious attempts to limit repetition in his third chapter, where he follows the same schema (presentation of Jesus's knowledge, Luke's redaction of the passage, resonance of the passage with Simeon's oracle, and implicit Christology) in each of the chief passages up for analysis. Despite some unavoidable repetitions in this section, Bullard says something new in connection to each pericope.

Although the target audience for this book is never identified explicitly, it must overlap substantially with the audience of the dissertation. Nonspecialists may be hampered, for example, by the fact that Greek citations are usually left untranslated. There is occasional slippage into word studies and statistics for vocabulary frequency in Luke or the New Testament, not all of it illuminating. There is also a great deal of summarizing what mainstream commentators (especially Bock, Bovon, Fitzmyer, Johnson, Green, Marshall, Noland, Plummer) say about the passages that Bullard takes up. These are sometimes helpful only indirectly—that is, when they show how the commentators' questions have little or nothing to do with Bullard's topic. There is a generally unquestioned, pervasive, problematic assumption in the book that a "Jewish" or "Jewish Christian" context exists (represented by the "OT" and "STJ"—the latter for "Second Temple Jewish literature") as meaningfully distinct from the "Greco-Roman" or "Hellenistic" context. A primary goal of the book is to determine which of the two contexts is the more appropriate background for understanding the presence of the thoughts of hearts motif in Luke (16). But this is too simple, too reminiscent of scholarship insensitive to the Hellenism in all Second Temple Jewish literature, most obviously in texts such as the Maccabean, Josephan, or Philonic corpora.

Bullard commendably attends to the differences between story and discourse, the role of the narrator and the knowledges of readers and characters, and diverging points of view but fails to engage literary-critical scholarship on narrative representations of cognition, so readers who come to this book looking for engagement with cognitive narratology or any of the varieties of scholarship under the umbrella term *cognitive science of religion* will be largely disappointed. Bullard's finding that Lukan thought representations generally function for the audience, not for the benefit of characters in the story, deserves more attention in conversation with critical scholarship on the narrative functions of thought representations undertaken by theorists such as Dorrit Cohn, Alan Palmer, and Lisa Zunshine. Bullard draws a contrast between Luke and the Fourth Gospel, where characters respond on the level of story to Jesus's preternatural ability to know thoughts (175–76), which would be well worth exploring in dialogue with narratological work on the functions thought representations can perform in various narrative genres, ancient and modern. Another missed opportunity is consideration of Lukan interior monologues in relation to ongoing conversations in classical and biblical scholarship about interiority and the nature of the self in antiquity (on which, see the Dinkler article noted above). If Bullard's project is not positioned to make major contributions to the study of the self or cognition in New Testament narrative criticism, however, it does an admirable job of complementing theological studies of Lukan Christology such as C. Kavin Rowe's *Early Narrative Christology: The Lord in the Gospel of Luke*, which is cited appreciatively and often throughout the book.

Peter: False Disciple and Apostate according to Saint Matthew, by Robert H. Gundry. Grand Rapids: Eerdmans, 2015. Pp. xx + 119. Paper. $20.00. ISBN 9780802872937.

Marius J. Nel, University of Stellenbosch

In this provocative book Robert Gundry argues that the Gospel of Matthew portrays the apostle Peter as a false disciple who publicly apostatized and therefore is destined for eternal damnation (vii). Gundry thus goes further than scholars who see Matthew's portrayal of Peter as being merely unfavorable or ambivalent.

Chapter 1 consists of a brief introduction in which Gundry defines the focus of his study as the portrayal of Peter in the Gospel of Matthew and not the historical, literary, or ecclesiastical Peters (2). A careful study of Matthew's redaction of Mark and his depiction of Peter in his narrative leads Gundry to conclude that, even though Matthew does not explicitly pronounce judgment on Peter, he consistently presents the evidence for him being a false disciple of Jesus (3). Gundry ascribes Matthew's reluctance to pronounce explicit judgement on Peter as being due to Jesus's prohibition of weeding out tares (false disciples) before the harvest (the consummation) and judging others (see 5:22; 7:1–2).

Chapter 2 indicates how Matthew does not, as is often assumed by scholars, give Peter a special position in his narrative prior to 16:13–23. Gundry, for example, argues that Peter in 4:18–20 is not given an honorific name by Matthew and that he is described as merely responding to Jesus's call as the other disciples had. Matthew also excludes Peter from important events such as the healing in 8:14–15. He is thus not central to every story that involved the disciples. While Peter is described in 10:2–4 as being the "first" in the list of apostles, being "first" is not necessarily a positive attribute in Matthew (9), since he emphasizes that the first will be "last" (19:29–30; 20:1–16). Peter being described as being first in 10:2 could thus point to him in fact being last and therefore lost (9). It is noteworthy that Matthew often speaks of Peter's failures. In the story of Jesus and

Peter walking on the sea (14:22–33), he depicts Peter as doubting if it is Jesus (14:28) who is walking on the sea and then almost drowning when he doubts again. Peter is also not included in the confession of the disciples in the boat that Jesus is truly the son of God (13). In 15:12–20 Matthew changes the question by the disciples in Mark about the meaning of the parables to that of Peter alone as their spokesperson. He also changes Jesus's response to his question into a rebuke as to how specifically Peter can still be ignorant of their meaning. Peter is thus not depicted in Matthew as the primary recipient and guarantor of Jesus's teaching.

Matthew 16:13–23, in which Peter figures prominently, is the focus of chapter 3. Gundry argues that Peter should not be given to much credit for his confession that Jesus is the Christ, the Son of the living God, since it simply indicates that he has caught up with the confession of the other disciples in 14:33 (16). His pronouncement of being blessed by Jesus also does not mean that he is saved. Significantly, Jesus also does not call Peter the bedrock on which he will build his church. Instead, the bedrock, as in 7:24, represents the words of Jesus, as is indicated by Matthew's shifting Jesus's second-person address of Peter to a third-person reference to his words. In this regard bedrock and the keys, used for opening or closing the door to the kingdom, have the same referent. The Matthean insertions into Mark's account (e.g., the command "Go behind me, Satan!" which recalls his account of the temptation of Jesus, and the designation of Peter as his "snare") consistently paints a negative picture of Peter (30).

Chapter 4 looks at Matthew's depiction of Peter from the transfiguration of Jesus up to the Garden of Gethsemane. By paying close attention to how Matthew redacted Mark, Gundry (31–42) reveals how Matthew emphasizes Peter's self-aggrandizing (17:1–8; 19:27–30; 26:31–35), failures (26:36–46), and angling for compensation (19:27–30), which resulted in him being sharply corrected by Jesus (17:24–27; 18:21–22). Matthew's redaction thus consistently depicts Peter as not exhibiting the superior righteousness required for entering the kingdom of heaven (see 5:20).

Chapter 5 focuses on Peter's denial of Jesus and Judas Iscariot's suicide, which for Gundry constitute the heart of Matthew's portrayal of Peter as a false disciple who apostatized (43). From 26:57 to 27:10 Matthew depicts Peter as reneging on his promise to suffer with Jesus (26:35) by emphasizing how he progressively distanced himself from Jesus (44). Not only does he watch the trail of Jesus from afar, but he wilts before a lone maid (26:69) and denies Jesus before all. Thereafter Matthew has him go out into the gateway (26:71), where he is confronted by another maid to whom he proclaims with an oath that he did not know "the man" (26:72). Matthew's doubling of Peter's oath taking casts him in an extremely bad light, since it implies that in line with Jesus's prohibition against oath taking (5:33–37) he has damned himself (50). After Peter denies Jesus a third time with the swearing of an oath, the cockcrow sounds, after which Matthew redacts Mark to emphasize that Peter went outside and wept bitterly (26:74–75). Gundry, however, does not interpret the adverb as intensifying Peter's repentance but rather as signaling his despair over his lost salvation (51). Supporting this interpretation, according to Gundry, are the numerous Matthean passages (8:12; 13:41–42; 13:49–50; 22:13; 24:51; 25:30), of which many are either inserted into otherwise parallel material (22:13; 24:51; 25:30) or appear in Matthew's unparalleled material (see 5:13; 13:48), which connotes weeping and the gnashing of teeth with eternal perdition in the outermost darkness (51). Peter is thus depicted as a false disciple who, in line with the warnings of Jesus, has been thrown into eternal damnation in the outermost darkness (52).

After surveying the various attempts of rehabilitating Peter (52–56) Gundry concludes than none has succeeded because they do not take note of the emphatically Matthean combination of weeping outside by the damned as an interpretative background for Peter's own weeping (56). For him it is not an indication of his repentance but rather of damnation (62). Combined with Matthew's topographical and chronological disjointed and distinct account of Judas's remorseful but hopeless suicide, Gundry concludes that Peter remained an apostate among true disciples in Matthew. The understanding of Peter's weeping as signaling his remorse, which leads to his reconciliation with Jesus, is to read Peter's portrayal in the other gospels into Matthew.

Chapter 6 surveys Matthew's omission of references to Peter occurring in Mark in a number of passages (9:23–25; 21:18–22; 24:3; 28:7) that contradict the commonly held view that Matthew highlights Peter as the apostolic first among equals and as the church's foundation. Chapters 7 and 8 focus on two related and intertwined Matthean themes, false discipleship and oppression, respectively, which strengthen the case against Peter. In these chapters Gundry argues that Matthew has a strong emphasis on the presence of false disciples in the church (79) and the reality of persecution. It is the latter that exposes falsity, since it is when they are persecuted that erstwhile disciples hide their profession of discipleship to protect themselves and in some instances, like Peter, even apostatize (90).

The last chapter recapitulates the way in which Matthew portrays Peter as a false disciple who publicly apostatized and some of the implications of this portrayal before the book concludes with an afterword. An important implication of Matthew's negative portrayal of Peter is that it points to an early date for his gospel, since it would have been difficult, if not impossible, to depict him in this negative manner after his martyrdom.

Through this brief but meticulously argued study, Gundry makes a strong case for the apostasy of Peter. While Gundry's conclusion will struggle to gain broad acceptance, it cannot be dismissed out of hand. A careful engagement with its specific exegetical conclusions is therefore called for. It is in this engagement that questions can, however, be asked of specific interpretations made by Gundry. Is it, for example, tenable that Matthew deliberately gives Peter no credit for his confession of Jesus as the Son of God in 16:16–17 becasue it is due to a revelation by God, and not an inner conviction, when he has Jesus calling him "blessed" in the same passage? If Matthew had in his narrative deliberately omitted Peter from the confession made by the other disciples in 14:33, it is not clear why he is given an opportunity to do so at all in 16:16. Would Matthew, in his redaction of Mark, not have made sure that there is no ambivalence in how his readers would perceive Peter (i.e., as a disciple who had never confessed that Jesus is the Son of God)? The same can be said of the interpretation by Gundry of Peter's weeping in 26:75 as signaling his anguish over losing his place in the kingdom of God. According to Gundry, the formula "weeping and gnashing of teeth" is used specifically by Matthew in 8:12; 13:41–42, 49–50; 22:13; 24:51; and 25:30 for those who lose their salvation. If the function of this particular formula is thus to signal that a person is lost, it is peculiar that Matthew has omitted the gnashing of teeth part thereof in his description of Peter's anguish. Does this omission not signal that Peter is not to be confused with those who are indeed destined for eternal punishment in Matthew? The argument that Matthew can explicitly depict Judas, but not Peter, as lost without contravening Jesus's prohibition of judging others (7:1), since Jesus, who has the authority to do so, had condemned Judas in 26:24, is also not convincing. Is Matthew, in making Peter's falsity apparent to his readers without himself declaring him lost, not simply thereby asking his readers to judge Peter themselves? It is thus not clear that Matthew's fear of transgressing Jesus's prohibition of judging others can explain why he does not explicitly declare Peter to be an apostate if he wants his readers to recognize and judge him as such. As is evident from these brief remarks, Gundry's fine study deserves a close and critical reading by all who have an interest in the study of Matthew.

The Metaphor of Shepherd in the Gospel of Mark, by Jogy Cheruvathoor George. European University Studies. Series 23: Theology 950. Frankfurt am Main: Lang, 2015. Pp. 266. Paper. €59.95. ISBN 9783631664476.

Wayne Baxter, Heritage College and Seminary

While scholars began mining the shepherd metaphor in the Hebrew Bible generations ago, examinations of this trope in the New Testament have a shorter history. The past decade has seen a heightened interest in the appropriation of this motif by the writers of the New Testament. With *The Metaphor of Shepherd in the Gospel of Mark*, Jogy Cheruvathoor George adds to the growing cadre of New Testament monographs that focus on the shepherd metaphor. This work represents George's doctoral dissertation completed in 2014 at the Pontifical Gregorian University in Rome, under the supervision of Massimo Grilli.

After a brief introduction to the nature and scope of his work, the book divides into two, two-chapter sections, each one revolving around Mark's explicit use of "shepherd" (ποιμήν). Part 1, "The Care of the Shepherd and the Incomprehension of the Disciples," begins with a careful survey of Mark 1:1–6:29: the prolegomena to the first occurrence of "shepherd" in 6:34. In the first chapter, "The Care for the Shepherdless," George focuses particularly on the deployment of "way" (ὁδός) because of its programmatic usage in Mark, occurring at key structural points in the gospel, as well as twice in the prologue, including the citation of Isa

40:3, a text that within its broader context (specifically, Isa 40:11) intersects with the shepherd metaphor. George maintains that further connections can be made between the metaphor and "way" through the evangelist's steady use of ἄγω (typically translated "lead") and its cognates, thereby evoking shepherding imagery in Mark's narrative. George shows through rigorous analysis how the first feeding account reveals the identity of Jesus as Israel's Shepherd. He argues, on the one hand, that Mark depicts Jesus as the one who shepherds God's people by nourishing them through his teaching (Mark 6:34b) and by miraculously providing for the crowd's physical needs through the multiplication of the loaves and fish (6:35–44). He asserts, on the other, that the evangelist's phrase "like sheep without a shepherd" alludes to Ezek 34:13–14 and Ps 23, which speak of YHWH shepherding his people by tending to their physical needs.

The second chapter, "The Care for the Gentiles and the Uncomprehending Disciples," offers a comprehensive examination of Mark 6:45–8:21. George identifies the linguistic and conceptual links between the first feeding miracle in 6:30–44 and the subsequent episodes of Jesus walking on the water (6:45–52), his healing of the Syrophoenician woman (7:24–30), the second feeding miracle (8:1–9), as well as the controversy with the Pharisees and Jesus's ensuing rebuke of his disciples (8:10–21). Key to George's exegesis of this section of the narrative is the gospel writer's use of the words "eat" (ἐσθίω), "bread" (ἄρτος), and "satisfy" (χορτάζομαι), for these terms evoke shepherding imagery (their Hebrew counterparts are associated with the metaphor in the Old Testament/Hebrew Bible), thus extending the shepherd metaphor beyond 6:30–44. George believes that, having revealed Jesus as Israel's Shepherd, the evangelist in 6:45–8:21, consequently, demonstrates how Jesus "manifested" his identity to his disciples: Jesus is the compassionate shepherd who sees his people's struggles, rescues and leads them to a place of safety and abundance, and extends his powerful shepherding to the gentiles. But they fail to recognize his self-revelation nor do they understand the true nature of his identity as Israel's Shepherd.

Part 2, "The Scandal and the New Communion," opens with the chapter, "The Smitten Shepherd and the Dispersion of the Sheep," which surveys Mark 8:27–14:25 in order to set the table for the second explicit occurrence of "shepherd" in 14:27. In this section the Markan Jesus reveals "the way" and how to participate in it. Once Jesus reaches the temple, his confrontation with the authorities sheds further light on his identity, but his opponents reject his message, resulting in the religious leaders' plot to kill him, thus introducing the passion narrative. In Mark's deployment of "taking," "blessing," "broke," and "gave," George observes resonances with the table fellowship Jesus offered the crowds in the two feeding miracles, thus evoking shepherd imagery in the Last Supper scene. George spends a great deal of time analyzing the evangelist's appropriation of the "stricken shepherd" prophecy of Zech 13:7 in Mark 14:27, believing that Mark has transposed the metaphor: from God's close associate who shepherded Israel but whose shepherding role terminates with his death that refines the remnant, to the beloved Son of God, the Shepherd of both Israel and the gentiles, whose death brings about eternal communion with his disciples and whose resurrection results in the reconstitution of his scattered followers.

The fourth chapter, "The New Beginning," outlines how Jesus the stricken shepherd's earlier prophecies of his followers' betrayal, dispersal, and denial (14:27–30) come to fruition in 14:43–52 and 14:66–72. The fulfillment of his predictions of resurrection and of his going ahead of his disciples takes place in Mark 16. That Jesus's resurrection corresponds to and fulfills his earlier prediction of the stricken shepherd means that, in George's view, Zech 13:7 also lies in background of the resurrection narrative. This shepherd imagery becomes further extended by Mark's use of "go ahead" (προάγω) in 16:7, because George believes that "going ahead" is characteristic of shepherds and shepherding imagery in the Hebrew Bible. Jesus, then, is the resurrected Shepherd who invites people to experience a new beginning by following him and proclaiming the gospel. George concludes his work by explaining the theological significance of the shepherd metaphor for Mark, noting how it contributes to the evangelist's Christology: Jesus Christ, the Son of God (1:1), is the Shepherd who teaches, nourishes, and leads his people; and to his Missiology: the metaphor serves as the literary vehicle to transition Jesus's mission from the Jews to the gentiles, while emphasizing the final universality of the gospel community.

George should be commended for his stimulating exploration into the shepherd metaphor. He does an excellent job of tracing the flow of Mark's narrative and how the passages in focus contribute to the wider literary panel in the story. His analysis of the text captures the highly interwoven nature of biblical narratives. I especially appreciate the discussion on how "the way" and "shepherd" motifs coalesce in Mark.

Given the nature of George's thesis—exploring the shepherd metaphor in a book where it only explicitly appears twice—I believe his study would have gained significant strength had he developed the foundation of his argument more extensively in his introduction. His delineation of the metaphor rests on its association with key words such as "satisfy" (χορτάζομαι), "gathering" (συνάγω), and "lead" (ἄγω). While George describes how the Hebrew equivalents for these terms are associated with shepherding imagery in the Hebrew Bible, his discussion is far too brief to be convincing. A case can surely be made, but, in order to make his argument, George needed either to expand the introduction or to devote the first chapter to building his foundation by tracing and assessing every occurrence of the Hebrew words in the Hebrew Bible and cross-referencing and evaluating their Greek equivalents in the Septuagint. As it is, the reader is left with nagging doubts about the extent to which these words actually do bear the shepherding imagery George claims. His work seems aimed more for a sympathetic audience than for a broader one waiting to be persuaded.

Although I enjoy how George works through the narrative, the shepherd metaphor too tightly controls how he reads the text. He tends to read Mark in light of the shepherd metaphor rather than seeking to understand the motif in light of the gospel as a whole. Thus he periodically overreaches in his assessment of the metaphor. For example, as he concludes his analysis of Mark 6:30–44, noting the evangelist's allusions to the food miracles wrought by Moses, Elijah, and Elisha, George asserts, "The image of Jesus as the Shepherd is the thread in which the narrator has constructed and bound all these OT images in this pericope" (82). Doubtless the shepherd metaphor resonates in the passage, but does it trump, say, the imagery of "prophet" that loudly echoes throughout 6:1–29 (the prophet without honor logion and the death of John the Baptist)? While YHWH shepherded his people under the aegis of Moses, Elijah, and Elisha, these figures are characterized first and foremost as prophets, not shepherds, in the Hebrew Bible. Although I found George's interfacing between the shepherd motif and "the way" of Isa 40:3 to be quite insightful, he seems to assume that Mark's way motif ought to be read in light of the shepherd metaphor. That the way motif, however, is part of the much larger and more significant Isaiah theme that reverberates throughout Mark (as numerous scholars, such as Marcus, Caneday, and Watts, have pointed out) suggests the opposite direction of influence. While generally on the right track, George's study would benefit from greater theological nuancing and restraint.

In the end, George offers a thought-provoking work. By not following the path of earlier and more expected explorations of the shepherd motif in Matthew and John, George blazes a unique trail in shepherd metaphor studies. His discussion of the intersection of the way and the shepherd trope opens the door to unexplored areas of how these two themes might interface in texts bearing much more explicit shepherding imagery, such as Matthew or John. Thus George's monograph points the way to future, fruitful study in this field.

Rejected Prophets: Jesus and His Witnesses in Luke-Acts, by Jocelyn McWhirter. Minneapolis: Fortress, 2014. Pp. x + 144. Paper. $29.00. ISBN 9781451470024.

David M. Miller, Briercrest College

This short volume is more than a fresh investigation of an important theme in Luke-Acts; it is also an interpretation of Luke-Acts as a Jewish-Christian text addressed to a "religious movement within Judaism" (7) whose members were still mourning the loss of the temple and bewildered by the tragic and surprising events that followed the coming of their Messiah.

In the introduction McWhirter describes how the book grew out of her experience teaching Luke's Gospel and attempting to integrate Luke's major ideas. Her solution, defended in the rest of the book, is to read Luke's narrative as a story of rejected prophets. She also states her guiding assumptions, including Luke's dependence on Mark and Q, his intimate familiarity with the Jewish Scriptures, and a date for Luke-Acts in the 80s or 90s, shortly after the First Jewish Revolt.

The first chapter situates the book in relation to other scholarship on prophecy in Luke-Acts. Luke's prophetic characterization of Jesus and his followers is widely recognized. What sets her contribution apart, McWhirter suggests, is her attempt to relate the "rejected prophet" motif directly to Luke's purpose and to reconstruct the questions in the minds of Luke's "sceptical" Jewish-Christian audience to which the story of Jesus and his prophetic followers provides convincing answers. According to McWhirter, characters in the narrative articulate the audience's actual questions—about the crucifixion of the Messiah, the widespread rejection of Jesus by Jews, the positive response of gentiles, and the destruction of the Jerusalem temple—and the narrative makes them thematic. Luke's answers appeal to fulfilled prophecy and to prophetic characterization in order to offer biblical precedent and to confirm that these events correspond to God's plan. McWhirter observes that Luke's use of scriptural allusions to defend its central characters and to persuade a "sceptical audience" resembles the way in which 1 Maccabees links its main characters to "biblical heroes" in order to legitimate the Hasmoneans as Israel's rightful rulers.

Luke's portrayal of Jesus as a prophet does not eclipse the title *Messiah*, and it is the idea of a crucified Messiah bringing salvation that, McWhirter suggests, Luke's Jewish audience found hard to grasp. The second chapter, then, addresses how Luke uses prophecy to confirm that the crucified Jesus is Israel's Messiah. Luke also associates forgiveness with fulfilled prophecy and with Jesus's prophetic role to show that Jesus the Messiah was able to forgive sins and in this way "to save the lost."

Chapter 3 considers parallels between the biblical prophet Samuel and Jesus and John the Baptist. Like Samuel, John's conception was a miraculous answer to prayer; the births of both are connected to God's sanctuary; both are depicted as Nazirites; and both experience God's favor. There are also connections within the infancy narrative between Jesus and Samuel: Mary's Magnificat in Luke 1 recalls Hannah's song in 1 Sam 2, and, like Samuel, Jesus is associated with the sanctuary both at his dedication and again at age twelve (Luke 2). According to McWhirter, the Samuel parallels contribute to Luke's characterization of John and Jesus as "trustworthy prophets who will carry out God's plan—a plan that centers on the temple and reaches out to include the poor and lowly" (32).

The next three chapters illustrate how Luke's depiction of Jesus as a prophet responds to his audience's questions about Jesus and the messianic age. Each chapter surveys one of Luke's central questions, discusses how Luke presents his answer as the fulfillment of prophecy, and argues that Luke legitimates it by linking Jesus to one or more different biblical prototypes.

Chapter 4 addresses connections between Jesus and the Elijah of 1–2 Kings, proposing that the Elijah parallels help legitimate the mission to gentiles. According to McWhirter, Luke claims that the inclusion of gentiles in God's salvation fulfills the prophecies of Isaiah and Joel, but it also recalls the actions of the biblical prophets Elijah and Elisha, to whom Jesus refers in his Nazareth sermon. These parallels set up the transition between Jesus and his disciples and confirm that Jesus's disciples, who extend the offer of salvation to gentiles, are Jesus's successors, just as Elisha was to Elijah.

In chapter 5 McWhirter argues that subtle links between Jesus and Moses in Luke's Gospel prepare for the explicit comparison with Moses in Acts 3 and 7 and underscore the penalty of judgment against those who fail to listen to Jesus, the prophet like Moses. Jesus's words and actions, however, correspond more closely to Jeremiah. The parallels legitimate Jesus despite his rejection by a majority of the Jewish people.

Chapter 6 explores how Jesus's prediction of the temple's demise draws on biblical prophecies about the destruction of the First Temple. These verbal echoes remind Luke's audience of biblical precedent and form part of Luke's response to Christian "anguish" about the recent destruction of Jerusalem and the Second Temple.

Chapters 7–9 discuss the function of Luke's prophetic characterization of main characters in Acts. In chapter 7 McWhirter focuses on the transition between Jesus and the apostles in general, and Peter in particular, by recalling the transition between Elijah and Elisha. To confirm the transfer of prophetic authority from Jesus to Peter and the apostles, Luke depicts Peter speaking and acting in ways that recall the prophetic speech and activity of the prophet Jesus.

In chapter 8 we find that prophets like Jesus, such as the apostles, Peter, and Stephen, are also rejected prophets like Moses. References in Acts to the "signs and wonders" that Jesus and the apostles perform link Jesus and his witnesses to the "signs and wonders" performed by Moses in Egypt. After the resurrection of Jesus, the Jews who had rejected Jesus during his earthly life are given a second chance to respond to Jesus as he is proclaimed by his witnesses in Acts, who are also prophets like Moses. These two rejections of Jesus parallel the two rejections of Moses described in Stephen's speech in Acts 7 and, from Luke's perspective, justify the recent destruction of Jerusalem by the Romans.

Chapter 9 takes up the theme of the extension of salvation to Gentiles. Any questions about Philip's baptism of the *gentile* Ethiopian eunuch are answered when Peter, whose authority as a prophet like Jesus is now well established, witnesses the Holy Spirit falling upon Cornelius's household. Subsequent parallels between Peter, Jesus, and Paul validate Paul's full-blown mission to gentiles later in Acts. By the end of Acts, readers recognize that Paul's fate corresponds to the fate of rejected prophets before him. Paul, for his part, remains faithful to his prophetic vocation, proclaiming the word to all who will listen.

In the conclusion McWhirter suggests that the particular constellation of issues Luke addresses in his two-volume work is best explained if Luke was "a Jew, writing for an audience of primarily Jewish Christians." She notes that concerns about the rejection and death of Jesus, the destruction of Jerusalem, and the inclusion of gentiles "are Jewish questions posed by Jewish characters," and Luke's attempt to reassure his audience through the use of prophecy and prophetic characterization "would appeal to Jews" (123–24). McWhirter also tackles the contemporary implications of Luke's message. According to McWhirter, the challenge to listen to Jesus and adhere to his message and mission remains relevant when it is heard as a message to contemporary Christians. But while Luke's answer about the temple's destruction originally "made sense" to a "Jewish minority within Judaism," it caused great harm after its original first-century Jewish setting was lost.

Rejected Prophets brims with insight. Even when McWhirter draws on earlier studies, her work advances the discussion by demonstrating that Luke's use of prophecy and prophetic characterization functions within the narrative to legitimate the gentile mission and to present Jewish rejection and the temple's destruction as part of God's plan. It is less clear, however, that Luke-Acts was composed as a direct response to a community struggling with precisely these questions. Although McWhirter's defense of a predominantly Jewish-Christian audience is proposed tentatively in the book's conclusion, she assumes throughout that the destruction of the temple, for example, was viewed as a tragedy by Luke's audience. Yet the fact that the Lukan Jesus laments the loss of Jerusalem in language that recalls Jeremiah does not mean Luke's audience still mourned its loss. Other explanations for Luke's interest in the temple's destruction are possible.

McWhirter's single-minded attention to prophecy can also exaggerate the importance of prophecy and overlook other topics of interest to Luke. McWhirter suggests, for example, that Jesus's forty days in the wilderness would have contributed to Luke's portrayal of Jesus as both a prophet like Elijah *and* a prophet like Moses. The possibility that the forty-day temptation recalls Israel's experience in the wilderness and contributes instead to Luke's emphasis in the immediate context on Jesus's identity as the Son of God is not discussed.

Although readers will doubtless quibble over specific aspects of its argument, *Rejected Prophets* is a valuable contribution to scholarship on prophecy in Luke-Acts and to the study of Luke-Acts in general. Specialists who are not persuaded by an approach that views Luke as a Jewish author writing within a Jewish context will still benefit from the careful attention to Luke's use of the Jewish Scriptures and to the explication of an important Lukan theme. Because it relates the theme of prophecy to other major themes in Luke-Acts, *Rejected Prophets* would work well as an introduction to Luke-Acts as a whole. The volume is accessible to beginning students who lack the original languages and who are unfamiliar with the historical context. More important still, McWhirter introduces Luke to her readers as a consummate storyteller and skillful reader of Scripture, illustrating at the same time how Luke's own work may be read with profit.

Cleansed Lepers, Cleansed Hearts: Purity and Healing in Luke-Acts, by Pamela Shellberg. Minneapolis: Fortress, 2015. Pp. x + 258. Cloth. $29.40. ISBN 9781451485240.

Kindalee Pfremmer De Long, Pepperdine University

Pamela Shellberg's *Cleansed Lepers, Cleansed Hearts: Purity and Healing in Luke-Acts*, in the Emerging Scholars series from Fortress Press, is a publication of her 2012 Marquette University dissertation, directed by Kevin Sullivan. The volume ably investigates a lacuna in scholarship on Luke-Acts, namely, a parallel between Luke 4 and Acts 10–11 and 15 created by Luke's use of two distinctive words, cleanse/clean (*katharizō, katharos*) and acceptable (*dektos*). Her book also helpfully examines ancient views of the condition of *lepra*, from medical, religious, and social perspectives.

In chapter 1 Shellberg observes that the Gospel of Luke mentions *lepra* frequently. Jesus twice speaks about the cleansing of *lepra* (Luke 4:23–27; 7:17–23), and he twice cleanses *lepra*-afflicted characters (Luke 5:12–15; 17:11–19). To show that these *lepra* references provide a model for divine acceptance of the gentiles in Acts (chs. 10–11, 15), Shellberg's method is eclectic: tradition-historical analysis, complemented by engagement with narrative, intertextuality, theology, and the ancient social context of *lepra*.

Chapter 2 investigates the phenomenon of *lepra* in the ancient world. Since the condition in the New Testament ought not be equated with Hansen's Disease, Shellberg employs the Greek term *lepra* instead of leprosy throughout the monograph. Her volume takes a constructivist approach, recognizing that language about illness is culturally constructed. Handbooks of ancient physiognomy, which lay out principles for judging character based on bodily appearance, do not list *lepra*, but its depiction may nevertheless intersect with physiognomic conventions. For example, in Leviticus the blemish-free skin of priests suggests moral purity. Mikeal Parsons and others have shown that Luke subverts physiognomic conventions related to other kinds of conditions and may do so with *lepra* as well. Physiognomy reflects a larger principle in the ancient world that the body and soul affect each other. Drawing on the work of Dale Martin (*The Corinthian Body*), Shellberg points out that for most ancient philosophers (even Plato, to a certain extent) the soul is not immaterial but consists of particles, vapor, or fluid interacting with the body. In ancient philosophy as well as Greek medicine, spirit (*pneuma*) also plays a role in perception, health, and illness, penetrating the body (and especially the heart) from outside through channels or passages (*poroi*), one of which is the skin. This perspective helps modern readers understand how the Holy Spirit can cleanse hearts (Acts 15:8–9). Disease may invade through *poroi* as well.

In medical texts, *lepra*—any number of skin afflictions characterized by an itchy or powdery thickening of the skin—occurs either through invasion through *poroi* or an imbalance of bodily fluids. If an indicator of therapeutic evacuation, it can signal serious or even fatal internal diseases. In Leviticus, the condition creates ritual impurity and is associated with death, even though the disease itself is not seen as not fatal. However, it does not signal divine displeasure. By contrast, the nonpriestly writings of the Septuagint often present *lepra* as resulting from divine punishment. Luke is more in line with the priestly tradition on this point. Both the Septuagint and the Hippocratic corpus use the word family of *cleanse* (*katharizō, katharos*) to describe the treatment or healing of *lepra*.

In chapter 3 Shellberg argues that the words *dektos* and *katharizō* align Jesus's speech in Nazareth (Luke 4) with the scene at Cornelius's home (Acts 10–11, 15). Just as God's acceptable year involves the cleansing of lepers (Luke 4:19, 27), so, too, the cleansing of gentiles (Acts 15:9; cf. 10:15; 11:9) relates to their acceptability to God (Acts 10:35). The word *dektos* can have a passive sense (acceptable to God) or an active one (God's blessing). Shellberg sees the latter as predominant in Luke (e.g., Luke 4:18–19, 24), having been drawn especially from Isaiah (49:8; 56:7; 58:5; 60:7; 61:2). The Isaianic passages in which *dektos* appears are filled with distinctive Lukan vocabulary: salvation/savior, light, release (*aphesis*), to do what is right, for all nations, to the end of the earth, light of the nations, eunuch, foreigner (*allogenēs*), and stranger (*allophulos*). Shellberg notes that the final three words on this list occur in the New Testament only in Luke-Acts (but this is also true of the phrases "to the end of the earth" and "light of the nations"). These intertexts define *dektos* as an acceptable time characterized by release from various kinds of oppression, setting the concept of *dektos* in the context of "the large sweep of the story of God's salvation, intended for Israel and extended to the nations" (146).

Chapter 4 explores the close association between cleansing and *lepra* in the Gospel of Luke. Both terms are ambiguous. *Lepra*, an uncertain boundary condition, may show either wasting or healing. So, too, the multivalent word *cleanse* blurs the meanings of healing and the restoration of ritual purity. Together, the two words convey Luke's concern with salvation: "how a body becomes *dektos* for God" through the divine *pneuma* that restores holiness to what is unclean (150). In Luke 2:22, *katharizō* connotes holiness, while in Luke 11:39–41 almsgiving cleanses by purifying a person (of greed) from the inside out, analogous to the evacuation of illness through the skin (which Shellberg argues is an aspect of *lepra*). Luke 7:22 ties the healing of *lepra*-afflicted people back to the Nazareth sermon and the story of Naaman's cleansing (ch. 4). In Luke 5:13, Jesus's touch and breath (from his spoken word) convey Jesus's *pneuma* into a *lepra*-afflicated man through *poroi*. In Luke 17:12–14, cleansing of ten *lepra*-afflicted men has eschatological significance, vis-à-vis Luke 7:22 and the distinctive word *allogenēs*, because Isaianic intertexts narratively link the *lepra*-inflicted and gentiles. In Acts, the word *katharizō* appears only in the context of Peter's dream or descriptions thereof (10:15; 11:9; 15:9). Just as Jesus cleanses the *lepra*-afflicted in the gospel, the Holy Spirit cleanses the hearts of the gentiles, warranting their inclusion with Jews as holy for God.

Chapter 5 revisits the Cornelius story in light of the previous chapters' findings. By means of cleansing stories earlier in the narrative, which have been about people, Luke prepares the reader to recognize that Peter's vision reveals the cleansing not of animals but of people (Acts 10:15; 11:9). Peter moves from a tentative insight about this point to a developed claim: God has cleansed the gentiles (Acts 15:8–9) by the Holy Spirit through faith, so that they are saved and accepted by God without distinction or partiality. Thus, the vision addresses neither circumcision nor table fellowship but rather Peter's anxiety about infidelity to the covenant principle of holiness/distinction. While no human act of purification or ritual can make unclean animals clean, God can do so, and the vision declares that God has done it. In *lepra*, the skin, a boundary between unclean and holy, "appears to be breaking down at the surface" (215), but Jesus, in whom the holy resides, brings the time of *dektos* and extends his *pneuma*, which first cleanses *lepra*-afflicted bodies (Luke) and then extends to "dissolve all boundaries and bring salvation to the ends of the earth" (218).

Pamela Shellberg makes a compelling case for a narrative parallel between the cleansing of *lepra* in the gospel and the cleansing of the gentiles in Acts and for *dektos* as a word that links the arrival of salvation to the gentiles with Jesus's programmatic statements about the year of the Lord's favor. On some smaller points, however, the author's argument goes beyond the evidence offered or lacks precision. With regard to therapeutic evacuation, for example, she notes that, because harmful substances may exit through *poroi*, including the skin, "*lepra* could be considered a therapeutic evacuation indicating serious internal and even fatally progressing illnesses" (82). This speculation finds no direct support in ancient medical treatises (at least, no evidence is provided for the reader). Later, in chapter 4, it is repeated as a fact undergirding her interpretation that *lepra*, like cleansing, is ambiguous because it could be a sign either of wasting or healing (i.e., therapeutic evacuation) (150) and that the cleansing of greed from the inside (Luke 11:37–41) reflects the ancient medical view of *lepra* as therapeutic evacuation (173). Her argument that Jesus cleanses a *lepra*-afflicted man by breathing into him the *pneuma hagiou* from the presence of God strikes me as similarly speculative, since the scene in Luke neither mentions breath nor emphasizes Jesus's speech (168, 180). With regard to the eunuch (Acts 8), Shellberg first views him as an Ethiopian Jew (67) but later he appears to represent foreigners (150). Her case related to Acts 10 would be strengthened by engaging alternative views, particularly arguments about distinctions between the words common and unclean.

Despite these concerns, Shellberg's primary thesis is persuasive. Her work makes a contribution by highlighting how salvation in Luke-Acts consists of restoration to wholeness, by increasing the evidence for reading Luke's two volumes as one narrative, and by adding to the case that healings in Luke's Gospel represent "glory to your people Israel" (Luke 2:32) (as I and others have argued). It also contributes to the ongoing project of understanding of how Luke-Acts weaves echoes of Israel's scriptures into the story to depict the arrival of the long-awaited divine visitation, so that the cleansing of gentiles and their acceptance by God becomes "a fulfillment of God's promises to Israel rather than a violation of any principles of holiness or distinction" (200).

Luke's Jesus in the Roman Empire and the Emperor in the Gospel of Luke, by Pyung Soo Seo. Eugene, OR: Pickwick, 2015. Pp. xiii + 194. Paper. $19.20. ISBN 9781498200547.

Frank E. Dicken, Lincoln Christian University

In this volume Pyung Soo Seo seeks to contribute to the ongoing discussion of the political outlook of Luke (and, to a lesser degree, Acts) by examining Luke's portrayal of Jesus's authority over against the authority of the Roman emperor, which makes up part of the sociocultural milieu of the Lukan writings. Seo's aim is to demonstrate that part of the subtext of the third canonical gospel is to demonstrate that Jesus's authority is greater than that of the emperor. The author presents his argument over the course of four chapters, plus an introduction and brief conclusion.

The introduction sets forth two aspects of Seo's argument. First, Seo understands Luke as an anti-imperial writing. He briefly surveys representatives of the two primary positions that have been taken with regard to Luke's political stance: *apologia pro ecclesia* (Cadbury, Conzelmann) and *apologia pro imperio* (Walasky); Seo believes that they are insufficient for addressing sociocultural realities surrounding the Gospel of Luke, particularly its implicit critique of imperial power. Second, Seo discusses the inseparability of religion and politics in the Roman world. Here he rightly argues that, while politics and religion were not entirely synonymous in antiquity, the two spheres were so closely linked that to examine one without considering the other is to make a categorical error. Along these lines, Seo critiques both Seyoon Kim (*Christ and Caesar*) and C. Kavin Rowe (*World Upside Down*) for what he believes is inconsistency on their parts for noting Jesus's universal lordship while maintaining that the Lukan vision is not anti-imperial. For Seo, to call Jesus Lord (or any other title held by the emperor, e.g., savior, benefactor) is to make an anti-imperial claim. This understanding of the political and religious dimensions of the first century is foundational to Seo's approach to Luke.

Chapter 1 of Seo's study is informed by sociologist Max Weber's three types of authority: charismatic authority, which is accepted on the basis of the individual's exceptional power and/or qualities; traditional authority, such as dynastic descent; and bureaucratic authority, which is granted by people in power (21–22). Seo believes that the birth narrative of Luke's Gospel demonstrates Jesus's charismatic authority, as he notes the widely accepted view that Luke shows Jesus to be superior to John the Baptist through a series of comparisons of the two in Lukan birth narrative. The differences in the circumstances and settings of the births of John and Jesus "correspond to their different missions which govern the degree of their authority" (29). According to Seo, Luke's passion narrative highlights Jesus's traditional and bureaucratic authority by positioning Jesus over against various rulers—the Jewish leaders, Pilate, and Herod—who hold traditional and bureaucratic authority. Seo points out that such rulers, as portrayed by Luke, derive their authority from sources other than God, unlike Jesus, and therefore possess authority that is inferior to Jesus's. Further, because these rulers hold political authority, Luke's depiction of Jesus as holding greater authority than they do forms part of the Third Evangelist's implicit critique of Roman Imperial power.

Chapter 2 turns to a comparison and contrast of Jesus's and Caesar's respective authority. Seo believes that Luke's portrayals of taxes and tax collectors adds to his anti-imperial stance. Seo seeks to show that Luke portrays the collection of taxes (Luke 2:1–2; 20:19–26; 23:3) and Jesus's interactions with Levi and Zacchaeus (5:27–32; 19:1–10) in a way that subverts the emperor's *imperium*. Seo defines *imperium* as the emperor's world domination and subsequent administrative power and *auctoritas* (the emperor's supreme authority over civil affairs in the empire). Specifically, Seo focuses on one aspect of the emperor's *auctoritas* in the Roman world: the responsibility for "morality in the Empire" (78). Tax collectors, as individuals operating under the emperor's authority, should have acted in moral ways if the emperor truly held moral *auctoritas*. However, Luke portrays them as acting in immoral ways (e.g., they are greedy and extort money). For Seo, this is an implicit critique of the emperor's *auctoritas*. In Seo's two case studies—Levi and Zacchaeus—only Jesus can correct the tax collectors' moral failings, thus diminishing Caesar's authority and amplifying Jesus's authority.

Seo focuses on the title "benefactor" as applied to both Jesus and Caesar in chapter 3. In order to make the contrast between Jesus and Caesar, Seo first identifies the emperor as a pagan king in Luke-Acts (Luke 3:1–2; Acts 17:7) and then describes Luke's depiction of kingly benefactors. For Seo, Luke depicts Jesus as the quintessential benefactor because Jesus is the greatest servant (106–9), in contrast to the emperor, who is not purely altruistic in his benefaction. Seo directly relates the title "savior" to "benefactor," seeing the two terms as essentially inseparable, because part of both Jesus's and the emperor's benefaction was deliverance from enemies and ensuing peace. This leads directly to Seo's fourth chapter.

Chapter 4 makes up a third of the volume (sixty pages). Here Seo builds on his initial discussion of Luke's portrayal of Jesus and the emperor as contrasting benefactors/saviors and addresses the related themes of victory, peace, and salvation. After demonstrating that Augustus Caesar was widely recognized as "savior," Seo then explains that Luke's presentation of Jesus as savior is "contracultural": Luke has constructed a culture in his writing "that mirrors and reverses the values" of the prevailing culture, "granting status and significance to its members" (129). Seo then turns to the Third Gospel to explore passages that portray Jesus as securing victory by his resurrection over both nonhuman (e.g., Satan) and human (e.g., the Jewish leaders, Herod) enemies. Jesus's victory ensures that his followers experience his peace and salvation. This stands in contrast to the emperor, who brought peace and salvation through his *imperium* enacted through violent means. Seo believes that Luke rejects violence as a means of procuring salvation and thereby shows the peace and salvation brought by Jesus to be superior to that of the emperor. A brief conclusion summarizes the foregoing discussion.

Seo's foray into empire criticism would benefit from greater detail in several instances. At times he does not provide sufficient justification for the interpretive decisions he makes. For instance, Seo states that, while Jesus and the emperor do not have direct contact in Luke-Acts, "the readers/hearers *probably* have in mind Luke's conclusion that the one who serves is the greatest in v. 27 [22:27] in connection with Jesus' victory over the emperor and other rulers" (114, emphasis added). This is an important conclusion for Seo at an important juncture in his argument, but he does not show his own readers why this is *probably* the case. As another example, Seo does not demonstrate how it is that Jesus triumphs over his human enemies by his resurrection; rather, this is assumed (139). Again, this is a weighty claim that is largely unsupported. As a final example, Seo makes the claim that the songs of Zechariah and Simeon in Luke 1–2 are programmatic passages but does not substantiate that claim. The role of programmatic passages in Luke-Acts is well-known, but Seo does not make his case in these instances. He could have expanded his argument in these places and others in order to make his case more effectively.

A second area where further explanation is needed from Seo is his methodology. Seo does address this issue in a footnote (19 n. 76), but he claims to be using various methods, not a single one. Some clarity on this matter might provide justification for the appropriation of, for instance, Max Weber's sociological categories of authority in chapter 1 or contra-culture theory in chapter 4. These are social-scientific methods in service of biblical studies, a long-standing practice, and Seo's study combines social-scientific study with a narrative/theological reading of Luke. Identifying some methodological parameters for his argument would prevent readers from having to guess what Seo is doing in each section of his discussion.

With these criticisms stated, I do want to commend Seo's book to scholars and students interested in empire criticism in New Testament studies. Luke and Acts (or Luke-Acts) have been widely recognized as some of the most politically charged writings in the New Testament. Over the past several decades scholars have moved beyond unnecessary dichotomies (the *pro ecclesia* and *pro imperio* approaches) to more nuanced understandings of Luke's interaction with the Roman Empire. This is where Seo makes his contribution. His interaction with the sociocultural setting of the Gospel of Luke and Luke's narrative and theological artistry combine to provide readers with a fruitful way of thinking about the subtext of Luke's portrayal of Jesus over against the emperor and empire as expressed in the accounts of taxes and tax collectors as well as the various titles and roles ascribed to Jesus.

JOHN

Creation Imagery in the Gospel of John, by Carlos Raúl Sosa Siliezar. Library of New Testament Studies 546. London: Bloomsbury, 2015. Pp. 272. Hardcover. $112.00. ISBN 9780567664242.

R. Alan Culpepper, McAfee School of Theology, Mercer University

This Edinburgh dissertation was completed in 2014 under the direction of Larry Hurtado and Helen Bond. Sosa Siliezar, a lecturer at several universities in Guatemala City, Guatemala, traces the identification of creation imagery in the Gospel of John to an article Sir Edwin C. Hoskyns published in 1920. Since then the theme has received occasional attention from Johannine scholars. In the introduction Sosa Siliezar reviews works published in the twentieth century: the dissertation by Terence Craig Voortman (1998); recent articles by Jeannine Brown (2010), John Painter (2007), Jan A. du Rand (2005), Hans Ulrich Weidemann (2010), and Mary Coloe (2011); and the dissertation by Anthony Moore (2010, published in 2013). Moore proposes a long list of "creation indicators" on the basis of which he argues that creation imagery is the main theme in the gospel and that John's signs are a "re-presentation of the days of creation in the Genesis sequence" (Moore, "The Theme of Creation in the Fourth Gospel," iii). In contrast to Moore, Sosa Siliezar argues that "John has intentionally included only a limited number of instances of creation imagery" (23), which he positions strategically in the gospel.

The major contribution of this dissertation is its methodological rigor. The author establishes a clear methodology for evaluating proposed creation imagery in the gospel, applies it to the most significant links that have been proposed between the gospel and Gen 1–2, and then offers suggestions regarding the function of creation imagery in its specific contexts in John and in the gospel as a whole. By the term *creation imagery* Sosa Siliezar designates "direct assertions about the creation of the world that are not dependent upon a particular OT text" (12) and instances where John may have used terms, images, or concepts from biblical traditions about creation. Assuming the "availability" of Genesis, he uses the critically reconstructed text of Genesis in the Göttingen LXX edition, which is important because he looks for verbal parallels between John and Gen 1–2 (the criterion of "significant similarities"). The third criterion Sosa Siliezar adopts is "prominence": Were these texts known in Jewish communities and used elsewhere in John, and do early Christian writers identify these references in John as creation imagery? Finally, he asks whether the proposed creation imagery coheres with John's line of argumentation. These criteria are essential because Sosa Siliezar applies them rigorously in determining whether instances of creation imagery that have been suggested by the authors listed above are legitimate or not.

Part 1 treats both the Prologue and John 17, since the two passages are closely related and both contain direct references to the creation of the world (1:3, 10; 17:5, 24). John evokes the Genesis account of creation in John 1:1–5 by means of the phrase *en archē*, by the reference *ho logos*, which appears elsewhere in creation discourse, and by the combination of *ginomai* and *pas*. John uses "life," "light," "darkness," and "to shine" differently, leading to the conclusion that, while it creatively deploys terms from Gen 1–2, John "is not making a direct reference to the Genesis narrative" through its use of these terms (42). Nor does Sosa Siliezar find compelling Mary Coloe's proposal that the structure of the Prologue resembles the structure of Gen 1:1–2:4a. The references to creation in Jesus's prayer in John 17 (vv. 5 and 24) function in ways similar to those in the Prologue, although without a clear reference to Gen 1–2. They highlight Jesus's existence with the Father prior to and apart from the created order.

Part 2 examines allusions to creation in John's account of Jesus performing the works of his Father (ch. 3), John's account of Jesus walking on the water and healing a man born blind (ch. 4), and the claim that John used the seven days of creation as an ordering principle for his gospel (ch. 5). Sosa Siliezar finds that in various references to Jesus's works (esp. 4:34, Jesus's being sent to "finish his work"; 5:36, completing works and the Sabbath; and 10:32, Jesus's performing "good works"), John makes use of creation imagery. Second Temple Jewish texts, particularly Philo, contain speculation about God's rest after creation; the Creator is still active after creation. Ancient interpreters (Irenaeus, Tertullian, and Chrysostom) also read some of these Johannine passages in relation creation. On the other hand, Sosa Siliezar rejects Hengel's suggestion that "Jesus finishes the work of creation and salvation on the cross and then he 'rests' in the grave" (100). The occurrences of *teleō* and *teleioō* in John 19:28–30 assert instead that the Scriptures are fulfilled through Jesus's death.

Two stories in particular employ creation imagery: walking on the water and healing the man born blind. John 6:19 echoes Job 9:8 LXX, where God alone walks on the sea. Surprisingly, Sosa Siliezar does not appeal to Ps 77:16–19, a hymn praising God for his work in creation: "Your way was through the sea, your path through the mighty waters, yet your footprints were unseen" (Ps 77:19). In context, Jesus's walking on the water in John 6 elevates him over Moses. Similarly, although there is no direct reference to Gen 2:7 in John 9:6, Jesus's distinctive act in making mud—the only time Jesus does so in the four gospels—resonates with the broader background in which "mud" (*pēlos*) is used in creation contexts (Isa 64:7 LXX; Job 10:9 LXX). Once again, ancient Christian interpreters support this connection (Irenaeus and Ephrem the Syrian). Sosa Siliezar suggests that the function of the creation imagery in this context is to support Jesus's claims in John 7–8: Jesus comes from the Father and existed before Abraham.

Various scholars have argued that the sequence of days in John 1:19–2:12 represent a week, corresponding to the week in Gen 1–2. Sosa Siliezar calls attention to the ambiguities of the sequence of days in John, especially in the search for a seventh day. Consequently, he concludes that "the claim that Jn 1–2 has been shaped by the seven days of creation in Gen 1–2 is not adequately supported by the evidence" (130). Likewise, the evidence does not support the arguments that have been advanced for the claim that John presents Jesus's signs (or the whole of the gospel) as a sequence of seven miracles that follow the seven days in Genesis. Evidence that ancient readers detected such a structure is lacking.

Part 3 addresses the purported instances of creation imagery in the Johannine passion and resurrection narratives. Sosa Siliezar argues that John's description of Jesus breathing on the disciples in John 20:22 echoes Gen 2:7, a verse that was cited widely in Jewish texts. In addition, at least three church fathers related 20:22 to this verse. The link between the two further supports the ideas introduced in the Prologue and earlier in the gospel. As a result, "the mission of the disciples should be regarded as universal in scope" (173).

Another interpretation that has been advanced from time to time reads the references to a garden in John 18 and 20 as allusions to the garden of Eden or Mary's confusion in thinking the risen Lord was the gardener as in a sense ironically true. Sosa Siliezar finds against the validity of both, primarily because of the difference in vocabulary in John, which uses *kēpos* rather than *paradeisos*. Second Temple Jewish texts do not refer to God or Adam as a farmer, John 15:1 uses a different term "vinedresser" (*ho geōrgos*) than 20:15 (*ho kēpouros*), and the suggestion that John presents Jesus as "the gardener of his paradise" does not appear until Jerome (*Homily* 87). Sosa Siliezar suggests, therefore, that if the references to a garden carry a further meaning, it is to a royal garden. John does not elsewhere refer to the expectation of a restoration of paradise.

In the conclusion Sosa Siliezar reiterates his thesis that John makes limited use of creation imagery at strategic points in the gospel and that they function to advance the Christology of the gospel in three ways: (1) John uses the creation imagery to portray Jesus in close relationship to the Father; (2) John uses this imagery to assert the universal significance of Jesus and his message and set him apart from John the Baptist and Moses; and (3) the creation imagery links past, present, and future, suggesting that Jesus is both the agent of creation and the agent of salvation and revelation. As further implications of his study, Sosa Siliezar contends that, since Jesus is so closely related to the Creator God, John does not advance a strict dualism. Moreover, John's creation imagery is found in all three editions of the gospel posited by von Wahlde.

Sosa Siliezar's work is admirably clear and methodologically consistent. He has brought a needed measure of order to the interpretation of this theme in John, and his work has the great strength of resisting the temptation to press an interpretation or thesis beyond the evidence that supports it. Pet interpretations may die hard, and one suspects that on the strength of recent work by such able scholars as Coloe, Painter, and Zimmermann debate will continue regarding some of Sosa Siliezar's findings. In particular, he may be too influenced by the lack of verbal parallels in some instances, especially since John has a penchant for varying terminology and using synonyms. One may also note that there is some methodological slippage between the two tasks Sosa Siliezar takes on: identifying instances of creation imagery and then analyzing its function in its immediate context and in the gospel as a whole. The rigor of his methodology is more evident in the first task than in the second, although his proposals regarding the function of this theme are generally persuasive. One might also ask that the development of the creation imagery in the wisdom tradition be given a greater role in this discussion.

Nevertheless, Sosa Siliezar has provided us with a valuable standard by which to assess the validity of proposals regarding allusions to creation in John, and his method might profitably be adapted to other readings of symbolism and double meaning in John also.

Abiding Words: The Use of Scripture in the Gospel of John, edited by Alicia D. Myers and Bruce G. Schuchard. Resources for Biblical Study 81. Atlanta: SBL Press, 2015. Pp. xvi + 284. Hardcover. $54.95. ISBN 9781628370942. Paper. $39.95. ISBN 9781628370935.

Beth M. Stovell, Ambrose University

Abiding Words: The Use of Scripture in the Gospel of John is an edited volume from the SBL Resources for Biblical Study series that focuses on new approaches to the use of Scripture in John's Gospel, as its title suggests. This volume emerged out of a suggestion by Mary Coloe at the Society of Biblical Literature Annual Meeting in San Francisco in 2011. Reading the work of Ruth Sheridan and Alicia D. Myers, Coloe suggested the need for an update on recent trajectories regarding Scripture use in John's Gospel. This in turn developed into a session on "John and Scripture" at SBL's Annual Meeting in 2012 in Chicago. Many of the chapters from this book were originally presentations at this conference, and the additional material was developed to supplement the key directions that these presentations took.

Myers begins the volume with an introduction that charts past scholarship on this topic and demonstrates the relevance of this volume both to continue and to advance past trajectories and to present new methodological approaches. Myers's contribution shows a keen awareness of the impact of this topic on issues not only regarding Israel's history and John's Gospel but also on issues such as Johannine sectarianism and claims of Johannine anti-Semitism. Myers explores past scholarship by grouping it under three main themes: "(1) the sources of John's references to Scripture; (2) the method of John's incorporation of these references; and (3) the sociological, theological, and rhetorical functions of the references" (4).

In many ways, Myers's themes in her introduction mirror the major sections of the book overall. The book is organized in three parts: (1) "The Form of John's Citations" examines citation technique, the use of quotation, and specific citation formulae; (2) "Social and Rhetorical Perspectives" explores sociological and rhetorical approaches to John's use of Scripture; (3) "Memory and Scripture in John" demonstrates how Israel's memory plays a key role in the development of John's Gospel through the use of allusions and how John uses imagery as a means to access memory and use it for rhetorical purposes in his gospel. Schuchard's conclusion reviews each of these three main parts to demonstrate the value of the current volume in its extension of past questions and suggestions for future steps in research based on this volume.

Part 1 consists of three chapters by Bruce G. Schuchard, William Randolph Bynum, and Michael A. Daise. Schuchard argues that John's use of Scripture indicates his use of an early Jewish Greek translation of the Hebrew Bible. For Schurchard, John is not simply an editor but also a rhetorician and careful storyteller (35). John's use of these citations is intentional and built into his overall gospel framework, which Schuchard proposes, against the general concensus, has its midpoint at chapter 10 rather than at chapters 11 or 12. Schuchard argues that this structuring of citations and the use of the Greek text lend themselves to the author's overall goal of presenting Jesus's work, person, and death to persuade hearers "to believe that Jesus is the Christ, the Son of God, so that believing, the hearer would have life in his name (John 20:30–31)" (41).

Bynum examines the form and function of John's use of Zechariah in the Fourth Gospel, specifically Zech 9:9 in John 12:15 and Zech 12:10 in John 19:37. Against a prevailing view of these citations as discrete uses, Bynum argues that John creates a literary *inclusio* using these two citations of Zechariah as "book ends" intended to signal a reading of John's passion narrative in light of the theological vision of Second Zechariah (Zech 9–14) (47–48). Through this *inclusio,* John applies the postexilic hope of God's salvation and a coming king to Jesus's passion, death, and resurrection. "Thus, in [John's] view, God has truly returned; the promised humble king has arrived; the new era of his lordship has begun; the era of renewal envisioned by Zechariah has come" (73). Considering his otherwise well-crafted argument, it was surprising that Bynum did not interact with Mark J. Boda and Stanley E. Porter's 2005 article, "Literature to the Third Degree: Prophecy in Zechariah 9–14 and the Passion of the Christ," which explores the same topic as Bynum's chapter.[1]

Daise examines the form and function of Scripture citation in John's Gospel by grouping clusters of citations that "share common lexical and thematic characteristics," including the language of "having been fulfilled," "introductory formulae explicitly ascribe[d] to Isaiah," and citations "cast as being 'remembered' by Jesus's disciples" (77). Daise focuses on this third category of "remembrance" formulae, namely, John 2:17/Ps 69:10; John 12:13/Ps 118:25–26; and John 12:15/Zech 9:9, arguing that they create an *inclusio* between John 2:17 and 12:13 and 15 that joins the start of Jesus's ministry at one Passover to the conclusion of Jesus's ministry at another Passover. Daise argues that this *inclusio* reverberates with motifs throughout the Book of Signs (John 1–12) that impacts John's Christology, pneumatology, and themes of a new creation.

Part 2 is the longest part of the volume and consists of four chapters by Jaime Clark-Soles, Alicia-D. Myers, Benjamin J. Lappenga, and Ruth Sheridan. Clark-Soles further develops on her 2003 book,[2] examining the social function of John's quotation of Scripture for his goals in his sectarian community. Using sociological categories and comparative social history, Clark-Soles applies this framework to John 12:37–41 and 15:25. She demonstrates that Scripture use in these passages emphasizes the differences between insider and outsider, aiming to encourage "fence-sitters" to complete allegiance (103–8), and promotes belonging through the language of hate for all associated with the world compared to love for one another (108–15)Whereas Clark-Soles's chief comparison is with sectarian Judaism, Myers uses Greco-Roman rhetoric (using Aristotle, Cicero, Quintilian, among others) as a starting point for examination of the rhetorical function of John's use of Scripture. Using John 1:19–34 as a test case, Myers argues that John

---

1. Boda and Porter include examination of all of the gospels rather than focusing only on the Fourth Gospel; however, they explain the implications of reading Zech 9–14 in these gospel accounts, just as Bynum does. See Mark J. Boda and Stanley E Porter, "Literature to the Third Degree: Prophecy in Zechariah 9–14 and the Passion of Christ," in *Traduire La Bible Hebraique,* ed. Manuel Jinbachian and Robert David, Sciences bibliques 15 (Montreal: Mediaspaul, 2005), 215–54.

2. Jaime Clark-Soles, *Scripture Cannot Be Broken: The Social Function of the Use of Scripture in the Fourth Gospel* (Leiden: Brill, 2003).

the Baptist is depicted as speaking with an Isaianic prophetic voice, incorporating John's Gospel into Israel's sacred story for the purpose of demonstrating Jesus's identity as the Son of God.

Lappenga examines the use of the term *zeal* in John's Gospel in light of early Jewish texts and demonstrates that, while "zeal for the temple" points to Jesus's actions in purifying the temple, it also points to the misplaced zeal of "the Jews" as they fail to acknowledge Jesus as the "true locus of God's presence" (152). In both cases Jesus is "consumed" by this zeal that characterizes the rest of the temple references in John 7–8 and the multidirectional use of Ps 69:9.

Sheridan uses the framework of metaleptic intertextuality (following Hollander and Hays)[3] to argue that the three Torah passages referenced in John 8:17 (Deut 17:6; 19:15; Num 35:30) leave a residing echo of their previous context of criminal context, including apostasy, blasphemy, and idolatry as they are used in John's Gospel. This echo creates a double motion in Jesus's references to "multiple witnesses" in John 8 in the context of John 7–8: (1) they counter the claims of Jesus as an apostate and an enticer to the idolatry of others (near to claims of blasphemy) (alluding to Deut 17:6); and (2) they turn the tables on "the Jews," shifting Jesus from the accused to the judge who points to the high crime of accusing someone falsely of apostasy (alluding to Deut 19:15) and has God, "the Father," as his "avenger of blood" (a theme of Num 35).

Part 3 is the shortest of the volume, containing only chapters by Catrin H. Williams and Jeffrey Brickle. Williams uses an interpretive framework based on social memory—emphasizing its role in forming and maintaining group identity—to examine the function in John's Gospel of three key figures in Israel's collective memory: Moses, Abraham, and Isaiah. Williams emphasizes that these social memories are not primarily written but exist in the oral tradition and the minds of John's hearers alongside their textual presence. Williams argues that the author of the Fourth Gospel uses these figures—so critical to Israel's memory—as three witnesses to Jesus's identity and earthly ministry as "the definitive revelation of God" (212). In this way, the author of the Fourth Gospel is able to "establish continuity with the past ... while "marking new 'beginnings'"(212).

Brickle's theory-driven chapter depicts John as an "intertextual memory artisan" (213) who uses memory arts as "a master storyteller and scribal purveyor of traditions 'new and old'" (214). Brickle states that the goal of this memory artisanship is "to radically shape and reshape the worldview, theology, and ethical construction of successive generations of Christian communities" (215). Using metaphors for memory arts of a "theatre," "an intersection," "a hypertext," "sympathetic resonance," "an image," "a mnemonic journey," and "a film or motion picture," Brickle examines the farewell discourse, the passion narrative, and the

---

3. John Hollander, *The Figure of Echo: A Mode of Allusion in Milton and After* (Berkeley: University of California Press, 1981); Richard B. Hays, *Echoes of Scripture in the Letters of Paul* (New Haven: Yale University Press, 1989).

epilogue alongside the prologue to demonstrate John's use of memory arts (222–33). One of Brickle's goals in this approach is to question typical print-culture approaches to John's Gospel and to move in a direction of orality and memory.

A strength of this volume is that it provides a helpful way into recent approaches to the use of Scripture in John's Gospel in the areas of form, function, social and rhetorical approaches, and new avenues into the impact of memory on John's Gospel (and thereby on the New Testament more broadly). However, a weakness of the volume is that it overlooks another trajectory of scholarship related to John's use of Scripture in the Fourth Gospel: linguistic approaches related to metaphor. Several recent scholars have used linguistic analysis to examine John's use of Scripture in John's metaphors, such as Jesus's kingship,[4] Jesus as the Lamb of God,[5] and Jesus as shepherd,[6] among others.[7] However, in fairness to the editors of this volume, they have not claimed that the trajectories they are exploring are the *only* approaches that have developed recently on this topic, but rather that these are the trajectories that they have chosen to explore more fully. Further, as Michael Daise points out in his contribution (75), studying John's quotation of Scripture now functions as a subfield of Johannine studies, and the focus of this book is on approaches where John's use of Scripture is the primary rather than secondary focus of a given study.[8]

In conclusion, this volume provides a helpful orientation to the most recent directions in the study of Scripture use in John's Gospel and a step forward for this topic. The style of writing, use of ancient languages, and methodological complexity of this work make it useful primarily to scholars within the fields of Johannine studies and intertextual studies. However, the editors have endeavored to make this volume accessible to students through translation and explanation throughout. Further, the use of social, rhetorical, and memory-related approaches may

---

4. See Beth M. Stovell, *Mapping Metaphorical Discourse in the Fourth Gospel: John's Eternal King*, Linguistic Biblical Studies 6 (Leiden: Brill, 2012).

5. Jesper Tang Nielsen, "The Lamb of God: The Cognitive Structure of Johannine Metaphor," in *Imagery in the Gospel of John: Terms, Forms, Themes, and Theology of Johannine Figurative Language*, ed. Jörg Frey, Ruben Zimmermann, Jan G. van der Watt, and Gabriele Kern, (Tübingen: Mohr Siebeck, 2006), 216–58.

6. Examples include Ruben Zimmermann, *Christologie der Bilder im Johannesevangelium: Die Christopoetik des Vierten Evangeliums unter besonderer Berücksichtigung von Joh 10*, WUNT 171 (Tübingen: Mohr Siebeck, 2004); and Ulrich Busse, "Metaphorik und Rhetorik im Johannesevangelium: Das Bildfeld vom König," in Frey, et al., *Imagery in the Gospel of John*, 279–318.

7. Stanley E. Porter provides a helpful survey of recent literary and linguistic approaches to John's Gospel in his "Study of John's Gospel: New Directions or the Same Old Paths?" in *Linguistic Analysis of the Greek New Testament: Studies in Tools, Methods, and Practice*, ed. Stanley E. Porter (Grand Rapids: Baker Academic, 2015), 277–306.

8. For example, in the metaphor studies discussed above the use of Scripture takes a secondary role to the main goal of metaphor analysis.

allow this volume a broader academic appeal. The cost of the volume in paperback makes it an affordable resource for any scholar's library.

Reconsidering Johannine Christianity: A Social Identity Approach, by Raimo Hakola. BibleWorld. New York: Routledge, 2015. Pp. xi + 175. Hardcover. $145.00. ISBN 9781138910232.

Cornelis Bennema, Union School of Theology

In this book Raimo Hakola employs social-identity theory to reexamine the nature of Johannine Christianity. The book contains seven chapters, of which chapters 3–6 are revised versions of earlier publications between 2005 and 2013. Each chapter is self-contained (they even have their own bibliographies); chapter 1 is foundational, chapters 2–3 are of a general nature, chapters 4–6 focus on particular episodes, and chapter 7 concludes the book.

Chapter 1 lays the groundwork for the rest of the book as Hakola explains how he understands the Johannine dualistic language. He claims that Johannine dualism is not a direct reflection of historical reality but a construction created by John. That is, both the gospel and the Johannine epistles are attempts to construct a secure social identity by creating imaginary symbolic worlds. Applying the three-world model developed by Kari Syreeni to the Johannine writings, Hakola claims that the relation between the world of the Johannine text and the real world is negotiated by John's symbolic world. In this, Hakola critiques two major groups in Johannine scholarship, both of which assume that John's narrative world is a direct reflection of the real world. First, while Hakola affirms the existence of a Johannine community behind the Johannine writings, he contends that there is insufficient evidence for a sectarian identity of a Johannine community persecuted by the diaspora synagogue (so Martyn, Brown, Meeks, and proponents of their views). Second, Hakola is fiercely critical of the proposal of Bauckham (and others, such as Klink and Bernier), which views John's Gospel as a reliable eyewitness account of and a theological reflection on the life Jesus. According to Hakola, the same methodological problem underlies the community hypothesis and the theory that the gospels are eyewitness testimonies: "Both theories have quite often led to unwarranted leaps from the narrative world of the gospels into the historical reality behind them" (21). Contrary to the majority of scholars who take Johannine dualism as a direct reflection of the historical reality, Hakola sees it as part of John's symbolic world. This also implies that various characters in John's narrative world are not necessarily referents of people in the real world. Since the Johannine writings show traces of intergroup behavior and reflect attempts to construct and secure a distinct social identity of a group of early Christians over against other groups, Hakola suggests that social-identity theory is an appropriate approach to understand these dynamics.

Chapters 2–3 form the background for more specific case studies in chapters 4–6. In chapter 2 Hakola assumes a diaspora setting for the Johannine writings and explores what this entails. Since this relates to the community hypothesis, Hakola interacts primarily with those who consider Johannine Christianity as a persecuted, sectarian community isolated from its sociocultural environment. Hakola's criticism has less to do with details in this model and more with the entire scenario of isolated Jewish diaspora communities with strict boundaries. According to Hakola, the available evidence suggests the existence of open, diverse, and nonhierarchical Jewish diaspora communities within "common Judaism." In such an environment, "it is preferable to take John's clear-cut dualism as an effort to construct a clearly defined social identity in a complex and diverse social situation rather than as evidence for the definite alienation of the community" (56). When Johannine Christians began distancing themselves from central Jewish identity markers such as the temple, Sabbath, circumcision, the law, and Moses, it caused a gradual alienation from fellow Jews to the extent that "they *felt* they were excluded from the synagogue even though there never was any formal decision to expel these believers" (60, emphasis original); "once a group of early Christians became socially more and more alienated from their fellow Jews and started to regard them as their opponents, the door was open to exaggerating their threat to the point where they became the source of persecution in the early Christian imagination" (61). Chapter 3 considers the relation between the gospel and the Johannine epistles. Contra many scholars who think that the epistles build upon the ideas presented in the gospel, Hakola argues that the similarities and differences between these writings are best understood by taking "the Gospel and the Epistles as independent witnesses of the shared tradition that is developed in different ways in different contexts" (68).

Chapter 4–6 provide specific case studies that demonstrate Hakola's approach. In chapter 4 Hakola examines John 11:47–53 using the concept of collective victimhood in social-identity theory to explain how the portrayal of Jesus as an innocent victim at the hands of Jewish authorities aided the construction of the social identity of Johannine Christians who increasingly abandoned their Jewishness and marginalized themselves from other Jews. Contra many scholars who contend that the confession of Jesus as the Messiah was the sole reason for expulsion from the synagogue, Hakola suggests that it was faith in Jesus as the Messiah *resulting in the abandonment of basic Jewish practices* that put the Johannine Christians on a collision course with other Jews. Hakola concludes that the sense of collective victimhood was appealing for Johannine Christians who felt persecuted by other Jews. Chapter 5 examines why the believing Jews are described as children of the devil in 8:31–47. He argues that these Jews could be seen as a symbolic representation of those who believed in Jesus as the Messiah (like the Johannine Christians) but continued to interact with diaspora synagogue communities (unlike the Johannine Christians). In order to preserve the distinctiveness of his group, John simplifies the diverse, complex social reality by using polarizing, dualistic imagery to caricature these other Jews. Chapter 6 deals with the character of Nicodemus. While agreeing with many scholars on the ambiguity of Nicodemus in John's narrative world, Hakola contends that Nicodemus as a Pharisee and a Jew may represent Jews in John's time who were sympathetic to Jesus. As such, the ambiguous character of Nicodemus may have helped Johannine Christians accept the ambiguities and uncertainties in their own world.

Chapter 7 summarizes the main arguments and results,and situates them in a broader scholarly context. In Hakola's own words, "I have claimed that John's dualistic view of the world should not be taken as a direct reflection of the isolation of the Johannine Christians from their surroundings but as an attempt to create a visionary world where those who believe in Jesus in the right way are much more clearly separated from others than they ever were in real life" (154). Hakola contends that a nonconfessional approach in the study of early Christianity, such as the social-identity approach, is superior to theological approaches because its results are assessable by everyone and not just by those sharing particular theological assumptions.

Hakola argues his case competently and cogently, and his creative argument provides an alternative to the two positions dominating the Johannine landscape today. Any serious student of the Johannine writings must engage with Hakola's views, and those interested in the interdisciplinary social-identity approach will also benefit from this study. I have four critical comments. First, I regard most methods as "neutral," so social-identity theory sheds light on sociological interactions within historical contexts but does not in itself indicate the extent to which a text reflects historical realities. In a sense, no text is an objective reflection of the real world. Any account of past events is *interpreted* history. But while John claims that his version of events in the real world is a truthful, that is, believable, presentation, Hakola essentially claims it is not because John imagines and exaggerates many aspects of the real world. It seems to me, however, that John's characterization of "the Jews," for example, is not very different from that of other Jewish groups in the Synoptics (see, e.g., Matt 23). I provide two examples where I read the evidence differently than Hakola and suggest a closer correspondence between the Johannine narrative world and the real world than Hakola would concede. In chapter 3 Hakola claims that the most obvious difference between the gospel and the epistles is that the former centers on the conflict between Jesus and "the Jews," whereas in the latter the term *Ioudaioi* does not feature at all (73). Hakola, however, fails to notice that the term *Ioudaioi* has already disappeared from the Farewell Discourses in John 13–17 (except for the isolated reference in 13:33). This might imply that the Johannine Jesus himself had already indicated that his conflict with "the Jews" would continue after his departure as the conflict between his followers and "the world." Early Christian writings such as Acts, 1 Peter, and Revelation, as well as church history to this day, testify to similar realities as we find in the Johannine writings. A second example that John's narrative world may reflect the real world more accurately than Hakola is willing to admit is in his treatment of Nicodemus. While Hakola sees Nicodemus as a representative of the social groups of Pharisees and Jews, I contend that in John's narrative world Nicodemus is representative of a particular group of people who were attracted by Jesus's signs but whose response to Jesus was defective or deficient. Various textual indicators suggest that 2:23–3:1 sets the stage for the Nicodemus episode so that Nicodemus represents the group in 2:23–25—not socially but in the way he is drawn to Jesus and responds to him. This could suggest a historical reality that, although Jesus was opposed by "the Jews" as a group throughout most of his ministry, not every individual in that group was hostile to Jesus.

Second, if Hakola is right and John's narrative world is a distorted version of the real world, would the early church have readily accepted the Johannine writings? Third, if we extrapolate Hakola's approach, no early Christian writing describing rival Jewish groups can be taken as a faithful account of the real world, whether the Jewish authorities in Jerusalem and diaspora synagogues in Acts, the Judaizers or non-Christian Jewish opponents in Paul's letters, or opposing Jewish groups in the Synoptics. Regardless of how long the process of the parting of the ways between Judaism and Christianity was, the implication of Hakola's hypothesis is that all early Christian writings invented a polemic that was worse than the actual reality in order to secure a distinct group identity. In fact, it would imply that the entire Jewish-Christian conflict may well be largely imagined by early Christians. I wonder whether Hakola is being overly suspicious of the correspondence between John's narrative world and the real world.

Fourth, Hakola assumes that John's Gospel is describing a version (imaginary or not) of the world in John's time, but why not take the gospel as a reflective account of events that took place fifty years earlier? It seems that we must still resolve whether the gospels reflect the *Sitz im Leben* of early Christianity in the late first century or that of the Palestinian situation in the time of Jesus and, related to this, whether the purpose for writing the gospels is to construct a distinct group identity that differentiates Christians from other Jewish groups or to describe the life of the central figure of Christianity in order to promote faith. In my view, social-identity theory could be used constructively to explain the sociological interactions between various groups in Jesus's time and arguably support a closer correspondence between the world of the Johannine text and the real world than Hakola would admit. John is undeniably a theologian who narrates how God incarnate has acted in history, and hence it seems appropriate that we use theological approaches to understand his writings. This does not mean we neglect or bypass the diverse social and historical realities. Nevertheless, my questions and disagreements do not detract from my appreciation for this well-argued, provocative book. It is a fine piece of scholarship.

My Flesh Is Meat Indeed: A Nonsacramental Reading of John 6:51–58, by Meredith J. C. Warren. Minneapolis: Fortress, 2015. Pp. x + 297. Paper. $44.00. ISBN 9781451490244.

Dana Robinson, Creighton University

Meredith Warren's book is a stimulating contribution to long-standing debates over the relationship of the canonical gospels to other Hellenistic literature and over the interpretation of one of John's thorniest passages. Warren approaches the Fourth Gospel with a well-established set of textual and literary methods but juxtaposes them in new and illuminating ways. As the title reveals, her primary interest is in the bread of life discourse, the controversial pericope in which Jesus insists that his followers must eat his flesh and drink his blood. In order to recover something of the original cultural resonances of this passage beneath the accretions of later sacramental theology, Warren looks outward to the Greek novels and, in particular, their appropriation of the tropes of hero cult. This is a familiar turn; other scholars have used generic conventions in Hellenistic narrative and biography to help locate John's treatment of Jesus. But Warren pulls on new threads to reveal a new web of meaning in John's narrative in which this passage is not a later addition but central to John's portrayal of Jesus's identity.

Chapter 1, "The Word Was Made Flesh," summarizes the relevant aspects of scholarship on the Gospel of John in general and John 6:51c–58 in particular. On the question of whether the bread of life discourse is to be understood as eucharistic or christological, Warren obviously takes the christological side, but in this chapter she carefully articulates her position vis-à-vis other scholars in both camps. Against the eucharistic side, she marshals demonstrations of John's overriding concern, throughout the gospel, with Jesus's identity as *simultaneously* human and divine, to argue that the pericope ought to be understood in this light, as part of a pattern within John's Gospel of using sharply marked physical signs to indicate divine identity. On the christological side, she distinguishes herself from scholars who suggest that the references to eating should be understood metaphorically as references to Christ's death. She argues that these interpretations do not go far enough in recognizing the extent to which John is bending generic expectations related to the establishment of hero cult in Hellenistic literature and using food language to make a strong statement about Jesus's identity as a divine-mortal being. Eating Jesus's flesh is still an important concept in this system, but it is neither sacramental nor completely metaphorical. To unpack this assertion, Warren devotes the next two chapters to analysis of the complex relationship between divine identity and sacrificial meals in the Hellenistic romance novels.

Chapter 2, "Second Only to Artemis," turns to the first half of the novelistic equation between divine identity and sacrificial meal. Identity is a major theme of the Hellenistic romances; important plot points turn on concealing or revealing the true parentage or identity of our intrepid heroines. But more significant to Warren's argument is the frequency with which romance heroines are mistaken for goddesses. She analyzes the epiphanic imagery surrounding them and the tendency of other characters "mistakenly" to worship them as goddesses. The effect of these "divine hints, ironic treatment, and disguise tropes" (92) is to suggest to the discerning reader that the heroine is being *mistaken* for who she is *in reality*. Warren concludes that this double ambiguity suggests a "simultaneous ontology in the narrative reality" (94) allowing the heroines to "straddle the boundary of divine and mortal." But it also reaches back to the epic tradition. By consciously echoing Homeric language of divine identification, the novels co-opt for their heroines certain cultural expectations surrounding sacrificial death of the hero.

Chapter 3 turns to these expectations in order to link the divine identity of the heroines with the patterns of death and consumption that mark the establishment of hero cult. In this, the most complicated stage of the argument, Warren asserts that "the association between the heroine and the divine reaches its climax at the moment of ultimate antagonism: human sacrifice" (118). In order to develop this pattern, she applies Gregory Nagy's work on divine antagonism and ritual symbiosis in hero cult to the narrative structure of the romance novels, then jumps into a lengthy discussion of the language and meaning of sacrifice in Greek and Roman religion and the taboos surrounding human sacrifice and cannibalism. The important conceptual link here seems to be that ritual consumption, and not the victim's death alone, is essential for the completion of certain types of sacrifice. In the case of hero cult and the romance heroines, the threat of human sacrifice evokes the imaginative possibility of human consumption—even when it is ultimately avoided. For Warren, the trope of human sacrifice becomes another way of evoking contemporaneity in the narrative: even when the heroines are not actually killed, the narrative creates suspense in such a way that they *are* killed—and eaten—in the anticipatory vision of the reader. This sacrifice confirms the identification between the hero victim and the divinity responsible for his or her death.

All of this is an elaborate set-up for the final chapter, "My Flesh Is Meat Indeed," where Warren brings these ideas to bear directly on John 6:51b–58 to argue that John "repurposes the sacrificial language of eating flesh and drinking blood in order to make Jesus' divine identity explicit" (191). John's innovation with genre comes into sharper view here. While the novels associate anthropophagy with divine identity by *not* describing the actual consumption but leaving enough ambiguity to make it real in the imaginations of the readers, John's Jesus makes the act explicit in the narrative. The shocking assertion that drinking his blood is necessary for his followers to have life does more, Warren argues, than simply weed out any squeamish disciples. It actually identifies Jesus as divine by collapsing divine antagonism, sacrificial death, and consumption into a single contemporaneous narrative event that creates identification between Jesus and God in the heroic mode.

So Warren concludes that this famous pericope "embeds a sacrificial ritual in narrative" (234); in other words, it draws on an established tradition of linking divine identity with sacrificial death, consumption, and cult formation *in narrative* in order to make a statement about Jesus's identity. Warren's insights into the ways that narrative ambiguity works to evoke double realities, both of time and of identity, are particularly valuable as demonstrations of the constructive power of absence and allusion. Warren uses the romance novels to construct a surprisingly sturdy bridge between the heroic mode of divine identification and John's narrative Christology, which uses grotesquely physical images of human sacrifice to evoke simultaneous death and life, consumption and nonconsumption, divinity and humanity.

In her contention that the sacrifice and consumption described in John 6 occur only at the level of narrative, Warren may overstate the separation between text and practice. The sacrificial trajectory of the romantic heroine follows the pattern of the establishment of a hero cult, but no cult of Chariclea or Leucippe is known to have existed. Warren's attempt to explain the bread of life discourse as equally contained by narrative—a "ritual in ink"—is immediately complicated by our knowledge that a cultic practice did exist among worshipers of Jesus. Warren's insistence on the separation is, of course, extremely useful as a heuristic device for focusing our attention on these literary constructions and stands as a necessary challenge to the tendency to reduce food language in Christian texts to overdetermined eucharistic references. But I suspect that this reading of the pericope as a dramatic and even shocking statement of divine identity has further implications for our understanding of early Christian cult practice as well as for other types of ritualized eating in narrative.

Raymond Brown, 'The Jews,' and the Gospel of John: From Apologia to Apology, by Sonya Shetty Cronin. Library of New Testament Studies 504. New York: Bloomsbury, 2015. Pp. xiii + 195. Hardcover. $112.00. ISBN 9780567470850.

R. Alan Culpepper, McAfee School of Theology, Mercer University

Written under the tutelage of David Levenson at Florida State University, this dissertation stands at the nexus of powerful currents in late twentieth-century New Testament scholarship: Roman Catholic biblical scholarship, the work and influence of Raymond E. Brown, and the growing awareness of the anti-Judaism of the Gospel of John. Cronin describes the evolution of Brown's interpretation of "the Jews" in the Gospel of John through the course of his writings and how he moved "from apologia to apology," recognizing the anti-Jewish intent and influence of these references. Along the way she notes the influence of other Johannine scholars, Jewish colleagues, and Vatican II on Brown, and in turn the ways in which he led the way in calling for recognition of John's anti-Jewish character.

The first chapter reviews Brown's life and career and sets it in the context of significant changes in the Roman Catholic Church. Divino Afflante Spiritu in 1943 opened the way for Catholic biblical scholars to engage in historical and literary criticism, and Brown himself was present at the 1963 session of the Vatican Council at which Nostra Aetate, which condemned anti-Semitism, was discussed. Later he was appointed to the Pontifical Biblical Commission in 1972 and again in 1996. While Brown's scholarship was rooted in the Church, he was also influenced by Protestant scholars, especially Rudolf Bultmann and C.H. Dodd, and later his colleague J. Louis Martyn, though he disagreed with each of these at various points. He also valued his contacts with Jewish scholars at the Jewish Theological Seminary during his years in New York.

Brown's publications on John in the 1960s established his position as one of the leading American and Catholic New Testament scholars. In *The Gospel of John and the Johannine Epistles*, a short book published in 1960, Brown interpreted "the Jews" as "the hostile Jerusalem authorities" and displayed no awareness of potential anti-Jewishness in the Gospel. In this first volume of his Anchor Bible commentary on John, published in 1966, Brown recognized that the term "the Jews" carried different meanings in different passages in the gospel and that its use was influenced by the evangelist's post-70 CE setting. Any changes in his views in the second volume of the commentary, published in 1970, are subtle at best but seem in line with his growing awareness. Still, Brown contended that the Jewish authorities were involved in the crucifixion of Jesus.

One of the anomalies Cronin notes is that Brown's greatest advances on these issues appeared in his brief, popular writings: an article published in *Worship* in 1975 and *A Retreat with John the Evangelist* (1998). In the former Brown rejected both the suggestion that offensive passages should be removed from the gospel and the uncritical adoption of hostile attitudes in it, noting "the fallacy that every position taken by an author of Scripture is inerrant" (Cornin, 73, citing Brown, 131).

In *The Community of the Beloved Disciple* (1979), Brown reconstructed the history of the Johannine community and speculated that the use of the term "the Jews" as a reference to the community's opponents in the synagogue originated with Samaritan converts who joined the community. The term was adopted by the community following their expulsion from the synagogue, when they no longer considered themselves Jews. For the first time Brown describes the hostility in the gospel as anti-Jewish (Cronin, 82, Brown, 42 n. 66).

Brown published a revised edition of *The Gospel and the Epistles of John* in 1988. In this edition Brown placed "the Jews" in quotation marks (as he had been doing since 1966) and summarized the community situation in the introduction.

Further development in Brown's thought is evident in his magisterial works published in the 1990s. In *The Death of the Messiah* (1994) Brown continued to maintain the involvement of Jews in Jesus's death but moved on to repudiate the condemnation of Jews by the Church in later centuries, quoting Nostra Aetate for the first time as exemplary of modern Christian attitudes toward Jews. Brown now addressed his readers directly about anti-Jewish sentiment. At the same time, he reiterated positions he took in *Community of the Beloved Disciple*, that the conflict with the synagogue reflects the gospel's setting, not the ministry of Jesus, and that "John's intent is hostile, deliberate, and incriminating towards 'the Jews'" (Cronin, 101). Cronin notes the irony that, while Brown's awareness of anti-Judaism in John culminates in *The Death of the Messiah*, John Dominic Crossan's *Who Killed Jesus* (1996) critiques Brown's treatment of anti-Judaism as insufficient. Brown never responded to Crossan in print.

Surprisingly in view of his earlier writings, Brown's 800-page *Introduction to the New Testament* (1997) does not contain a separate section or discussion of anti-Judaism in John. In contrast, concern over anti-Judaism pervades the last book published before his death, *A Retreat with John the Evangelist* (1998). In this slim volume Brown allows the evangelist to speak in the first person, to claim that he was not John the son of Zebedee and that his characters represent different types of responses to Jesus. The evangelist says he never intended his gospel to fuel hatred for the Jews in later centuries, "and I sincerely regret that my words were applied to them" (Brown, 71; Cronin, 123). Brown's awareness of John's anti-Judaism therefore grew steadily over the decades, and he moved from explaining it to apologizing for it. In this popular volume at the end of his life, Brown characterizes Vatican II as the most important religious event of his lifetime.

Cronin also reviews two works that were published after Brown's death in 1998: *An Introduction to the Gospel of John* (2003), edited by Francis J. Moloney, and *Points de vue divers sur les juifs dans Jean* (1997), which was Brown's assignment for the preparation of the document, *The Jewish People and Their Sacred Scriptures in the Christian Bible*, that was published in 2001. In the former Brown claims that, while John is the most Jewish book of the New Testament, by the time it was written the Johannine community no longer considered themselves Jews. Hence this very Jewish gospel was in fact anti-Jewish. Brown restates his position in *Points de vue*, and Cronin shows how much of Brown's writing was reproduced in *The Jewish People and Their Sacred Scriptures*.

In the conclusion Cronin sets Brown's work in the context of biblical scholarship on John, surveying the treatment of "the Jews" in commentaries and articles published during his career. What emerges is the uniqueness of Brown's work in three respects: "(1) his commitment both to historical criticism and the continuing value of the Gospel of John, (2) his direct handling of the potential anti-Judaism in the text *and the early date that he began to do this in comparison to others*, and (3) the way he impartially reports historical events without passing judgment on the first-century communities" (Cronin, 181). Brown was the first to begin to deal with anti-Judaism in John (as early as 1970), and his sensitivity to this issue continued to grow throughout his career.

Cronin's careful analysis of Brown's writings as they deal with "the Jews" in John and John's anti-Judaism brings to light Brown's unflinching honesty in historical interpretation, his fidelity as a Catholic scholar, and his sensitivity to John's influence throughout the centuries of Christian condemnations of Jews. She defines the various ploys other scholars have used to deny or soften the issue and shows how Brown (and others) rejected these attempts to deny John's anti-Judaism. Hers is a mirror in which we see not dimly but clearly, and that in itself is a significant contribution to Johannine scholarship and Christian efforts to address the anti-Judaism and supersessionism latent and overt in the Christian scriptures. One can also applaud her gracious refusal to take a position of superiority because of her later vantage point when treating both Brown and others. See, for example, her comment that "there is much that a more complete revision [of *The Gospel and the Epistles of John*, 1960 and 1988] would have changed" (93) and her response to the absence of any direct address to readers of Robert Kysar's *The Maverick Gospel* against adopting John's hostile attitude: "it seems that this was something progressive on Brown's part and not something that necessarily has to be seen as a deficiency in Kysar's approach" (160).

Two minor points of critique: While Cronin treats Martyn's *History and Theology in the Fourth Gospel* and its influence on Brown deftly and in detail, she does not point out that one of the major differences between Martyn and Brown is that Martyn maintained that the entire process of the expulsion of Johannine believers from the synagogue (and the coming of the Greeks [in John 12:20–21] and the gathering of others who are not of this fold [10:16]) is to be understood as intra-Jewish, while (as she correctly says) Brown maintained that by the time the gospel was written the evangelist and his community no longer regarded themselves as Jews. Second, Francis Moloney's name is unfortunately misspelled throughout.

Cronin understandably does not treat the literature on John and Judaism published after 2000, but there have been significant additions to the field in the past sixteen years, especially: Bieringer et al., eds., *Anti-Judaism and the Fourth Gospel: Papers of the Leuven Colloquium, 2000* (2001); Adele Reinhartz, *Befriending the Beloved Disciple: A Jewish Reading of the Gospel of John* (2001); Raimo Hakola, *Identity Matters: John, the Jews, and Jewishness* (2005); Nina L. Collins, *Jesus, the Sabbath and the Jewish Debate* (2014); Jonathan Numada, "Interpreting Johannine Anti-Judaism in Light of Hellenistic Diaspora Jewish Social Identity and Cultural Memory" (McMaster, PhD diss., 2016); and the papers presented at the 2015 conference on "John and Judaism" at Mercer University (SBL Press, forthcoming). Regardless, readers seeking to understand the interpretation of "the Jews" in John in contemporary scholarship should start with Cronin's lucid study.

ACTS

Paul in Athens: The Popular Religious Context of Acts 17, by Clare K Rothschild. Wissenschaftliche Untersuchungen zum Neuen Testament 341. Tübingen: Mohr Siebeck, 2014. Pp. xix + 215. Cloth. €89.00. ISBN 9783161532603.

Troy M. Troftgruben, Wartburg Theological Seminary

Clare K. Rothschild is Associate Professor of Theology at Lewis University (Romeoville, Illinois), editor of several book collections (e.g., *Apocalyptic Imaginations*), and a prolific author of many articles, essays, and book-length studies (e.g., *Luke-Acts and the Rhetoric of History*). True in this book and elsewhere, her written contributions reflect judicious reading, clear argumentation, and substantial dialogue with New Testament scholars and classicists. These traits make Rothschild a significant voice in New Testament studies whose writings from the last dozen years speak for themselves.

In *Paul in Athens*, Rothschild credits her study to a suggestion of Hans Dieter Betz: "that Paul viewed himself as, in part, a cult transfer figure" (ix). She finds the same dynamic at work in Luke's presentation of Paul, specifically the Areopagus speech of Acts 17:22–31. Despite the seemingly ad hoc nature of Paul's visit to Athens, Rothschild identifies the passage as a climactic narrative moment that builds on a nexus of traditions around the figure of Epimenides: "Beginning with the traditional attribution of Acts 17:28a to Epimenides, the study hypothesizes that Luke makes Paul speak in character (i.e., προσωποποιΐα) in order that he might 'appear' at the highpoint of the narrative as this ancient Cretan seer, the individual accredited with transferring Cretan Zeus worship to Athens.... [This] met one of the author's most important literary goals, namely to present Paul as the early Christian cult transfer facilitator *par excellence* (κτίστης, οἰκιστής), a representation Luke knew, at least in part, from Paul's self-descriptions in his letters" (4).

In addition to front and back matter, *Paul in Athens* comprises nine chapters and an appendix. Chapter 1 (the introduction) persuasively introduces the book's thesis. Scholars have long regarded Paul's speech in Athens as both a high point of Acts but also a muddled mix of traditions. Rothschild argues that its primary significance lies not in Paul's engagement with philosophical traditions but in Luke's portrait of Paul as a cult transfer facilitator.

Chapter 2, "History of Research," reopens a question widely dismissed by New Testament scholars of late: whether the citation of Acts 17:28a ("In him we live and move and exist") may be credited to traditions surrounding Epimenides (the *Epimenidea)*. The attribution held sway among interpreters both ancient (e.g., Theodore of Mopsuestia) and modern (e.g., Kirsopp Lake), until two twentieth-century voices (M. Pohlenz, H. Hommel) shifted attribution toward Stoic sources. Rothschild challenges this status quo attribution, due especially to the historic prevalence of the *Epimenidea* and Luke's lack of clear interest in Stoicism. Furthermore, Paul's activity in Athens parallels Epimenides closely: "For Luke, *both* Paul and Epimenides are strangers from afar summoned to Athens to fix a mistake; *both* announce that the tomb of their god is a lie; and, *both* transfer eastern cult traditions to Greece through Athens" (24).

Chapter 3, "Text and Translation," gives Rothschild's assumptions about Acts and her text and translation of Acts 17:16–34. Following Pervo, she places Acts in early second-century Asia Minor but associates it with ancient historiography. Rothschild also notes that many English translations wrongly emphasize the presence of philosophers (v. 18) and a presumed antagonism between Athenians and Paul.

Chapter 4, "*Epimenidea* in the First Two Centuries C.E.," generates a portrait of Epimenides from ancient sources: a popular poet, philosopher, and legislator, as well as purifier and "Greek seer *par excellence*" (37). Most relevant to Acts are two particular notions. The first entails Epimenides being summoned from Crete to Athens to eradicate a plague. By advising Athenians to sacrifice on the Areopagus, he purified the city. "Hence even to this day, altars may be found in different parts of Attica with no name inscribed upon them, which are memorials of this atonement" (Diogenes Laertius, *Lives* 1.110). The second tradition entails a fifty-seven-year nap taken by Epimenides, after which he awoke, identifying him as divinely favored and loosely associated with resurrection ideas.

Chapters 5 ("The Areopagus Speech") and 6 ("Bracketing the Areopagitica") are the book's most exegetically substantial. In the former Rothschild interprets

Paul's Areopagus speech in view of Epimenidean traditions and Greco-Roman literary topoi. She argues that Paul's association with the Areopagus, references to an altar "to an unknown god," the identification of an unnamed deity, the statement in verse 28a, and an emphasis on resurrection are all clear allusions to the *Epimenidea*. In the sixth chapter she characterizes Paul not merely as accused (like Socrates) but genuinely as a proclaimer of foreign divinities (Acts 17:18, 20). Rothschild argues that the surrounding narrative has several archaic elements (Areopagus, Dionysius the Areopagite, Damaris) that evoke the distant past of classical Athens. Collectively, the two chapters suggest that Luke portrays Paul as an "Epimenides *redivivus*" figure welcomed by distinguished members of the ancient Athenian high court (107).

Chapter 7, "Acts and *Epimenidea*," reflects broadly on commonalities between the Paul of Acts and the *Epimenidea* to show not literary dependence but "that the Lukan Paul fits the general paradigm of an ancient cult transfer figure" (108). Rothschild briefly names fourteen points of contact, some of which are more compelling (e.g., call stories) than others (e.g., tattoos). Even if some of the similarities are not overwhelmingly pronounced, the chapter rightly addresses the question of larger narrative parallels between these traditions.

Chapter 8, "God in Transit: Paul Transfers Christianity to Athens," builds on the work of Elizabeth Gebhard to argue that Luke "models Paul's missionary activity in Acts 13–28 on the conventional literary pattern of cult transfer narratives" (121), a pattern readily visible in the *Epimenidea*. While admitting that "Luke does not slavishly adhere to the prototype" (124), Rothschild shows where Gebhard's ten elements of the cult transfer pattern (crisis, oracle, command, embassy, difficulties, arrival, welcome, accommodation, opposition, temenos) may be discerned in Paul's activity in Acts 16–17 (transfer to Athens) and Acts 21–28 (transfer to Rome). "The purpose of Luke's reliance on the formula is to highlight Christianity's safe, successful, peaceful, and legal transfer to Europe and beyond" (131).

Chapter 9 is more provocative than its title ("Conclusion") suggests. After summarizing the preceding chapters, an "epilogue" on Crete associations in Acts argues that "Luke" was a Cretan who adopted the persona of Titus. Based on Titus's historic association with Troas (2 Cor 2:12–13), absence in Acts, and shifts to first-person language at Troas (Acts 16:8, 11; 20:5, 6), Rothschild suggests that "an author adopting Titus' persona" wrote Acts, "explaining the depiction of Paul as the Cretan hero, Epimenides" (136). An appendix follows on the significance of "sleep" language in Luke's narratives and the *Epimenidea*.

Paul in Athens is a model of superb scholarship: focused, refined, researched, and clearly argued. Characteristic of her work, Rothschild's book perceptively illumines features of Acts that resonate with literary topoi from the Greco-Roman world. Aimed at scholarly audiences, her work reflects emerging points of consensus in Acts studies—as a second-century work, influenced by various literary traditions, intentionally reflective about Paul's legacy—and builds on these with her own original contributions. These traits make *Paul in Athens* a work of gravitas that merits careful consideration by all interpreters of Acts.

Where *Paul in Athens* argues for the *Epimenidea* as influential to Acts 17:16–34, the book is persuasive. Rothschild's larger claim—that Luke portrays Paul as a Christian cult transfer facilitator par excellence—is argued effectively but may not persuade all readers. Potential obstacles lie not in inherent flaws in her argument but in whether it truly explains the larger narrative terrain of Acts. For example, that "chapter 17 is the climax of the Book of Acts" (120) is possible but not unambiguously clear. That Luke depicts Paul's missionary work as "a series of cult transfers" (131) is also a constructive reading but with its own abiding questions, such as the role of Philippi in Acts 16:11–40, the role of Paul's custody experiences in Acts 22–26, and whether Paul truly transfers Christianity to Rome in Acts 28:11–31. (The suggestion that Luke was Cretan is equally interesting, with its own set of accompanying questions.) Also, the book's use of "succession" and "transfer" language for its thesis is a potential strength for its clarity and consistency (120, 131) but at the same time has significant (potentially negative) implications for the narrative's view of the movement's Jewish roots at the ending. Challenges aside, the refinement, balance, research, and clear reasoning that accompany Rothschild's arguments make *Paul in Athens* a compelling study for even the most skeptical readers.

Paul in Athens is a work of fine scholarship that reflects broad awareness, new advances in scholarship, and a constructive interpretation that challenges traditional assumptions about Acts 17:16–34 and the narrative's engagement with the *Epimenidea*. For these very reasons, interpreters of Acts will reckon with, learn from, and be indebted to Rothschild's study for many years to come.

The Topos *of Divine Testimony in Luke-Acts*, by James R. McConnell Jr. Eugene, OR: Pickwick, 2014. Pp. xii + 322. Paper. $29.60. ISBN 9781620327555.

Kyle R. Hughes, Atlanta, Georgia

In this book, a revision of a doctoral dissertation completed at Baylor University under the supervision of Mikeal Parsons, James McConnell explores the function of divine testimony in Luke-Acts. Employing the tools of rhetorical criticism, McConnell aims to read Luke's appeals to the testimony of God, in both word and deed, against the backdrop of the ancient topos of divine testimony. Utilizing a close reading of both Hellenistic narratives and key passages in Luke-Acts, McConnell identifies the central function of this topos in Luke-Acts, as in Hellenistic narratives in general, as marking divine approval (or disapproval) of a particular character or characters.

The book is divided into seven chapters. After an introductory section that sets out the author's method (ch. 1) and provides a basic understanding of how ancient rhetorical handbooks conceived of divine testimony (ch. 2), the heart of the book follows the Lukan pattern of "word and deed" in examining divine testimony through both utterances (chs. 3–4) and actions (chs. 5–6), in each instance analyzing first Hellenistic narratives more broadly and then Luke-Acts specifically. The book concludes with a summary and avenues for future research (ch. 7).

In chapter 1 McConnell sets out his methodology, which he identifies as "that of rhetorical criticism, combined with a close reading of the text in order to discern the persuasive structures within the narrative as well as a vehicle to understand how the text would have been received by first-century auditors" (21). McConnell also provides a brief history of research concerning the use of Scripture and the miraculous in Luke-Acts, contending that his contribution will bring these two areas of New Testament scholarship into dialogue with the subject of rhetorical topoi in order to produce a new understanding of how Luke conceives of authoritative testimony.

Chapter 2 surveys the writings of ancient rhetoricians and concludes that, whereas modern biblical scholars often understand a topos in a literary sense, referring to a stock theme or cliché, the ancient sense of the term included an understanding of a topos (Latin *locus*) as "a source of proofs, used in composing a speech for the purposes of defending or prosecuting one accused of some crime" (24). Within this forensic understanding of topos, McConnell is particularly interested in what Cicero calls *external arguments* and what Aristotle terms *inartificial proofs*, which depend not on what is particular to the subject matter being argued but rather on sources outside the case itself, such as the testimony of witnesses or authorities. In light of Cicero's dictum that "external arguments depend principally on authority" (38; cf. *Top.* 4.24), it comes as no surprise that the ancient rhetoricians believed divine testimony to be a particularly persuasive source of such proofs. To further support this claim, McConnell produces a wealth of examples of the topos of divine testimony, in both words and deeds, found in ancient speeches and treatises.

Chapter 3 turns to the subject of how the topos of divine testimony functions with respect to divine utterances in Hellenistic narratives. Specifically, McConnell concludes that divine testimony "was used in narratives to legitimate or denigrate characters portrayed in those narratives" (75). McConnell takes pains to demonstrate that ancient narratives such as histories and biographies were written for persuasive purposes and that therefore we should not be surprised to find this rhetorical topos in this particular genre; indeed, the bulk of this chapter is dedicated to providing evidence of just this phenomenon, analyzing in turn examples of three forms of divine testimony: through direct divine speech, through an inspired intermediary, and through oracles. Though in every case the "overarching function" of this form of divine testimony is to portray a character as either pious or impious, the specific purposes of the testimony in a given narrative can include encouraging, affirming, commanding, and warning a character, as well as explaining a divine act or providing a prophecy that will later be fulfilled (120).

In chapter 4 McConnell turns to divine testimony through utterances in Luke-Acts, having justified in the previous chapter the comparison of Luke-Acts with Hellenistic histories and biographies by defending the position that Luke-Acts is likewise best understood as a "persuasive narrative" (79). Also as in the preceding chapter, McConnell organizes the instances of divine testimony through utterances in Luke-Acts into those made through direct speech, through an inspired intermediary, and "through reference to and the citation of Jewish scripture" (121), here standing in for the oracles of Hellenistic narratives. This last category, which takes up the majority of the chapter, is justified on the basis that an ancient audience "would have understood scripture references in the same way as references to oracles in contemporary Hellenistic literature" (140); both would be recognized as divine speech, and both would often, albeit not always, be prefaced by introductory statements (174). McConnell concludes that in Luke-Acts, as in Hellenistic writing, divine testimony through utterances has the primary purpose of characterizing someone with respect to that person's piety or lack thereof; in other words, the rhetorical purpose of this kind of testimony is to enable the audience "to experience the divine perspective of the character in question" (176).

Chapter 5 returns to his study of Hellenistic narratives, this time with attention to divine testimony as expressed through deeds. Drawing on Ciceronian categories, McConnell provides examples of the various ways by which the gods could express such testimony, including through objects and events in the heavens, the appearance and paths of birds, sounds and fire from heaven, dreams and visions, signs and portents in creation, and the examination of entrails. Across these various categories, divine testimony through deeds "generally … serves as warnings, commands, encouragement, and prophecies of coming events" (225); within a specific narrative context, it often functions more specifically as a means of expressing the gods' approval or disapproval of certain characters (225–26). Divine testimony through deeds thus functions in much the same way as it does in the case of utterances; the two forms of the topos therefore have considerable overlap in terms of their significance as a vehicle for developing characterization in a way that would have been readily understood by an ancient audience.

In chapter 6 McConnell applies the above insights gleaned from Hellenistic narratives to analyze how divine testimony through deeds functions in Luke-Acts. He identifies examples of divine testimony from each of the categories of divine deeds set out in the previous chapter with the exception of examining entrails; the majority of examples are, of course, the many dreams and visions found in the book of Acts. McConnell notes that the topos of divine testimony functions within Luke-Acts in the same ways observed in Hellenistic narratives, again emphasizing the "fundamental" purpose of expressing either sanction or disapproval for various characters (263).

In a concluding chapter McConnell summarizes his argument and then proceeds to set out, in narrative order, the various and profound ways in which divine testimony features in Luke-Acts, serving to convince the ancient auditor of God's approval of characters such as John the Baptist, Jesus, and members of the early church, and thus, by extension, their actions as well. In sum, "the main characters in the combined narrative of Luke-Acts are described throughout by God's testimony" (275), such that "the cumulative weight of [this evidence] would have been readily understood by the ancient audience" (276). In the final accounting, therefore, the topos of divine testimony functions in Luke-Acts just as it does in much of Hellenistic literature insofar as it is designed to persuade auditors to form certain conclusions about the guilt or innocence, piety or impiety, of different characters.

McConnell's book is a fine example of how rhetorical criticism can better illuminate our understanding of particular aspects of the New Testament, in this case the topos of divine testimony in Luke-Acts. The obvious strength of this book is McConnell's clear and thorough presentation of this topos in Greco-Roman materials. As a result, McConnell makes a convincing case that an educated ancient auditor would understand and find persuasive Luke's use of divine testimony. If this book could benefit from one improvement, however, it would be the presence of a stronger comparative element. In the introduction McConnell notes that "it may be necessary to compare the Lukan passage with its parallels in Mark and/ or Matthew in order to discern the specific focus in Luke" (18). Indeed, such an approach would help shed light on the extent to which Luke's use of this particular topos is a unique feature of his writings. Unfortunately, over the course of McConnell's book, the other gospels (and other early Christian writings besides Luke-Acts) essentially fade from view, and McConnell seems to admit as much when he concedes that future research could expand on his work by carrying out "the investigation of other NT documents for this same phenomenon" (277). That being said, this slight deficiency does not detract from the fact that McConnell has produced a meticulously researched, carefully argued book that will be of great service to not only students of the gospels but also anyone looking for an example of how to convincingly utilize rhetorical criticism.

PAUL AND THE PAULINE EPISTLES

2 Corinthians, by George H. Guthrie. Baker Exegetical Commentary on the New Testament. Grand Rapids: Baker Academic, 2015. Pp. xxv + 710. Hardcover. $49.99. ISBN 9780801026737.

Craig Keener, Asbury Theological Seminary

This work by George H. Guthrie, Benjamin W. Perry Professor of Bible at Union University, is a splendid contribution to the Baker Exegetical Commentary series to which it belongs. Like many of the other volumes, this one is characterized by evangelical identity, willingness to engage critical scholarship in a friendly way, and commitment to serve the church.

This commentary offers consistent treatment throughout. Many commentaries today (including one of my earlier ones) offer spottier treatment of some passages than of others. Toward the end of their project some also seem to run out of interest or, probably more often, the remainder of their allotted word count. By contrast, Guthrie paces himself, consistently offering careful attention to grammatical detail even in the less-used or controversial passages.

The commentary will prove useful in courses based on either the Greek or the English text. Guthrie's extensive attention to grammatical detail, including the specific character of grammatical cases and the like, make this work quite suitable for a Greek exegesis course focused on 2 Corinthians. At the same time, its prose is easy to follow and read, and all Greek is transliterated and translated after each use, making it accessible for the user less familiar with the language. Guthrie employs diagrams and discourse analysis where relevant; the visual charting of grammatical and rhetorical elements at points (e.g., the parallel rhetorical structures in 6:4–5 on 326, 6:14–16 on 351, 11:22 on 551, and 11:27 on 562) is designed to help readers follow more easily.

Guthrie provides healthy attention to both Jewish and gentile Greco-Roman sources, emphasizing in his introduction both Paul's wider Greco-Roman context and Paul's own identity as a messianic Jew. These interests include discussion of ancient leadership values in Corinth (14–17), a matter that naturally figures into Paul's need to defend his ministry in this letter. Guthrie especially draws attention to the wider stylistic and theological context of Paul's letters and the context of early Christianity more generally, as well as the Old Testament context that formed a major theological and rhetorical source for early Christianity.

Guthrie consistently remains respectful toward the range of scholarly options and makes judicious choices among them, usually in ways that take most account of the specific context in 2 Corinthians. One can often learn about a commentator's orientation and openness to other views by examining the range of voices with which she or he interacts. I often establish initial impressions about a work by surveying its index as well as scanning sample pages. In this case, Guthrie's author index lists roughly four hundred modern authors, and there are at least several others (such as J. D. Crossan) whose names the indexer missed.

Guthrie engages a wide range of scholarship. Authors of sociohistorical and sociorhetorical studies include Bruce Winter (eighteen times), H. Dieter Betz (sixteen times), Peter Marshall (twelve times, including his seminal *Enmity in Corinth*), L. L. Welborn (twelve times); H.-J. Klauck (six times), with multiple references also to other experts such as Christopher Forbes, Margaret Mitchell, and Jerry Sumney. Jerome Murphy-O'Connor's generally historically oriented works appear sixteen times; Gordon Fee appears six times. Closely engaged with the Greek text, Guthrie cites extensively Bruce Metzger (twenty-three times), Ceslas Spicq (fifty-nine times), and Daniel Wallace (thirty-five times).

Following a growing trend in scholarship, Guthrie allows more space for earlier voices such as Augustine, Jerome, and Calvin than do some previous commentators; he properly and often credits Gerald Bray's collection of patristic sources on 2 Corinthians. Guthrie also engages the standard commentaries, at greatest length the massive works of Murray J. Harris, then Margaret Thrall and Victor Paul Furnish. Additionally, Guthrie interacts significantly with Barnett, Barrett, Garland, Hafemann, Keener, Martin, Matera, and Witherington, and often, though less so, with Bruce, Belleville, H. Betz, Hughes, Lambrecht, Plummer, J. Scott, and Windisch. The shorter commentaries by Colin Kruse and

Frederick Danker appear four and five times, respectively (though Danker's concise work supplies surprisingly fresh insights for its size).

Guthrie thus engages conversation partners from various theological and exegetical perspectives. Admittedly, some older works are less represented; Rudolf Bultmann's work, including his commentary, appears only five times; Dieter Georgi only four; E. Bernard Allo's work is missing. More surprising, James D. G. Dunn appears only once, and some other scholars, such as David deSilva and J. David Hester Amador, do not appear at all. As is painfully obvious, however, today's secondary literature is too vast to engage it all, and on the whole Guthrie's wide range of engagement merits appreciation, especially because he appears much more careful than some other scholars to credit all his sources.

Regarding specifics, Guthrie's introduction examines at some length Paul's interaction with the Corinthians before the letter (17–23). He dates 1 Corinthians in late 53 and 2 Corinthians in 54/55 (18). Following a trend of a number of recent commentators, Guthrie argues at some length for the letter's unity (23–32). He examines the arguments for various divisions, especially the likeliest one at 10:1, but highlights significant elements of literary continuity and prefers rhetorical explanations for the breaks. He also offers his own *inclusio* of at least "nine terms and phrases" from 1:1–7 that recur in 13:11–13; some of these terms are hardly rare, but others, such as παρακαλέω and ἅγιοι appear to strengthen his case.

While supporting the unity of the letter's two main sections, Guthrie does not deny differences of emphasis or interest between them. He examines at special length reasons for the preponderance of the first-person plural in most of 2 Cor 1–9, in contrast to that of the first-person singular in chapters 10–13 (32–38). Guthrie contends that Paul speaks largely for a ministry team earlier but shifts to a personal appeal in 10–13. Here it seems to me that 2:14–7:4, which defend Paul's apostleship and yet employ mostly the plural, should seem more comparable with chapters 10–13. Nevertheless, Guthrie is correct that the "I" in these later chapters becomes more specific.

Regarding the "opponents" (45–46), Paul's rivals are Jewish Christian, as Paul is, but not necessarily like the Jewish Christian opposition in Galatia. Here they are Hellenistic Jews from the sophistic tradition; Guthrie follows especially Bruce Winter's significant *Philo and Paul among the Sophists* here.

Guthrie is careful in his handling of evidence. For example, he notes the scarcity of examples of ἀπόστολος in the LXX but connects the verb cognate with the later Jewish institution of the *shaliakh*. He freely recognizes that some elements of this institution cannot be documented in the first century and thus is satisfied to contend simply that these ideas *may* have been in use in first-century Hellenistic Judaism.

Pastors will find helpful the pastorally sensitive and often cross-culturally relevant reflections at various points in the commentary (e.g., 339–400, 499–500). Although these appear merely as samples in discrete sections, they do invite readers to engage the text at a fresh level of understanding, even if primarily by way of illustration. Considering concrete implications that texts from a different setting might offer our own contexts often helps us enter more sympathetically the texts' implied worlds. Occasional citations from Mark Twain (94), Wendell Berry (291), and others further provide some lively variety in the text.

For some conclusions regarding various sample points in the letter: The contrast in 3:6 does not denigrate the law but instead contrasts those dependent on their own ability to observe the law with the experience of the Spirit, shared by Moses and new covenant believers (198–200). The new creation in 5:17 refers not merely to individual believers but to the entire new order in Christ of which they are a part, inviting an eschatological basis for evaluation (308). The spiritual warfare language of 10:3–7 is directed especially against Paul's opponents (472). Paul may depict himself in the third person in 12:2–4 partly to keep the focus on his weakness rather than risk boasting (581). Guthrie believes (probably rightly) that the thorn in Paul's flesh most likely reflects Paul's frequent experience of being persecuted (591).

Guthrie's commentary is a suitable textbook on 2 Corinthians, especially for a seminary-level or upper undergraduate exegesis or English Bible course. It has more space to work with than more compact commentaries (including, for example, the Augsburg commentary by Frederick Danker and my own for Cambridge) and is more accessible than the most comprehensive volumes (such as the magnificent works of Margaret Thrall [ICC] and others). Certainly scholars as well as pastors will learn from Guthrie's judicious choices and scholarly insights.

1 and 2 Thessalonians, by Richard S. Ascough. Phoenix Guides to the New Testament 13. Sheffield: Sheffield Phoenix, 2014. Pp. 99. Paper. $19.95. ISBN 9781909697577.

Jeffrey A. D. Weima, Calvin Theological Seminary

This brief introduction to 1 and 2 Thessalonians is written by Richard Ascough of Queen's University, Kingston, Canada. Ascough's academic career has focused on ancient associations in Macedonia and how they inform our understanding of the social context of Paul's letters to the Thessalonians and, to a lesser extent, also to the Philippians. His stated purpose in this latest addition to the Phoenix Guides to the New Testament is to offer not a detailed commentary of 1 and 2 Thessalonians but "an overview of the historical development of the Christ group at Thessaloniki while demonstrating how these two letters inform the historians' craft of (re)constructing social structures and theological developments" (5). The book's brevity, avoidance of technical terms connected with the academic study of the New Testament, cleverly worded headings, and colloquial writing style indicate that it is aimed not narrowly at scholars but at a wider audience of those interested in the Bible and the formation of the early Christian church.

The volume contains six chapters, the first four of which deal with 1 Thessalonians and the final two with 2 Thessalonians. Chapter 1 reconstructs the founding of the Christ group at Thessaloniki, drawing not on the account of Acts 17, which

Ascough considers for the most part historically unreliable, but on the text of 1 Thessalonians and information gleaned from archaeology. Ascough paints a vivid picture of the "Paul party" (Paul, Silvanus, and Timothy) arriving in Thessaloniki and working in tough conditions in a leather shop in the industrial section of the inner city. There they shared an apocalyptic message with coworkers that asserted that their hearers were in imminent danger of God's wrath but could escape if they would only abandon their allegiance to idols and instead serve the "living and true God." After a period of intense debate with the Paul party, an already well established association of shopworkers made the collective decision to commit themselves to the God and Christ proclaimed by their three new coworkers from the east.

Chapter 2 focuses on various details related to the composition of 1 Thessalonians. The letter was not authored by Paul alone but all the members of the Paul party: "We should imagine that Paul and others were together in a room brainstorming ideas and arguing about policies and procedures, while a scribe took notes, mentally and on a wax tablet, that he would later craft into a rhetorically effective written presentation" (20). After briefly outlining the structure of 1 Thessalonians according to the epistolary conventions of that day, Ascough raises the issue of whether 2:13-16 is authentic, concluding tentatively that this passage was not part of the original letter but added sometime after the destruction of the Jerusalem temple in 70 CE. The chapter ends with a review of rhetorical criticism and an outline of the letter based on this method.

Chapter 3 takes up the first of two key themes that run through the whole letter: the affirmation of the relationship between the Paul party and the Christ group in the city. This key theme is treated in three major sections of the letter. In 2:1–20 the Paul party is very much concerned with defending their decision to leave Thessaloniki while reassuring the Christ group of their deep and abiding interest in their wellbeing. In 1:2–10 the three authors remind the Thessalonians not only of how their extant relationship was established through the missionaries' preaching of the gospel but also of how the Thessalonians received and responded to that gospel. In 5:12–22 the focus shifts away from the relationship between the Paul party and the Thessalonian Christ group to the nature of leadership within the group itself.

Chapter 4 addresses the second of the two key themes in the letter: the advice given to the Thessalonians on how to remain faithful in the face of moral challenges and their impending mortality. These topics were brought to the authors' attention by the Thessalonians themselves, most likely in a letter brought to them by the recently returned Timothy, and are taken up in four sequential passages. In 4:1–8 there may be a specific yet unnamed infraction behind the exhortations against sexual misconduct, but the focus of the authors' response is on the impact sexual ethics has on community relationships. In 4:9–12 the picture emerges of a workers' association that expresses deep care for all of its members but does not want to get involved in the machinations of benefaction typical of such groups in that day. In 4:13–18 and 5:1–11 the letter writers address the Christ group's loss of hope that their deceased members would be saved at the coming of Jesus and their question about when Jesus will return.

The final two chapters concentrate on 2 Thessalonians. Chapter 5 is almost entirely taken up with issue of this document's authenticity. Ascough considers several matters related to this issue, such as the meaning of a letter "as though from us" (2:2), the autograph greeting of 3:17 with its claim to authenticity, the letter's unique vocabulary and stylistic features, and both its similarities and differences with the first letter. It is not until chapter 6, however, that Ascough finally reaches a conclusion (again tentative): "To my mind there is enough evidence to indicate that 2 Thessalonians is not authentic, and was written by person or persons unknown a generation or two after Paul's death, but genuinely felt that what they were writing is in keeping with the spirit of Paul and his companions.... 2 Thessalonians was written to a Christ group in the city who were facing somewhat changed circumstances in a later generation" (72). The rest of the chapter examines the letter's three central topics in light of the presumed post-Pauline situation: the encouragement of Christ followers who are undergoing significant suffering at the hands of their enemies (1:3–12 and 2:13–3:5); the correction of some misunderstanding and the calming of some apprehension around the timing of Jesus' return (2:1–12); and advice about certain members of their group who are creating disturbances and refusing to share in the work that is the basis of the community's financial support (3:6–15).

The book closes with a brief epilogue that traces the church's history in the subsequent centuries as well as the place of both letters in the canonical process.

The biggest strength of this guide is its use of inscriptions pertaining to voluntary associations and how information about these ancient groups sheds light on various aspects of the Christ group in Thessaloniki. Commentaries on 1 and 2 Thessalonians have made little or no use of the parallel of associations with early Christian communities, so this is an area where the book makes a unique contribution. This volume also provides a very readable overview of what are often referred to as "introductory matters" pertaining to 1 and 2 Thessalonians. Ascough does a commendable job in presenting complicated and technical debates on several scholarly issues in a concise and user-friendly manner that the nonspecialist can readily grasp and appreciate.

Not all of the book's claims, however, are persuasive. For example, the mention of cosenders does not require a conclusion of coauthors. In fact, there are several compelling reasons for viewing Paul as the primary and authoritative voice in the letter. The rejection of Acts 17:1–10 in the reconstruction of the Christ group in Thessaloniki is justified by details in that account that do not fit with information contained in 1 Thessalonians. Yet since Ascough concedes that "very few scholars think that the writer simply invented everything in Acts" (3), it would have been helpful to hear more about what information from that account he does recognize as historically reliable. On the question of whether 1 Thess 2:13–16 is a later interpolation, Ascough claims that nothing is lost with the removal of this passage "since 2.12 and 2.17 fit together well with no disruption of the argument" (25). Yet the emphatic personal pronoun that opens 2:17 ("But you...") would be unnecessary and even slightly awkward if it follows immediately after 2:12, which already shifts the focus away from the Paul party to the Christ group ("who calls *you* into his kingdom and glory"). The "now concerning" formula that opens 4:9 is simply a topic marker (see also its occurrence in 4:13 and 5:1) and does not require the existence of a written letter from the Christ group to the Paul party with a set of specific questions. In the absence of any explicit reference to such a letter (as in 1 Cor 7:1), it is better to view the four subjects addressed in 1 Thess 4:1–5:11 as the response of the Paul party to the oral report about the church from Timothy (3:6). Ascough rightly sees in 2:1–20 the concern of the Paul party to defend their personal integrity (apologetic function) rather than to present themselves as a positive example for their readers to imitate (paraenetic function), as is so often asserted by recent commentators. But he fails to follow the strongest textual reading in 2:7a, rendering this verse as "we were *gentle* among you" instead of "we were *infants* among you" (so NA28) and thus misses the powerful metaphor of how the Paul party acted as "innocent as infants" during their mission-founding visit to Thessalonike. The question addressed in 5:1–11 is not so much about the timing of Jesus's return as it is about the fate of *living* believers on the day of the Lord (in contrast to 4:13–18, which deals with the fate of *deceased* believers at Jesus's return). This passage comforts readers in the knowledge that God has not destined them to experience "wrath" on that day but "salvation" and eternal life (5:9–10)

In summary, Ascough has written a brief and user-friendly overview of the formation of the Christ group at Thessaloniki and of important introductory issues involved in the two letters addressed to this church. This book provides a helpful first step in preparing the modern reader for a deeper analysis of 1 and 2 Thessalonians.

Framing Paul: An Epistolary Biography, by Douglas A. Campbell. Grand Rapids: Eerdmans, 2014. Pp. xxii + 468. Paper. $39.00. ISBN 9780802871510.

Matthew V. Novenson, University of Edinburgh

It is probably fair to say that current scholarly discussion of the apostle Paul concerns itself relatively little with the classic question of the chronology of Paul's letters. Indeed, with the significant exception of Gregory Tatum, *New Chapters in the Life of Paul* (2006), one is hard-pressed to point to any major technical treatments of the topic since the turn of the millennium. (By contrast, the second half of the twentieth century saw a flurry of monographs on Pauline chronology from the distinguished likes of John Knox, Charles Buck and Greer Taylor, Robert Jewett, Gerd Lüdemann, Rainer Riesner, and Jerome Murphy-O'Connor, to name a few.) Douglas Campbell worries that the current neglect of this aspect of critical *Einleitung* is yielding corrupt interpretations of the Pauline epistles. He writes, "My massive project on justification [*The Deliverance of God*, 2009]... was also an education into the problematic interweaving of theological and biographical concerns within current Pauline scholarship. I learned that a particular account of Paul's life—including, most importantly, a particular account of the production of his letters—was being used to buttress a particular account of his soteriology. This was not in itself objectionable, but it was being done dishonestly, or at least sloppily" (xvii). *Framing Paul* is Campbell's effort to put theological interpretation of Paul on a firm footing.

The book's macrostructure is elegantly simple. Chapter 1, "An Extended Methodological Introduction," explicates and defends the approach taken in the book. Campbell begins by appealing to J. Christiaan Beker's rubric of contingency and coherence in the Pauline corpus (*Paul the Apostle*, 1980) both as an accurate description and as a puzzle in need of a solution. Campbell proposes that the only hope of parsing the coherent from the contingent in Paul is to articulate a chronological and biographical "frame" for the letter corpus as a whole; hence the book's title. (For his crucial concept of framing, Campbell appeals to Jacques Derrida, but not to any specific work by Derrida. He cites Barbara Johnson's 1977 essay "The Frame of Reference," which treats Derrida's "The Purveyor of Truth." But Derrida's "Parergon" also suggests itself as a point of reference.) Finally, Campbell cites John Knox's *Chapters in a Life of Paul* (1950) as a methodological model, but one in need of modification and completion. Campbell follows Knox in bracketing out the Acts of the Apostles entirely and in taking 1 and 2 Corinthians and Romans as a fixed point and then fitting other epistles in as it is possible to do so. This decision determines the remainder of the table of contents.

In chapter 2, "The Epistolary Backbone: Romans and the Corinthian Correspondence," Campbell takes 1 and 2 Corinthians and Romans—the three longest letters of Paul, all universally recognized as authentic, each of which refers to Paul's collection of money from his gentile assemblies for the holy poor in Jerusalem—as an anchor for his project. Here he establishes only a relative chronology: 1 Corinthians, then 2 Corinthians, then Romans. On the assumption that Paul's actual itinerary unfolded according to his stated intentions in 1 and 2 Corinthians, Campbell places all three letters in the space of roughly one year. In chapter 3, "Augmenting the Backbone: Philippians and Galatians," Campbell turns first to Philippians. Because he sees close thematic parallels in it to both 1 and 2 Corinthians and Romans, Campbell proposes that Paul wrote Philippians from Corinth shortly before he wrote Romans, also from Corinth. Campbell then treats Galatians, and on the grounds of the profile of Paul's opponents therein locates it, too, in the same busy year of letter-writing from Corinth. At the end of chapter 3 Campbell makes a key move in establishing an absolute chronology, arguing from Paul's reference to his escape from Damascus during the kingship of Aretas in 2 Cor 11:32–33 (summarizing his detailed case in *JBL* 121 [2002]: 279–302). By coordinating with Josephus, *A.J.* 18, Campbell argues that this escape must have happened in 36–37 CE, and by aligning this with Paul's reference to his Arabian-Syrian period in Gal 1:17–18, identifies 51–52 CE as the time of composition for all five letters discussed to this point.

Chapter 4, "Locating the Thessalonian Correspondence," assumes the authenticity of 1 Thessalonians and argues for the authenticity of 2 Thessalonians, leaning especially on computer-assisted stylometric studies by Anthony Kenny, Kenneth Neumann, David Mealand, and Gerard Ledger. Furthermore, by identifying in 2 Thess 2 (the "man of lawlessness" passage) a reference to the plan for a cult statue of the emperor Gaius in the Jerusalem temple, written, Campbell thinks, during or soon after the event, he dates both 1 and 2 Thessalonians to 40–42 CE, effectively moving the earliest literary evidence for Christianity up, relative to the majority view, by about a decade. Chapter 5, "Locating Philemon, Colossians, and 'Ephesians,'" argues that not only Philemon but also Colossians and Ephesians are authentic and that all three were written and sent together ("a single epistolary event") from Paul imprisoned in Asian Apamea to the Lycus Valley assemblies in Colossae and Laodicea, not to Ephesus. Campbell dates these three letters to 50 CE, some eight or nine years after the Thessalonian correspondence and a year or two before 1–2 Corinthians, Galatians, Philippians, and Romans. On Campbell's chronology, as of 50 CE Paul had not yet encountered the Teacher (Campbell's term, modified from J. Louis Martyn's plural) and his gospel of gentile circumcision, which explains, for Campbell, why Colossians and Ephesians do not speak in terms of "works of law," "justification," and "the faith of Christ."

To this point in the book Campbell has ruled ten out of ten epistles authentic, but in chapter 6, "Locating Titus and 1 and 2 Timothy," at last he finds evidence of pseudepigraphy. He treats Titus first, finding it suspect on stylometric grounds (the only one of the thirteen letters to meet this criterion) and on account of Zenas and Apollos's supposed travel route via Crete (Titus 3:13), which Campbell judges so impractical as to be fictitious. First Timothy passes the stylometric test but fails on account of anachronisms: the reference to a Lukan word of Jesus as scripture (1 Tim 5:18) and the anti-Marcionite slogan "antitheses of falsely so-called gnosis" (1 Tim 6:20–21). Second Timothy fares slightly better, but the impractical itinerary in 2 Tim 4:19–21 and the Lukan-sounding list of Paul's sufferings in 2 Tim 3:10–11, among other details, lead Campbell to judge all three Pastoral epistles pseudonymous. He finds confirmation for this view in Marcion's ten-letter *Apostolikon*, which Campbell thinks Marcion inherited rather than made. Thus ends the epistolary biography. An eight-page conclusion summarizes the main findings of the book. A three-page appendix plots these findings on a timeline. The back matter concludes with helpful indices of modern authors, subjects, and ancient sources.

As will already be clear, the conclusions at which Campbell arrives via this process are not uncontroversial. By his reckoning, there are ten authentic Pauline letters (all but the Pastorals), all of them written between 41 and 52 CE. Second Thessalonians is authentic and roughly contemporaneous with the plan for a cult statue of Gaius in the Jerusalem temple in 40 CE. Colossians and Ephesians are both authentic and in fact are earlier than 1–2 Corinthians, Galatians, Philippians, and Romans. But *sogenannte* Ephesians is actually the letter to the Laodiceans mentioned in Col 4:16. The tearful letter mentioned in 2 Cor 2:3–4; 7:8 is canonical 1 Corinthians, and canonical 2 Corinthians is a literary unit, not a composite of any other letters or letter fragments. Likewise Philippians, but Phil 3:2–4:3 is a lengthy quotation from a previous letter of Paul to the Philippians. Philippians and Romans are both written to combat the influence of the Teacher, the same person responsible for the crisis that occasioned Galatians. Further, all three of these letters were written in the space of a single year, 51–52 CE. Only 1 Timothy, 2 Timothy, and Titus are pseudonymous, hailing from the mid-second-century Marcionite controversy.

Readers will have to weigh Campbell's arguments for each of these conclusions one by one. I find some more compelling than others. (In regard to the whole, Campbell's procedure of establishing one possibility at a time, each one resting upon the last, sometimes tempts one to diminishing confidence in the emerging composite picture.) Just here, it may be helpful to highlight some of the key methodological decisions that underlie his reasoning. For one thing, Campbell insists that all thirteen canonical letters must be presumed authentic until proven otherwise (see 15–18 on radical doubt). Significantly, however, he does not extend this principle to noncanonical 3 Corinthians, Laodiceans, Alexandrians, and Correspondence of Paul and Seneca, all dismissed in a single note (25 n. 30). In assigning dates and provenances to letters, he leans heavily on Charlotte Hartwig and Gerd Theissen's theory of *Nebenaddressat*, "addressees alongside," the idea that Paul uses the writing of a letter to an assembly elsewhere (e.g., Romans) as an occasion to instruct the assembly *from which* he is writing (e.g., Corinth) (see 52–55 and passim). This hypothesis allows him to assign dates and places to letters for which we would otherwise lack them. Campbell also makes much of the social condition of incarceration, in particular—via modern analogies including Dietrich Bonhoeffer and Martin Luther King Jr.—the idea that "incarceration is a fertile space for reflection and literary work, especially by (literate) activists" (269), to explain certain literary features of Colossians and Ephesians. Because he gets considerable mileage out of these and other methodological decisions, readers must pay close, critical attention to the methodological introduction in chapter 1.

The question of the chronology of Paul's career is an important one, and Campbell has given us one formidable—but not the only possible—answer to it. I wonder, however, whether this question is the logical prerequisite that Campbell insists it is. He writes, "Any valid Pauline interpretation in any historical respect must begin with a workable account of the letters' circumstances in relation to one another. We must tell the story of their interrelated composition. This is the sine qua non of all valid historical interpretation of Paul" (12). This seems to me overstated. Certainly, those interpretations that depend on particular relations among the letters (e.g., the claim that Paul's parousia hope waned over time) stand or fall on the chronology of the letters. But other kinds of interpretations are not thus bound. (Admittedly, virtually any discussion of the disputed letters does require the kind of prolegomena that Campbell here advocates.) Again, Campbell worries, "How much current Pauline exegesis is mistaken because the historical story of the letters it presupposes is corrupt? The figure might be disturbingly high" (12). Well, maybe, but the figure also might be innocuously low, and I rather suspect the latter. Most bad interpretation of Paul, it seems to me, is bad not because of faulty chronology but because of more pedestrian failures of reasoning (anemic knowledge of historical context, myopic theological commitments, and so on). On the other hand, lots of good interpretation of Paul—including much that is recognized as such by Campbell—manages to get by with only a rough, provisional idea of the chronology of the letters.

If this is the case, then we do not need *Framing Paul* for all the reasons Campbell tells us we do, but we do benefit a great deal from it nonetheless. It is now an essential point of reference for all subsequent work on Pauline chronology. What Knox was for the 1950s or Lüdemann for the 1980s, Campbell is for the 2010s. If his pleas for the authenticity of 2 Thessalonians, Colossians, and Ephesians manage to win the day, he will have brought about a revolution. But even if they do not, he will have contributed a landmark work of critical introduction.

Keeping the Feast: Metaphors of Sacrifice in 1 Corinthians and Philippians, by Jane Lancaster Patterson. Early Christianity and Its Literature 16. Atlanta: SBL Press, 2015. Pp. 218. Paper. $32.95. ISBN 9780884140658. Hardcover. $47.95. ISBN 9780884140672.

Timothy A. Brookins, Houston Baptist University

Jane Lancaster Patterson's *Keeping the Feast* represents another contribution in a steady stream of studies that examine New Testament authors through metaphor theory (see Bonnie Howe 2006; Beverly Gaventa 2007; Jennifer Houston McNeel 2014). As aptly summed up in the book's subtitle, the work focuses on metaphors of sacrifice in 1 Corinthians and Philippians. The book stems from Patterson's doctoral dissertation (written under Victor Paul Furnish and defended at Southern Methodist University in 2009) but represents the fruit of several years of reflection and conversations with students and colleagues since that time.

The book begins with a succinct but helpful introductory chapter disclosing Patterson's methodological approach and background assumptions. Her approach is both cognitive/ rhetorical and historical/social. On the cognitive/ rhetorical side, she is concerned with how Paul's metaphors and their "entailments" (the various related moods, images, and meanings that cling to them [10]) function within the context of 1 Corinthians and Philippians as literary wholes and how these metaphors in total context impact the moral formation of his audiences. Patterson assumes that sacrificial references in Paul's letters, as in most of the New Testament, are mostly metaphorical, not literal in reference. This, however, does not mean that Paul rejected the continuation of Jewish sacrificial practices or the ongoing legitimacy of the temple cult. Indeed, the prophets of the Jewish scriptures had also referred to sacrifice metaphorically.

On the historical/social side, Patterson's purpose is to (re)define Paul's sacrificial metaphors in the terms in which they were understood in their original Jewish and Greco-Roman contexts. Whereas virtually no one in the developed world today has any firsthand experience with sacrificial practices, they were diverse, widespread, and universally familiar in Paul's world and thus served as a fruitful source for metaphorically based paraenesis. Here Patterson introduces a major underlying thread in her argument: familiarity with sacrifice today in general derives from church dogma, which tends, erroneously, to reduce all sacrifice to sacrifice of atonement.

Chapter 2 develops further Patterson's understanding of sacrifice as metaphor in Paul's rhetoric. Here she reviews various stages in the development of metaphor theory, from ancient times to the recent works of I. A. Richards, Paul Ricoeur, Eva Kittay, and, most notably, George Lakoff and Mark Johnson, whose work she identifies as her "main guide" (20). In keeping with recent theory, Patterson suggests that metaphors do not simply describe similarities between things but in fact *create* similarities, enabling listeners to conceptualize what is less familiar (e.g., a community) in terms of what is more familiar (e.g., one body with many parts). Thus Paul uses metaphors creatively and *provisionally*, often mixing them. Following Ricoeur and Kittay, Patterson also suggests that metaphors have to be interpreted within the context of whole discourses or even whole works. In this respect, a metaphor used in one context may resonate, with its various systematic entailments, throughout an entire work and may thus shape interpretation even in contexts where the metaphor is not explicitly invoked. This observation sets up Patterson's main argument in the book: a single metaphor sits at the heart of each of these letters, Philippians and 1 Corinthians, helps organize it, and reverberates through its various sections. (Patterson assumes the basic literary integrity of both of these letters.)

Chapter 3 defines ancient sacrificial practices and their entailments in greater detail. The Greco-Roman "commensal" sacrifice centered around a common meal; such occasions were characterized by conviviality and rejoicing. The "covenantal" sacrifice, by contrast, centered around oath-keeping and emphasized the violent consequences of oath-violation. Similarly, sacrifices in the Jewish cult fell into two major categories: dedicatory/ thanksgiving sacrifices and propitiatory/atoning sacrifices. In Patterson's judgment, Paul's sacrificial metaphors in Philippians resonate with the Greco-Roman commensal sacrifice and the largely overlapping Jewish category of *shelamim*, or thanksgiving sacrifice. Paul's sacrificial metaphors in 1 Corinthians, on the other hand, are structured around the Jewish Passover rituals. Patterson reiterates here a point that she reprises frequently throughout the book: despite speaking of sacrifice consistently in *metaphorical* terms, Paul did not reject literal practice of the Jewish cult.

Chapter 4 explores sacrifice as an object of study since the nineteenth century. Patterson's main purpose in this chapter is to call into question the contention of those who have viewed the practice of sacrifice across history in evolutionary terms. For Patterson, a spiritualized or inward interpretation of sacrifice (e.g., the "sacrifice of a contrite heart") need not be more advanced than, and is certainly not exclusive of, a more literal orientation toward sacrifice. While it is true that literary elites, who generally viewed sacrifice "reflectively" rather than naively, often "critiqued" sacrificial practice, stressing perhaps its higher moral meaning, they often argued simultaneously for continuance of the literal practice. Such was Philo, and such was Paul. (Actually, Patterson seems to give conflicting signals on how reflective Paul was, in one place suggesting that sacrifice itself was not an "object" of his thought but merely a "tool" [8], but in another classing him with the "reflective," "the interpreters," the "entrepeneurs" who reflected on the meaning of sacrifice.)

Chapters 5 and 6, focused respectively on Philippians and 1 Corinthians, constitute the center of the book. In chapter 5 Patterson argues that Paul's sacrificial metaphor in Phil 2:6–11 represents a *shelamim*, or thanksgiving, sacrifice and that understanding this section as such is the "key to most of the letter's ethical councils" (87). Entailments of the *shelamim* sacrifice, according to Patterson, include "holiness, friendship, morality, reciprocal self-giving, the relationship between suffering and joy, and commerce between heaven and earth" (115). Thus Christ's submission to slavery, humiliation, and death for the sake of others demonstrates what the *shelamim* offering was all about and instantiates the paradigm that Christians themselves are to emulate. Within this schema, reciprocal service gives way to joy. Self-sacrifice gives way to exaltation. These themes reverberate throughout the remainder of the letter.

At the center of 1 Corinthians, by contrast, is a Passover metaphor (5:8: "Therefore, let us celebrate the festival, not with the old yeast, the yeast of malice and evil, but with the unleavened bread of sincerity and truth"). According to Patterson, the entailments of Passover include "eating, freedom and slavery, covenant, cleanness, belonging, holiness, and community" (120) but *not*—and this is one of the main contentions of Patterson's book—atonement (62, 133–34). In other words, the Passover metaphor was about a common moral life, the unity of Jew and gentile in purity of life, in "unleavened" conduct. For Patterson, the Passover metaphor then reverberates from here throughout the letter, its echoes sounding out in every section, sometimes loudly, sometimes only faintly.

A seventh chapter reiterates the book's main arguments and casts a quick glance in the direction of Romans. In summary, a single kind of sacrifice organizes Paul's moral counsels in each letter, the *shelamim* sacrifice in Philippians and the Passover rituals in 1 Corinthians. In Romans, however, Paul's focus is on God's *justice*, or rather on God's *justice*, on what *God* has done to reconcile the world to himself. The Yom Kippur ritual of Lev 16 features in Rom 3:21–26 and appears more faintly in 6:5–6 and 8:3–4. In a helpful concluding sentence, Patterson sums up the book: "When the cultic and sacrificial metaphors are heard with all their complex resonances, one can discern more clearly how Paul used them persuasively to shape the ethical reflection of his communities over time. The cultic metaphors are far from decorative tropes, but rather carry a great deal of the freight of Paul's moral counsel" (172).

Patterson's work makes a valuable contribution to the field. She has joined a host of others who recognize the essential, and indeed inescapable, role of metaphor in theological discourse. Her contention that Paul organized his instruction in each letter around a single, central metaphor is admirable for its attention to the whole discourse (or letter) as constitutive of the "context" and certainly has some theoretical as well as practical plausibility. On the other hand, I could not help but feel that the study lacked somewhat in methodological controls, which resulted often in what appeared to be somewhat arbitrary interpretive judgments. Patterson's enumeration of the entailments of each sacrificial complex seemed somewhat selective. For instance, her characterization of the scapegoat ritual at Yom Kippur as "far from being the paradigmatic Jewish sacrifice" and as "an anomaly" (71) seemed a convenient way of sidelining atonement as a possible entailment. Moreover, the alleged links, or "resonances," are often faint or underdetermined; for example, "puffed up" (1 Cor 4:6) need not be a "leaven" metaphor, for this language was a widespread trope for "haughtiness" in Greco-Roman literature; "unblemished" (Phil 1:10; 2:15) could easily be connected with Yom Kippur and atonement (LXX Lev 23:12, 18) rather than *shelamim* sacrifice; and the contention that the pattern of suffering followed by exaltation, embodied in Phil 2:6–11, is to be understood in relation to Jewish sacrifices of thanksgiving hardly seems the most obvious association. In short, while Patterson has contended admirably for a certain consistency in the picture in each letter, her analysis exhibits a certain methodological laxity and could be tightened up by better controls. How does one reduce complex descriptions of sacrificial rituals in various texts into discrete entailments? Can such entailments be numbered? When can we assume that passages occurring in distant contexts within a text are in fact associated in meaning or that one (perhaps underspecified) text should be interpreted in the light of the other? How does one identify a true semantic "reverberation"? How can we be sure that our interpretation of the "whole discourse" through a single metaphorical "key" does not just impose organization on the text from the outside? If, as Patterson states, Paul "mixes his metaphors remorselessly" (160), in what way are we justified in interpreting underspecified texts as reverberations of one (distant) metaphor rather than of any one of the other metaphors employed?

These problems perhaps owe something to the limitations of more cognitive-rhetorical approaches themselves, which by their nature involve attempts to "get into the minds" of the original authors. However, Richard Hays's outstanding work on echoes of Scripture in Paul and now also the gospels (work that has definite similarities to what Patterson is doing) demonstrates how sophisticated and methodologically sound such attempts can potentially be. With better controls, projects in this vein are certainly worth advancing further.

Wealth in Ancient Ephesus and the First Letter to Timothy: Fresh Insights from Ephesiaca by Xenophon of Ephesus, by Gary G. Hoag. Bulletin for Biblical Research Supplements 11. Winona Lake, IN: Eisenbrauns, 2015. Pp. xii + 258. Hardcover. $49.50. ISBN 9781575068299.

Susana de Sola Funsten, Los Angeles, California

In this book Hoag refocuses attention on how modern interpreters should understand the teachings on wealth in ancient texts such as 1 Timothy. More specifically, Hoag aims to explore whether 1 Timothy encourages Christians in the early Christian communities to conform to or deviate from the dominant and established cultural expectations regarding wealth. To this end, he examines a selection of passages from 1 Timothy related to this topic (2:9–15; 3:1–13; 6: 1–2a, 2b–10; 6:17–19). The approach gathers information on the social context for 1 Timothy from the usual ancient sources and compares this with information from *Ephesiaca*, the ancient Greek novel by Xenophon (also known as *Epehesian Tales*).

Chapter 1 introduces the narrative outline of *Ephesiaca* along with an extensive discussion on different theories regarding its author and date of composition. Hoag aligns his views with those of James O'Sullivan, who, through extensive linguistic and compositional analyses of *Ephesiaca*, argues that it was very likely written sometime in the mid-50s CE.[1] It is worth mentioning that this chapter does not contain even a superficial survey of the authorship and date of composition of 1 Timothy. It is not until the "Summary and Conclusion" that Hoag explains that "the authorship of 1 Timothy was avoided because it cannot be determined conclusively…, and my attention remained solely on the contents of 1 Timothy" (227). Regardless of the overarching goals of this study, it is regrettable that Hoag circumvented this important discussion because one of the main premises in this book is that both 1 Timothy and *Ephesiaca* were written in similar time periods by the apostle Paul (1 Timothy) and Xenophon of Ephesus (*Ephesiaca).*

The method employed in this analysis is a slightly modified version of Vernon Robbins's sociorhetorical approach. Chapter 2 presents the social setting and cultural values of the wealthy in Ephesus. Chapters 3–7 take up selections from 1 Timothy and proceed with investigations of: (1) "inner texture," especially identification of language and word patterns; (2) "intertexture," that is, interactions between the language and themes in both texts; (3) "ideological texture," the social location of individuals and groups and their function within the text; and, finally, (4) "sacred texture," or the relationship between humans and the divine. Each analysis of the "textures" is followed by a brief summary, and each chapter ends with a helpful general summary. The stated objective of the sociorhetorical approach is to determine "how the terms and themes in the teachings on riches [in 1 Timothy] may have been understood in antiquity" (21).

---

1. James N. O'Sullivan, *Xenophon of Ephesus: His Compositional Technique and the Birth of the Novel*, Untersuchungen zur antiken Literatur und Geschichte 44 (Berlin: de Gruyter, 1995).

Chapter 2, "The Social Setting and Cultural Rules of the Wealthy in Ephesus in the First Century CE," is an excellent and thorough review of the history of Ephesus, particularly its rise to the position of an important and wealthy city in the first century CE. A key contributing factor was its legendary connection to the goddess Artemis, a link that had many advantageous political, economic, and social ramifications. The temple built in her honor (the Artemisium) was a famous pilgrimage site in antiquity. The Artemisium was also the center of the city's civic, financial, political, and religious life. In such a multicultural and multi-ethnic society as Ephesus, there is no precise way to identify who were the wealthy. Nevertheless, archaeological evidence confirms what is also true for other cities in the Mediterranean world, that wealthy individuals and their families were deeply engaged in the dynamics of patronage and benefaction. As per the dominant cultural norm of this period, prominent and wealthy citizens were expected to pay for projects and events on behalf of the city, including the activities surrounding the worship of Artemis, the city's patroness. In return, they were awarded honors, social status, and prominent positions in civic, religious, and economic activities. The narrative of *Ephesiaca* confirms this social context even more vividly. As Hoag points out, "the rich *owned* Ephesus, and … Ephesus *owned* them. Failure to follow social and cultural rules put people at risk of losing their identity and place in society in relation to the gods and the people" (60).

The topic of chapter 3 is 1 Tim 2: 8–15, with a specific focus on 2: 9–10, the instructions regarding women's adornment where Hoag detects commandments relevant to the handling of wealth. An interesting and informative survey of the primary and secondary literature on women's adornment in the ancient Greco-Roman world exposes some of the many controversies involved. The survey confirms what is by now widely known, that cultural and social expectations for women in antiquity required that they behave virtuously, dress modestly, and participate actively in religious cults. There were, of course, many differences on how to define what was considered virtuous or modest in reference to women. Nevertheless, Hoag draws our attention to women's participation in religious life by focusing on the depiction of Anthia, the primary female protagonist in *Ephesiaca* and a daughter of an aristocratic Ephesian family. As a daughter of an aristocratic family and a participant in the sacred rites of Artemis, Anthia is described in *Ephesiaca* as dressed in specific attire (fine clothing) and sporting a "braided" hairstyle. The Greek word for "braided," πλέγμασιν, a rare word in ancient and New Testament literature, is also used for the for the forbidden hairstyle in 1 Tim 2:9. This linguistic correspondence between the two texts provides Hoag with a basis for arguing that the instructions to women in 1 Timothy are aimed at wealthy aristocratic Ephesian women who, like Anthia in *Ephesiaca*, are expected to engage in the cult of Artemis (79). Thus, according to Hoag the instructions to women in 1 Timothy would be perceived as radically counter-cultural not only in their command to observe modesty but even more so in the exhortation that they should abandon their customary and expected behavior as worshipers of Artemis.

Chapter 4 focuses on the subjects of greed and stewardship, also found in the lists of qualifications for leaders in 1 Tim 3: 1–13. The presence of virtue and vice lists in 3:1–13 and their similarities to virtue and vice lists found in ancient Greco-Roman and Jewish literature have led many scholars to see these as evidence of tendency within early Christian communities to conform to dominant Greco-Roman cultural values. Hoag purports to show otherwise. First, a review of epigraphic evidence from Ephesus shows that religious leadership positions were obtained through family connections, not merit, skill, or qualification. Epigraphic evidence also confirms that riches gained improperly (greed) was a concern in the community. The narrative of *Ephesiaca* mirrors the epigraphic evidence showing that leadership roles in religious cults were handed down and preserved within the wealthy families of high status. The *Ephesiaca*, however, does not provide strong or convincing evidence to support the notion that greed was a problem within this firmly entrenched system. This is at the same time interesting but not surprising. As a work of fiction, the *Ephesiaca* likely depicts an idealized situation with enough content from real life to make the narrative elements easily resonate with its intended audience. According to Hoag, the *Ephesiaca* may be considered an example of sacred writing (*hieros logos*). As such, its role was not only to entertain but also to communicate the expected rules and values important for the citizens of Ephesus to assimilate and observe, especially the wealthy. Taking this perspective into account, Hoag argues that 1 Tim 3:1–13 gives wealthy Ephesians a very different set of expectations, ones that drastically severed the link between wealth, honor, status, and religious leadership.

Chapter 5 focuses on 1 Tim 6:1–2a, specifically on how masters and slaves are to behave toward one another. Although these verses do not explicitly refer to issues of wealth, Hoag includes them here because they reflect ideas about benefaction, a topic relevant to wealth. The scholarship on these two verses is controversial, inconclusive, and tends to take one of two positions. In one, the masters are addressed as benefactors; in the other, the slaves are addressed as benefactors. Because both positions have certain validity, Hoag's strategy is to work with a third hypothesis, which identifies "God as the benefactor." A review of ancient evidence along with the *Ephesiaca* clearly shows that the typical cosmology in antiquity was characterized by a steeply hierarchical ordering of relationships between the human and divine, with the god or gods at the top, followed in descending order by free people, slaves, animals, and material objects. In this system, blessings and gifts naturally flowed from the deity on down to the lower levels of being. Hoag reasons, therefore, that 1 Tim 6: 1–2a can be understood as calling slaves to serve their masters, not because slaves or masters would benefit from this behavior, but rather because both masters and slaves are recipients of God's beneficence. According to this logic, slaves who serve and honor their masters also honor God, the ultimate Benefactor. To advocate such an attitude would be deeply controversial and countercultural in the actual social and cultural world of the *Ephesiaca* and 1 Timothy.

Chapter 6 focuses on 1 Tim 6:2b–10, regarding false teachers and godliness. In 1 Timothy false teachers are identified by erroneous teaching and greed, especially behavior that uses religion as a means for personal gain. Reading these verses in light of *Ephesiaca*, Hoag encourages us to imagine that the intended audience for these verses are the wealthy religious leaders of Ephesus, who were profoundly invested in keeping their roles within the status quo, especially in the worship of Artemis. Hoag also invites us to appreciate the difficulty of this demand and the fear that it would elicit since the well-being of the city was deemed to be entirely dependent on the careful attention to the worship of its patroness.

Chapter 7 spotlights 1 Tim 6:17–19 addressing the rich with specific commandments on how to handle wealth. Again, using *Ephesiaca* as a lens, Hoag concludes that 1 Tim 6:17–19 is a call for the wealthy in Ephesus to radically alter their lifestyles and behavior in society. The rich are commanded to live simply, to stop being haughty, to refrain from engaging in patronage and benefactions, and to share their possessions with everyone equally regardless of their social location. Throughout the chapter Hoag contends that 6:17–19 has wealthy Ephesians in view, whose lives were enmeshed with the cult of Artemis and whose wealth was probably stored in the Artemisium. Viewed from this perspective, one can gain an even more vivid appreciation of the radical nature of the message in theses verses.

At the end of the book, one is rewarded with a helpful summary and conclusion, reinforcing the idea of the value of using *Ephesiaca* as a source of information for interpreting New Testament texts. Hoag also concludes that, contrary to the arguments of influential scholars such as Hans Conzelmann and Martin Dibelius, the teachings on wealth in 1 Timothy are consistent with other teachings on wealth in the rest of the New Testament.

There is much to commend in this book, especially the extensive gathering of information from ancient sources (literary, historic, archaeological, numismatic, and other) for each of the topics in the selections from 1 Timothy. There are some areas, however, in which I perceived some gaps, which may be explained by limitations of space. In chapter 3, for example, regarding women's adornment, it is disappointing that Hoag did not engage further with the scholarly discussions on gender and authority structures in the ancient world. It seems clear that clothing, hair styles, or handling of wealth are only tangentially related to overarching issues, especially boundary setting specifically as it applies to females. In chapter 5, regarding the instructions to masters and slaves in 1 Tim 6:1–2a, it seems important to mention that these verses are the natural conclusion of a household code starting at 5:1. Because of this, it is regrettable that Hoag glossed over the relevance of ancient household codes for understanding these verses. My final criticism has to do with the congruence between 1 Timothy and other texts in the New Testament on matters regarding handling of wealth. It seems there is an important omission, perhaps an inadvertent one, that this book includes no mention of any similarities between the messages on wealth in 1 Timothy and the rest of the Pauline literature. This is especially conspicuous when one of Hoag's main assumptions from the start is that 1 Timothy was written by the apostle Paul. A relatively minor quibble is that, given the extensive references to *Ephesiaca*, it might have been judicious to add the text in its entirety as an appendix at the end of the book.

Reading Romans in Context: Paul and Second Temple Judaism, edited by Ben Blackwell, John Goodrich, and Jason Maston. Grand Rapids: Zondervan, 2015. Pp. 192. Paper. $19.99. ISBN 9780310517955.

Günter Röhser, Rheinische Friedrich-Wilhelms-Universität Bonn

„Reading Romans in Context" ist ein Text- und Studienbuch, welches Abschnitte aus dem Römerbrief mit zeitgenössischen Paralleltexten vergleicht. Wie der Untertitel ausweist („Paul and Second Temple Judaism"), liegt der Fokus dabei ausschließlich auf dem frühen Judentum; pagan-hellenistische Vergleichstexte werden wohl als für Paulus nicht relevant erachtet.

In einem Geleitwort begründet Francis Watson (einer der beiden Widmungsträger des Bandes) ein solches „reading in context" mit der frühchristlichen Praxis selbst, ohne die uns die meisten dieser (jüdischen) Schriften überhaupt nicht erhalten geblieben wären.

Im Vorwort geben sich die Herausgeber (und das gilt auch für die meisten Mitautoren) als ehemalige Doktoranden der Durham University (UK) zu erkennen, und in einer Einführung suchen sie eventuelle Vorbehalte aus dem eigenen, evangelikalen Umfeld gegenüber der Beschäftigung mit deutero- und außerkanonischer Literatur auszuräumen und geben einen kurzen Überblick über den relevanten historischen Zeitraum (eine unkritische Nacherzählung der biblisch-jüdischen Geschichte vom Exodus bis ins Jahr 70) und die Literatur des Zweiten Tempels.

Die einzelnen Kapitel sind immer gleich aufgebaut und beginnen mit einer kurzen Einführung in das Thema des folgenden Textvergleichs (zumeist unter Aufnahme des vorderen Kontextes im Römerbrief wie auch der vorhergehenden Kapitel des Buches). Es folgt die Präsentation des frühjüdischen Vergleichstextes unter bestimmten, kursiv hervorgehobenen Gesichtspunkten und anschließend die Durchführung des Vergleichs unter diesen Gesichtspunkten mit dem Abschnitt aus dem Römerbrief. Abgeschlossen wird das Kapitel jeweils durch Hinweise „for further reading": weitere frühjüdische und paulinische Texte zu demselben Thema, englische Übersetzungen und kritische Textausgaben, Sekundärliteratur (eine jeweils knappe, aber treffende Auswahl). Am Ende des Buches stehen ein Glossar (in dem Begriffe, die im Text fett hervorgehoben sind, erläutert werden), ein Mitarbeiterverzeichnis sowie Stellen-, Themen- und Autorenregister. Der Band ist also sehr gut erschlossen und sorgfältig ediert.

Im Folgenden werde ich die Kapitelüberschriften wörtlich (inkl. *Kursivierung* der Pseudepigraphen) aufführen und jeweils anschließend den Inhalt bzw. das Ergebnis des Vergleichs durch den betreffenden Autor bzw. die betreffende Autorin kurz charakterisieren.

1. „*Psalms of Solomon* and Romans 1:1–17: The ,Son of God' and the Identity of Jesus." Thema ist die Identität Jesu als Davids- und Gottessohn. W. Hill ver-

gleicht den königlichen Messias aus PsSal 17 mit der Darstellung Christi in Röm 1 und stellt „an ironic reversal of many of these features of the psalm" (35) fest.

2. „Wisdom of Solomon and Romans 1:18–2:5: God's Wrath against *All*." J. A. Linebaugh behandelt das Thema von Gottes Zorn über Götzendienst und Unmoral der Menschen. Während Weish 13–15 in dieser Hinsicht Israel von Nicht-Israel unterschieden sieht, ist für Paulus Israel in die Geschichte des Abfalls von Gott hineinverflochten.

3. „*Jubilees* and Romans 2:6–29: Circumcision, Law Observance, and Ethnicity." S. Whittle konfrontiert die Beschneidungsgesetzgebung von Jub 15 („am Fleisch") mit der Beschneidung des Herzens („im Verborgenen") bei Paulus, durch welche – nicht ohne Aufnahme einer entsprechenden biblischen Tradition von der Bundeserneuerung, wie sie in Jub 1,23f selbst vorliegt – eine Möglichkeit der Gesetzeserfüllung auch für die Heiden eröffnet wird.

4. „4QMMT and Romans 3:1–20: Works of the Law and Justification." J. Maston und A. Sherwood wenden sich der Frage nach den „Werken des Gesetzes" zu. Während im Qumran-Text deren Tun „zur Gerechtigkeit angerechnet wird" (also zur Rechtfertigung führt), ist dies für Paulus ausgeschlossen, weil die ganze Welt vor Gott schuldig dasteht und deshalb niemand durch (das Tun von) Werke(n) Gerechtigkeit erlangen kann. Vor allem aber muss nach Paulus auch für diejenigen, die außerhalb der traditionellen Bundesbeziehung stehen, Gerechtigkeit erreichbar sein.

5. „The *Epistle of Henoch* and Romans 3:21–31: The Revelation of God's Righteousness." J. A. Linebaugh stellt hier zwei gegensätzliche Verständnisse von „Gerechtigkeit Gottes" vor: Während 1Hen 92; 93–105 für die jetzt leidenden Gerechten und die jetzt auftrumpfenden Sünder „an eschatological reversal of fortunes" (60) ankündigt, verkündigt Paulus eine ganz andere Art von Gerechtigkeit: diejenige, die den Gottlosen kraft der Erlösung durch Christus aus Gnade in die Rechtfertigung durch den Glauben einbezieht.

6. „Sirach and Romans 4:1–25: The Faith of Abraham." Hier werden zwei unterschiedliche Abraham-Bilder gegenübergestellt: M. J. Kamell vergleicht Sir 44 (Verheißungsempfang aufgrund von Treue und Gehorsam gegenüber dem Gesetz und in der Versuchung) mit Röm 4 (Verheißungsempfang aufgrund der Gerechtigkeit des Glaubens).

7. „*Community Rule* and Romans 5:1–11: The Relationship between Justification and Suffering." Die Gemeinderegel und Paulus stimmen nach M. D. Mathews darin überein, dass Leiden ein Kennzeichen der wahren Gläubigen und Gerechten und deshalb ein Grund zur Freude ist. Für Paulus vergewissert es jedoch vor allem die Gläubigen ihrer Hoffnung auf zukünftige Herrlichkeit, weil es ein Leiden in der Gemeinschaft mit Christus ist (vgl. 8,17).

8. „Philo of Alexandria and Romans 5:12–21: Adam, Death, and Grace." J. Worthington stellt die Frage: "How do Philo and Paul interpret Adam's sin and death and the effect on his progeny?" (81) Antwort: Während nach Röm 5 das Sünden- und Todesverhängnis durch Adam in die Welt kam, steht dem in der Schrift „De opificio mundi" „Philo's very dark but still less tragic view" (85)

gegenüber: Gen 3 wird philosopisch-allegorisch ausgelegt, damit der Mensch nicht wie Adam der Versuchung erliegt, sondern die Vernunft die Kontrolle über die Seele behält!

9. „Wisdom of Solomon and Romans 6:1–23: Slavery to Personified Powers." J. R. Dodson vergleicht den narrativ-rhetorischen Einsatz von Personifikationen sowie das Verständnis des Todes des „Gerechten" („Sohn Gottes") in Weish und bei Paulus.

10. „Sirach and Romans 7:1–25: The Human, the Law, and Sin." J. Maston stellt der ausweglosen Situation des Menschen unter Sünde und Gesetz nach Röm 7 das Konzept der menschlichen Autonomie und Willensfreiheit von Sir 15 gegenüber.

11. „*4 Ezra* and Romans 8:1–13: The Liberating Power of Christ and the Spirit." Thema ist die eschatologische Freiheit von Sünde und Tod. Während diese nach 4Esr 6 erst in der Zukunft zu erwarten steht („Herzensverwandlung"), für die Gegenwart aber die eigene Willenskraft und das Gesetz gegeben sind, sieht Paulus jene Ziele bereits in der Gegenwart durch die Gabe des Geistes Christi verwirklicht. In dem Beitrag von K. B. Wells sind besonders die vergleichenden Schaubilder bemerkenswert.

12. „The *Greek Life of Adam and Eve* and Romans 8:14–39: (Re-)creation and Glory." Der Beitrag von B. C. Blackwell beleuchtet den engen Zusammenhang von Herrlichkeit, Gerechtigkeit und Unsterblichkeit des Menschen, deren Verlust und deren Wiederherstellung auf der einen Seite sowie Verderbnis und Wiederherstellung der ganzen Schöpfung auf der anderen Seite sowohl in der Genesis-Erzählung von grVitAd als auch bei Paulus.

13. „Philo of Alexandria and Romans 9:1–29: Grace, Mercy and Reason." Sowohl im dritten Buch von Philos „Legum allegoriae" als auch in Röm 9 findet sich eine Beispielreihe mit biblischen Personen, bei denen Gottes Segen bzw. Fluch jeglichem menschlichen Werk vorausgeht. O. McFarland legt dar, wie Philo dies mit der lobens- bzw. tadelnswerten Beschaffenheit ihrer „Naturen" oder ihren zukünftigen Handlungen erklärt, während Paulus auf das erbarmende, scheinbar willkürliche Erwählungshandeln Gottes (auch zugunsten der Heiden) im Rahmen der Heilsgeschichte verweist.

14. „Philo of Alexandria and Romans 9:30–10:21: The Commandment and the Quest for the Good Life." D. Lincicum zeigt in seinem Beitrag, dass Philo in seiner Auslegung von Dtn 30,11–14 LXX (in „De virtutibus" 183–84: „very good instructions for repentance") wesentlich näher an dem ursprünglichen Sinn des Textes bleibt (124: „holistic acceptance of the law") als Paulus in Röm 10,6–8 (Botschaft des Glaubens). "Paul, like Philo, may be seen to offer a proposal for how Deut 30:11–14 leads to the good life, but the precise content of that good life clearly differs" (127).

15. „Tobit and Romans 11:1–36: Israel's Salvation and the Fulfillment of God's Word." J. K. Goodrich vergleicht „Israel's eschatological story line" (130) in Tob 14,3–7 (Text nach dem Sinaiticus) mit der Darstellung bei Paulus und stellt wichtige Unterschiede im Ablaufplan („Three-Stage Fulfillment") fest.

16. „4 Maccabees and Romans 12:1–21: Reason and the Righteous Life." B. C. Dunson formuliert als Themafrage: "For Paul, how does transformation of the mind lead to transformation of behavior and emotions?" (136) Für den philosophisch beeinflussten Autor von 4Makk reichen dafür geschöpfliche Vernunft und Gesetz, wohingegen für den Apostel die Erneuerung von außen kommen muss – von Gott, durch den Heiligen Geist.

17. „Josephus and Romans 13:1–14: Providence and Imperial Power." Was das Verhalten gegenüber dem Staat betrifft, so zeigt D. Pinter „a common pattern of opinion" zwischen Josephus und Paulus (149): Die Regierenden haben ihre Autorität von Gott, man ist ihnen Steuern und Ehrerbietung schuldig.

18. „1 Maccabees and Romans 14:1–15:13: Embodying the Hospitable Kingdom Community." 1Makk 1–2 (sowie 4Makk 5) dienen N. K. Gupta zur Illustration der Bedeutung von Speisevorschriften für jüdisch-judenchristliche Identität – eine mögliche Ursache für die Spannungen zwischen „Starken" und „Schwachen" in Rom.

19. „Tobit and Romans 15:14–33: Jewish Almsgiving and the Collection." D. E. Briones erfasst das Verhältnis zwischen der Almosentheologie des Tobitbuches und der paulinischen Kollekte mit Hilfe eines „three-way relational pattern" (160). Während in Tob 4 und 12 ein reziprokes Verhältnis zwischen Almosengeber und Gott besteht (Belohnung), sieht Paulus ein solches zwischen Judenchristen und Heidenchristen – mit Gott als „a common source of grace" (165).

20. „Synagogue Inscriptions and Romans 16:1–27: Women and Christian Ministry." S. Mathew schließlich zieht Synagogeninschriften (also keine literarischen Texte wie zuvor), in denen Frauen führende Rollen und Positionen zugeschrieben werden, zur Illustration ehrender Aussagen von Paulus über führende christliche Frauen in Röm 16 (Empfehlung der Phöbe und Grußliste) heran. "By recognizing these women and attributing to them the roles and titles that he does, Paul goes as far as, if not beyond, other Jewish communities by allowing and even encouraging women to serve in leadership positions" (171).

Auch wenn die Vergleiche hier nur verkürzt wiedergegeben werden konnten, ist doch deutlich, dass sie vor allem auf den Unterschied zwischen Paulus und der Literatur des Zweiten Tempels abzielen. So sagt es auch der Umschlagtext: „to see firsthand what makes Paul a distinctive thinker in relation to his Jewish contemporaries." Das ist völlig legitim, solange man weiß, was man tut. Denn es liegt auf der Hand, dass das Ergebnis eines Vergleichs immer von dem abhängt, *womit* man etwas vergleicht. So macht es natürlich einen Unterschied, ob man Röm 1–2 mit der Weisheit Salomos oder z. B. mit der Anthropologie der Hymnenrolle aus Qumran (1QH) vergleicht; ob man Röm 3 mit der Epistel Henochs oder mit der heilschaffenden Gerechtigkeit Gottes in anderen Texten des frühen Judentums vergleicht; ob man Röm 4 mit Sir 44 oder mit Texten vergleicht, die Abraham als Vater der heidnischen Proselyten vorstellen; ob man die paulinische Kollekte mit einem karitativen Almosen oder dem Almosen der „Gottesfürchtigen" für Israel vergleicht; usw. Jeweils erhält man ein anderes (Gesamt-)Bild von Paulus.

Wenn man diese Voraussetzung immer im Auge behält, stellt der vorliegende Band ein wertvolles Hilfsmittel für die Auslegung des Römerbriefs dar. Er
ist ein Arbeitsbuch im besten Sinne—was auch durch die zahlreichen Schaubilder unterstrichen wird und vielleicht auch durch den linksbündigen Druck (kein
Blocksatz) zum Ausdruck kommen soll. Man kann den Einsatz im akademischen
Unterricht nur wärmstens empfehlen.

Corinthian Wisdom, Stoic Philosophy, and the Ancient Economy, by Timothy
Brookins. Society for New Testament Studies Monograph Series 159. New
York: Cambridge University Press, 2014. Pp. xv + 264. Hardcover. £60.00. ISBN
9781107046375.

Devin L. White, Candler School of Theology, Emory University

Corinthian Wisdom, Stoic Philosophy, and the Ancient Economy is the engagingly written—and ultimately persuasive—revision of the author's 2012 Baylor
University dissertation. Scholarly consensus has long held that Paul wrote 1 Corinthians in response to a crisis that was caused, at least in part, by the wisdom of
the Corinthians. Most today would agree that this wisdom was sophistic rhetoric.
Over seven chapters, Brookins advances a refreshingly contrarian thesis, arguing
that the Corinthians' wisdom was a Christianized Stoic philosophy.

In a succinct introduction, Brookins couples his thesis with a summary of
modern scholarship on the wisdom of the Corinthians. His survey of the literature is clear, concise, and an able introduction to the project's thesis. "The 'wise
man' among the Corinthians," Brookins argues, "is less the 'sophist' than he is the
'Stoic'" (7). In fact, "the divisive 'wisdom' of the Corinthians … can be accounted
for as a *Christian development of Stoic philosophy*, arguably without remainder"
(4, emphasis original).

In chapter 2, perhaps the study's most important chapter, Brookins delivers
a withering review of the rhetorical hypothesis. He offers two particularly salient
criticisms. First, proponents of the rhetorical hypothesis rely upon an insufficiently
critical mirror-reading of 1 Corinthians. Second, alleged rhetorical terminology,
including key phrases such as ἐν σοφίᾳ λόγου (1:17) and ἐν ἀποδείξει πνεύματος
(2:4), is better read as ancient philosophical terminology. To make this point,
Brookins surveys the uses of these and related lexemes in first-century sources,
finding that in the vast majority of cases these terms or their Latin cognates refer
to philosophy and philosophers.

As noted when explaining his own methodology in chapter 3, Brookins aims
to avoid insufficiently critical mirror-reading. Instead, he suggests, any search for
the wisdom of the Corinthians has three tasks. First, it ought to identify quoted
Corinthian language in the epistle. Second, it should search for patterns unifying the range of seemingly unrelated topics Paul addresses throughout the letter
(sexual standards, food offered to idols, and procedures for corporate gatherings).
Finally, if steps one and two indicate significant overlap between the Corinthians'

slogans, problematic practices, and any particular ancient school of thought—such as rhetoric or Stoic philosophy—the reader ought to consider whether the social world of ancient Corinth makes it likely or unlikely that the Corinthian community had encountered that school of thought.

Brookins is obviously correct that it is historically preferable to privilege the Corinthians' own words and actions over Paul's second-hand perception of the Corinthian situation. Accurately identifying Corinthian slogans is notoriously difficult, however, so Brookins devotes the remainder of chapter 3 to cataloguing and interpreting likely slogans. On the basis of these slogans, as well as the topics Paul addresses throughout the epistle, Brookins arrives at a list of five topics he feels reflect the viewpoint of the Corinthian wise person: wisdom and the nature of the wise person; the concept of freedom; indifference; the primacy of the intellectual/spiritual over the physical; and intracommunal distinctions drawn on the basis of intellectual/spiritual status. Each of these five topics, Brookins notes, are paralleled in Stoic discourse.

Brookins thinks it insufficient simply to identify parallels between the Corinthian community and first-century Stoicism. His method demands that he also establish that some Corinthians could have received a rudimentary Stoic education. Thus in chapter 4 he demonstrates that Stoicism was a part of the first-century Corinthian milieu and that the Corinthians themselves were likely to have encountered it. Brookins here provides an up-to-date treatment of the question of the community members' socioeconomic status. Against those scholars who have argued for an impoverished Corinthian community, Brookins upholds the post-Theissen consensus that the members of the Corinthian community represented a cross-section of the socioeconomic profile of greater Corinth. Since first-century Corinth contained a sufficiently large number of well-to-do persons, at least some recipients of 1 Corinthians could have received a cursory Stoic education, perhaps in a gymnasium.

Chapter 5 surveys all of 1 Corinthians, pointing out correlations between Brookins's five-point summary of the Corinthian wise person's position and the behavior Paul attributes to the community. Especially convincing is his discussion of the Stoic concept of "freedom," which works well to explain the rationale of the man who has taken his father's wife in 5:1–13. In the course of this chapter, Brookins demonstrates that Paul, throughout the whole of the letter, appears to be interacting with the views of stoicizing Christians.

Chapters 6 and 7 round out the study, as Brookins connects his Stoic hypothesis with other trajectories in research on the Corinthian correspondence and restates the study's major arguments and conclusions. His conclusions regarding Paul's own relationship with Stoicism are particularly insightful. Although Paul was not a Stoic philosopher, he argues, Paul might have accidentally sounded like one to an audience familiar with Stoicism. This audience in turn might have assumed that Paul himself was advocating some features of Stoic thought, perhaps the very features of Stoic thought (e.g., freedom) that raised such a furor in the community.

Some readers will take issue with minor components of Brookins's argument. For example, several verses that Brookins reads as Corinthian slogans may well have originated with Paul, not the Corinthians. This is especially so in the case of 1 Cor 2:15, which distinguishes between the "spiritual" and "psychic" persons (πνευματικός and ψυχικός). Contra Brookins, it seems the distinction between πνευματικός/ψυχικός distinction is more likely Hellenistic Jewish than Stoic. Similarly, the contrast between the infant and the mature person (νήπιος and τέλειος) is not, as Brookins claims, "a distinctively Stoic contrast" (168) but a contrast between levels of personal maturity common in Greek and Roman educational literatures of all levels. Brookins does acknowledge that some of the texts he identifies as Corinthian slogans are open to speculation, and the reader should bear this caveat in mind.

Besides these relatively minor and debatable points, *Corinthian Wisdom* does leave one potentially significant issue unexamined. Brookins provides no discussion of distinctively Stoic views of rhetoric. This may strike some as a problematic omission, since some scholars of ancient philosophy have argued that Stoic sages integrated rhetoric into their philosophical curriculum. Catherine Atherton has helpfully reconstructed Stoic rhetoric's distinctive features by examining ancient descriptions of Stoic rhetoricians in action ("Hand over Fist: The Failure of Stoic Rhetoric," *CQ* 38 [1988]: 392-427). If Stoics did have specific rhetorical expectations for their sages, it becomes possible that some Corinthians measured Paul against Stoic (rather than sophistic) rhetorical standards.

In the final evaluation, Brookins's thesis is convincing. *Corinthian Wisdom* should be essential reading for any grappling with the historical backdrop to 1 Corinthians. It is erudite, forcefully written, and, in the end, probably correct. The rhetorical hypothesis, in its conventional form, is shown to be as open to question as its antecedents, the gnostic and Hellenistic-Jewish hypotheses. Equally importantly, Stoic doctrines (e.g., the freedom of the sage) seem likely precursors to the behavior Paul describes in 1 Cor 5. At the very least, no careful scholar can any longer simply assert, without explaining the reasoning behind the assertion, that the wisdom fracturing the Corinthian community was sophistic rhetoric. At most, Brookins has hit upon the better-reasoned, historically plausible counter-hypothesis that should replace the rhetorical hypothesis as our understanding of the wisdom of the Corinthians.

Paul's Divine Christology, by Chris Tilling. Foreword by Douglas Campbell. Grand Rapids: Eerdmans, 2015. Pp. xxiv + 322. Paper. $30.00. ISBN 9780802872951.

Chris Kugler, University of St. Andrews

This is the first Eerdmans edition of Tilling's 2012 WUNT volume (2/323), which itself was a lightly revised version of his PhD thesis written under the supervision of Max Turner at the London School of Theology. In this stimulating monograph, Tilling argues, in interaction (and basic agreement) with Hurtado,

Bauckham, and Fee in particular, that a hitherto unappreciated constellation of features in Paul, and the way in which this constellation relates to the same constellation in ancient Judaism, reflects the most all-embracing and fundamental category of Pauline Christology: the "Christ-relation." For Tilling, the Pauline "Christ-relation" is the "*pattern of ... language in Paul* [that] *is only that which a Jew used to express the relation between Israel/the individual Jew and YHWH*" (73, emphasis original).

This edition begins with a stage-setting foreword by Pauline luminary Douglas Campbell (x–xix), followed by two prefaces (xx–xxiii). Beginning in chapter 1 (1–10), Tilling provides clarification of the terms and concepts that he will use throughout, as well as an overview of the shape and concerns of the following argument. The *Forschungsgeschichte* of chapter 2 (11–34) is especially valuable. The survey begins from the Reformation and works its way to the time of publication. In particular, Tilling rightly notes the two key issues—(1) the nature of Jewish monotheism and (2) Paul's Christology in relation to such—and the shift which occurred in the 1970s from seeking a Hellenistic background to Paul's Christology to seeking a Jewish one (15–21). Tilling contends that all studies, notwithstanding their strengths, unduly focus on "titles" and/or isolated "themes" (22–27), "christological exegesis" (28–29), "Paul's experience" (29–30), and/or the alleged cultic "worship" of Jesus (30–32). For Tilling, the all-embracing (and much more appropriate) "pattern of Pauline themes relevant to the divine-Christology debate has not yet been sufficiently grasped" (33).

Before we learn what this pattern is, Tilling focuses on three of the most important representatives for an early high Christology: Fee, Hurtado, and Bauckham (34–62). Notwithstanding his appreciation for the positive gains of Fee's work, Tilling registers major criticisms: Fee's division of the "person" and "work" of Christ is inappropriate (35–36); his emphasis on preexistence, in reaction to Dunn, is unhelpful (36–37); he fails adequately to deal with the "subordination" texts (39–40); and he lacks conceptual and semantic clarity at certain points (40–41). More generally, Tilling argues that Fee's decision to structure certain elements of his Pauline Christology according to christological titles is likewise a weakness (43–47). As to Hurtado, along with the appreciative comments, Tilling makes the following criticisms: Hurtado does not "grasp the breadth of Christ devotion in Paul's letters" (57); (2) Hurtado's use of the category of "Christ devotion will not suitably cover the range of phenomena necessary to grasp" (57); and his emphasis upon "cultic worship" has ultimately proven indecisive (59–61). Having noted the gains of Bauckham's work, Tilling's central criticism, following that of Chester's, is the fact that figures other than the God of Israel sometimes share in the features of Second Temple Jewish monotheism that Bauckham claims strictly demarcate the unique divine identity (19–21).

As to Tilling's thorough treatment of Hurtado and Bauckham, one should note the following points. (1) Hurtado has never written a Pauline Christology; therefore, Tilling's claim that Hurtado has not attended to all of the Pauline evidence is somewhat beside the point. (2) Hurtado's contention that, by and large, "cultic worship" is the most important indicator of divinity in the ancient world remains convincing. (3) Likewise, Bauckham's claim that certain features of ancient Jewish monotheism demarcate the unique divine identity remains convincing. The fact that certain figures sometimes "trespass" this territory does not prove that the territory does not exist but rather that certain Jewish texts *intend* to indicate that certain figures temporarily participate in the unique divine identity without themselves being inextricably identified with it. Tilling rightly argues that none of these figures provides a full precedent for Pauline Christology (196–233), but this hardly makes them totally irrelevant to an appreciation of such.

In chapter 4 (63–74) Tilling helpfully disambiguates the debates about Second Temple Jewish monotheism (63–72), arguing in particular that "biblical faith in the one God is fundamentally about the exclusive *relational* allegiance of Israel to this one God" (67, emphasis original). This conception obtained both for later Second Temple Jews and for Paul (67–72). Importantly, this emphasis upon the relational (one might have expected the word *covenantal* more often) nature of Pauline (and Second Temple) monotheism provides a fresh angle from which to observe Paul's Christology: "*this pattern of Christ-relation language in Paul is only that which a Jew used to express the relation between Israel/an individual Jew and YHWH*" (73, emphasis original).

Tilling then launches into a major exegesis of his foundational text (ch. 5: 75–104), 1 Cor 8:1–10:22. In particular, and in a way that is representative of his entire thesis, he argues that "*Paul, having opened his argument in a way which expresses true faith in the one God as the relational commitment of believers to this one God over against idolatry, goes on to speak explicitly and continually of the relation between risen Lord and believers over against idolatry. Furthermore, he details this Christ-relation with the terms and categories drawn from complex of themes and concepts that, in the Jewish scriptures, describe the relation between Israel and YHWH over against idolatry*" (76, emphasis original). Amidst impressive grammatical and text-critical arguments (77–81), discussions of Paul's intertexts (81–85), the text's historical exigency (87–89) and innumerable incisive judgments of exegetical detail, Tilling convinces.

Moving to the rest of the undisputed Pauline material (105–80), Tilling contends that the Pauline letters reflect the Christ-relation pattern at point after point. From Paul's "goals," "motivations," and "passionate affections" to sundry other features of his christological rhetoric, the Christ-relation pattern corresponds to the Jewish God-relation pattern.

Chapter 7 (181–87) argues that the pattern of data that Tilling calls the Christ-relation is a pattern that Paul would have recognized and of which he made conscious use. Following chapter 8 (188–95), in which Tilling assesses 1 Cor 16:22 from the perspective of the Christ-relation, he considers the import of three Second Temple Jewish texts: Sir 44–50, the Similitudes, and Life of Adam and Eve (196–233). To summarize a complex argument, Tilling contends that these three texts, far from challenging his case for a Pauline divine Christology, actually support it. The Christ-relation pattern in Paul corresponds far more closely to the God-relation pattern in these texts than to the exalted conception of the high priest (Sir 50), the Son of Man (Similitudes) and/or Adam (LAE).

Chapters 10 (234–52) and 11 (253–57) gather together the conclusions of the foregoing arguments in a helpful summary. In the final appendix (258–72), Tilling provides a very thoughtful discussion of the potential bridges that his focus on the Christ-relation might build between the worlds of biblical studies and systematic theology.

In sum, the book is stimulating and at times stunning, thorough and detailed, attentive to exegetical minutiae and to larger historical and theological movements. Its central contentions, moreover, convince. As to the points of criticism, however, the following should be said. One wonders whether the absence of any discussion of messiahship was deliberate. Likewise, the reader will find no discussion of Adam and/or image Christology, which is a considerable lacuna. One wonders whether Tilling omitted such discussions because he does not see how they might relate to—or perhaps he thinks that they are simply incompatible with—his emphasis on the Christ-relation. I, however, think these features are perfectly compatible. This also relates to Tilling's discussion of "intermediary figures" (196–233). The presupposition seems to be that, if one wants to argue for a fully divine Christology, such a person needs to distance Paul's Christology from associations with such figures. This reflects, I suggest, a misunderstanding. In ancient Judaism, not least because of a widespread, high theological anthropology, figures other than God sometimes participated in the unique divine identity. One need not diminish the force of these texts in order (rightly) to contend that Paul's Jesus is far more thoroughly and inextricably identified with the unique divine identity than any of these figures ever were.

The Ritualized Revelation of the Messianic Age: Washings and Meals in Galatians and 1 Corinthians, by Stephen Richard Turley. Library of New Testament Studies 544. London: Bloomsbury, 2015. Pp. ix + 198. Hardcover. $100.99. ISBN 9780567663856.

Craig L. Blomberg, Denver Seminary

As with many of the LNTS volumes, this is a revised doctoral dissertation, written under John Barclay at the University of Durham. Turley is now professor of fine arts at Eastern University in Pennsylvania along with teaching theology, Greek, and rhetoric at Tall Oaks Classical School in Delaware. His multidisciplinary interests and expertise are clearly evident in this book.

After outlining the major approaches to studying religious ritual in general and then in Paul in particular, Turley defends his "agreement with performance- and practice-based theories and their emphasis on the role of the ritualized body in the formation of social order" (23). Throughout he finds Ray Rappoport's studies particularly generative of the kind of study he wants to undertake of baptism and the Eucharist in Paul.

Turley's key texts for studying Pauline thought on baptism are Gal 3:26–29 and 1 Cor 6:11 and 12:13. Applying both form criticism and speech-act theory, he determines, contra James Dunn and Gordon Fee, that these texts are talking about literal baptism in water, not as salvific in and of themselves (cf. 1 Cor. 10:2), but as metonymic of the larger process of salvation. As with performative speech more generally, the act of announcing one's allegiance to Jesus publicly in the context of one who proclaims one to be baptized is constitutive of the act itself. That baptism is a very body-involving ritual personalizes the act all the more, but in the corporate context of the body of Christ—the church. The internal response to God of faith becomes externalized, giving it a "public objective value" (42). In the context of Galatians' apocalyptic worldview, baptism also pronounces the arrival of the new age in general and in the life of baptizand. In short, "Christian baptism did nothing less than reveal ritually another world," and "the uniqueness of this ritually revealed world accounts for the uniqueness of the social arrangements" in Gal 3:28 (55). A "temporally recalibrated body" thus "mediates a comparably recalibrated social order" (560).

If Galatians focuses on the theological newness of the newly baptized, 1 Corinthians highlights their ethical newness. The vice list of 6:9–10 outlines what some of the Christians in Corinth had been, but now the arrival of the new age, ritualized in their baptismal washing (v. 11), shows that they have left these vices behind through the gift of the Holy Spirit. Of course, not everyone follows through on these commitments, but in baptism they have accepted an obligation to do so. "To behave in a manner that violates this cosmic state and the obligations inherent therein is not only a denial of the Corinthians' pneumatic identity in Christ, but indeed a betrayal of the very Spirit of God given to them in order to fulfill their baptismally established obligations" (73).

The verse 1 Cor 12:13 adds the verb *potizein* into the lexical mix of key concepts. All the baptized Corinthian believers have been given the Spirit to drink: "saturated in his outpouring" (Beasley-Murray). With Ezek 36 in the background, the purifying function of the ritual again comes to the fore, again in the context of the arrival of the new covenant. "Through the formation of ritualized bodies, abstract concepts are made substantial and thus comprehensible, being experienced by the ritual participant as something inseparable from his or her self" (97).

The same dynamics are operative with the celebration of early Christian table fellowship. We do not know that the Eucharist per se was in view in Gal 2:1–10, but table fellowship clearly was. Here Turley argues that the traditional perspective gets the better of the new perspective in explaining why the issue was so inflammatory, far more so than any merely intramural Jewish debate would have been. With "participatory performance indispensable to the attribution of sanctity to any discourse," Peter's refusal to continue to eat at table with gentile Christians amounts to a wholesale denial of the Christian claim that a new age has arrived, that the Spirit is equally available on identical terms to all persons across the standard humanly erected sociological divisions, in short, that the gospel is true! After Peter's enjoyment of unreserved table fellowship with these gentiles, he is under *obligation* not to shrink back from his previous commitments.

Turning to 1 Cor 8–10, Turley shows that the recent trend in some circles to interpret Paul as not countenancing the consumption of idol meat under any circumstances simply cannot do justice to the nuances of his argument nor his overall thesis on behalf of Christian freedom. When Paul foregoes his privileges, it is always voluntarily. Unlike baptism, which is a once-for-all ritual, the Eucharist is a recurring one, consistent with its past, present, and future symbolism. While some think Paul is countering an overly realized eschatology in Corinth, Turley argues that at least here "Paul is seeking to correct the Corinthians' *under*-appreciation of the eschatological nature of their ritual of commensality" (152). What further distinguishes this ceremony from baptism is the contrast between the "cup of the Lord" and "the cup of demons" (10:21), which together "represent nothing less than two incompatible ritually revealed cosmologies" (159).

For the reader unfamiliar with some of the literature on ritual with which Turley interacts, this work can at times require some heavy slogging. But it is well organized, with clearly identified results that repay the effort needed. It is of a piece with the growing body of New Testament scholarship that recognizes the importance of studying the phenomenon of embodiment in numerous contexts. Turley's conclusions frequently mediate between unnecessary either/or options: the sacraments as salvific versus having nothing to do with salvation, for example. Turley also reminds us that Louis Martyn's approach to Paul's thought as apocalyptic continues to contribute fruitful insights in possibly unexpected areas. "Baptism and the Lord's Supper," Turley has shown, "forged a ritualized composite that *revealed*, and *incorporated* Christians into, a unique messianic conception of time" (174). But this does not mean that Turley rejects a participationist approach to Paul's thought, for the corporate and embodied dimensions of his approach to these two rituals require that to be part of the mix as well. Further, they have ethical implications, obligating the participants to act in ways consonant with their new identities in this new age.

Small quibbles could always be raised at a few points. Is Turley assuming a credobaptistic understanding of Paul? If so, should it not be defended rather than merely assumed against the paedobaptistic alternative? If not, does sprinkling a baby who cannot yet believe rather than immersion of a believer not at least partially change the function of the ritual embodied in baptism? If the Eucharist is likewise so constitutive of a believer's very identity, shouldn't Turley wrestle with the ways of participating in it that Paul thinks potentially bring judgment on oneself, especially if they involve neglect or mistreatment of the poor (11:17–34)? Couldn't an intramural Jewish debate in Antioch still have included disagreements over the apocalyptic question, "what time is it?" even if perhaps not quite to the same degree as on the "old perspective's" interpretation? And when Turley decides that *pistis Christou* and its synonyms represent objective rather than subjective genitives because of the stress on the rituals attached to *believers'* bodies, couldn't a stress on Jesus's faithfulness, even unto his very bodily death, which

Paul suggests we are potentially to imitate, also accomplish that same function, even if again perhaps not quite to the same degree? At the end of the day, I find Turley's conclusions more convincing nevertheless.

Paul's Ekklesia as a Civic Assembly: Understanding the People of God in Their Politico-Social World, by Young-Ho Park. WUNT 2/393. Tübingen: Mohr Siebeck, 2015.

Bradley J. Bitner, Oak Hill College

In Paul's world the term *ekklēsia* "already told its own story."[1] Its basic tale was one of political community—of assembly, of participation (or exclusion), of decisions taken, and of embassies sent and received. But just how the ecclesial story unfolded, both in its internal- and external-facing aspects, depended largely on the constitution and the context of a given *ekklēsia*. It was a term with a deep historical and wide cultural and geographical pedigree. When applied to early groups of Christ-believers, *ekklēsia* was potentially implausible—even provocative—in the ears of first-century auditors. For modern readers of Paul's epistles, the origins, resonances, and social and theological dynamics of *ekklēsia* continue to puzzle.

A recent contribution to the longstanding debate over the meaning and implications of ἐκκλησία comes in the form of this slightly revised 2012 dissertation completed under the supervision of Hans-Josef Klauk at the University of Chicago. Park, now Professor of New Testament at Hanil University and Theological Seminary in Jeonju, South Korea, examines Paul's use of the term to designate the groups of Christ-believers that he founded and to which he wrote. He insists on its sociopolitical resonances and refuses to capitulate to the Hellenism/Judaism divide in his exegesis. In this, Park adds to a growing body of scholarly work that largely seeks to go beyond a genealogical to an analogical, spatially contextualized, and multivalent approach to the meaning of *ekklēsia* in the *corpus Paulinum*.[2] Like

---

1. E. A. Judge, "Did the Churches Compete with Cult Groups?," in *Early Christianity and Classical Culture*, ed. John T. Fitzgerald, Thomas H. Olbricht, and L. Michael White (Leiden: Brill, 2003), 501–24.

2. A recent sampling includes: Paul Trebilco, "Why Did the Early Christians Call Themselves ἡ ἐκκλησία?" *NTS* 57 (2011): 440–60; George H. van Kooten, "'Ἐκκλησία τοῦ θεοῦ': The 'Church of God' and the Civic Assemblies (*ekklēsiai*) of the Greek Cities in the Roman Empire: A Response to Paul Trebilco and Richard A. Horsley," *NTS* 58 (2012): 522–48; Yonder M. Gillihan, *Civic Ideology, Organization, and Law in the Rule Scrolls: A Comparative Study of the Covenanters' Sect and Contemporary Voluntary Associations in Political Context* (Leiden: Brill, 2012); Korinna Zamfir, "Is the ἐκκλησία a *Household* (of God)? Reassessing the Notion of οἶκος θεοῦ in 1 Tim 3.15," *NTS* 60 (2014): 511–28; Bradley J. Bitner, *Paul's Political Strategy in 1 Corinthians: Constitution and Covenant* (Cambridge: Cambridge University Press, 2015); Anna C. Miller, *Corinthian Democracy: Democratic Discourse in 1 Corinthians* (Eugene, OR: Pickwick,

many such studies, Park spends much time in the Corinthian correspondence but does not limit his analysis to those epistles.

As Park stresses in his introduction, he is after both intention and reception; he wants to understand Paul's meaning in employing *ekklēsia* as well as "what the word implied to the first Christians, both those who were under his influence and those who were in a discordant relationship with him" (1–2). His approach is to follow the terminological trail, first through the classical and Hellenistic worlds (ch. 1), then through the LXX and Second Temple sources (ch. 2), and, finally, into (primarily) the Pauline epistles (chs. 3–5). Yet throughout, Park generally avoids a "word study" approach, attending rather to the sociopolitical and contextual dynamics of *ekklēsia*.

Beginning with classical Athens, Park provides a summary of scholarship on the *ekklēsia* as the civic assembly within the ancient *polis*. Leaning heavily on Aristotle, Park highlights the civic functions of the political assembly: it was a popular council with powers relating to decrees, judicial sentences, elections, embassies, and the exchange of honor. The *ekklēsia* was a public assembly convened in public space. Participation was fundamental to the form of life centered on the *ekklēsia*. In assembling some of the lexical signals that cluster around this civic form of life from the time of Athenian democracy onward, Park also briefly notes *koinōneō* (13–14), *metechō* (15), and *politeia* (16–17; see 105, 211 in relation to Phil 1:27; 3:20), although his focus on these constellations does not in every case guide his later exegesis. An *idiōtēs* had no formal standing or sanctioned voice as such in assembly but might nonetheless be present and unofficially vocal (17–18). Park nods toward 2 Cor 11:6 (17 n. 90) here but nowhere comments on what connection this observation might bear to what Paul's instructions regarding the *idiōtēs* in 1 Cor 14:16, 23–24 might tell us about his *ekklēsia* as civic-like assembly.

The importance of the LXX and early Jewish backgrounds to (Paul's use of) *ekklēsia*, and especially its relation to the *sunagōgē*, form the focus of chapter 2. Here Park reminds us that, even at the lexical level, *ekklēsia* is not merely a gathering but a "civic assembly" (67). Pointing especially to the evidence of Ezra and Nehemiah, Park further argues for a kind of constitutional conception of *ekklēsia* as "not only a cultic gathering, but also a political assembly" (76). When the Maccabean literature, Philo and Josephus are added to the postexilic narratives, the picture of *ekklēsia* that emerges is of an official and regular assembly comprising "active participants in their civic community," (79) engaged in diplomacy and exercising judicial functions (82–83). These literary representations of the Jewish constitution (*politeia*) in action find their "archetype," Park argues, in the Sinai *ekklēsia* (89; see Deut 31:30). Where such *ekklēsia* language and action especially cluster in later Jewish-biblical narrative, it tends to be at "structurally crucial" and even eschatologically charged junctures (e.g., the dedication of Solomon's

_____

2015); Richard Last, *The Pauline Church and the Corinthian Ekklēsia* (Cambridge: Cambridge University Press, 2016).

temple in 2 Chr 6; the polemic against intermarriage in Ezra 9:1). Jesus's statement about building his *ekklēsia* in Matt 16:18 therefore becomes "a politically sensitive remark" (91). That he makes this statement en route to Jerusalem also coheres, for Park, with an overwhelmingly "Jerusalem-centric" focus of *ekklēsia* references and discourses in the LXX and early Jewish literature. Philo, perhaps above all, in his universalizing of the Mosaic *politeia* and its associated *ekklēsiai*, provides an analogue to early Christian—and particularly Pauline—usage (96). This chapter in particular is a helpful synthesis of some earlier research and offers several insightful and relevant observations.

In chapter 3 Park turns to consider Paul's use of the term and concept of *ekklēsia*. "Epistolary dynamics" account for a significant portion of this usage. That is, writing from a distance, "Paul utilized the political capacity of this word to establish his letters' recipients as the honourable citizens in an *ekklēsia* and relied on the diplomatic nuances of this word to locate his *ekklēsiai* in the web of translocal relationship [*sic*]" (124). In so doing, Park suspects, Paul was largely drawing on a new or modified *ekklēsia* tradition that predated him, one originating with Matthew's Jesus (Matt 16:18) and the "Jerusalem community." Where Paul adapts this usage is especially in speaking of the new, christocentric, gentile, and local (plenary) communities, their "officials," and in responding to what he conceives as abuses within the *ekklēsia tou theou*. For Paul, "*ekklēsia* was predominantly a local congregation in a city, which meant that there was one *ekklēsia* per city" (100). Park challenges the notion that Paul's use of *ekklēsia* (especially in Corinth) sounds primary notes either of "house church" or of "voluntary association" (100–101). Rather, the "civic nature" of *ekklēsiai* is the central and "consistent core" of Paul's ecclesiology" (133). Paul's bold application of this *ekklēsia* conception to gentile groups generated "substantial conflict" in light of the centrality of Jerusalem for the early Jewish-Christian movement (135). Ephesians 2:11–12 (post-Pauline for Park), with its articulation of *ekklēsia* as "Gentile participation in Christ in the political privileges of the Israelites," encapsulates the ultimate triumph of the Pauline ecclesiological paradigm (149-50). Chapter 3 includes a robust engagement with many exegetical texts and issues.

Park tightens the textual and geographical focus in chapter 4 by examining the conflict within the Corinthian *ekklēsia*. In his correspondence with Corinth, Paul employed *ekklēsia* "in its full socio-political sense" to rhetorically create a "symbolic universe" and a resultant "Christ-confessing community" (151–52). Paul's use of "gathering in assembly" (*sunerchomenōn ... en ekklēsia*, 1 Cor 11:18) points unequivocally, in context, to a considerable spatial aspect contributing to the conflict concerning the Lord's Supper (11:17–34). Conceding the "imaginative" (even if plausible) nature of any archaeological reconstruction of Corinthian *ekklēsia* space, Park nevertheless prefers something like Murphy-O'Connor's or Horrell's hypotheses (i.e., the model of the villa at Anapologa or that of commercial-domestic space within an *insula*). He thinks this spatial reality, whatever it may have been, correlates importantly with the *ekklēsia* inequalities and subsequent conflict because the space was private but the gathering and the meal were public

(165). This "social problem" is to be distinguished from Paul's interpretation of space and place (as in Økland's *ekklēsia* = ritual space; *oikos* = material space). For Park, Paul's solution to the spatially and socially generated conflict was the application of *ekklēsia* language and dynamics most clearly to the *plenary* assembly in Corinth, whereby its divinely constituted and unified nature were stressed. Yet, given that there were almost certainly "two levels of worshipping groups in Corinth: the whole *ekklēsia* and the house churches" (169), and given that Paul was less clear in confirming "house groups as *ekklēsiai*" in each instance in the Corinthian correspondence, the result of Paul's strategy in 1 Corinthians was rather an "incomplete" compromise (176). Although the *ekklēsia* was fundamentally public, private spaces continued to allow for habits of social class that, when surfacing, led to conflict. In sum, this complex interplay between gathering spaces and social status account for Paul's epistolary response and strategic deployment of *ekklēsia*.

In chapter 5 Park continues to reflect on these dynamics in relation to the Corinthian and Macedonian evidence. He rightly notes that Paul evinces a concern for "common convention" (*synētheia*, 1 Cor 11:16 [179]) among the assemblies. By introducing a differential comparison with the Thessalonian and Philippian correspondence, Park builds on the approach of scholars such as John Barclay. He cautions against too quickly generalizing from the Corinthian ecclesial model. Park examines the evidence for social status and "inner structures" of the Corinthian and Macedonian *ekklēsiai*. He knows he is treading on contested and difficult methodological territory as he engages debates over the "new consensus," yet he weaves together exegetical observations, socioeconomic models (including the so-called economic scales proposed by Scheidel, Friesen, and B. Longenecker), archaeological evidence, and information from Acts to probe the social strata and dynamics of the early Pauline *ekklēsiai*. In the end, Park wants to moderate the new consensus view, suggesting that—especially with regard to the Thessalonian and Philippian groups—the epistolary and social historical data suggests few, if any, members with even moderate surplus (ES4 or higher). He links this argument with the observations that in the Macedonian epistles Paul is more concerned with so-called leadership structures, employing some administrative and financial terminology and principles also used with reference to voluntary associations (*collegia*). Nevertheless, Park rejects *collegia* as model for the Pauline assemblies, preferring to see them as a helpful analogy, particularly in the self-understanding of the Philippian and Thessalonian groups (208–15). On this basis he proposes considering the Corinthian assembly/ies as households characterized by "economic independence," whereas the Macedonian assemblies operated more closely to the "economic interdependence" of the *collegia*. Park then briefly suggests the potential of testing these approaches against later developments in early Christianity such as 3 John and the Didache, where the social dynamics of funding and communal structures are also briefly foregrounded.

Any future editions of this volume would benefit greatly from closer editing—typographical and other errors accumulate at times to the point of distraction—and from a more robust Greek subject index. But despite these shortcomings, Park has produced a stimulating study that rightly warns against undervaluing the civic-political connotations of *ekklēsia* in Paul. His treatment of the Jewish-biblical trajectories of *ekklēsia* in conjunction with various Greco-Roman resonances is a major methodological strength. Furthermore, his tendency to range widely within the Pauline corpus (and Acts) allows him to work toward a global view of the evidence. Simultaneously, however, such a broad scope means that in many cases Park's exegetical engagement with any one text or passage (even within the Corinthian correspondence) is quite limited and leaves many issues unexamined. Sometimes the focus on *ekklēsia* language elides other pertinent contextual features. Neither in Park's treatment of 1 Cor 4:17 nor Acts 11:26 does he reflect on why *teaching* is a fundamental Pauline activity in *ekklēsia* or how this might (or might not) relate to his earlier observations on the *ekklēsia* as a civic assembly in both the Greco-Roman and Jewish traditions. Elsewhere the same kind of terminological focus leads Park to overreact: he thinks Økland has overemphasized ritual dynamics of *naos* in 1 Corinthians and thereby emptied *ekklēsia* of its sociopolitical import in her treatment. But Park himself virtually ignores the intimate links between the terms and cultural concepts that dominate 1 Corinthians (e.g., the nexus among *ekklēsia*, *koinōnia*, and *naos* in 1 Cor 1:1–9; 3:5–4:5). Finally, in his discussions of multiple *ekklēsiai* within certain cities and yet Paul's preference to conceive of these as one plenary assembly, Park does not go on to consider the translocal networks or communications among the Pauline *ekklēsiai*. In each of these examples, Park's preparatory work in Greco-Roman and Jewish patterns of civic assembly might easily have allowed him to probe further Paul's constructions of *ekklēsia*; doing so would have strengthened even more his solid contribution.

Exploring Philemon: Freedom, Brotherhood, and Partnership in the New Society, by Roy R. Jeal. Rhetoric of Religious Antiquity 2. Atlanta: SBL Press, 2015. Pp. xxix + 230. Paper. $30.95. ISBN 9780884140917. Hardcover. $45.95. ISBN 9780884140931.

Timothy Gombis, Grand Rapids Theological Seminary

This is the first volume to be released in a new SBL Press series called Rhetoric of Religious Antiquity. Roy R. Jeal's *Exploring Philemon: Freedom, Brotherhood, and Partnership in the New Society* is a sociorhetorical commentary. Sociorhetorical interpretation is regarded as an "analytic," rather than a method, in that it "evaluates and reorients its strategies as it engages in multifaceted dialogue with the texts and other phenomena that come within its purview" (from the editorial foreword [xi]). The commentary, along with subsequent volumes, analyzes the text from three angles of approach, or perhaps it is better to say that it takes three passes at the text. First, the author analyzes the "rhetography" of the text, a term that blends "rhetoric" with "graphic" to come to grips with how the ancient text moves its audience(s) through depictions, images, and mental pictures. Second, the author analyzes the various textures at work in and through the text, including the text's "inner texture, intertexture, social and cultural textures, ideological texture, and sacred texture" (xii). Third, the commentary discusses the rhetorical force of the text as an example of the emerging discourse of a developing community within the Mediterranean world. That is, the commentary interprets "how emerging Christian belief systems blended graphic imagery and reasoned argumentation into newly configured Mediterranean discourse" (xii). These three passes at the text, each viewing the same text through different lenses, do not merely repeat the same conclusions but aim to come to a "comprehensive view of the features and the effect—the rhetorical force—of the letter as it emerged in its ancient setting" (xviii).

In Jeal's view, what distinguishes sociorhetorical interpretation as an "analytic," or perhaps "a range of analytics" (2), is that a method employs a formula and follows identifiable steps in order to produce predictable results within a predetermined framework. This analytic, alternatively, "is a kind of 'multiple accounts evaluation' that analyzes (and reanalyzes) texts using features of rhetorical, social, and cognitive reasoning in order to help interpreters learn how the texts being examined function to influence thinking and behavior" (2). The aim is "to discover phenomena in the texts as they emerge in their social, anthropological, and rhetorical contexts and as they bring about religious and theological cognition" (3). Ultimately, then, the goal is to "identify, analyze, and interpret what the text and the arguments *do* and *how they go about doing it*" (2). That is, Jeal's analysis is concerned with the rhetorical force of the Christian discourse that was emerging among the early Christian movement in the first century. This mode of engaging texts takes the classical rhetorical handbooks seriously but goes beyond them, recognizing that early Christian texts such as Philemon are quite different from public speeches in political assemblies or the law courts (4).

The bank of vocabulary used in sociorhetorical interpretation has been developed by participants in the Rhetoric of Religious Antiquity study group of the SBL, under the leadership of Vernon Robbins. Because some terms may be new to many readers, Jeal helpfully provides a glossary at the beginning, explaining such terms as "argumentative texture" ("The reasoning that occurs inside a text") and "rhetorolects" ("An elision of 'rhetorical dialect' that refers to the emergent modes of discourse created by early Christ-believers").

The commentary proper begins with an introduction (1–37) that covers some familiar ground (author, audience, situation, etc.) but includes an analysis of the letter's rheterolects, rhetography, and textures. Here Jeal states that Philemon is a "wisdom text" in that it "has a wisdom goal, and has a view toward wisdom space" (7). This has to do with how Christians are called to live wisely according to the new "in Christ" space they inhabit while also inhabiting the Mediterranean world. Wisdom is about "doing good in the world and about living faithfully, fruitfully, and ethically" (7). Against the assumption that Philemon does not present much of a theology or theological vision, Jeal states that the theological richness of the letter is seen in its rhetorical goal of the formation of an alternative community living into the fullness of having new identities as "holy ones" (33). One of the benefits of a sociorhetorical approach is that it reveals how the letter theologizes as it presents "the nature of the new life, the new society, the communal life, the ecclesial life, the new existence, of Christianity" (34).

The introduction is followed by a section of the commentary that analyzes the letter's rhetography (39–54): the visual manner in which the world of the text is constructed. While the sets of metaphors and relationships receive due treatment by commentators on Philemon, the benefits of the sociorhetorical approach are seen in that Jeal asks what these modes of expression are doing and discusses how they are doing their work. They create a new space within which Christian life and action are to be envisioned. Beyond merely noting the decision that Philemon faces as an individual abstracted from an intensely complicated social situation, Jeal is able to be alert to the array of networks of connection and relationship the "in Christ" reality generates and how the new world into which Philemon has been brought, along with Onesimus and Paul (among others), sets the table for the way forward. A translation of the letter follows this section (55–56).

A "textural commentary" makes up the bulk of the volume (59–200), representing the second step in the analysis. After a brief discussion of the entire text's "repetitive texture," (59–62), Jeal analyzes the various textures of the letter's opening, middle, and closing. This is not a typical commentary into which one can easily parachute for a brief discussion of this or that verse. Jeal treats larger units of text at several different points in distinct ways and in such organic fashion that the considerations of various aspects of the text cannot easily be consulted for a "quick take" on the meaning of this or that expression. The value of this approach, however, is seen in Jeal's discussion of the intertexture of slaves and slavery (138–52), drawing upon scriptural conceptions of slavery and treatments of slavery by other writers and thinkers in the Greco-Roman world. Analyzing the texture of Paul's discussion in this frame leads Jeal to claim in several places that Paul implicitly but strongly advocates for Philemon to manumit Onesimus (32, 140, 200–201). A final portion of this section is a consideration of "ideological texture," in which Jeal discusses his own ideological approach to the text, Paul's ideology, and other values that must be acknowledged, since the interpretive enterprise is not purely mechanical. The final part of the volume contains the third step of analyzing the letter: a discussion of the letter's rhetorical force as emergent discourse (203–10).

This is a substantial volume on Philemon, and the resetting of the analysis of Paul's rhetoric goes beyond merely rehashing familiar interpretations in new language. Because the character of Philemon as a religious text that emerges from the first-century Christian movement determines and orients the rhetorical terms, frames, and labels, Jeal's work is far more helpful than many previous rhetorical analyses of New Testament letters. Perhaps this is what the author meant by "methods" that produce predictable results, "rhetorical criticism" in the sense of labeling various portions of text with terms that come from the classical handbooks. The approach represented in this volume seems appropriate to the material, and the flexibility of the analytic, being refined by repeated encounters with the text, commends it further.

If You Call Yourself a Jew: Reappraising Paul's Letter to the Romans, by Rafael Rodriguez. Eugene, OR: Cascade, 2014. Pp. xix + 317. Paper. $29.60. ISBN 9781625646804.

Philip Esler, University of Gloucestershire

Rafael Rodríguez has already distinguished himself as a scholar of memory and orality in connection with the Jesus tradition in *Structuring Early Christian Memory: Jesus in Tradition, Performance, and Text* (London: T&T CLark, 2010) and *Oral Tradition and the New Testament: A Guide for the Perplexed* (London: Bloomsbury, 2014). Now he turns his creative attention to Romans in *If You Call Yourself a Jew: Reappraising Paul's Letter to the Romans*, a work he describes ("half-jokingly") as writing "accidentally" in consequence of having to teach a graduate-level course on the text in 2010.

The principal stimulus for the production of this book (ix) was that, during his work on Romans, Rodríguez changed his mind about the character of its audience. Whereas he had previously shared the majority view that Paul wrote to an audience of Jews and gentiles, he came to agree with Stanley Stowers, Andrew Das, Runar Thorsteinsson, and some others that Paul was writing solely to a gentile audience. In particular, he hit upon the view that when Paul says "But if you call yourself a Jew..." (Rom 2:17) he actually also meant a gentile here, more precisely "a gentile proselyte to Judaism," not "an ethnic Jew" (ix). It will be immediately apparent that this idea allowed Rodríguez to have his cake and eat it: it enabled him to urge that the figure addressed in Rom 2:17 was both a gentile *and* a Jew (whatever those words might mean). I will return to this issue below.

Nevertheless, and with admirable determination, Rodríguez then set about testing this thought on the entire text of Romans in its order of writing. The book contains fifteen substantive chapters: (1) "Introduction: Paul the Apostle to the Beloved Gentiles of Rome," which briefly covers the broad character of Pauline theology and the recipients and purpose of Romans; (2) "The Gospel, the Power of God: Paul Begins to Write," on Rom 1:1–17; (3) "The Wrath and Impartial Judgment of God: Gentiles in Pauline Perspective," on 1:18–2:16; (4) "Introducing the Gentile Proselyte: A Gentile Who Calls Himself a Jew," on 2:17–3:20; (5) "The Righteousness of God Apart from Torah: Or, Not a Law-Free Gospel," on 3:21–4:25; (6) "Christ, the New Adam: Undoing the Curse of Death," on 5:1–21; (7) "Baptized, Buried, Raised: Freed from Sin, Enslaved to Righteousness," on 6:1–23; (8) "*Nomos*, Flesh, Spirit: The War Waging Within," on 7:1–25; (9) "Creation Renewed by the Spirit: Security in the Presence of God," on 8:1–39; (10) "Israel and Christ: Paul's *Pathos* for the People of God," on 9:1–29; (11) "Israel and Christ, Pt. II: Torah's *Telos*," on 9:30–10:21; (12) "(Re-)grafted Olive Branches:

The Persistence of Hope," on 11:1–36; (13) "Living Sacrifices: One Body, Many Members," on 12:1–13:14; (14) "The Offering of the Weak: Paul and the Particular Assemblies in Rome," on 14:1–15:13; (15) "In Sum ... The End of Paul's Rhetoric and of His Letter," on 15:14–16:27. In each chapter Rodríguez supplies a fresh translation of the passage in view that reflects his exegetical views; he thus provides his own translation of the whole letter. Rodríguez addresses a very large array of textual data, touching on most of the scholarly topoi in a measured, lucid, and fair-minded way.

Anyone familiar with Rodríguez's earlier scholarship will expect this process to produce an array of new and interesting ideas to be thrown into the broad mix of Romans research, and so it proves here. While it is not feasible—in the space and genre of a review such as this—to mention all of these ideas, I survey some (while counseling others to read this stimulating book for themselves). Afterward I will offer some reservations that might be expressed about this project.

Rodríguez's central idea, on the *Ioudaios* addressed in Rom 2:17, is set out on pages 48–61. Rodríguez argues that "Paul still imagines a gentile in vv. 17ff., only now this gentile has taken on the yoke of Torah" (49). He follows Thorsteinsson in seeing here "an individual of gentile origin who wants to call himself a Jew" (50). He suggests that "*The choice between an actually Jewish interlocutor in Rom 2:17–29 and an ethnically-gentile-religiously Jewish interlocutor will prove to be the fork in the road for our reading of Romans as a whole*" (51, emphasis original). Although Rodríguez favors the latter option, it is important to note that he considers the person referred to at Rom 2:17 as actually circumcised (50) and as a "proselyte" (53, "the gentile proselyte"). Forced by Rom 2:27 to concede that the person addressed in 2:17 is a "transgressor of Torah through the letter and the circumcision," Rodríguez produces the ingenious idea (57–61) that the transgression involved is not the fact of circumcision (denying that would be impossible) but that a gentile was not circumcised on the eighth day as prescribed in the Law (Gen 17:12; Lev 12:30). Perhaps as he develops this idea, however, Rodríguez might refer to some evidence for the idea that a law *requiring adult Israelites to circumcise their sons* on the eighth day could be, or ever was, invoked as a bar, or indeed have any relevance, to adult non-Israelites wishing to join Israel and willing to be circumcised to do so. For Rodríguez, then, in Rom 1:18–2:29, Paul is addressing the depraved immoral pagan, in 2:1–16 the elitist moralizing pagan, and in 2:17–29 the gentile proselyte to Judaism. When he comes to Rom 4:1 ("What then? Shall we claim to have found Abraham our forefather according to the flesh?"), Rodríguez interprets this as a natural question, "given that Paul imagines himself to be speaking with a proselyte to Judaism" (90).

In relation to Rom 7, Rodríguez proposes, "Paul imagines himself as addressing a gentile audience that is positively disposed toward Torah" (127). In this context he considers the famous I-voice in Rom 7:7–13 (130–38) that, he argues, continues on to verse 25. This is not Adam's voice, nor is Paul speaking in his authorial voice or as a representative of Israel (133–35). Rather:

Paul has repeatedly raised the specter of a gentile proselyte who has submitted
himself to Torah's authority as a means to achieve self-mastery. Now Paul speaks
as that character [in an example of *prosopoiia*]. ... Paul dons the *persona* of a
gentile who has taken on Torah only to find that, rather than self-mastery, Torah
has led him to a deeper, more vivid awareness of his enslavement to his passions
and desires. (137)

This interpretation allows a fresh interpretation of the difficult words of Rom 7:9:
"I once lived apart from Torah."

Rodríguez explains Paul's unexpectedly positive attitude to Israel expressed
in Rom 9:1–5 on the basis that "this only makes sense if Romans 1–8 has focused
narrowly and exclusively on the *gentiles'* reconciliation with God" (172, emphasis original). Thus he approaches the matter quite differently from those (myself
included) who think that at this point he turns to the vast majority of Israel who
(unlike Judean members of the Christ-movement in Rome) have not turned to
Christ. Paul will argue that God has not abandoned his people Israel in favor of
the gentiles (172). He pursues this view through a detailed examination of Rom
9–11.

When Rodríguez comes to Rom 14–15, with its signs of tension between
the strong (usually thought to have some connection with gentiles) and the weak
(usually thought to have some connection with Jews), Rodríguez invokes his
overall view of a purely gentile "encoded audience," especially here following the
arguments of Andrew Das (in *Solving the Romans Debate* [Minneapolis: Fortress,
2007]) and argues that "Romans does not address the problem of Jewish practices
per se but rather the observance of Jewish practices *by gentiles*" (259, emphasis
original). In relation to the collection, Rodríguez makes this point (290), consistent with his argument overall: "In Rom 15:30–33 we have a genuine appeal for
inter-ethnic unity, as Paul (a Jew) appeals to his readers (gentiles) for their prayers
as he takes an offering from Macedonia and Achaia (more gentiles) to the believers in Judea and Jerusalem (more Jews)."

Rodríguez submits that the "greetings" in Rom 16:3–16 "do not provide an
obstacle to our reconstruction of Paul's audience as thoroughly gentile" (293),
which they might otherwise appear to do since there are some Jews mentioned
in these verses. Following Runar Thorsteinsson, although the idea was initially
expressed by Stanley Stowers and has been ably developed by Andrew Das, he
proposes that the second-person plural form was a form of indirect salutation
whereby Paul asked the actual addressees of his letter to greet other people (i.e.,
not his addressees) on his behalf (293–94).

Two areas call for closing comment. First, at the heart of Rodríguez's argument
is an ambiguity surrounding his "ethnically-gentile-religiously Jewish interlocutor" in Rom 2:17–29 (51) mentioned above. Is this person a Jew (or Judean) or
not? Here Rodríguez's failure to interrogate the nature of the identities in view,
a failure he shares with many in the guild, causes difficulty. He clearly believes
that someone who has been circumcised and adopted other Judean customs

remains ethnically gentile even though "religiously" Jewish. Rodríguez considers a proselyte is only religiously Jewish. He presumably takes this view because of the persistence of the notion that the *Ioudaioi* of our sources were adherents of a religion, Judaism, whereas in fact (whether you call them Jews or Judeans) they were members of an ethnic group (which did include religious beliefs and practices but only as part of a larger, more inclusive identity). Becoming a Jew/Judean through circumcision and adoption of Jewish/Judean customs meant adoption of Jewish/Judean ethnic identity, not the adoption of a separable and separate Jewish religious identity (which was nonexistent in the first century CE just as surely as Judaism is a category error for this period). A statement by Philo dealing with treatment of the proselyte (*prosêluton*) and related to Lev 19:33–34, to which Steve Mason has alerted me, brings out the truth of the matter, that a proselyte transfers from some other ethnic group to the Judean one, with pellucid clarity (*Virt.* 102–103):

> When he (Moses) has made laws concerning fellow members of the *ethnos* (*peri tôn homoethnôn*), he considers that incomers (*epêlutas*) should be considered worthy of every careful concern because they have left behind their blood-relations (*genean tên aph' haimatos*), their homeland (*patrida*), their customs (*ethê*), the sacred rites and the temples, gifts and honours of their gods, and they have undertaken a noble migration (*apoikia*) from mythical inventions to the clarity of the truth and the worship of the one and truly existent God. He directs those from the (Judean) *ethnos* to love the incomers, not only as friends and relatives (*sungeneis*), but as themselves, in body and soul, in physical matters acting in common as far as possible, in matters of understanding, grieving and rejoicing over the same things, so that although divided in parts they seem to be a single living being fitted together, and sharing a common nature (*sumphuêis*) in fellowship (*koinonia*) brought perfectly together.

In consequence, it is questionable whether an interlocutor of the sort postulated by Rodríguez did, or even could, have existed in the first-century CE Mediterranean world.

Second, the lynch pin of Rodríguez's argument, the view that Paul was writing only to gentiles, for which he relies upon creative and impressive arguments advanced by Stowers, Das, and Thorsteinsson, cannot be reconciled with the evidence of Rom 16 within the larger context of the letter. In the greetings section of Rom 16—a chapter conclusively established by Harry Gamble as part of the original letter—Paul sends instructions to greet (*aspasasthe*) twenty-five named Judeans and non-Judeans, and no one disputes that these were all Christ-followers (and we might add Aristobulus in 16:10). An earlier suggestion of mine (*Conflict and Identity in Romans* [2003], 118) that Judeans "may have approached 50%" of the total has been scoffed at by Das (Sol*ving*, 90), but I am unsure why. Even Das (*Solving*, 90–91) has to concede that at least five of the people mentioned in Rom 16 were Judeans (Prisca, Aquila, Andronicus, Junia, and Herodion). For most scholars, this is the end of the story; we have a mixed audience.

But Stowers (*A Rereading of Romans: Justice, Jews, and Gentiles* [New Haven: Yale University Press, 1994], 33) very helpfully brought into the discussion the feature of many ancient letters wherein the author asked the recipient and addressee of the letter to give greetings to a third party (not a recipient or an addressee). Das has also adopted this view (*Solving*, 89–90). Yet it remains highly unlikely for Rom 16. First, it assumes accepting that in Rom 16 Paul has not named a single person for whom he was writing this letter and intending to hear it read, but twenty-five persons, some Judean (even including his close friends Prisca and Aquila) and some non-Judean (the wrong sort of gentile Christ-follower perhaps?), whom he was not addressing. This alone stretches the bounds of credibility. Second, Paul must have done this in spite of the fact that at the outset he had addressed his letter "to all God's beloved in Rome, who are called to be saints" (Rom 1:7), that is, not to one particular person or group of persons of the same type (such as "religiously Jewish" gentiles on Rodríguez's approach), but to every Christ-follower. Putting these two considerations together produces a third factor, that when the twenty-five Judean and non-Judean Christ-followers who are named in it heard about this mammoth letter that had arrived in their city they would have understood, on the Stowers/Das argument, that they were not part of God's beloved in Rome and not called to be saints, for Paul had addressed all such people when he wrote the letter but he had excluded them from his consideration when he did so. In a culture permeated with honor and shame, it is hard to see why Paul would have disgraced them so. These twenty-five Christ-followers were intended recipients of this letter.

Rather than mechanistically applying a feature of Greek letter-writing to Rom 16 (i.e., the assertion that those greeted are nonaddressed third parties), we need to relate the greetings section to the particular circumstances of the letter. First, there is the likelihood that Phoebe (Rom 16:1) was going to carry the letter around the various Christ-movement groups in Rome and that it was appropriate for Paul to name the various people he knew of in each such group as she did so. Yet a second circumstance should also be considered. In the context of a letter where Paul was trying to bring Christ-movement subgroups in conflict together under their superordinate identity in Christ (see my *Conflict and Identity in Romans*), his injunction to greet X and Y went beyond a greeting simply *from him* to them in that it additionally entailed that *they must each be accepting and welcoming of the other*. While this idea would repay further consideration, its prima facie appeal is underlined by the last injunction in the series, "Greet one another with a holy kiss" (Rom 16:16), immediately followed by a warning against people who cause dissension (16:17–20).

Anyone who, like Rafael Rodríguez, spends real time working on Romans learns to appreciate the astonishing richness of its argument and the enormity of the mind that produced it. Nothing in these concluding comments is meant to detract from the creative contribution to Romans research that Rodríguez has made in this book, nor from the stimulation he has provided to fresh engagement with the inexhaustible depths of this Pauline letter.

GENERAL EPISTLES AND HEBREWS

Hebrews, by Mary Ann Beavis and HyeRan Kim-Cragg. Wisdom Commentary 54. Collegeville, MN: Liturgical Press, 2015. Pp. 334. Hardcover. $49.49. ISBN 9780814682043.

Bryan J. Whitfield, Mercer University

With this volume in the Wisdom Commentary series, co-authors Mary Ann Beavis and HyeRan Kim-Cragg ably fill a gap in the feminist interpretation of Hebrews. Although other feminist scholars have provided chapter-length treatments, until now there has been no comparable book-length commentary. These authors argue that Hebrews is "a submerged tradition of Sophia" (203) and seek to demonstrate that its foundations lie in Jewish wisdom literature (especially the book of Wisdom). They aim to recover the implications of that tradition for the appreciation and critique of Hebrews.

In keeping with the goals of the series, the volume engages feminist voices from various social locations. The two lead authors are Beavis, a Canadian biblical scholar, and Kim-Cragg, a Korean-Canadian practical/pastoral theologian with expertise in the theology of worship and religious education. Other contributing authors include two Filipina biblical scholars, Ma. Maricel Ibita and Ma. Marilou Ibita, and three other Canadians: Jewish studies scholar Justin Jaron Lewis, First Nations poet Marie Annharte Bake, and biblical scholar Nancy Calvert Koyzis. As lead co-authors, Beavis and Kim-Cragg have written the main text, while all seven authors provide text boxes, sidebars, and interpretive essays that are interspersed throughout. These additions allow the authors to explore various perspectives on the text and give their work a multilayered, almost talmudic feel. At times this device places disagreements between the authors in the foreground. Beavis, for example, supports the NRSV's inclusive-language translation for Heb 2:6–7 (which is quoting Ps 8:4–8), while Lewis argues that the NRSV's language obscures both the meaning of the psalm quotation and the midrashic interpretation of it that the author of Hebrews develops (21).

The authors' introduction lays out their approach to Hebrews and surveys traditional matters of introduction. They review the authorship of Hebrews, giving particular attention to the case made for Priscilla. In the end they find no unequivocal evidence for any specific author but advance the hypothesis of collective authorship based on the use of the authorial "we" and the parallel to co-sponsored Pauline letters (lviii–lxii). Concluding that 1 Clement, which they date to 96 CE, uses Hebrews as a source, they assign that date as a *terminus ad quem* for Hebrews. but they do not take a position on whether it should be dated before or after the fall of the temple (lxii–lxiii). They conclude that Heb 13:24 is evidence for a Roman destination (lxiv–lxv), and they stress the homily's connections with Hellenistic Judaism, especially that of Alexandria, concluding that a Platonic worldview shapes the writing (lxvii). Viewing the audience as a congregation made up of both Jews and gentiles, they locate the genre of Hebrews as a homily or homiletical midrash and outline the homily as an alternation of scriptural exposition and exhortation (lxviii–lxxii). They then review eight major interlocking themes of Hebrews: the pilgrimage of faith, the persistence of faith, the perfecter of faith, the high priesthood of Christ, the earthly servant Christ, sacrifice and atonement, covenant, and true worship (lxxii–lxxxiv).

The authors structure the body of the commentary in six sections (Heb 1–2; 3–4; 5–7; 8:1–10:18; 10:19–12:29; and 13:1–25). In keeping with the approach of the series, the authors treat the entire text of Hebrews in blocks of material rather than providing a verse-by-verse analysis. That approach strengthens attention to the rhetorical shape of the writing as a whole and enables readers to grasp the flow of the argument of Hebrews easily. The authors bypass more technical issues, although they often stress intertextual allusions and echoes. In the place of more specialized discussion, they give voice to the intersecting issues of gender, power, class, and ethnicity that the text and the world in front of the text raise (xvii).

In their treatment of Heb 1–2, for example, the authors explore the hymnic nature of the prologue (1:1–4) but note the problem the language of sonship and inheritance poses for feminist readers, a concern they counterbalance with the story of the daughters of Zelophehad, the only explicit discussion of inheritance rights in the Torah (3). They point to the ambiguity of Heb 1:5, where the verb translated "begotten" may also be translated "gave birth to" (9–10) and argue for a reading of 1:6a ("when he brings the firstborn into the world") that images "God in the role of mother or midwife in the context of royal adoption" (10). But most significantly, they find the homilist's opening argument grounded in the biblical creation account, "especially as filtered through the Wisdom tradition" (23). Several sidebars enrich the main text: Beavis's discussions of the proto-feminist Katherine Bushnell and Lewis's Jewish perspective in particular. The chapter also includes two pieces from Annharte (out of a total of thirteen, one for each chapter of Hebrews), poems of traditional sacred stories of the First Nations that provide a postcolonial critique and counterpoint to the other voices.

The remaining chapters unfold in a similar pattern. Alongside their exposition of the text, the authors discuss rabbinic traditions about the wilderness generation and the gendered traditions surrounding the New Moon festival, and Kim-Cragg provides a sidebar discussion of a similar Korean women's ritual, Ganggangsullae. The authors underscore the parallels between Wis 7:22–26, 30 and Heb 4:12–13, both texts that feature the penetrating activity of the word or of wisdom. Lewis explores the midrashic technique of *gezerah shavah* in Heb 4:1–16 (46–47). Beavis and Kim-Cragg argue that the discussion of priesthood in Heb 5–7 constitutes the final groundwork for the subsequent chapters. They note that the focus on Jesus's suffering (5:8) may lead to problematic interpretations supporting abuse or oppression (55–56), and they judge the author's rhetoric in 5:11–6:12 to be coercive and manipulative (63–64).

The discussion of Heb 8:1–10:18 develops the central theme of the new covenant, grounded in Davidic covenant with its unconditional promises. But the authors warn that interpreters must repudiate attempts to use this text in the service of anti-Judaism. They explore the reverence for the tabernacle in Jewish tradition, noting the role of women in its construction (88–90), then summarize the argument of Hebrews regarding the contrast of Christ's sacrifice with earthly rituals in the tabernacle. The chapter closes with an interpretive essay by Kim-Cragg that explores cross-cultural, postcolonial, and ecological perspectives on blood and sacrifice (100–107) and a final essay by Ma. Maricel Ibita that critiques and reappropriates the idea of "Christ's sacrifice once for all" from a feminist perspective (108–22).

In their discussion of the subsequent paraenetic section, the authors stress the text's focus on the faithful endurance of God's people (123). But here, as in their discussion of Heb 6:1–12, they critique the homilist for abusive rhetoric. A call to endurance can trivialize oppression and lead to a distorted perspective on suffering, especially for women, as Kim-Cragg makes clear in her study of this issue in Korean feminist theology (131–34). More positively, the authors' treatment of Heb 11 stresses the role of women in the list of scriptural heroes. In particular, the authors highlight the translation of 11:11, arguing that Sarah, not Abraham, should be understood as the subject (143–45). But they also note postcolonial scholars' critique of the conquest of Canaan and of the valorization of Rahab (150–53). The images of God as a father enacting painful discipline on his children (12:4–13) and the threatening exhortation of Heb 12:25–29 that "undermines the celestial vision of the heavenly Zion" (162–68) also prove problematic for feminist readers.

In their discussion of the final exhortations in Heb 13, the authors highlight the role of hospitality (13:2) and the implications of the fluidity of the pronouns in the concluding verses for the question of authorship (184–88). The volume then concludes with Ma. Marilou Ibita's essay that reveals the dynamic of women providing hospitality and at the same time needing hospitality, a dynamic she finds in both the biblical narratives and in the lives of Filipina domestic workers today (189–201).

The clarity of the exposition and the inclusion of diverse voices prove positive contributions of this commentary, but this treatment of Hebrews is not without its limitations. Some discussions, such as the connection of baptism to Heb 1:5–7, appear only loosely connected to the larger argument. The authors engage most major English-language commentaries on Hebrews, but there are some puzzling omissions, including the volumes of William Lane and Luke Timothy Johnson. Equally puzzling is the lack of engagement with the substantive work of female scholars on Hebrews, including Gabriella Gelardini, Ellen Bradshaw Aitken, and Amy L. Peeler.

These weaknesses aside, with this volume Beavis and Kim-Cragg and their collaborators clearly advance the state of feminist scholarship on Hebrews. Their focus on connections between Hebrews and the book of Wisdom, their willingness to reconfigure our understandings of sacrifice, and their model of collaborative scholarship all hold promise for further work on this "word of exhortation."

Written To Serve: The Use of Scripture in 1 Peter, by Benjamin Sargent. Library of New Testament Studies 547. London: Bloomsbury, 2015. Pp. x + 225. Hardcover. $120.00. ISBN 9780567660855.

Abson Joseph, Indiana Wesleyan University

In *Written to Serve* Benjamin Sargent seeks to offer a corrective to what he views as a lacuna in recent research on 1 Peter: "no study has yet attempted to offer a definition of 1 Peter's general approach to Scripture" (2). Sargent surveys key contributors in the scholarship on 1 Peter's use of Scripture, then uses William Schutter's work as a starting point to shed additional light on the matter. He endeavors to accomplish his goal by answering several key questions: "How might the biblical hermeneutic or hermeneutics of the epistle be characterized?" "How does the apparent scriptural hermeneutic of 1.10–12 relate to the use of Scripture in the epistle?" "Where does Peter's use of Scripture come from?" "What exegetical culture does 1 Peter operate within?" "What are the implications of Peter's use of Scripture for contemporary biblical scholarship?" (2–3). He uses the introduction to offer preliminary answers to these questions and to provide an overview of the study as a whole.

In chapter 1, "1 Peter 1.10–12: A Hermeneutical Statement?," Sargent undertakes a detailed study of the statement to provide "a new understanding of its significance for the use of Scripture in the epistle" (18). Sargent argues against the view espoused by many recent studies in 1 Peter and advances that the theological narrative alluded here is one of discontinuity. He identifies a Petrine theory of Scripture that views prophetic utterances as being concerned to one time or circumstance in particular that lies beyond the prophets' own reality. In other words, Scripture is seen as oriented exclusively toward the audience that received the epistle (19–21, 30, 33). He proposes that "Scripture ought to be heard as directly addressing the situation of the communities, just as Peter assumes in practice in the epistle" (48).

Chapter 2 focuses on "Formal Citation of Scripture in 1 Peter." Sargent discusses several approaches to what constitutes a citation or quotation. He highlights the complexity in determining the nature of a citation and favors the reader-response approach that locates the validity of a citation primarily in whether or not the audience recognized a quotation from Scripture as such and the extent to which a quotation disrupts the flow of the narrative and stands out as an appeal to a higher authority (52–54). Thus Sargent is able to identify eleven citations in 1 Peter. He analyzes each citation in detail, discussing the source, form, and function in 1 Peter. He engages relevant scholarship on each passage and considers the view that the principal hermeneutical idea of 1 Pet 1:10–12 is christological in nature as inadequate vis-à-vis how Scripture is interpreted in the letter. He acknowledges that 1 Peter does have a christological or kerygmatic interest but argues that it is more significant to view 1 Pet 1:10–12 as establishing an understanding of Scripture that is both kerygmatic and paraenetic (98–99; see also 29).

In chapter 3, "Allusion to Scripture in 1 Peter," Sargent uses some of Michael Thompson's criteria for identifying allusions, both acknowledging the hypothetical and speculative nature of that process and the difficulty in assessing textual allusions and explaining the reason to study the quotations and allusions separately (100–101). He makes a distinction between the numerous possible allusions to *texts* present in 1 Peter and the two allusions to *events*: the flood and Sarah's obedience. Sargent interacts with the recent scholarship on 1 Peter in the process and uses his discussion to reinforce further his claim that "Peter has no concerns relating what texts may have meant to Israel in the past: they are exclusively oriented towards the suffering and glories of Christ and the service of the communities" (100).

Chapter 4, "The Exegetical Background to the Use of Scripture in 1 Peter," locates the use of Scripture in 1 Peter within the "cultural milieu of sectarian Jewish apocalyptic" (147). Sargent surveys the scholarship on 1 Peter that explores the relationship between the epistle and Qumran literature highlighting the hermeneutical similarities between the two (148–56). These similarities include: "a common sectarian matrix," "the use of internal interpretation: where Scripture is explained from the perspective of someone who inhabits the text and speaks with its voice," and "the relation between biblical material and the communities for which it is interpreted" (160–61). For Sargent, Peter's hermeneutic is both sectarian and primitive. He concludes the chapter with an excursus surveying the discussion on the authorship of the letter, only to suggest that the study has nothing to add to the discussions. However, he argues that the internal evidence strongly suggests dating the epistle within the first decades of the Christian church (168).

In chapter 5, "1 Peter and Theological Interpretation of Scripture," Sargent discusses the implications of the determinate meaning of Scripture in 1 Peter he proposes. He highlights and critiques the works of I. Howard Marshall, Francis Watson, and Joel B. Green, among others, in their attempts to relate Peter's use of Scripture to a contemporary biblical hermeneutic. He acknowledges the contributions of their research and pushes back against the notions that suggest that Peter's use of Scripture is characterized by anything other than determinacy (172–77). Sargent goes on to discuss the nature, role, and use of determinate meaning in the history of interpretation and in contemporary discussion on hermeneutic. He acknowledges the difficulties and challenges in applying the approach to determinate meaning that he identifies in 1 Peter to a contemporary approach to Scripture (186). However, he hopes that its use in 1 Peter may contribute to a theological understanding that frees the concept from its negative association with historical criticism and that biblical scholars and theologians may still find it instructive.

Sargent's treatment is crafted well. He exhibits dexterity in bringing together key conversation partners and demonstrates awareness of past and current scholarship on the use of Scripture in 1 Peter. He engages other scholars critically and shapes his argument carefully. His definition and extensive treatment of the quotations and allusions are helpful contributions. He is aware of the potential areas of weakness in his argument and attempts to address them. He has succeeded in his endeavor to offer a detailed study of the use of Scripture in 1 Peter.

Sargent's desired contribution to the scholarship of 1 Peter is also the main area of concern and weakness of this project. He is aware of this predicament, as is attested by the questions he raises in the conclusion (194). Sargent's main argument, which he reiterates throughout, is that Peter views Scripture as having a single meaning and that meaning applies solely and exclusively to a single group, to the Christian communities he is addressing (4). Further, there is no continuity between Israel and Peter's audience. Sargent is correct in highlighting Peter's focus on Scripture's meaning for his audience, but he overstates his case by pushing for an exclusive/determinate meaning in Peter's use of Scripture. How can Peter adequately relate the meaning of a text without understanding its original implications?

Sargent describes Peter's hermeneutic as primitive. He questions the depth of knowledge and/or understanding of the Old Testament Peter's audience possess (56). He questions Peter's knowledge of the same (63–64, 135). He goes so far as to argue that Peter lacks the exegetical sophistication attested in Hebrews, the Acts of the Apostles, and Paul (5, 8, 68, 118, 163, 177). He is ambivalent but crafts his argument in a way that creates reasonable doubt on these issues (62–63). Sargent clarifies that his description of 1 Peter is not intended to be derogatory, but one wonders if it is not at least prejudicial. If Peter and Paul share this "primitive and sectarian" approach, on what bases is Peter more primitive? Sargent needs to do more to establish why Peter lacks the knowledge or/and exegetical sophistication exhibited by Paul, Hebrews, and others.

Further, Sargent builds much of his case against the notion of continuity and against Peter's awareness of the meaning of Scripture for Israel on arguments from silence. Sargent's engagements with other scholars and/or with the text often ends with his claim that there is no evidence or there is no way to say for certain that Peter had this or that in mind, or that his audience would understand (41, 56, 62–63, 101). For example, he raises the question: "How can we be sure that the possible allusions detected by scholars today really were read or heard as such in the first century" (101). However, the same question can be asked of Sargent: How can we be sure they were not?

Lastly, one wonders the extent to which Sargent's agenda to free *determinacy* from the negative association with historical criticism has affected his study of 1 Peter. It would have been more helpful to this study if Sargent had focused on the implications of the limitations of determinacy of Scripture and its application in contemporary hermeneutics rather than simply raising the questions.

Repetition in Hebrews: Plurality and Singularity in the Letter to the Hebrews, Its Ancient Context, and the Early Church, by Nicholas Moore. Wissenschaftliche Untersuchungen zum Neuen Testament 2/388. Tübingen: Mohr Siebeck, 2015. Pp. xiii + 276. Paper. €84.00. ISBN 9783161538520.

Amy Peeler, Wheaton College

Nicholas J. Moore's revision of his University of Oxford doctoral dissertation argues a simple point: repetition in the Epistle to the Hebrews is not a "uniform theme" (209); rather, "Christ's one-off sacrifice is determinative for the particular construal of repetition in any given case" (116). The simplicity of Moore's focus allows him to achieve wide-ranging ends, making contributions to church history, ecclesiology, and the exegesis of Hebrews.

Hebrews has often played a role in debates about repetition and ritual in the church, and Moore captures his readers at the beginning of his work by analyzing the longstanding and widespread assumption that the author of Hebrews roundly disapproved of "vain repetitions." Many have previously seen Hebrews uniformly arguing that repetition is ineffective and associated with earth (as opposed to heaven) or the old covenant (as opposed to the new). Because Moore wants to argue against these assumptions, he clarifies the scope and meaning of repetition. First, utilizing the work of Mary Douglas and Catherine Bell, he clarifies that repetition is not the same as ritual; second, he argues that Hebrews' interest in repetition centers on efficacy. Moore then charts the efficacy of repetition on a five-point scale from situations where repetition can annul efficacy to instances where repetition can create efficacy. This differentiation will allow him to clarify Hebrews' various approaches to repetition.

Before Moore focuses on Hebrews, however, he sketches the plausible historical limits of the letter and analyzes four streams with which "an educated first-century Hellenistic Jew" would have been familiar (the Old Testament, Jubilees and Qumran, Middle Platonism as represented by Philo and Plutarch, and early Christianity) and their various approaches to repetition, uniqueness, plurality, singularity, and totality. Moore argues that Hebrews' "thought on repetition" is unique in its historical setting; however, it seems the same could be said about any Second Temple document if enough aspects of repetition were considered. This historical context does, however, prepare the reader to appreciate the nuance with which Hebrews treats the theme.

Chapter 3 moves to texts that come after Hebrews to investigate "the origins of a negative reception of repetition" (67), by treating Christian response to repeated repentance, baptism, and sacrifices. The sources treated here support the first part of Moore's thesis: these early Christian writers, like Hebrews, do not view repetition solely as negative. When they do speak against repetition, it is because the repetition compromises the singularity "associated with crucifixion, repentance, and baptism." Hence, these authors reflect positively on "the singularity of the Christ event and its application to ongoing Christian practice" (88). Moore's choice to place this chapter before his exegetical ones allows the focus to remain on Hebrews alone in the second half of the book, but readers might be better able to appreciate the moves made in the early Christian writers after having thought about Hebrews' treatment of repetition.

Analysis of repetition in Hebrews then follows in three movements: revelation (ch. 4), repentance (ch. 5), and ritual (ch. 6). Like other commentators before him, Moore argues that the author of Hebrews intends no stark contrast between the prophets and Christ. Instead, the prophets' words prepare for and are brought to fulfillment in Christ; moreover, God repeats (!) their words in the new covenant. Moore proceeds to argue that the very plurality of the message "is fundamental to enabling the audience to comprehend the full magnitude of the Son's character and achievements" (105). Hebrews creates diversity in the text it reads, especially chronological difference in Pss 8 and 95 to show their culmination in the Son. One wonders, however, if Moore's argument falls prey to thematic slippage here—the introduction of plurality in the textual quotations does not seem quite the same as repetition. Nevertheless, the point stands with regard to revelation that Hebrews has a positive view of repetition, which is integral to the form of this early sermon.

Hebrews holds quite the opposite opinion with regard to repentance. In chapter 5 Moore treats the warning passages in Hebrews and concludes that this New Testament author believes genuine Christians can apostatize either through ongoing sin or a single act of rejection; if they do, repentance is unrepeatable. Moore refrains from softening Hebrews' message here by suggesting ways this stringency fits with the rest of the canon, although he showed in the third chapter how some church fathers made this move. In light of such serious consequences, repeated listening to the word of God becomes all the more necessary.

It is not only the repetition of the word that Hebrews encourages but sacrifices as well. In other words, Moore reads Hebrews as being largely positive concerning ritual, but in order to argue that point Moore first must show how the author of Hebrews holds up the singular uniqueness of the priesthood and sacrifice of Christ. For the two sections of this chapter (priesthood and sacrifice), Moore initially establishes the argument that the author of Hebrews is operating with a vision of an actual heavenly cult. With that in view, Moore shows that Christ's priesthood is both ontologically and epistemologically prior to the Levitical priests. He exists before them, and when he inaugurates his priestly service, he shows their system to be ineffective. The problem with them is not simply their plurality, but their plurality reveals they are subject to the weakness of death and therefore cannot solve humanity's problem of mortality.

Similarly, the difference between the offering of Christ and the blood of animals is not simply that Christ's is singular and the others multiple, but animals cannot be willing or obedient and therefore cannot be perfect, whereas Christ "in his perfect obedience becomes the perfect sacrifice" (175). Moore arrives then at a summative point: "Repetition gains negative connotations and is used rhetorically to great effect only in contrast to Christ—the uniqueness of his priesthood and the singularity of his sacrifice" (178). In the final part of the chapter, he makes a convincing argument that Hebrews uses the phrase διὰ παντός as a way to refer to the *tamid*, the daily sacrifice. The author calls his community to offer regular sacrifices of praise "on the basis of the reality and accessibility of the heavenly cult" (204).

The concluding chapter returns to Moore's chart of efficacy to discover that Hebrews largely treats repetition positively or at least neutrally, as evidence that the familiar view of Hebrews and repetition presented referenced at the beginning of the monograph was incorrect. With regard to the exceptions to the largely positive rule—repetition of basic teaching and repentance—when Hebrews views repetition negatively, it does so because "Hebrews is not out to denigrate repetition but to promote the excellency of Christ" (211).

In closing, Moore engages with Kirkegaard's notion of repetition to highlight the unimaginable gift nature of the second covenant and the attitude of openness to it that the readers should cultivate. Finally, Moore closes with some implications from his study: historically it shows more distance than proximity between Platonism and Hebrews and suggests a post-70 date; theologically, it can be used to support the ongoing ritual practices of the church.

Despite a few qualms with overstatement or arrangement mentioned above, I find *Hebrews and Repetition* to be a thought-provoking and valuable work. Moore is especially helpful in demonstrating Hebrews' appreciation of the Old Testament cult. For example, in his analysis of Heb 9:6–8, the inaccessibility of the holy of holies stands in contrast to the continual accessibility of the outer tent (180). He draws out the logic: "if an entrance once a year represents restricted access, then an entrance once-for-all surely means *even less* access" (184, emphasis original). The description of both parts of the tabernacle indicates that the author seeks to compare more than just the Yom Kippur offering and Christ's offering. The author is describing, not denigrating, the sacrifices, because he then goes on to use the daily sacrifice as an example of the continual prayer he urges his audience to practice. Hebrews' disagreement with the Levitical sacrifices lies not in their repetition but in their innate inadequacy, in light of the sacrifice of Christ. On the other hand, the example of their continual access to God can and should be replicated by the present New Covenant community.

Repetition in Hebrews masterfully elucidates this key theme in the letter. With clear, witty prose, interdisciplinary engagement, and thorough conversation with primary and secondary literature, Moore has corrected a widespread but incorrect assumption about Hebrews and its view of repetition.

James: Diaspora Rhetoric of a Friend of God, by Margaret Aymer. Phoenix Guides to the New Testament 17. Sheffield: Sheffield Phoenix, 2015. Pp. ix + 86. Paper. $19.95. ISBN 9781909697607.

Carla Swafford Works, Wesley Theological Seminary

In this succinct guide to James, Margaret Aymer, formerly of the Interdenominational Theological Center but now at Austin Presbyterian Seminary, seeks to rescue James from lingering perceptions that the epistle is devoid of theology or that it is only concerned with general paraenesis (35). In contrast to Martin Luther's characterization of James as "a right strawy epistle" or to Dibelius's assertation that James "has no theology at all," Aymer proposes reading James as "a theological writing that weaves together theology and praxis of a community into a homiletic epistle that is not so much an explanation of Christianity for outsiders as it is a guide to Christian communal life for insiders" (36). Aymer interprets the epistle as "an ancient encyclical" that serves as a call to action for a migrant people. In doing so, she takes seriously the audience's setting in the "diaspora" (Jas 1:1) and emphasizes the social and cultural power dynamics and perils faced by the audience and navigated by the epistle's author.

As part of the Phoenix Guides to the New Testament, the volume succeeds in offering an overview of the epistle's content as well as a brief survey of the history of interpretation, questions about its authorship, and considerations about the audience, but this book does so much more than give an overview. Aymer makes the text come alive in its context by placing a spotlight on an audience who would struggle to live faithfully in the midst of a "host community" (66). Furthermore, Aymer draws implications for those who read this first-century diaspora rhetoric as scripture today by asking, "What happens when contemporary Christians, reading this ancient migrant writing, adopt this migrant stance as the lens through which they interpret their world?" (2).

The book is arranged in five chapters with a brief introduction to the volume. Chapter 1, "Questions of Identity," provides a clear overview of the discussions and key concerns regarding authorship, the history of the epistle's acceptance in the church, the possible time of its writing, and the issue of genre. After weighing the evidence, Aymer sides with church tradition that links authorship to James the brother of the Lord Jesus. Chapter 2, "Listening to James," argues that the epistle does have a structure, not the structure of a letter, but of an ancient speech (19). Aymer shows the benefit of reading James as a community would have heard it read out loud. She takes the reader through the sections of this speech and emphasizes the rhetorical flair that is often missed when reading the text silently. Instead, she allows us to see James as a "wordsmith" who plays with words, uses stylistic repetition, and links the text with alliteration (21). The benefit of listening to the text is also the hearing the connection of larger themes that weave throughout the letter. Themes of justice, endurance, action, freedom, and true religion draw the speech together (22–23), and these are introduced in the beginning of the letter. Aymer then works closely with the Greek as she "hears" the rest of the epistle, demonstrating the advantages of listening to this text as a speech. The end result is reading James as a "tightly constructed homily with themes that overlap" (30).

The final three chapters of the book focus on Aymer's interpretation of this epistle as a theological exhortation to a people of faith who live in another culture, a world that has competing systems of justice and power. Chapter 3, "That True Religion: Theology and Ethics of James," reveals the theological core that supports the epistle's call to action. The chapter considers the praxis of faith in light of

James's many metaphors of God and near silence regarding Jesus (36-43). Aymer raises questions about the relationship of faith to James's eschatological vision, a vision that gives rise both to hope and to warnings for the community of faith. This chapter establishes the connection between James's theology and his exhortation for the believers to live out their faith.

In chapter 4, "James and Kyriarchy," Aymer considers James's instruction in light of the power dynamics of the audience's culture. According to Aymer, the message of James both offers critique to the kyriarchy of his culture, especially concerning matters of class and economics, and reflects and preserves some of the cultural norms, particularly surrounding gender and sex. In consideration of the community's prejudice against the poor, Aymer writes, "James goes beyond naming these poorest of the poor 'honorable', he argues that God has chosen these destitute women and men to be models of the kind of faithfulness that clients typically show their patrons. These poorest of the poor are, according to James, heirs of God's own kingdom (2.5)" (54). James casts a vision of an alternative kingdom in which Jesus, not Caesar, is Lord (60–65).

Finally, in the last chapter, "James as Migrant Writing," Aymer argues that James's audience is constantly navigating two cultures: their home culture and their host culture. By "migrant writing," Aymer means "a text that purports to be written to, for, or by migrants; it gives some counsel regarding how those migrants might interact with their home and host cultures" (66). The epistle provides for this first-century audience a "particular migrant strategy for dealing with a host community" (66). In this regard, the letter itself, Aymer proposes, is "a kind of diaspora space, where cultures collide and commingle and where tradition is invented" (66). Taking seriously the liminal status of migrants who experience disassociation both from their home culture and their host culture, Aymer shows how James navigates the tension between "the world," a place where the poor are abused and the rich receive preferential treatment, and the "kingdom," where the impoverished will be enriched and justice will reign (70). At the end of this chapter, Aymer draws implications for those who claim James as a sacred text: "for Christians, who enter into a scriptural relationship with James, this epistle affects their identity, their understanding of the nature of God and their relationship to God, as well as how they ought to live" (78). How they ought to live, Aymer has argued, can be summed up quite nicely by Jas 2:17: faith without works is dead.

This volume provides an excellent overview of James and restores a reading of this letter that weds theology and praxis for the concerns of real communities who are navigating a world that is not their own. Aymer demonstrates the benefit of probing into the life of the intended audience, even when that audience is not given a specific location by the author. She has shown how reading James as "diaspora rhetoric" helps us hear this epistle as a call to practice faith in a world of competing values. The attention given to the theology of the letter and to its structure provides a well-balanced counterargument to the lingering perceptions of James as an unstructured set of exhortations with little to no theology.

Although Aymer corrects Luther's influence in some ways, this book perpetuates the sharp dichotomy between Paul and James. Aymer professes the desire to read James for James, without the baggage of comparison (36). This is a laudable goal. However, again and again she includes brief comparisons intended to show how the Pauline epistles differ from the Epistle of James (23–24, 26, 36, 47, 71). The comparisons often make assertions about all Paul's letters with little concern for the context of each writing. For example, in the comparison of the hierarchy of leadership between James's community and Paul's churches, Aymer cites the leadership titles of the Pastoral Epistles as the offices that would be common to all Paul's churches (47). She groups all the Pauline epistles together as missives written to teach "theological tenets" to so-called "outsiders" (36), whereas James, Aymer claims, is concerned for insiders to live out their faith. To Aymer, this difference represents the diversity of the early church at the time that James was written (26). By portraying Paul as interested only in teaching theological components of the faith and not in praxis (36), however, she neglects to see the parallels with Paul's letters, which she also deems as "migrant writings" (66–67), as missives that wed theology and ethics. Notwithstanding, Aymer's reading of James is thought-provoking. This volume will be an excellent addition to a textbook list for seminarians and graduate students, but it is also accessible to the pastor who wants to linger longer in the study of the Word.

James, 1 and 2 Peter, and Early Jesus Traditions, edited by John S. Kloppenborg and Alicia J. Batten. Library of New Testament Studies 478. London: Bloomsbury, 2014. Pp. xx + 234. Hardcover. $112.00. ISBN 9780567420534.

Pheme Perkins, Boston College

A selection of the seminar papers offered in different years to the SBL section on 1–2 Peter and James will inevitably be somewhat disconnected, even though the volume editors made their selection based on the broad topic of "Jesus traditions" employed where one least expects them. Given Professor Kloppenborg's long-standing interest in the redaction of the sayings source Q and its early sociohistorical context, one might expect all nine essays in this volume, five on James and two each on 1 Peter and 2 Peter, to equate "early Jesus traditions" with Q. But in fact the authors take divergent positions on that question as it relates to these writings. For the two essays on 2 Peter, "early Jesus traditions" means the extent to which its author knows the Gospels of Matthew and John. Watson on 1 Peter dismisses any direct dependence on Q or Matthew in favor of a more diffuse set of commonly known traditions about Jesus's teaching and passion. Horrell's treatment of 1 Pet 2:21–25 suggests that this sort of early Jesus tradition has been "scripturalized" by clear allusions to Isa 53.

That leaves James, a work that mentions Jesus Christ only twice (1:1; 2:1), neither clearly tied to any tradition about Jesus at all, to bear the weight of investigating whether or not one can find traces of Q absent dependence on Matthew and Luke. If that thesis could be argued with a reasonable degree of probability, then it would bolster the case for a "Q gospel" circulating widely enough to be treated as an independent entity. The editors admit in their joint introduction that one cannot demonstrate a dependence on Q as reconstructed from Matthew and Luke. The best one could hope for is to detect the presence of some more developed form of Q. Paul Foster's essay takes on that challenge directly but reaches the conclusion that our evidence does not provide unambiguous support for the hypothesis. Patrick Hartin's piece can only argue for it by drawing back to a broader perspective, arguing that James has enlarged a concept of "wholeness" that is found in Q. Similarly Alicia Batten presumes that echoes of Jesus tradition are Q but demonstrates that James has a sophisticated, "urbanized" philosophical recasting of its material. David Kaden presents a comparable analysis with a more detailed comparison to Stoic sources. Finally, the most challenging of the papers on James by Dale Allison outlines the elephant in the room: Can we even assume that the audience of James recognized any of this material as "Jesus tradition" rather than a more generic wisdom collection?

Not surprisingly, the editors' introduction defaults to such broader language as studying how Judean and Greco-Roman influences shaped or shared Jesus tradition as it was remembered. Or that in discussing Jesus traditions one need not focus on the earliest Jesus material. One has much to learn from these often neglected writings from the end of the first- or early second-century texts as well. Each of the three epistles has recrafted its material in ways that reflect a distinctive understanding of piety appropriate to the shifting socioeconomic location of its audience. The various strategies employed by their authors to render an inherited tradition relevant to new audiences provide additional insight into the rich diversity of the early Christian movement.

Chapter 1, by Paul Foster, "Q and James: A Source-Critical Conundrum," engages the question of whether or not James has employed Q head on, listing the data at its fullest in table 1. The reader immediately sees that all twenty-four examples have some link to Matt 5–7 or its Q versions. After a brief survey of key moments in prior scholarship on Jesus tradition in James beginning with Mayor's 1892 commentary to demonstrate that there is no consensus position to account for the phenomenon, Foster analyzes the Greek text of the eight most striking examples in detail. He concludes that, while one can discern a clear interest in some form of Jesus's sermon, the parallels are admittedly not very exact. It is entirely possible that James is aware of Matthew and perhaps even Luke. The fact that his material can all be associated with Jesus's sermon makes haphazard selection from a more diffuse mass of remembered Jesus sayings unlikely. However, one cannot reach any definite conclusions about the source from which James takes its material.

In chapter 2, "Wholeness in James and the Q Source," Patrick Hartin shifts to a much less precise methodology for treating the James and Q question. Comparing "big picture" theological concepts in which Hartin also relies on generalizations about Jewish monotheism and specious comparisons between an alleged Jewish view in which God is the origin of both good and evil, while James stresses the essential goodness of God, is highly problematic. Nor do the similarities alleged between James and Q carry much force, given the lack of specific linguistic ties between the two. "Wholeness" or "single-heartedness" and "perfection" is certainly an important ethical value in James. Perhaps exploration of its roots in Jewish traditions that also stem from a comparable intellectual milieu would provide the bridge that Hartin's thesis requires. Absent that, he must default to asserting that, although Q does not use the language, it has the same concept. But such assertions do not support the assertion that Q and James are from "a similar framework or milieu" in any but the vaguest sense.

Dale Allison's "The Audience of James and the Sayings of Jesus" (ch. 3) puts the question of how or even if an audience would perceive the material that we identify as "Jesus traditions" to be such. He adopts earlier suggestions by John Kloppenborg that it is possible to understand James as employing the rhetorical tactic of *aemulatio*, recasting an earlier tradition in one's own words. This rhetorical practice requires an audience capable of discerning the intertext being paraphrased. Allison points to Jas 3:7–9 and its obvious allusions to Gen 1 without precise verbal correspondences as further evidence for *aemulatio* in James. From this perspective as well as his conviction that James belongs in the early second century, Allison concludes that it may well know Matthew and even Luke. He ventures further in explaining why there is not a more direct mention of Jesus in relationship to this material positing that James envisaged an audience that embraced Jews in the diaspora who were not Christians.

Chapter 4, Alicia Batten's "The Urbanization of Jesus Traditions in James," and chapter 5, David A. Kaden's "Stoicism, Social Stratification, and the Q Tradition in James: A Suggestion about James' Audience," both extend the discussion of the actual or implied audience to an urban world in which both rhetorical and philosophical topoi were the intellectual currency of the day. Focusing on examples in Jas 4 and 5, Batten detects the presence of a common trope that contrasted all the evils of urban life and its competitive violence that crushes the poor with the rustic virtues or the countryside. She also concurs with scholars who detect examples of Stoic psychagogy in James. David Kaden, a student of Kloppenborg's, develops the Stoic thesis in more detail with the added twist of drawing on some comparable material in *Hermas* that James's diaspora is early second-century Rome. His argument is problematic in its presentation of Epictetus as the Stoic in question and then suggesting that one draw a socioeconomic profile for James that incorporates Epictetus.

Both chapters on 1 Peter provide important methodological insights into how the picture of Jesus is reshaped as it is being remembered among Christians a generation later. In "Jesus Remembered in 1 Peter? Early Jesus Traditions, Isaiah 53, and 1 Peter 2.21-25," David Horrell suggests that his example has some relevance to the larger debates over "historical Jesus" or "remembered Jesus" that necessarily incorporates Christology. He then presents a very compelling case that the treatment of Jesus's suffering in 1 Pet 2:21–25 incorporates into the memory of

Jesus's passion echoes of Isa 53 that are not part of the gospel narratives. In chapter 7, "Early Jesus Tradition in 1 Peter 3.18–22," Duane Watson tackles the web of Jewish traditions behind this passage. In addition to Isa 53, he lays out the recasting of Gen 6–8 especially as represented in 1 En. 6–16 apparent in verses 19-21. So far many scholars would agree. However, Watson presses the "early button" by positing that Enoch material would only have been known in Aramaic-speaking Judea in the first century, dating its other canonical witnesses Jude (55–60 CE) in that setting, 2 Peter (80–90 CE) in Rome, and consequently 1 Peter to Peter or circles around him that knew the Judean material.

In "The Gospels of Matthew and John in the Second Letter of Peter," Terrance Callan adopts the general dating of 2 Peter to the second century (125 CE). He takes on objections against reliance on Matthew for the transfiguration allusion in 2 Pet 1:16–18 and compares its free use of Matthew with the same flexibility in its use of Jude and of Gen 6. An apparent echo of John 21:18 in 2 Pet 1:14 leads him to explore other echoes of the Fourth Gospel. Though it seems rather distant, Callan hears John 15:1–17 in 2 Pet 1:3–11. The final chapter, "The Testimony of Peter: 2 Peter and the Gospel Traditions," by Gene Green, incorporates another methodological perspective, epistemology, to highlight the relationship between testimony and knowledge. Testimony requires witnesses who are also involved in and offering interpretation about events. Ancient rhetorical theory concurs in its understanding of testimony. Green concludes by applying this fuller picture of testimony and witness to the Petrine self-presentation in 2 Pet 1.

Because it takes students out of their "comfort zone" for historical Jesus traditions, Q, and canonical gospels, the essays in this volume provide excellent methodological pedagogy for a number of issues in New Testament criticism today. However, narrative and reader-response criticism as applied to such pseudonymous epistolary traditions might require more precision with the "audience of" argumentation. To what extent can one make the move from an audience implied by the text to what these essays presume as the socioeconomic description of an actual community?

REVELATION

The Woman Babylon and the Marks of Empire: Reading Revelation with a Postcolonial Womanist Hermeneutics of Ambiveilence, by Shanell T. Smith. Minneapolis: Fortress, 2014. Pp. xii + 211. Paper. $49.00. ISBN 9781451470154.

Margaret Aymer, Austin Presbyterian Theological Seminary

Feminist, womanist, and postcolonial hermeneutics rarely function collectively to undergird an argument. Shanell Smith's monograph models how this combination opens new avenues for research. Smith analyzes Rev 17–18 informed by all of these hermeneutics. Her work exposes an interpretative lacuna: the privileged African American woman. Such a person reads from a location of privilege and oppression simultaneously. She is at once embedded in and a victim of empire. In response, Smith proposes the neologism ambi*veil*ence as a disruptive, self-interrogatory hermeneutic. Using this hermeneutic, she reads woman Babylon as both slave and empire. Further, she reads herself, her privileged African American female location. Her reading raises questions of solidarity *and* self-awareness, privilege *and* oppression. Her scholarship provides a helpful tool for liberative readers of biblical texts.

Smith begins her work by raising troubling questions for self-reflective biblical interpreters: "what happens when the text reflects back to you aspects of your identity with which you either have not come to terms or refuse to embrace? … How can you read the Bible 'with caution and resistance' when what you read implicates you in the very things that may 'offend' or 'threaten the dignity' of others?" (2). Smith answers these questions by using exegesis to frame a hermeneutic discussion. Her exegesis is solid, as will be evident, but this is not, primarily a book about exegesis. Smith's work aims to provide an answer for her questions. To do so, she must engage in constructive biblical hermeneutics.

Smith's first chapter begins by introducing womanist and postcolonial hermeneutics. At the beginning Smith introduces womanist theologians, then considers postcolonial thought. Smith then turns to her hermeneutical neologism, ambiveilence. Both Dubois's "veil" of double-consciousness and Bhaba's postcolonial "ambivalence" shape this hermeneutic. Dubois's metaphor describes the "twoness" of being both "an American, a Negro" (57). Such "double-consciousness" inhibits self-consciousness for African Americans. Morrison's assertion that the veil may be self-protective complicates Smith's argument. One could use the veil to shield oneself from unacknowledged social locations. Smith argues that both can be true. The veil could be imposed and/or self-imposed. In either case, the veil inhibits self-consciousness.

To Dubois's veil, Smith adds Bhaba's postcolonial concept of colonial ambivalence (64). She rejects "the binary of the colonial relationship," (i.e., colonizer versus colonized). Instead, she posits that complicity and resistance coexist "in every colonized subject" (64). For Smith, this ambivalence applies also to biblical texts. A hermeneutical frame of ambivalence moves her "past the impasse whereby one part of the biblical text appears to be purely anti-imperialistic literature, and the other … reflects empire" (66).

Smith's resulting hermeneutic of ambi*veil*ence includes but exceeds both Dubois and Bhaba. First, it includes a gendered analysis that privileges African American women's experience. Second, it is intentionally activist rather than simply theoretical. With Dubois, ambi*veil*ence recognizes the veil of double-consciousness. However, ambi*veil*ence insists upon lifting that veil, for the sake of self-consciousness. On one side of the veil sits the imperial privilege of the global north; counterpositionally sits the gendered, racial, and class oppression of African American women. Here also one hears Bhaba's colonial ambivalence. Reading from a place of ambi*veil*ance requires interrogation of self and biblical texts. It requires examining the reinscription of empire in texts. It also requires reading in light of African American women's experiences. Such a reading necessarily resists misogynistic voices, even those in the minority.

Smith aims unapologetically at liberation and transformation: "A hermeneutics of ambi*veil*ance helps to highlight the ways in which one's own 'historical [and contemporary] experience of subjectivity' or one's aiding and abetting in the subjectivity of others may be reflected in the text" (69). She intends this hermeneutic to "lead the interpreter to engage in honest self-reflection, with the goals of coming to a fuller understanding of the self, and the desire to help others prevail over their oppressive conditions" (69).

Chapter 2 engages "scholarly conversations" about the "Great Whore." Smith begins by engaging the feminist conversation. Here she highlights the work of Schussler Fiorenza and Pippin. These represent the "dichotomy … in the "Great Whore debate" … that [Smith] seek[s] to dismantle" (90). Should Babylon be read as an imperial, oppressive city, as posited by Schussler Fiorenza, or should she be read as a victimized woman, as Pippin would argue? Smith's hermeneutic of ambi*veil*ance, and her autobiographical reflection, argue for both truths (91). Smith continues by engaging African American interpretations of the Great Whore. These argue, to different degrees, that Revelation represents a "minority report" (104). John of Patmos "writes in the interest of marginalized people against oppression" (104). Smith's ambi*veil*ence suggests a more nuanced reading. She insists that "John does not present a minority report in the *full* sense, but rather a masculinist one" (104). A full minority report would not reinscribe imperial and patriarchal misogyny.

Chapter 3 lays out, briefly, Smith's perspective on the *Sitz im Leben* of Revelation to John. For those familiar with scholarship around Revelation, much will be familiar here. One may be forgiven for skimming through it. The chapter demonstrates that Smith's work takes seriously contemporary scholarship concerning Revelation. Further, it serves as background for the exegetical work of chapter 4, which represents Smith's reading of Rev 17 and 18. Here she takes on John's "*masculinist* minority report" (131). John clearly presents a critique of imperial power. However, he presents that critique "in feminine flesh. John's detailed and vivid destruction of the *woman* Babylon (17:6), includes humiliation via the exposure of her naked body, the feasting on her flesh while she still has breath, and the burning up of whatever of her remains" (131). In this, Smith agrees with Pippin's assessment.

Smith goes on to argue persuasively that the woman Babylon is a brothel slave. She attends to πορνή, the word written on Babylon's forehead. This she reads as "a mark of ownership" within the context of Revelation (131). For Smith, Babylon's tattoo marks her as a slave, a brothel slave. Here Smith differs from other interpreters. Others have treated Babylon as if she were a ἑταῖρα, a courtesan. The difference is control over one's own body. The πορνή was forced have sex; the ἑταῖρα had more freedom of choice. Smith takes great care in outlining the implications of Babylon's slave status. She is "under the control of two pimps": the beast and John of Patmos (142). Both exploit her body to their own ends, John robing and disrobing her as he pleases (149). Further, her fancy dress should be understood as one of the "tricks of the trade" (146–47). Finally, Smith points out that John attributes words to her that she never actually says. This practice "is another way of abusing her and concomitantly enforcing her silence" (148). Smith in no way negates that Babylon represents the oppressive power of Rome. Ambi*veil*ence requires that she attends to the woman Babylon as *both* victim *and* oppressor.

Toward the end of chapter 4, Smith engages the womanist aspect of her hermeneutic. She intentionally reads slave woman Babylon in light of African American women's experience. There are two sides to this veil. On the first, woman Babylon is a victim of empire (154–67). Smith draws parallels between Babylon and African American enslaved women. They both experienced the *ab*use of their bodies. They both lived with a lack of physical control over their bodies. They both experience danger and death from the marking of their skin. On the other side of the veil, woman Babylon is a participant in empire (167–71). Here the experiences of privileged African American women attend. Smith self-interrogates here. She speaks of her own participation in privilege as an African American woman of the global north. The end of the chapter completes the act of "rending the veil." Smith advocates for that self-consciousness that the veil inhibits. She must "come face to face in … an unclouded mirror" (174). Self-consciousness dictates that she must acknowledge herself as a victim of and participant in empire.

Smith concludes with further thoughts about the implications of ambi*veil*ence for the interpreter. Her hermeneutic "necessitates … not only a critical investigation of a text, but also, and more importantly, a willingness to be read and exposed by the text" (181). Here she moves into waters that make historical critics uncomfortable. The work Smith proposes is not merely "interpretative business; it is personal and interpersonal" (184). Some may dismiss that as not really "exegetical," yet even the most "objective" historical criticism has always already been personal and interpersonal. Unlike these, Smith owns and names what is at stake for her. The ambi*veil*ent interpreter must engage in a self-conscious rending of the veil. She must name the ambivalences that these ancient texts expose in her. She must take seriously the ways in which (hashtag) black women's lives matter within the interpretative enterprise. And she must do so for "the well-being of all people" (184).

Smith's work presents a helpful, nuanced interpretative lens. Her ambiveilent hermeneutic resists the either/or-ness of earlier discourses. It exposes the veil occluding the paradox many wish to resist. A text, and an interpreter of texts, can both liberate *and* oppress simultaneously. This applies to more than one veil. Smith's work challenges any attempt to make texts or interpreters univocal. This would have been true even had Smith not engaged womanist thought. But she does engage womanist thought as part of her hermeneutic. As she does, she exposes yet another veil. Smith wrestles, perhaps more than her predecessors, with the ambi*veil*ence of privilege. This project represents not only a new interpretative proposal. It represents Smith's own coming to self-consciousness about her veil. Smith realizes that her African American women's experience is not unilateral. She, too, can be both victim of and participant in empire. Finally, a gentle warning: Smith's clear and poetic prose is intentionally activist. Self-consciousness is only part of her project. She means to expose her readers also. Smith's argument holds up an "unclouded mirror" to her audience. Her work challenges us. What is your veil? How does the text read you? And what do you need to rend for "the well-being of all people" (184)?

Revelation's Hymns: Commentary on the Cosmic Conflict, by Steven Grabiner. Library of New Testament Studies 511. New York: Bloomsbury, 2015. Pp. ix + 254. Hardcover. $112.00. ISBN 9780567656766.

Peter S. Perry, Lutheran School of Theology at Chicago

Steven Grabiner received his PhD from the University of South Africa in 2013 and is now adjunct professor at Southern Adventist University and president of the mission organization Outpost Centres International. His dissertation under Dirk van der Merwe has been published with slight revisions as *Revelation's Hymns: Commentary on the Cosmic Conflict*. His thesis is that the cosmic conflict between God and Satan is the primary background for interpreting the hymns of the book of Revelation. This cosmic conflict, he argues, has been minimized in recent scholarship by overemphasis on past historical events, especially conflict with the Roman Empire. He suggests that situating the hymns within the conflict between God and Satan better explains the particular details of each hymn.

The general structure of the book is typical of dissertations: overview of study, method, interaction with scholarship, analysis of pertinent texts, and conclusions. Chapter 1 lays out the aim of the book and provides an overview of the study. Grabiner includes a discussion of the sources of the hymns, reviewing a few positions on the relationship of Revelation's hymns to acclamations and honors in the Roman Empire. He acknowledges the arguments of scholars such as Edgar Krentz, David Aune, and David Seal but argues that the Old Testament should have priority for understanding the function of the hymns.

In Chapter 2, "Hermeneutical Perspective," Grabiner gives a brief overview of narrative criticism, leaning primarily on the work of James Resseguie. His main interest in narrative criticism seems to be a communicative construct of implied reader and implied author. This allows him to assert an implied reader "who would know things not specifically stated within the text.... From a narrative-critical approach, the actual reader is to read the text from the standpoint of the IR" (16). In this way, Grabiner argues that his construction of an implied reader, especially the priority of some background knowledge over other knowledge, is prescriptive for every reader. Although narrative setting is critical to Grabiner's argument, he does not discuss its significance until the next chapter.

Some general questions about Revelation are addressed in "Literary Considerations" (ch. 3). Grabiner does not take a position on the identity of John, using narrative criticism to constrain the question to the implied reader's awareness of the author as mediated through the text. The genre of Revelation is mixed: epistle, prophecy, and apocalypse. Grabiner's focus is on prophecy, and one can detect his concern that the message of Revelation not be constrained to Christians in the Roman Empire but have "special prophetic significance for the church throughout the ages" (27). Grabiner pictures the heavenly events as taking place within a heavenly throne room, which he equates with the heavenly temple. This is critical to his argument: throughout the book he assumes that the implied reader will see a divine council in every reference to the throne room or temple and the presence or absence of Satan in every divine council. For example, Satan is "a being who was once closely connected with God and had full right to heavenly council.... the temple is the place where the divine council met. It was in this location that the war in heaven began" (59–60). Whenever the throne room or temple is mentioned or implied, Grabiner suggests the implied reader will be aware of Satan and the cosmic conflict with God.

Chapter 4, "Conflict and Theodicy," develops the picture of Satan that Grabiner believes is implied throughout Revelation. Leaning on Sigve Tonstad's *Saving God's Reputation*, he sees the conflict with Satan in Rev 12 as pivotal. He argues that throughout Revelation Satan is portrayed as "vying for supremacy, and not simply in the Roman Empire, but throughout creation" (37–38). The throne is always a symbol of conflict: Satan is claiming God's right to rule. Every reference to a divine council (e.g., the throne, twenty-four elders) reminds the implied reader of Job 1–2 and Zech 3, where Satan attends the council accusing God and God's people. Thinking of the divine council, the implied reader also is reminded of the fall of "this anointed cherub (Ezek 28.14)" and the "'star' that is 'fallen from heaven' (Isa 14.12)" (56–57). Thus for Grabiner, every possible evocation of the setting of the divine council simultaneously evokes both the presence and the fall of Satan, in other words, the cosmic conflict.

Chapters 5–7 play out this reading in the hymns of Revelation. Chapter 5 looks at the hymns of Rev 4–5. The cosmic conflict is present in these hymns through their parallels with Rev 12–13. The Lamb and a head of the beast are slain. The relationship of God and the Lamb is paralleled by the dragon and beast. The beast receives power and a place on the throne from the dragon. The implied reader, Grabiner suggests, will read the hymns of Rev 4–5 through these correspondences. For example, when implied readers hear power, authority, honor, and glory given to God and the Lamb, they will be mindful of Satan's claims to power, authority, honor, and glory.

Chapter 6 examines the hymns of Rev 7, 11, and 12. As in previous analyses, Grabiner connects references to the throne room to a divine council that assumes conflict with Satan. Further, the reference to white robes in Rev 7 echo the festal clothing given to Joshua in Zech 3:3–5 (119). The "kingdom of the world" (Rev 11:15) does not refer to Rome's rule but Satan's rule over the world that has now been transformed into "the kingdom of our Lord" (134–35). Revelation 12 is where the cosmic conflict is most clear. Grabiner reads Michael in Rev 12 as an angelomorphic Christ in order to picture more clearly the conflict between God/Christ and Satan rather than simply one of God's agents and Satan.

Chapter 7 develops these themes in the hymns of Rev 15 and 19. The temple setting of Rev 15 evokes the divine council and the council's concern about Satan's rebellion. Those who have conquered the beast sing the song of Moses against the claims of Satan, the slanderer and accuser. For example, when they sing that God's ways are just and true (15:3), it is against the implied accusations of Satan that God's ways are unjust and false. The hymns celebrating the fall of Babylon in Rev 19 recall Satan as the force behind the great city. "Thus, while Babylon will have historical connections to political and religious systems that fight against the worship of God, the larger imagery in the text is that of the war in heaven" (201).

Grabiner summarizes his argument in chapter 8 ("Summary and Conclusion"). He again lifts up his concern that the cosmic conflict with Satan is underplayed in modern scholarship. "Too frequently this theme is left underexposed in an attempt to relate the document back to the historical context of the time of composition" (224). His analysis shows that "the function of the hymns is to participate in the refutation of Satan's accusations" (225).

I am sympathetic to Grabiner's concern that focus on the Roman Empire may downplay the way Revelation reveals that the Roman Empire is a part of a larger conflict between God's forces and Satan. The history of interpretation of Revelation demonstrates that Christians have not felt constrained to apply it only to the Roman Empire but to many different empires and institutions. The multivalent and evocative imagery in Revelation has not and probably will not be constrained by our attempts to keep it contained in the first century. Grabiner's argument is a helpful reminder that John sees the conflict with Rome as a part of a larger conflict with Satan that reminds readers of other historical conflicts, such as with Babylon. Apocalyptic, in its cosmic, spiritual, and moral dualism, assumes this larger conflict even as it engages a present historical one.

That being said, Grabiner's execution of his argument is unpersuasive and weakened by method, analysis of Revelation as story, and engagement with scholarship. Grabiner's argument was dependent on accepting the premise that an implied reader who knows everything he or she is supposed to know would deduce implied connections with a divine council constructed primary from Job 1–2, Zech 3, Isa 14, and Ezek 28. Grabiner needs a more comprehensive theory of communication and especially of intertextuality, rather than narrative criticism, to make a case that there are details of the hymns that can be explained only by an intertextual network with these Old Testament passages. In addition, Grabiner never discusses that these are hymns and assumed to be sung or chanted. How does this genre and oral media influence the reception of these "texts" by an implied reader?

The oversight of analysis of hymns as hymns is compounded by a failure to assess the linear structure of the book. Grabiner assumes that the implied reader has simultaneous access to the whole book, for example, that the reader has the conflict in Rev 12–13 in mind when reading Rev 4–5. While this may be true for someone who has long studied the text, narrative criticism generally asserts the linear telling of story: rising conflict, climax, and resolution. It is unpersuasive that the cosmic conflict is fully known from the beginning of Revelation when it is revealed beginning in chapter 12. Any exposition of the conflict in Revelation needs to account for the way it is revealed.

Grabiner's engagement with scholarship further undermines his argument. One of the best engagements is the dialogue with Fekkes on Isa 14 that expresses Fekkes's interpretation and objections to Grabiner's thesis and then answers them (57–59). But other key scholars do not receive consistent or deep engagement. Adela Yarbro Collins's work (both *The Combat Myth* and *Crisis and Catharsis*) deserve fuller treatment. For example, she argues that Satan's role as accuser is subordinate to his role as warrior in Rev 12 (*Combat Myth*, 161). This is found nowhere in *Revelation's Hymns* and undermines a critical part of Grabiner's argument. Grabiner does refer occasionally in footnotes to Klaus-Peter Jörns's *Das hymnische Evangelium*, one of the most comprehensive books on Revelation's hymns, but never engages Jörns's arguments about the functions of these hymns.

With the weaknesses of method, analysis of Revelation as story, and engagement of scholarly sources, *Revelation's Hymns* fails to persuade that the cosmic conflict provides essential background to understanding Revelation's hymns.

NEW TESTAMENT AND BIBLICAL THEOLOGY

Beyond Bultmann: Reckoning a New Testament Theology, edited by Bruce W. Longenecker and Mikeal C. Parsons. Waco, TX: Baylor University Press, 2014. Pp. x + 372. Paper. $59.95. ISBN 9781481300414.

Matthew V. Novenson, University of Edinburgh

This is an unusual sort of book, and all the more interesting for it. The brainchild of its editors, Baylor University colleagues Bruce Longenecker and Mikeal Parsons, it offers a collaborative (not to say consensus) retrospective on Rudolf Bultmann's very important *Theology of the New Testament* some seventy years after its initial publication. As the book's subtitle suggests, a number of the contributors also take the opportunity to theorize the possibility of a New Testament theology in our own late modern or postmodern context. The book is therefore both a conversation with a past master and a workshop on the future of a discipline.

The list of contributors is a who's who of leading senior scholars of the New Testament, all of whom have reckoned elsewhere with the problem of theology in biblical studies. With the exception of one standout mid-career scholar (Kavin Rowe), they are all current or emeritus post-holders of distinguished chairs of New Testament in Sweden (Samuel Byrskog), Switzerland (Jörg Frey), Germany (Udo Schnelle, Angela Standhartinger), Britain (John Barclay, Richard Bauckham, James Dunn, Larry Hurtado, and Francis Watson), and the United States (Richard Hays, Luke Timothy Johnson, and Wayne Meeks). (Interestingly, the book is dedicated to Beverly Roberts Gaventa and N. T. Wright, two scholars who one imagines could easily have been contributors themselves.) Readers may notice that the list is also entirely white and almost entirely male, which we may charitably assume has more to do with the demographics of the field than with any conspiracy on the part of the editors.

The book comprises thirteen chapters arranged in two asymmetrical parts. Part 1, entitled "Bultmann by the Book," is made up of eleven essays corresponding roughly to the successive chapters of Bultmann's *Theology of the New Testament* (with some reshuffling especially around Bultmann's part 3: "The Theology of the Gospel of John and the Johannine Epistles"). These essays are: Samuel Byrskog, "The Message of Jesus"; C. Kavin Rowe, "The Kerygma of the Earliest Church"; Udo Schnelle, "The Kerygma of the Hellenistic Church Aside from Paul"; Richard B. Hays, "Humanity Prior to the Revelation of Faith"; John M. G. Barclay, "Humanity under Faith"; Jörg Frey, "Johannine Christology and Eschatology"; Richard Bauckham, "Dualism and Soteriology in Johannine Theology"; Luke Timothy Johnson, "The Rise of Church Order"; James D. G. Dunn, "The Development of Doctrine"; Larry W. Hurtado, "Christology and Soteriology"; and Wayne A. Meeks, "The Problem of Christian Living." The reader quickly finds that these several essays do rather different things with their respective sections of Bultmann's *Theology*. As the editors explain in the preface, "[The contributors'] task was not to assemble an overview of publications that have appeared since Bultmann's day, but to reflect on the viability of Bultmann's contribution in light of developments within New Testament studies since that time. They were not asked to shape their reflections in relation to a structural template, nor to conform to a single interpretation of Bultmann" (viii). This is a perfectly sensible editorial policy, but the consequence is that some essays (e.g., Frey, Hays) focus on critical engagement with the honoree, while others (e.g., Bauckham, Schnelle) feature more of the contributors' own interpretations of the primary texts, and still others (e.g., Johnson, Meeks) take up the gauntlet of theorizing New Testament theology. The reader must therefore pay close attention to how each contributor chooses to dialogue with his assigned bit of Bultmann.

Part 2, "Bultmann in History and Theology," comprises just two essays supplying relevant historical contexts for understanding Bultmann and his project. Angela Standhartinger's "Bultmann's Theology of the New Testament in Context" provides an intellectual history of Bultmann's work in the period 1933 to 1952, focusing on the question how the *Theology* relates to the political setting of German National Socialism and the Second World War. Francis Watson, in "Bultmann and the Theological Interpretation of Scripture," contextualizes Bultmann's development of certain key theological concepts (kerygma, theology, fallenness, salvation-event, and faith) vis-a-vis his contemporary interlocutors, especially Karl Barth, Martin Heidegger, and Wilhelm Kamlah.

These lattermost essays skillfully highlight the vexed issue—which courses just below the surface of the whole book—of naming the criteria by which we, working in the twenty-first century, judge Bultmann's *Theology* to be a success, failure, or otherwise. Watson, for instance, rises combatively in defense of Bultmann: "For some, lacking theological interest or competence, the theological orientation is already sufficient to call the whole work into question. For others, the problem lies not with theology but with Bultmann himself, notorious as the great demythologizer and archskeptic. Yet these are old, tired, and unfruitful responses to this figure, whose best work retains its potential to challenge and provoke" (272). The editors, one senses, share Watson's reverence for the honoree, even invoking at one point the analogy of the *ma'aseh merkabah* (!): "The rabbis of old warned that studying the mysteries of the divine throne room was both important and dangerous, and that only people with maturity of years and character should explore those perilous mysteries. Something similarly might be said to a lesser degree of the study of Bultmann" (viii). I think I see the point of the analogy, but surely it strains the "to a lesser degree" clause to breaking point. Bultmann was no god, let alone God.

He was, however, possessed of a truly great theological mind, as a number of contributors remind us. Thus Richard Bauckham: "Reading Bultmann's interpretation of the Gospel of John, even in the light of the kinds of critique that must be applied to it at the present day, is still an exhilarating experience. As an attempt at a truly theological interpretation of the Gospel, it has few rivals" (133). And Luke Timothy Johnson: "Bultmann's is the only version of the odd enterprise in intellectual history called 'New Testament theology' that is truly grown-up; other entries in the field pale in comparison" (156). John Barclay, writing in a similar vein, comments, "It is not clear if there is anyone alive today competent to match Bultmann's achievement" (99). Barclay's interesting comment invites further reflection. We might well ask whether it is indeed the case that no one has yet matched Bultmann's achievement, but the answer would depend entirely on how we define the achievement and what we allow to count as matching it. It is a valuable exercise to compare closely Bultmann's New Testament theology to that of, say, Georg Strecker, or G. B. Caird, or Udo Schnelle, and to have to explain precisely what, if anything, makes Bultmann's superior. In this connection, I recall that Daniel Boyarin has called N. T. Wright's recent *Paul and the Faithfulness of God* "the Bultmann for our age," and it strikes me that Wright's book (and the series of which it is part) is both impressive and objectionable in many of the same ways that Bultmann's *Theology* is.

If, however, we concede that no one has yet matched Bultmann's achievement, then we might ask whether this is because we are all "lesser mortals" (Kavin Rowe's phrase at p. 37) or because Bultmann's achievement is not worth matching. The latter possibility is not really in the spirit of the book, but Wayne Meeks gives it serious consideration in his essay, advancing the "impious" hypothesis that "'New Testament theology' is a category mistake. The New Testament does not have a theology. The second-order procedures by which the practices that constitute the Christian community must be ordered and corrected in every generation—the procedures we name 'theology' and 'ethics'—are ours to carry out, and we must take responsibility for them and for the ways in which we may use the New Testament (and the Old) in the process" (229). If Meeks is right (which would of course require further discussion to establish, but which seems to me distinctly possible), then the lack of any twenty-first-century New Testament theology to rival Bultmann's is no indictment upon us. In fact, it might actually be a sign of disciplinary progress. Which is not to say that Bultmann was not great (perhaps greater than any New Testament scholar since) or that his *Theology* is useful only as an artifact of mid-twentieth-century scholarship or that theological interpretation of the New Testament is impossible or inadvisable. As someone who was required as a graduate student to read Bultmann's *Theology* in full and who requires my own graduate students to read it in full, I heartily agree with the editors' admonition that it "does not deserve to become a treasure trove to be raided for the odd quotation here or there. Instead, it deserves to be read carefully and for profit within the guild of New Testament scholarship" (ix). But for what kind of profit, exactly? That is the question. *Beyond Bultmann* poses this question as sharply as any other book in recent memory has done, and it should therefore be welcomed warmly and read widely.

EARLY CHRISTIANITY AND EARLY CHRISTIAN LITERATURE

Others and the Construction of Early Christian Identities, edited by Raimo Hakola, Nina Nikki, and Ulla Tervahauta. Helsinki: Finnish Exegetical Society, 2013. Pp. 344. Paper. €30. ISBN 9789519217611.

Benjamin H. Dunning, Fordham University

Others and the Construction of Early Christian Identities is the culmination of a research project at the University of Helsinki, 2010–2013. The essays generally cohere in exploring how ancient authors used discussions of religious "others" to further various projects of self-definition. Many of the essays are also engaged with what is termed a "social identity approach" to ancient texts, according to which "images of others serve to construct and maintain distinct social identities rather than reflect social reality in any straightforward manner" (15). Following an introduction by the editors, the book is divided into three parts.

Part 1 contains four essays examining the interactions, both social and rhetorical, of early Christians with a variety of Jewish groups. In "Pharisees as Others in the New Testament," Raimo Hakola takes up the question of why New Testament texts sometimes portray the Pharisees unambiguously as Jesus's opponents while in other moments depict them as more sympathetic to the emerging movement. Hakola argues that we should consider the work that different textual depictions of the Pharisees do to shore up a secure notion of identity for communities of Jesus followers. As he demonstrates convincingly through an analysis of Q, the canonical gospels, and Acts, both negative and positive portraits of Pharisees play their part in "a struggle to create a secure social identity" for early Christians (65).

In the following essay, "The Flexible Apostle: Paul's Varied Social Identifications in 1 Corinthians 9 and Philippians 3," Nina Nikki also uses a social-identity approach to engage critically with New Perspective scholarship (most especially Mark Nanos), arguing that in both these passages Paul demonstrates his willingness to navigate multiple social identities in flexible and contextual ways, none of which can be considered "false" in any simple or straightforward sense.

"Questions of Identity, Otherness, and 'Jewishness' in Ephesians' Scholarship," by Minna Shkul, responds to the recent scholarly emphasis on the Jewishness of Jesus, Paul, and the early movement by noting that this emphasis, while welcome, exacerbates the gap between New Testament texts and the eventual, largely gentile church, wherein "the cultural positioning of the pseudonymous letters" becomes an especially acute question (105). Shkul explores this question specifically with respect to Ephesians, unpacking the range of stances that scholars have taken on the question of the letter's "Jewishness." She argues that we need to attend in more nuanced ways to processes of both "selection and deselection" (124) with respect to the text's negotiation of Jewish cultural heritage.

Rounding out the book's first section, Mika Hynninen examines aspects of the early Christian claim that Christ was murdered by the Jews in "Creating the Murderers of God: The Case of the *Gospel of Peter*." After an extensive discussion of social-identity theory, Hynninen posits that an actual historical conflict "between Christians and Jews" lies behind the apocryphal text (156) but that social-identity theory can help put a finer point on that conflict, clarifying how the author extends a specific negative experience into "a trait of the whole community" (159). In this way, the proximate other is figured negatively in the interest of shoring up the in-group's identity in positive terms.

The second section of the book turns to the issue of intra-Christian polemic. In "How to Expose a Deviant? Resurrection Belief and Boundary Creation in Early Christianity," Outi Lehtipuu argues that debates over the resurrection of the dead proved to be "particularly useful for boundary drawing" among various early Christian groups (166). The essay focuses on the Treatise on the Resurrection and the Testimony of Truth, using a sociological perspective on questions of deviance to compare and contrast the two texts and situate them in a larger early Christian conceptual landscape regarding resurrection. Lehtipuu intriguingly poses the question of how the author of each text would have viewed the perspective on resurrection espoused in the other one—"would he have been one of 'us' or one of 'them'" (189)—and chooses to leave the question open, while noting points of theological common ground and also divergence.

In "Ignorant People, the Fool and Pagans: Intra-Christian Polemic and Portrayal of the Other in *Authentikos Logos*," Ulla Tervahauta offers a close reading of *AL* 33:4–34:32 (also known as *Authoritative Teaching*). The author notes that the passage in question deals differently with "ignorant people" than with the subsequently criticized "foolish person" and argues that in view here are "two different responses to spiritual struggle" (197). The essay then analyzes how these two critiques are situated within a set of "relatively tolerant" (if still generally critical) reflections on pagan religious practice (212).

The final essay in this section is "Christian Identity and Intra-Christian Polemics in the Pseudo-Clementines," by Päivi Vähäkangas. While cognizant of the scholarly literature critiquing "Jewish Christianity," the author concludes that the category remains heuristically helpful for classifying the *Recognitions*—albeit with the important caveat that the category be carefully circumscribed to signify nothing more than the intersection of a positive valuation of Jewish praxis, a set of beliefs that can be designated "Christian," and a claim to connection with the early community of (Jewish) Jesus followers in Jerusalem.

The book's third and final section addresses the broader ancient cultural contexts in which early Christian polemics against various others took place. Niko Huttunen's "In the Category of Philosophy? Christians in Early Pagan Accounts" argues that not all Roman authors treated Christianity in purely negative terms. The analysis provides close readings of passages in Epictetus, Marcus Aurelius, Lucian, and Galen, exploring especially the ways in which ancient non-Christian associations between Christianity and philosophy led to relatively tempered conclusions regarding the former, even as Christianity remained in many of these contexts the "other" of philosophy.

The final two essays are closely related and, according to the acknowledgments, had their genesis in a different research project. In "Danger and Delusion: Ancient Literary Images of Religious Prejudices," Marika Rauhala traces the limits of acceptance in ancient Greek and Roman religion and looks at the role of negative images—especially those of feminization and foreignness—in buttressing the imagined sobriety of the established religious order. Maijastina Kahlos's "Nocturnal Rituals as an Othering Device: The Long Life of Fears and Labels in Ancient Polemic and Legislation" follows a similar thread but concentrates on nocturnal practices. Kahlos traces the history of suspicion around these practices, demonstrating convincingly that such suspicion was not inevitable or automatic but specific to particular political configurations and social and rhetorical contexts. The essay is expansive in its scope and helpfully brings in both later texts (e.g., Augustine, Jerome, Sulpicius Severus) and Roman legal materials to offer a different (if complementary) perspective on the questions examined throughout the volume. As a result of this range, Kahlos is able to trace an interesting shift in the rhetorical uses of these suspicions as Christians became more visible within Roman society and eventually came to occupy a position underwritten by imperial power.

In general, the essays in the volume do not attempt to be comprehensive in their engagement with previous scholarship that has taken up similar theoretical problems. Instead, each essay tends to focus its scholarly engagement on the secondary studies most relevant to its more narrow topical focus. This is fair enough. But the cumulative result is that a reader unfamiliar with the field could easily complete the volume and still be without much sense of the degree to which questions of self-definition, otherness, and the constructive work performed by rhetoric have been previously explored in New Testament and early Christian studies from a broad range of methodological perspectives. Furthermore, while the editors signal their awareness that "neither various forms of early Christian discourse nor language in general reflects history in a transparent way" (11), at times individual essays draw conclusions about social reality or appeal to the authority of empirical studies in ways that could benefit from further theoretical justification. The appeals to theory work best when used in focused and delimited ways to illuminate a particular point of textual analysis; they are less satisfying when predicated on broad sociological generalizations about how human beings behave across time and place. And while this reviewer very much appreciated the authors' repeated acknowledgment of the problems associated with terms such as *Jewish* and *Christian*, especially with respect to the earliest texts, the pragmatic (if qualified) use of them anyway sometimes runs the risk of begging certain questions about identity—and indeed, perhaps questions that would seem to be central to the volume's concerns.

On the whole, the essays are strongest when engaged in close and careful reading of the primary texts—and there are many moments of real and valuable insight. Thus specialists will want to consult individual essays, and the volume as a whole is well worth a careful reading. At the same time, the continual focus on in-groups and out-groups that the social-identity approach sets up may at times lend itself to an overly dualistic perspective on early Christianity and its others, thereby obscuring some of the ambivalence—that is, an interplay of disavowal, desire, and identification both with and against—that characterized so many early Christian projects of self-formation.

The Sentences of Sextus, by Walter T. Wilson. Wisdom Literature from the Ancient World 1. Atlanta: Society of Biblical Literature, 2012. Pp. xiv + 478. Paper. $51.95. ISBN 9781589837195. Hardcover. $71.95. ISBN 9781589837270.

Justin M. Rogers, Freed-Hardeman University

The work under review introduces and provides text, translation and commentary on the *Sentences* of Sextus. The *Sentences* is a Christian composition originally written in Greek sometime between the late second and early third century CE. The author is otherwise unknown, but Origen already mentions both the title of the work and the author of the collection (*Cels.* 8.30).

Wilson's inaugural volume in the Wisdom Literature from the Ancient World series sets the bar high for subsequent publications. The volume depends heavily on the earlier edition and translation of Henry Chadwick (*The Sentences of Sextus: A Contribution to the History of Early Christian Ethics*, Texts and Studies 5 [Cambridge: Cambridge University Press, 1959]) and supersedes that of Richard A. Edwards and Robert A. Wild (*The Sentences of Sextus*, SBLTT 22 [Chico, CA: Scholars Press, 1981]). Despite the accessibility of both of these editions, modern academic publications on the *Sentences* have been relatively rare. For this reason, secondary scholarship is referred to only occasionally in Wilson's volume.

The paucity of modern publications on the *Sentences* of Sextus does not match the ancient reception of the work. Origen declares that "the multitude of Christians read" the work (*Cels.* 8.30), and the *Sentences* was popular in Christian circles well into the Middle Ages. This is partially due to Rufinus's attribution of the collection to Xystus II, a bishop of Rome martyred in the Decian persecution. In addition to the original Greek and the Latin of Rufinus, versions have been discovered in Coptic (from Nag Hammadi), Syriac, and Armenian.

The *Sentences* exerted a profound influence on the early church. Origen quotes the *Sentences* explicitly for the view that castration is advisable (*Sentences* 13, 273), a position Origen himself rejects (*Comm. Matt.* 15.3). The work also figured prominently in the debate between Jerome and Rufinus. Although Jerome can quote the *Sentences* approvingly (*Jov.* 1.49), Rufinus's Latin translation was met with Jerome's criticism of the *Sentences* as a pagan collection (e.g., *Ep.* 133.3). There is some truth to the claim, as the *Sentences* is heavily dependent on two Pythagorean collections, the *Sententiae Pythagoreorum* and the *Clitarchi sententiae*. The moral austerity of Pythagoreanism was attractive to the early Christians, and the *Sentences* offers us an example of how a Christian author would adapt such material to his specific value system.

The original form of the *Sentences*, on which Wilson's volume is based, consists of 451 numbered verses. These can alternatively be divided to yield approximately 490 maxims or gnomes (γνῶμαι). An additional 159 sayings were added later in the manuscript tradition sometime between the translation of Rufinus (late fourth century) and the Syriac versions we now possess (early sixth century).

Wilson opens his volume with forty pages of introduction. He begins by listing three major contributions the work can make to modern academic inquiry: the *Sentences* offers us a formative chapter in the development of the Christian wisdom tradition; it offers us a window into the early development of Christian asceticism; and it helps us to assess the Pythagorean influence on early Christian ethics.

After discussing the importance of the work for the ancient Christian tradition (1–4), Wilson briefly surveys the state of the text in its versions (4–7). He then turns to a sketch of the reception history of the work, focusing on opinions regarding authorship (7–10). A source-critical discussion forms the longest subsection of the introduction (11–29). Herein Wilson sketches the complicated relationship between the *Sentences*, the earlier Pythagorean collections, and the later *Ad Marcellum* of Porphyry. Wilson is able to extend and correct the earlier source-critical conclusions of Chadwick. After briefly considering the morphology of the collection, the introduction closes with a useful summary of the major themes of the work (32–40).

Although the survey is appropriate in its length and content, the reader will perhaps notice Wilson's focus on the Greek and Latin fathers. Such a focus is understandable, but one might wish for a sketch of the reception history of the work in the Syriac or Armenian tradition as well.

The bulk of the volume (41–425) consists of Greek text, English translation, and commentary on the sayings. Wilson aims at an authoritative, critical edition of the *Sentences*, and his product appears sound. The two extant Greek manuscripts (Π and Υ) form the basis for the text, although the ancient versions are routinely cited in the critical apparatus. Wilson is unafraid to critique the textual judgments of his predecessors but keeps text-critical comments to an appropriate minimum in the commentary. The English translation is both sufficiently literal and readable. Wilson opts for traditional translations of familiar terminology (e.g., "flesh" for σάρξ; "virtue" for ἀρετή) even when these are not the most meaningful (e.g., μεγαλοψυχία as "greatness of soul"). No blame may be assigned, however, since the commentary elucidates all technical terms.

Although there is no discernible structure to the *Sentences* as a whole, the work generally seems to be grouped according to common words or themes. Wilson thus subdivides the *Sentences* into over fifty thematic or verbal units, commenting on each unit as a whole. This approach makes the commentary manageable, but it is not without difficulties, as Wilson himself acknowledges. For example, some literary units are consistent and easily discernible (e.g., vv. 15–21 on the world or vv. 122–128 on prayer), while others appear jumbled (e.g., vv. 76–82D, in which most gnomes concentrate on the danger of wealth, but vv. 80–82a on prayer).

As is the nature of gnomic literature, the *Sentences* can be repetitive. Wilson neither repeats his comments nor passes over the parallels but generally balances his commentary to provide additional contextual insight to repeated gnomes. This makes the commentary an excellent reference tool for those seeking information on one literary unit or individual aphorism.

Overall, the commentary is appropriate in length, detail, and subject matter. Wilson's greatest strength is his routine quotation of parallel maxims from ancient authors, almost always in English translation. Biblical wisdom literature, school texts, Philo, Seneca, Clement of Alexandria, Porphyry, and a host of others are routinely cited to illustrate the contents of the *Sentences*. Wilson does not generally claim that these authors shared common sources, but the parallels help to illustrate the ubiquitous nature of similar wisdom sayings in the Greek tradition.

The volume concludes with a bibliography (427–36) and indices, including an index of Greek words (437–45), of primary texts cited (446–67), of modern authors cited (468), and of subjects discussed (469–78).

Wilson's contribution is well designed and well executed. Although the *Sentences* of Sextus has yet to receive the attention it deserves, it can be hoped that Wilson's work will provide a starting point for a variety of research paths. The volume is a recommended reference tool for all students interested in the history of Christian ethics and wisdom traditions, the beginnings of the Christian ascetic movement, and the influence of Pythagoreanism on early Christianity.

City of Demons: Violence, Ritual, and Christian Power in Late Antiquity, by Dayne S. Kalleres. Oakland: University of California Press, 2015. Pp. xii + 374. Hardcover. 95.00. ISBN 9780520276475.

Sarah E. Rollens, University of Alabama

City of Demons is a sophisticated examination of the rhetoric of demon possession and exorcism in late antiquity. Whereas other studies have treated the many references to such occurrences rather homogenously, as if they were all identical phenomena, here Dayna S. Kalleres explores how the rhetoric works in the *specific, local* contexts in which it emerges. Her focus is on elite urban church leaders who are demonologists and/or exorcists. Under this lens, she aims to analyze the discourse of demons and ritual prescriptions, which she locates in the wider practice of diabolization, described as the "construct[ion of] the undeniable reality of a spiritual warfare in which stronger Christians must engage in direct battle against demons" (2). This discourse, she argues throughout, contributes to the identity formation of early Christians through constructing a world of spiritual conflict in which demons constantly attack true believers.

It is necessary to carefully contextualize such a dense and nuanced project. The guiding question for Kalleres's analysis is: "What happens when church leadership diabolizes its surrounding animistic environment?" (21). She is wary of scholarly efforts to explain away references to demons by rendering them merely discursive phenomena. "In our own effort to avoid reductive reading," she explains, "we will attend to the category of ritual practice" (5). Focusing on ritual practice allows her to accept the reality of demons in their antique social setting without letting contemporary, personal beliefs affect the analysis. She views her study as a corrective to portraits of late antique Christianity that depict the tradition as a superstitious corruption of an earlier form, as well as portraits that had located the focus of demon discourse in the wilderness as opposed to the cities. Her investigation will also supplement the study of the social and political roles of the bishop in late antiquity, since scholars all too often reduce these figures to rather secular authorities in the "disenchanted space" (13) of the city.

Although I will attempt to outline her investigations here, there are numerous particulars that such a short review will no doubt overlook. The book is organized by following three bishops who engage in diabolizing rhetoric. Part 1 explores John Chrysostom in his urban setting of Antioch. Kalleres describes Antioch as a city enchanted with supernatural agents. Inhabitants had a smorgasbord of ritual practices from which they could choose to manage these agents' effects. Despite their social differences, all of the inhabitants "participate in a loosely shared understanding of Antioch's supernatural powers" (28). It was a city "pulsating with spiritual powers" (31). This conclusion is based on not only ancient literature that speaks to the diversity of gods among the city's inhabitants but also the physical structure of the city itself: Antioch contained architecture and physical space that presumed the presence of a variety of supernatural agents. Even if temples or shrines had fallen out of use by late antiquity, their physical presence remained influential. "As people move around and through the city's imposing religious remains," Kalleres argues, "these structures—regardless of their state of decay—still continue to imprint their ritual and religious lives" (33). The customs associated with various festivals, though in decline, lingered in the cities, too. Kalleres uses the example of Libanius's dream of human sacrifice in a temple devoted to Zeus to explore the various social processes and ritual practices one might undertake in Antioch to make sense of an incident of supernatural communication. Various magical amulets and texts also attest to efforts to manage the supernatural. Thus there is an interesting kind of democratic agency that is well supported in this period: "While the human body is always in danger of suffering victimization in some kind of demonic attack, a person has the ability to defend him/herself and fight back through his/her own ritual manipulations" (48). This, in turn, creates a "marketplace" for such apotropaic objects, as well as for ritual experts.

It is within this urban setting that John Chrysostom tries to draw boundary lines among these practices in order to keep Christians oriented toward the rituals of the church. Rather than denying the efficacy of non-Christian practices, John's strategy is to *diabolize* them, to maintain that they are permeated with the demonic. Using a mildly Stoic framework that sees the individual's proper cognition as a capacity that much be carefully managed, John claims that participation in non-Christian rituals allows demons to influence the Christian's faculty for perception. The images that John uses in his rhetoric are imbued with violence. "The mind/soul is penetrated, injured, raped, mutilated, and scarred by demons; it transforms into a festering wound, a diseased and leprous entity" (58). He also suggests that demons conspire behind and animate weddings, civic festivals, theatrical performances, and even Jewish customs. In this way, his rhetoric diabolizes these ordinary phenomena to which Christians were otherwise very attracted. In keeping with the common understanding that all Christians participate in the body of the church, such demonic infections were contagious to other Christians as well.

The result of this demonic influence on the Christian soul is immorality. Moreover, if Christians do not manage their faculties properly, they are complicit in this depravity. But all is not lost, since John describes how Christians can fight back. Their weapons are primarily baptism and the Eucharist rituals, which "work to fortify rational thought and free will" (59). Baptism was an especially transformative ritual that "sealed" (85) the soul from demonic attack, restored one's cognitive faculties, and turned one into a Christian soldier. Kalleres suggests that these rituals became a kind of "ecclesiastical prophylactic" (59) that allowed the Christian to be in the urban environment but unaffected by it. Thus John is rhetorically constructing the Christian identity as one with a certain combative disposition toward the external world. In fact, as Kalleres goes on to show, John argues that the "strong" Christians in the community had an *obligation* to confront their enemies in the public sphere before exorcising the demons that animated them. She illustrates this promotion of spiritual warfare with John's rhetoric against Judaizers and Jews in Antioch.

Part 2 analyzes Cyril's influence in Jerusalem in a similar fashion. Kalleres begins this portion of the book with the tension that stemmed from Jerusalem's fraught history as both the Holy City and Aelia. She gives particular attention to the changes to the physical landscape in the city that were inaugurated under Hadrian when he transformed Jerusalem to reflect the political and cultural hegemony of Rome. Jerusalem's long history of conquest determined how its inhabitants understood these changes, and apocalyptic discourse had previously allowed them to ruminate on and make sense of Rome's ever-imposing presence. Apocalyptic texts such as 4 Ezra and 2 Baruch reflected on past conquests and spoke of "a holy but hidden city that continue[d] to exist untouched by Rome" (127). Only certain people (the one who received the *apokalypsis*) could access the spiritual reality of the city.

Such apocalyptic ideas were mobilized again by Cyril in the fourth century, in response to Constantine's lavish and self-aggrandizing building projects in the city, in order to help the inhabitants distinguish between being residents of an earthly, imperial city and an eternal, holy city. Most have assumed that Constantine's actions benefited only Christianity, but Kalleres wants to look for "dissenting voices" that can help explain "Cyril's more radical diabolization of religious space in Jerusalem" (142). She highlights the Bordeaux Pilgrim as a text that witnesses to "Christians in dialogue, if not conflict with, imperial and ecclesiastical directions for Aelia's transformation" (142).

Cyril used the apocalyptic notions of true spiritual, revelatory perceptions to train his Christians to see past the physical city in their midst, which he maintained was animated by demons, to discern the Holy City. This discerning was, in fact, *obligatory* for baptized Christians. "If one can ritually engage the correct biblical texts at the proper time and place within the Holy City and under the right bodily conditions," Kalleres argues regarding Cyril's training, "space and time fracture just enough to allow a sensory glimpse into biblical realities" (153). This training required Cyril to evoke graphic visualizations in baptizands and to guide them through rituals of exorcism that involved "a kind of visual calisthenics" (165). If they were successful, they transformed themselves into apocalyptic prophets who were able first to truly perceive Christ's sacrifice and then to grasp the Holy City that is occluded to others. Just as John Chrysostom had argued that demons affected the Christian's proper perception, Cyril also claimed that demons influenced a person's cognition and kept one from discerning the true Holy City. He thus counseled baptizands to avoid certain parts of the city where they were especially vulnerable to demons. Yet when they were properly fortified, they became not only prophets but also soldiers who could engage with their enemies in an apocalyptic showdown.

What Cyril was also doing, Kalleres contends (drawing upon Catherine Wessinger's work on millennialism and violence), was marking boundaries between insiders and outsiders among the inhabitants of Jerusalem and encouraging his flock to police them. She proposes two ways that Cyril creatively blended his own political enemies into his apocalyptic rhetoric. First, she suggests he was inspired to rail against false prophets and other deceivers in response to the influence of Acacius, who was his competition and was responsible for his exile. Second, he developed his notion of "antichrist" in response to the emperor Julian's plans to rebuild the Jewish temple; Julian was symbolized by the antichrist who was bent on destroying Christians. Acacius and Julian were both existential problems, from Cyril's vantage point, and by incorporating them into his apocalyptic drama, he was able to diabolize them through a context of violence.

Part 3 looks at Ambrose of Milan, who used diabolizing strategies to undercut Arian Christians' claims to authority among Milanese Christians. Although it is shorter than parts 1 and 2, its argument is just as complex. The mid-fourth century inaugurated a conflict of authority in Milan between Arian Christians and Nicene Christians, manifesting especially in conflict over ecclesiastical space. This all came to a head during the so-called basilica crisis of 386, when Ambrose supported the Nicene Christians in defending sacred spaces in Milan from Arians. What was at stake for him was the very real contamination of holy space (the altar), which linked the Christian directly to the sacred. The anxiety was thus: "What happens, then, when someone who has reinscribed the wrong creedal formula approaches a church's altar in order to participate in the Eucharist? What kind of otherworldly entities may they invite to the altar setting if they speak the wrong words or the Arian creedal formula rather than the Nicene words?" (221). Embedded in this anxiety was Ambrose's rhetoric of diabolization: contaminating sacred space potentially allowed demons access to them. For Ambrose, the cleansing of baptism protected Nicene Christians from potential contamination. Interestingly, though they represented a clear threat, the presence of demoniacs at holy sites and their reactions in such spaces simultaneously attested to the *power* of particular locations—and the truth of the factions associated with them, as when demoniacs in Milan "conveniently" (231) pronounced to the truth of Nicene beliefs and vilified Arian doctrine.

This is a tour de force of Christian demon rhetoric in late antiquity. Kalleres's bottom line in these three case studies is that "urban ecclesiastical and Episcopal leaders gain power and authority in and over their city through diabolizing others' forms of ritual and rhetoric" (202). Specialists of late antique Christianity should certainly read and consider her nuanced treatment of demons, church politics, and urban Christian groups. With such erudite case studies, there are hardly any shortcomings. If pushed, one could observe that the notion of violence and ritual were generally undertheorized in this book. When it comes to violence, in almost all cases Kalleres is dealing with the *discursive representation* of violence, not actually violence, and she does not reflect much on the relationship between the two. As for ritual, it is also a category that she tends to assume is self-evident. The only rituals that she focuses on are officially sanctioned church practices such as baptism and Eucharist. It is clear that some of the textual evidence that she discusses evinces other "folk" practices in these urban settings, but they are given less attention than the rituals promoted by bishops. Careful reflection on the categories of ritual and violence, especially since they are critical to this study and are featured in the book's title, would have thus been welcome, but even in their absence *City of Demons* is truly an impressive work.

The Text of Marcion's Gospel, by Dieter T. Roth. New Testament Tools, Studies and Documents 49. Leiden: Brill, 2015. Pp. ix + 492. Hardcover. $220.00. ISBN 9789004245204.

H. A. G. Houghton, University of Birmingham

A new scholarly edition of the evidence for Marcion's Gospel has long been a desideratum. In this volume Dieter Roth rises magnificently to the challenge of assembling and evaluating the fragments preserved in a range of early Christian writings, offering a reconstruction and commentary that should become the point of reference for all subsequent work on the Euangelion. Roth goes beyond the ninety-five-year-old edition of Adolf von Harnack in numerous ways, pointing out his predecessor's inconsistencies and errors, highlighting unwarranted assumptions, adducing some new information about the sources and their transmission, and developing a scheme for indicating levels of confidence within the reconstruction. Since the submission of his doctoral thesis in 2009, Roth has published several articles addressing well-known issues associated with Marcion's text, such as its relationship to the canonical version of the Gospel of Luke, its form of the Lord's Prayer, and the language in which it was known to Tertullian. Now, after extensive revision and expansion, comes this edition of the text adhering to the highest standards of meticulousness and transparency.

The first main chapter, on the history of research, shows how the biblical text of Marcion has exercised scholars since the late seventeenth century. The provocative theses recently put forward by Matthias Klinghardt and Markus Vinzent have antecedents in earlier debates about the relationship between Marcion's Euangelion and the Gospel of Luke. Although Roth tries to avoid presuppositions about the origin of Marcion's text, he shows that the consensus that Marcion abbreviated the canonical Luke, as suggested by a variety of ancient sources, derives from many decades of argument and counterargument. In addition to Harnack as his main dialogue partner, Roth engages with recent work on Marcion's Gospel by David S. Williams and Kenji Tsutsui; Jason BeDuhn's English reconstruction and translation of 2013 appeared too late to be incorporated into the main text of this book, although it is occasionally mentioned in footnotes. Roth acknowledges his debt to the methodology of Ulrich Schmid's work on Marcion's Apostolikon, with which the present study forms something of a diptych.

The principal sources for the Euangelion are Tertullian's *Adversus Marcionem* and Epiphanius's *Panarion*, with the Pseudo-Origenic *Adamantius Dialogue* coming a distant third. A handful of references are also made by writers such as Ephrem the Syrian and the Armenian Eznik of Kolb, but these are shown to be of minimal textual value. Thirty pages of tables in chapter 3 lay out the attestation of the Euangelion based on each verse of canonical Luke, of which 486 are preserved in witnesses to Marcion's text (86). The relative importance of the sources corresponds to the number of verses they present (summarized on page 5): Tertullian attests 438 verses, Epiphanius 114 verses, and the *Adamantius Dialogue* 75 verses, while ten other sources account for 33 verses.

Roth adopts a rigorous and empirical approach, restricting himself to the surviving data. For the fullest possible analysis, he also takes account of variations in the transmission of the New Testament and the patristic sources. He shows that there is insufficient evidence to identify any extant gospel fragments, including Papyrus 69, as copies of Marcion's Gospel (46). Earlier suggestions about the contents of the Euangelion that were justified by appeals to Marcion's theology are rejected, with several shown to rest on flimsy evidence (e.g., 363, 394). One of Roth's notable improvements on Harnack is his insistence that only material explicitly attested by ancient sources to be missing from Marcion's Gospel is identified as an omission (or, as indicated less prejudicially in his reconstruction, Not Present). All other verses of canonical Luke are simply to be marked as Not Attested, regardless of the cases that may be made for their theological consonance or otherwise with Marcion. Another strength of Roth's analysis is his contention, again following Schmid, that the understanding of an author's citation habits is essential to evaluating the evidence for the text that the author quotes. For Tertullian in particular this means that variations in conjunctions, word order, the position of pronouns and the use of the future tense are more likely than not to have been introduced by him rather than preserve the form of text in his copy of the Euangelion. (The same appears to be true more generally of early Latin versions of the gospels.) In all sources, the preference for Matthew in the early church indicates that, where this gospel differs from Luke, agreements with Matthaean wording may have been introduced at the point of quotation. This is not to deny that copies of the Euangelion and even Marcion's text itself may have included Matthaean forms, but the evidence for harmonization toward Matthew makes it difficult to reconstruct this securely from the sources for Marcion. Conversely, Roth takes agreements with Luke against Matthew at points where Tertullian may be quoting from Marcion as confirmation that this is indeed evidence for the Euangelion (e.g., 144). Some might object that this could result in an amplification of the overlap between the reconstructed text of Marcion and canonical Luke, but it is justified by the demonstration of the distinctive nature of the citations in *Adversus Marcionem* and the attested relationship between the two gospels.

The middle five chapters of the book treat each source in turn. Roth begins by examining verses that are cited by Tertullian in *Adversus Marcionem* and at least one other work, in order both to identify features of Tertullian's citation practice and to isolate readings that may derive from Marcion's Gospel. This is followed by a consideration of the verses of the Euangelion that appear only in *Adversus Marcionem*, with subsequent chapters devoted to Epiphanius, the *Adamantius Dialogue*, and the shorter sources. The quotations are cited in full at the head of each section of commentary: Greek and Latin are given in the original language, and information about textual variants within the patristic work is included in the footnotes. It is striking to discover that, as in his translations of Origen's commentaries, Rufinus substituted a different biblical text in his Latin translation of the *Adamantius Dialogue* and even attempted to make this pseudonymous work appear more like a work of Origen (349–52). Roth's detailed commentary engages fully with earlier scholars and editions, although it should be noted that quotations from these are normally not translated: a reasonable command of German is needed to appreciate the discussion fully.

The culmination of the extensive commentary is the reconstructed text, verse by verse, in chapter 9. Conscious of debates about the status of editorial texts, Roth emphasizes that this is not necessarily the "original text" of the Euangelion but the *"best attainable text for Marcion's Gospel according to the sources"* (4, emphasis original). Four levels of confidence are indicated typographically: bold for "secure" readings, bold and italic for "very likely" readings, roman type for readings of "slight confidence," and italic alone for "possible" readings. Phrases for which the word order is uncertain are placed within curly brackets. Although Roth's commentary is arranged by source, he makes it simple for users to locate his relevant discussion by including the appropriate section numbers at the beginning of each verse; the reconstruction can also be read in conjunction with the tables in chapter 3 that give a synoptic overview of sources. In addition, the book is furnished with extensive indices: readers wishing to annotate their critical editions will find extremely useful the lists of places where Roth considers the IGNTP apparatus of Luke or Nestle-Aland 28 to be problematic (491).

In his judicious evaluation of citations and transparent discussions, Roth shows himself to be master of an extensive body of material. While he is often critical of earlier work, a constructive tone is maintained throughout. The book is generally very well presented, with few typographical errors (although there is a higher incidence of these in chapter 7, particularly in Latin); in the reconstructed text, just four letters are to be corrected: δουλεύειν the second time in 16:13, Καίσαρος in 20:25, ὥρθριζεν in 21:38, and ἤρξαντο in 23:2. Most readers are likely to consult discussions of individual passages, but Roth is to be congratulated on making the commentary readable in its entirety. In addition, although this is primarily a work of textual scholarship, there are numerous pointers to matters of broader interest. These include verses that were particularly important to Marcion (e.g., Luke 18:19) and those that are key to determining the relationship between the Euangelion and the canonical text of Luke (e.g., Luke 4:43 and 16:16). The examination of the reliability of the sources for Marcion's Gospel is also pertinent to the use of patristic citations in reconstructing the text of the New Testament: Roth demonstrates both why and how the evidence of each source must be evaluated before its inclusion in an apparatus, no matter how tempting superficial parallels or unusual readings may appear.

In sum, this comprehensive and admirable study offers a solid foundation for further investigations. Anyone who chooses to take issue with the reconstructions advanced here will need to justify them as compellingly as the discussions in Roth's commentary. At a time when Marcion has again risen to the forefront of scholarly attention, the present volume is set to be a contribution of lasting value.

A Modest Apostle: Thecla and the History of Women in the Early, by Susan E. Hylen Church. Oxford: Oxford University Press, 2015. Pp. xiii + 182. Hardcover. $74.00. ISBN 9780190243821.

Kate Wilkinson, Towson University

In *A Modest Apostle: Thecla and the History of Women in the Early Church*, Susan E. Hylen grapples with two examples of early Christian literature that both frustrate and delight, 1 Timothy and the Acts of Paul and Thecla. She positions her argument as a response to a standard narrative "among Christians who promote gender equality in the Church" (2). This narrative emphasizes the freedoms and leadership roles of women in the primitive church, subsequent subordination as church institutions developed, and the relocation of women's leadership to celibate, ascetic communities. In this narrative, 1 Timothy and the Acts of Paul and Thecla represent two early second-century points of view on women's role in the church, views put forth by two distinct communities. The community responsible for the Acts of Paul and Thecla, possibly a female community, allows and even celebrates women's teaching, traveling, and heroic leadership. On the other hand, 1 Timothy represents a community attempting to delegitimize this model of women's leadership. Hylen argues that this model oversimplifies the picture of gender and leadership in both texts. She suggests that the two are better read as complementary options deriving from a field of cultural norms that included both feminine leadership and strictures on feminine behavior. Women's modesty and women's leadership were not mutually exclusive. Hylen reminds us that Christians in the third, fourth, and fifth centuries easily accepted both texts rather than viewing them as mutually exclusive visions of gender and leadership.

A Modest Apostle is organized into an introduction, four chapters, and a conclusion. The chapters cover norms for feminine behavior, both modest and active, in the first centuries of the Roman Empire, then an analysis of 1 Timothy, an analysis of the Acts of Paul and Thecla, and an examination of the reception of Thecla by later Christian authors. The introduction provides an overview of previous interpretation, especially early feminist interpretations of 1 Timothy and the Acts of Paul and Thecla, and more recent accounts by scholars such as Virginia Burrus and Kate Cooper. Hylen addresses theoretical problems such as the relationship between text and history, the concept of cultural norms, and the meaning of the public and the private in a Roman context. Most interesting is her brief discussion of women's agency in historical and cultural context. Hylen calls on both Sherry Ortner and Saba Mahmood to argue that "ancient women who exerted power may be understood to embody—rather than resist—social expectations for their behavior" (13). Despite this early foray into Mahmood's strong criticism of feminist scholarship that conflates resistance with agency and prioritizes a proto or emergent liberal subject, Hylen tends to contrast modesty and leadership in her following analyses and clearly discovers women's agency in their leadership rather than in their modesty (89, 122). Hylen reads both modesty and leadership as feminine norms that ancient Christian women embodied but finds them conflicting or paradoxical norms. Modesty constrains, while leadership provides opportunities for agency. Given Mahmood's argument that the practice of modesty requires agency, I would have expected Hylen either to explicitly differentiate her own interpretation or follow Mahmood's insights more closely.

Hylen's first chapter, "Virtuous, Active Women in the Greco-Roman World," gives a good overview of the roles, limitations, and opportunities for women in the first century BCE through the second century CE. She discusses wealth, patronage, marital roles, childbearing, and civic and domestic virtues. The discussion is especially useful for thinking about the place of upper- and upper-middle-class women but too often conflates "women" with "women of means." A discussion of the roles and responsibilities, and especially the sexual vulnerability, of slave, noncitizen, and freedwomen would have been a welcome addition.

In her chapter on 1 Timothy, Hylen puts the letter into conversation with Livy's *History* and Plutarch's *Advice to the Bride and Groom* and *On the Virtues of Women*. She argues against the view that 1 Timothy must be read as a response to a specific "heretical" group of celibate women. She gives a strong account of the ways that criticisms of women's inappropriate action were often used to discredit opponents in the ancient Greco-Roman context and reminds that these criticisms need not match any realities. Just because 1 Timothy criticizes women's inappropriate speech does not mean that women were regularly teaching and preaching. Alternatively, exhortations to modest speech might simply reflect agreed-upon ideas about the cultivation of specifically masculine and feminine virtue. Feminine silence is a practice that promotes marital harmony, from Plutarch's point of view. He does not, in fact, expect women to refrain from speaking altogether, since their wise speech is necessary for good household management. Hylen follows her discussion of the requirements for feminine modesty in 1 Timothy with an analysis of the possibilities for women's leadership implied by the text. She analyzes the roles of female deacons, widows, and married women. Her argument against the idea that marriage necessarily implied a limitation of a woman's capacity to lead is particularly strong. Hylen's rejects the overly simplified notions that celibacy must increase a woman's freedom while marriage must limit that freedom. She rightly emphasizes the increase in social and civic status that marriage, and especially childbearing, brought upper-class women in Greco-Roman antiquity. She concludes that the shared cultural norms expressed in 1 Timothy were contradictory—as gender norms in any society tend to be—and that the letter need not be read as an overwhelming condemnation of women's leadership roles within the church.

The Acts of Paul and Thecla has often been interpreted as an expression of support for early Christian women's leadership and independence. Hylen counters this, perhaps naïve, feminist reading of the text and emphasizes instead the many ways in which its heroine conforms to norms for feminine modesty. She focuses on Thecla's early silence followed by her demonstration of wise and self-controlled public speech. While Hylen does not see Thecla as the embodiment of a community of independent, celibate women, neither does she view Thecla as a cypher for masculine theological debates. She rejects Kate Cooper's view that civic leadership versus apostolic authority were the key issues at stake in the Acts and insists that the tale tells us about women, not just about male authors' agendas. Her argument would be improved by paying as much attention to the issue of rhetoric in the Acts of Paul and Thecla as she does in her analysis of 1 Timothy. Hylen hardly notes conventions of the romance genre to which the Acts belong. For example, Thecla's early silence is ambiguous. Is it the silence of a modest unmarried girl sitting at her window or the silence of a romantic heroine trapped by a love spell? The play of eroticism and chastity in Thecla's relationship with Paul complicates the notion of Thecla's conformity to feminine norms.

The chapter on the reception history of 1 Timothy and the Acts of Paul and Thecla is a particularly compelling piece of the argument. Hylen demonstrates that later Christians, especially those whom we might expect to reject any texts in support of women's leadership, enthusiastically embraced the Thecla narrative. Thecla and 1 Timothy lived happily side by side in the early church, without any particular "domestication" of Thecla's leadership. She continues to be celebrated for her teaching, heroism, virginal virtue, and baptizing activities. With the exception of Tertullian, church fathers found her orthodox and exemplary. In other words, those who more closely shared the gender norms surrounding both women's modesty and women's leadership did not, in general, find 1 Timothy and the Acts of Paul and Thecla incompatible.

In sum, Susan E. Hylen's book is a welcome addition to the literature on Christian women's roles in the second century CE. It will not end all debate over the interpretation of either 1 Timothy or the Acts of Paul and Thecla, but it will certainly hold an important place in future discussions. The book is well-written and clearly organized and should be of real interest to advanced students, academics, and the educated clergy.

Der Kommentar Cyrills von Alexandrien zum 1. Korintherbrief: Einleitung, kritischer Text, Übersetzung, Einzelanalyse, by Konrad Zawadzki. Traditio Exegetica Graeca 16. Leuven: Peeters, 2015. Pp. xxviii + 615. Hardcover. €105.00. ISBN 9789042930452.

David Kneip, Abilene Christian University

Scholars interested in patristic exegesis have enjoyed a steady flow of publications over the last several years on the topic: studies of individual authors, overarching examinations of interpretive trends, new translations of patristic commentaries, and so on. However, those translations (and the resultant studies) are not always based on critical editions of the ancient works. With his new edition, translation, and analysis of Cyril of Alexandria's commentary on 1 Corinthians, Konrad F. Zawadzki makes a significant contribution to the field of patristic exegesis and takes a step toward correcting the problem of uncritical editions.

Zawadzki's book is a revised version of his dissertation submitted in Trier. The value of the volume begins with its edition, which deserves some explanation. First, while there have been three different modern editions (all in the nineteenth century) of Cyril's commentary on 1 Corinthians, each had a problematic manuscript basis. In contrast, Zawadzki gathers *all* of the manuscripts, weighs their value (some are imperfect copies of others), and considers *all* of them in his edition. As it happens, there are two manuscripts that are the best of the lot, and Zawadzki leans on these primarily; when only one manuscript has a particular pericope, he prints that one, but when two have all or part of it, he prints them both in parallel columns. Second, Cyril's commentary does not exist in its original form in Greek; rather, it only survives in the catena tradition, in several cases with specific reference to the particular volume of Cyril's original commentary. Zawadzki does not engage in sustained discussion of the problems associated with the authenticity of catena texts, but he does analyze the selections presented in light of the challenges of the catenae, including which verse a particular marginal comment may refer to. In my own judgment, the dogmatic material displayed in the commentary and Zawadzki's discussion of it are sufficient in this case to indicate that the texts are reliably Cyril's.

In terms of its contents, the book as a whole is broken up into four main parts. First, Zawadzki provides a lengthy introduction, including material on the manuscript tradition, the breakdown of catena materials by chapter of 1 Corinthians, comments on the modern printed editions, and a discussion of the date of the commentary's composition, its genre, its addressees, its written style, and its place in the larger body of Cyril's exegetical works. Zawadzki then proceeds to Cyril's commentary itself, presenting the Greek text(s) on the left-hand page of each opening and the German translation(s) on the right-hand page. The third primary portion of the text is essentially a commentary on Cyril's commentary, proceeding selection by selection according to the catena manuscripts; in fact, in many ways this is the most important part of the book, both in quantity and quality, as Zawadzki spends nearly half of his entire page count unfolding for his readers Cyril's exegesis of 1 Corinthians. Finally, the book concludes with a substantial summation, including what Zawadzki sees as the central themes of the commentary and his understanding of Cyril's exegetical procedures and commitments.

The book itself is a handsome volume, well-bound and on good paper; these features are not surprising for a production of a major European publisher. Further, I found only a handful of typographical errors, a welcome sight in a book of over 600 pages! The typefaces (Roman and Greek, with an occasional "other") are sufficiently sized and easy to read, both in the primary text and in the footnotes, and the text is organized on the page in a way that is easy for the reader to follow. The back matter includes many helpful resources, including an extensive bibliography of ancient and modern sources, multiple appendices, and multiple indices. In short, the entire book is produced in such a way that scholars can use it effectively and with ease.

Beyond the elements already noted, there are still more aspects of the book to commend it, of which I will mention two. First, Zawadzki provides the first translation of Cyril's commentary on 1 Corinthians into a modern language, apart from those fragments available in Judith Kovacs's 2005 volume on 1 Corinthians in the series The Church's Bible. For many scholars and students, both in patristics and New Testament studies, simply having a translation of Cyril's commentary will be a welcome addition to their libraries, whether of Cyril's works, patristic exegesis, or Pauline studies. On the whole, the translation is quite good, although, naturally, some scholars will want to quibble with this or that translation. In terms of translation theory, Zawadzki's would qualify as a "dynamic equivalence" translation; the translation represents the Greek well but also reads as good, contemporary, scholarly German. Happily, Zawadzki is appropriately consistent in translating the terms that were most important for the fourth- and fifth-century debates about Christology and the Trinity: "Gott," "Sohn," "Logos," "Natur," and so on.

Second, as Zawadzki shows via the translation and elucidates in his comments, Cyril is not restricted to a single exegetical approach but rather employs many interpretive strategies, from simple paraphrase (like a homiletician), to etymological analyses, to historical explanation of the first-century situation in Corinth, to comments about the text's meaning for contemporary theological debates, to pastoral encouragements for his audience. This demonstration on Zawadzki's part corrects some modern descriptions of Cyril's exegetical predilections (as shown in the book's part D) and also puts a further nail into the coffin of the traditional (and false) Antiochene-Alexandrian binary with regard to exegetical strategies. In terms of Cyril's theological applications, we also see how much relevance he saw in the dogmatic discussions of his day, as Zawadzki points out how skillfully Cyril is able to weave contemporary theological questions into his commentary. In fact, as Zawadzki says, "So kann Paulus im Kommentar Cyrills als jemand erscheinen, der Arius und Nestorius kritisiert…" (557).

Given the broad scope of the book, there is very little missing that a scholar might reasonably expect from a book of this type. If there is indeed a desideratum in terms of the book's approach, it is that Zawadzki does not engage at much length the broader conversations about patristic exegesis (e.g., questions of "figural exegesis"), nor does he spend much space placing Cyril's practices in the context of other ancient exegetes. However, the depth at which he engages Cyril's *own* work will allow for future work on those very topics.

There is one aspect of Zawadzki's argumentation that I found unconvincing, namely, his repeated assertion that the commentary was written during the Nestorian period (that is, after the beginning of the Nestorian controversy in 428), rather than before it, like almost all of Cyril's other exegetical writings. There is a long section on this topic (37–60), in which Zawadzki builds his argument primarily on Cyril's terminology regarding and manner of speaking about Christ: the "natures" of Christ, that Christ is not "divided," that Mary is "Theotokos," and so on. Zawadzki attempts to argue that these syntactic tendencies are clues for dating the text during the Nestorian period. However, there are at least three counterarguments. First, Cyril never names Nestorius in this commentary; granted, an argument from silence is not particularly strong, but in his other anti-Nestorian writings, Cyril is often quite ready to explicitly name his opponent. Second, "Theotokos" is rightly associated with the Nestorian controversy, but it is not restricted to it; in fact, it had been used in Egypt for approximately one hundred years by that point, if not more. Finally, and most importantly, in this commentary Cyril simply does not talk about Christ in the same way that he does in the anti-Nestorian writings. There is similar terminology, to be sure, but he uses words such as "nature" in different ways; I would argue that the christological thought found here represents an intermediate stage between that of Athanasius's *On the Incarnation* and the later, more developed Christology of Cyril's conflicts with Nestorius. The best comparison (in my mind) is with Cyril's pre-Nestorian *Commentary on John*, which contains much of the same christological thought, uses much of the same terminology, and (incidentally) also does not name Nestorius.

However, while this last point is important for Cyrilline studies, this volume has many virtues and will be useful for many people. For Cyril scholars, it provides a critical edition and translation of one of Cyril's neglected works, hopefully opening the door for more studies like this in the future and enhancing our ability to further our understanding of Cyril as an exegete, pastor, and theologian. For scholars of patristic exegesis, the book gives us more raw material to study, as well as introductory investigations into the commentary itself. For New Testament scholars, the volume provides a window into the ways that ancient Christians interpreted the Pauline epistles, thus enriching our understanding of 1 Corinthians.

Christianity in Roman Africa: The Development of Its Practices and Beliefs, by Robin M. Jensen and J. Patout Burns Jr. Grand Rapids: Eerdmans, 2014. Pp. liii + 670. Cloth. $55.00. ISBN 9780802869319.

Allen Kerkeslager, Saint Joseph's University

This lengthy volume will be an instant classic. In mostly catalogue form, it surveys practices, rituals, and theological debates primarily from the late second century to mid-fifth century in the churches of regions now embraced by modern Algeria, Tunisia, and western Libya (omitting ancient Cyrenaica). The book is the product of a full decade of collaboration in seminars, papers, and site tours by contributors who already have outstanding records of scholarship. Although the English style is clear and the use of untranslated foreign words is limited, the origin in professional society activities is preserved in its presumptions of specialized knowledge. The result is too technical for most undergraduates. However, it will prove illuminating to advanced readers and merits repeated consultation as a reference tool.

The introduction surveys the sources and themes that will be addressed in the remainder of the book (xlv–liii). It also acknowledges the debt to W. H. C. Frend and others in its methodology of "correlation of archaeological and literary evidence." Chapters 1–3 survey the history of Christianity in Roman Africa up to the Arab conquest (1–85). Chapter 4 summarizes the archaeological evidence for Christianity in the targeted region and period (87–163). Combined with 153 excellent site drawings and color plates, this represents one of the book's most distinctive and valuable contributions. Chapters 6–12 survey Christian ritual practices in Roman North Africa, including baptism (165–231); church services and the Eucharist (233–93); penance (295–361); activities of clerical offices and orders (363–439); marriage, virginity, and widowhood, including both ritual and quotidian features (441–89); funerary rituals (491–517); the cult of the martyrs (519–51); and daily practices related to prayer, food, economics, and affirming one's Christian identity (553–99). Chapter 13 draws together the implications of the previous chapters (601–21). These are summarized in what may be the closest to a unifying main thesis that the book's catalogue form allows: "The major crises and conflicts … were all focused on the preservation of the holiness of the church and its identity as the assembly of those being saved" (601). The volume closes with a bibliography and indices of places, monuments, and subjects.

The book makes a number of significant contributions to the study of Christianity in Roman Africa. First, it achieves its goal of providing a synthesis of the literary and archaeological evidence for Christianity in the period and region. Each of the main chapters on rituals (chs. 5–12) is organized chronologically and focuses primarily on the evidence from Tertullian, Cyprian, and Augustine. Each of these chapters concludes with sections devoted to the "correlation" of archaeological and literary evidence and the "correlation" of theology and practice. The unique disciplinary contribution of archaeology is often marginalized by subjugating the archaeological evidence to the interpretive guide of written sources (a principle made explicit on 519), but the outcome goes beyond mere correlation to the more impressive achievement of integration.

Second, the collaborative effort of multiple authors has ensured that the treatment of the sources is generally defensible and rarely marred by tendentious interpretation. This is further insured by stubbornly staying close to the ancient literary and archaeological sources. The emphasis on summary and synthesis of primary sources unfortunately limits the development of bold arguments or a truly groundbreaking overarching thesis. However, the advantage of this approach is that the summaries will preserve their utility for generations.

Third, the rigorous focus on the primary source material is complemented by extensive documentation that establishes the book as an ideal starting point for research on the topics addressed in the book. The detailed summaries of primary sources, numerous references in the text, and extensive footnotes make it a goldmine of information. The book will provide an encyclopedic resource for anyone who wants to learn where to find more about conflicts between the Donatists and

Caecilianists, Augustine's views on marriage, Christian burial practices, or a host of other topics.

Since the book so admirably achieves its goals, any mild criticisms must be restricted to pointing out the limitations imposed by these goals and its catalogue form. First, the canonicity of Tertullian, Cyprian, and Augustine as the defining voices of Christianity in Roman North Africa remains unchallenged by the choice to use their works as an organizing principle. The book's treatment of the three patristic figures is so careful and exhaustive that it reveals more than enough evidence to suggest that they do not adequately represent the diversity of African Christianity. Even Cyprian with all his emphasis on bureaucratic order turns out to resemble the Montanists in his claims to direct revelation (382–83). Citations and allusions in the works of the three major figures indicate that they also owe a great debt to persons who are not easily identified. These include the unknown authors of Jewish and Christian apocrypha and pseudepigrapha, who tend to play a more prominent role in histories of early Christianity right next door in Egypt. However, the book is comprehensive enough that one does catches glimpses of sources with more diverse worldviews (e.g., martyrological tales; 523–30).

Second, despite the masterful use of sources from the larger cultural context, the book's image of church development sometimes appears more compartmentalized than might have been suggested by a more comparative approach. Discussion of forces of change concentrates largely on persecution from the outside and disputes over beliefs and practices within the churches. Other dynamics that might have been more fully explored are implied in the similarities observed between Greco-Roman funerary rituals and Christian rituals (126–28, 491, 505–8, 530–31); the unmentioned undertones of typical Greco-Roman assumptions about pollution in Cyprian's views of contamination and purity (177–78, 255–58); the numerous precedents for Christian penance in civic practice, voluntary associations, and Judaism; the barely mentioned dialogue between Augustine and contemporary philosophy; or hints of connections between the supererogatory powers of Christian martyrs, magic, and Greco-Roman tales of heroic deaths (381–82, 521–51).

Third, the chosen emphasis on catalogue and description of practices and beliefs severely limits the opportunities for capitalizing on modern methodologies that might have helped to explain and understand these practices and beliefs. The authors cannot be charged with lack of awareness because such methodologies are occasionally implied in tantalizingly brief allusions. For example, the passing reference to the "liminal state" of penitents under Augustine echoes Victor Turner (355). But the generative questions of symbolic anthropologists make no major appearance in the discussions of schisms and other conflicts. Likewise, the performative aspects of human behavior emphasized by sociologists and other theorists failed to arouse more evocative treatment of the rich theatricality of the many rituals surveyed in each chapter. More recent cognitive science approaches also may have suggested more exploration of the inner workings of mysticism and other types of religious experience that were frequently expressed in the context of prayer, fasting, vigils, cult of the dead, and other practices surveyed in the book. The limited use of such methodologies in a book that devotes so much space to social conflicts, rituals, and other topics ideally suited to their application represents a missed opportunity for provoking deeper understanding and broader appeal.

Of course, no book can do everything. The limitations imposed by the chosen focus, format, and approach do not detract from the book's stellar accomplishment in doing what its authors set out to do. They have produced a truly magnificent synthesis of the most relevant primary sources. It will be indispensable for all future research on the topics it addresses. Given its modest price, no collection of works on early Christianity, Roman history, or ancient North Africa can afford to be without this encyclopedic, impeccably researched, and consistently reliable resource.

HISTORY OF INTERPRETATION

Handbook of Women Biblical Interpreters: A Historical and Biographical Guide, edited by Marion Ann Taylor; associate ed., Agnes Choi. Grand Rapids: Baker Academic, 2012. Pp. xviii + 585. Hardcover. $44.99. ISBN 9780801033568.

Alice A. Keefe, University of Wisconsin–Stevens Point

Gerda Lerner's classic work, *The Creation of Patriarchy*, opens with an important salvo: "Women's history is indispensable and essential to the emancipation of women." Why is this? Because without any collective memory of resistant and critical foremothers, each generation of women has had to start from scratch in identifying, analyzing, and critiquing the restrictive patriarchal ideologies of their time and place. This absence of collective memory especially characterizes the situation of women who have read and interpreted the scriptures throughout Christian and Jewish history; each pondered and wrote about the scriptures without knowledge of the insights of other women interpreters and without even knowing that other women had ever done the same. Even in the late twentieth century, feminist biblical interpreters have operated with little or no knowledge of their foremothers in the work of biblical interpretation. We (contemporary feminist biblical scholars) have had to study and write as if we were the first women in history to ask gender-inclusive questions of the biblical texts or to challenge patriarchal or misogynistic readings of them. The burgeoning field of reception history has been of little help in identifying women biblical interpreters in history; standard treatments of the history of biblical interpretation leave the impression of an almost exclusively male club. Happily, in recent decades feminist scholars have begun to fill in some of the missing pieces. In 1993, Gerda Lerner offered one of the earliest efforts to write a history of women's reception of the Bible in her chapter on "One Thousand Years of Biblical Interpretation" in *The Creation of Feminist Consciousness*. Subsequent work from feminist scholars trained specifically in biblical reception history have followed, including Marla J. Selvidge's

Notorious Voices: Feminist Biblical Interpretation 1500–1920 in 1996, Joy A. Schroeder's *Dinah's Lament: The Biblical Legacy of Sexual Violence in Christian Interpretation* in 2007, and *Recovering Nineteenth-Century Women Interpreters of the Bible*, edited by Christiana de Groot and Marion Ann Taylor, also in 2007. Now these and other historical and thematic studies are complemented by a new reference work, edited by Marion Ann Taylor with associate editor Agnes Choi, *Handbook of Women Biblical Interpreters* (2012). Situated at the intersection of biblical reception history and women's history, this volume clearly demonstrates that there is indeed a history of women reading and interpreting the Bible and provides us with a substantive guide to its scope, diversity, and complexity.

This handbook offers entries on 180 women biblical interpreters, Christian and Jewish, from the patristic era to the mid-twentieth century, arranged alphabetically. The handbook excludes second-wave feminist biblical scholars such as Phyllis Trible or Elisabeth Schüssler Fiorenza; among the criteria for inclusion in this handbook were that the woman interpreter had to be dead and active in her work prior to the 1970s, when women gained access to graduate education in biblical studies and employment as professors within the academy. A third criterion for inclusion was that a woman interpreter be representative, in the senses of either being representative of work being done in her historical era or representative of particular methodological approaches or concerns. Although there are many more records of women interpreting the Bible after the sixteenth century due to the expansion of printed Bibles and literacy, the editors strive for chronological balance, including abundant entries on interpreters from the patristic and medieval eras. Each entry includes pertinent bibliographic data, examines the interpreter's contexts and hermeneutical methods, and highlights key themes explored in her work. A brief bibliography accompanies each entry, guiding readers to primary sources and selected secondary sources.

This handbook encompasses a tremendous variety of women interpreters. Some were well known in their own time and are well remembered today, such as American abolitionist Angelina Grimke, while others were relatively unknown and have since been forgotten, such as the nineteenth-century Anglican author Mary Cornwallis. Some were honored in their own time for their erudition and piety, such as Marcella and Birgitta of Sweden, while others were persecuted as heretics, such as Marguerite Porete. Some were nuns, and some were laywomen. Some were Protestant or Catholic, some were Jewish, and some were secular intellectuals, such as Mary Wollstonecraft. Most of the women included are Europeans or European Americans, but also included are Juana Inés de la Cruz and several African American women, including Jarena Lee and Sojourner Truth. Some were highly educated and could read Greek or Hebrew; others relied entirely upon inspiration for their interpretive insights and might even be illiterate, such as Margery Kempe. All faced the challenge of justifying their interpretive acts as they dared to cross the boundary into the male preserve of biblical interpretation. Many claimed divine authorization through the medium of visions, dreams, or other forms of divine inspiration. Others staked out their right to interpret based upon some intellectual principle, such as the teachings of Reformed theology. All in all, this volume offers a rich treasure trove for the student of women's religious history.

The women included come from a wide variety of social, religious, and historical contexts, but despite this diversity their common situation as women reading and interpreting the Bible in patriarchal cultures led many to engage with similar themes, texts, and concerns. Many turned their attention to key prooftexts for male supremacy, such as Gen 2–3, 1 Tim 2, and Eph 5:21–33, and offered counter-readings that anticipated many of the insights of contemporary feminist biblical scholars. For example, long before Trible's rereading of Gen 2, both Christine de Pizan (fifteenth century) and Moderata Fonte (sixteenth century) argued that Eve's creation out of Adam's flesh, compared to Adam's creation out of the dust, indicated that Eve was the crown of creation, not a derivative and inferior being. Defending women's right to study, teach, and preach, nineteenth-century interpreters such as Phoebe Palmer and Jarena Lee invoked the memory of Mary Magdalene as the first to preach the good news of the resurrection. The early twentieth-century women's activist and biblical scholar Anna Lee Starr presented Jesus as the emancipator of women and questioned whether all of Paul's writings were equally inspired. Biblical texts involving sex and sexuality also were interpreted in "proto-feminist" ways. Who knew that the seventeenth-century Venetian nun Arcangela Tarabotti long ago challenged those interpretations that blamed Dinah and Bathsheba for the sexual transgressions committed against them, rather than pinning the guilt on the lustful Prince Shechem or King David? Or that in the eighteenth century Ann Francis, a vicar's wife in England, published her own translation and imaginative interpretation of the Song of Solomon? The entries give particular attention to evidence of gendered exegesis in the work of their subjects, attending to the places where an interpreter is conscious of the difference her gender makes in her work of interpretation. While not all the women surveyed used gendered exegesis or addressed specifically female concerns in their writing, the overall effect of this volume is a clear testimonial to women's resistance and perseverance over many centuries in the face of patriarchal ideologies that denigrated women's intellectual capabilities and denied to them the authority to teach or preach.

Over ten years in the making and drawing together contributors from diverse fields—women's studies, biblical studies, religious studies, English, and history—this handbook is a monumental achievement and will be the standard guide to women's reception history for years to come. This volume will be an important addition to reference-room collections as well as personal libraries. Students will appreciate the easy access to authoritative yet accessible overviews of these brilliant and sometimes prophetic women, many of whom have rarely been celebrated or studied. Researchers of reception history will also appreciate the scripture index, subject index, and chronological list of women biblical interpreters at the back. Feminist scholars of all types will appreciate this work's documentation of a long history of courageous women insisting on their own authority to reread the very scriptures used to subordinate and silence them.

The Rediscovery of Jewish Christianity: From Toland to Baur, edited by F. Stanley Jones. History of Biblical Studies 5. Atlanta: Society of Biblical Literature, 2012. Pp. xii + 248. Paper. $33.95. ISBN 9781589836464.

Jeffrey L. Morrow, Seton Hall University

For far too long the roots of the modern historical-critical method of biblical studies have been traced to Germany in the eighteenth or nineteenth centuries. One important, but too often neglected, aspect of the earlier history of historical biblical criticism is the way in which English biblical exegesis, and particularly that found among English Deists, influenced later German biblical scholarship.[1] *The Rediscovery of Jewish Christianity: From Toland to Baur* is thus a very helpful corrective to this common but incorrect assumption. This volume focuses on the specific issue of "Jewish Christianity" and the ways in which so much of modern scholarly discourse on Jewish Christianity is indebted to John Toland (1670–1722). Traditionally, scholars have located the origin of scholarship on Jewish Christianity in the work of Ferdinand Christian Baur (1792–1860).[2] Prior to coming to German scholarship, however, such study was initiated among English intellectuals, in particular Toland and Thomas Morgan (ca. 1680–1743). It was especially through Johann Salomo Semler (1725–1791) that such nascent English biblical criticism became known in the world of eighteenth- and nineteenth-century German biblical scholarship.

The Rediscovery of Jewish Christianity is the fifth volume in the Society of Biblical Literature's relatively new and exciting series History of Biblical Studies, the main purpose of which is to provide the first English translations of key works of nineteenth-century and early twentieth-century biblical scholarship that have thus far never been published in English translation. In light of the series aim, *The Rediscovery of Jewish Christianity* stands apart from other books in the series in three ways. First, despite including excerpts from Toland's work, in just over seventy pages, this volume is not primarily the publication of an earlier work of biblical studies. Rather, the majority of the volume, the first more than 160 pages, is devoted

---

1. Some histories of biblical scholarship have pointed this out, but they remain exceptions to the rule. Such helpful studies that discuss the ways in which earlier English exegesis came to Germany and influenced German biblical scholarship include Scott W. Hahn and Benjamin Wiker, *Politicizing the Bible: The Roots of Historical Criticism and the Secularization of Scripture 1300–1700* (New York: Herder & Herder, 2013); John Rogerson, *Old Testament Criticism in the Nineteenth Century: England and Germany* (Philadelphia: Fortress, 1984); and Henning Graf Reventlow, *Bibelautorität und Geist der Moderne: Die bedeutung des Bibelverständnisses für die geistesgeschichtliche und politische Entwicklung in England von der Reformation bis zur Aufklärung* (Göttingen: Vandenhoeck & Ruprecht, 1980).

2. See, e.g., the comments in Anette Rudolph, "Die Judenchristen in Justins Dialog mit Tryphon," in *StPatr* 36 (2001): 300–302; and Joan E. Taylor, "The Phenomenon of Early Jewish-Christianity: Reality or Scholarly Invention?" *VC* 44 (1990): 314. These examples are included in the present volume (139 and nn. 5–6).

to contemporary scholarly essays on the book's topic. Second, unlike others in the series, Toland's work does not represent nineteenth-century or early twentieth-century biblical scholarship but rather late seventeenth- and early eighteenth-century biblical exegesis. Finally, whereas the series is primarily devoted to producing the first English translations of these texts, the piece from Toland that the authors include from *Nazarenus* was initially published in English, even though it was his own English edition of his earlier French work (45). The series is also intended for monographs on the history of biblical scholarship, and this present book, albeit an edited volume and not a monograph, fits that description fairly well.

The first part of the volume, "Background," is composed of a single essay, Matti Myllykoski, "'Christian Jews' and 'Jewish Christians': The Jewish Origins of Christianity in English Literature from Elizabeth I to Toland's *Nazarenus*" (3–41). Myllykoski's contribution does a superb job of situating the concepts of "Christian Jews" and "Jewish Christians" in the English literature prior to the Baur's later German work. The author utilizes the wealth of sources available from the Early English Books Online website, which boasts "digital facsimile page images of virtually every work printed in England, Ireland, Scotland, Wales and British North America and works in English printed elsewhere from 1473–1700" (3 n. 2).[3] Myllykoski's study of the phrase *Christian Jews* within this literature allows him to write: "The use of the term *Christian Jews* in the period before 1700 is surprisingly coherent. In biblical scholarship, it characterizes the ethnic Jews who joined the Jesus movement and who for a time continued to observe the Mosaic law" (14). When it comes to the phrase *Jewish Christians*, however, Myllykoski discovers a different historical context, specifically the political debates between Arminians who supported Charles I and the Puritans who opposed him (20). Toland's work brings to this earlier discussion a historical treatise that seems to be an apologia for the Unitarian or Socinian views in contrast to the more traditional visions of early Christianity. One of Myllykoski's insights, which I have found to be true even beyond this time period, in works from other regions and in other languages, is that the "anti-Catholic atmosphere among many Englishman found expression in texts whose authors—among other peculiarities—regarded Catholic and Jewish practices as essentially similar. Therefore, the Catholics also resembled Jewish Christians and Christian Jews of the early church" (4–5).

Part 2, "John Toland and the Rediscovery of Jewish Christianity," begins with Pierre Lurbe's "John Toland's *Nazarenus* and the Original Plan of Christianity" (45–66). Lurbe explains the origin of Toland's famous work, *Nazarenus*, which is the main text on which this volume focuses. He shows that, although Toland wrote *Nazarenus* in English, he based it upon an earlier text that he wrote in French, namely, *Christianisme Judaïque et Mahométan*. This earlier French text was a portion of a more expansive work, *Dissertations diverses de Monsieur Tolan-*

---

3. The website may be accessed at http://eebo.chadwyck.com/home. It is a truly magnificent resource for anyone interested in English texts from this time period.

dus, which he dedicated to one of his most significant patrons, Prince Eugene of Savoy.[4] Toland's work became especially important for drawing attention to apocryphal New Testament literature, in this case the Gospel of Barnabas. Toland argues that the Gospel of Barnabas is a "Mahometan" gospel (52 n. 17), which he claims to have discovered.[5] Lurbe argues that this allowed Toland to reconfigure the history of early Christianity in a way vastly distinct from how it was traditionally envisioned.

Next is Matt Jackson-McCabe's "The Invention of Jewish Christianity in John Toland's *Nazarenus* (67–90). Jackson-McCabe's essay details the significance of Toland's early use of "Jewish Christianity" in *Nazarenus*. Jackson-McCabe argues that:

> the category "Jewish Christianity," if supported by historical argumentation, was a byproduct of Toland's attempt to lay claim to the mythic source of Christian authority—Jesus and the apostles—for his own Enlightenment ethos of rationality, universal humanity, and tolerance. The concept of "Jewish Christianity," in other words, was an invention of ecclesiastical apologetic discourse and Christian myth. (70)

Jackson-McCabe underscores how Toland viewed Islam as a form of Christianity, what he called "Mahometan Christianity." The notion of Jewish Christianity became for Toland an "apologetical construct" (80), as was his concept of Mahometan Christianity, for the purpose of defending a form of religious toleration in Europe (80–89). Thus, Toland's turn to Jewish Christianity, was the result not of a scientific-historical investigation but rather of Toland's own theo-political agenda, his "humanistic reclamation of Christian myth" (89).

After this we have F. Stanley Jones's "The Genesis, Purpose, and Significance of John Toland's *Nazarenus*" (91–101). Jones's brief essay does a good job situating Toland's *Nazarenus* in historical context, particularly in the context of Toland's other works and his politics. Jones points out, in light of *Nazarenus*'s genesis in Toland's earlier French *Christianisme*—a key fragment of which exists from 1698—that it appears that Toland already had his notions concerning Mahometan Christianity prior to finding the Gospel of Barnabas in 1709 (93–94). For Toland, the practice of history becomes the means of achieving his political ends, by exposing "the origin of prejudice" (95), historical inquiry can help lead to religious toleration, which Jones maintains is the main purpose of *Nazarenus* (96). Significantly, Jones identifies "this insight that the first Christians

---

4. The actual name in the dedication was the Prince's pseudonym, Megalonymus.

5. Toland's actual words, which Lurbe provides in a footnote, are worth reproducing here: "I. IN *the first place you'll find the succinct history of a* NEW GOSPEL, *which I discovered at Amsterdam, in the year* 1709. *It is a* Mahometan Gospel, *never before publicly made known among Christians, tho they have much talkt about the Mahometans acknowledging the* Gospel" (52 n. 17, citing *Nazarenus*, ii).

were Jewish Christians and were also the first heretics may be said to be the catalyst behind modern critical study of the New Testament and Christian origins" (99). It might be putting it too strongly to label this "insight" as "the catalyst" to modern historical-critical New Testament scholarship, but it certainly was an important contribution. Other earlier works—such as Spinoza's 1670 *Tractatus theologico-politicus*, as well as Richard Simon's 1689 *Histoire critique du texte du Nouveau Testament*, 1690 *Histoire critique des versions du Nouveau Testament*, and 1693 *Histoire critique des principaux commentateurs du Nouveau Testament*, which Johann Salomo Semler brought into German—played important roles in this regard.[6]

Part 3, "From Toland to Baur," begins with Matt Jackson-McCabe, "'Jewish Christianity' and 'Christian Deism' in Thomas Morgan's *The Moral Philosopher*," (105–22). In this essay Jackson-McCabe brings Thomas Morgan's work into discussion. He shows how Toland's contemporary Morgan was likewise an important early figure in the history of scholarly discourse on Jewish Christianity. He emphasizes how Morgan's work, within a couple of decades of Toland's *Nazarenus*, functioned similarly to Toland's work, both linking nascent historical criticism with "the theological apologetics of Enlightenment Christianity" (120).[7] Jackson-McCabe concludes that, "much like Toland, Morgan used the tools of critical historiography to authorize his humanistic, rationalistic religious views by identifying them as the pristine original Christianity of Jesus and the apostolic era while simultaneously delegitimating the traditional religion of his opponents as a corrupt deviation from that original" (121).

After Jackson-McCabe we come to F. Stanley Jones's "From Toland to Baur: Tracks of the History of Research into Jewish Christianity" (123–36). This essay, along with the next one, are perhaps the most significant in the volume because they situate the present discussion in its history, genealogically tracing

---

6. See, e.g., Marianne Schröter, *Aufklärung durch Historisierung: Johann Salomo Semlers Hermeneutik des Christentums* (Berlin: de Gruyter, 2012), 86–90; Justin Champion, "Père Richard Simon and English Biblical Criticism, 1680–1700," in *Everything Connects: In Conference with Richard H. Popkin*, ed. James E. Force and David S. Katz (Leiden: Brill, 1999), 39–61; Pierre-François Moreau, "Spinoza's Reception and Influence," in *The Cambridge Companion to Spinoza*, ed. Don Garrett (Cambridge: Cambridge University Press, 1996), 408–33; and John D. Woodbridge, "German Responses to the Biblical Critic Richard Simon from Leibniz to J. S. Semler," in *Historische Kritik und biblischer Kanon in der deutschen Aufklärung*, ed. Henning Graf Reventlow, Walter Sparn, and John Woodbridge (Wiesbaden: Harrassowitz, 1988), 65–87. Indeed, Toland himself was influenced by Spinoza and Simon—he explicitly cites Simon in *Nazarenus* and explicitly responds to Spinoza's thoughts in other works. For more on this influence, see, e.g., Hahn and Wiker, *Politicizing the Bible*, 487–541. Semler was key in bringing Simon's works on New Testament scholarship into German.

7. He goes so far as to suggest that "the rise of critical scholarship on the New Testament itself, insofar as it proceeded from the same mythic assumption, was just as intimately bound up in post-Enlightenment ecclesiastical apologetics" (120 n. 72).

the influence of Toland's work to Baur, who is usually credited as originator of this particular scholarly discourse. Semler emerges as one of the key mediators of English Deistic intellectual currents into the German academy. Jones summarizes this history as follows:

> Rejected and refuted in detail by [Johann Lorenz] Mosheim, Toland's ideas were known to Semler and appropriated under the concept of two "parties" with distinctive canons in early Christianity. [Johann Karl Ludwig] Geiseler refereed Semler's position to distinguish his own. Baur hammered out and modified his views with continual reference to Geiseler's overview until he finally arrived at the position ascribed to Semler but ultimately indebted to Toland. Toland's "Jewish Christianity" then became known as Baur's "Judenchristenthum." (133–34)[8]

David Lincicum's "F. C. Baur's Place in the Study of Jewish Christianity" (137–66) continues this discussion, focusing especially on Baur's work. Interestingly, Lincicum points out how the eighteenth century happened to be a time when English works were in hot demand in Germany; there was thus an increase "in the reading, sales, and translation of English books in Germany" at that time (142). Near the end of his essay Lincicum mentions "a striking confluence between anti-Catholic rhetoric and anti-Jewish rhetoric in Baur's reconstruction of early Christianity" (159).[9] This appears to be the *pathos* of much of historical biblical criticism, at least of the eighteenth- and nineteenth-century mode—or rather, one of the *pathea* of historical criticism: the implicit (or explicit) denigration of Judaism, and thus Catholicism, which was often the veiled target behind Protestant biblical scholarly attacks things Jewish in the eighteenth and nineteenth centuries. The volume closes with two lengthy excerpts from Toland's *Nazarenus*, first the preface (169–85), then "Letter I" (187–242).

The Rediscovery of Jewish Christianity is a fine contribution to the history of modern biblical scholarship. The field is in sore need of more such works. It would be a great benefit to have many other volumes such as this one, including excerpts of a major early figure in biblical criticism, with scholarly essays situating that scholar and work within the scholar's broader historical context, as well as within

---

8. Although Jones mentions that Semler resided in the very home of his teacher Siegmund Jacob Baumgarten (1706–1757) and that Semler there witnessed Baumgarten's defenses of English Deistic thought (which contrasted from Baumgarten's formal public lectures and publications), as well as that Semler helped Baumgarten in reviewing English Deistic literature (124 and 127), Jones does not mention that Semler apparently translated some of these English Deistic works into German under Baumgarten's direction and inspiration. For comments to that effect, see J. C. O'Neill, *The Bible's Authority: A Portrait Gallery of Thinkers from Lessing to Bultmann* (Edinburgh: T&T Clark, 1991), 39–40. Needless to say, Semler was immersed in English Deistic intellectual literature, particularly concerning biblical interpretation and theology.

9. He writes further, "In fact, Judaism provides a direct inheritance to Catholicism in the form of its hierarchy and external institutions" (159).

the history of scholarship itself. Anyone interesting in the study of Jewish Christianity, the history of New Testament scholarship, Toland, or Baur will appreciate this wonderful volume. This is a book I know I will return to in the future. I heartily recommend it.

The "Nocturnal Side of Science" in David Friedrich Strauss's Life of Jesus Critically Examined, by Thomas Fabisiak. Emory Studies in Early Christianity 17. Atlanta: SBL Press, 2015. Pp. x + 219. Paper. $29.95. ISBN 9781628371086. Hardcover. $44.95. ISBN 9781628371093.

Jeffrey L. Morrow, Seton Hall University

With *The "Nocturnal Side of Science" in David Friedrich Strauss's Life of Jesus Critically Examined*, Thomas Fabisiak has made a significant contribution to studies of Strauss, but also to the history of historical Jesus studies and to the history modern biblical criticism more broadly speaking. This present volume, the author's 2014 Emory University doctoral dissertation, is quite impressive considering that origin. Fabisiak's dissertation is one of those rare dissertations that makes a truly important contribution to the field.

Fabisiak includes, very early on in his introduction (1–22), a marvelous anecdote relating to an exorcism of sorts performed by a modern theologian that could serve almost as a parable for the book's topic:

> "In the name of Reason, to which power is given over all specters; in the name of Science … before whose light all deceptive images vanish; in the name of Christianity, which has purified the air of all evil spirits, I command you, demon who does not exist, depart from this sick woman!" She suddenly interrupted this solemn address and, in her crude Swabian dialect, she dealt the learned necromancer a flood of abuse. … "You human ass, you think I'm afraid of your filthy talk? Get out of her unless you want what's coming to you!" The noble exorcist hurried sheepishly away. (1–2)[1]

The remainder of the introduction situates David Friedrich Strauss's (1808–1874) work in his social, theological, philosophical, and historical context. He underscores the complexity of the issues, showing how "the struggle between 'philosophy' and 'theology' is also a struggle about what Christianity is in its essence—and how it will define and be defined by a modern, secular, or rational age" (6). Fabisiak thus begins his introduction with an important discussion of Enlightened "disenchantment" and persistent cases of exorcisms in Germany (1–6). He proceeds to examine Strauss's most famous work, *Das Leben Jesu* (7–10), as well as its place within the history of New Testament criticism (10–13). Fabi-

---

1. The quotation is taken from Fabisiak's modified translation of Friedrich Wilhelm Krummacher, *An Autobiography*, trans. M. G. Easton (New York: Carter & Brothers, 1869), 208–9.

siak then provides an overview of Strauss's discussion of "ghosts" and demons in *Das Leben Jesu* (13–20). After a discussion of the turn to examine the "nocturnal side" of religious history, namely, regarding what we might think of as occult, paranormal, or mystical phenomena (20), he concludes with a brief overview of his volume (21–22).

In chapter 1, "Strauss on the Science of the Nocturnal Side of Nature" (23–67), Fabisiak covers Strauss's work on issues relating to ghosts, demons, clairvoyance, and the like regarding the "nocturnal side of nature." Fabisiak mentions how "German romantic medicine and natural philosophy shaped the scientific study of phenomena like ghost seeing and clairvoyance" (25), and this is the context in which he situates Strauss's work. Romantic thinkers of the time, such as Friedrich Wilhelm Joseph Schelling (1775–1854), resisted Enlightenment "fragmenting tendencies" (30). Under the influence of Friedrich Schleiermacher (1768–1834), Strauss's romanticism was tempered by Schleiermachian dialectic. These combined influences helped Strauss take the religious and mystical experiences of common folk seriously, even as his method demystified them.

In the second chapter, "The Nocturnal Side of Strauss's Historical Critique of Miracle Stories" (69–102), Fabisiak takes a closer look at Strauss's examination of the gospel miracle stories in *Das Leben Jesu*. Fabisiak emphasizes how Strauss's work on the nocturnal side of nature—his studies of contemporary accounts of demon possession and mystical phenomena—affected Strauss's gospel criticism when it came to the miracle accounts. Fabisiak explains how "the architectonics of souls and bodies that underlies Strauss's writings on the nocturnal side of nature is tied up with the questions of immanence and eschatology that obsessed him throughout his career" (101). As he had approached his contemporaries claiming to have experienced supernatural phenomena, so with the figures in the New Testament; Strauss trusted that they had experiences but limited those experiences to the result of nature, such as the human nervous system.

In chapter 3, "Strauss on Myth and the Nocturnal Side of Nature" (103–39), Fabisiak situates Strauss's New Testament criticism within the context of the late eighteenth- and early nineteenth-century theories of myth and their role in biblical studies, including the "mythic school" (e.g., Johann Gottfried Eichhorn [1752–1827]). Strauss relied upon these earlier romantic notions of myth, especially that of biblical scholar Wilhelm Martin Leberecht de Wette (1780–1849), whom Strauss credited "with bringing the romantic conception of myth fully to bear on the Bible" (109). The final sections of this chapter take up the ways in which Strauss applied the work of various philosophers—Georg Wilhelm Friedrich Hegel (1770–1831) and Immanuel Kant (1724–1804)—to his work on the Bible. Fabisiak concludes that "Strauss takes up aspects of romantic thought and draws on his experience with the nocturnal side of nature. In the process, he defines a scientific and demystifying approach to religion" (138).

The fourth chapter, "The Nocturnal Side of Christian and Modern Origins" (141–76), examines how Strauss's work on the life of Jesus from the gospels, and particularly on the apocalyptic aspects of Jesus in Strauss's work, functions as a criticism of modernity. Much as Johann David Michaelis (1717–1791) had rendered the Old Testament ancient, strange, and different, as a distant ancient Hebrew cultural artifact, for his contemporaries, Strauss made Jesus distant as "an unfamiliar ancient thinker" (143) to his contemporaries.[2] Many of Strauss's contemporaries and immediate predecessors (e.g., de Wette) considered Jesus a forerunner (or even founder) of the Enlightenment. As Fabisiak explains, "In German idealism, the historical Jesus reemerges from the crucible of criticism in a transfigured form: he is a symbol, image, or ideal of modern rational *Bildung*" (158). Strauss makes this view impossible with his apocalyptic Jesus. Strauss thus links modernity with the Protestant Reformation, not with Jesus. *Das Leben Jesu* thus "operates in effect as a critique of modern reason" (161).

Fabisiak's conclusion, "Strauss's Visions of Modernity and Historical Science" (177–98), builds on the chapters that came before and pulls together Strauss's views concerning modernity and the importance of historical science. In the end, it is clear that Strauss's "critical writings in the 1830s emerged in a context where speculative idealism and romanticism still converged with popular religious belief to shape scientific discourses and methods" (178). He therefore did not reject the experiences of Jesus's disciples concerning alleged miracles such as Jesus's bodily resurrection, even though Strauss did not concede these actual miracles could have taken place. Rather, he located the experience of the miracles to psychological elements in the experiencers.

One of the many areas of received scholarly opinion that Fabisiak challenges is the all too often assumed association of "the rise of the modern, secular era with the 'disenchantment of the world'" (3). Fabisiak's work challenges this gross oversimplification. As he explains up front, "This rationalization and demystification was not a straightforward process, however. The relationship between science and faith or secularity and religion remained complex and tangled throughout the period" (3).[3] One of the most important but far too often neglected insights Fabisiak brings to the fore is the role of the modern state in the new modern biblical studies. Relying upon earlier studies like those by Michael Legaspi (*The Death of Scripture*) and Jonathan Sheehan (*The Enlightenment Bible: Translation, Scholarship, Culture* [Princeton: Princeton University Press, 2005]), Fabisiak observes how "scholars transformed the Bible from a sacred Scripture into a uniquely privi-

---

2. On Michaelis's work here, see Michael C. Legaspi, *The Death of Scripture and the Rise of Biblical Studies* (Oxford: Oxford University Press, 2010), which Fabisiak cites in his work, e.g., 11 n. 28 and 127 n. 63.

3. He likewise explains how, "In the dominant strains of eighteenth- and early nineteenth-century German philosophy, it was commonly believed that modern, secular, or scientific disciplines and forms of life evolved out of the heart of Christianity" (6). Strauss and others will pose a challenge to this, but it helps to underscore some of the complexities involved in these discussions.

leged cultural text. Their work defined the university, in the place of the church, as the proper sphere in which to understand religion and Scripture; it helped to shore up civil authority against religious insurrections and to shape the secular state" (11).[4] Importantly, Fabisiak does not shy away from what might be more controversial or provocative insights regarding these complex scholarly/institutional/political relationships, as when he points out:

> Although *Aufklärers* [Enlighteners] opposed religious intolerance and political tyranny, their work often served the interests of an absolutist state. German state officials and aristocrats enthusiastically embraced and supported the *Volksaufklärung* [popular Enlightenment]. It played a crucial role in state formation…. Those who were not ready to be inducted into the enlightened public sphere … were subjected to a different, often more painful model of reformative education …. campaigns of popular Enlightenment in the churches and schools went hand-in-hand with a growing discourse on religious pathology and the rise of the asylum. Medical, psychological explanations of religious disorder transformed potential threats from inspired charismatics into objects of education, psychiatric treatment, and imprisonment. (65–66)

In his discussions regarding the history of modern biblical criticism, Fabisiak shows himself well aware of the subtleties of the history, and he eschews the often incorrect assumptions biblical scholars too often make in regard to the history of their own discipline. Contrary to so many textbooks locating the birth of modern biblical criticism to eighteenth- or nineteenth-century Germany, as if it sprang *ex nihilo* from the mind of erudite German academicians, Fabisiak is well aware of the earlier influence of biblical exegesis and hermeneutics of English Deists (10–12 and 76–78). What was new for me was the context of specifically Swabian Pietism for understanding Strauss and many of his contemporaries. Without lapsing into reductionism, Fabisiak underscores "the importance of Swabian Pietist and theosophical traditions … [as the context] in which Schelling, Hegel, and later Strauss began their careers…. [This helps] to complicate any oversimple or triumphalist narrative of secular disenchantment" (36 n. 35).

Finally, his focus on Strauss's *Das Leben Jesu* is helpful considering just how influential that work proved in New Testament scholarship, and really the whole of religious and theological studies of the time, as Fabisiak justly notes, "Strauss's attempt [in *Das Leben Jesu*] to carry out a historical critique without 'presuppositions' defined an ethos and rhetoric of *Wissenschaft* in the fields of history and theology" (69). Along with other works that made the turn to myth theories, Strauss aided in the scholarly shift that occurred, where the focus was no longer

---

4. In this context, Fabisiak mentions, "The rise of secular science from the Enlightenment to the present is bound up with the troubled lives of modern institutions—the state, the university, the asylum, and capitalism" (21).

centered on the events themselves in history but rather on the narratives within the texts under study (107).

This volume makes an important contribution to the history of modern biblical criticism and the history of historical Jesus studies in particular. It will be of great interest to anyone who is concerned with the formative history and intellectual context for modern biblical criticism, modern New Testament studies, and the study of the historical Jesus. Fabisiak's work on David Friedrich Strauss's *Das Leben Jesu* helps uncover the complex influences that led to his historical biblical hermeneutic and poses a serious challenge to overly simplistic accounts of secular disenchantment. Fabisiak's work is a sophisticated bringing together the religious history of nineteenth-century Germany, major eighteenth- and nineteenth-century German philosophical trends, historical Jesus studies, and the history of biblical scholarship in the nineteenth century in light of its immediate history from the seventeenth through eighteenth centuries, as well as the early history of psychological sciences and their relation to the "nocturnal side" of nature.

1–2 Samuel, 1–2 Kings, 1–2 Chronicles, edited by Derek Cooper and Martin J. Lohrmann. Reformation Commentary on Scripture, Old Testament 5. Downers Grove, IL: IVP Academic, 2016. Pp. liv + 745. Hardcover. $40.00. ISBN 9780830829552.

John Herbst, Regent University

From the publication of the first volumes of the Ancient Christian Commentary on Scripture in 1998, we have seen a substantial increase in the number of "theological" commentaries and commentary sets. Instead of trying to place the biblical writings into their historical contexts à la the historical-critical method, these works read the scriptures within a canonical setting, trying to fit passages into a greater theological scheme. The Reformation Commentary on Scripture continues this approach by compiling selected commentary from a broad range of Reformation-era writings.

This is not to say that Reformation exegesis coalesced around unified aims and methods. The volume under review shows that Reformation-era commentary on the books of 1 and 2 Samuel, 1 and 2 Kings, and 1 and 2 Chronicles displays "the depth and richness of exegetical ferment that defined the Reformation Era" (xxi). Yet as far as biblical interpretation goes, the best of this volume lies within its *theological* reflection on individual passages.

I think that this is what Richard Muller, quoted in the introduction, must have had in mind when he wrote that, while the historical-critical method can often correct the errors of "traditionary" readings "the conclusions offered by historical-critical exegesis may themselves be quite erroneous on the grounds provided by the exegesis of the patristic, medieval, and reformation periods" (xliv). (This is the worst that this volume has to say about the historical-critical method; a number of modern theological commentaries are much harsher.) The introduction consequently describes the mining of Reformation exegesis as "retrieval for the sake of (spiritual) renewal." But beyond historical interest, the items most profitably "retrieved" lie amidst the Reformers' efforts to contextualize biblical passages into the whole of scripture and theology.

The general introduction begins with a helpful description of the development of scriptural exegesis from the church fathers through the Middle Ages. Building upon the work of Origen and Augustine, medieval commentators searched for the *quadriga*, the four meanings of each passage: literal, allegorical, moral, and anagogical (this last relates to the use of temporal realities to discern spiritual facts). Because these nonliteral interpretations often had little objective basis, Thomas Aquinas and Nicholas of Lyra began to stress the primacy of the literal sense, thus paving the way for the Reformers' work. For the Reformers, Lyra was especially popular, so that the commentaries in this volume regularly reference his work.

To help us sort through the different Reformation approaches, the introduction describes eight separate "schools of exegesis." The best represented of these by far is "Luther and the Wittenberg School," which, by my estimation, accounts for no less than 50 percent of the entries. The key method here was elucidated in 1521 by Philipp Melanchthon in *Loci communes* (Common Places), referenced repeatedly though this volume. The *Loci communes* approach identifies the primary argument of a given passage, then uses the result to develop doctrine. The introduction lists a number of German Lutherans who used this method, including the most prolific contributor to this volume, Melanchthon's student Johannes Bugenhagen. But the *Loci communes* approach extended beyond the German Lutheran sphere so that advocates included people such as seventeenth-century Anglican priest John Mayer, another prolific contributor.

A second shorter introduction introduces Reformer approaches to the subject of this volume, 1–2 Samuel, 1–2 Kings, and 1–2 Chronicles. Following Luther, the Reformers much preferred Kings to Chronicles, so that the Chronicles chapters of this volume are much shorter than those of the other books. We find further description of the *Loci communes* method, which is appropriate, given its dominance in the entries. As the pre-Enlightenment Reformers had not developed the tools to offer much on issues we associate with modern lower and higher criticism, the editors' decision to stress *Loci communes* commentary was wise, as this sort of work will surely have the most value for modern readers. This second introduction stresses above all the diversity of the commentators with respect to confessional perspectives, methodology, and exegetical results. Recognizing a "plurality of perspectives" (xlix) is crucial for the editors: readers should not use this work to find "right answers" (l) but instead should note what the Reformers found to be worthy of commentary. This introduction then closes with an overview of the principal contributors and their perspectives.

Next comes the commentary itself: six chapters, one for each of the six biblical books covered in this volume. Each chapter begins with a brief introduction to the book in question, followed by selected Reformation-era overviews of the book. The book is then broken down into sections of biblical text that average a chapter or two. The biblical text is rendered in the English Standard Version (ESV). There follows a short summary of the general approach of the contributing Reformers. Next comes selected Reformer commentary, usually a single long paragraph in length, but sometimes more. Reformer commentary is sometimes grouped according to subsections of the text. For example, the work on 1 Kgs 8 is broken down into subsections on 8:1–13, 14–53, 54–61, and 62–66.

Following the commentaries is a map of Europe at the time of the Reformation, a ten-page Reformation timeline, biographical sketches of the contributors and related figures, a bibliography, and indices of authors and writings, subjects, and scripture. The biographical sketches are especially helpful. The entries for the 90 percent of contributors with whom I was unfamiliar are well prepared, on a par with those in reference works such as *The Oxford Dictionary of the Christian Church*.

The second introduction highlights the work of the most famous Reformation figures, Martin Luther and John Calvin. I assume that the editors stressed Luther out of historical interest, as his comments in this volume rarely display theological heft. For example, Luther's comments describing his strong preference for 1 and 2 Kings ahead of 1 and 2 Chronicles entirely lack objective reasoning. We learn what Luther thought, but from exegetical, theological, and devotional points of view Luther's conclusions without supporting evidence do not help much. Downplaying Chronicles based on Luther's preferences is no better than pushing aside James for the same reason. Throughout this volume Luther plainly shares his opinions but rarely gives a supporting argument.

Calvin's contributions are much more erudite, as out of all the Reformers his methodology is closest to the modern historical-critical method. His commentary here comes largely from sermons he preached on 2 Sam 1–13 in 1562 and 1563. Unfortunately, no one else from his "school" ("the Geneva Reformers") is represented in this volume, except perhaps for Calvin's admirer and foil, Jacobus Arminius. We see Calvin's theological depth in his comments on 2 Sam 6, in which God kills Uzzah for catching the ark as it falls from the cart. Calvin recognizes the apparent injustice of God's action but then instructs us to take care not to act beyond our appointed office. Calvin notes as well that, while Uzzah's execution appears to be immoral, we must accept that God's understanding of justice will always be greater than our own.

I appreciate the substantive commentary by all surrounding the Elijah cycle. The work on 1 Kgs 19 ("Elijah and the Lord") and 2 Kgs 2:1–12 ("Elijah Taken to Heaven") are among the highlights of the volume. The 2 Kgs 1–12 commentary contains fascinating explanations of the symbolic meanings of various elements in the passage: dividing the waters; Elisha's request for a double portion; Elijah's ascent to heaven. As for 1 Kgs 19, some commentators criticize Elijah's lack of faith, while others stress a God who encourages his servants as they go through difficult times. The editors highlight the use of this passage to discuss a "true church existing without definable structure," but I especially enjoyed a piece from the Calvinist Puritan Thomas Adams, who likens Elijah's story to his recent history of

England. Adams sees God's power in his judgment of Henry VIII, King Edward, and Queen Mary, followed by the "still voice" during the reign of Queen Elizabeth.

Overall, this volume is fun, particularly if one likes church history. Historical-critical exegesis may be the flavor of the day, but there is certainly room for more theological/ traditional biblical interpretation, particularly with respect to the Old Testament. Perhaps even more than its companion Ancient Christian Commentary on Scripture, Reformation Commentary on Scripture: Old Testament is a nice introductory tool to guide our historical and theological reading.

HERMENEUTICS AND METHODS

Borderline Exegesis, by Leif E. Vaage. Signifying (on) Scriptures. University Park: Pennsylvania State University Press, 2014. Pp. xiii + 201. Cloth. $58.46. ISBN 9780271062877.

Jacqueline M. Hidalgo, Williams College

A rewarding and challenging read, *Borderline Exegesis* records an "ongoing struggle to know a good life" (2). Leif Vaage searches for other, better worlds by carefully reading biblical texts in critical conversation with our contemporary world. Blending traditional literary-, source-, and historical-critical tools with more contemporary liberationist, biographical, and postmodern strategies, Vaage interprets selections from Job, Matthew, James, and Revelation as passages that overturn "common sense" about what constitutes the good life. Although this book includes four essays that previously were published in Spanish, these essays are not mere translations; they have been significantly transformed.

Vaage situates himself as a borderline exegete, a subject who has moved between the bounds of North Atlantic biblical scholarship, his family background in Christian Norway, and his work in Peru. Yet the borderline of Vaage's exegetical method refers to more than the borders between cultures, nations, religions, or languages. Vaage defines borderline exegesis as a pursuit of hope that points the exegete toward "the edge that opens onto a yet undefined and thus unbounded possibility" (157). While this book still privileges an examination of biblical litera-ture over a thorough investigation of the author's worlds, Vaage unapologetically reads with the poor and oppressed, especially from Latin America.

The introduction and its illuminating notes define key terms, questions, and approaches that inform the book. Vaage describes biblical texts as "public places" from and through which peoples have sought answers to some of life's most press-ing questions, such as "Why must we suffer as we do? And why is there never enough of virtually everything? Is this the only possible way for the world to be? As good as it gets? What hope is there?" (14). Emphasizing a practice of "progres-sive unknowing" (5), Vaage underscores the fundamental otherness of the ancient worlds that produced biblical texts. However, Vaage's historical study aims to uncover other possible worlds and open up "alternate future[s] in the present" (9).

The first chapter examines Job 38:1–42:1–6. According to Vaage, modern readers' concentration on Job's innocence/guilt misdirects our attention from the text's critique of anthropocentrism. Carefully analyzing some of the symmetries between Job's complaint and God's response, Vaage teases out how images of non-human nature matter in God's rhetoric. Life is harsh for all creation, and human life gains no special "priority" over anything else (53); this realization transforms Job. Moreover, a perception of humanity as a noncentral part of a larger creation may be most urgent in our current ecological crisis.

Chapter 2 shifts to a discussion of human embeddedness within the social worlds we manufacture. The core texts informing this chapter are Jesus's teachings in Matthew (5:3–7:27; 10:5b–42; 13:1–52; 18:1–35; 20:1–16; 23:1–25:46), with special attention devoted to the Sermon the Mount (5:3–7:27). Comparing Matthew with Q and Luke, Vaage argues that Matthew's Sermon attacks Roman cultural elevation of the self-controlling free adult male head of household who pursues his own glory by dominating and subduing others. The Sermon criticizes such competitive winning and finds no shame in losing. Here Vaage sees common ground between Matthew's appraisals of Roman domination and contemporary Latin American critiques of neoliberal capitalism. The Sermon's ethic is connected to the central economic premise of the "Our Father." Lack of daily bread and debt are the main concerns, and these concerns find their root in "developmental" economics that favor the long-term gain of some while exploiting many others.

Vaage then breaks up his biblical exegesis with "a scriptural biography," a meditation on the broader socialities that have shaped his engagements with biblical texts. The structural centrality of this interlude is impactful, providing a richer accounting of how the Bible means "scripturally" for Vaage. He became a biblical scholar in part because of a pursuit of the power that enveloped particular discursive arguments in and around the Bible. Recalling a piece he wrote in Lima in 1992, he describes how the Bible is actually a "weak" text. For Vaage, the Bible's greatest power comes in readerly interactions, when we turn to the biblical texts as sites for excavating the "thus far unconsidered" (104).

Chapter 3 searches for the unconsidered in the Epistle of James and finds that systemic change also requires daily actions and individual subjective transformation. Vaage classifies James as having an ascetic orientation that he defines as "an embodied struggle to live 'against the grain' of a dominant 'normal' world in a given cultural setting" (107). Vaage depicts a Roman free elite male culture that performed and maintained dominance through the speech practice of "boasting," and he suggests that James employs a concentric structure that emphasizes the power of ascetically controlled, nonboastful speech. Modifying Hegel's master-slave dialectic, Vaage identifies James's "Christians" as "two-souled" (122) people pursuing alternate subjectivities. He differentiates "alternate" from "alternative" in order to describe the ongoing struggle of James's subjects who seek to opt away from dominant modes while sill living within them.

The fourth chapter turns to Revelation as an act of collective dreaming that registers an "unlost" desire for transformation even when repression seems unceasing (126–27). This chapter does not presume the biblical text always offers a liberating ideal. Following Stephen D. Moore, Vaage describes Revelation as narrating a divine coup that merely replaces the Roman emperor with God. Thus, the utopian ending cannot be the dream we most need. Looking elsewhere, Vaage examines ruptures in Revelation's dreamscape, focusing on the interludes between the sixth and seventh seal in 7:1–17 and between the sixth and seventh trumpet in 10:1–11:14. These moments interrupt Revelation's cycles of violence and in so doing offer a "borderline of hope" (128). He also fruitfully examines a moment of Peruvian rebellion against Spanish colonial rule that helpfully underscores how "the dreamscape inhabited by the extra-textual reader" significantly impacts what one finds in Revelation and how one uses it (138).

Vaage briefly concludes his book by redefining borderline exegesis and the necessities of hope in the face of environmental crisis. Although he describes biblical studies as a fundamentally "colonial science" that maps the mythology of imperial nation-states, he claims that biblical texts are open to "the deep play of an unconstrained and ideally unconstraining signification" (153). Therefore, the peril and promise of reading the Christian Bible resides in diverse meaning making.

Among the great strengths of this book is its recognition of the complexities of assumptions and pluralities of perspectives that exist between and within different cultural worlds. Nevertheless, though he is someone who reads so intentionally with and for the poor of Latin America, he only incorporates a few stories from his time in Peru, mostly by way of analogy. A future project might integrate more of these narratives from Peru as an equal conversation partner with the biblical material. For instance, one might ethnographically read with communities by directly asking them about what better possible worlds they imagine in and around the Bible.

Greater critical conversation with feminist, Latin American, and North American minoritized scholars might have furthered Vaage's borderline thinking because many of these scholars conceptualize an even more open and unsettling "borderlands" in which hemispherically American subjects encounter and wrestle with the Bible as a consequence of exploitative, violent cultural contact. For instance, Vaage's study of James's "two-souled" subjects might have been further augmented through explicit conversation with W. E. B. DuBois's notions of "double consciousness" and the "veil" and Gloria Anzaldúa's "mestiza consciousness." Place-aware Jewish critics who interpret Job after the Shoah or Latin American and U.S. Latina/o critics who attend specifically to class and migration in biblical studies have dramatically questioned when and how we can look for hope in the Bible; their practices open up new lines of hopeful reading even as they challenge the practices of power and authority that envelop many engagements with biblical texts. For example, looking at Matt 20:1–16, Vaage compellingly describes the landowner as just, but such a reading might have drawn out more layers of signification had the chapter weighed interpretations such as the one Jean-Pierre Ruiz provides in *Readings from the Edges* (2011). Thinking with contemporary U.S. immigrant day laborers, Ruiz refuses to identify the landowner with God and instead imagines Christ as one of the laborers, an approach that opens up new questions about signifying play on authority and the "kingdom of God" within the parable. Ruiz's book also raises questions about broader practices of scriptural authority and authorization that could have complemented Vaage's search for hopeful borderlines in and around biblical material.

Borderline Exegesis is a valuable contribution to our field's proliferation of reading practices. This book should spark further conversation about how and why we persist in reading biblical texts, and it will be a model that can inspire others. Ever seeking that borderline of hope, Vaage proves that engagements with biblical texts may yet take us to unexpected places, even or especially if these places offer up uncharted, multivalent, and contradictory possibilities.

Reading the Bible Ethically: Recovering the Voice in the Text, by Eric Douglass. Biblical Interpretation Series 133. Leiden: Brill, 2014. Pp. 301. Hardcover. €115,00. ISBN 9789004282865.

Walter Brueggemann, Columbia Theological Seminary

Eric Douglass (Randolph-Macon College) has written a discerning analysis of the complex interaction between the author and the reader of a text. He concludes that the act of interpretation is a "conversation" between two partners. But in order to have such a conversation, the author and authorial intent must be acknowledged and taken seriously. Thus his book pivots on the intentionality of the author, as the book resists the several deconstructive strategies now popular that champion the disappearance of the author. Among the issues that concern this discussion are the distance between "what the author planned to say and what the reader actually creates" and the reader's bias that is propelled by desire. The term *ethically* in the title means for Douglass to take authorial intent seriously and not to transpose it into the text that the reader desires.

Douglass offers two chapters on the significant work of the author. The author writes with an intention to say something specific. The author, second, writes to engage with a particular public audience, the intended audience. Third, by the use of language that is inherently generative, the writer is capable of "generating entire structures of new-ness" (52). The result may be a new way of thinking that is not reducible to existing cultural ways of thinking. The work of the writer in bringing words (objects) together in new configuration is, in this jargon, "supervenience" that reflects the subjective agency of the author. The result is a fresh word that is a reconfiguration according to the imagination of an active intentional agent.

The second group of chapters in the book is devoted to analysis of the act of reading. In Douglass's purview, the reader begins to read with "an initial guess," whereby the reader anticipates the genre of the text and so the likely message of the text or at least the orbit in which the message can be received, understood, and interpreted. Such an initial guess, however, often is not correct because the author may surprise. The reader's initial guess, however, is sometimes too powerful, so that it can suppress the textual design and intent of the author. When the initial guess is recognized as incorrect, the reader can adapt to attend to what is on offer in the text that the reader has initially suppressed. Adaptation by the reader permits attention to the text that is then no longer controlled by the initial guess of the reader.

When the reader's guess goes awry, the outcome is a cognitive disjunction that requires a second guess. Thus the reading is not contained in predictable genres but requires an authentic subject who exercises freedom who is not fully controlled by the initial guess, by the text, or by cultural context. The capacity of the reader to exercise such freedom makes it possible for the reader to reengage the text and so to produce a new object that meets the reader's intended desire. The exercise of such freedom yields the "history of reception" through which a generative text results in many different readings that are influenced by the desire, context, and social location of the reader. Douglass recognizes that the reader may indeed so dominate the text as to reproduce what the reader intended all along, and we have ample evidence of this procedure. With reference to the Bible that is Douglass's concern, this constitutes the practice of knowing what the biblical text says even before we begin to read it. The challenge for the reader is to recognize the unfamiliar in the text that does not yield readily to such an initial desire.

The reader's enormous capacity to exercise power and freedom may yield textual activity in a way that "the text floats free, and can exceed the author to 'mean' things that she—quite literally—could not even imagine" (104). Douglass offers an acute analysis of such reading wherein texts float free in two modes. On the one hand, the work of Kant and Hume has resulted in new criticism, Russian formalism, narratology, and structuralism. On the other hand, the trajectory of Nietzsche and Derrida has resulted in deconstruction and radical forms of reader response. In both trajectories the outcome is private language that becomes monologic, as the reader dominates the text and overpowers the intention of the author. The sustained practice of such a procedure is as though the author has no voice in the world, no shaping power over the world, and eventually no significance for the reader. The antidote to the reader's monologic truth is to participate in a broader dialogue with a voice other than our own that is not finally malleably adaptable to our will as reader.

The burden of this book is to insist that the author must be seen as fully a partner in the work of the text. In an appeal to Martin Buber and Emmanuel Levinas, Douglass allows that the author is indeed a "thou," an active, engaged, intentional subject; this thou is able to be a revelatory presence in the life of the reader who jars settled comfort zones. With a vigorous appeal to Bakhtin, Douglass urges that ethical reading is dialogical reading that honors an intention other than our own, an intention that may violate initial expectations. It follows that ethical reading hopes for and embraces "the ideal communicative situation" of Habermas.

The implication of this proposal for reading is that the reader must pay some attention to the identification the author and the author's voice. Among the strategies for such attentiveness to the author, consideration may be given to the biography of an author. In this discussion reference is made to the biography of Paul and the way what we know of his life illuminates his letters. Attention may be given, moreover, to the author's "way of living" because we may expect from the author a consistency of authorial behavior. We may attend to the "'future author," that is, the author's subsequent disclosures of intention and interpretation, that for which the author as a free agent may continue to hope. While the point is suggestive, Douglass is aware that such an author, even with attention to bibliography, way of living, and future, is still a construction of the reader, a matter about which we have ample evidence in the many "historical quests" in New Testament scholarship.

I have found this to be an instructive book. Some of it is expressed in rather esoteric terms that might be articulated clearly. One might wish, moreover, that the author had gone further to trace out the implications of his argument in a mode of social criticism. It occurs to me that the unrestrained constructiveness of the reader amounts to a form of commoditization. In the absence of a resisting voice in the text, everything can be reduced to utilitarianism that serves ideology. In the end, the "author" and the "reader" are actual selves. Surely reading is an event in which an actual self meets another actual self with an alternative will. Such a meeting is especially important as an alternative to narcissism that takes inordinate freedom to create a private world of private talk to serve a private interest.

Before I finish, I suggest that the argument of this book is not unlike the great thesis of my teacher, James Muilenburg, in his defining SBL presidential address of 1968 on rhetorical criticism. Muilenburg wanted in his address to resist the reductionism of genre analysis (here "initial guess") and to insist that the text is not traffic in predictable knowable genres but is in fact the utterance of a real historical self. Douglass's argument might usefully be related to the terms of Muilenburg that are more familiar in the guild. (But maybe that is an initial guess on my part that wants to be too familiar.) The deep modern "turn to the subject" is challenged by critical work that seeks to hear and honor that other voice that bears witness another reality beyond the one we already have in hand.

Reading the Bible Intertextually, edited by Richard B. Hays, Stefan Alkier, and Leroy A. Huizenga. Waco, TX: Baylor University Press, 2015. Pp. xiv + 334. Hardcover. $49.95. ISBN 9781481303552.

Josh Mathews, Western Seminary

In November 2004 a group of scholars convened at Johann Wolfgang Goethe-Universität in Frankfurt am Main for a conference titled "Die Bibel im Dialog der Schriften." Under the supervision of Stefan Alkier and Richard B. Hays, the seminar's papers were compiled into a volume with the same title as the conference and with the subtitle *Konzepte intertextueller Bibellektüre*. Subsequently, the nine essays that had been written in German originally were translated into English and included together with the other four essays, which had been written in English for the conference and translated into German for the earlier publication. An additional essay on methodology by Stefan Alkier was also added to this 2009 English edition, which was reprinted in 2015.

The topics and approaches represented in these essays covers an array of interdisciplinary perspectives. They all relate in one way or another to the theme of the seminar, in which the dialogicality conceptualized by Mikhail Bakhtin is applied in various ways to the biblical canon and to the interaction between the Old and New Testaments and other texts outside the canon. Corresponding to the English title, the concept of intertextuality as it is presented here draws upon the poststructural literary theorist Julia Kristeva's notion of *intertextualité*, which is itself a development of Bakhtin's dialogicality. This is the nexus around which the various essays in the volume are gathered.

The book is organized into four main parts. Part 1 introduces the project by laying the methodological foundation and by surveying some of the historical precedent for intertextual approaches to the Bible. In the second section, which makes up the core of the book, the authors apply the principles of intertextuality to the interpretation of particular biblical texts. Part 3 considers intertextuality beyond the canon, and, finally, part 4 concludes the collection with another essay by Alker on the relationship between intertextuality, semiotics, and New Testament studies.

In different ways the two essays of part 1 establish parameters for the contributions that follow. Alkier begins by locating the discussion within the framework of semiotics, identifying Kristeva's conception of intertextuality as a starting point for his outline of the concept's history. This historical overview provides the backdrop against which Alkier explains his own approach to intertextuality in biblical studies, which he applies in a reading of Mark 4. This essay broadly introduces the manner in which the other contributors conceive of intertextuality and utilize it in their interpretive work, thereby differentiating "intertextuality" as it is used throughout the essays from other construals of the term. On the one hand, this statement is likely to encounter no disagreement: "Through the intertextual connection of the canon, it is hermeneutically justifiable to read and interpret every biblical writing in light of every other biblical writing." On the other hand, some might not continue on to Alkier's conclusion that "the canon shows itself to be a field of play on which, from a limited inventory of signs, there emerges in the act of reading an unlimited number of possible combinations and effects of meaning" (12).

In chapter 2 Steve Moyise also begins with Kristeva in order to survey the history of approaches to the New Testament's use of Scripture. Moyise, whose approach aligns generally with the others in the volume, takes intertextuality to imply that meanings of biblical texts, rather than being fixed, are able to be revised as they interact with other texts. He considers several examples of Old Testament references within the New Testament and seeks to offer a balanced approach in which both author-centered historical criticism and theories of

intertextuality derived from poststructuralism are brought together to complement one another and in which their extreme forms are deemed unsatisfactory
for studying Scripture. One could be left wondering if Moyise has adequately
demonstrated nonarbitrary parameters for employing the constraints of historical criticism to guard against the infinite interpretive possibilities allowed by
some forms of intertextuality.

The first essay in part 2, by Michael Schneider, applies intertextual readings
to 1 Cor 10. Relying on the thought of Umberto Eco, Schneider moves from an
intratextual reading to an intertextual reading. He draws hermeneutical and theological implications from Paul's engagement with the Pentateuch to elicit new
interpretive discoveries for the readers of Paul's letters. Methodological discussion
is interspersed along the way in an attempt to demonstrate the strength of this
kind of intertextual reading, namely, "the integration of traditional research with
newer reader-oriented questions into an overall hermeneutical concept" (52).

Eckart Reinmuth's task in chapter 4 is to engage in an intertextual reading
of Rom 1:18–28 against the backdrop of the Adam story in Gen 1–3. Reinmuth
formulates a nuanced understanding of allegorical reading, understood in terms
of intertextuality. This is meant to demonstrate the way in which New Testament authors allude to Old Testament texts by the use of narrative abbreviation,
resulting in revised meaning that "thus participates in the allegorical discourse of
ancient Judaism" (61).

The next chapter is written by Leroy Huizenga, who also oversaw the translation of the book's English edition. Here Huizenga considers the Gospel of Matthew
from the perspective of Jewish intertextuality in general and Isaac and the Akedah
story of Gen 22 in particular. Huizenga seeks not only to demonstrate that Matthew's Gospel does in fact bear resemblances to the Pentateuch's Isaac narratives
but also to intimate what kinds of interpretive implications—related to Matthean
temple motifs or soteriological models, for instance—might follow from this dialogue between portrayals of Jesus and Isaac.

In her essay entitled "Paul as User, Interpreter, and Reader of the Book of
Isaiah," Florian Wilk locates her piece with respect to Alkier's expression of
intertextuality as definitively decentering the author and recentering the interwo-
venness of texts. In concert with the other writers in this volume, she distinguishes
her perspective and use of intertextuality from production-oriented perspectives,
although she offers little methodological explanation for this distinction. From
this starting point she surveys intertextual examples, specifically considering the
formative process of Paul's intertextual appropriation of Isaiah.

Chapter 7 is Richard Hays's essay on Luke-Acts in intertextual dialogue with
several Old Testament passages. This exhibits a hermeneutical strategy whereby
Luke insistently and skillfully represents "*narrative continuity*, linking the story
of Jesus seamlessly with the much longer narrative of God's promises to Israel"
(116). At its core this Lukan message is one in which the portrayal of Jesus as a
countercultural liberator becomes paradigmatic for the church as a countercultural community juxtaposed over against both Judaism and the Roman Empire.

The final chapter of this main section deviates from the pattern slightly in that its author, Marrianne Grohmann, considers an intertextual dialogue between two Old Testament texts instead of between the New Testament and the Old. She explores Ps 113 in relation to the Song of Hannah in 1 Sam 2:1–10, registering nuanced observations from both the Hebrew and Greek textual traditions. Although many exegetical analyses have identified links between these two passages, they have typically not been conducted from the perspective of intertextuality, at least as it is presented in her essay and the others in this collection.

The essays in part 3 all expand the purview of the study by exploring intertextuality that includes the biblical canon and also reaches beyond its boundaries. First, George Aichele posits the potential for intertextual dialogue between canonical and noncanonical texts, using as an example Conan of Cimmeria, the mighty warrior from the movie *Conan the Barbarian* and the stories upon which the movie was based. Most notably, "Conan's crucifixion scene opens up an intertextual nexus," suggests Aichele, "a virtual hypertext link with crucifixion scenes in the Gospels and Elsewhere." This intertextual phenomenon functions such that "the stories of Christ not only interpret Conan, but Conan's stories also interpret Christ" (153).

Continuing with this expanded notion of extracanonical intertextuality, Peter von Möllendorff relates Lucian's *True History* to the Christian apocalyptic writing of Revelation in the New Testament, though the weight of the investigation is much more focused on the former than the latter. Next, Thomas A. Schmitz considers sixth-century Greek poet Nonnus of Panopolis in relation to his Christian tradition. After these few examples of extracanonical intertextuality, chapters 12 and 13 shift to focus again more directly on methodological issues. Magdolna Orosz revisits Kristeva and Bakhtin to apply elements of semiotics to the intertextual analysis of texts, and Hans-Günter Heimbrock employs Gilbert Ryle's notion of "thick description," as formulated by Clifford Geertz, to view the Bible in terms of practical theology.

Finally, Stefan Alkier draws the collection to a conclusion by outlining the basic motivating convictions, theoretical foundation, and methodological decisions of a semiotic program for New Testament studies.

The goal of this project, generally speaking, is to gather an interdisciplinary group of scholars in like-minded discussion around a certain conception of intertextuality, or at least a certain range of possible formulations of intertextuality within which one can speak of it constructively in relation to biblical studies. Throughout intertextuality is consistently construed, as Grohmann states in her essay, as an interaction between texts and readers that, on the one hand, "contributes explanations of relationships between texts and, on the other hand, reflects the contribution of readers to the meaning of texts" (122). In this way, the hermeneutical approach is presented as a way "for postmodern interpreters to restore lines of conversation with the church's classic premodern traditions of interpretation" (xiii).

This approach to intertextuality is juxtaposed, at times subtly and at times overtly, over against other understandings of the concept. Its construal here appears to be intended as a promising alternative, or perhaps a corrective, to either of two other general approaches: (1) coopting the term *intertextuality* to describe the kind of research already being done related to sources and backgrounds of biblical texts, or to *Traditionsgeschichte* approaches; or (2) using it to refer to the process of discerning when terms, themes, or theological concepts form connections between canonical texts, a process that serves as easy rationalization for more traditional Christian approaches to reading the Old and New Testaments synchronically as a unified whole. The kind of intertextuality envisioned in these essays is to be understood against the backdrop of those two approaches.

The efforts of this volume in this regard are successful, insofar as the essays do supply many arguments and examples of the particular conception of intertextuality accepted by the contributors. Nevertheless, some readers may find a lack of delineation to be an obstacle to either clarity or acceptance of the proposed perspective. Individuals who fall into one of the other two categories mentioned in the above paragraph will perhaps be hesitant to accept key points of the methodologies assumed in these essays. Those readers would certainly benefit from the book's exegetical and theological insight regardless of disagreement with aspects of methodology. However, they might do well to read something else that introduces or demonstrates some of the hermeneutical presuppositions prior to working through these essays. Hays's *Reading Backwards* might be a helpful companion.

Iconographic Exegesis of the Hebrew Bible/Old Testament: An Introduction to Its Method and Practice, edited by Izaak J. de Hulster, Brent A. Strawn, and Ryan P. Bonfiglio. Göttingen: Vandenhoeck & Ruprecht, 2015. Pp. 383. Hardcover. €45.00. ISBN 9783525534601.

Michael B. Hundley, Central Washington University

Iconographic exegesis first burst onto the scholarly scene in 1972 with the publication of Keel's *Die Welt der altorientalischen Bildsymbolik und das Alte Testament* (translated into English in 1978 as *Symbolism of the Biblical World*). *Iconic Exegesis of the Hebrew Bible/Old Testament* carries the study of images further into the mainstream of biblical scholarship as a textbook most suited to graduate students, designed "to provide readers with a template for doing iconographic exegesis and incorporating images into all of their subsequent interpretive work." This is especially welcome, as scholars often misuse or underutilize the ample ancient Near Eastern imagery available to illumine the thought world of the Hebrew Bible. The volume contains an introduction and eighteen chapters written by multiple authors, divided according to the tripartite division of the Hebrew Bible: Pentateuch, Prophets, and Writings. Each aims at methodological clarity, offers specific analyses that illumine the benefits of and model iconographic exegesis, and concludes with an assignment for readers. Of the many worthy entries, this review gives particular attention to the introduction and the chapters in the first section.

In the introduction the editors define iconographic exegesis as "an interpretive approach that explains aspects of the Hebrew Bible with the help of Ancient Near Eastern visual remains" (20). They argue that ancient Near Eastern images may be productively applied to the study of biblical texts for three primary reasons: (1) the volume and comparability of the images; (2) images, like texts, are "constitutive components of any culture's symbol system," providing "window into the cultural, social, religious and political world that lies behind the Old Testament" (21); (3) images and texts are linked. They continue by identifying three major aspects of image-text relationships: congruence, correlation, and contiguity.

> If image-text congruence identifies the existence of common motifs between visual and verbal artifacts and if image-text correlation seeks to explain the level and degree of interaction that produces such congruence, then image-text contiguity seeks to historicize those interactions through discernible lines of influence and/or plausible mechanisms of contact and interaction. (25)

The editors then offer a brief and illustrative example of their method from Isa 63. An overview follows on working with images, including the types of images, their sources, and their analysis.

De Hulster (ch. 1) begins the Pentateuch section by bringing iconography to bear on the Priestly creation story. He makes the important observation that ancient Near Eastern images commonly function more as thought pictures that communicate concepts rather than literally trying to represent their subject matter. For example, Egyptian images often "combine multiple, sometimes mutually exclusive, vantage points in a single unified frame of reference" (47). De Hulster then turns to a comparison of ancient Near Eastern images of the cosmos with the literary imagery in Gen 1–2:4a. He concludes that, while the cosmos is generally understood to be tripartite in the ancient Near East (heaven, earth, and netherworld), Gen 1 focuses on the earth with no mention of the netherworld and a concept of heaven that is less a physical location and more a concept stressing divine supremacy.

In chapter 2 Strawn addresses the portrayal of humanity as the image of God in Gen 1:26. He begins by commenting on the subjective and personal nature of comparison before comparing the biblical image especially with Mesopotamian visual analogues. He notes several points of comparison especially between the biblical image and Mesopotamian royal inscriptions and iconography, while stressing the nonviolent nature of the biblical image, which contrasts with the violent rhetoric of Neo-Assyrian royal ideology. He acknowledges divine violence in the Bible, yet argues that it goes against the Priestly design of the cosmos and suggests that the dominant violence in the Bible is exercised on behalf of those in need.

Staubli in chapter 3 considers the Akedah in Gen 22. While he argues against widespread human sacrifice in the ancient Near East, he identifies a common constellation of images: "(1) a god, menacing (2) a human, before (3) a goddess, with (4) a recumbent sheep or goat above the human victim" (99). He argues that Gen 22 is founded on a similar constellation in which (1) a deity (Elohim) asks for (2) a human sacrifice, while (3) another deity (YHWH) represented by a messenger (4) provides an animal substitute. The reception history of the Akedah also continues to use the same constellation of images. It would help to explore how biblical monolatry leads to a recontextualization of the constellation such that a single god seemingly works at cross-purposes, an idea wrestled with in subsequent exegesis.

In chapter 4 Strawn looks to Egyptian iconography to illumine the biblical references to YHWH's strong hand and outstretched arm. He adduces images of Pharaoh smiting his enemies, suggesting military violence and dominance, alongside images of deities extending an arm of blessing to humanity. While he argues that the latter is a better match for the biblical image, he suggests that both may be operating in the Bible, even simultaneously. Defeating an enemy simultaneously rescues one needing deliverance.

In chapter 5, de Hulster and Strawn turn to mixed divine metaphors in Deut 32, using ancient Near Eastern images that blend conceptual categories as an explanatory tool. They note the Egyptian mixing of human bodies and animal/symbol heads and *Mischwesen* (hybrid creatures) that represent a complex and often frightening admixture of forms. *Mischwesen* in particular are "category-jamming, sense-overwhelming" figures that are suitable analogues to the divine language of Deut 32 as they mediate and reveal the divine while simultaneously "protecting the deity's divinity by constraining the imagination as they transgress imaginative categories" (131–32). However, while the authors are correct to note that images may help the audience visualize this imagery, literary descriptions often transcend categories far more than visual representations to such an extent that they are not meant to be visually imagined or even fully conceptualized (see, e.g., the description of Ninurta in STT 118 rev).

Schmitt (ch. 6) begins the section on the Prophets by helpfully extending iconographic exegesis to architectural remains using Rapoport's categories of fixed, semifixed, and nonfixed features of the built environment. De Hulster (ch. 7) identifies the Egyptian ureaus serpent and the often winged mount of the weather god as analogues to the biblical seraphim and cherubim, respectively. He likewise suggests that angels were identified as winged beings because of their association with the winged seraphim and cherubim and especially their role as beings who traveled between heaven and earth (in later Christian reception, angels are also associated with the Roman victory goddess Nike). He concludes by hypothesizing about the reason for angels. Hunziker-Rodewald (ch. 8) addresses the enigmatic reference to thrones in Sheol in Isa 14:9. Buried Syro-Palestinian royal statues used in sacrificial practice suggest that they were associated with an ancestor cult. She argues that Isa 14 turns this image on its head, offering a biting satire of a Babylonian king. De Hulster (ch. 9) associates the monument and the name in Isa 56 with a standing stone that materialized the memory of the name, positing that the ban of divine statues led to a culture of material commemoration. De Hulster and Strawn (ch. 10) compare Isa 60 and Persian period iconography, which they argue are both instantiations of Persian imperial propaganda. Staubli (ch. 11) argues that literary texts such as Ps 67 or Zech 1:8–6:15 can be read as a type of image and that Zechariah's vision of a lampstand flanked by two figures corresponds with ancient lunar iconography. Bonfiglio (ch. 12) compares the Persian royal archer imagery with descriptions of YHWH as archer in Zech 9, arguing that the biblical imagery represents a blending of concepts related to the divine-warrior literature and royal-archer iconography.

Strawn (ch. 13) begins the Writings section by adducing visual parallels to the psalmic references to real and metaphorical lions used to describe the wicked, YHWH, and the self. LeMon (ch. 14) argues that the iconic structure of Ps 63, particularly related to winged images of YHWH, "correspond[s] simultaneously to (1) the iconography of the winged sun disk as a god of order and justice who protects the king, especially in military contexts; (2) the winged sun disk emanating liquid nourishment from heaven; and (3) the winged goddesses suckling and protecting royal figures" (276–77). He posits multistability, in which images simultaneously convey two different interpretations, as a way of understanding the multivocality of YHWH's winged form. While true to some extent of visual images, he may find more explanatory power in literary images, which follow different rules and allow for and even encourage multistability. LeMon (ch. 15) continues by examining divine violence in Ps 81 and ancient Near Eastern iconography. He appeals especially to Egyptian and Egyptian-influenced royal smiting imagery, which portray the moment before the fatal blow is struck. LeMon contends that Ps 81 adapts the imagery such that YHWH, not Pharaoh, stands poised to dominate, while the enemies of Israel await YHWH's deadly violence and Israel await the divine benevolence. He further argues in light of the iconography that the difficult expression *hiphil šwb* + hand + *'al* should be translated as "'to rear back one's hand over (an enemy)' in a menacing gesture" (291). Strawn (ch. 16), after examining potential iconographic parallels, suggests that biblical authors use the fear of YHWH to connote pure terror and appropriate worship, as both are predicated on the divine power and ability to inflict punishment on those who may disobey him. De Hulster (ch. 17) suggests that iconographic exegesis may profitably inform biblical translation, using Song 7:2–6 as a test case. He adopts a pleonastic approach, which "retains formal features of Hebrew poetry" as it "makes accessible for contemporary readers the 'mental furnishings' that undergird the imagistic quality of much poetic language" (319). Staubli (ch. 18) extends beyond the Protestant canon to include an analysis of the celebration in Jdt 15:2–3 involving twigs.

The editors and publisher of *Iconic Exegesis of the Hebrew Bible/Old Testament* are to be commended for a well-produced volume. The majority of the chapters are of high quality, interesting, and informative. They show the range and applicability of iconographic exegesis both in terms of its breadth and the

diversity among interpreters. The chapters are generally clear and methodologically transparent, allowing the reader access into the scholarly studio. They are
also helpful in their dual focus. While they often address specific textual issues,
their approach more broadly illumines and models how iconographic exegesis
can be used to address myriad larger issues, including metaphor, literary imagery,
emotion, architecture, violence, ritual, and translation.

As with any edited volume presenting multiple positions, there is ample room
for scholarly disagreement (e.g., regarding the debatable reference to a physical
monument in Isa 56, the text's somewhat apologetic tone regarding biblical violence,
and the inclusion of cherubs and seraphs as exemplars of angels). While the authors
take pains to express the value of comparing texts and images, they could do more
to note the differences between these media, which often follow different rules and
are often "read" differently by their audiences. For example, whereas major gods are
often visually depicted as aesthetically pleasing and primarily anthropomorphic,
texts often describe the gods in visually unimaginable terms, expressing their greatness by transgressing otherwise discrete categories and stretching the mind's ability
to comprehend (e.g., the description of Marduk in the Enuma Elish and Ninurta
in Lugal-e). In other words, a monstrous visual image of a major deity would be
unpalatable, while a monstrous textual description of the same deity may be considered necessary. However, these quibbles are indicative of the ever-evolving and
variable state of the field, and this introductory volume invites readers to make
further contributions to it. Overall, this volume is highly recommended for all who
are seeking easy access to the world of iconographic exegesis.

TEXTUAL CRITICISM AND TRANSLATION

*Galatians to Philemon according to the Syriac Peshitta Version with English Trans-
lation,* translated by J. Edward Walters; edited by George A. Kiraz. Surath Kthob.
Piscataway, NJ: Gorgias, 2013. Pp. 216. Cloth. $150.00. ISBN 9781611438932.

James F. McGrath, Butler University

This volume, containing the Pauline epistles from Galatians through Philemon in a bilingual edition in Syriac and English, is one of a number of volumes
recently added to the series that Gorgias Press has been publishing under the overarching heading of The Syriac Peshitta Bible with English Translation, or Ṣurath
Kthobh. In this volume the Syriac text has been prepared by George Anton Kiraz,
who also provides a foreword, while the English translation and introduction are
by James Edward Walters. The Syriac text included in the volume is essentially
that of the British and Foreign Bible Societies 1920 edition, with some corrections.
Since this text is widely available on its own, including online, and the corrections
are few and minor, the component of this book that will be of the greatest interest
is the English translation.

Syriac is still not a language in which New Testament scholars can universally be assumed to be competent, yet the translation of the New Testament into a dialect of Aramaic involves a move into a language that is quite similar to that spoken by Paul and other New Testament authors, as well as a world of thought that retained not only linguistic but also certain cultural elements that would have been close to aspects of Paul's own heritage. It is therefore a welcome contribution to have a translation that seeks (for the most part) to stick closely to the wording and ideas as expressed in the Syriac translation, highlighting those aspects that differ from the wording or nuances of the Greek texts, while not doing so in a rigidly literal manner that makes the resulting English text awkward or stilted— something that is no small accomplishment in and of itself.

The introduction to the volume explains the approach to translation that has been adopted and provides a list of key instances of agreement between the Peshitta and either the majority text or other witnesses, while (even more significantly) highlighting and discussing those points at which the Peshitta offers unique readings (xxii–xxvi). A number of these are especially noteworthy, as they provide evidence of what are unlikely to be scribal errors but are more likely interpretations of the Greek text. In some instances the question of how the Greek text came to be rendered that way is as impossible to answer as it is fascinating, as in Phil 2:16, where, in place of the Greek phrase usually rendered "holding fast to the word of life," the Syriac means "in order that you might be salvation for them" (xxiv–xxv). In other cases we can well understand the rationale for a change, for example, Gal 3:8, where the Peshitta makes it God rather than Scripture that knew ahead of time and proclaimed to Abraham (xxiii).

The discussion of the translation of important Pauline terms such as righteousness/justice and faith/faithfulness interacts (albeit briefly and indirectly) with both historic and contemporary discussions of these subjects among New Testament scholars. The choice to offer the rendering "the faithfulness of Jesus the Messiah" is noteworthy, given the amount of recent scholarly attention to and debate concerning how to best render the Greek phrase πίστις χριστοῦ. The decision to render the word ܗܝܡܢܘܬܐ as "faith" when referring to Abraham's response reflects Walters's understanding of "Paul's apparent point that the human response to the faithfulness of the Messiah is faith in the Messiah" (xii). Of course, one can argue that the response of Abraham is itself expressed not only in terms of *belief* or even *trust* but also *faithfulness*. But whatever an interpreter's view on that matter, the discussion of this subject in the introduction, as well as its incorporation into the translation itself, highlights the relevance of the volume not only to those interested specifically in Syriac studies but to all interpreters of Paul's letters and thought.

There are a number of points at which the translation is open to dispute, and if the reader does not know Syriac (or perhaps, at the very least, investigate the range of meaning of a term with the assistance of detailed lexical aids), he or she might not realize that it is not the Syriac text that is taking sides in certain debates but the translator. One instance of note is Phil 2:6, where the word ܚܛܘܦܝܐ renders the Greek word ἁρπαγμός. Whatever one's view of the meaning of the Greek, which has itself been hotly debated, the Syriac term has connotations of seizing by force. The rendering "something to be exploited" (67) thus appears to be driven by theological considerations related to Christology rather than a mere interest in conveying the sense of the Syriac as precisely as possible. It is worth noting that the rendering provided can be found in Michael Sokoloff's edition of Carl Brockelmann's lexicon. There (442) the root meanings are given, such as "spoil," "plunder," and "booty," but specifically for Phil 2:6 the proposed rendering is what we also find in Walters's translation: "he did not regard this as something to be exploited." However, the Latin editions of Brockelmann (see 109 of the first edition and 227–28 of the second) appear to lack an equivalent to the rendering of Phil 2:6–11 provided in the Sokoloff edition. This seems to confirm that the proposed rendering of the word in this New Testament context may reflect recent theological debates, not the connotations of the Syriac word in its ancient context. Yet the latter is precisely what New Testament exegetes need from the English translation of the Syriac.

It ought to be emphasized that the preceding example does not represent a typical occurrence. By way of contrast, we might consider Phil 3:7–8, where the Greek includes the word σκύβαλον, meaning "excrement." The Syriac renders it—as have numerous English versions—with a word meaning "loss." Thus, that familiar wording does not represent the translator's sensibilities regarding an expletive but fidelity to the Syriac. Also of interest is Phil 2:6, where the Greek, which refers to the "form of God," is rendered by the Syriac as the "image of God," which might lend support to those who argue that this hymnic passage is best understood as contrasting Jesus with Adam.

The concern is that the reader who consults the volume and who does not know Syriac may be misled at times into thinking that the Syriac provides support for a particular understanding of the Greek text or interprets the text in particular ways, and will not be able to distinguish those instances where it truly does from those where the rendering relates more tendentiously to the Syriac.

In still other cases the choice of rendering in English is surprising, but a more literal rendering is offered in a footnote. I am not referring to the many instances that provide a faithful English conveyance of the meaning of the Syriac idiom, while the latter is rendered more literally in the footnote (see, e.g., 89). In some instances it is simply unclear why the English was rendered as it was or why the more literal rendering in the footnote was not given in the main body of the translation text. One example is the English text of 1 Tim 1:10, which refers to "illicit sex," whereas a literal rendering, as indicated in the footnote, would be "those who lie with men" (129). Another is Titus 3:9, where the English text has "about the Law," while a more literal rendering, "of the scribes," is given in a footnote (175).

There are also postscripts to the letters that are present in the Syriac text but that are not rendered into English. Also, while I noticed no typographical errors either in the Syriac text or in the English, the mistaken heading "Ephesians Ch.6" is given where it ought to say "Galatians Ch.6" (29, 31).

Despite the concerns voiced above in relation to a small number of crux passages that are the focus of much scholarly discussion and debate, and so perhaps would inevitably be controversial however they were rendered, the translation on the whole aims for fidelity to the Syriac and clarity in the rendering thereof into English. Provided that it is used cautiously and judiciously, the translation by Walters will offer access to the meaning of the Syriac Peshitta to scholars and other interested readers. The Syriac Peshitta provides important evidence of early Christian interpretation of the Pauline corpus within a context that stood not just culturally but also linguistically close to Paul's own background. Thus it is my sincere hope that not only this volume, but the series as a whole, will be given the attention it deserves by New Testament scholars.

The Antioch Bible: The Gospel of Luke according to the Syriac Peshitta Version With English Translation (Syriac Edition), translated by Jeff W. Childers; edited by George A Kiraz. Piscataway, NJ: Gorgias, 2013. Pp. 300. Cloth. $150.00. ISBN 9781463202415.

David A. Smith, Duke University

The decision by the editors at Gorgias Press to publish the Antioch Bible is one for which both scholars of antiquity and those who worship in the Syriac tradition may be deeply grateful. In the wake of the present, massive displacement of persons, the loss of life, traditions, and cultural artifacts in the war-plagued land of Syria and much of the surrounding Middle East, this series preserves, arranges, and makes newly available for a variety of readers the central cultural and religious heritage of Syriac Christianity. One may thus hope that the volumes of this series will be acquired by many libraries of universities and theological schools, alongside such works as the *Gorgias Encyclopedic Dictionary of Syriac Heritage* (2011). One may also be confident that, inasmuch as the Peshitta itself has had as "its primary purpose … to serve the basic needs of ecclesial communities who worship God in the Syriac language" (xviii), the publication of *The Syriac Peshitta Bible with English Translation* will be, as Childers envisions, useful "for the purposes of study, personal devotion, and liturgy" (xx). The publication of the Syriac text of the Peshitta alongside a fresh, readable English translation will, of course, facilitate the academic study of the Syriac language and the particular character of the Syriac version of the Bible—a rich offering indeed. For all of this the editors, Jeff Childers, George Kiraz, and Andreas Juckel deserve supreme thanks.

The present volume on the Gospel of Luke includes a forward by George Kiraz on the arrangement of the Syriac text, which Kiraz has prepared and modified slightly from the 1905 edition published by the British and Foreign Bible Society, which was itself based on the critical text compiled by P. E. Pusey and G. H. Gwilliam in 1901. As in the BFBS edition, the text is presented in the present volume in East-Syriac Nestorian script (see xiv–xv). The text is far easier to read than BFBS editions currently available, and the Antioch Bible series greatly improves upon the BFBS layout by following a consistently right-to-left format, clothed in a beautiful, gold-inscribed magenta binding. As with the earlier BFBS edition, the critical apparatus of Pusey and Gwilliam is absent, a fact that improves readability for nonacademic readers but hinders scholarly inquiry. The brief preface by Kiraz, in which he explains succinctly a number of small adjustments and corrections to the BFBS text, is followed by a detailed and helpful introduction by Childers, in which the general character and history of the Peshitta version of the Bible in general and of the Gospel of Luke in particular are discussed, together with a selection of readings from the Peshitta version of Luke that are noteworthy either as witnesses to the form of the original gospel text or for their theological significance within Syriac Christianity.

The English translation itself exhibits a close fidelity to the Syriac source text, attempting to reproduce in English the meaning of the Syriac while allowing for a "dynamic equivalence" that avoids overliteral constructions that may be awkward for English readers. At times, however, the translation seems overly concerned with this potential problem of awkwardness. For example, Childers explains his rendering of Luke 1:24 (ܣܘܡ ܪܐܬܐ ܝܗܒ ܡܢ ܪܐܡܐ) as "after that time" instead of "after those days" because the latter phrase is though to be awkward (xx–xxi). I do not find the phrase to be unnatural at all, just as the translators of the NRSV did not. Moreover, the Syriac phrase, which closely follows the Greek Μετὰ δὲ ταύτας τὰς ἡμέρας, reflects Luke's deliberate utilization of a biblical idiom (compare, both in Syriac and in Greek, Exod 2:23; Judg 11:4; 1 Kgs 17:7; Dan 1:18; cf. Acts 9:19l 15:36l 21:15). Childers's adjustment of this biblical idiom to a simpler English one at 1:24, 1:39, 2:1, and 5:17 is within the parameters of dynamic equivalence, but these choices result in the loss of an important resonance in the textual encyclopedia of the Syriac source text. The same must be said of the decision to collapse certain instances of hendiadys into simpler constructions (as in Luke 5:31, where ܐܡܠ ܐܡܪܐ ܣܥ ܪܐܠܐ is rendered simply as "Jesus answered them" instead of the more exact "Jesus answered and said to them"), since hendiadys is a common feature of biblical narration in Hebrew, Greek, and Syriac (so Gen 31:43, 2 Sam 14:19, 1 Macc 2:19, and especially the New Testament gospels and Acts). This resistance to formal equivalency thus obscures certain important linguistic features of the Syriac text, features that the original translators of the Peshitta chose to reproduce from their source texts and that, when read in the study or heard in the liturgy, are important for the literary cohesion of the Syriac canon.

Childers's admirable English translation is, nevertheless, a great improvement over older "literalizing" translations of the New Testament Peshitta into English, such as that of George Lamsa, which tend, on the whole, toward an orientalizing emphasis on what are felt to be the distinctively Semitic features of the Syriac text. Although the text, of course *is* semitic, the point, as Childers rightly observes, is that, "unless one is very familiar with Syriac linguistic idiom and the semantics of words in their ancient contexts, highly literal renderings of the Peshitta can obscure the meaning and create misunderstandings" (xix). Childers's restraint in such literal renderings is thus an important strength of this translation. His translation is also distinguished from the work of Lamsa and others by its lack of involvement in the debate over the question of whether the gospels were written first in Aramaic, of which Syriac is a later and distinctive dialect. This viewpoint has often given the work of New Testament Peshitta translation an apologetic character, as the Syriac version has been thought to give readers access to an original, unhellenized Christianity. Childers himself eschews any attachment to the theory of Aramaic primacy, observing instead that most modern New Testament scholars understand the Syriac gospels as translations of works written in Greek (xv–xvi). For Childers, then, the Peshitta text provides an early and important window into the story of the gospel texts and the communities who received, translated, and preserved them.

As Childers discusses in depth, the Peshitta is an important witness to the text of Luke. The Syriac versions of the gospels frequently share the readings of the so-called Western text-type of gospel manuscripts in Greek, and while Childers ably discusses and exhibits this affinity, he helpfully draws attention to the close association between the Peshitta text of Luke and the Byzantine family of texts (xxx). This complexity is important for ascertaining the significance of the Peshitta for New Testament textual criticism. Although Childers's careful text-critical discussion is necessarily selective and confined to an introduction, readers who approach this volume with text-critical questions in mind will not be disappointed, though they will need to make use of other works, such as the important study of P. J. Williams, *Early Syriac Translation Technique and the Textual Criticism of the Greek Gospels* (Gorgias, 2004). Even still, as Childers observes, "Gaining a clear picture of the character of the Peshitta text within the context of its Old Syriac and Diatessaronic ancestry on the one hand, and the Greek tradition on the other, awaits the publication of a critical edition of the Peshitta Gospels" (xiv).

The publication of a critical edition of the Peshitta is, indeed, highly desirable. What a close reading of the present volume reveals, however, is that such a critical edition needs not only a thorough text-critical apparatus but also, perhaps, the sort of cross-referential marginal apparatus present in the recent Nestle-Aland critical editions of the Greek New Testament, and/or—heaven help us—the more exhaustive but nearly impenetrable critical apparatuses of the Göttingen *Septuaginta*. If such an accomplishment were achieved, the reader could, perhaps, observe in the critical notes a reference to the Peshitta's partial deviation at Luke 3:4 from the Greek text of Luke in favor of the Syriac form of Isa 40:3. Similarly, an apparatus might invite the reader at Luke 8:54 to compare the Lukan form of Jesus's command to the little girl to the Peshitta's Markan form at Mark 5:41, since, in notable contrast to the Greek texts, the two Syriac gospels share the same reading (as is especially appropriate, since there is no need for a comment about how to translate the Aramaic phrase ܩܘܡ ܛܠܝܬܐ into Greek at Mark 5:41). As it is, such desiderata are beyond the scope of the Antioch Bible project, which has the more simple and pressing task of making the received text of the Peshitta accessible, with a clear translation and thorough introduction, to academic and religious communities. In this worthy goal it overwhelmingly succeeds.

Codex Sinaiticus: New Perspectives on the Ancient Biblical Manuscript, edited by Scot McKendrick, David Parker, Amy Myshrall, and Cillian O'Hogan. Peabody, MA: Hendrickson, 2015. Pp. 352. Hardcover. $84.95. ISBN 9781619706477.

S. Matthew Solomon, New Orleans Baptist Theological Seminary

This collection of essays emerged from an international conference and seminar on Codex Sinaiticus from 6–8 July 2009, at the British Library. The conference coincided with the launch of the digital Codex Sinaiticus (available at www.codexsinaiticus.com) on 6 July 2009, the culmination of nearly a decade of work by an international group of scholars. The main thrust of the project was the conservation, imaging, transcription, and development of a website wherein the world would have unprecedented access to the oldest, most complete Christian Bible. Contributions in this volume are made by a wide range of scholars, including scholars in the fields of biblical studies, palaeography, philology, classical and Byzantine studies, theology, and Septuagint studies, as well as archivists, conservators, librarians, research fellows, and the archbishop of Sinai.

The collection of essays is divided into five major sections: the codex's historical setting, the Septuagint (LXX) portion of the codex, the New Testament and Shepherd of Hermas portion of the codex, modern histories of the codex, and how the codex is being used and studied today.

Harry Gamble leads off with an essay situating the codex within its fourth-century setting. He describes physical aspects of the codex, noting its unique shape and ground-breaking format, representing "a great leap forward" in terms of book production (4–5). Gamble argues also that the format of the codex may suggest that the contents therein were to be highly regarded. Lastly, he suggests that the codex was likely commissioned and produced for an affluent, well-educated, and pious individual as a patronal gift to a church or as a personal copy, which is in contradistinction to the long-held belief espoused by Skeat that the codex was more than likely one of the fifty ordered by Constantine (7–12).

Section 2 includes essays from three scholars concentrating on the LXX portion of the codex. Emanuel Tov compares the LXX portion of Sinaiticus to Codices Alexandrinus (02) and Vaticanus (03). He concludes that the distinctive features of the LXX portion when compared to 02 and 03 more than likely represent differences between Christian traditions. Rachel Kevern describes the process by which fragmentary portions of the codex were digitally reconstructed (down to the pixel level) in the LXX portion of the codex. Kevern states that in all thirteen fragmentary leaves needed to be reconstructed, including the new finds from 1975. Albert Pietersma compares the text of Psalms in the codex to the original Greek text. While he argues that the Psalms are riddled with mistakes in Sinaiticus (43), he concludes that new evidence since the days of Rahlfs demand a new study of the codex as a witness to the Old Greek text of Psalms.

Section 3 is much larger and contains eight essays on the New Testament and Hermas portions of the codex. Eldon Jay Epp's essay represents the keynote address of the conference with added material for publication. Epp situates the discovery of the codex in its mid-nineteenth-century environment, that is, what the text-critical world looked like when the codex was entered into textual criticism. Epp's masterful essay examines Sinaiticus's precursors: Codex Bezae (05), 02, and 03. When the text of Sinaiticus was made widely available, it overshadowed the previously popular 02 and 05 and for a brief time took attention away from the elusive text of 03. Epp's important and clearly laid out appendixes detailing the history of research of the major codices as well as the history of critical editions is an extraordinarily valuable contribution to the field.

David Trobisch next demonstrates how the publication features of Sinaiticus help to explain how the New Testament came together as a singular publication (94). Trobisch points to a single archetype for the New Testament as we know it, an argument that needs more space in this essay but can certainly be found in his other writings. Klaus Wachtel's chapter on the correctors of Sinaiticus contains an interesting section in which he concludes that Sinaiticus's purpose was to serve as an exemplar for creating further texts because it contained corrections from holy martyrs Pamphilus and Antoninus. Wachtel devotes the rest of his essay to corrector C^a, who Milne and Skeat argued corrected his text toward the Byzantine tradition. Wachtel demonstrates that this is not necessarily the case and that the situation of the Byzantine text during the time of the C^a corrections was fluid.

Juan Hernández Jr. analyzes the Apocalypse of John included in the codex. He argues that some textual variants (e.g., a change from "creation" to "church" in Rev 3:14 to avoid Jesus being part of the created order) found within the Apocalypse can act as commentary on the text, although these were more than likely not changes made by scribes while copying the text but probably were present in the exemplar.

Chapters 9 and 10 examine the work of scribes who copied the text of Sinaiticus. Peter Head analyzes the work of Scribe D especially in the New Testament leaves of the codex. Head analyzes the different methods Scribe D employed to end a line. He concludes that Scribe D could be labeled as "the 'best' scribe of one of the best surviving manuscripts (MSS) of the Greek Bible" (135). Amy Myshrall analyzes handwriting and argues that the writing that has traditionally been ascribed to Scribe B could actually be the handwriting of two scribes, which she labels B1 and B2. She further suggests that work on the codex could have been divided up into two teams: Scribes A and D on one team and Scribes B1 and B2 on the other.

Chapters 11 and 12 conclude the section on early Christian writings, dealing with the Shepherd of Hermas. Dan Batovici analyzes the physical aspects (quire structure and numbering, titles and subtitles, and paragraphing) of Hermas. He then argues that Hermas appears exactly like other biblical books copied by Scribe B, with nothing pointing to it simply being an appendix and not part of the biblical text. Archbishop Damianos of Sinai discusses the significance of the discovery of Hermas among the new finds of 1975, wherein portions of the codex were newly discovered at Saint Catherine's Monastery. In his introduction, Archbishop

Damianos reminds his readers of the less-than-ideal situation surrounding the codex's displacement during the nineteenth and twentieth centuries.

Section 4 contains four major contributions to the study of Codex Sinaiticus, detailing its modern history, including its "discovery" and the events surrounding the relocation of its parts. Christfried Böttrich, in his essay, summarizes both sides to the story. On the one hand, the Western, Protestant telling of the story of the discovery of the codex had as its hero Tischendorf who rescued the manuscript and advanced scholarly study. On the other hand, the Eastern, Orthodox telling of the story had Tischendorf as the villain, conning and stealing Sinaiticus through treachery. Böttrich rightly states that both perspectives are one-sided and wrong. In the rest of his essay, he examines the details surrounding the Russian government's intentions and Saint Catherine's expectations in regard to the final landing spot for the codex, where a flawed but final decision was made in 1869.

Nicholas Fyssas examines Russian correspondence from the Sinai archives in his essay, providing a short review of what happened with Sinaiticus since 1844, with newly discovered details in some instances. Straight away he asks critical questions about Tischendorf's account of his discovery of the codex. Although he makes allowances for Tischendorf simply being a product of his time, Fyssas challenges Tischendorf's account of the discovery of the codex on two fronts. First, he demonstrates that storing manuscripts in baskets was a common practice, as seen in iconography and in the few finds discovery of 1975, where manuscripts were found in baskets. Also, he points out how illogical it is to think that monks would burn animal skins, as they do not burn easily and would produce a horrible smell. Fyssas further hints that the portion of Sinaiticus that Tischendorf took back with him to Leipzig after his first visit could have been taken without consent, as on his second and third trips the major portion of Sinaiticus was made unavailable to him even though others had seen it before Tischendorf returned. A newly discovered document points to the fact that the larger portion of the codex was always meant to be simply *a loan* with the goal of completing the facsimile version on which Tischendorf was working. Fyssas interacts further with documents during the period from 1859 to 1869, when the large portion of the codex was in storage in Russia without being formally donated to the tsar. Complex social differences between East and West during this time period cloud the intentions of both parties in terms of proper ownership of the codex. In the end, rubles and awards were given to Saint Catherine's along with a freeing-up of finances in return for the donation of Sinaiticus to the tsar. Fyssas, however, reproduces the receipt for rubles and awards by the monastery that makes no mention of receiving these as rewards for Sinaiticus. What becomes abundantly clear from Fyssas's essay is this: the situation surrounding current ownership and whereabouts of the various portions of Sinaiticus was never what was envisioned by Saint Catherine's leadership initially, despite the modern spirit of cooperation. This essay alone makes the volume worth reading.

William Frame synthesizes events surrounding the purchase of the codex by the British government, noting that British Museum trustees initially contributed

£7,000, then raised an additional £53,563 to qualify for a matching gift from the government, whose final cost was £39,437. Panayotis G. Nikolopoulos provides the last chapter of section 4, providing a report on the new finds of 1975 from Saint Catherine's Monastery. More than eleven hundred codices have been identified, more than eight hundred of which are Greek. With the find, the library at the monastery has become one of the most important libraries for Greek majuscule manuscripts. Notable for textual critics, two new types of majuscule scripts were identified among the finds, both dating to the ninth century.

Section 5 contains six chapters that detail modern study of Sinaiticus. Chapter 17 presents a physical description of the codex, examining specifically the British Library folios. The parchment used was mostly calf and sheep and of the highest quality, with only few visible blemishes, suggesting the codex was meant to be lavish. The pages were pricked and lined in order to keep text neat and tidy. Scribes used high-quality red, brown, and black ink throughout the codex.

Hieromonk Justin of Sinai adds to the discussion of the modern treatment of Sinaiticus. In his chapter he recalls the efforts to conserve and photograph the new finds manuscripts, including the new fragments of Sinaiticus found. The facilities of the library at the monastery were in dire need of upgrade toward the beginning of the Sinaiticus project, and construction was slowed due to unforeseen circumstances. So, conservators from various settings devised ingenious ways to restore, conserve, and photograph fragments of Sinaiticus. In this process, Nikolas Sarris discovered a fragment of Sinaiticus in the binding of another later Greek manuscript from Sinai, which he details in a short section of this chapter.

One of the benefits of the project to the wider public has been a digital transcription of the codex. T. A. E. Brown describes the process by which the codex was transcribed electronically. For the New Testament portion of the codex, the team adapted existing data from the Institute for New Testament Research in Münster. For the Old Testament and noncanonical works, the team compared standard-edition base texts to the new digital images, resulting in an electronic transcription of the codex. Additionally, the team had to tag the text to account for various correctors and the physical layout of the codex. The various transcriptions were then reconciled, and the codex was consulted in places where doubt remained. Once the transcriptions were finished, they were converted into an XML format for electronic publication. Peter Robinson further describes the next step in the process of making the electronic transcription of a text into an electronic edition of the actual codex, a complicated process with extraordinary results. Robinson situates the achievement of the electronic book within its modern context, examining the pros and cons of creating an electronic edition, eventually explaining why a project such as the Codex Sinaiticus project should not be attempted in the same way again. David Parker explains in further detail the exact nature of the electronic transcription of the codex in his chapter, spending a decent amount of space discussing the transcription process of the new finds.

Steve Walton devotes the final chapter to the importance of Sinaiticus for contemporary Christianity. He suggests that Sinaiticus shows us an early example of how the Christian community fully supported Jewish Scriptures as Christian Scripture. Also, he suggests that an examination of the work of the different scribes and correctors on the codex demonstrates that biblical interpretation is primarily a communal exercise. He ends with a comparison of Qur'an manuscripts to New Testament manuscripts, wherein it is shown that revision and suppression of variant texts of the Qur'an occurred during the seventh century. Sinaiticus helps us to see that, even though Byzantine manuscripts flourished in later times, there was no systematic suppression of Alexandrian or Western texts. Walton is correct in noting that the codex is not simply for academics. It is a manuscript that tells a story that should resonate with contemporary Christians.

One of the major contributions of this collection of essays can be seen in the chapters that find common ground in the story of Sinaiticus's history. For too long, only Tischendorf's story has been told, an account that has been disputed by Saint Catherine's Monastery, among others. Documents uncovered in Sinai and Russia have been examined in this volume, filling in some of the gaps during the tumultuous period between the years 1859 and 1869. As a result of the project, a shared way of describing the history of the codex has emerged (xvii). While the circumstances surrounding the continued absence of the codex from Saint Catherine's are not ideal, the codex's story has now been told as honestly as possible, given the extant documents now available.

This collection of essays serves as a valuable contribution to several fields. While not a completely comprehensive compendium, *Codex Sinaiticus: New Perspectives* serves as a nice complement to existing studies on the text and physical features of the codex and further advances the field with new information and analysis. Much work remains to fully understand and appreciate such an important manuscript. The Codex Sinaiticus Project, however, has made future study both possible and exciting.

Arabic Versions of the Pentateuch: A Comparative Study of Jewish, Christian, and Muslim Sources, by Ronny Vollandt. Biblia Arabica 2. Leiden: Brill, 2015. Pp. xviii + 330. Hardcover. €115.00. ISBN 9789004289918.

John Kaltner, Rhodes College

Translation of the Bible into Arabic is a topic that has not generated a great deal of interest or excitement in the field of biblical studies. Arabic manuscripts containing biblical texts were often consulted in earlier centuries, but this was because Arabic grammar books written in European languages were nonexistent and Arabic translations of the Bible were a useful alternative for study of the language. Generally speaking, scholars have tended to view Arabic versions of the Bible as secondary to resources such as the targumim and the Peshitta because they were not translated directly from the original languages. Copies of the entire Bible in Arabic are rare and late, and they were typically written in response to the rise of printed Bibles in European languages. For a long time, printed editions of the Bible in Arabic, such as the Constantinople Polyglot of Eliezer Soncino (1546) and the London Polyglot (1653–1657), were the main sources for scholarly work before attention began to shift to the medieval codices more recently. To this day, serious study of the Arabic biblical tradition has been undertaken by very few despite the fact that there are more versions of the Bible in Arabic than in any other known tradition.

With this book, a reworking of his 2011 University of Cambridge dissertation under Geoffrey Khan, Ronny Vollandt attempts to more fully integrate the Arabic versions of the Pentateuch into the scholarly conversation and to show how biblical studies can benefit from a consideration of them. He calls his contribution "philological groundwork," and it is clear that he has spent considerable time toiling in the field and sifting through its soil. He draws upon the evidence found in approximately 150 Arabic manuscripts that contain the entire Pentateuch or portions of it, most of which are presently found in Europe while the rest are in the Middle East.

The details surrounding the first translations of the Bible into Arabic remain largely unknown. Muslim sources from the early centuries of Islam claim that some Jewish and Christian communities in Arabia quoted the Bible in Arabic, and some pre-Islamic Arab poets sometimes cited biblical traditions, but there is no evidence to suggest that the earliest Muslims had direct access to the biblical text written in the language. Vollandt argues that the Bible was first written in Arabic during the second half of the ninth century, with the earliest translation activity involving liturgical texts commonly used in synagogues and churches and works that had a great deal of popular appeal, such as the wisdom writings. Many of the Jewish texts were written in Judaeo-Arabic, which presents the Arabic in Hebrew letters. The Jewish community adopted Arabic in the eighth and ninth centuries, and it was the towering figure of Saadiah Gaon (d. 942) through his Judaeo-Arabic Bible translation known as the *Tafsīr* who had the greatest influence on the future development of the Arabic Bible among Jews. On the Christian side, the Melkite monks associated with the monasteries in the Sinai Peninsula and Palestine pioneered Arabic translation of the Bible in the ninth century. The Syriac-Orthodox Church of the East also played a key role early on, with other groups such as the Egyptian Coptic Church not compiling an Arabic translation of the Bible until the twelfth century.

The volume under review has two main parts, the first of which offers a descriptive analysis of the linguistic background via a review of the manuscripts and the various groups behind them. Vollandt categorizes the translations based on their *Vorlagen*, and he spends most of the book discussing those translated from Syriac. He identifies three different types within this category, with the one he labels Arab[Syr]1 being the earliest. It is written primarily in Classical Arabic and is based on the Peshitta, with one of its important features being frequent usage of vocabulary that is also found in the Qur'an. A related group of manuscripts that he identifies as Arab[Syr]2, which was quite popular and eventually supplanted Arab[Syr]1, tends to avoid the use of terms related to the Qur'an. A third set, which he calls Arab^{Syr}3, falls between the other two in its usage of vocabulary related to Islam. Vollandt's other main families of manuscripts are those from Hebrew (primarily through Saadiah's Judaeo-Arabic *Tafsīr*), those from the Syro-Hexapla, those from Greek, and those from Coptic.

The chapter on Muslim use of the Arabic Pentateuch is an interesting examination of how the following four prominent Muslim scholars referred to and quoted from the first five books of the Bible: Ali Ibn Rabban (810–865), Ibn Qutayba (828–889), al-Tabari (839–923), and Ibn Hazm (994–1064). These sources sometimes cite the Pentateuch for apologetic purposes in order to argue for the supremacy of Islam or to claim that Muhammad's coming was foretold in the Bible, and they provide important evidence for when the biblical text was translated into Arabic. According to Vollandt's analysis of their writings, both Ibn Qutayba and al-Tabari were using the translation found in Arab^{Syr}1, and this is one of the reasons why he dates that form of the text to the second half of the ninth century. Ibn Rabban's quotes from the Pentateuch are similar but not identical to Arab^{Syr}2, so he might have been familiar with it at a prewritten stage.

The second part of the book is a linguistic and exegetical study of Arab^{Syr}1, the two most important witnesses of which are Sinai MS Ar., dated to 940, and Oxford, Bodleian Library, MS Hunt. 186 from a little bit later. Arab^{Syr}1 occasionally follows the LXX rather than the Peshitta, and diacritical dots are sometimes misplaced in both manuscripts. The latter feature, in addition to other scribal errors in the Sinai manuscript, suggests to Vollandt that it might be the work of a nonprofessional copyist. He examines the translation technique under the headings of syntax, vocabulary, particles/morphemes, and style. The analysis makes it clear that the translators responsible for Arab^{Syr}1 were more concerned with remaining true to the target language rather than the *Vorlage*. For example, in Syriac more variation in word order within a sentence is permitted than in Arabic, but Arab^{Syr}1 consistently follows the rules of Classical Arabic in its rendering. Where the Syriac *Vorlage* and Arabic grammar agree, Arab^{Syr}1 goes along with the sentence order of the former. But where it would lead to a violation of the standard rules of Arabic, Arab^{Syr}1 adjusts the word order and presents it in a different way than it appears in the Syriac. The same concern for the rules of Classical Arabic grammar is also seen in the way Arab^{Syr}1 translates particles from the Syriac and sometimes introduces ones that are not present in the *Vorlage* but are necessary in Arabic. Regarding vocabulary, Arab^{Syr}1 avoids cognates in favor of semantic synonyms, and it contains very few foreign words that are not found in the Arabic lexicon. Muslim literature has influenced the translation a great deal, primarily through the use of words and expressions found in the Qur'an. Interestingly, anthropomorphisms related to the deity that would be offensive to Muslims are usually translated literally in Arab^{Syr}1. In his section on style, Vollandt discusses the presence of additions, omissions, and substitutions in Arab^{Syr}1. The analysis throughout the book is thorough, and Vollandt displays a firm grasp of prior scholarship. One minor point needs correction: despite Vollandt's claim otherwise (195), Cain is not mentioned by name in the Qur'an. The book concludes with two appendices. The first one provides an inventory of the manuscripts consulted for the study, and the second lists the chapter divisions that are found in Arab^{Syr}2 and Arab^{Syr}3.

Vollandt has succeeded admirably in his goal of arguing for the importance and relevance of the Arabic versions in biblical scholarship, and it is hoped that he and others will build on this work by engaging in similar studies of other sections of the Bible. Brill's recently launched Biblia Arabica series, of which this is the second volume to appear, will serve as an excellent forum for such future efforts.

BIBLE AND CULTURE

Ice Axes for Frozen Seas: A Biblical Theology of Provocation, by Walter Brueggemann; edited by Davis Hankins. Waco, TX: Baylor University Press, 2014. Pp. vi + 424. Cloth. $59.95. ISBN 9781481302180.

Joy A. Schroeder, Capital University and Trinity Lutheran Seminary

Ice Axes for Frozen Seas: A Biblical Theology of Provocation is a collection of eighteen essays, articles, and addresses composed by Walter Brueggemann between 2008 and 2012. The anthology is edited and introduced by his former student Davis Hankins. The volume's title has its origins in a National Public Radio interview in which Brueggemann quoted Franz Kafka, who said that one should read "only books that bite and sting us," since a "book must be the ax for the frozen sea within us" (quoted on 1). Throughout this book Brueggemann uses his own lively interpretation of biblical texts to break open and challenge frozen or calcified ideologies that, in his view, sustain and bolster the power of "Pharaoh"— a designation for heartless political and economic systems that quantify resources, labor, and production without regard for responsibility to humans, creation, or God the creator.

Hankins' introductory chapter sets Brueggemann's work in sociopolitical and theoretical context. It is not incidental, says Hankins, that 2008, the date of the earliest essays, marked the beginning of the global economic recession, the election of Barack Obama, and the rise of social movements that sought less economic stratification, for each of the collected essays "more or less directly responds to the ensuing experiences of both ongoing crisis and hope for change" (4). Readers interested in critical theory will appreciate Hankins's discussions of Brueggemann's debts to French philosopher Gilles Deleuze and Argentine political theorist Ernesto Laclau.

The eighteen essays, of varying lengths and addressed to differing audiences, are grouped thematically. Six essays were published previously or concurrently in other venues. Part 1, "Poetic Cadences That Create Hope," begins with two lectures originally addressed to Lutheran bishops. The first, "Conflicted Human Agency," treats Ps 30, highlighting the "chutzpah" and rhetorical strategy of the psalmist who challenges God to respond by reminding YHWH that the deity's honor will be diminished among the other gods if YHWH does not honor the covenant and rescue the speaker (27–28). The psalmist's supplication is both a challenge to the deity and an act of hope. The second address, "Conflicted Divine Agency," examines the poetic divine speech found in three passages from Second Isaiah (54:7–8; 49:14–18; 40:27–31) in which "YHWH runs the gamut of emotion that moves from hope to anger, and back to hope, always one more time" (65). The essay "Misbegotten Hope" reads the Songs of Zion through the lens of postcolonial theory. Brueggemann urges readers to challenge the ideology of "chosenness" (of king, city, and temple) embedded in these psalms. In "Poems vs. Memos," Brueggemann examines the "memos," workflow charts, and "committee reports" for Solomon's construction of the temple and the palace (1 Kgs 4–7) and Pharaoh's building projects (Exod 5). He argues that poetry, such as that found in 2 Sam 20:1, 1 Kgs 12:16, and the songs of Moses and Miriam, is "*thick* with subversive possibility" (98), able to resist the totalitarian memos of Pharaoh and Solomon that quantify human labor and production at the expense of dignity and freedom. The final essay in the section, "Biblical Language," relishes God's self-praise in which "God unembarrassedly offers self-doxology in which YHWH struts before the nations and before the other gods" (120), language that "has a counterpoint in God's impatience and irritation with all that does not conform to YHWH's self-celebrating governance" (121).

Part 2, "Narrative Complexities That Challenge," begins with "Food Fight," an essay that contrasts the ideology of the anxious, food-hoarding Pharaoh—a system of food production, distribution and monopoly that regards the world as a closed system of limited resources—with a theology of gratitude that trusts in God's abundance. Brueggemann observes that grain, wine, and oil, "the three great money crops in the ancient world" frequently mentioned together in Hebrew scripture, are used by the Christian church as "sacramental tokens"—oil for baptism, bread and wine for Eucharist (163). "Departure without Arrival" is a brief tribute to Peter Ochs and the Scriptural Reasoning movement. A pair of essays, "The Nightmare of Amnesia" and "The Antidote to Amnesia," deals with scriptural passages that accuse the Israelites of forgetting God and their covenantal responsibilities (e.g., Hos 4:6; 13:6). The antidote to amnesia is offered by grandparents, whose "primal function" is to help their grandchildren remember. The purpose of the Egyptian plagues was so that grandparents would tell the story to their grandchildren (Exod 10:2). "Double Agency" deals with the complexities of biblical accounts that suggest that there were two agents of the forced migration of Judeans under Babylonian rule: the Babylonian king and YHWH, who used Nebuchadnezzar as an agent of punishment; however, some in the migrant community, especially in subsequent generations, resisted the strict "Deuteronomic calculus" that suggested that permanent exile was just punishment for the "sins" of their parents (242, 245). Here Brueggemann also identifies pro-Babylonian "accommodators" (Jeremiah, Baruch, and Shaphan) and anti-Babylonian "resisters" (Ishmael of the royal family), drawing parallels to the experiences, challenges, and dilemmas negotiated by contemporary displaced persons, who might well need to "accommodate or perish," while avoiding the "uncritical accommodation without resistance [that] will inevitably result in the loss of historical identity" (246).

Part 3, "Legal Covenants That Coalesce," proposes "Sabbath," "neighborly community," and "neighborly economy" as urgently needed responses to contemporary economic policies that are unjust toward humans and the earth. The biblical deity is vexed by unjust human behavior and calls people into covenantal "neighborly" relationships. In "From Narrative to Policy," Brueggemann deals with the connection between the exodus narrative and the legal codes in Deuteronomy that enjoin leaders, food producers, and slaveholders to act with compassion for the poor and enslaved precisely because the Israelites themselves had been slaves and sojourners. Brueggemann calls for U.S. society to draw on the more promising, liberating parts of its own narrative—which inspire "practices of peace and prosperity with liberty and justice for all" (252)—rather than the more "truncated" version of the American founding narrative that fails to challenge "a market ideology and an aggressive practice of market control and a monopoly of natural resources" (254). In "The God Who Gives Rest," Brueggemann puts forward Sabbath as a countercultural alternative, offering rest to the earth, humans, and animals. The three-day festival proposed by Moses and Aaron (Exod 5:1–2) was "no innocent act of piety" but "rather a performance of an alternative allegiance that would substantively delegitimate Pharaoh" (281). "Covenantal Risks and Rewards" contrasts the "public morality of the village economy," exemplified by Naboth, the vineyard owner wronged by the royal family in 1 Kgs 21 (302), with the "Baal system of commodity exchange" (301) and "the Jerusalem system of dynasty and temple, epitomized by Solomon" (305). Acknowledging that it is "a leap from there to the Occupy Wall Street movement," Brueggemann nevertheless draws parallels between ancient and contemporary times, since Wall Street represents a culture of commodity, and the Occupy movement, according to Brueggemann, "voices a yearning sense that the economy could be ordered differently," in a more neighborly way (319).

Part 4, "Imaginative Provocations That Compel," begins with the essay "Testimony," addressed to preachers. The role of "witnesses" in biblical, historical, and contemporary settings is to break the silence enjoined by coercive empires or communities. These individuals "set in motion processes that run well beyond their own utterance" (328). Brueggemann calls on preachers to let "the old testimony against ancient empire become the contemporary testimony against the dominant contemporary ideology, whereby the old, old story becomes the new, new song" (333). "Obedience," a keynote address delivered at Andrews University's commemoration of Dr. Martin Luther King Jr., draws parallels between Moses and King. Brueggemann enjoins the students to "Dream," "Depart," "Travel light with easy bread," and "Live for the neighborhood" (346). "Slow Wisdom," a lecture delivered at Baylor University, ponders the complex situation of universities, which, on the one hand, "run the risk of alliance with the interests of might, wisdom, and wealth," but should also be settings where "slow wisdom" may be cultivated and the cries of the suffering may be heard in the humanities, social sciences, economics, and earth sciences (364). In "Bail Out," written in November 2008 as a reflection on the financial crisis and subprime loan rates, Brueggemann recommends theological responses to the economic crisis, commending "covenantal existence," generosity, and trust in divine abundance as an answer to the autonomy, anxiety, and greed that he regarded as the foundations of the economic crisis (375–77). In the final essay, "Jubilee," Brueggemann suggests that the fiftieth anniversary of Walmart (2012) would be "a splendid occasion for a Jubilee year" and an opportunity for the giant store chain to "pause in its rough and tumble of economics to give back for the sake of the neighborhood" (381).

In this volume Brueggemann demonstrates the remarkable ability to make interesting the biblical texts that many readers might find tedious, such as the lists of workers, supervisors, and supplies in 1 Kgs 4–7, as Brueggemann reveals the ideology of the text and a picture of Solomon as "the quintessential generator of memos that were designed to advance and sustain royal and legitimacy" (90). Since this is a collection of essays rather than a monograph, the book's arguments do not develop in a linear progression. Rather, the reader finds Brueggemann circling again and again to the same images and insights, reworking and often repeating ideas. This could be frustrating to readers who wish for a finished monograph in a fully organized and developed state. Others, including this reviewer, may appreciate the essay format, both because the essays are manageable in length (each can be read in one sitting) and because the collection provides a glimpse into how this distinguished biblical theologian develops and works out his ideas over time.

Rethinking Biblical Literacy, edited by Katie Edwards. London: Bloomsbury, 2015. Pp. xiv + 218. Paper. $39.95. ISBN 9780567050984.

Valarie H. Ziegler, DePauw University

When I first examined the table of contents of *Rethinking Biblical Literacy*, I was dismayed. Some of the topics have already received numerous scholarly treatments—after all, *The Simpsons* is in its third decade, *Lost* ended in 2010, and if there was a time when Madonna was not, I do not remember it. Other chapters explored areas unfamiliar to me, such as Irish biblical literacy. Still others examined subjects I wasn't eager to probe, such as the chapter on comedian Eddie Izzard's "room for poo."

Despite that inauspicious beginning, I am happy to report that I not only enjoyed this book but also learned a great deal from it. Editor Katie Edwards has assembled one of those rare anthologies that actually goes somewhere. *Rethinking Biblical Literacy* offers significant challenges to those of us with traditional training in biblical studies and religious studies.

The book juxtaposes what Edwards calls the "ubiquity of the Bible in popular culture" (x) with the widespread perception (delineated most famously by Stephen Prothero in *Religious Literacy: What Every American Needs to Know—*

and Doesn't, 2007) that biblical literacy is declining. If fewer people are familiar with the Bible, *Rethinking Biblical Literacy* asks, Why do we see so much Bible around us, from blockbuster films (*Noah* and *Exodus*, 2014) to spray-can urban street art?

Defining biblical literacy is critical to this discussion. If literacy means a close knowledge of biblical texts, narratives, and characters, then many Westerners are indeed less conversant with the Bible than they used to be (though there is considerable disagreement about just when the golden age of biblical literacy reigned). But if literacy refers not simply to knowing content but also includes engaging the Bible in other ways (through art, music, comedy, video, computer applications, and the like), then the Bible remains omnipresent in Western culture. *Rethinking Biblical Literacy* offers a variety of assessments of these popular appropriations of the Bible.

The book is organized into three sections. Part 1, "Located Literacies," presents case studies that reveal a decided unfamiliarity with biblical texts. The first chapter examines the state of biblical literacy in Ireland. Author Maire Byrne contends that reading the Bible has never been critical to Irish Roman Catholic identity, that curricula about the Bible in Irish schools focus on the Bible as talisman rather than text, and that, consequently, in Ireland the Bible is "rarely allowed to enter 'normal' life, where literacy is more easily gained" (19).

The situation in England is different. In "What the Bible Really Means: Biblical Literacy in English Political Discourse," James G. Crossley argues that English politicians reference the Bible constantly by purporting to reduce the Bible to what it "really means." These meanings are invariably identical to the speakers' current political agendas. Both Crossley and Iona Hine (in ch. 3, "The Quest for Biblical Literacy: Curricula, Culture and Case Studies") marvel at the social capital Britons confer upon the King James Bible, whose four hundredth anniversary was celebrated in 2011. The KJV is so tied to English cultural and literary identity that even the atheist Richard Dawkins proclaimed that those who had not read the KJV were "verging on the barbarian" (32). In 2012 the Education Secretary provided every English state school with an embossed King James Bible, not so much for students to read but rather as a relic to admire. Hine wonders if there are any meaningful projects that might encourage people to read the Bible for themselves.

Part 2, "Visual Literacies," includes chapters on *Lost*, street art, Madonna, and *The Simpsons*, all arguing that popular culture can advance biblical literacy. Matthew A. Collins delineates the intriguing ways that the television series *Lost* (2004–2010) incorporated biblical themes, characters, and textual references into its puzzling storyline. Desperate to solve the series' riddles, viewers discussed biblical themes at length at fan websites. Thus, Collins concludes, mainstream television can function as "a tool for promoting biblical literacy" (87).

Next, Amanda Dillon examines a number of amateur street artists who critique social injustice by referencing biblical characters in their art. Dillon challenges readers to expand their understanding of biblical literacy to include visual applications emerging from the passionate lives of ordinary people. Street art, she asserts, democratizes and revitalizes biblical interpretation.

Alan W. Hooker also examines visual imagery in his chapter on Madonna's 2012 "Girl Gone Wild" video. Madonna claimed she wanted to "stop the lies and hypocrisy of the church" (121), and Hooker's thick description skillfully connects the video's lyrics and images to the Catholic understandings of creation, gender, and atonement Madonna repudiated. Madonna emerges here as a sophisticated biblical interpreter. Hooker's thesis that "biblical literacy can be much more than text" and that viewing "Girl Gone Wild" is "in itself an act of biblical literacy" (139) is well taken.

Part 2 concludes with Robert J. Myles's "Biblical Literacy and *The Simpsons*." Myles argues that *The Simpsons* often "provides a satirical challenge to the dominance of the Bible and religion" (146) in American culture but occasionally "misses an opportunity for criticism" (157).

The two case studies in Part 3, "Popular Literacies," argue that popular-culture treatments of the Bible can make scripture accessible to interpreters in uniquely powerful ways. In her chapter on *The Girl with the Dragon Tattoo* (2005), Caroline Blyth notes that the novel ties five gruesome murders of women to texts from Leviticus. Blyth says that the juxtaposition of the novel's horrific gender violence with ancient Israel's Holiness Code overwhelmed her with "the pervasiveness and the normalization of socially sanctioned violence within the Levitical law codes," particularly as they marginalized, controlled, and threatened women (173). No scholarly study of the Bible had ever produced such a visceral effect in Blyth, who in closing implores academicians to bring popular culture into conversation with the Bible "as a new and infinitely valuable way of knowing these ancient texts" (183).

In the final chapter, "A Big Room for Poo: Eddie Izzard's Bible and the Literacy of Laughter," Christopher Meredith examines Izzard's 1997 "Glorious" stand-up comedy tour. Izzard lampooned Genesis's depiction of God shutting Noah and his family, their animals, and their food into an enclosed space on the ark, without access to the outdoors, for over a year. What, Izzard asked, did Noah do with all the excrement that piled up? That the Noah story fails to consider this very practical question amuses Izzard's audience and subverts the authority of the biblical narrative. But, Meredith contends, a secular audience's willingness to mock the Bible has the paradoxical effect of demonstrating the Bible's "continued cultural currency by trading laughs against it" (207). Ironically, the Bible has become a "recognizable cultural necessity that modern, mainstream society would rather forget about but is irredeemably attached to" (194). If, Meredith concludes, those concerned for biblical literacy accepted the loss of the Bible's authority in this secular age and fretted less about "preserving a serious paternal metaphor in the midst of a decentralizing of biblical dissemination," they would recognize that "biblical literature remains in social and cultural circulation," though "the metaphor is not as serious as it once was" (211).

I suspect that most readers of this review are academicians who, like me, associate biblical literacy with a scholarly understanding of the biblical text. We are suspicious of amateurs' interpretations and not likely to regard Madonna videos as useful in understanding ancient narratives from Genesis. Basically, we are hesitant about the project this book sets before us—rethinking biblical literacy—because, while we may enjoy studying the Bible in popular culture, we do not believe popular culture has anything to teach us about the Bible.

Nevertheless, this book drew me in. Part 1 played to my prejudices, demonstrating that, yes, Britons have a high regard for the King James Bible, and English politicians are good at using the Bible for their own purposes. Nevertheless, no one in this section seemed to have a clue about how to read the Bible intelligently.

Part 2 made me think, especially the chapters on *Lost* and Madonna. *Lost* fan websites provide clear evidence that viewers engaged the Bible to make sense of the series, and Collins's discussion of the series's allusions to Naomi and Ruth, Jacob and Esau, Cain and Abel, Yahweh and Satan, the exodus, and the good shepherd prompted me to rethink all those biblical images in light of *Lost's* narrative. Finally, if Madonna is really doing the critique of Gen 2–3 and of atonement theory that Hooker describes in "Girl Gone Wild," she is brilliant.

Part 3 made me think even more. Years ago I began but never completed *The Girl with the Dragon Tattoo* because I was sickened by the misogyny the novel depicted. Blyth's discussion of the Levitical Holiness Code in light of the novel made me feel—and fear—the sexism and implicit violence of Levitical laws in ways that I had not for years. As for Eddie Izzard, I must confess I had never heard of him prior to reading Meredith's chapter. Izzard sounds funny, and his work provides Meredith a useful platform to argue that much of the current angst about declining biblical literacy is really discomfort about nonexperts discoursing/drawing/videoing/joking about ancient texts to which we have devoted our scholarly lives. That is an issue I will continue to process.

RECEPTION HISTORY

Moses: The Man and the Myth in Music, by Helen Leneman. The Bible in the Modern World 61. Sheffield: Sheffield Phoenix, 2014. Pp. xi + 300. Cloth. $80.00. ISBN 1909697443.

Siobhán Dowling Long, University College Cork

In recent times, there has been an increasing interest among biblical scholars in writing about or citing examples of musical interpretations of biblical narratives in their published works and/or edited volumes. But despite the growing interest, the "new method" of interpretation continues to be viewed with varying degrees of suspicion, more often than not, by those who know very little about music or, worse still, by those who think they know more than they do. Given that the Bible has been interpreted in music for centuries, it is important to note that there is nothing "new" about this "new method," except to say that in recent times, and thanks to Helen Leneman's pioneering work, it has come to the attention of those now working in biblical studies. Musicologists and theologians have long since known about and commented upon the use of the Bible in music, a point that testifies no doubt to the existence of a serious neglect in biblical studies. This neglect however, is being addressed slowly but surely in publications such as the one under review, including others like it, and in a variety of new biblical commentaries recently published or in press at this time.

Helen Leneman's latest book, *Moses: The Man and the Myth in Music*, is the third in a trilogy of musical interpretations of biblical narratives and one that seeks to uncover the richness of musical retellings about the man Moses and his relationships with characters Zipporah, Miriam, and Aaron. Leneman's other two works are *The Performed Bible: The Story of Ruth in Opera and Oratorio* (2007) and *Love, Lust and Lunacy: The Stories of Saul and David in Music* (2010), both published by Sheffield Phoenix. As a scholar of musicology and biblical studies, I respect Leneman's work, knowing that the musical analysis, including her knowledge of the Hebrew Bible, is 100 percent accurate and reliable. So, when Leneman speaks about the mellow tonality of D Flat major or the bright tonality of B major, there is no question as to the veracity of these statements. The objective of her discussion of the music is to shed light on the biblical narrative in a way that uncovers the pathos of the ancient story. Leneman notes in all three volumes that she is a scholar, a musician, and a performer (i.e., a singer and a pianist), and this, too, is testament to her knowledge and discussion of the music found within this book. Interestingly, and unlike her other two volumes, Leneman speaks about her experience of chanting the narratives when she chants Torah alternately in Hebrew and in English in her synagogue, as well as during the annual Passover Seder, which as Leneman points out, "took on a special meaning during the course of writing this book" (xiv–xv). The present volume, then, does exactly what it says it does on the cover in its treatment of the reception of narratives of Moses in music, namely, in operas and oratorios from the nineteenth and twentieth centuries, including a discussion of Handel's well-known eighteenth-century oratorio, *Israel in Egypt* (HWV 54, 1738).

The type of musical analysis found in Leneman's *Moses: The Man and the Myth in Music* contrasts sharply with the textual analysis in *Handel's Israelite Oratorio Libretti: Sacred Drama and Biblical Exegesis* (Oxford: Oxford University Press, 2012), by Deborah W. Rooke, a work that purports to treat Handel's oratorio libretti in isolation from the music. Many reviews of this monograph have noted Rooke's grave neglect of Handel's music, highlighting also the notable absence of her treatment of other oratorios: *Israel in Egypt, Joshua, Alexander Balus, Belshazzar* and the *Occasional Oratorio*. A review (*Music and Letters*, 2012 93:602–5, http://ml.oxfordjournals.org/content/93/4/602.extract) by the respected Handelian expert, musicologist, and Cambridge scholar Ruth Smith, author of *Handel's Oratorio's and Eighteenth Century Thought* (Cambridge: Cambridge University Press, 1995), notes Rooke's neglect of Handel's music and the absence of the aforementioned oratorios. Smith also points out that Rooke was "insufficiently versed in the material she has undertaken to analyse" (602), as evidenced in the list of "errors" (604), and the "astonishingly selective," "skewed," and "superficial" accounts (603). By way of contrast, Leneman's expertise in music, alongside her scholarly treatment of the biblical narrative in music, shines through time and time again in *Moses: The Man and the Myth in Music*, as it does in her two other volumes. Leneman's approach, unlike Rooke's, places her discussion at the very heart of reception history.

The book is divided into nine chapters (1–251), with a prologue titled "Prelude" and a concluding chapter titled "Postlude." It contains two helpful tables "Musical Retellings" (253) and "Voice Types" (254) and four appendices, "Charting the Musical Retellings" (255–57), "Miriam's Song" (258–66), "Moses in Musical Theatre" (267–79), and "Annotated Music" (280–89), as well as bibliography of musical works" (290–91), a bibliography (292–97), and an index (298–300).

Chapter 1 (1–7), titled "Musical Notes," presents an overview of the musical genres discussed in the book, namely, opera and oratorio, including a section on the nature of music, voice types, and Jewish music, followed by a short conclusion. Content on the development of the "English Oratorio," the genre of oratorio invented by Handel, would have been an interesting addition in this chapter. Chapter 2 (8–61) presents a very helpful overview of the sixteen works discussed in the book, which includes some well-known and some obscure musical works by a broad range of composers, beginning with Handel from the eighteenth century and moving on to Hummel, Marx, David, Bruch, Hast and Massenet, Rossini, Rubinstein, Perosi, and Orefice from the nineteenth century, and Weill and Schoenberg from the twentieth century. This chapter includes interesting facts about each work, such as biographical details for each composer, biblical references upon which the musical work is based, voice settings for various biblical and extrabiblical characters within each musical work, the existence or nonexistence of musical scores, the availability of recordings and DVDs, including one or two links to YouTube, as well as interesting points raised in the accompanying liner notes, which are very often written by well-known scholars in the field of musicology. Chapters 3–9 follow a similar outline in each one, beginning with a brief summary of the biblical narratives selected (ch. 3: Exod 1–2; ch. 4: Exod 3–5; ch. 5: Exod 6–12; ch. 6: Exod 14–15; ch. 7: Exod 16–17; 19–20:25; ch. 8: Exod 32; and ch. 9: Numbers, Deuteronomy, and the death of Moses), followed by a commentary on the biblical narratives, a discussion of the music, and a short conclusion. Since part of the challenge of writing in this area involves making the discussion of the music accessible to the non–musically literate reader, a glossary of musical terms at the back of the volume would have been a welcome addition for those unfamiliar with the vast number of technical musical terms mentioned in the book. While the musical analysis in chapters 3–9 is perhaps best suited for a musically literate reader, the overview of works in chapter 2 serves as a good introduction both to those literate in music and to those with no musical background.

A frequent criticism of the "new methodology" is the lack of argument present in books such as *Moses: The Man and the Myth in Music* and other books of a similar nature. While this is true on one level, it rather blatantly misses the point as to what the author is attempting to do, namely, to uncover the pathos of the ancient story through a musical interpretation. Leneman summarizes this point as follows on the back cover "Through music, the listener can hear and also feel the suffering of the Israelites; the passion of Moses as leader, liberator, and even lover; the intensity of Miriam's vision and commitment; and the whole range of emotions experienced by every character that inhabits this story." If readers want arguments in favor for and against reception history or to explore current debates in biblical studies, then they will be disappointed and ought to seek out other books written on these themes. However, if they want to know something more about the pathos of the narratives of Moses, then this book is a good place to start. Readers are encouraged to listen to some or all of the available recordings on CDs or YouTube so that they can uncover for themselves the pathos within the biblical narratives about the man Moses. The editors of Sheffield Phoenix are to be congratulated once again for another handsome production, for the fine attention to detail, and for the care given not only to Leneman's *Moses: The Man and the Myth in Music* but to every book published by this press.

Reception History and Biblical Studies: Theory and Practice, edited by Emma England and William John Lyons. Library of Hebrew Bible/Old Testament Studies 615. London: Bloomsbury, 2015. Pp. 296. Hardcover. $120.00. ISBN 9780567660084.

C. L. Seow, Vanderbilt Divinity School

There has been a strong and rapidly widening current of projects since the 1990s on the Bible and reception history, broadly so-called. Arguably the most ambitious is the *Encyclopedia of the Bible and Its Reception* (2009–), with thirty volumes projected and twelve volumes published so far. Alongside this are several more circumscribed works, including the *Dictionary of the Biblical Tradition in English Literature* (ed. D. L. Jeffrey, 1992), *Blackwell's Companion to the Bible and Culture* (ed. J. F. A. Sawyer, 2006), *A Concise Dictionary of the Bible and Its Reception* (J. F. A. Sawyer, 2009), *Oxford Handbook of the Reception History of the Bible* (M. Lieb et al., 2010), *Bible and Music: Influences of the Old Testament in Western Music* (Max Stern, 2011), *Dictionary of the Bible and Western Culture* (ed. M. A. Bevis and M. J. Gilmour, 2012), and *The Bible in Music: A Dictionary of Songs, Works and More* (Siobhan Dowling Long and J. F. A. Sawyer, 2015). The last five years alone saw the founding of several new journals dedicated to reception history: *Relegere: Studies in Religion and Reception* (2011–), *Biblical Reception* (2012–), *Postscripts: The Journal of Sacred Texts and Contemporary Worlds* (2012–), and *Journal of the Bible and Its Reception* (2014–). De Gruyter launched two book series: Studies of the Bible and Its Reception (nine volumes since 2013) and Handbooks of the Bible and Its Reception (two volumes in 2016). The series to which the volume under review belongs, Scriptural Traces: Critical Perspectives on the Reception and Influence of the Bible, has published six volumes since 2013, with at least another volume due out this year. All these, together with various commentaries, monographs, and articles, indicate that reception history is no longer a niche-area of research but a significant new (though not entirely new!) frontier in biblical scholarship, as it has been in classics and other disciplines that have similarly engaged reception theory.

As one might expect at any frontier, there are a myriad challenges and not a little chaos that come with the excitement of new possibilities. Participants justify their venture and call on others to join the cause. There are questions of identity, clarification of objectives and strategies, challenges of cohesion amid diversity, forays into further territories, and attempts to provide guidance for newcomers. All these are on display in this collection of essays by sixteen scholars in various stages of their careers.

The introductory essay, by Emma England and William John Lyons, characterizes reception history as offering a "garden of delight," an apt metaphor in many ways, not least for the rich variety of growths that one encounters in the volume. Yet some readers may bristle at the depiction of biblical scholarship in its traditional manifestation as the cultivation of an odd bonsai tree, presumably because it is a highly controlled cultivation and, in the view of the editors, stunted. Here, and occasionally in other essays, one discerns an apologetic posture in the attempts to justify broadening the field in this way and to distinguish the reception-historical approaches from the historical-critical approaches that have dominated the academy (the stunted bonsai) as "leaving little of itsnarrow remit untouched and with much repeated ad nauseam" (3). Even those who wish, despite their training and predilections, to participate in the cultivation of this garden are portrayed as "dilettante wanderers, who have somewhat heroically left their academic comfort zone behind them, even if for only a little while" (6), while the approach championed by reception historians is said to creative, as if other forms of biblical scholarship are not. As the academy has seen before, enthusiasm for the promise of a new direction leads to eager proclamations of the death of the old and the beginning of the new, with the new being the means by which biblical studies might be saved from its imminent, inevitable, and much-deserved demise. This is perhaps not the most welcoming way to start, no way to invite broad participation in the cultivation of the garden.

The metaphor of a garden may also prompt one to observe that this garden, while indeed delightful, is not entirely so. Amid the beautiful plants are weeds, even noxious weeds, "growths" (receptions) that are not delightful but can be ugly, puzzling, difficult to appreciate, obnoxious, even dangerous (such as receptions that have nefarious consequences). Historians of biblical receptions surely ought not to overlook such realities of the Bible's effects.

Susan Gillingham's essay offers a different metaphor in her defense of the project. She turns the put-down of reception history as "biblical studies on a holiday" into an opportunity to extol the delights and rewards of a holiday—an eye-opening experience, a broadening of one's hermeneutical "horizons," as it were, as one encounters new cultures, new languages, and different histories. She acknowledges that more work is needed on "the theoretical theological underpinnings" (22) and disciplinary coherence but pleads that it is early days yet. For now, she says, the discipline is largely pragmatic, focusing as it does on "assessing the *performative* nature and the practical *impact* of biblical texts" (23, emphasis original). All this is true enough. Yet not all contributors will agree that the theoretical underpinnings, or indeed the subject of research, need to be theological. Indeed, some of the essayists in the volume, along with other advocates of this approach, have suggested that one of the strengths of reception history is precisely that it goes beyond confessional interests, beyond an essentialist view of "*the* Bible." This is not to say that one cannot be theological, only that not all reception histories need to be. Moreover, for Gillingham "it is important to *start* with the Hebrew text … [and] some understanding of the possible composition of the text its earlier setting" (20, emphasis original). She insists that it is "always the text" that is at the center of reception, and when "the text" disappears, one is no longer dealing with "the reception of the text" but more with "the reception of interpreters" (21). In this regard, Gillingham's approach shows the greatest continuity with historical criticism, at least in terms of procedure: first the biblical text, then the reception of that text. Yet her formulation begs the question of what is meant by "the text" and whether the biblical text in Hebrew (or Greek) is the necessary starting point of every reception-historical investigation—assumptions that other contributors dispute. Her procedure may be understood to imply that "biblical exegesis," in the traditional sense of the designation, is the primary task of any reception history, whereas later receptions are add-ons, a view that other contributors also challenge.

Like Gillingham, Roland Boer uses the metaphor of travel. He speaks of "the lure of the road" and the sheer pleasure ("eroticism") of encountering news areas of inquiry—the "intersections of myriads of disciplines"—as one ventures from "home," in his case, his habitation in the classical methods of biblical studies. In such forays, Boer avers, a biblical scholar does not leave behind the skills and tools acquired from "home." Rather, one brings them to bear in the new adventures on the road, namely, for him in this case, the exploration of topics as far from his "home" as Lenin, Calvin, and the music of Nick Cave. His prior training leads to an approach that is "intimate" (close-reading), "immanent" (engaging the objects of study on their own terms, with their own approaches), "comparative" (analyzing the object of study with others), "genealogical" (tracing the trajectories of approaches and points of view), and "constructive" (asking the "so-what" question). Biblical scholars bring their skills and experience to the project.

James Harding implicitly challenges Gillingham's two-step approach. He asks: "Can a distinction be made between first and second stages in interpretation, that is, between the study of texts *in their original historical contexts* and their *subsequent history of reception* actually be maintained? And why should the former be essentialized as *the* point of coherence for the discipline?" (35, emphasis original). Harding asserts here, as he has elsewhere, that "there is no such thing as Biblical Studies," and reception history contributes to this conceit. By this he means that there is such a plurality of methods and cross-fertilizations with other disciplines that there are no longer any disciplinary boundaries that define "biblical studies." So biblical scholars must be humanist scholars and engage all areas of the humanities—a direction that is salutary and productive, as his exemplars show. Still, biblical scholars in general do have a common subject of study, the "horizons" of which they must investigate, as Jauss might say, with their "horizon of expectation," not least the substantial reservoir of knowledge and assumptions they share with others of the same academic ilk. Be that as it may, Harding rightly insists there is no such thing as "the original text," as even textual criticism cannot recover any *Urtext*, only multiple versions that one must take seriously as "first." There can be no distinction between "text" and "reception," for everything that biblical scholars do is, in fact, reception history; even historically oriented approaches are "reception-historically conditioned" (41).

On this score, Brennan Breed corroborates Harding's claim, for Breed, too, points out that recent textual critics are increasingly cognizant of the fact that "the Bible did not originate from pristine manuscripts, and neither was there one consistent line of authorship or editing that culminated in the communal authorization of a final, authoritative manuscript" (97). So there is no single discoverable biblical text that must be the starting point of research. Drawing on French philosopher Gilles Deleuze's analogy from the field of ethology, an animal behavioral science that focuses on the potential action of each species, Breed argues that reception history, like ethology, is not linear. Rather, like an ethologist, one should focus on what each species actually does and can potentially do. Accordingly, one gathers, the task of the scholar of the reception of the biblical tradition is not so much to construct a linear metahistorical narrative but rather to do many reception-historical investigations as part of a vast system of connectivity.

Caroline Vander Stichele also draws on Deleuze to make the point of interconnectivity, more specifically his collaborative work with Félix Guattari, in developing the rhizome as a hermeneutical metaphor. Like the analogy of ethology, the rhizome theory allows for multiple points of entry into the study of an object's roots and offshoots. Just as a rhizome does not have a center and the parts are connected in nonhierarchical ways, reception aesthetic has neither beginning nor an end, only a network of interconnected parts, with each part offering a potential locus of interest. So doing reception history is akin to surfing the internet. At the same time, Vander Stichele calls upon the literary theory of intertextuality, specifically as developed by Jonathan Culler, which is not confined to evidence of sources and influences in any given text but rather "anonymous discursive practices, codes of whose origins are lost, that make possible the signifying practices of later texts" (Culler quoted on 80–81). For Vander Stichele, such a broad understanding of intertextuality allows the scholar of reception history to explore the relation between any given interpretation and its "cultural reservoir." At the same time, she employs Mieke Bal's notions of "preposterous history" in her book *Quoting Caravaggio* (Chicago, 1999), which problematizes the "idea of the precedent as origin by considering the later work as an active intervention in the earlier work, rather than as a passive recipient" (83). The idea that later artists often reference earlier works allows scholars of reception history to connect intertextuality and iconography. All this is, of course, in line with the "horizon of expectations" that Hans Robert Jauss posits, along with his insistence on both diachrony and synchrony.

Breed's ethological model and Vander Stichele's rhizomatic one, both important for the theory of reception history, are played out in the other essays. Jonathan Cameron argues in his essay that reception history is always open-ended, constantly evolving, liminal, and multidimensional. Indeed its most important contribution to biblical studies is that "it refuses to allow the written word to define its borders" (76).

Like Gillingham and Boer, Ian Boxall uses the metaphor of travel, in this case, his own journey to (re)discover Patmos, a journey in which he encountered travelers from the past, many of whom became his guides in reading his biblical text. The guides to whom Boxall refers are in the main those from Christian *Auslegungsgeschichte*, and his "standard resources" are those used in church history. His conclusion is one that scholars of *Auslegungsgechichte* often underscore, that "precritical" interpreters were often exceedingly careful readers capable of remarkable insights, often gained by exploring the interstices of the received text and raising interesting alternative questions that might prompt one to reread the text and consider possible ways it might mean. Yet the purpose of such investigations—including the history of Jewish interpretation, one might add—is not just to find old-yet-fresh insights and new questions, is it? Might it not, for instance, show how meanings have changed or may have been created? One might also find meanings and lessons in the intersections of competing histories of interpretation—Jewish, Christian, and Muslim. Clearly, Boxall—as Gillingham as well—subsumes *Auslegungsgeschichte* under the rubric of reception history, even though some scholars of *Auslegungseschichte* would not consider much of what historians of reception do to be *Auslegung*, and indeed some practitioners of reception history do attempt to distinguish the two, even if not terribly compellingly. Several sections of the Society of Biblical Literature Annual Meeting, too, reflect this tension between the history of interpretation and the history of reception. Yet none of the essays in this collection address the issue.

Moving in the opposite chronological direction as Gillingham and Boxall, Helen Jacobus begins not with the Bible but with contemporary music, in this case Leonard Cohen's reception of an ancient Jewish liturgical poem that draws not only from the Bible and rabbinical antecedents but also sources unbeknownst to Cohen and even the liturgical poets, as well as ancient Near Eastern astrological traditions. Likewise, Michael Gilmore begins not with the Bible but with John Lennon's song "God," which makes neither reference nor allusion to the Bible, and then studies two receptions of Lennon's "God" that in vastly different ways biblicize Lennon's "God." In a somewhat similar fashion, Lyons begins with two modern musical receptions of the Apocalypse of John: Blind Willie Johnson's

"John the Revelator" (1930) and Martin Gore's version of "John the Revelator" performed by Depeche Mode in their 2005 album, *Playing the Angel.*

Just as there are no methodological borders in reception history, so there are no cultural ones. While the majority of essays engage the reception of the Bible in the West, Masiiwa Ragies Gunda and Gerald West focus on the Bible in Africa, and they do so using different strategies. Gunda's piece is on the impact of the Bible in Zimbabwe amidst the interplay of social and political forces as it is played out in the highly charged national sanction on homosexuality. West's investigation of the use of the narrative of Jephthah's daughter in Judg 11 among a distinctive socioreligious group highlights the issue of multiple layers of reception in any given context.

West's essay reinforces the point that reception history has no disciplinary or cultural boundaries, for his is an approach that draws on cultural anthropology and the sociology of religion. The call for such interdisciplinarity is precisely what Ibrahim Abraham insists that those who study the reception of the Bible in modern music must do. He contends that biblical scholars, by virtue of their training, still tend to privilege the production of texts and the literary analyses thereof. If one were truly committed to reception, he seems to say, one must consider not only those who produce the musicians but those who consume it. By contrast, a sociology of religion approach considers the fact that the consumers of the music have entirely different sets of assumptions and interests than the producers. The consumers of modern music inspired by the Bible may in fact be entirely secular and have neither knowledge of nor regard for any religious message that the producers of the music may have had in mind. The essays of West and Abraham thus point to an irony in most reception-historical studies, namely, that the focus on receptions are also productions. The emphasis is still on production and the study of the product. Should reception historians not also consider the horizons of the consumers of the products who do not themselves produce for public consumption, perhaps through sociology and cultural anthropology? For those who investigate the reception of the Bible in the present, would it not be methodologically desirable to study the ethnography of the consumers? In a more utilitarian way, Emma England urges the deployment of resources of the field of digital humanities, a prospect that may bring great rewards, though one that for most may seem utterly forbidding.

Such is life at the frontier, it seems. Even as the eager and hopeful would-be pioneers are striving to define their identity and cohesiveness, there are critical voices from without but also from within that in various ways call attention to the shortcomings of the project and, worse yet, seem to proclaim its demise: "the end of reception history" (James Crossley) and "the end of biblical interpretation" (Samuel Tongue), echoing similar refrains from other quarters. Yet these rhetorical flourishes should perhaps not be understood as prophetic doom oracles. Rather, they are rhetorical defenses against external challenges—in Crossley's case, a resistance to attempts of opponents to set disciplinary boundaries; in Tongue's case, a demurral to the over-easy distinction between the religious and the secular. What Harold Bloom calls "the anxiety of influence" (see Gilmour's use of the theory in his essay) is in evidence here: the Oedipal impulse of new writers to highlight the originality of their own proffers over against their predecessors.

As a whole, this volume is a rich and valuable one, in many places advancing and nuancing the discipline and offering many stimulating examples of the payoffs of such approaches. Yet one wonders if it is a volume directed mostly at those who are practitioners and those who are already open to it—the somewhat heroic dilettantes. It would be most unfortunate if the apologetic and polemical tone here and there will keep the substantive contributions from receiving the broad hearing they deserve. Given the repeated emphasis in the essays on the contingent and provisional nature of reception-historical studies and the recognized need for humility and collaboration in the enterprise, it is disconcerting to find the occasional othering of ideological and methodological adversaries as rigid "gatekeepers" (69–72), characterized as "achingly unsophisticated" (64) and "rather juvenile" (66). One is reminded of the caricature of young Elihu who comes lately to dismiss the elders as providing no real answer to the problem at hand. The sage counsel of Jane Tompkin's "Fighting Words: Unlearning to Write the Critical Essay" (*The Georgia Review* 42 [1988]: 588–90) remains a still much-needed reminder to us all that form and tone do matter in productive scholarly discourse. To continue the editor's opening metaphor, those who tend "the delightful garden" should not see their task as "guerilla gardening, with small rebellious groups sowing its seeds" (3). Rather, they proudly point to the beautiful blossoms and delectable fruit that the garden yields and show the care with which they tend the all the plants, including the old-yet-beautiful bonsai.

Have You Considered My Servant Job? Understanding the Biblical Archetype of Patience, by Samuel E. Balentine. Studies on Personalities of the Old Testament. Columbia: University of South Carolina, 2015. Pp. xxi + 287. Cloth. $54.95. ISBN 9781611174526.

Jeffery M. Leonard, Samford University

Perhaps it should not be surprising that the biblical book whose language is most difficult is the book for which our language of description falls most miserably short. Job is a complex book, to be sure, but it is much more than that. It is a haunting book, an unsettling book, a book that teeters between shoring up faith and stripping faith away. Most of all, it is an irresistible book. As Samuel Balentine confesses in the preface to this outstanding volume, "Once you enter into it fully, you never escape" (xi).

The lure of Job's ambiguities was as powerful for ancient interpreters as it has been for moderns. A wealth of interpretive paraphrases, commentaries, sermons, allusions, paintings, illustrations, plays, novels, and poems attests to the abiding attraction of this singular biblical work. In this study, Balentine traces this reception history of Job, charting the course of the book's interpretation as it has passed through the hands of one generation of readers after another. The result is a work that highlights Job's place in the intellectual and spiritual lives of the book's inheritors while at the same time raising (or raising again) fundamental questions about the book itself.

As part of the Studies on Personalities of the Old Testament series, this volume is naturally centered around the characters who populate the biblical story—Job, of course, but also Job's wife, his friends, the satan, and God. In part 1 of the study (13–110), Balentine considers the characters of the didactic tale that frames the book (Job 1–2; 42:7–17). In part 2 (111–220) he turns to the cast of the poetic dialogues that form the book's heart (Job 3:1–42:6). Balentine's approach in the book is exemplified by his first chapter, "The Job(s) of the Didactic Tale." Here he begins by focusing on the tension that exists between the patient Job of the book's prose and the rebellious Job of its poetry. Faced with the dilemma of explaining Job's great suffering and the scandal of his protests against God's judgment, many early rabbinic commentators raised objections to Job's righteous status and remained skeptical of his participation in the world to come. Most ancient interpreters, though, tended to dismiss or ignore Job's protests, giving greater weight to his patient endurance. The Septuagint's translation of the book represents an early softening of the excesses of Job's outbursts. The Testament of Job goes much further, dramatically recasting the story as a contest between Job and Satan in which Job knows in advance he will suffer and yet does so willingly and patiently while never complaining against God. Echoes of this vision of Job are evident in the church fathers as they treat Job as the "athlete of the Church" who exemplifies the heroic battle for God against Satan. It is this depiction of Job as saintly warrior that dominates Gregory the Great's influential sixth-century work, *Moralia in Job*. For Gregory, Job is the "true soldier of God" whose outbursts in the middle of the book are no more than expressions of passion in the face of suffering, responses parallel to Christ's own passion. Drawing upon Astell's work, Balentine notes that this image of Job as God's soldier led to his becoming the patron saint for the medieval knightly orders and model for their "heroic virtues."

The approach Balentine takes in this first chapter becomes the template for the remaining chapters. In "God and the Satan" he walks readers through the transformation of the Joban Satan from servant of God to grotesque enemy, while noting the simultaneous tendency to minimize God's own complicity in Job's suffering. He marks a dramatic reversal of these trends beginning with Goethe's *Faust*, as Satan is, if not redeemed, at least presented in a more sympathetic light and as attention is increasingly turned to the dark side of a deity who allows Job's torment "for no reason."

In "There Was Once a Woman in the Land of Uz," Balentine contrasts the common presentation of Job's wife among the church fathers as an Eve-like temptress inspired by the devil with more sympathetic accounts that emphasize her own suffering and the comfort she offers her husband. He notes that only in the modern period has Job's wife finally been given her own voice in works from authors such as Roth, MacLeish, and Frost. Here she appears less as comforter than as the voice of righteous anger, an anger Job's own character appears too passive or too impotent to offer himself.

As early interpreters tended to suppress the outbursts of the dialogues' defiant Job, Balentine turns in "Job's Words from the Ash Heap" to the antecedent voices of protest against innocent suffering in Mesopotamian literature. He then lays the groundwork for his consideration of modern protests against divine injustice through a lengthy consideration of the Promethean myth, both in its original setting in ancient Greece and in its revival in the works of Goethe, Byron, the Shelleys (Mary and Percy), and Milton.

In "God on Trial," Balentine highlights the dilemma Job faces as conscience demands he bring suit against God but practicality insists God cannot be brought before the bar. He explores these same issues in the works of two twentieth-century Jewish authors, Franz Kafka's *The Trial* and Elie Wiesel's *The Trial of God*, both of which wrestle with Job and the trial motif. The Joban dilemma is particularly sharp in Wiesel's play, for though God is placed on trial for abandoning his people during a pogrom, the trial is set only in a *Purimspiel*. The protagonist, Berish, who has lost his community and his family, rails against God's injustice but knows "putting God on trial, however serious, is nothing more than a game" (147).

In "Job's Comforters," Balentine notes the varied ways in which Job's friends have been understood by interpreters, from the positive assessments of Maimonides and Calvin (especially for Elihu) to their depiction as torturers and inquisitors in the plays of Gelber and Levin. Balentine draws particular attention to the influence of the Joban dialogues on debates over theodicy in the eighteenth century. Like Job's friends, Leibniz and Pope insisted that primary truths about God's justice must prevail against the contingent truths of an individual's personal experience of suffering or injustice, even in a case such as Job's. Against these two stands Voltaire, who saw in the devastating Lisbon earthquake of 1755 a shattering of Pope's notion that "Whatever is, is right." With Job, Voltaire felt it better to protest the present state of affairs than to bow to the notion that "All's well."

In "'Then the Lord Answered Job out of the Whirlwind,'" Balentine considers the formidable challenges of the divine speeches that conclude the poetic dialogues. As elsewhere in his writings on Job, he suggests the divine speeches may be read as attempts not to cower Job into silence but to elicit from him continued challenges against injustice. For most early interpreters of the divine speeches, Behemoth and Leviathan were inextricably tied to Satan or the antichrist. Hobbes's seventeenth-century use of Leviathan as a positive depiction of an all-powerful monarchic state represented a sharp break with this negative portrayal. More important for biblical interpreters, though, is the sustained use of Joban imagery by Melville in his masterwork, *Moby Dick*. Through both Ishmael's and Ahab's pursuit of the Leviathan, Balentine explores Melville's own grappling with a God whom he could not deny but whom he also could not accept.

Balentine concludes with a discussion of the book's epilogue and the difficult theological and literary problems it circumscribes. Here he focuses especially on Jewish works that wrestle with the problem of undeserved suffering: Perets's *Bontsey Shvayg*, Greenberg's poem, "Y. L. Perets and Bontsye Shvayg in the Warsaw Ghetto," Leivick's *In the Days of Job*. The highlight of the chapter, though, is his consideration of the novels written by Elie Wiesel in the wake of the Holocaust, works he cautiously acknowledges bring him "as close to the inner sanctum of Jewish history as a Gentile may be permitted" (213). Balentine treads carefully and perceptively through these deep waters.

To read Balentine's work and to observe the ease with which he moves from early postbiblical interpretation to Byzantine and Renaissance art to Enlightenment philosophy to modern literary works is nothing if not a humbling experience. Whatever criticisms might be offered of the book are hardly more than quibbles. The lack of artistic reproductions in a work so rich in description of the visual arts, the cumbersome use of endnotes rather than footnotes, an unnecessary detour here or there (most notably, perhaps, the overlong discussion of Hobbes's *Leviathan*)—these are hardly worth mentioning when compared to the excellence of the volume as a whole. With this work, Balentine has produced a companion to his other works on Job which students of the biblical text will surely want to consider.

Between Biblical Criticism and Poetic Rewriting: Interpretative Struggles over Genesis 32:22–32, by Samuel Tongue. Biblical Intepretation Series 129. Leiden: Brill, 2014. Pp. xii + 292. Hardcover. $149.00. ISBN 9789004270404.

Anthony C. Swindell, Jersey, Channel Islands, United Kingdom

This is in many ways a very specialist study, confining itself to interpretative issues over the narrative account in Gen 32:22–34 of Jacob wrestling with the angel as handled in the post-Enlightenment period and concentrating on a handful of selected modern poems. At the same time, it seeks to place the hermeneutical issues that it uncovers at the very heart of the debate over the status of the Bible as a bi-canonical document in our pluralistic age.

Chapter 1 is a persuasive account of the growth of "The Poetic Bible" in the eighteenth and nineteenth centuries under the influence of critics Lowth and Herder and the poets Blake, Wordsworth, and Coleridge. It led broadly to the concept of the cultural Bible, with its outworking recently in the celebrations over the four hundredth anniversary of the King James Bible. Chapter 2 moves swiftly on to impact of theory on biblical studies in the shape of the writings of the literary theorists Jacques Derrida and Mieke Bal and biblical scholars Yvonne Sherwood and Stephen Moore. In this case, the outworking is *The Postmodern Bible* of 1995 and its aftermath. The issues at play include the validity of literary-aesthetic responses to the Bible in the wider context of the reader-response approaches to the text and the impact of the critiques offered by gender and postcolonial studies.

This leads Tongue to single out Gen 32:22–32 as a suitable case study, beginning with Emily Dickinson's poem, "A Little East of Eden," which finds the God of patriarchy taken off balance.

Chapter 3 then prepares the ground for Tongue to set out his concept of poetic paragesis, using the ideas of Derrida and de Certeau to outline an understanding of poetic biblical rewritings as examples of the encounter between postmodern insights into the multivocality of *all* literature and the highly guarded site known as "the Bible."

Chapter 4 explores a range of examples of theological interpretations of the Gen 32 text, including the Targums, Justin Martyr, Ambrose, Luther, and Calvin, with the mystery over the identity of Jacob's antagonist central to most readings. Significantly, Herder's Romantic pastoralism consigns the whole episode to the realm of dreaming. This chapter then proceeds to discuss the "double canonicity" of the Bible as both fossilized sacred text and as the platform for poetic retellings that discover within it various forms of alterity. Poems by Alden Nowlam, Yehuda Amichai, and Jamie Wasserman are recruited to demonstrate the spaces of *différance* or of iconoclasm that orthodox readings of the Bible exclude.

Chapter 5 investigates the "male gaze" as a component in the deciphering of the text, using David Kinloch's poem in Scots dialect, "Jacob and the Angel," to highlight the below-the-belt nature of the blow suffered by Jacob as a guide to patriarchal masculinities. In the end, Tongue argues that it is the undecidability of the events at the River Jabbok that are the key to the text's potency, rather as Todorov claimed that fantastic narratives depend for their charge on the uncertainty generated by hovering between naturalistic and supernaturalistic explanations.

This study champions deconstruction as the path to engagement with the text of Gen 32:22–32. The incompleteness of the road to religious canonization (Is the final form of the biblical hypotext found in some early codex, in the Vulgate, or in some modern translation?) is grist to the mill, as is the permeability to the wider culture of the words used in any vernacular translation. We are invited to value insights into how meanings are generated over and above the validity or even the richness of particular meanings. It is a powerful hermeneutical emetic. Yet we need to remember that there have been long historical periods in which the text of "the Bible" has been fixed and stable. We need also to recall that some of the most witty and contrarian of literary rewritings of the Bible belong to the premodern period. Think of Chaucer or Boccaccio. It is also an inescapable fact that many literary rewritings integrate other components of the Jacob story (the birthright episode, the ladder etc.) intertextually with this one. This is particularly evident in Jenny Diski's novel *After These Things* (2004), where the wrestling episode becomes a psychological response to Jacob's dealings with Laban and the prelude to his reunion with Esau. The final reservation that I would express is that Tongue's choice of rewritings to bolster his argument concentrates almost exclusively on poems, as opposed, for example, to novels or plays. This matters because of the distinction that the literary theorist Mikhail Bakhtin makes between poetry, which he designates as "inherently monological," and the polyphony of the novel (see his *The Dialogical Imagination* trans. Caryl Emerson and Michael Holquist [Austin: University of Texas Press, 1981], 275–300). It is precisely the polyphony or multivocality of Rabelais or Dostoevsky that prevents their writings from being commandeered to support an iconoclastic teleology—or any other teleology.

Tongue has done us a great service in delivering a trajectory that takes us from the Romantic formulation of the poetic Bible through to the current standoff between historical-critical studies of the biblical text and the challenge presented by one version of reception studies. The narrative of Gen 32:22–34 lends itself well to the exposure of the fissures in patriarchal religion illuminated by the modern poems that the author has chosen to foreground. Tongue's overall approach amounts to a hermeneutical detoxification of the reception history. To balance the picture we now need (for want of a better term) a "Jacob-through-the-ages" literary study that allows the contradictions and twists and turns in the reception history (not just in the hypotext itself) to become manifest, avoiding a prescriptively selective approach to the extant literary tradition. This, however, will depend upon the acceptance that empirically there has been a stable text, or at least series of stable versions of the biblical text or hypotext, to which successive literary rewritings have responded.

Indexes

AUTHORS AND EDITORS

REVIEWERS

PUBLISHERS

New and Recent Titles

FIGHTING FOR THE KING AND THE GODS
A Survey of Warfare in the Ancient Near East
Charlie Trimm
Paperback $89.95, 978-1-62837-184-0   748 pages, 2017   Code 060394
Hardcover $109.95, 978-0-88414-238-6   E-book $89.95, 978-0-88414-237-9
Resources for Biblical Study 88

EARLY JEWISH WRITINGS
Eileen Schuller and Marie-Theres Wacker, editors
Paperback $44.95, 978-1-62837-183-3   316 pages, 2017   Code: 066006
Hardcover $59.95, 978-0-88414-233-1 E-book $44.95, 978-0-88414-232-4
The Bible and Women 3.1

WHEN TEXTS ARE CANONIZED
Timothy H. Lim, editor
Paperback $29.95, 978-1-946527-00-4   188 pages, 2017   Code 140359
Hardcover $44.95, 978-1-930675-95-7   E-book $29.95, 978-1-930675-99-5
Brown Judaic Studies 359

PEDAGOGY IN ANCIENT JUDAISM AND EARLY CHRISTIANITY
Karina Martin Hogan, Matthew Goff, and Emma Wasserman, editors
Paperback $49.95, 978-1-62837-165-9   424 pages, 2017   Code: 063548
Hardcover $64.95, 978-0-88414-208-9 E-book $49.95, 978-0-88414-207-2
Early Judaism and Its Literature 41

REDESCRIBING THE GOSPEL OF MARK
Barry S. Crawford and Merrill P. Miller, editors
Paperback $89.95, 978-1-62837-163-5   708 pages, 2017   Code: 064520
Hardcover $109.95, 978-0-88414-204-1 E-book $89.95, 978-0-88414-203-4
Early Christianity and Its Literature 22

GOSPEL JESUSES AND OTHER NONHUMANS
Biblical Criticism Post-poststructuralism
Stephen D. Moore
Paperback $24.95, 978-1-62837-190-1   164 pages, 2017   Code 060691
Hardcover $39.95, 978-0-88414-252-2   E-book $24.95, 978-0-88414-251-5
Semeia Studies 89

SBL Press • P.O. Box 2243 • Williston, VT 05495-2243
Phone: 877-725-3334 (toll-free) or 802-864-6185 • Fax: 802-864-7626
Order online at www.sbl-site.org/publications